MW01253034

Plato and Myth

Mnemosyne

Supplements

Monographs on Greek and
Latin Language and Literature

VOLUME 337

The titles published in this series are listed at brill.nl/mns

Plato and Myth

Studies on the Use and Status of Platonic Myths

Edited by

Catherine Collobert
Pierre Destrée
Francisco J. Gonzalez

BRILL

LEIDEN · BOSTON
2012

Library of Congress Cataloging-in-Publication Data

Plato and myth : studies on the use and status of Platonic myths / edited by Catherine Collobert,
Pierre Destrée, Francisco J. Gonzalez.
    p. cm. – (Mnemosyne. Supplements, ISSN 0169-8958 ; v. 337)
    Based chiefly on a conference held in May 2008 at the University of Ottawa.
    Includes bibliographical references (p.   ) and index.
    ISBN 978-90-04-21866-6 (hardback : alk. paper) 1. Plato–Congresses. 2. Myth–Congresses. I.
Collobert, Catherine. II. Destrée, Pierre. III. Gonzalez, Francisco J., 1963-

B395.P517 2012
184–dc23

2011042778

This publication has been typeset in the multilingual "Brill" typeface. With over 5,100
characters covering Latin, IPA, Greek, and Cyrillic, this typeface is especially suitable for
use in the humanities. For more information, please see www.brill.nl/brill-typeface.

ISSN 0169-8958
ISBN 978 90 04 21866 6 (hardback)
ISBN 978 90 04 22436 0 (e-book)

Copyright 2012 by Koninklijke Brill NV, Leiden, The Netherlands.
Koninklijke Brill NV incorporates the imprints Brill, Global Oriental, Hotei Publishing,
IDC Publishers, Martinus Nijhoff Publishers and VSP.

This book is printed on acid-free paper.

MIX
Paper from
responsible sources
FSC
www.fsc.org   FSC® C004472

PRINTED BY DRUKKERIJ WILCO B.V. - AMERSFOORT, THE NETHERLANDS

CONTENTS

PART I

REFLECTIONS ON THE NATURE OF PLATONIC MYTHS

PART II

APPROACHES TO PLATONIC MYTHS

LIST OF CONTRIBUTORS

Luc Brisson is directeur de recherche at the CNRS.

Claude Calame is directeur d'études at EHESS, and chercheur attaché at Centre Louis Gernet de Recherches Comparées sur les Sociétés Anciennes.

Catherine Collobert is Professor of Philosophy at the University of Ottawa.

Pierre Destrée is chercheur qualifié at the FNRS, and Associate Professor of Philosophy at the University of Louvain (Louvain-la-Neuve).

Monique Dixsaut is Emerita Professor of Philosophy at the University of Paris I-Panthéon Sorbonne.

Louis-André Dorion is Professor of Philosophy at the University of Montreal.

Radcliffe G. Edmonds III is Associate Professor of Greek, Latin and Classical Studies at the Bryn Mawr College.

G.R.F. Ferrari is Professor of Classics at the Berkeley University of California.

Francisco J. Gonzalez is Professor of Philosophy at the University of Ottawa.

Elsa Grasso is maître de conférences in Philosophy at the University of Nice.

Christoph Horn is Professor of Ancient Philosophy and Practical Philosophy at the Institut für Philosophie of the University of Bonn.

Annie Larivée is Professor of Philosophy at Carleton University of Ottawa.

Kathryn Morgan is Professor of Classics at the University of California, Los Angeles.

Glenn Most is Professor of Ancient Greek at the Scuola Normale Superiore at Pisa, and Professor of Social Thought at the University of Chicago.

Christopher Moore is Lecturer in Philosophy and Classics, and Ancient Mediterranean Studies at Penn State University.

ELIZABETH PENDER is Senior Lecturer in the Department of Classics at the University of Leeds.

CHRISTOPHER ROWE is Emeritus Professor in the Department of Classics and Ancient History at Durham University.

HAROLD TARRANT is Professor of Classics at the University of Newcastle.

FRANCO TRABATTONI is Professor of History of Ancient Philosophy at the Università degli Studi of Milano.

GERD VAN RIEL is Professor of Ancient Philosophy at the Institute of Philosophy of Leuven University.

ACKNOWLEDGEMENTS

Most of the essays included in this volume are based on papers given at a conference held at the University of Ottawa in May 2008, in the context of the Research Group in Hellenic Thought. The other essays were especially written for this volume.

The conference was organised by Catherine Collobert. The organizer is grateful to the SSHRC (Social Sciences and Humanities Research Council of Canada) for its generous financial support.

The editors would like to give special thanks to Gabriela Cursaru and John MacCormick for their excellent work in preparing the manuscript; and to Laura de la Rie, Peter Buschman, Caroline van Erp, and Irene van Rossum for their patience and friendly professionalism.

NOTE

Since the theme of this volume should also be of interest to those who are not specialists in either Ancient Philosophy or Classical Studies, the editors have decided to avoid using Greek fonts in the text for the most part, but to add quotations in Greek in footnotes.

INTRODUCTION

Catherine Collobert, Pierre Destrée and Francisco J. Gonzalez

This volume seeks to show how the philosophy of Plato relates to the literary form of his philosophical discourse. Myth is one topic whose importance for the study of Plato is only now beginning to be recognized. Reflection on the uses and role of myth in Platonic thought is indeed essential not only for understanding Plato's conception of philosophy and its methods, but also for understanding more broadly the relation between philosophy and literature, given that myth is in the first place a poetic discourse. We can distinguish between two types of relation between philosophy and poetry: 1) a relation of critique and conflict and 2) a positive and constructive relation. We could add a third relation which is one of exclusion. Yet if philosophy excludes the literary art, as Peirce would have it, Plato would be no more a philosopher than is Montaigne.

The divide between philosophical discourse and literary or poetic discourse has haunted philosophers from the very beginning and up to contemporary developments. What we witness today is either a radicalisation of this divide or its annulment by way of bringing into question the categories that made the differentiation possible, as in the case of Derrida. In treating literature as something fundamentally other, philosophy seeks to associate itself with science. If this is a possible orientation for philosophy, it is not the only one. The other possible orientation is on the side of literature. While Plato might appear to have inaugurated the relation of conflict, his philosophy is in many respects an example of overcoming the conflict. Plato's philosophy in effect presents itself as a poetic philosophy. Plato is a writer in the literary sense of the word. Not only did he write dialogues, but he also created myths whose ambiguous epistemological status reflects the ambiguity of the relation between philosophy and literature itself.

Deceptive, fictional or mimetic, myth in its relation to *logos* defined as reasoned discourse appears at once as both same and other. *Logos* easily becomes myth and vice versa. Plato blurs the boundaries and the difference becomes less pronounced: myth becomes an integral and constitutive part of philosophical discourse. While not a verifiable discourse, myth possesses a truth content that makes of it an object of interpretation. This means that Plato possesses the key to the philosophical interpretation of the images that he creates and that he sometimes places this key in the hands of Socrates who transmits it to us. To take this key in hand is to commit ourselves to a hermeneutical task that gives us access to certain truths. It is always possible that these truths to which a myth gives us access are not of the same order as those to which dialectical reasoning gives us access. In other words, while some myths complement dialectic argumentation and in this sense illustrate conceptual discourse, others appear to transcend reasoned discourse in providing a synoptic view of an inaccessible reality, such as the eschatological myths that conclude a dialogue.

Myths raise important methodological questions with regard to the capacity of language to represent reality and of discourse to persuade. If a myth is in some cases more persuasive than a reasoned discourse, this apparently would not be the case for an audience of philosophers who place more trust in reason than in imagination and who distrust stories of questionable morality. A case in point is precisely the number of scholars who refuse to take into account the myths in Plato's dialogues. On the other hand, the diversity of ways in which Plato uses myth suggest, if not the complete absence of a theory of myth, at least the absence of a coherent theory. This does not mean that there is no coherent usage of myth and no coherent function attributed to myth.

This volume comprises twenty chapters, which elucidate the various uses and statuses of Platonic myths in the first place by reflecting on myth *per se* and in the second place by focusing on a specific myth in the Platonic corpus.

The first part of this volume is dedicated to questioning from various angles what are Platonic myths, how we could identify them and interpret them.

The three first chapters investigate as a starting point the vexed question of the *muthos-logos* distinction. In 'Plato's Exoteric Myths,' Glenn W. Most elucidates the intricacies of the relation between *muthos* and *logos* in Plato's dialogues by establishing a set of eight criteria, which eventually allows him to offer a provisional repertory of the Platonic myths. These criteria thus are tantamount to various characteristics of a Platonic myth: (1) it is monological, (2) its narrator is older than his listeners, (3) it is said to belong to oral sources, (4) it is unverifiable, (5) it derives its authoritative quality from the tradition, (6) it has a psychagogic effect, (7) it is descriptive or narrative, and (8) it is located at the beginning or at the end of a dialectical exposition. Most further tackles the problem of the addressees of Platonic myths, thus addressing the more general question of the reception of the exoteric Platonic works.

Monique Dixsaut in her 'Myth and Interpretation' attempts to explicate the new definition of *muthos*, with which Plato provides us, to pave the way to illuminate Plato's various uses. A specific difference between *logos* and *muthos* lies in the enigmatic form of the latter. In consequence, a *muthos* in order to be understood calls for an interpretation. However, this is not true of all myths but only of the Platonic ones—Plato, Dixsaut argues, regards *allegoresis* as a waste of time on the grounds that traditional myths are 'the products of human imagination'. Dixsaut identifies three rules of non-allegorical interpretation that the interpreter should follow: he must 'know himself,' 'identify whom the myth is about,' and be aware that 'the message of the myth is prescriptive, not cognitive'. She further applies these rules to Plato's myths.

The question as to how to interpret Platonic Myths is revisited by Harold Tarrant. In his 'Literal and Deeper Meanings in Platonic Myths,' he maintains that the surface meaning of Platonic myths should not be rejected on the grounds of the existence of a deeper meaning. He supports his view in relying on the Neoplatonists' hermeneutics. Even though Platonic myths comprise fantastic elements, they can be both taken at face value and considered to convey a deeper meaning. The fantastic elements may constitute markers for the addressee to look for a deeper meaning. Tarrant examines several myths from *Protagoras*, *Meno*, *Gorgias*, and *Pheado* and especially the myths of judgement, in addition to the *Timaeus-Critias* to argue for a double meaning in Plato's myths, that is, the literal and deeper meanings.

The next three chapters examine the status of the Platonic myth from the perspective of the Platonic art of writing. In 'Freedom of Platonic Myth,' G.R.F. Ferrari investigates the truth status of Platonic myths, first in eschatological myths like the *Gorgias* and, second, in the *Timaeus*. Approaching the relation between *logos* and *muthos* from Plato's perspective, that is, as a writer concerned with plot construction, allows Ferrari to argue that, 'the gradient between *logos* and *muthos* in his dialogues is—for Plato, though not for his Socrates—a formal rather than a substantial matter'. With the same fruitful approach, Ferrari tackles the status of the *Timaeus* as both a *muthos* and *logos*. As he argues, when Plato chooses 'to frame cosmology as cosmogonic myth' he means 'to render unmistakeable his sense of the limitations of cosmology as a philosophic pursuit' while nonetheless providing us with an explanation of the cosmic order intended to convince us of the beautiful order that is the cosmos.

Catherine Collobert in her 'The Platonic Art of Myth Making: Myth as informative *Phantasma*' addresses the issue by propounding a definition of myth that does not fall into Plato's own criticism of the poets as image-makers. Regarding the myth as verbal image, she argues that a Platonic myth consists of an informative *phantasma* that is distinguished from a *doxastic phantasma*. As a grasping of appearances, the latter is produced by the poet and sophist, who may not be aware of their art of illusion out of ignorance. As she maintains, 'by contrast, the philosopher shapes his image so as to point to the specific features of the original he intends to illuminate'. In consequence, the Platonic myth as a philosophic *phantasma* is shaped after a representation of truth and hence as a transfer of the *skhêma* of truth. This is why the knowledgeable image-maker to whom Socrates alludes in the *Sophist* is in fact the philosopher, who is 'a true manipulator of images', as she has it.

In 'Spectacles from Hades. On Plato's Myths and Allegories in the *Republic*,' Pierre Destrée argues that Platonic myths are not in principle very different from what Plato calls 'images', or 'comparisons', which were labelled 'allegories' by the interpretative tradition. Against a recent trend in recent scholarship which takes myths to be a purely intellectual tool in the framework of a philosophical argumentation, he defends the traditional view that myths, and images or allegories are primarily aimed at emotionally touching their audience by addressing the irrational part of their soul. Through reviewing the central images and myths of the *Republic*, he demonstrates that these forms of writing are to be conceived of as protreptical ways by which Plato aims at motivating his audience; in the *Republic*, this aim consists in motivating them, mainly through Glaucon who is the main interlocutor of Socrates, to adopt a philosophical life, and also (but both things are the two faces of the same coin) to pursue a morally good life.

The second part of the volume is dedicated to various Platonic myths and demonstrates the wide range of possible approaches to them.

The first two chapters investigate the myth of Prometheus in the *Protagoras* from two different perspectives. In 'The Pragmatics of 'Myth' in Plato's Dialogues: The Story of Prometheus in the *Protagoras*,' Claude Calame argues that we should read Plato's myths in a pragmatic way, and not, as is usually done, as if they were to be read apart from their enunciation context; in order to understand the function and role of these myths, one should take their narrative context into account, as well as their dramatic framework. This interpretative stance is exemplified with the Prometheus myth which Calame compares to other versions of the same myth of the foundational role of the hero Titanus. Thus, reoriented by the Protagoras which Plato puts on stage and in interaction with Socrates, the muthos in the sense of efficacious narration is explicitly substituted for the logos in the sense of dialectical discourse with the purpose of sustaining the opposed arguments of the dialogue's two protagonists on the subject of the teachability of virtue: there can be no 'myth' without 'poetic' recreation and without the discursive form that grants it its practical effect. The myth is neither substance nor fiction.

In his 'Religion and Morality. Elements of Plato's Anthropology in the Myth of Prometheus,' Gerd Van Riel argues that even though the debate on Protagoras' own authorship of this text is still open, this myth expresses a number of anthropological points which represent Plato's own doctrines. In other words, the myth should be read as part of Platonic philosophy, and not just as a stunning example of sophistic argumentation with which Plato disagrees. This point is made by clarifying the role of the myth within the *Protagoras*, and by pointing out a number of objective links between Plato's Prometheus story and other Platonic dialogues, namely the *Laws* and the *Politicus*. Those objective links concern Plato's attitude towards religion and his analysis of the political virtue of abiding by the law. Strikingly, however, Socrates and Protagoras draw opposite conclusions from the content of the myth. On the basis of this analysis, this contribution aims to point out the specific function of the myth in this dialogue: the myth establishes the common anthropological ground on which both discussants (Socrates and Protagoras) will rely to make their own case. This does not mean that the myth reveals a factual truth (as this never seems to be the case in Platonic myth). Rather, it represents an a priori agreement that is not submitted to a dialectical discussion, but taken for granted as a basic starting point from which divergent conclusions will be drawn.

Myths of judgment in the afterlife play an important and recurrent role in Plato's dialogues; accordingly, five chapters offer various readings of these myths which appear in different guises and contexts in the *Gorgias*, the *Phaedo*, and the *Republic*.

The first two contributions deal with the myth of the *Gorgias*. In 'Whip Scars on the Naked Soul: Myth and *Elenchos* in Plato's *Gorgias*', Radcliffe Edmonds offers a reading of the myth which insists on its link with Socrates' practice of the *elenchos*. Many scholars have interpreted the horrific image of the Great King disfigured like the basest slave by the marks of the whip when appearing before Rhadamanthys as a threat of hell-fire designed to convince the skeptical Callicles that justice pays 'in the end.' Socrates' myth, however, does not supply a missing part of the argument for a just life by threatening afterlife retribution. Rather, the graphic images of the judgment illustrate the process of the Socratic *elenchos* as a way of judging how to live a just life in this world. Plato carefully manipulates the traditional mythic details in his tale of an afterlife judgment to provide an illustration, in vivid and graphic terms, of the workings of the Socratic *elenchos*. Not only does this myth, in reforming judgment in the afterlife, illustrate through narrative the contrasts between Socrates' *elenchos* and the rhetorical arguments of his interlocutors, but the description of the judgment and punishment as the examination and healing of a soul scarred with wounds and disease illuminates the effects of the *elenchos* on the interlocutors.

In 'The Status of the Myth of the *Gorgias*, or: Taking Plato Seriously', Christopher Rowe attempts to resolve the puzzle set up by the paradoxical way Socrates is introducing the myth, i.e. introducing it not as a myth or story but as something he believes to be true. The puzzle consists in the fact that even if Plato's Socrates is supposed to believe in such things (which is already something of a stretch), in fact much of the story, and many of its most important elements, are plainly invented for the occasion. How then can Socrates regard it as 'true'? The solution offered appeals to a particular thesis about how Plato is to be read, according to which he is capable of simultaneously operating with two different sets of premises, and two different ways of understanding the world: that of his opponents or interlocutors, and his own. What Socrates is describing at the end of the *Gorgias*, Rowe proposes, is *his* quite unorthodox ideas of judgement, punishment, and suffering, dressed up and disguised as a novel story about Hades, which his audience will immediately understand (even if, like Callicles, they do not believe it), even while they miss—as we serious readers should not—the truth hidden beneath its surface.

In the *Phaedo*, Plato offers various arguments for the immortality of soul and completes the discussion with a myth of the afterlife. In 'The Rivers of the Underworld: Plato's Geography of Dying and Coming-back-to-Life', Elizabeth Pender explores the details of the extraordinary description of the underworld this myth provides us with, especially Plato's description of the rivers of Tartarus. Pender shows how carefully the myth and rivers are placed within the composition of the dialogue as a whole, and how the rivers and the underworld geography function as places of punishment and so contribute to the myth's teleological vision of a universe founded upon principles of balance, interchange and inescapable justice.

In one of two papers in the collection specifically devoted to the Myth of Er, Annie Larivée ('Choice of Life and Self-Transformation in the Myth of Er') suggests that, rather than seek to uncover some static meaning in the myth, we regard it instead as a thought experiment meant to be used creatively by the reader. This thought experiment, which involves imagining a choice of possible lives premised on the counterfactual idea that external circumstances of life are in our control, serves as a tool of self-knowledge.

Specifically, it can do so in two ways: 1) imagining past lives helps us become aware both of the kind of life we wish to leave behind and the kind of life we aspire to; 2) imagining that our current external life conditions are the product of our choice encourages us to actively use these conditions as a means of transforming ourselves. Here myth, with the imaginative play it sets free, turns out to be essential to the Socratic project of self-knowledge.

In his 'Combating Oblivion: The Myth of Er as both Philosophy's Challenge and Inspiration', Francisco J. Gonzalez focuses more on the unusual content of the myth to show how it is in tension with the project of the *Republic* as a whole. Rather than describe the world beyond, the Myth of Er describes a place of transition where human souls, neither fully disembodied nor yet embodied, gather after their sojourn in the heavens or the underworld, eager to choose a new life and thus re-enter the world of becoming. The depiction of the choice, furthermore, identifies the lives chosen with their external circumstances, makes the comparison of lives thereby extraordinarily complex, grants the 'chance of the draw' an inescapable role in determining the range of one's choices, and makes oblivion an essential condition of entering the life one has chosen. In these ways, the myth describes what evades a rational account not because it constitutes a divine reality beyond the grasp of reason but because it constitutes a human-all-too-human reality that cannot be controlled by reason. The myth thus represents everything against which the philosopher must continually struggle in that pursuit of justice for which the rest of the dialogue provides the ideal model.

With the *Symposium*, the *Phaedrus* is probably the most literary dialogue written by Plato; no wonder that myths play here an important role. Three chapters are devoted to them. In his 'The Myth of Theuth in the *Phaedrus*', Christopher Moore offers a detailed analysis of the Myth of Theuth that shows how Socrates can use myth to convey a particular lesson to a particular interlocutor. The lesson is that composing and memorizing speeches presupposes rather than furnishes wisdom or understanding. This is a truth that could evidently be conveyed without a myth and Socrates indeed insists, when Phaedrus objects to his making up stories, that the truth conveyed is what matters, not the source. If Socrates nevertheless chooses to present his lesson in the form of a myth, this is primarily because Phaedrus' character, as it is depicted in the dialogue, seems both especially receptive to myths and uncritical in his reception of them. Socrates' task is therefore to recount a myth that will sufficiently puzzle Phaedrus so as to provoke him to think about its message. The particular myth Socrates tells, in depicting two gods discussing the value of writing, might in addition reinforce the connection between speaking and pleasing the gods suggested elsewhere in the dialogue. Finally, if Plato chose to have Socrates address a myth- and speech-loving interlocutor like Phaedrus, that may be because he suspected that there is a little bit of Phaedrus in all of his potential readers.

In 'Myth and Truth in Plato's *Phaedrus*', Franco Trabattoni seeks to show that while Plato does not see the traditional myths that have simply been handed down to us as having any claim to truth, he believes that the philosopher can use myths of his own creation to express the truth. Yet Trabattoni also argues for a much stronger thesis: that the philosopher *must* use myth to convey the truth when this truth is a metaphysical one, since such truth lies beyond the limits of dialectical reasoning. Dialectic can establish that metaphysical entities such as the soul and the Forms exist, as well as demonstrate negative claims about them, but it cannot give our knowledge of them any positive content. It can arrive at the threshold between the physical and the metaphysical, but it cannot cross that threshold to give a positive description of the 'place beyond the heavens'. That task therefore falls to myth. A myth of course cannot 'demonstrate' the truth it expresses, but this only shows that in our embodied state our grasp of metaphysical reality can never be more than partial and 'irrational'.

In 'Theriomorphism and the Composite Soul in Plato,' Kathryn Morgan focuses not on any of the mythological narratives, but rather on what she calls 'mythologized images' of the soul. If these images visualize the soul in animalistic form and as compounds in which it is hard to determine what belongs to the soul and what belongs to the body, this is due to our own embodied state. While thus reflecting the limitations of our embodied perspective, however, the deficiencies of these images are also intended by Plato to provoke us to reflect on these limitations. Thus Morgan argues that we *should* press the details of an image like that of the chariot in the *Phaedrus* precisely in order to confront its inadequacies, e.g., the lack of any clear analogues for the technical, inanimate features of the image such as the reins and the chariot. If due to our embodied state we must resort to metaphorical language to express the nature of the soul—and here Morgan appears to be in agreement with Trabattoni—Plato also uses that language in such a way as to make us recognize its inadequacy.

The myth of the 'creation' of the world in the *Timaeus* is among the most commented Platonic myths, and the two chapters dealing with it are an answer to Myles Burnyeat's new, and challenging reading of it. Elsa Grasso ('Myth, Image and Likeness in Plato's *Timaeus*') grants the validity of

Burnyeat's argument that the property of being 'eikôs' attributed to Timaeus' cosmological 'myth' should not be interpreted as a defect of being merely 'likely' afflicting all discourse about the sensible world, but rather as the virtue of being 'reasonable' to which such discourse can and should aspire. In the bulk of her paper, however, Grasso seeks to restore what is lost in Burnyeat's translation of 'eikôs' as reasonable: the connection to image (eikon). Timaeus' myth is an image of a world of becoming that is itself the image of being, as well as being an image of that demonstrative, certain discourse that has being as its object: in both cases the myth aspires to be a better rather than a worse image. Grasso also shows the complexity of the kind of image at work here: neither analogy nor allegory, in which image and original are kept clearly distinct, it tends instead to blur the boundaries in the way metaphor does. Also, the way in which a myth is an image is not so easily distinguishable from the way in which a *logos* is an image. One finds oneself in a hall of mirrors where the sharp oppositions usually taken to define Platonism lose their relief.

In his 'Why is the *Timaeus* called an *eikôs muthos* and an *eikôs logos*?', Luc Brisson also challenges Burnyeat's reading by insisting that for Plato the truth-status of a discourse depends on the ontological status of its object. A myth or *logos* is *eikôs*, he argues, because its object is an image of true being. Unlike Grasso, however, Brisson does insist on a distinction between myth and *logos*, taking the former to be a 'tale' concerning origins beyond our experience (such as the genealogy of the gods, the world, and ourselves) which as such cannot be true or false, and the latter to be an account of what is accessible to experience (such as the current structure of the world). The *Timaeus*, he suggests, moves back and forth between myth and *logos* in these senses without settling for one or the other. Both, however, can only be *eikôs* because the sensible world that is their object is only an image.

Probably the most difficult myth to interpret among Platonic myths is the one Plato offers in his *Stateman*. In 'Why two Epochs of Human History? On the Myth of the *Stateman*', Christoph Horn argues that this myth differs considerably from what we know from other narratives to be found in the Platonic dialogues. It is neither a direct nor an indirect epistemic use which characterizes this myth. Plato rather tells it as a condensed doctrinal sketch of his political philosophy and his theory of history. As to the interpretative puzzle of whether the myth presupposes two or three stages of human history, Horn defends the traditional interpretation according to which the myth presupposes only two, not three stages of human history, and raises several objections against the three-stages-interpretation advanced by Brisson and Rowe. He concludes with the contrast between the politically ideal epoch of Cronos and the suboptimal era of Zeus which is the crucial point of the *Statesman*'s myth.

Taking as its starting point Glenn W. Most's classification of what should count as a Platonic 'myth' in the first chapter, the last chapter of the volume aims to expand it. In 'The Delphic Oracle on Socrates' Wisdom: a Myth?', Louis-André Dorion offers a detailed answer to the old question of whether the famous story told by Socrates at his trial before the jury in the *Apology* is a fiction. He argues not only that this story is a fiction invented by Plato, but also, and more importantly, that we should consider it a Platonic myth since it adequately satisfies all the criteria offered by Most's proposal. The Delphic oracle myth can be said to be a myth of origins, as are other myths of this kind in Plato's dialogues.

In the present volume we thus seek to understand, under different headings and from different perspectives, how and why Plato's philosophy incorporates myth into its very practice. Since the creator of myths can be considered a type of poet, this project situates itself within the broader problem of Plato's critique of poetry in relation to his own work as a poet. The present volume can therefore be seen as a continuation of the volume *Plato and the Poets* edited by Pierre Destrée and Fritz-Gregor Herrmann. We can only hope that these volumes will in turn inspire others, as we are far from believing that a question that has been with us since Plato composed his poetic and philosophical masterpieces over two thousand years ago will be settled here.

PART I

REFLECTIONS ON THE NATURE OF PLATONIC MYTHS

CHAPTER ONE

PLATO'S EXOTERIC MYTHS*

Glenn W. Most

Already at the very beginning of Greek literature, Homer takes pains to transform the transmitted *muthos*, the traditional body of legends concerning men and gods, which he and his audience received from their predecessors as their cultural patrimony, according to the concept of *logos*—rationality, humanity, appropriateness, probability—which was doubtless not only his own but also shared with many of his contemporaries: he explains the inexplicable and he suppresses the monstrous; as Longinus noted (9.7), he humanizes the divine and he idealizes the human. And so too later, Homer's initiative was followed by all his successors: in every generation of Greek culture, poets, philosophers, and ordinary listeners struggled to find some kind of mediation between the given, generally accepted, and yet sometimes simply intolerable *muthos* on the one hand and the inquisitive, ambitious, and never fully satisfied *logos* on the other.

But no one before Plato assigned to the problematic relation of *muthos* and *logos* so central a role in his thought as Plato did. This is already made clear lexically by the fact that a number of invented compound words, without which we ourselves can no longer even imagine conceptualizing this problem, are attested for the first time in Plato's works, and indeed were most likely coined by him: *muthologia* appears eight times in his writings, *muthologêma* twice, *muthologikos* once, *muthologeô* as many as seventeen times.

It is not surprising that Plato's many readers have always been perplexed by the questions not only of Plato's attitude towards the traditional Greek myths but also of the place of *muthos* within Plato's own works.[1] For no other Greek thinker attacked the traditional myths as violently as Plato did;

---

* This article is a revised version of Most (2002).

[1] Besides the works cited in the following notes, see also on Plato's myths for example Stewart (1905), Stöcklein (1937), Levi (1946), Edelstein (1949), Loewenclau (1958), Pieper (1965), Hirsch (1971), Findlay (1978), Janka and Schäfer (2002), Partenie (2009), and the articles in the present volume.

and yet no other ancient philosopher has inserted so many striking and unforgettable myths into his own works as he did. How is such an apparent contradiction to be explained? Diogenes Laertius reports (3.80) that some people thought that Plato uses too many myths—but then he goes on in the same (textually not unproblematic) sentence to justify their use by Plato in terms of their deterrent effect upon unjust people. Whether or not we wish to adopt his explanation (as we shall see later, worse ones could be and have been offered), this passage is an important testimony which proves that already in ancient times some readers had recognized this problem and attempted to come to terms with it.

The problem was rendered all the more acute by the fact that Plato's own linguistic usage regarding the relation between *muthos* and *logos* is quite inconsistent. On the one hand, a number of passages show beyond any doubt that at least in some contexts he intends *muthos* and *logos* to be thought of as being strictly alternative to one another. For example, Protagoras offers his listeners the free choice between a *muthos* and a *logos* (*Prot.* 320c); then he begins with what he calls a *muthos* (320c) and later goes on to what he terms a *logos* (324d). And yet other passages violate such a clear terminological distinction. Aristophanes calls his celebrated myth of the spherical men in the *Symposium* not a *muthos* but a *logos* (*Symp.* 193d); and in the *Gorgias*, the very same speech of Callicles can be considered by some as a *muthos*, but also by Socrates as a *logos* (*Gorg.* 523a, 526d–527a).

Thus it seems indispensable to differentiate between *muthos* and *logos* in Plato's thought; but it turns out that to do so is, at least terminologically, not possible in a clear or unambiguous way. Various passages in Plato's works provide contradictory indications about just how we are to understand the opposition between *muthos* and *logos*. Is the philosophical *logos* itself a *muthos*, or is the *muthos* a kind of *logos*, or rather the exact opposite of *logos*? Is the difference one between discourses that are inferior and superior, or bad and good, or false and true, or probable and true, or changing and changeless, or else is it a matter of something quite different? Is the difference one of objects or one of modes, or both, or neither? It is not hard to find passages in his works that point in one or the other of all these directions.

The hermeneutical discomfort engendered by this combination of urgency and difficulty has led many scholars to seek some single unambiguous criterion that would allow them to identify once and for all those parts of Plato's text which could be considered myths. In most cases, they have limited themselves to single features of either form or content; but one cannot say that the results obtained in this way have been fully satisfactory.

On the one hand, Couturat (1896) and Zaslavsky (1981) tried a purely formal approach, locating in the simple appearance of the word *muthos* a sufficient criterion for the presence of a myth—and yet the results show that Plato uses the word to mark passages that no reader except Couturat and Zaslavsky has ever considered to be myths, while some of the most famous Platonic myths (like the end of the *Gorgias* or the story of the invention of writing in the *Phaedrus*) are never called *muthos* by Plato. Croiset (1895, 288; 1896) sought a different formal criterion in the use of extended, uninterrupted speeches—but the *Symposium* for example consists of eight such speeches, of which only one or two (Aristophanes' and part of Diotima's) can be considered mythic. On the other hand, the complementary approach, defining particular parts of the text as myths on the sole basis of their content, has hardly been more successful, either because the features of content that were invoked were too vague (so Frutiger [1930], 36–37) or because the same features are found in many non-mythic passages as well and their relation to the mythic character of the myths remains unclear (so Morgan [2000], 37).

It is not hard to understand why such one-dimensional attempts to define the Platonic myths tend to fail: for our own modern concept of *muthos* arose out of the intellectual developments and cultural needs of the last several centuries and hence corresponds only partially to the ancient understanding of the term.[2] Any attempt on our part to speak of Plato's myths is necessarily anachronistic and represents an intrusive projection of our own notions into his texts, one which he could at best only partially have even understood, let alone approved. Only an approach that flexibly combines formal criteria with features of content and that above all remains critically aware of its own inescapable anachronism can hope to do justice both to Plato's ancient texts and to our modern ideas.

In comparison with the one-dimensional approaches in terms of either form alone or content alone mentioned hitherto, it seems better to try to develop further an interpretative strategy which we could call discursive and which goes back to Gaiser (1984) and especially to Brisson (1994). These latter scholars based their analysis not exclusively upon the conceptual content of the various passages in question nor upon recurrent lexical signals, but instead upon the concrete conditions of the communicative situations of the speakers and their listeners, whose pragmatic linguistic interaction with one another constitutes the unmistakable dra-

---

[2] I have discussed this general question in Most (1999).

matic quality of the Platonic dialogues. If we apply to the Platonic corpus the eight such discursive criteria which I suggest here for determining those parts of the Platonic dialogues which can be identified as Platonic myths in our sense (Appendix A), they allow us to establish a repertory of at least fourteen such passages (Appendix B). To be sure, these eight criteria are not likely to be completely uncontroversial. Some of them (though not all) admit occasional exceptions; but this means only that they should not be applied mechanically, but flexibly, tactfully, and with a modicum of self-irony. And of course the resulting repertory may well be subject to criticism, modification, and perhaps also further enlargement; but it is my suggestion that this group comprises all those texts which most easily, unambiguously, and unanimously can be counted as Platonic myths.

1. *Platonic myths are almost always monological.* Against the background of the more or less lively dialectical conversations that fill most of the pages of the Platonic corpus, the myths are differentiated in the first instance by the fact that they are presented orally by a single speaker without any interruption at all by his listeners from beginning to end. The only exception is found in the *Statesman*, where the narrative of the Eleatic stranger is repeatedly interrupted by his listener Socrates—but this exception is in fact hardly serious, for we easily understand that it is virtually impossible to restrain Socrates' exuberant discursivity, and in any case his interruptions never furnish objections or questions to the speaker but only confirm and encourage him. By contrast, in terms of the typology proposed here *Laws* 3.676b–682e is not an example of a myth narrated dialectically but, instead, of the dialectical analysis of a myth which is presupposed here and, precisely, is not narrated.

2. *Platonic myths are probably always recounted by an older speaker to younger listeners.* The speaker's comparatively advanced age is treated with respect by his listeners—otherwise it would be impossible to understand why, in the middle of the typically lively exchange of a Greek conversation, the other interlocutors suddenly fall silent and are willing to listen to one person for a long time without ever interrupting him. The difference in age between speaker and listeners is particularly emphasized in the *Statesman* (268d) and *Protagoras* (320c). The only possible exception is Aristophanes' myth in the *Symposium*; but if, as some scholars think, he was born in 460 BC, then at the imagined time of the dialogue he will already have been 44 years old, and, in any case, in this entertaining and variously anomalous situation,

a brilliant comic poet might well have sought a particular comic effect by permitting himself to pretend to be older than he really was.

3. *Platonic myths go back to older, explicitly indicated or implied, real or fictional oral sources.* Even if it seems highly probable, or even evident, to us that a certain myth was invented by Plato, he likes to pretend that it is a genuine excerpt from the real reservoir of oral legends present in Greek culture: so for example in the *Statesman* (268e–269b, 271a–b). The most circumstantial indications of a supposed tradition are found in the Atlantis myth of the *Timaeus* and *Critias*: the chain of oral transmission leads without interruption from Egypt, via Solon, Dropides and the older Critias, all the way to the younger Critias. But in other cases too, Plato likes to name allegedly reliable authorities and specific sources: priests, priestesses, and Pindar in the *Meno* (81a–b); Er in the *Republic* (X, 614b); ancestors in the *Statesman* (271a). In other dialogues where no specific source is actually named, the speaker claims to have heard the myth from other people (and hence not to have contrived it himself): so *Phaedo* 107d ('it is said'), *Gorgias* 523a, 524a ('he says,' 'having heard'), *Phaedrus* 274c ('hearing from earlier people,' 'I heard'), *Laws* 4.713c ('we have received the report'). And many of the figures and narrative schemes in Plato's myths, even the probably invented ones, are familiar from the customary Greek repertoire of traditional legends and popular tales: Zeus, Prometheus, Epimetheus, Hermes (*Protagoras*); Zeus, gods, giants (Aristophanes in the *Symposium*); stories of humans and animals, of creation, violence, transgression, and retribution.

4. *Platonic myths always deal with objects and events that cannot be verified.* Whatever ordinary humans can know by testing their experience and can communicate to others is strictly excluded as possible material from the Platonic myths. Either the myths deal with the very first things, deriving present circumstances aetiologically from the earliest times (the original judgment of the dead in the *Gorgias*, the origin of political communities in the *Protagoras*, the invention of writing in the *Phaedrus*, human sexuality and the birth of Eros in the *Symposium*, the periods of world history in the *Statesman*, Atlantis and the creation of the world in the *Timaeus*, again Atlantis in the *Critias*, the time before the first state in the *Laws*). Or else they deal with the very last things, supplying an eschatology for events after death: so in the *Phaedo, Gorgias, Meno, Phaedrus* and *Republic*. In either case, the mythic report cannot be subjected to empirical verification but must be taken on faith.

5. *Platonic myths generally derive their authority not from the speaker's personal experience but from the tradition.* For this very reason they are not subject to rational examination by the audience. Sometimes it is explicitly indicated that Plato's myths are open to being doubted by skeptical listeners: so in the *Gorgias, Phaedrus,* and *Statesman.* Or else, symmetrically, an unswerving belief in them can sometimes be stubbornly maintained against any possible doubt: so in the *Phaedo, Gorgias, Statesman,* and *Laws.*

6. *Platonic myths often have an explicitly asserted psychagogic effect.* Over and over it is explicitly indicated that listening to a myth produces great pleasure: so in the *Phaedo* ('I would hear with pleasure,' 108d), *Protagoras* ('more delightful,' 320c), *Symposium* ('I enjoyed listening to what you said,' 193e), *Republic* ('more pleasantly,' X, 614b). But the myth's appeal to its listeners' emotions goes beyond providing them with delightful entertainment: it can also supply them with a strong motivating impulse towards performing action, one capable of surpassing any form of rational persuasion (*Statesman* 304c-d, *L.* II, 663d-e). Even if Socrates is not completely convinced himself that the myth of life after death he recounts in the *Phaedo* is true, nonetheless he holds fast to it, using it like a magical incantation that fills him with confidence (*Phd.* 114d).

7. *Platonic myths are never structured as dialectic but instead always as description or narration.* The dialectical parts of Platonic dialogues are organized in terms of a variety of logical procedures: examination of premises, search for contradictions, *dihairesis* and *synagoge.* By contrast, the Platonic myths are structured either synchronically as the description of the co-existing parts of a place (so in the *Phaedo, Gorgias,* and *Republic*) or, more often, diachronically as the narration of the successive episodes of one or more larger actions (so in the *Protagoras,* in the myth of writing in the *Phaedrus,* in the *Symposium,* in the myth of Atlantis in the *Timaeus* and in the *Laws*). In this regard (and not only in this regard), the myth of the creation of the world in the *Timaeus* is a notorious problem: already in the 4th century BC scholars contemporary with Plato or only slightly later than him were arguing about whether he intended this myth to be understood as being synchronic or diachronic.

8. *Platonic myths are always found either (a) at the beginning of an extended dialectical exposition or (b) at the end of one.* (a) A Platonic myth often has the function of opening a section of logical analysis whose beginning is explicitly signalled. In the *Meno* a new beginning is said to be made with

the myth (79e–81e). In the *Protagoras* the sophist first tells a *muthos*, and when that is over he goes on to supply a corresponding *logos*. The myth of the invention of writing in the *Phaedrus* is followed by a dialectical analysis of the disadvantages of this technology. After telling his myth of the spherical humans in the *Symposium*, Aristophanes himself supplies his own *dihairesis*, classifying the kinds of human eros. Later in the same dialogue, Diotima begins with a myth of the birth of Eros, then goes on to give a philosophical dialogue and lecture. In the *Statesman* too, a new beginning is explicitly signalled by the myth (268d). (b) Or else the myth concludes an extended dialectical portion of the text, often so that the results that have already been obtained by logical means can now be repeated impressively in a mythical form: so in the *Phaedo, Gorgias, Phaedrus, Republic, Timaeus, Critias* and *Laws*.

With the exception of this eighth feature (to which we shall return later), all the other characteristics I have indicated are thoroughly typical of the traditional myths which were found in the oral culture of ancient Greece and which Plato himself often describes and indeed vigorously criticizes. This fact raises a difficult and fundamental question: what is the exact relationship between Plato's philosophical myths and the customary myths of the Greek culture that surrounded him? I would like to conclude by making a few tentative suggestions regarding this perplexing and often discussed problem.

   Let us approach Plato via the detour of his greatest student.[3] It is well known that Aristotle composed some of his works for the students and colleagues who worked with him in the Lyceum and others for people outside. Aristotle himself refers to the external writings with such terms as *exôterikoi* (8 times), *ekdedomenoi* (once), *enkyklia* (twice) and *en koinôi* (once); starting in the 2nd century AD (Lucian, Galen), the corresponding term *esôterikoi* is found for the internal writings. The difference in kinds of addressees of the two groups of writings was evidently related to a difference in their literary character: Aristotle's reputation, in the first centuries after his death, for the elegance and literary finish of his works does not correspond to the tightly argued, severe style of his transmitted writings; and, particularly interesting in the present context, we know from a fragment of his *Eudemus* (44 Rose) that at least this one exoteric work contained a myth, while some fragments of his *Peri eugeneias* (91–94 Rose) make it manifest that this was a

---

[3] Cf. especially Dirlmeier (1962), 5 ff.; also Usener (1994), Cerri (1996), Dalfen (1998).

dialogue. Both these features are entirely lacking in Aristotle's esoteric writings. Of course this does not in the least prove that myths and dialogues characterized all of Aristotle's exoteric writings; but at least it demonstrates that these features, which were entirely excluded from the esoteric writings, could make an appearance in the exoteric ones.

In general terms, the case of Plato is strikingly similar. Whatever our view of the Tübingen school, it is generally agreed that Plato too produced two different kinds of instruction for two different kinds of addressees: on the one hand the written texts we still read, all without exception dialogues and many containing myths; on the other hand his oral teachings for his students and colleagues in the Academy (there are also conflicting reports about at least one example of oral teaching for a limited external audience, the lecture 'On the Good'),[4] about whose literary form we know little or nothing for sure but which there is no reason to think were anything other than difficult in content and dry in style, presupposing considerable philosophical preparation in their listeners and containing neither dialogue nor myths.

Of course there are evident differences between the specific ways that Plato and his best student conceive of the nature of exoteric and esoteric writings and the distinctions between them: for Plato, esoteric communication is oral (this is not only his practice, but it is also theorized in the *Phaedrus*); for Aristotle it too is written, like his exoteric works (though we presume, no doubt rightly, that he read out these texts to his students). It is not accidental that Plato is said to have nicknamed Aristotle *Anagnôstês*, 'the reader' (*Vita Aristotelis Marciana*, 6; *Vita Aristotelis Vulgata*, 5; *Vita Aristotelis Latina*, 6), for literacy is a more ineluctable feature of Aristotle's world than it is of Plato's. And the *fata libelli* made the destinies of the two authors' writings exactly complementary: in the case of Plato it is only the exoteric writings that have been transmitted, whereas his esoteric teaching is only reported to us indirectly and incompletely; in the case of Aristotle it is only the esoteric writings that are well represented in direct transmission, whereas the exoteric publications that made him famous in the centuries after his death have survived only in scant fragments.

In his writings, Plato himself gives striking examples of how he conceives of both kinds of transmission of philosophical teaching. Anaxagoras is evidently for Plato a notorious example of exoteric publication (*Ap.* 26d–e, *Phd.* 97b–c): his writings are for sale at the public market and can be bought by

---

[4] The most important testimonia are conveniently assembled in Gaiser (1968), 441 ff.

anyone with enough interest and money; the buyer reads the writings aloud, from the philosophical text speaks not the author's voice but a different, not necessarily a philosophical one (cf. *Phdr.* 275e). By contrast, Zeno demonstrates paradigmatically in the *Parmenides* (127b–e) an esoteric transmission of knowledge: although he entrusts his doctrines to a written text, he does not communicate them by publishing and disseminating it, but instead he reads out orally from his manuscript to a small and carefully chosen group of listeners in a private place.

To generalize cautiously from Plato's differentiation between these modes of philosophical communication, we might say that exoteric philosophical writings must compete in the literary market-place not only with other philosophical writings for the attention of philosophically trained readers, but also with other literary texts of all sorts for the attention of a philosophically untrained public. But the most important kinds of literary works that could be found at the Greek market-place at that time were drama (tragedy and comedy) and epic poetry (above all Homer and Hesiod), both kinds characterized above all by myth and dialogue. If this was so, then a shrewd author who wanted to make sure that his writings would seem interesting and attractive not only to philosophers but also to non-philosophical readers will have ensured that they prominently displayed the same kinds of textual features that the unprofessional readers expected from the books they set out to buy.[5] Esoteric writings, by contrast, possess a high degree of monopoly within a limited discursive space and can restrict themselves to few addressees without having to worry too much about competitors. In short, exoteric writings are directed to a broader and more heterogeneous audience including non-specialist readers, esoteric ones to a smaller and more homogeneous audience comprising fewer readers but better trained ones.

To be sure, no author is exposed entirely without defence to the conditions of the literary market-place, and to a certain extent every author creates the readers he needs. But Plato and Aristotle seem to have concluded that if they wished to change the minds of their contemporaries they would have to first attract them with the bait of the very same literary devices to which they were accustomed—and then to redirect them in a completely different, philosophically satisfactory direction.

Of course the fact that Plato's and Aristotle's exoteric writings were also directed to non-philosophical readers does not mean that in their

---

[5] On Plato's relations to the poets, see now Crotty (2009).

authors' eyes they were philosophically worthless. For why bother to write them at all, and so many, and with such extraordinary care, if they had no philosophical value? Moreover, Aristotle often refers in his esoteric writings to his own exoteric publications, and calls the later 'useful' twice, and he also refers no less than seventeen times to Plato's dialogues—surely he would not have done so if he had known that his teacher regarded them as philosophically worthless.

But then just what was, in Plato's view, their philosophical value? In the *Phaedrus*, Socrates says that the only value of written communication is to remind someone who already knows the truth (275c–d, 278a); but it is hard to imagine that Plato intended his exoteric writings exclusively for internal use in the Academy, merely to remind his more forgetful students about the doctrines he had already transmitted to them orally. For why then would he have taken such pains with their literary character,[6] and how then could we explain their immediate and continuing enormous impact on outside readers like Xenophon and Isocrates, starting already in the first decades of the 4th century?

It seems more plausible to assume that Plato wrote his dialogues not only for philosophically trained readers but also, and perhaps above all, for potentially interested external non-experts, i.e. for young men (and their parents) who wanted to know what they should do in life. He wanted these writings to reach not only people who had already made the decision to devote themselves to the philosophical way of life but also, and perhaps above all, non-philosophical readers, and to convince these that their life would be less valuable if they did not study (Platonic) philosophy. In other words, Plato's dialogues were intended at least partially as parainesis and protreptic.[7] In order to reach these readers, Plato had to study, master, deploy—and then invert the most successful strategies of literary communication in contemporary Greek culture. Dialogue and myth he learned not only from Alexamenus of Styrus and Zenon (Diog. Laert. 3.48), from the Sophists and Sophron, from the mysteries and the Orphic texts—but above all from Attic tragedy and the epic poems of Homer and Hesiod, both of them genres politically institutionalized at Athens as the predominant literary forms at that time. In Plato's eyes, both genres used their linguistic beauty, their appeal to the emotions, and their unquestioned authority to transmit a dangerously false image of man and the world. In his dialogues,

---

[6] On Plato's literary artistry see especially Nightingale (1995).
[7] Cf. Festugière (1973) and especially Gaiser (1959).

he seems to have been trying to provide a philosophically correct version of both genres, using their potentially perilous means to transmit salubrious doctrines. That is why Plato can call his *Republic* and his *Laws* a good myth (*Rep.* II, 376d; VI, 501e; *L.* VI, 752a; VII, 812a) or term the latter work the best tragedy (*L.* VII, 817b).

In Plato's project of educating a new philosophical audience, his dialectic and his myths are closely bound together. It is not at all the case that only dialectic represents the true philosophy in Plato's writings: instead, Plato's myth and his dialectic are complementary and interdependent. We should recall here the eighth criterion of myths in Plato's writings indicated earlier (Appendix A8): they always stand either at the end or at the beginning of an extended dialectical exposition. On the one hand we move repeatedly in Plato's writings from the narration of a myth to an analysis of its meaning, and on the other hand the severe construction of a logical *dihaeresis* and *synagoge* repeatedly leads into a myth. Both forms of discourse are necessary because, although each one is unmistakably different from the other, nonetheless each one offers a complementary access to truth. Without *logos* there would be in Plato's writings no proofs, no analysis, no verifiability, no intellectual conviction; but without *muthos* there would be no models, no global vision, no belief, no emotional motivation.

Because no man is exclusively a philosopher and above all because none of the non-professional readers whom Plato seems to have wished especially to reach with his dialogues was exclusively a philosopher, both discursive registers, *logos* and *muthos*, are indispensable in Plato's writings. The ancient view, reported by Diogenes Laertius, that Plato's myths were intended to deter unjust men, is probably not completely wrong but only partially true: most likely they were intended not only to help to deter people who were making the wrong choice in life, but also to attract people who might yet make the right one. To achieve this effect, Plato had to use both dialectic on the one hand and myth and dialogue on the other. As a result, his own writings can best be described by a term he himself most likely invented: they are all forms of *muthologia*.

And yet, there can be no doubt that in the end Plato is not fundamentally a myth-teller but a philosopher. For all the frequency with which there are found in his works those lexical combinations of *muthos* and *logos* in which *muthos* forms the first part, *logos* the second (and in which, by the laws of Greek grammar, what is involved is a form of *logos* involving *muthos*), it is striking that there is not a single instance in any of his writings in which *logos* forms the first part, *muthos* the second (and in which, by the same laws, what would be involved would be a form of *muthos* involving *logos*): Plato may well be constructing a *muthologia*, but he is doing so within the horizon, and by the constraints, of *logos*.

APPENDIX A

Proposed Criteria for Distinguishing Platonic Myths

1. Platonic myths are almost always monological.
2. Platonic myths are probably always recounted by an older speaker to younger listeners.
3. Platonic myths usually claim to go back to older, explicitly indicated or implied, real or fictional oral sources.
4. Platonic myths always deal with objects and events that cannot be verified.
5. Platonic myths generally derive their authority not from the speaker's personal experience but from the tradition.
6. Platonic myths often have an explicitly asserted psychagogic effect.
7. Platonic myths are never structured as dialectic but instead always as description or narration.
8. Platonic myths are always found either (a) at the beginning of an extended dialectical exposition or (b) at the end of one.

APPENDIX B

A Proposed Provisional Repertory of Platonic Myths

– *Phaedo* 107c–114c: the Underworld and the structure of our earth.
– *Gorgias* 523a–527a: the Underworld.
– *Protagoras* 320c–323a: the anthropology of politics.
– *Meno* 81a–c: the immortality of the soul.
– *Phaedrus* 246a–257a: the nature of the soul.
– *Phaedrus* 274b–275b: the invention of writing.
– *Symposium* 189c–193d: the origin of sexuality.
– *Symposium* 203b–204a: the birth of Eros.
– *Republic* X, 613e–621d: the myth of Er.
– *Statesman* 268e–274e: the periods of the world's history.
– *Timaeus* 20d–25e: Atlantis.
– *Timaeus* 29d–92c: the creation of the cosmos.
– *Critias* 108e–121c: Atlantis.
– *Laws* 4.713a–e: pre-political life.

CHAPTER TWO

MYTH AND INTERPRETATION*

Monique Dixsaut

When invited to clarify his views on myth, Paul Valéry confessed to a certain 'recalcitrance of mind':

> I was unable to orient myself in my own disorder, I did not know what I should get hold of to plant my beginning into before developing the vague thoughts aroused by the chaos of images and recollections, the number of names, and the welter of hypotheses.[1]

How indeed could one orient oneself when coming to deal with a term—*muthos*—whose very denotation is uncertain, and which every attempt at specification seems to render a little more unspecified? The reason why the mind feels recalcitrant about speaking on the topic of myth (as mine certainly does) is because it senses a sort of incompatibility between its most rightful demands and what it is faced with. To quote Valéry once more,

> what perishes under the slightest new attempt at precision is a myth. Submitting it to scrutiny, subjecting it to the manifold converging attacks the wakeful mind deploys, you will see the myths dying.[2]

The critical eye does not only cause myths to die, it also makes the very concept of myth evaporate: 'Is it not dispersed, partly in the names, partly in the epic, proverb and theogony, and in fable and genealogy?'[3]

It might nevertheless be hoped that, if narrowed down to Plato's *Dialogues*, these problems about the definition and function of myth would be easier to resolve, but one soon discovers that here to the polysemy of the term one must add its ambivalence. Is it a legend, a fairy-tale which makes us lapse into second childhood,[4] or the narrative of an event, belonging

---

* Translated by Kenneth Quandt, with the collaboration of Jean Dixsaut.
[1] Valéry (1957), 964.
[2] Ibid.
[3] Detienne (1981), 326.
[4] Each and all of those who have set out to determine the number and kinds of beings there are 'seem to treat us as children to whom they are telling a story' (*Soph.* 242c).

to a primordial age, that determines the nature and structure of the universe as well as mankind's passions, activities and destinies?[5] The spectrum of the meanings and values of *muthos* stretches between these two extremes. Plato can just as soon use the term 'myth' for the tales of traditional Greek mythology as for those of his own writing, whether derived from mythology or not; as soon for stories that are fantastic as for stories that are probable; as soon for harmful as for noble lies. Not forgetting the question of understanding why he, who was the first to oppose *logos* to *muthos*, could himself make such abundant use of myth in his own writing.

The opposition to *logos* is, I fear, an unavoidable starting-point if one wishes to elucidate the new sense Plato gave the term *muthos*. *Logos*, however, is a term no more univocal than *muthos*. If, as it is said at the end of the *Theaetetus* and in the *Sophist*,[6] *logos* designates 'speech,' the phonetic expression of what has been an interior and silent discourse, then surely a myth cannot be passed along except by a *logos*. As the words *muthologein* and *muthologia* show, there does exist at least one sense of *logos* compatible with *muthos*, i.e., a certain sort of *logos* that can perfectly well have a *muthos* for its content.

Are we then to admit that *muthos* and *logos* are opposed only if *logos* means dialectical *logos* as it is defined in the *Republic* (510b), a *logos* that moves through ideas to arrive at ideas? The Hegelian formulation of that opposition is certainly the clearest of all: myth, being speculatively impotent, resorts to and wakens sensory images suitable for representational thinking whereas *logos* moves through concepts alone.[7] Plato's own use of myth would then be 'a concession to the world of senses and imagination,' to be accounted for by the fact that philosophy was then still in its infancy: myths belong to the pedagogy of the human kind. In its Hegelian rendering the opposition is drawn so radically that it entails not only that whatever is not dialectical is, regardless of its charm, to be banished from Plato's philosophy, but that whatever is not dialectical should be considered as mythical. From a slightly different perspective, the 'new interpretation' supported by

---

    [5] Such as the story told by Timaeus.
    [6] Socrates says in the *Theaetetus* (206c7–d5) that *logos* must mean one of three things, 'the first being the utterance of one's thought by means of vocal sounds with names and verbs' (τὸ μὲν πρῶτον εἴη ἂν τὸ τὴν αὑτοῦ διάνοιαν ἐμφανῆ ποιεῖν διὰ φωνῆς μετὰ ῥημάτων τε καὶ ὀνομάτων) or, as the Stranger puts it (*Soph.* 263e7–8), 'the stream which flows from the soul through the lips with sound is called *logos*' (τὸ δέ γ' ἀπ' ἐκείνης ῥεῦμα διὰ τοῦ στόματος ἰὸν μετὰ φθόγγου κέκληται λόγος).
    [7] Hegel (1832–1887), XIV, 189.

the believers in the unwritten doctrines holds that Plato 'viewed all his writings as myths,' as 'philosophical poetry'.[8]

By adopting verifiability and unverifiability as the criterion by which to distinguish *logos* from *muthos* and thereby giving *logos* a larger extension, Luc Brisson seeks to avoid this kind of conclusion.[9] A statement would be verifiable if its referent, whether it lies in 'the world of intelligible Forms' or in the sensible world, is accessible through an 'act of intellection' or an 'act of sensation,' respectively. Neither act could grasp the referents of any myth. The dividing line would then no longer be drawn between dialectical and non-dialectical but between intuitive and discursive. To verify would be to apprehend immediately the extra-discursive reality mentioned by the *logos*. The verifiability-criterion can be valid in the sensible world, since a perception can serve to prove or disprove an opinion.[10] Bur the notion of an intellectual intuition closely modelled on sensible intuition seems to run counter to the passages in the *Republic* where 'it is the *logos* itself that, by its dialectical power, comes in contact with the highest section of the intelligible' (511b3–4)[11] and where it is repeatedly stated that dialectic is the 'only path' by which one may reach the intelligible beings and the Good itself.[12] Moreover, to think that dialectical *logoi* could be verified by an act of intellection seems to me to contradict as well the correction that Socrates articulates in his comparison with the eclipse of the sun (*Phd.*100a1–3): he who examines the beings within the medium of arguments (*en logois*) deals no more with images than he who examines them within experience. In other words, they both deal with images, and consequently there is no direct grasping of intelligible realities.

The main objection, however, is that for Plato one and the same statement can be called a *logos* or a *muthos* according to whether one believes it to be true or false.[13] When Mircea Eliade advances what he calls the 'least

---

[8] Reale (2004).

[9] Brisson (1982), 125–137.

[10] See e.g. *Phlb.* 38c–39a: if the walker came closer to the thing he sees from afar, perception would be enough to enable him to identify it.

[11] Τὸ τοίνυν ἕτερον μάνθανε τμῆμα τοῦ νοητοῦ λέγοντά με τοῦτο οὗ αὐτὸς ὁ λόγος ἅπτεται τῇ τοῦ διαλέγεσθαι δυνάμει.

[12] This is not the place to dispute that question, but see *Rep.* 533c and 534c; cf. Dixsaut (1999).

[13] Cf. *Gorg.* 523a1–2: ἄκουε δή, φασί, μάλα καλοῦ λόγου, ὃν σὺ μὲν ἡγήσῃ μῦθον, ὡς ἐγὼ οἶμαι, ἐγὼ δὲ λόγον. Belief cannot of course be a criterion to differentiate *muthos*, since I can believe in some stories (about historical facts, for instance) and think they are true, as well as it might seem to me, and to Plato, impossible and nuisible to believe in the *muthoi* Homer tells about the gods (cf. *Rep.* II and III).

imperfect' definition of the myth, he is intent on stressing that myth is considered a 'true story' because it always refers to realities.[14] A cosmogonic myth is 'true' because the existence of the world corroborates it; a myth about the origin of death is true because man's mortality proves it; and so forth. A veritable *logos*—a dialectical *logos*—is always true, but a myth can also say true things: the tales we tell children 'are surely as a whole false, though there are true things in them too' (*Rep.* 377a3–5),[15] and our tales are also useful when we speak about ancient things impossible to know and 'try to liken our lie to the truth as best as we can' (382c10–d3).[16] The fact that a myth is necessarily a fabrication does not imply it is false. But if myths happen to be true it is because an inspiration makes them able to 'touch something of the truth,' and consequently they can express truths only in a 'blended way resulting nevertheless in a discourse which has some claim to plausibility' (*Phdr.* 265b6–7).[17]

1. On the Interpretation of Myths

That is why I think disregarding the point of view of truth and adopting instead that of *meaning* or signification is an approach to the difference between *logos* and *muthos* both less questionable and more fruitful. For truth is another term that in Plato is too polysemic to serve as a criterion: does one mean ontological truth? or propositional? or even a kind of verity that is merely verisimilar? A dialectical *logos* is not only true, it controls its own *meaning* by bringing into question and correcting the signification of each of the main terms it uses, and it can also give an account of all the moves it had to make in order to discover what a certain being truly is. On the other hand, a *logos* that expresses an opinion either affirms or denies something about something; understanding this sort of *logos* depends on the familiarity one has with the language spoken and on some well- or ill-founded representation of what it refers to. Neither of these two types of *logos* is enigmatic. Whether dialectical or doxic, and whether true or false, a *logos* does not provoke the question 'What can it possibly mean?' nor does it allow a suspicion to arise that it might possess a hidden meaning.

---

[14] Eliade (1963), 16.

[15] πρῶτον τοῖς παιδίοις μύθους λέγομεν; τοῦτο δέ που ὡς τὸ ὅλον εἰπεῖν ψεῦδος, ἔνι δὲ καὶ ἀληθῆ.

[16] ἀφομοιοῦντες τῷ ἀληθεῖ τὸ ψεῦδος ὅτι μάλιστα, οὕτω χρήσιμον ποιοῦμεν.

[17] ἴσως μὲν ἀληθοῦς τινος ἐφαπτόμενοι ... κεράσαντες οὐ παντάπασιν ἀπίθανον λόγον.

But there exist some utterances that by virtue of their inspired character lead us to realize they are saying something more or something different
from what they are saying. These disclose their meaning only upon interpretation. The *Dialogues* offer many examples. In order to understand the
oracle of Apollo, Socrates conducts his inquiry by questioning and analysing
the answers of those who are believed to be wise (*Ap.* 21b sqq.); he has come
to grasp the meaning of his familiar 'demonic sign' (*Phdr.* 242b–c); he is
able to give Protagoras a lesson on how to interpret a poem of Simonides
(*Prot.* 342a–347a), just as he works at deciphering certain ancient maxims
that he cites in the *Phaedo*;[18] and if he has no doubt about what the lady
in white appearing in his dream wishes to tell him (*Cr.* 44a–b), he has in
his prison certain dreams whose meaning he tries to elucidate but which
remains uncertain (*Phd.* 60e1–2).[19]

And yet he categorically refuses the endless task involved in the interpretation of the traditional myths:

> PHAEDRUS: But you, Socrates, in the name of Zeus, do you believe the story to
> be true?
>
> SOCRATES: If like the wise I were to disbelieve it, I would not be exceptional.
> Like them I could advance a scientific interpretation and say that it was a
> Boreal wind that made her [Orytheia] fall from those rocks nearby when she
> was playing with Pharmaceia, and because this was how she died she is said
> to have been seized by Boreas.[20]   (*Phdr.* 229c6–7)

If acting 'like the wise' and not believing in this menagerie of monsters
and other outlandish things (*atopiai*) entails that one 'attempts to reduce
every one of them to the standard of probability'[21] by 'means of some
crude skill or other' (*agroikôi tini sophiai chrômenos*) the attempt would
require much too much time—maybe even every waking moment. Socrates
rejects the practice of physical allegorising which had become prominent
before the time of Plato for the simple reason that he does not have time
to waste in providing a 'justification' for the fantastical by translating it

---

[18] *Phd.* 62b, 63c, 67c, 69c, 70c, 81a, 107d. See Dixsaut (1991), 48–65.

[19] ἀλλ' ἐνυπνίων τινῶν ἀποπειρώμενος τί λέγοι.

[20] εἰπὲ πρὸς Διός, ὦ Σώ-κρατες, σὺ τοῦτο τὸ μυθολόγημα πείθῃ ἀληθὲς εἶναι; — Ἀλλ' εἰ
ἀπιστοίην, ὥσπερ οἱ σοφοί, οὐκ ἂν ἄτοπος εἴην, εἶτα σοφιζόμενος φαίην αὐτὴν πνεῦμα Βορέου κατὰ
τῶν πλησίον πετρῶν σὺν Φαρμακείᾳ παίζουσαν ὦσαι, καὶ οὕτω δὴ τελευτήσασαν λεχθῆναι ὑπὸ τοῦ
Βορέου ἀνάρπαστον γεγονέναι.

[21] αἷς εἴ τις ἀπιστῶν προσβιβᾷ κατὰ τὸ εἰκὸς ἕκαστον (229e2–3), Hackforth's translation (1972
[1952]), 24.

into natural terms.[22] For this kind of translation moves from unreal figures toward 'realities' that are no more real, in fact, since they are only sensible images. This kind of allegorical interpretation in effect reinforces a belief in the reality of what is mere image, a belief in the truth of what seems to be likely. Better is a naive faith (*pistis*) in what is unlikely,[23] in images that are not copies of an intelligible paradigm but mere fabrications of human imagination, phantasmagorias of poets; one can credit these only fleetingly and as a matter of play.

It is better not to seek to comprehend something that has nothing comprehensible about it. The function of all mythology is precisely to shield the incomprehensible from any demand for justification, to accept its existence while stripping away all its terrifying aspects, thanks to the endless supply of images that issue forth from the free play of imagination. In Greek mythology, says Creuzer, the heavy seriousness of the dawn of time has degenerated into a free play of fantasy. Socrates decides therefore to take the traditional myths at their face value, and to adopt in respect to them the same attitude adopted by the survivors of great catastrophes, who in their *naïveté* 'accepted as true the things that were said about gods and men' (*Laws*, 679c2–8).

The allegorical interpretation of myths will never teach anyone anything, and merely substitutes the likely for the unlikely. And yet it is an allegorical method that this same Socrates applies to the nouns of his language in the very long etymological section of the *Cratylus*, without any sign of being disheartened by the hugeness of the undertaking. The crude skill of the *Phaedrus*, called here Euthyphro's 'demonic skill' (*daimonia sophia*, 396d), descends upon him suddenly and causes him to break forth into prophecy. The method of etymology does have an affiliation with the prophetical, the oracular, the poetical, the mythical—with all the types of utterances that elude a spontaneous, immediate understanding. It is a method favoured by every kind of exegesis, given the presupposition that an 'original' wisdom (*sophia*) is packed within the words of the language, a wisdom that it is the task of another wisdom (*sophia*) to spell out and make clear. It reveals what is supposed to be the authentic and fundamental speech that had been deposited, in a concentrated form into each word. In etymologies you

---

[22] The *Cratylus* takes place at a time when the theory and practice of etymology, together with those of allegorical interpretation, are on the increase; see Pépin (1990), § IV and § V, and Dixsaut (1990), 59–70.

[23] Cf. πειθόμενος (230a2) which stands in contrast to εἰ ἀπιστοίην (229c6), εἴ τις ἀπιστῶν (229e2).

may hear the voice of the origins, and this voice must be heard because the etymological meaning, transcending all the meanings-in-use, is the true meaning of the word, deriving its profundity and its authority from its mythical authors: the Gods, the Muses, the Ancients, the sages. According to etymological interpretation language is a rich repository of symbols, and only secondarily a system of signs.

However, if one gains nothing by seeing in the rape committed by Boreas the action of the North wind, one also gains nothing by making the natural aptitude to 'run' (*thein*) the etymology of 'gods' (*theoi, Crat.* 397b–c). At the beginning of his prophesying, Socrates specifies that his inquiry will not really bear on the gods but 'on whatever opinion that men may have had (*hên pote tina doxan echontes*) about them when they gave them their names' (*Crat.* 401a4–5), 'it is obvious that he who first established the names assigned them according to what he thought things to be' (436b5–6).[24] The series of etymologies will show how language brings along with it an 'unconscious metaphysics,'[25] that of universal flux. It is this small unnoticed error at the beginning (436d)—the identification of Nature with incessant flux—that the giver of names has assumed as an implicit principle when shaping all the other terms. Thus what is doing the speaking in language is nothing but the truths and errors of opinion. To assert that everything in language relies on opinion does not at all mean that language always begets falsehood. Language only inherits, and passes on, *opinions*, opinions that can be true or false, inspired or ill-inspired. The play on *mantike/manike* or on *eros/pteros* proves nothing; for Plato a word's etymology is no proof but in jest, though one can use it to point at the path to be followed when inquiring into the meaning of a word. Just as the wish to signify is not realized once and for all in language, so the will to give meaning to the world and to the life and death of men is not realized in myths, and yet that is precisely the claim being made by allegorical exegesis. Just as one finds at the core of words but human opinions, one finds in myths but the products of human imagination. Naive credence is then for Socrates the best way to avoid taking the myths seriously.[26]

---

[24] οἷα ἡγεῖτο εἶναι τὰ πράγματα, τοιαῦτα ἐτίθετο καὶ τὰ ὀνόματα.

[25] Bergson's phrase. He often uses it to refer to an experience which fixes and oversimplifies all things as opposed to that which grasps them in real duration and change. His criticism of language is akin to Plato's, but the metaphysics language conveys is the very opposite of what it is for Plato.

[26] The same decision is repeated in *Tim.* 40d7–8: 'we must be persuaded by those who have spoken in former times' (πειστέον δὲ τοῖς εἰρηκόσιν ἔμπροσθεν) about the gods of traditional religion and their genealogies.

The *Timaeus* (71a–72b) brings up an entirely different mode of interpretation, when it comes to deciphering signs sent by the intelligent part of the soul to the irrational part during divinatory dreams. Recognizing that the mortal soul can be guided only by images and simulacra, the god, says Timaeus, conferred upon a certain organ, the liver, the power to receive and reflect images that come not from external objects but from the immortal part of the soul. In order to apprehend them the soul must be purely receptive, must have no self-initiated movements, and must be in an unconscious state (*aphrosune*). Its power of divination (*manteia*) allows the part of the soul that has no share of reason (*logos*) or reflection (*phronesis*) 'to come in contact (*proshaptoito*) somehow with truth'—in the *Phaedrus* (265b7), Socrates also said of the discourses he had just made that they had 'touched' (*ephaptomenoi*) something of the truth. But the irrational soul comes in contact with a sort of truth through images whose meaning can only be grasped by means of a particular *techne*, the prophetic art. This passage from the *Timaeus* is the first instance of distinction between divination and prophecy. The meaning he gives to the term *prophetes* is not the usual one, 'he who speaks in the name of another':[27] instead, he has it refer to the rational interpreter of divinatory delirium, whose art consists of understanding the meaning of the prescription and to discriminate (*krinein*, *Tim.* 72a4) the good from the bad. This is just what Socrates does in the *Crito* (44a) when he interprets his dream about the lady dressed in white: he understands that in announcing him his death, she announces him nothing bad, since the most important thing is not to live but to live well.

For after all to what kind of truth is the epithumetic part of the soul able to accede? And what true things can simulacra possibly contain? Mantic is the means that thought adopts for guiding the actions that have their source in the appetites. Images and simulacra therefore embody prescriptions. Divination is a prescriptive art, not a cognitive one. It is not a correct perception of present, past or future events. The truths enclosed in images are not true because of their conformity to experience; 'touched' by the desiring soul, they impose on it an orientation that is right but unreasoned, they are

---

[27] The few occurrences of *prophetes* in the *Dialogues* follow the common use ('spokesman'): this is true of the *prophetes* in the myth of Er (*Rep.* 617d2, 619b3, c4), of the cicadas, *prophetai* of the Muses in the *Phaedrus* (262d4); and of Socrates, the *prophetes* of Protarch and Philebus (*Phlb.* 28b8). The distinction between *mantis* and *prophetes* may have been implied in *Charm.* 173c, considering it is deleted in Socrates' 'dream'. See Dixsaut (2003).

principles on which correct actions can be based. When intelligently guided, the appetitive part instinctively avoids the bad and chances upon a due measure.

The truths conveyed by divinatory dreams are always personal. They announce the good or the bad as it pertains to *someone*. In the *Phaedrus* (242c, cf. *Ap.* 31d), Socrates says that his daemon is not a high-ranking daemon yet it gives him all the insights he needs, and gives them only to himself, who is then no better than an illiterate who only knows the letters that make up his own name. Solving a riddle is coming to understand to whom it pertains. 'Man' is the response to the riddle of the Sphinx; 'the philosopher' is the key to the maxims 'difficult to understand' Plato cites in the *Phaedo*: the life that is pure is a metaphor for the purification of philosophy, and the initiate and the bacchant are metaphors for the philosopher; the sojourn among the gods is a metaphor for thought's contact with the intelligibles. Such sayings make no sense *per se*, and do not even deserve being believed in or passed down, except to those able to make sense of them. But interpreting them does not amount to extracting a meaning that venerable sages have hidden there but to exploit them as media for a new meaning. The generosity that Socrates shows in the way he transforms ancient guesswork into metaphors can also go by the name of irony.

The prophet, says Timaeus, will never grasp what the symbolic images or utterances signify unless he is 'sound in mind' (*sôphrôn*), or has come back to his senses: the same man can be a *mantis* while he is asleep and a *prophetes* when he is awake. To divinatory *mania* is opposed the *sôphrosunê* that the *prophetes* needs. This *sôphrosunê* requisite to the prophetic art cannot be reduced to not being delirious: it is the *sôphrosunê* prescribed by the Delphic inscription. It consists of knowing oneself and attending to one's own concerns. Before being able to interpret any oracle the prophet must first decipher the oracle which enjoins 'Know thyself'. The dream that had kept on coming throughout his life, Socrates says in the *Phaedo* (60e–61b), offers a good example of this rule, as it presents Socrates with a difficult problem of interpretation: is he to understand that he must doubt, at the very moment of his death, the thing of which he was certain through his entire life, the identity between 'philosophy' and the highest work of art (*mousikê*)? Why should the god not be satisfied with the music that is 'the highest'? Why does he insist on a 'popular music'?

Socrates had at first understood the dream to be encouraging him to continue on the same path. This first interpretation entailed a proud refusal to write: why write like a writer when one *thinks* like the divine being that the philosopher is? The reason for it becomes clear as death draws near: while it is enough for a deity to communicate his utterances and dispatch his oracles, a man must have an awareness of his limitations, know himself, and have the humility to engage in writing. Apollo told him to compose and Socrates obeys in the end. One might sense, in the shift from the first interpretation to the second, that Plato is taking an opportunity to remind us, through the voice of Apollo, that there is no other way a man can participate in immortality than by this labour, all too human and hardly divine, of composing and writing. In any event Socrates' hesitation shows that interpreting means supplying a meaning, not discovering it (the dream could have either meaning, or it could have both). If one succeeds in finding the word that solves the riddle, that word is never the last word; one knows well that man is a much more terrifying enigma than the oracle for which he serves as the solution.

To summarize up to this point: myth belongs to the category of utterances that need to be interpreted. That it can be and must be interpreted in order to be understood is what opposes *muthos* to *logos*. This can also serve to distinguish between two species of myths: those that are not worth the trouble required by any interpretation, and those that repay the effort one chooses to invest in trying to grasp their meaning. One hardly needs to add that the latter are for Plato the ones that he composed himself. Allegory, as the 'attempt to redeem myth,'[28] fails to interpret myths except by taking them as allegories, which comes to seeing myth as the sensible translation of intelligible truths: any act of decoding presupposes a previous encoding. So an allegorical theory does not credit mythology with any intrinsic value, though it recognizes that the signification attributed to myths by the practice of an allegorical method has some theoretical truth.[29]

This is precisely the kind of interpretation Socrates protests against; he does not take the outlandish creatures of traditional mythology seriously enough to spend his time deciphering them or arguing whether the tales are true or false. But the reflection in the *Timaeus* on interpreting divinatory dreams furnishes precious indications for isolating the three rules of non-allegorical interpretation. The interpreter must (1) know himself; (2) make out *whom* the message is talking about; and (3) be aware that what he sets out to decipher is prescriptive and not cognitive.

---

[28] Pépin (1990), 45.
[29] *Id.*, 74.

I will now attempt to see whether applying these three rules to the myths we find in the *Dialogues* opens up avenues of exploration or leads to dead ends.

2. On Myths as Interpretations

2.1. *The Interpreter Must Know Himself*

In the only passage where one finds Plato presenting something like an *ars interpretandi*, self-knowledge is seen as a prerequisite to determining the signification of an enigmatic vision or utterance. The problem is that it was precisely in the name of self-knowledge that in the *Phaedrus* Socrates refused to waste his time examining 'extraneous matters' (*allotria*, 230a1):

> I myself have certainly no time at all to give to those things. The reason, my friend, is this: I am not yet able to 'know myself' as the Delphic inscription enjoins. It seems to me ridiculous to examine extraneous things as long as I am still ignorant of that. And so I let those things go and accept the current beliefs about them: as I was just saying I submit to examination not those things but myself. Am I some savage beast more twisted and fuming with pride than Typhus, or a tamer and simpler animal, whose nature participates in some divine, un-Typhonic destiny?[30]   (229e4–230a6)

Socrates has better things to do than interpret myths because myths will not help him come to know himself. But he is not content merely to quote the Delphic maxim, he adds an interpretation of it: the alternative, savage beast or gentle animal tamed and taking part in the divine, is not at all implied by 'Know Thyself'. The interpretation is distinctly Socratic (or Socratic-Platonic), as is proven by the fact that 'know' (*gnônai*) is immediately glossed as 'examine' (*skopein*). Socrates sends packing the monstrous figures of the Centaurs, the Gorgons and the Chimaera, but these may not be so extraneous after all since it is possible that Socrates, or more accurately his soul, might have some kinship with the savage creature Typhon is. His self-knowledge seems to have something to learn from the way that myths represent certain forces, forces to which he cannot be altogether sure his

---

[30] ἐμοὶ δὲ πρὸς αὐτὰ οὐδαμῶς ἐστι σχολή· τὸ δὲ αἴτιον, ὦ φίλε, τούτου τόδε. οὐ δύναμαί πω κατὰ τὸ Δελφικὸν γράμμα γνῶναι ἐμαυτόν· γελοῖον δή μοι φαίνεται τοῦτο ἔτι ἀγνοοῦντα τὰ ἀλλότρια σκοπεῖν. ὅθεν δὴ χαίρειν ἐάσας ταῦτα, πειθόμενος δὲ τῷ νομιζομένῳ περὶ αὐτῶν, ὃ νυνδὴ ἔλεγον, σκοπῶ οὐ ταῦτα ἀλλ' ἐμαυτόν, εἴτε τι θηρίον ὂν τυγχάνω Τυφῶνος πολυπλοκώτερον καὶ μᾶλλον ἐπιτεθυμμένον, εἴτε ἡμερώτερόν τε καὶ ἁπλούστερον ζῷον, θείας τινὸς καὶ ἀτύφου μοίρας φύσει μετέχον.

soul has no relation. To know oneself one must know one's soul and to know one's soul one must know what a human soul is. This passage in the *Phaedrus* recalls the image in Book 9 (588c–e) of the *Republic*, where the human soul is 'likened to one of these many natures the tales say to have existed in olden times, such as the Chimaera, Sylla, Cerberus and the throng of others in which many forms grew naturally together in one (*sumpephukuiai ideai pollai eis hen genesthai*)'. Every human soul is inhabited by forces (figured by the shapes, *ideai*, of a hydra, a lion and a man respectively) that can be tame or wild. The figure of Typhon is in the *Phaedrus* the symbol of the inhuman element in man, but there is also in him something participating in the divine: such an association endows man with a nature in no way less fantastic than that of the Centaur. What is presented by Socrates as an alternative is in fact an absurd and monstrous co-existence.

The outcome of the confrontation between these contradictory forces is never assured, and so it is not necessarily a human soul that will be found inside a body that has a human shape, since what characterizes the human soul is its ability of both 'becoming like the divine so far as it can' (*Tht.* 176b–c) and 'leaning toward one or another animal nature' (*Pol.* 309e2–3).[31] '*If* by chance the education turns out to be correct and the inner nature is benign, man can become the most gentle of animals; *but if* his upbringing is neither adequate nor appropriate he will be the most ferocious of animals ever to roam the earth' (*L.* 766a).

Any man can glimpse in myths the instability of his species and the uncertainty of his nature, and get an inkling that there is in himself more of the infra-human and of the supra-human than there is of humanity. There can be uncertainty during the life he is presently living as to which force it is that prevails within his soul, but the sequence of incarnations reveals which of those forces has won out, as well as revealing the absence of any essential difference between human souls and the souls of animals and those of gods. This is what the 'reincarnations' of the *Phaedo* mean (81e–82b), where the ruling principle is that the souls will go into creatures similar to themselves, that is to the nature of their habits and practices during their previous lifetime. Whence we have a burlesque parade consisting of asses (e6), of wolves, falcons and kites (a4–5), and of bees, wasps and ants (b6–7), setting up the topology of the myth at the end where 'each type of soul will see that the place it is destined to go is determined by its habitual way of life'.

---

[31] ἀποκλινεῖ μᾶλλον πρὸς θηριώδη τινὰ φύσιν.

These two principles (the absence of any essential difference between human souls and the souls of animals and of gods, and the link between the choice of a way of life and the following reincarnation) are found again in the Myth of Er, and in the ironic metamorphoses at the end of the *Timaeus* (90d–92c). The descending evolution of the species, from the human species to the species of fish, needs only slight changes. A similar uncertainty—though this time it concerns the mode of existence of those living under a divine shepherding—colours with irony the depiction of a supposed Golden Age: will it be a state verging on peaceable animality, with men passing their time drinking and eating, and sharing stories like the ones the Stranger is now telling about them, or will it be the condition of divine men, who give themselves over to philosophy (*Pol.* 272b–d)? In either event the peaceful and domesticated animal living in the age of Kronos becomes, once the world is left to itself, a savage beast, and the more savage as its technical intelligence is greater.

The *Phaedrus* (246c–d) presents yet another possible anthropology; there the human species is not a higher animal species but a species endowed with the lowest kind of divine soul, a soul whose wings have lost their feathers. A human soul is simply a soul that 'by an unfortunate turn of luck' (*tini suntuchiai*, 248c6) has become forgetful and heavy, and has fallen. Precisely because of the perplexity they betray, it is myths that cast the most light on the human condition, since they correct the error of contrasting men as mortal with gods as immortal while requiring you to ask in any given encounter, 'Is this is a man?'[32]

It is at least certain that our soul, as opposed to divine souls, is not made solely of good elements; it is a blend of whose proportions even the god and his servants who composed it have but an imprecise knowledge (cf. the increasing impurity of the mixture in *Tim.* 41d). And it is also certain that we do not inhabit the true Earth and do not live in the age during which the world was entirely under the control of gods.

But what world do we inhabit? In which age do we live? It is not only the nature of man that is amenable to alternative conceptions: '*if* ... *if instead* ...',[33] the questions extends to the universe as a whole: 'Now *if* really (*ei men dê*) this world is beautiful and if the Creator is good, it is obvious that he was looking off to that which is eternal; *but if* (*ei de*) the opposite—one can't even say it without committing an act of impiety—it is toward that

---

[32] This of course alludes to Primo Levi's *Se questo è un uomo* (2005 [1947]).
[33] Besides *L.* 766a just quoted, see *Pol.* 272b8, c5: εἰ μὲν ... εἰ δὲ.

which comes to be and passes away' (*Tim.* 29a2–4). It is not impossible that man is just an animal; not impossible that the cosmos is just a chaos subject to chance and necessity; and not impossible that we are living during the world's evil epoch, in which mankind has not yet invented a political order capable of overcoming a state of nature consisting of a war of all against all—since for Plato the majority of existing constitutions do nothing more than perpetuate this state.

Myth alone is able to point to this depth of chaos or non-sense that subsists and persists. It is not the fictions myth presents that are fantastic, but the fact that man so easily accommodates himself to the lack of sense of his own existence and of the world he lives in. If the interpretation of myths is based on self-knowledge and contributes to it, it is because myth alone is able to make *visible* the senselessness of it all.

2.2. To Understand the Meaning
of a Myth Is to Identify Whom the Myth Is About

Intelligence and right opinion constitute the whole range of knowledge; their objects are the only objects of cognition, or for that matter are the only ones to be called 'objects'. As a consequence, attempts to determine which objects belongs to mythical discourse proper tend to assign to the latter a domain of 'intermediate' realities—that is, souls, since they are objects neither of intellection nor of perception. This is the position of Cassirer, taken up by many others in different forms. Hirsch's position is a little different: myth can speak about anything, but whatever it speaks about it relates to the soul and the soul's experience. Myth would then be 'the story of the experiences (a story that for *logos* remains paradoxical) that the soul has of the unity of its origins and its destiny, a unity whose duration continues beyond time and exceeds all becoming.' It is 'the expression (*Ausdruck*) of life and its problems'.[34] Myth can indeed speak about anything. The intelligible Forms are presented in all their glory in the myth of the *Phaedrus*: Justice, Temperance, and Science (247d) nourish the wings of the soul and the divine thought, and Beauty shines forth with the most vivid clarity. On the other hand the 'probable myth' (*eikôs muthos*) which makes up the *Timaeus* speaks of the sensible world and all that it contains, including souls. There is no class of things that either requires or excludes being spoken of mythically.

---

[34] Hirsch (1971), x.

But myth speaks in a different way, and if it speaks in a different way it is because the myth-teller is *seeing* differently. As K. Reinhardt so excellently puts it, myth arises out of a vision and a *pathos*.[35]

'Seeing' is indeed what myths are all about in Plato. The *Gorgias* ends with the story of how Zeus required the judges in the after-life to adopt a new point of view. Zeus decides that man, 'naked and dead,' will be judged by a judge who is himself naked and dead, 'viewing the soul in itself by means of his soul alone' (523e3–4). His decision reveals how unjust is the justice of this world when viewed by a kind of seeing that does not allow itself to be influenced by appearances and false testimony but is able to look directly at what is invisible, namely the soul. The image this myth gives of true justice, this dream of a world where each person would be judged for what he is— for what his soul is and not for what he appears to be or possesses—seems to have very little relation (not to say none) with the several approaches to the Idea of Justice we find in the *Republic*. The viewpoint of Zeus in the *Gorgias* on the way justice had been rendered 'before,' and the measure he adopts for guaranteeing that judges have a just viewpoint—this story (*muthos*) does not present in images what is the aim of the *Republic*: a definition (*logos*) of the Form of Justice. Rather, the myth shows how inevitably unjust are the judgments passed by judges who are not dead and not naked.[36] Most of all we are to perceive and feel and believe that the only unavoidable penalty, in the face of which there is no chance of impunity, is that which the choice of an unjust life inflicts on the soul.

Commenting on the myth of Gyges (359d–360b), Lévinas sees in it 'the impunity of a being alone in the world',[37] a being for whom the world is a spectacle in which the others are nothing but means or obstacles to his self-gratification. This world, where nobody speaks to anybody and nobody sees anybody, is in fact the absence of a world—a desert. In his 'solitary liberty, uncontested therefore and unpunished,' the shepherd is a being 'who sees those who look at him without seeing him and knows that he is not being seen'. The fact of not being seen reveals to him a greater power: being able not to see. One must be able not to see others in order to be capable of murder and usurpation.

The myths at the end of the *Phaedo* and the *Republic*, in the *Phaedrus* and the *Statesman*, not to mention the *Timaeus*, widen the angle of vision and

---

[35] Reinhardt (2007), 133–134.

[36] 'Unjust' according to true opinion: a judgement taking into account the power or the wealth of the accused is not found, or felt, 'just' by any social standard.

[37] Lévinas (1971), 62.

present us with a grand spectacle. The narrator has, or rather *is*, a view of the whole, because he gazes down from above or from the outside of what he describes. He makes us see what he alone can see, but also what others see from their several vantage points and how they see it. To be viewing from above or from below, from the outside or the inside, and having a vision of the whole as opposed to a partial vision, are not incidental matters in the myths of Plato. Much has been made of the fact that Plato often confers the myth onto a foreign voice: those of Protagoras the Abderitan, Diotima, priestess of Mantinea, Er native of Pamphylia, the Egypyian priest of Sais and Timaeus of Locri, the Eleatic or the Athenian Strangers; even Socrates, in the only dialogue where he 'crosses the frontier' and tells a long story, which would be taken by anyone, Phaedrus says, 'for a stranger being shown the country by a guide' (*Phdr.* 230c8). Such is no doubt Plato's way of indicating that the story being told has been borrowed from a variety of sources, and more generally that it is always made to originate in the imagination or the memory of *others*.

But it seems to me equally important to take into account the fact that *relating a myth is to make us see*. 'So, envision some men' (*idê gar anthrôpous, Rep.* 514a2–3), Socrates enjoins Glaucon at the beginning of the myth of the cave; Glaucon replies: 'I see' (*horô, ephê*) to which Socrates repeats: 'see, then' (*hora toinun*, 514b7–8). 'Here is how one would see this earth if one viewed it from above' (*Phd.* 111b5–6). 'We have introduced this myth so that it might be shown (*endeixaito*) ... so as to see (*idein*) more clearly' (*Pol.* 275b). It is necessary that someone sees if he is to make us see, someone who is entirely identified with the perspective he adopts; it is his perspective that creates the spectacle we are given to see.

In the *Phaedo* our Earth is measured from an elevated perspective, and our existence thereby takes on a putrid character. Submerged 'in an air so very heavy that it deprives everything around us of its colour and deprives our eyes of their clarity of vision,' our Earth has 'a diseased and eroded' character.[38] By opening an upper region of the Earth, the myth restores the true proportion according to which the world is structured and denounces the illusions that belong to each of the partial views within. There results a relativisation of all points of view and a hierarchy of partial viewpoints: at the bottom, the viewpoint of the fish-men living in the region of the sea; then that of the men who inhabit the crevices of the earth, living in groups like frogs beside a pond; and finally that of the bird-man who can see the

---

[38] Reinhardt (2007), 105.

true Earth and the true hierarchy of the elements within it and thus can give them their veritable names. The limitation that belongs to each locale only renders more praiseworthy the rare attempt of a wise fish to see what the 'frogs' (men) see; and the rare attempt of a wise man to see what the birds see: at all levels the 'wise' make the effort to raise their heads.

But a world no less unknown opens up beneath. Er the Pamphylian must hear and observe 'everything there is in that place' (*Rep.* 614d2–4).[39] First he sees the movements of souls, crossing each other as they come and go. As in the *Phaedo* and in the *Phaedrus*, the myth supplies the expanse of space needed for their voyages and it structures the space according to their differences. Er's mission is to report back all that he sees, but he recounts much more than he could ever have seen, for he recounts what souls recounted to him about what they saw on their different voyages and he describes what those that arrived in middle of the light saw when they contemplated the structure of the entire universe. But the one spectacle that he affirms was really worth seeing (*tautên gar dê ephê tên thean axian einai idein*, 619e7) is the spectacle of the souls choosing their lives. The verb *idein* is then repeated five times, from 619e to 620d, as if Er could not believe his eyes.

As to the myth of the *Phaedrus*, it unfolds a splendid spectacle, but we are not too sure where we need to stand to see it in its entirety. Clearly the vantage point is a place that is not of this world, and not of any world, since it is not the location in space that determines the seeing, but rather the seeing that engenders the space wherein what it sees might be placed. The power of seeing proper to each category of souls thus appears to be the cause of the differences between the souls, whether of gods, of beasts, or of men. I do not believe there is a need to develop the point any further: vision, in this myth, is what is at stake and is the reward of all the movements of the souls, since here vision is their nourishment (247d4).[40] Though 'only the soul that has beheld truth may enter into this our human form' (249b6–7) so that all men, from the philosopher down to the tyrant, must have seen something of the Forms, some of them have had a fuller vision and can recall it. During the journey with her god, the soul looked down upon what we now assert to be and raised the eye towards what truly is. The recollection of that journey is the experience of reminiscence (249c2), the single experience that still connects to its original condition the mutilated soul which has lost its plumage.

---

[39] καὶ διακελεύοιντό οἱ ἀκούειν τε καὶ θεᾶσθαι πάντα τὰ ἐν τῷ τόπῳ.

[40] θεωροῦσα τἀληθῆ τρέφεται καὶ εὐπαθεῖ.

The *Timaeus* in a sense pushes the theme of viewing to its limit, since it invites us to see our world as the image of what the Demiurge actually sees. As to the Cave, I'm not sure there is any valid reason for calling it an allegory rather than a myth, at least if, instead of endlessly discussing its correspondence to the sections of the Line and thereby focusing all attention on its topology, one is willing to agree that its subject-matter is the alienation and the liberation of a prisoner's outlook, and that the essential points are the changes a prisoner goes through according to the various orientations of his vision.

It seems however there are good grounds to call the Platonic myths allegories, especially the Cave: Plato himself provides an interpretation, at the end or even in the course of presenting them. And yet how does Socrates answer when Glaucon remarks that it is a really strange image (*atopon eikôna*) he is recounting, and that he is showing him really strange prisoners? 'They are like us' (*homoious hêmin*, 515a5). His response does not render explicit some hidden meaning; these two Greek words are not the *logos* Socrates has made into a *muthos*. The prisoners are like us only because Socrates sees 'us' as prisoners. It is from his point of view that the similarity exists, and in order to understand the myth one has to share that point of view: the interpretation of the myth he is telling consists, for Socrates, of saying that this myth is the product of his interpretation. As H. Blumenberg notes, when it comes to a Platonic myth 'the antithesis between creation as primary and hermeneutics as secondary does not apply'.[41]

The Cave speaks of 'us,' not of man generically nor of mankind as a whole, but of those confined within the prison engendered by their own self-ignorance and self-alienation. What the prisoners have in common is their state of *apaideusia, apaideusia* is the perspective that compels to see 'us' as prisoners. The myth is meant to persuade us to turn our heads around, to get up and leave.

This 'us' is not the same as the one about whom Socrates declares that having saved the tale could save us in the end, if we are persuaded by it (*Rep.* 621b8–c1).[42] The myth of Er addresses all those—most likely the great majority of us[43]—who, although they have chosen justice, are not absolutely convinced that they have thereby chosen happiness also. The myth is meant

---

[41] Blumenberg (2005), 53.

[42] μῦθος ἐσώθη καὶ οὐκ ἀπώλετο, καὶ ἡμᾶς ἂν σώσειεν, ἂν πειθώμεθα αὐτῷ.

[43] According to *Phd.* 90a1–2: 'Utterly good men, and utterly bad ones are very few in number, the great majority stands in between' (τοὺς μὲν χρηστοὺς καὶ πονηροὺς σφόδρα ὀλίγους εἶναι ἑκατέρους, τοὺς δὲ μεταξὺ πλείστους).

to persuade them of the necessary connection between the two, justice and happiness, that is, to persuade them of the immortality of the soul, since if their life in this world were all there is and were the only life they should have, then the connection between justice and happiness would truly not be evident.

Featherless biped, heavenly plant, prisoner in a Cave, or for that matter an image within the great image that is the cosmos: one can grant that all the Platonic myths speak of human life, that they play with the possibilities of resolving the mystery: 'What is man'? To interpret a myth truly is to understand *whom* it is talking about, as is stated by the second rule. To say this is not to assign myth a particular object—man is not an object, it is a question—but a particular kind of vision: myths can see and speak of every thing, but whatever they look at is turned into a spectacle because every thing is viewed from the outside. So every thing becomes 'extraneous,' including the Forms: when seen, they are not considered as intelligible but as beautiful, and including one's own self since each prisoner sees but a shadow of himself on the wall. Myths express the human, all-too-human way of seeing every single thing, which is to tell oneself stories about it and thus see only images, whether visual or spoken. There exists a right as well as a wrong use of images and the use made by his three great eschatological myths is for Plato undoubtedly right.

With their long perspectives or their elevated points of view, with their calculations involving thousands of years, myths make us move in an infinite space and in a time that lengthens life by countless multiples, and thereby introduce countless occasions for downfall and redemption. The cycle of the world-ages and of the incarnations of souls, the expanse of space in which they make their voyage and encounter one another, this expanse in which the procession of the gods wings its way on high and the heart of Tartarus beats below—all this introduces the distance and detachment needed for the free play of fantasy. By widening the field of vision and transporting it into a space where the place each soul is destined to occupy some day has been predetermined, a place it will have chosen unknowing, the different geographies are tantamount to a table of destinies. To inscribe these destinies into space makes it visible that death is powerless to cancel the differences. Our souls will inhabit regions that resemble them, desolate or overcrowded, on ground shifting and stagnant if they live in the middle, turbulent and inescapable for those whose soul resembles the wave and vortex of Tartarus, boiling or icy for those who are subject to the influences of anger or hatred. The geography of the *Gorgias* is fairly simple, while that of the *Phaedo* is more elaborate; it is the sphere of the earth that in the *Phaedo* is constructed to assign a place to the human souls while in the *Phaedrus* it is the entire universe, but the message is the same: the life hereafter is a metaphor for this life here. It is not so much a matter of setting out punishments as it is of presenting a typology of souls. Myth in Plato can work like an incantation, but it also comes with a heavy dose of irony.[44]

Chaos does exist, justice is not a thing of this world, things just keep coming and going, men keep suffering and endlessly die, and yet there is no reason to view the whole affair as tragic. One must not take seriously something that does not deserve it: 'Surely human affairs are not of such great worth that one should take them very seriously; but we are forced to take them seriously—and that's bad luck!' (*L.* 803b). Er the narrator tells us what a narrator feels when he sees men choosing their (next, but most probably present) life: 'nothing was more pitiful nor more ridiculous nor more astonishing' (*Rep.* 620a1–2).[45] Pity and ridicule are also present in the myth of the Cave.[46] Traditional myths give a tragi-comic vision of human existence; the narrative of the Platonic myths has an ambivalence and irony that give them their light touch.

Their purpose is less to make us believe that just retribution exists than to give us a way to perceive the crushing absurdity in the way men live their lives. The element of fantasy in the discourse introduces a kind of distance that allows one to realize that nothing is more fantastic than the form men impose on their own existences. It is therefore a matter of describing with exactitude what men do with their souls and with their lives, the way they imprison themselves in ignorance, the tortures their foolishness inflicts on others and on themselves. What makes the account seem fabulous is that man is a fabulous beast, an animal whose monstrousness can be cast in an indefinite number of fantastical images. One must only observe and describe—there's no need to invent anything. The choice of one's life is incomprehensible even to the man who is making it, though he is no less responsible for his choice. The choice he makes has been preceded by an infinity of choices: the moment of the first choice is absolutely impossible to determine. Whether in the multiplicity of his previous lives or in a single

---

[44] At the end of his § IX on 'Myth,' Friedländer (1969 [1954]), 171–210 writes: 'Thus we gain a final perspective in which the myth appears akin to irony, both revealing and concealing'. Cf. also Reinhardt (2007), 43–46.

[45] ἐλεινήν τε γὰρ ἰδεῖν εἶναι καὶ γελοίαν καὶ θαυμασίαν.

[46] Once out of the Cave the prisoner takes pity on his former companions (τοὺς δὲ ἐλεεῖν); while his eyesight is still dim and unsteady, 'would not they find him ridiculous?' (ἆρ' οὐ γέλωτ' ἂν παράσχοι, 517a2).

life, always, one has already chosen before choosing what he wants to do with his soul and himself. But who is it that makes the choice? Who is responsible for preferring what he prefers without knowing why he prefers it? An ignorant, obviously—but what about his ignorance, has he chosen it? and how could one chose to be ignorant unless out of ignorance? There is something inexplicable about all this, and what myth and myth alone can do is to *show* it, and thereby make visible the disconcerting strangeness of the utterly familiar. Thus, it does what no other kind of utterance can do: it sets before us the incomprehensible and at the same time exempts it from needing a justification. In this way it leaves only one alternative open: one must either try to impart some sense, or accommodate to non sense.

2.3. *The Message of a Myth Is Prescriptive, Not Cognitive*

Early in the *Phaedo* (60c) Socrates is composing a *muthos* in the manner of Aesop. If Aesop, he says, had reflected on the way pleasure inevitably follows on pain he would have made a fable about it. The succession is an empirical fact, duly verified by the feelings in Socrates' leg, but one would never compose a fable about it unless he had reflected on its inherently illogical aspect. According to logic opposites exclude each other; but in Socrates' fabrication their necessary succession becomes the result of some god's hope to reconcile contraries, an intention visualized in the image of their sharing a single head. At one stroke the myth makes the absurdity perceptible and suppresses it through the device of a divine intervention.

With its play on sense and non-sense, cosmos and chaos, the presence or absence of the divine (of the divine intelligence, that is), mythical utterance has as its goal to persuade the irrational part of the soul with the help of images. The rhetoric it uses is affective, not argumentative: in this, myth has a function analogous to that of the divinatory dreams that intelligence sends to the appetitive part,[47] whether it is to terrorize—and the eschatological myths certainly have a dissuasive purpose—or to soothe the rebellious and obstinate part of the soul with consoling promises. Er makes us see that it is possible to rise above the element of chance and misfortune that all human life brings with it, and to reconcile fate and choice, necessity and freedom. However, myth not only enjoins us to orient our conduct properly. It also brings us to correct the erroneous names we give things. And in this it has a

---

[47] The influence proceeding from the reason can strike terror into the appetitive part, or rather use sweetness and make it thrive in gentleness of mood (*Tim.* 71b–d); on the fact it is in both cases in a state of divination, see Dixsaut (2003), 275–291.

dialectical function. It makes evident, not by demonstration but by reaching an elevated perspective, that our mistaken denominations go along with the narrowness of our vision.[48] If we 'raise our heads'—or turn them—we will no longer mistake for reality what is mere simulacrum, for happiness sheer heteronomy, we will no longer confuse the good statesman and the divine shepherd, and so forth.

But every myth Plato composed is meant above all to persuade us of the power of intelligence, a power we must imprint on whatever rebels most strongly against it, in the most disorderly places of the cosmos, the city, or the human soul.

In his second speech in the *Phaedrus*, after having shown the connection between intelligence, eros and reminiscence, Socrates declares that 'none of our earthly poets has ever sung, nor ever will sing, an hymn to this supercelestial place that is worthy of it' (247c3–4). And yet to compose such an hymn is not at all impossible, since Socrates says one must dare to do it, and does it. The philosopher makes himself a myth-maker in order to celebrate the divinity of intelligence and the glory of the intelligible region, and also to show the fantastical and absurd aspects of human life. Like Socrates in his prison, the philosopher can compose Aesop's fables as well as hymns to Apollo. But in doing so, he no longer speaks what pleases gods but what pleases his fellow-slaves.[49]

---

[48] As shown by such phrases as: 'the period which we call a lifetime' (*Phd.* 107c), 'the various objects which we now call "beings"' (*Phdr.* 247e, cf. 249e), 'the thing to which we have given the name of "heavens" or "world-order"' (*Pol.* 269d7–8). See also *Pol.* 286b sq.: the myth of the revolutions of the Universe is said to be as long as the 'ontological' passage of the *Sophist*, but also as useful to help us 'become better dialecticians'.

[49] Cf. *Phdr.* 273e–274a.

CHAPTER THREE

LITERAL AND DEEPER MEANINGS IN PLATONIC MYTHS

Harold Tarrant

1. The Hermeneutics of Myth among Later Platonists

While this paper will seek to explore the meaning of Plato's issues in terms
that would have been more familiar to those we usually refer to as 'Neoplatonists' than to us, it does not arise from an unqualified commitment to
what they have to say about Plato's myths or about the interpretation of
Plato more generally. However, there were among them serious and scholarly readers who had studied these issues at a time of greater awareness
of religious texts relevant to the hermeneutics of myth in Plato's own day.
Although some of them were disconcertingly imaginative and had strange
religious ideas of their own, the contributions of Porphyry and Olympiodorus early and late in this period deserve our attention, while others
still worked with distinctions and principles from which we can learn. Ultimately I shall argue that the idea present from Iamblichus to Proclus, that
Plato's myths are to be understood at a deeper level *while not rejecting
their surface reading*, can be applied successfully to some or all of Plato's
myths.

Without pretending that Plato himself had any invariable concept covering everything to which we should today refer to as his myths, or that
muthos was necessarily the term that he would have given to such a concept, I wish to begin with that slippery term itself. Its meaning is flexible and
culturally loaded, and its potential for confusing those who live beyond the
culture is therefore great. While I approach the Platonic *muthos* against the
background of Neoplatonic hermeneutics, I shall not pretend that the Neoplatonists were themselves exempt from misunderstandings arising from
cultural difference. They too had to struggle to immerse themselves in the
cultural world of ancient Greece just as we do. They too were liable to misunderstandings. I wonder, though, whether it should not now be suggested
that in one respect they had an advantage over us. The hermeneutics of
myth had for generations been a philosophical subject, going back at least to

Plato's own time, as our growing understanding of the Derveni papyrus and its consistently allegorical interpretation of an Orphic mythical text demonstrates.[1]

The important part played by myth within Platonism *as a philosophy* (and not just within certain writings of Plato) had long before been recognized by Plutarch, who did not shy away from recreating his own myths in the Platonic tradition (as in the *De Genio Socratis* or the *De Facie in Orbe Lunis*) or from explaining further traditional myths from within the Platonic tradition (as in the *De Iside et Osiride*). There is some evidence to suggest that he saw himself as working here in the tradition of those who learned from Plato himself, such as Xenocrates or Heraclides, not as an innovator. What is certain is that when Plutarch sought to offer us a myth there was no suggestion at any time that he must recreate *a Platonic myth* in the same way that one might seek to spell out Platonic doctrines in different words. The stories themselves are quite different, but they are told to illustrate, or covertly to suggest, some of the beliefs that Plutarch claimed to share with Plato. They are ideally intended to be different reflections of the same basic truths, pulling the right strings to move us in the right direction, immersing the reader in a world that she was culturally conditioned to respond to.

Shortly after Plutarch, Numenius applied similar rules to the understanding of Homeric and Platonic texts, arguing from the unsatisfactory nature of the surface meaning that Homer's Cave of the Nymphs passage (frs 30–32 des Places) and Plato's Atlantis (fr. 37) alerted the attentive reader to a need for allegorical interpretation.[2] Similarly he offered symbolic interpretations of individual terms or names (frs 38, 57, 58). Numenius was ultimately the inspiration of a string of allegorical interpretations of Atlantis among Plotinus' friends Origenes, Amelius, and Porphyry, and this last seems to have reported for later Neoplatonists, including Proclus, the terms in which the debate occurred between these allegorisers and the anti-allegorisers. Porphyrian tradition represented the debate as between those who took the

---

[1] It is tempting to claim that Proclus sometimes did interpret Orphic writings in a manner consistent with the allegorical interpretations of the Derveni author and his times, seeing the Orphic Zeus as intelligent divinity (*in Tim.* III, 228.12–15; cf. PDerveni XVI, 9–15, XVIII, 9–12) as well as a demiurge (*in Tim.* I, 317.18–19; cf. PDerveni XVI, 9–15), and offering an Orphic etymology of Ouranos (*in Tim.* III, 174.7–12; cf. *in Crat.* 100, p. 63.8–10) that does not accord with that of the *meteôrologoi* of Plato's *Cratylus* (396b–c) but *might* agree with the damaged text of PDerveni XIV, 12, since Ouranos too must be named from his function.

[2] The role of Numenius here is discussed in Tarrant (2007), 39–40, and in connection with Atlantis story in particular 70–77.

Atlantis story as *historia* and those who thought it was *muthos*.[3] The terms *historia* and *muthos* are never explained, but *muthos* clearly referred to a story that is not intended to be taken literally, but should rather be read as an allegory. A *historia* was therefore a story that one reads literally. During this period the literary world, of which Porphyry's teacher Longinus was an important part, distinguished between *muthos* and *historia* in a manner described by Alan Cameron:

> *muthos* is a story containing *fantastic* elements, which one cannot believe if one takes it at face value, and its meaning must therefore be sought at a different level;

> *historia* on the other hand contains nothing totally impossible, and can thus be taken at face value, though this does not by any means imply that such a story will actually be true.[4]

This dichotomy, at least as it applied to Platonic myths, was subsequently rejected by Iamblichus, for whom the Atlantis myth was both a magnificent allegory of the constant opposition, at all levels of reality, between *peras* and *apeiron*, and something that was not such that its superficial meaning had to be rejected.[5] As emerges at various points of Proclus' commentary too,[6] none of Plato's claims were entirely impossible. There was both a deeper meaning *and* the possibility of understanding the story at face value.

The importance of keeping open the plausibility of a surface meaning emerges also, I believe, in a passage of the *Commentary on the Republic* (II, 354.24 355.7) to which Kathryn Morgan has drawn attention.[7] Proclus is anxious to deny that myths should be regarded as simply fictional, stating 'things that are not,' and to affirm that Plato thought that their preservation was valuable, *qua* interpreters of 'things that are'. Most importantly, 'they spontaneously lead those who believe/trust (*peithomenois*) them back up to the truth of things that are, although they teach without rational considerations (*eikotôn*) or demonstrations, as if in unison with our unperverted intuitions about things'. What should be noticed is that the belief or trust cannot be a belief in the deeper truth to which it will ultimately lead, so that it must presumably involve a response to what is immediately apprehended. Even so, it cannot be a wholly mistaken belief or trust that sets us

---

[3] See below for further details.

[4] See Cameron (2004), esp. 90–91.

[5] Proc. *In Tim.* I, 77.24–80.8 = Iambl. *in Tim.* fr. 7 (Dillon, [1973]).

[6] E.g. Proc. *In Tim.* I, 177.22–31, 181.21–182.2.

[7] Morgan (2000), 281–282; in order to bring out the required emphases I offer my own translation below, but I have used Morgan's for comparison.

on this road to enlightenment, but one that recognizes a conformity with our deeper beliefs, as an image conforms with its original or as a particular conforms to the universal. Even if Proclus does not here go so far as to claim that we must first take on trust the literal truth of the surface meaning, he considers it vital for the proper uplifting action of the myth that our response to its obvious meaning should not be one of doubt and mistrust. This explains why it is so important to him that the myth of Atlantis should not have a surface meaning that provokes immediate disbelief.

This innovation has been linked with a distinction between Platonic and poetic myth as it appears in Olympiodorus *On the Gorgias* (46.4–6),[8] whereby poetic myth is *impossible* to approve at face value, so that understanding it literally renders one liable to be harmed by it, although sophisticated people are driven more directly towards the intended deeper meaning; whereas philosophic myth may be approved at face value also, making it far easier to overlook the deeper meaning.

At first sight the view that I associate with Iamblichus, Proclus, and Olympiodorus looks perilous. If Plato's myths can be understood both literally and non-literally, then one must seek a double meaning for every myth in Plato. But how does one recognize a passage as 'myth' (and so know to look for a double meaning) unless Plato has especially labeled it as such, which is not his consistent practice? On this principle every Platonic text with which the interpreter chose to find some opaque meaning might be claimed as a myth, and then be de-mythologized and re-mythologized at will. However, the position that they resisted was scarcely any better, denying as it did that *any myth* can be understood at the surface level. Everything that one disagreed with in a Platonic text could conveniently be labeled 'mythical' and treated as symbolizing something that one finds less worrying. Even so, just because a hermeneutic principle applied to Plato's myths is hazardous, this does not necessarily mean it is wrong.

2. How to Recognize a Myth: Some Clues in the *Protagoras*

In these circumstances we require some means of recognizing what is a myth in Plato and what kind of de-mythologizing might therefore be legitimate. The sharpest distinction between *muthos* and *logos* is to be found in the *Protagoras*. Protagoras himself makes the distinction (320c2–4), gives a reason for choosing to begin with *muthos* (c6–7), and signals his move

---

[8] See Tarrant (2007), 83.

to *logos* a little later (324d6–7). So we have clearly contrasted examples of this character's *muthos* and his *logos*. Both constitute parts of Protagoras' explanation of the problems posed by Socrates concerning the vexed claim to teach civic excellence. A key factor in Protagoras' initial choice of *muthos* is his *seniority*. It seems that *muthos* is more charming just as long as the speaker is older or in some other sense more senior than his listeners. The Eleatic Stranger may tell a myth-like story early in the *Statesman*, but his seniority to young Socrates is not in question. Likewise Phaedrus will always defer to Socrates in the *Phaedrus*. But in many dialogues Socrates does not tell such stories until at the close he has earned by debate the right to be taken more seriously. Whereas he will not be surprised if Callicles reacts to the final myth of the *Gorgias* as if it were some old lady's tale (527a), his newly established credibility adds to the readers' confidence, however puzzled they may be, that there must be an important message here.

The social dynamics of myth, then, are such that one expects to be able to classify tales told by the old to the young as myths. Myths must travel from generation to generation, and require that storytellers should ordinarily be older than their listeners. This of course has implications for the status of the Atlantis story, which has supposedly been passed down from the old to the young within Critias' family (20e, 25d–26c), as from the mature Egyptians to the child-like Greeks (22b). Critias' claim that his tale is *pantapasin alêthês* seems to misdiagnose the beast with which he is dealing, whereas Socrates' welcoming the fact that it is a genuine *logos* and not an invented *muthos* (26e) is not without its irony.[9] On the other hand, following best ancient practice,[10] we should not take Timaeus' remarks about his own creation-story being a *muthos* too seriously. In actual fact he is *apologizing* to Socrates that he may not be *consistently* able to offer an accurate and uncontroversial picture. We should expect no more, thinks Timaeus, but that does not stop him aiming higher. Socrates seems to be the senior figure here, if anything, and we do not have the correct social situation for Timaeus to be using a myth. In fact he much more often calls his aim an *eikôs logos*,[11] leaving any

---

[9] Hawtrey (1983).

[10] For a discussion of Proclus' treatment of the *eikôs muthos* theme see Martijn (2006).

[11] Eight cases as opposed to three (29d2, 59c6, 68d2); at both 59c and 68d Timaeus is indicating that he has gone into quite enough detail on a particular matter, about which he has spoken in a distinctly un-myth-like manner. In both cases he suggests that it is now clear by what comparisons one might proceed further while preserving the *eikôs muthos*, insisting at 68d that calls for greater clarity would demonstrate an ignorance of human cognitive weakness. So the term *muthos* has a function in discouraging us from taking matters of detail as reliably established, but it has no role in the description of Timaeus' actual discourse.

suggestion of modest aims to the term *eikôs*. And at very least the creation-story offered by Timaeus is not consistently delivered in the manner that we expect of a myth.

But let us return to Protagoras' distinction for a moment. What else is it meant to accomplish? Could 'Protagoras' intend that his myth will result in a different kind of cognition from that which his *logos* yields? I think this is extremely unlikely, first because 'Protagoras' is the last Platonic character who should be seen as having such an aim. He ought, surely, to be aiming to make a change in what is 'true for us,' without any suggestion that what had previously been true for us was false. At best he could be replacing our inferior perspective with a better one, saying 'Consider it [not as you previously considered it, but] in the following way'.[12] He is telling us what we ought to think;[13] and that he should not be surprised that *arête* is teachable.[14] He can of course hope that Socrates learns,[15] but in the end it is a matter of what one thinks.[16] *Logos* is not meant to have any more powerful or lasting an effect over Socrates than *muthos*. Throughout Protagoras has been aiming to charm the gathering into abandoning disbelief, and this is exactly what is achieved in Socrates' case.[17]

Furthermore, the two are supposed to explain the two parts of his answer to Socrates' worries, the myth explaining why *politikê arête* is something Athens expects to find in any citizen, and the *logos* suggesting how this wide distribution is compatible with the view that it originates with teachers, and originates best with *special* teachers. The two parts need to be complementary, and the first part of the explanation must explain and represent excellence in such a way as to make an answer to the second possible: above all as a particularly valuable universal *technê*. Together the two parts will impart a certain understanding of the kind of thing that *arête* is and the advantages of employing teachers to enhance it. That is clear, I believe from the closing remarks: 'This, Socrates, is the kind of myth and *logos*[18] that I've told you [to show] that excellence is teachable and that the Athenians consider this to be the case' (328c3–4).

There is, however, a major difference in the way that the two kinds of material will contribute to the aim. The *logos* argues from ordinary

---

[12] ὧδε γὰρ ἐννόησον (324d7).
[13] οἴεσθαί γε χρή, ὦ Σώκρατες (325c4).
[14] ἀλλ' οὐ χρὴ θαυμάζειν, ἀλλὰ πολὺ μᾶλλον εἰ μὴ διδακτόν (326e4–5).
[15] τοῦτο αὖ μάθε (326e7).
[16] οἴει ἄν τι ... οἶμαι μὲν οὔ, 327b5–7; οὕτως οἴου καὶ νῦν, 327c4–5; οἶμαι, 328a1, b1.
[17] κεκηλημένος, 328d4; πέπεισμαι, e3.
[18] καὶ μῦθον καὶ λόγον.

human experience directly towards the conclusion that Protagoras desires, giving the impression that Protagoras himself believes whatever the *logos* claims. The *muthos* on the other hand needs only to have a certain part of its message accepted, and there is no expectation that the great agnostic himself would be committed to all the material within it, involving as it does a number of gods and other mythical figures. It does not really matter whether *politikê arête* is a gift of some god called Zeus. What matters is that it should be something analogous to the various crafts, except that it is for good reasons universally distributed; that like those crafts it should be exclusively human; and that it should be the particular gift that enables us to live in *polis*-like communities. However, the fact that the message is delivered in such a deeply embedded cultural framework enabled the listener to respond in such a fashion that she feels this gift also to be providential—a vital part of the structure of our world, more so than any of the other crafts since everybody must have it. What Protagoras finds to be important in the myth emerges at 323a–324c, which offers various considerations that support the specific conclusions that this excellence is universally distributed and that it is properly developed by some kind of instruction.

While always allowing that Plato himself had an interest in this story and would have chosen details that suited his wider themes,[19] when one considers what 'Protagoras' has hoped to achieve by the story, one has to ask whether it is any more than the basis for *one possible explanation* for how political excellence is both universally distributed among humans and properly acquired only through the learning process. He will in fact only require one possible explanation to evade the difficulties that Socrates has raised concerning the claim that political excellence can be taught. Details may be needed for *this particular explanation*, but Protagoras merely requires that excellence should work in a manner *somehow similar* to that which he has outlined in his story. No claims are ever made for its truth, provenance, or conformity with Greek tradition. Hence the account of our origins and all the divine machinery have no role to fill in the subsequent debate, until such time as Socrates has triumphed and earned the right to use the myth for his own purposes at the close of the dialogue (361c–d). The myth has supplied a framework within which excellence might be considered; the myth is used for such purposes by those with a fatherly point to make.

---

[19] These clearly include the importance of forethought in our lives, the craft-like nature of *arête* and its privileged position over other crafts as a source of salvation.

3. The *Meno* and *Gorgias*

At first sight the *Meno* is similar, in so far as the senior character brings in, but does not seem to depend upon, some traditional Greek religious materials, alluding to the doctrines of a certain kind of priest and priestess (81a), poems of Pindar and other poets (81b–c), the story of Daedalus' statues (97d–e), and Homer's Teiresias (100a). The latter two cases are only illustrative examples, and Socrates famously refuses to commit himself to any of the details of the religious doctrines immortalized in poetry (86b). However, Socrates has earlier said of the poetic and priestly *logos* that he believes in its truth,[20] a stronger claim than any made by Protagoras for his myth. The major part of this *logos* involves the transmigration of an eternal soul, whose importance for Platonic works usually seen as late 'early' or early 'middle' period could only be doubted by the most extreme advocates of a non-doctrinal reading of Plato. The dialogue cannot build on the foundation of such a doctrine, since the reactions of young 'Meno' at 81a7, a9, and e3–5 suggests that he has no interest in sharing Socrates' belief, or indeed any theological belief. Instead Socrates attempts to show him by empirical means that knowledge is recollection in some meaningful sense. Both themes, that of the birth-cycles of an immortal soul and that of its associated ability to somehow 'recollect' something vital to proper living, are taken as serious Platonic doctrine throughout antiquity, beginning with Aristotle's *Eudemus* (fr. 5) and certain pseudo-Platonic works.

The apparent closeness of the *Gorgias* and the *Meno* makes it logical to turn next to the former. This also reflects my belief that the part of the *Gorgias* relevant to our theme, though possibly not the arguments with Gorgias and Polus, do follow both *Protagoras* and *Meno*.[21] Material of a mythical character is prepared for by Callicles' illustrative use of a scene from Euripides' *Antiope*, where the character Zethus chastises his brother Amphion, the mythical king of Thebes, to the music of whose lyre the walls of Thebes were built (485e–486c). Callicles' speech sees Euripides' reworking of this myth as something with a strong message for his contemporaries, regardless of any quasi-historical basis it might have. As if in answer, myth is first used by Socrates at 492e with Euripides' line suggesting that humans may have

[20] ᾧ ἐγὼ πιστεύων ἀληθεῖ εἶναι ἐθέλω, 81e1–2; cf. 81a8.
[21] For a two-stage view of the composition of the *Gorgias* see Thesleff (1982), and now in greater detail Thesleff (2007).

misunderstood life and death, a line suggestive of transmigration, since it implies that our present life is a 'death,' a break from the real 'life'. Socrates 'would not be surprised if Euripides is speaking the truth in this passage'.

The Water-Carriers myth is then immediately introduced, with the intention that it should illustrate the pointlessness of the life of the profligate. The clever interpreter who has explained this to Socrates gives an allegorical interpretation of the myth, whereby it depicts the state of soul of foolish humans, who have souls that 'leak,' and are doomed to go on trying to make good the loss by supplying what is missing through an equally defective vessel, an intellect suffering from disbelief and forgetfulness. Various elements here, including (i) the use of spurious etymology to equate an element in the myth with something quite different in the interpretation, and (ii) the campaign against the dissolute life, remind one of the author of the Derveni papyrus, and particularly of column V. At V.6, we read roughly as follows: 'Do they doubt the terrors of Hades at all?'[22] Then the concept of being worsted by pleasure appears, for at lines 8–10 there we read something along the lines of: 'For because they are vanquished by sin and by pleasure in general they neither understand nor believe. And disbelief and failure to understand are [the same; for if they do not] understand they do not come to know either'.[23] The dissolute life seems to lead to disbelief (*apistia*), a fault central to the interpretation of the Water-Carriers myth (493c3), while lack of understanding (or failure to learn, *amathia*) may possibly be related to forgetfulness (*lêthê*) in the same line.

It is most important that the interpreter who explains the Water-Carriers myth identifies Hades itself with the unseen soul (493b4–5), so that the message is by no means confined to another existence, and everything to do with our psychical life in this one, apparently urging us not to become incurably incontinent. Indeed, it is Callicles' reform in this life that Socrates

---

[22] ἆρ' "Αδου δεινά τι ἀπίστουσι. There may be punctuation before a question-word τί, and there are uncertainties over the first word; from multi-spectral imaging kindly shown to me by Apostolos Pierris of the *Institute for Philosophical Research at Patra*, I gather that there is a hint of οὔκουν [τε at the end of the previous line, ἆρ' is uncertain, and one may be correct in preferring the ἐν that one might have expected.

[23] ὑπό [τε γὰρ] ἁμαρτίης καὶ [τ]ῆς ἄλλης ἡδον[ῆ]ς νενικημέν[οι, οὐ] μανθ[άνο]υσιν [οὐδὲ] πιστεύουσι. ἀ[πι]στίη δὲ κἀμα[θίη ταὐτον· ἢν γὰρ] [μὴ μα]νθάνωσι μη[δ]ὲ γινω[σ]κωσ[ιν ... Square brackets here follow Kouremenos et al. (2006). Further restoration of this column, assisted by the use of multi-spectral photography, may prove interesting. However, any recent text illustrates all that is here important to me. An important monograph now tackles the relationship of the Derveni Papyrus to the *Cratylus*, and particularly to the names of the gods: Anceschi (2006).

too is trying to bring about: 'It at least shows what I want to get across to
you, if I am somehow able, persuading you to change your mind, and instead
of your insatiate and unrestrained life to choose the life which is sufficient
and capable of dealing with whatever circumstances' (493c4–8). This use
of a myth about the underworld as a direct reflection of the circumstances
of living human beings involves a process denoted by the verb 'mutho-
log-ize' (*muthologein*), a centaur of a word that acts almost as a framing
device (493a5, d3). Since Callicles has declared himself impervious to myth,
the next illustration, though clearly related and 'from the same training-
ground,' involves no use of it. We must wait until the final pages for another
myth.

This final 'myth' is actually considered a *logos* by its narrator (523b2), just
like the poetic and priestly *logos* of the *Meno*. This may remind one that
in late antiquity a *muthos* had been expected to differ from a *historia* in
having elements that were impossible or fantastic in order that it might turn
the mind to search for a deeper meaning. The myth has failed to achieve
its purpose if it does not rapidly cause the listener to undertake the search
for a deeper meaning. In the *Meno* and *Gorgias*, unlike the *Protagoras* that
involves a pair of unseemly divinities and a time beyond the reach of human
memory, the narrator is willing to treat as *logos* what his interlocutor will
write off as simple *muthos*. Perhaps Iamblichus had noticed such passages
when he claimed that a Platonic myth could be valid or plausible both at
a deeper level and when taken literally. Perhaps, in referring to the story
as 'very fine' at 523a1, as when speaking at *Meno* 81a8 of a *logos* that is
'true and fine', Socrates is suggesting the pair of qualities expected of a
logos that is also a *muthos*. Perhaps, in fact, in using the verb mutho-log-
ize (*muthologôn*), 'Socrates' had already deliberately hinted at the double
status of the Water-Carriers myth.

What seems certain is that 'Socrates' is meant to feel that tales of judgement in the underworld do reflect an actual truth, and that the story that he
offers at the close of the dialogue (regardless of details) does have *some point*
when taken literally, since the story follows immediately after claiming that
the greatest evil is to arrive in Hades with a soul infected by a plurality of
crimes (522e3–4). The myth is immediately followed by a declaration of
trust,[24] and a reference to 'these *logoi*'. 'Socrates' comes to various conclusions about the nature of death and the way we should live as a result of
it. To ignore this context is to pretend that Plato can be something other

---

[24] πιστεύω ἀληθῆ εἶναι, 524a8–b1.

than a Platonist. Little in this myth runs counter to Plato's notion of the correct depiction of divinities, and it shows these divinities working towards a more rational and fairer universe. Zeus has both providential intentions and divine powers of perception. Venerable humans behaved honourably, but could be deceived.

However, we should not forget that the Water-Carriers myth had earlier been meant to have a primary application to this present life, and that talk of the underworld in the original myth had been interpreted as applying to the unseen world of the human soul here and now. This ought to colour our response to any subsequent myth about what goes on in Hades, so that it is easy to imagine the myth implying in part that our real judgement of present lives, our own and other people's, can only for so long be deceived by the richness of our bodily surroundings. So one should therefore ask *exactly* what it is that Socrates would claim to believe.[25] Does he *believe* that the role of the gods has been exactly as specified, and that Kronos (explained at *Cratylus*, 396b as pure intellect)[26] had presided over a regime of unfair punishments and rewards? Does he *believe* that mortals once had foreknowledge of their deaths as stated by Zeus at 523d5–7? Does he *believe* in the chronological sequence he proposes? It seems to me that the myth spins out a story that is only supposed to offer an explanation of how things actually are, and I have Olympiodorus (*in Gorg.* 48.2–3) on my side. He claims that clothed and naked judgements are ever taking place, clothed in the bodily world, naked on the soul's separation:

> The interpreters have not been able to grasp this because they have traversed the depths of Plato's language; for he says this clearly and emphatically, and nothing other than this.[27]

Where then does he say any such thing? Olympiodorus is referring to the conclusions that Socrates has drawn from the myth at 524b–526d. These reflect not upon how things have been, but on how things are. Death is the

---

[25] Since writing what follows I have had the opportunity to read Sedley (2009), who ultimately offers a choice between two interpretations of the final myth, one 'purely symbolic,' the other finding a more literal truth in parts of the account of underworld punishment, a choice somewhat 'underdetermined by the text'. Such lack of determination seems to me to be characteristic of Platonic myths more generally.

[26] The Derveni Papyrus, regarding the cosmos as the product of intelligent causation in the Anaxagorean tradition, had already explained the name as signifying 'striking intellect' (κρούων νοῦς, XIV.7).

[27] *In Gorg.* 48.3 *ad fin.* (trans. Jackson, Lycos, and Tarrant [1998]); unless a negative has somehow disappeared, the implication is that many interpreters have been perpetually looking too deeply into the text in the search for a hidden meaning, presumably looking for symbolism in the meaning of individual words.

separation of soul and body, after which soul and body continue for a time to
have separately the same characteristics as they had when united, bearing
the same scars. These make a post-death judgement of the soul easy enough,
allowing the proper punishment of the curable, the eternal torment on the
incurable, and occasionally the reward of especially deserving cases. It is
only after this passage that we meet the real declaration of belief (526d4),
and this calls into question, I believe, the meaning of the declaration of
belief back at 524a8–b1. 'I trust that it is true.' What in this context can 'true'
mean?

It certainly does not mean that the myth proper was literally true in every
detail, and that there was a time when the judgement process altered exactly
as specified. It surely does mean that the story has an important message
to convey about the present. The most important truth is surely whatever
the story seeks to explain.[28] Truth claims made for myths are not ordinarily
claims about the accuracy of details of the story, interpreted literally, but
claims about its overall meaningfulness. It has something to teach us if
only we will listen. The final myth of the *Phaedo*, if that is what it is, fits
this notion well. Without affirming that this is as things are, 'Socrates' gives
the kind of account that a believer in the immortality of the soul ought to
give (114d). The reader is probably quite puzzled by many of the details, but
one cannot help recalling that the prophetic swan only sings—and sings
most beautifully—just before its death. And Socrates serves the same god
of prophecy (84e–85b). If this is the case, then Socrates' swansong too can
be expected to reflect insights into the nature of the world to which he is
departing. Maybe Socrates has earned the right to be taken seriously here;
maybe there is more in the detail than meets the eye. Ultimately I would
sum up my position on the myths of judgement as follows:

A. Myths of Judgement, while their detail may be unconvincing if taken
   literally, aim to impart a serious message in which one may legitimately believe;
B. The most important message, expounded by a combination of words
   and images that seek to express something of which there is actually
   no visible image, concerns the rewards and punishments of correct

---

[28] In much the same way Proclus, after telling us of the 'historical' approach to the
Phaethon myth affirms that: 'It is a basic requirement that the conflagration should have happened (for that is the reason for the story's being told), and that the reason given for it should
be neither impossible nor something that could easily occur.' (*in Tim.* I, 109.17–19, Tarrant's
translation [2007]). The only historical truth required for the 'historical' interpretation of a
myth was that the event explained by the story happened! Myths exist for the *explanandum*.

conduct in the unseen life of the soul here and now, and much of the detail will be chosen not because it is supposed to be literally true of the other world, but because it somehow illuminates Plato's theories about our conduct in this life;

C. Since the unseen life of the soul is not something that is ended by its separation from the body the message may be suspected of having some application also to the world beyond;

D. While as a tale of the world beyond it is most readily classified as a *muthos*, as something designed to reflect the arguments concerning our present situation it might rather be classified as a *logos*; hence its status is complicated, and dependent upon how it is viewed.

If this is so, then there may be other myths in the corpus that admit of a similar two-tier interpretation. Even if Protagoras insists on the radical division of myth and *logos* in his great *rhêsis*, there was scarcely a Platonist in Antiquity who did not see a serious voice of Plato behind the part that was myth, and for Proclus the myth was the only part of the dialogue important enough to have input into his *Platonic Theology*.

4. THE *TIMAEUS-CRITIAS*

Here I consider just one other work, the *Timaeus-Critias*. What would our theory mean for the truth claims made by Critias for the Atlantis-story and assented to by Socrates? Today there are few Platonists or Classicists who take them seriously at face value.[29] The claim that Iamblichus paid most attention to was Critias' 'true in all respects' at 20d8, but not even he interpreted this as 'true in every detail'.[30] Rather he took it to mean 'true at every level,' so that it had both its more important metaphorical meaning and a surface plausibility: because it accurately reflected the paradigm, there would, in infinite time, be some time when the paradigm was instantiated in this particular fashion. Later Platonists who took this view did not offer anything that we might refer to as historical or geographical 'evidence,' and indeed it seems unimportant to their view, which sees the literal truth as an image of the universal one,[31] to maintain that it *had happened* rather

---

[29] See now Morgan (2000), 261–271; Vidal-Naquet (2007).

[30] The principal passages for the position on Atlantis taken by Iamblichus, Syrianus, and Proclus are its introduction at *in Tim.* I, 77.24–80.8; its recapitulation at I, 130.10–132.30; and the concluding remarks about the story and its narrator at I, 191.3–192.27.

[31] *in Tim.* I, 79.22–28.

than that it *will happen*. What Iamblichus was at pains to argue was that nothing in the claims made in the story was beyond the bounds of plausibility.[32] I doubt that Plato ever meant us to think in this way, for I doubt that he ever meant us to rely on Critias' infallible judgement about a story told to him in his youth by an ageing family member, but more important is Socrates' response at 26e4–5, about it not being a *plastheis muthos* but an *alêthinos logos*. Proclus sees this as little more than corroboration of his broadly Iamblichan position:

> Then again, we should infer from this passage too that the story of the Atlantides was not a fiction, as some believed, but both a 'historical' study and one with special relevance for cosmic creation as a whole. So even the details he gave about the size of Atlantis should not be condemned as mythical fictions by those who virtually confine the earth to within a narrow strait.[33]

Even if one is as blind as Proclus to signs of irony, we have seen good reasons for not making too much of the terms *logos* and *alêthinos*. The latter is in any case better chosen to suggest that this is *truly a logos* than that it is *a true logos*, while the former need mean no more and no less than it meant at *Meno* 81a, 81d, and *Gorgias* 522e and 524b. It would be suggesting not the literal truth of details but the meaningful explanation of something genuinely in need of explanation. But might it be that the sense is further specified by the corresponding denial that it is 'not a manufactured *muthos*'? In one sense the evidence would suggest that it had been manufactured, and that Plato has drawn on all kinds of happenings, some recent like the inundations of Helike and Boura, some more distant and plausibly the object of folk-memory; and that he has manufactured a composite story out of details that are true or meaningful in their own proper contexts. Little can be done to justify Critias' claim that the story is 'in every way true' (*pantapasin alêthês*) in the sense that he himself intends, yet Plato could view it as reflecting a deeper overall truth, while offering a plurality of more straightforward lessons in its fragmented parts. Overall we have a charter myth that purports to establish the Socratic state as the true heritage of every Athenian;[34] but in fact the reader, no doubt looking for the shot of pride that public eulogies were accustomed to supply,[35]

---

[32] See here the preliminary statement of the position at *in Tim.* I, 76.17–18: 'Some do not rule it out that things could have happened in this way'; and the denial that any aspect of what was related was impossible at I, 190.9.

[33] *in Tim.* I, 197.19–24, trans. Tarrant (2007).

[34] Cf. Morgan (2000), 264.

[35] Morgan (2000), 266.

misses out on the promised detail that was expected to glorify the works of the ancient Athenians: the foreshadowed story is never told. Meanwhile the story of Timaeus tells us rather of that ancient 'state' that is the true heritage of all human beings, and the state to which we should all aspire. That state is our heritage insofar as we are souls in need of inner justice, not insofar as we are soul-body composites, and not insofar as we are citizens.

Plato left the status of Critias' story intentionally unclear. The identity of Critias himself (let alone of the missing guest at the beginning of the dialogue) seems impossible to settle on the basis of what we are told, and the question of whether the work is unfinished is another enigma. It seems certain that Plato would have expected many readers to accept most of what was said about Athens and Atlantis, at least in the beginning and before the story progresses to a level of detail that is incompatible with its supposed origins, at face value. It seems highly probable that he wanted others to be left perplexed about what he intended. The first wave of allegorical interpreters looked to explain the mythical 'war' in terms of two kinds of soul, or two kinds of *daimones*, or competing soul-circuits to explain this myth. The focus from Numenius to Porphyry was on the dangerous moment of souls coming into generation, souls that had previously endured no interruption to the smooth running of their circuits, no break with their earlier idyllic existence. The cataclysmic moment engulfed all in a sea of generation, wiped out all but a trace of memory, and destroyed our paradise as 'Zeus spoke'. The vivid images of the demise of Athens' enemies was thus interpreted as applying to an unseen realm. The *Republic* had used the analogy of justice in the vividly-depicted city to explain justice in the soul; the *Timaeus* too had urged us to model our souls on a visible cosmic paradigm just as the demiurge had modelled the cosmos itself upon an earlier paradigm; might not the *Timaeus-Critias* frame be hinting at something about the soul too?

It may perhaps be so, but appealing to microcosm-macrocosm analogies is a double-edged sword. There had never been an intention to exclude a political message from the *Republic*, still less to exclude the cosmic message from the monologue of Timaeus. Analogies work best when they are founded upon an actual or at least a possible model. For instance, we should not be taken in by Socrates' account of his own intellectual midwifery if his picture of physical midwifery were completely fictitious. If Critias' story cannot be historically true *per se*, it must nevertheless supply a meaningful account of the kind of clashes between states that do actually occur, and one in which the thinking individual can recognize *some* truth. To that extent

Iamblichus was right. A Platonic myth must be meaningful on two levels, the one more superficial and sufficiently in accord with our cultural or empirical expectations to strike us as offering a plausible lesson, the other deeper and covertly trying to convey something of which the first-time reader will not be conscious. The truth of the latter will belong to a different metaphysical order than any truth in the former. Only if the superficial meaning seems familiar to us will we allow the deeper meaning to influence our lives. Even so, Iamblichus was equally right to avoid insisting that the superficial meaning must reflect a single sequence of historical truth from the past, accurately recorded by a dutiful Solon from impeccable Egyptian records. There is surprisingly little in Proclus' *Commentary* about the provenance of the story, and no attempt to demonstrate the surface meaning by geographical, historical, or archaeological means.

A Phaedran Conclusion

If Iamblichus came close to appreciating the double-edged workings of Platonic myths it must be possible to see why. No dialogue seems to hint quite as much at the hermeneutics of myth as the *Phaedrus*. Early in the dialogue it is Phaedrus who seems to lack respect for the surface meaning of the myth of the rape of Oreithuia (daughter of Erechtheus) by Boreas (the North Wind), calling it a 'piece of mythologizing' (*muthologêma*, 229c5) and being keen to discover Socrates' attitude to what he seems to regard as the important intellectual question of the status of myths. If Phaedrus expected Socrates to declare his enthusiasm for either its obvious physical explanation (whereby a girl is blown off rocks and killed) or any other allegorical meaning then he must have been disappointed. Though he would not find it odd that somebody should doubt the story and search for a natural explanation, he thinks of such an impulse as potentially involving unending labours, because there are always further myths to challenge the interpreter's ingenuity. Such interpreters he finds too clever and industrious, while their aim is ill-directed (*ou panu eutuchous andros*, 229d4). Clearly he does not think they get myths right, even though they approach them from the point of view of likelihood (*kata to eikos*, 229e2), but he does not really explain why, merely indicating that his priority is self-knowledge, and that this leaves no time for such speculations as deal with what is alien to him. He therefore avoids these speculations, takes these stories in the conventional sense (*peithomenos tôi nomizomenôi peri auton*, 230a2), and investigates his own nature.

Two things seem missing here. The first is any clear statement about what the conventional sense is, and the second is whether his acceptance of the stories concerned is expected to enhance his understanding about his true self. The omissions seem important, the former because from the *Euthyphro* (6a–b) through to the *Republic* Socrates has been a doubter of many traditional stories, and the latter because as we have seen interpreters had already been relating myths concerning Hades to the unseen life of the soul (*Gorg.* 493b). Here in the *Phaedrus* the remarkable thing is that the Socrates who affirms that he trusts in the myth in the conventional manner immediately gives a hint that the physical imagery of the myth might in fact have some bearing for his own inner search.

With an allusion to the 'tresses of the hundred-headed Typhôs',[36] the traditional *father* of the winds (Hes. *Theog.* 869–870), Socrates asks at 230a4–6 whether he might be 'an animal more multi-tressed than Typhon and smokier (*epitethummenos*)'. Whatever Plato might have wished to signify by this term (and it is tempting to translate 'over-blown'), it is another use of *tuph*-termology (perfect participle of *epituphomai*), leading on to a third use with the other half of Socrates' question: whether he is really a gentler and simpler animal, by nature sharing in some divine and puff-free (*atuphos*, 230a6) gift. In this last case the only natural reading of the *tuph*-term is an ethical and psychological one, implying the absence of delusion vanity (*tuphos*), so that the wind-associations have somehow metamorphosed into a soul-association, which in turn looks forward to the image of opposing forces within the complex soul (253d1–e5), and to the questions of the simplicity or complexity of those being addressed that the scientific orator must address (277b–c). Whatever Socrates thought of the literal truth of the tale of Boreas and Oreithuia it has led him to think of the stormy and gentler forces within the human self, Boreas no doubt of a more typhonic one, and Oreithuia perhaps, with her associations with Attica and girlish play, with a gentler one. An uncritical attitude towards the literal meaning of a myth is by no means incompatible with reflection upon what it might mean *for oneself.*

Now Iamblichus must have been familiar with the use of *Phaedrus*, 229d–e by pre-Iamblichan literalists to argue against allegorical interpretation.

---

[36] Ar. *Clouds*, 336: whether Plato is alluding directly to the play or to dithyrambic poetry there criticized, one is immediately invited to be thinking of storm-clouds. Note that *Clouds*, 337 continues with the phrase 'crook-taloned birds that swim the air,' a remarkably threatening phrase by which to refer to clouds, and strongly suggesting avian raptors that seize and carry off their prey in their talons. It is conceivable that this and other dithyrambic phrases used here appeared in a retelling of the Boreas and Oreithuia myth.

Proclus (*in Tim.* I, 129.11–23) records the use of d3–4 as a general argument by those who resisted the allegorical interpretation not only of the Atlantis-story but also of Platonic myths in general. Then, after two further arguments, a final argument is recorded that bears some resemblance to e2–4, only offers the specific example of those who waste time explaining away everything untoward in Homer. So one can scarcely doubt that Iamblichus would have had to take the warnings of this passage into account. Perhaps he was also impressed by the literalists' second and third arguments, that Plato's style of communication was mostly direct, and that allegorical interpretation is unnecessary where a passage's presence still can be explained adequately when it is taken literally. But he might still have seen how 230a could be used to suggest the presence of a second meaning, relevant to soul. And he might also have noted the absurdity of having Socrates take as straightforward historical truth both versions of a myth that according to Socrates had alternative physical locations (229d1–2).

There is a further passage in the *Phaedrus* which is likewise relevant to the value of the surface-meaning, for Socrates' remark, following Phaedrus' suggestion that he can easily invent stories from Egypt and elsewhere, also has some significance for Platonic myths in general. People of long ago, he claims, being more naive than Phaedrus' generation, were content to respond to oracular utterances as the pronouncements of oak and stone just as long as their message was true (*Phdr.* 275b–c). While superficially a simple endorsement of the literal reading, the case cannot in fact be that simple. If a myth's provenance was irrelevant, and the only question was whether or not this was how things were, then one should hardly ignore the fact that much of the myth of Theuth had made claims about where it came from and the super-human status of the participants (274c–d). One must assume that it was not to any of this that Phaedrus needed to pay attention, but only to the basic message encapsulated in the words of Thamous with which it concluded. Phaedrus certainly understands this to be Socrates' point, and accepts at 275c3–4 that writing is much as Thamous has claimed. Questions of the accuracy of historical detail in the story of Theuth are irrelevant to the dialogue and not worthy of the reader's energies. Like the very written records that are the subject of the tale of Theuth, such detail has no independent educational value and cannot serve to teach us what we had not already once known (*Phdr.* 275c–d), whereas Phaedrus can recognize the truth of the final message from within himself. In the words of Thamous (275a5–6), Theuth has 'found not a recipe for memory but for recollection,' and Phaedrus at c3–4 gracefully accepts Socrates' reminder.

Myth is simply part of the armoury that the scientific writer will have available for reaching the minds of others. It is giving us instruction neither in history nor in physics, and neither its literal details nor any scientific interpretation can offer us instruction. It may readily be accepted as something meaningful and to be trusted, but it cannot communicate to us any propositions that are to be learned and believed, for it would mean different things to different people (275a7–b2). Expecting to receive truths into ourselves from outside sources will end in disappointment, for meaning is something that we must find through recollection from within ourselves (a2–5).[37]

It is in no way strange, then, if Plato's myths are not in need of any decoding process. As they are told, simple and unsophisticated, they retain the ability to become relevant to us by our rediscovering meaning within us. Decoded by the allegorists they can only try to tell us something, losing their ability to serve as a catalyst for our self-discovery. Iamblichus, however, does not try to tell us what myth teaches but what it gives an image (*eikôn*), symbol (*sumbolon*), or indication (*endeixis*) of. He had seen that Plato's myths require the reader's initial trust, that we are expected to respond to them as something that is in some sense true, and that their educational value is not to be held in question. Only thus could they retain the power to stimulate further understanding of ourselves the microcosm and of the universal macrocosm in which we live.

---

[37] The *Phaedrus* had begun with an emphasis on the importance of self-knowledge in the very context of the interpretation of myth (229e–230a), and even those who deny the authenticity of the *Alcibiades I* (130e) may still accept the notion that Plato sees the self predominantly as the soul. As for 'recollection' its dominant meaning at 275a appears to belong to this world, yet its appearance here will still recall the centrality of the 'recollection' of a different world which the soul may access in the myth at 250a–e.

CHAPTER FOUR

THE FREEDOM OF PLATONIC MYTH

G.R.F. Ferrari

The myth of final judgment in Plato's *Gorgias* is unusual among Plato's eschatological myths. Although it bears quite as many hallmarks of traditional myth as do those of the *Phaedo* and *Republic*, Socrates refuses to classify it as a 'myth' or 'tale' (*muthos*), despite having no hesitation in so classifying his other eschatological myths. Callicles, he has no doubt, will regard what he proceeds to say not only as a tale (523a) but as an old wives' tale (527a)—a reaction that would fit with Callicles' earlier refusal to be persuaded by images and allegories (493d), as well as with his iconoclastic naturalism (482c–486c). If Callicles is not one to swallow the conventional moral pieties by which the unambitious live, he will hardly give ear to traditional stories about the underworld and its punishments for conventional transgressions. Socrates, however, insists on classifying what he has to say about the final judgment as a *logos*, an 'account,' on the grounds that the things he is about to say, he will say 'as things that are true' (523a).

Since there is nothing in the content of the myth to render it especially unmythical, and since, at its conclusion, Socrates issues a caveat about its complete veracity that is similar to the one he attaches to the *Phaedo* myth (114c), I assume that Socrates' unusual insistence that what he is saying is *logos* rather than *muthos* is provoked by the need to pre-empt Callicles' unusually strong scepticism. He is saying, in effect, 'you, Callicles, ought to pay attention to this story—though I doubt that you will—because it isn't *just* a story, but tells the truth'. By the same token, if it is due to the special circumstances in the *Gorgias* (rather than to any quality of this myth in particular) that Socrates decides to make explicit the fact that he regards the story as a *logos*, this gives us reason to assume that he feels the same way about similar stories that he never calls anything other than *muthos*. Socrates' idiosyncratic declaration in the *Gorgias* can thereby open a window onto the nature of Platonic myth in general.

1. THE PHILOSOPHER'S FREEDOM

Readers will forgive me if I attach the beginnings of my argument directly
to the conclusion of an earlier study of mine, which examined the tripartite
soul of Plato's *Republic*. I drew a comparison there between the choices
made by the philosopher in the course of his life and those made by the
disembodied souls described in the *Republic*'s eschatological myth, the
myth of Er, when the moment comes for them to express their preferences
with regard to the kind of life they wish to lead in their next incarnation.
How rich do they wish to be? How learned? How famous? Would they
rather be an athlete or an intellectual, a woman or a man, a humble citizen
or a tyrant? They are given the opportunity to weigh the effect that each
of their choices will have on their souls, and thereby on the happiness or
unhappiness they will experience in their next earthly life (*Rep.* 618d–619a).
Each soul must draw a lot to determine how early in the process its turn
to choose will arrive, a constraint which may limit the range of choices
available when its turn eventually comes. But this limitation is never drastic
(see 619b), and no further constraint is imposed. Each soul is completely free
to choose from the possibilities on offer at the time.

Clearly, some things that such a soul can choose—the circumstances
of its birth, for example—the living philosopher could not. The crucial
point of resemblance, however, is that, as described in the *Republic*, the
philosopher is a person who makes all his choices in life with a view to how
they will affect the condition of his soul. The philosopher does not look to
the consequences of those actions in the larger world except to the extent
that those consequences have an effect on his soul's good health (see esp.
Rep. IX, 591c–592b). The result is that all the choices such a person makes
are entirely within his power. It is not that the philosopher refuses to act in
the larger world or to seek to have an effect upon it; what he refuses to do
is to stake his happiness, the health of his soul, upon such effects as he may
hope to achieve in that world. The world may stymie those hopes, just as
the lottery may fall out badly for the disembodied souls. Nevertheless, for
the philosopher, as for those souls, the opportunity to choose for happiness
is always available. And when the philosopher chooses, he chooses as freely
and as directly as if his soul were already outside of its body.

That the philosopher is able to act in life as does the disembodied soul in
the myth of Er is a claim that can readily be extended to the *Gorgias* and its
myth. The moral that Socrates draws there from his myth is that he should
work to present as healthy a soul as he can to the judges of the dead, and
that in order to achieve this goal he should live 'practising truth,' an activity

which makes him the best he can be (526d), and which he is happy to equate with 'practising virtue' (527d). In order to work on his soul, he tells Callicles, he sets aside those things which count for honours among most men (526d). That is to say, he sheds from his concern the very range of things that Zeus in the myth demanded be shed by those proceeding to final judgment, the 'clothes,' as he put it, that tend to distort judgment: the fine figures they may cut, their material wealth, their family connections (523c). They must be stripped of their bodies and judged naked, judged simply for their souls.

Socrates' practice of truth thus, in effect, strips him of his body, to the extent possible, while he is still in it. He does not wait for final judgment, but is his own judge and jury. He thinks freely. Nevertheless, he remains aware that this is a freedom achieved in the teeth of the world from which it abstracts, and that the world is under no obligation to cooperate. Socrates may *think* without arrest, but he acknowledges to Callicles that this does nothing to prevent him from being bodily arrested, dragged into court on false pretences, perhaps even punched on the nose with impunity (486b, 527c).

Contrast the kind of freedom that Callicles supposes himself to exemplify. As a 'natural man,' he will force the world to cooperate, to bend to his will, and describes the action as that of freeing oneself from enslavement to convention and social inhibition (484a). Callicles believes it possible to live entirely for the social and political world and yet still live 'naturally' (*kata phusin*, 483e). Despite bringing out the contrast between nature and convention, his Great Speech contains no language to suggest that the way to overcome convention is to strip its veneer, or pierce its mask; such are not his metaphors. What the natural man does to evade convention is to shake it, tear it apart, trample it (484a). The result is that his natural excellence becomes 'manifest' and 'shines out' (484a).[1] The natural man does not seek to manipulate appearances; he seeks to appear to others in his natural glory.

From a Socratic perspective, however, the grand reputation and the other social goods that Callicles seeks to obtain by living in the light—in the public, competitive spaces of the city (484d, 485d, 486d)—amount to nothing more than a veneer of excellence after all. What looks like mastery of the social world is in reality no better than enslavement to it, since Callicles' natural man must focus entirely on controlling it, on bending it to

---

[1] *anephanê.* Callicles strikes this verbal note several times in the course of the speech: *apophainei,* 483c; *exelampsen,* 484b; *lampros,* 484e; *ariprepeis,* 485d.

his will (see esp. 513a–d). Socrates, by contrast, believes that a better way to attempt to live free and fine is to do what can be done well with domains that are already wholly within your control, and which, for reasons independent of their being within your control, are worthy of your attention and care. One of these domains, as we have seen, is that of the philosopher's choices in life. Another, I now wish to propose, is that of myth.

2. SOCRATIC STORYTELLING

Let us take the *Gorgias* myth first from Socrates' perspective, the perspective of the character telling it within the dialogue. In what sense does it constitute a domain that is wholly within his control? Not in the sense that he has invented the tale: after all, he declares it something he has heard and been convinced by (524b, 526d). Its cast is made up of traditional gods and heroes, and some of its features Socrates attributes directly to Homer. The sense in which it is a domain wholly within Socrates' control emerges at the moment when Socrates has finished telling the initial story of how Zeus instituted the judgment of the dead. At this point, announcing himself convinced of the truth of this narrative that he has heard, Socrates proceeds to 'draw inferences' from it (524b). These inferences are not conclusions so much as they are statements of what is required by the story if it is to make sense. Death, he reasons, must involve the clean separation of the soul from the body; otherwise, Zeus's judges could not judge without prejudice, as the story requires. Furthermore, if the soul is to be judged naked, it must bear judgeable signs that are independent of the body it once wore. Just as the bodies of the recently deceased retain the marks that they bore or acquired in life, argues Socrates (notice *ara*, 524d), so too do their souls (524b–d).

Socrates' procedure at this point is, in effect, to take the world of this story and make it his whole world, inhabit it to the exclusion of all else. Let Callicles consider it an old wives' tale; Socrates will entertain no scoffing that pokes at the foundations or origins of the narrative. (Compare his reaction when Phaedrus implicitly accuses him of inventing his Egyptian tale at *Phaedrus*, 274b.) The narrative itself is his foundation, in the sense that it provides the unquestioned background against which he elaborates his thoughts about punishment and reward in the afterlife. This is not to say that he rules out entertaining objections to particular points thrown up by that elaboration. An example would be his claim that the majority of incurable souls in Tartarus are those of assorted potentates and politicians.

The very fact that he calls Homer in as 'witness' for this point suggests that he regards it as a more open question, more in need of defence, than the tale of judgment within which it features.[2]

By insulating the world evoked in his narrative from those who would sweep it aside, Socrates turns it into his sandbox, where he is free to play to his heart's content. This world imposes its constraints, of course (the sandbox has walls); but they are internal constraints only. Socrates has chosen, freely, to be convinced by this story, and, having chosen, is free to explore and to make further sense of its world in whatever way strikes him as best.

And *why* does he find the story convincing? If, with Terry Irwin,[3] we assume that Socrates finds assurance through the myth that the world reflects his moral views, then we may well complain, as Irwin does, that its being a moral tale constructed out of his moral views is hardly a good enough reason for him to believe the myth—not if it makes claims about the world, rather than just expressing his moral views. Irwin attributes this position to Socrates because of how he refers back to the arguments with Gorgias, Polus and Callicles after the myth is done (527a–b). Socrates announces there that it would not be surprising for us to share Callicles' dismissiveness of the myth, were we able to find something better and truer. But as things stand, his three interlocutors, among the wisest men in Greece, have been unable to show that any way of life is better than the one that Socrates has recommended, and which seems also to be of benefit in the afterlife. Socrates' moral views, not theirs, are the views that, here at the end of their discussion, have survived attack and stand firm.

Socrates neither says nor implies here that the dialectical arguments preceding the myth are also what prove the myth to be true, and constitute the basis on which he claims that it is true.[4] The connection between those arguments and the truth of the myth is less direct. Introducing the myth, Socrates calls it a 'very beautiful' or 'very fine' account (*mala kalou logou*, 523a). He finds it beautiful, presumably, because it expresses his belief in justice. Now, this is the same Socrates who has just defended his way of

---

[2] Augustine's procedure in Book 12 of the *Confessions* is comparable: there he encourages a plurality of interpretations of the bible provided they do not come from unbelievers, since all interpretations must be consistent with the truth—that is, with Christian doctrine.

[3] Irwin (1979), 248.

[4] *Pace* Dodds (1959), 385: 'Socrates really bases his appeal on the preceding ethical arguments'; Irwin (1979), 248: 'the myth rests on the independent moral argument of the dialogue'; Morgan (2000), 159: 'The truth of the myth stands or falls by the success of the previous arguments'.

life against three opponents, and emerged triumphant; therefore he is fully entitled to find the myth beautiful, and, believing it beautiful, want to take it to be true—even while appreciating that its beauty does not guarantee its truth. Furthermore, until an opponent shows up who can dislodge him from his convictions, there is nothing to prevent him trusting that the myth is in fact true, so far as it goes. (With Dodds,[5] I take *Phaedo*, 114d as our fullest indication of how far that would be: while no man of sense would insist that the afterlife must be just as Socrates has described, that it is either this way or something like this is an assertion worth venturing.) Not that Socrates can *prove* it true: the 'something better and truer' cannot be the dialectic that Socrates has just taken them through, since he regards this 'something' as a thing that they have not been able to find. Rather, it would, presumably, be the account that a divine being could give of these matters.[6] But in the God's absence, Socrates will put his trust in what he finds beautiful.

When Socrates turns at 527a from the admission that the myth would be worthy of deprecation were we able to find anything better and truer to the reminder of his interlocutors' earlier defeat in dialectic, he does so with the phrase 'but as things stand' (*nun de*). This phrase, I take it, implies something like the following ellipsis (which I here insert into the gist of Socrates' words rather than translating in full): 'But as things stand <I intend to hold by the truth of this story, for all that it falls short of what we might most wish to find, since> as you see, the three of you, for all your wisdom, were unable to defeat me in argument'. Socrates is explaining why he counts himself entitled to accept as true a story whose limitations he has just admitted. There is no need to foist on him here the quite implausible claim that his earlier moral arguments directly prove the world to be as the myth describes it.[7]

Nor, on the other hand, need we go to the opposite extreme, and deny that Socrates is deriving any support at all for the truth of the myth, even indirect support, from his success in argument—as does Joachim Dalfen.[8] In Dalfen's view, Socrates' implicit claim at 527a–b is that both the myth and the arguments are the best of their kind that he has so far been able to discover, and deserve to be trusted, in their different ways, for that reason. Now, while it is true that, in other dialogues, Socrates speaks of following the

---

[5] Dodds (1959), 376.

[6] Compare *Rep.* 382d, *Phdr.* 274c.

[7] Socrates' insistence that his myth is a *logos* does not imply, then, that he places myth and *logos* on a par. His insistence implicitly asserts his right to regard his story as true, despite its being a story rather than an argument.

[8] Dalfen (2004), 499.

strongest argument he can find at any time, implying thereby that he may well find a better at some later time, Dalfen makes Socrates at *Gorgias*, 527a–b evaluate his tale and his argument more evenhandedly than is warranted by the text. Of his tale, Socrates is quite deprecatory; he sounds like a man who hankers for the something better and truer, in the light of which his own tale would look shabby. Of his dialectic, Socrates is downright boastful: his thesis has held fast, through repeated argument, against the assaults of three of the wisest men in Greece.[9] Socrates does not end the *Gorgias* with a global caveat; he ends it with a claim of entitlement to imaginative freedom.

3. PLATONIC FICTION-WRITING

Now let us take the myth from Plato's perspective, the perspective of the writer. There is a strong possibility that, unlike his character Socrates, who denies originality (and whose denial we have little reason to doubt), Plato is himself the creator of the myth's most striking and important narrative feature: the storyline that derives the need for souls to be judged naked from an earlier, unsatisfactory practice of judging people on their dying day, while they were still alive and in possession of their social assets.[10] Nevertheless, and as was the case for Socrates within the fiction, the sense in which the myth constitutes a domain of freedom for Plato does not depend on his having invented it. Let him have heard it from the very lips of Archytas; once Plato has decided to incorporate it into the dialogue he is writing, it comes entirely under his own control. This is not to say that the inherited material, to the extent that it is inherited, imposes no constraints; but nothing outside of the material itself need affect how Plato chooses to deal with it.

When it comes to how the myth relates to the discussion that precedes it, however, there is an important difference in the situations of Plato the writer and of the Socrates within his dialogue. Socrates in the dialectical exchanges has to secure agreement from his opponent at each turn, as he proceeds from question to question, point to point. If his opponent shifts his ground—as Callicles, for example, often does—Socrates must adjust his line of questioning accordingly. Throughout the series of exchanges,

---

[9] True, he looks back on the dialectic at 509a with his usual claim not to know the truth of these matters. But rather than anticipate being controverted by some future discussant (always a possibility, of course), he touts his long-standing record of total victory in every discussion on this topic.

[10] On this point, see Dodds (1959), 375–376.

Socrates has an argumentative goal that he is striving to reach; but he cannot be presumed to anticipate his opponent's every move—the places where his opponent will balk at agreement, or shift his ground, or even withdraw his cooperation entirely. The fictional Socrates is arguing live, and adjusting to a live interlocutor as he goes. When he comes to tell the myth, however, his opponent's agreement is no longer required; indeed, Socrates tells the story to an audience whose contempt of such things he openly acknowledges.

(This is not to say that Socrates has forgotten his audience. By telling this myth to Callicles' face, and especially by elaborating its punishments for the greatest tyrants, he is doing two things at once, both of them with Callicles in view: he presents a picture of natural, violent justice that, considered abstractly, ought to appeal to Callicles; but he then casts a Calliclean hero in the role of principal offender against that justice. It is the verbal equivalent of giving Callicles the punch on the nose that he had so gleefully anticipated for Socrates. For that very reason, though, it is a final gesture. It neither seeks nor requires any comeback from Callicles.)

Plato, by contrast, is not working with a live audience, but writing the script for the entire dialogue: its dialectical bouts, its mythical narrative, and everything else besides. This act of writing is, for him, what the telling of myth is for Socrates: a domain that is wholly within his control—the third such domain that we have met with in this investigation.[11] Although the dialogue is packed with arguments, what it amounts to overall is a story. Plato is writing a drama, and the drama has a plot. The premise of the plot is that Socrates must win his arguments. Plato decides what obstacles to put in his way, and when to remove them—that is, he decides what concessions will be made by Socrates' opponents. Often enough, those concessions may be of a sort that would seem unwise, in retrospect, to the person who made them, as they seem unwise to us who read and judge them. If Socrates is engaging in dialectic rather than eristic, his arguments need to be valid; but they do not also have to be sound (although, of course, they may be), nor does he have to strive to make them so (although, of course, he may).[12] And

---

[11] Compare Jacques Derrida's *aperçu* about the Egyptian myth in the *Phaedrus*: oral transmission of a tale is the nearest Socrates ever gets to written publication. See Derrida (1972), 172. Notice also that, were Socrates not a dialectical conversationalist but a pure philosophic theorist, his argumentation would be as much a domain of freedom for him as is his mythtelling. But Plato chose not to portray him as that sort of philosopher; nor to write as that sort of philosopher himself.

[12] Compare the account of Aristotelian dialectic, and how it differs from eristic, at one extreme, and demonstration, at the other, in Smith (1997), xiii–xxi. An eristic argument may

if Plato is constructing a plot rather than directly propounding a philosophic theory, then for him, too, soundness of argument (or the attempt at it) is not a constraint; rather, it is among the elements that he can incorporate, freely, into his plot.

To take a straightforward example: the valid argument that Socrates deploys to controvert Gorgias in the first section of the dialogue depends on the claim that one who has learnt matters of justice is a just man, in the same way that one who has learnt matters of carpentry is a carpenter. But this claim is only true if the learning and knowledge in question is practical—the kind of knowledge that can be neither taught nor learnt, but only imparted and acquired, as it may be through apprenticeship to a master—rather than technical—the kind of knowledge that can be written in a book. That is to say, the conditions under which the argument would be sound as well as valid transcend anything that is even spelled out, let alone justified, either in this or in subsequent arguments contained in the dialogue. That is one way in which the argument invites us to thought.

When Plato's writing is approached in this spirit, the gradient between *logos* and *muthos* in his dialogues is—for Plato, though not for his Socrates—a formal rather than a substantial matter. He will have had many good, writerly reasons for shifting from fictional dialectic to fictional story-telling (as he shifts also, on occasion, to fictional speech-making, fictional history, fictional cosmology, fictional reportage, fictional lecture, and so on). But they are all just grist for his dramatic mill. It is the whole dialogue that carries his intention.[13]

When I emphasize Plato's freedom as a writer, I do not mean that he experiences no constraints. The constraints of plot-construction are considerable for any writer, and all the more so when a major part of the plot consists of arranging dialectical exchanges in such a way that Socrates can

---

also be valid, but it will never be both valid and sound: on this issue see Dorion (1995), 215. In *Topics* VIII, 11 (161a24–33), Aristotle says outright that dialectic of the gymnastic or peirastic types may contain false premises.

[13] And just to be clear: nothing in the view I propose here excludes the possibility that Plato's intention for a dialogue as a whole is the intention to get a philosophic position across to his readers. So, for example, in Ferrari (2007) I make much of how differently Plato chose to picture the three-part soul at the different stages of his argument in the *Republic*, and how these differences will fail to receive their due weight from a reader who assumes that, because Book 4 contains the *Republic*'s most technical and rigorous argument having to do with the soul, it therefore contains Plato's last word on the topic in this work. Nevertheless, the position I attribute to Plato as a result of attending to the plot-movement of the dialogue as a whole is, after all, a moral psychology. It is a philosophic view of the soul that the *Republic* gives us reason to accept.

win, while also elaborating the dialogue's philosophic themes. But as with Socrates playing in his mythical sandbox, these constraints are all internal, and arise only from the writing.[14] And when I assert that the writing constitutes a domain wholly within Plato's control, I have not forgotten the irony of his situation, as one who writes for publication. That the written work, once published, escapes the control of its author to an alarming degree is a theme that Plato himself was, as readers of the *Phaedrus* know, among the earliest of writers to express within one of his writings. Publication is the equivalent, for Plato, of Socrates' decision to invite others to prepare their souls as he prepares his (*Gorg.* 526e)—with the difference, however, that writing and publication separate into two moments what for the character Socrates proceed concurrently.

But all such talk of writerly freedom may be thought anachronistic. Did the world not have to wait until the Romantic period before it heard its artists celebrate their artistic freedom and individual creativity? Is it not the case that when the ancients, Plato among them, write about the artistic process, their key term for it is *mimesis*, and that what such *mimesis* is mimetic of, in their view, is the external world? How, then, can it be correct to propose that Plato as a writer was subject only to the internal constraints of plot construction?

It is not at all my intention to make Plato a Romantic *avant la lettre*. Nor do I deny that the mimetic artist, in Plato's formulation and in Aristotle's after him, must attend to the world around us if he wishes his plots or his paintings to succeed. Aristotle in the ninth chapter of the *Poetics* famously distinguishes the poet from the historian on the grounds that the historian tells what happened, while the poet tells the kinds of things that could happen, whether because they are likely or because they are inevitable. If this formulation binds the poet less firmly to the world than it does the historian, it binds him to it nonetheless. For consider: the inevitability or likelihood that Aristotle has in mind here is that of the succession of events that constitute a fictional plot. Let Homer pit his Odysseus against monsters as fabulous as you please, still, his hero's fears, stratagems, and eventual escapes must be plausibly motivated and brought off for the episode to properly engage its audience. The action will be plausible if it is recognizably human; and it will be recognizably human if the connections between events are those generally found in life.

---

[14] Compare the approach that Norbert Blössner takes toward reading Plato in Blössner (1997), and the summary that he gives of that approach in Blössner (2007), 375–384.

But here is the crucial point: if we take his task as a whole, the action that the poet imitates is something that he makes, not something that he finds. The poet is a maker of plots. That is why Aristotle is at pains to distinguish the unity proper to a plot from the unity that accrues to an individual's life-story merely by virtue of its being one person's story (*Poetics*, §8); and why he can declare a preference for plausible impossibilities over possible implausibilities (*Poetics*, 1460a26–27). The poet, if we take his task whole, is not imitating life but creating a new life—creating a plot that, by virtue of the plausible connections that link its beginning to its middle and end, comes to have the organic unity of a 'living creature' (*zôion*, 1459a19–21). (Aristotle seems to have inherited this idea and this image from Plato, *Phdr.* 264b–c.) Where the poet chooses to begin, where he chooses to end, and by what events he chooses to connect beginning to end: this is the zone of his freedom. The connections he employs must be plausible, and the constraint of plausibility binds the poet to the real world; but such plausibility is merely instrumental to the goal of constructing a plot that will have the effect the poet intended.[15]

Let the poet have inherited unalterable plot-points from his culture, as the Greek tragedians did, writing plays mainly on traditional themes from myth; let him be required to attend to the empirical realities of human behaviour; still, these are only ingredients that he puts into his mix. (Think how different the *Electra* of Euripides is from the *Electra* of Sophocles.) The cake he is baking from that mix is his story; what the poet does is to make stories. And in this task, he is alone, and he is free. He depends on no other man for his success (but only for a successful reception), nor can the world prevent him from achieving it (although the quality of his ingredients may). He is assembling parts into a whole, and by his sense of that whole his task is determined.

The reason it is easier to make this case from the text of Aristotle than from anything to be found in Plato is that Plato is himself writing fiction. When he writes about poetry, it is not in order to provide dispassionate analysis of the art. Most often, he has a social agenda in mind; and always, his views are not directly stated. Nor does any dialogue contain an analysis of plot-construction, however indirect. (*Phdr.* 264b–c, just mentioned, comes closest, since it insists on the organic unity of any piece of artful writing. It applies to all writing, however, not to stories alone; and is in any case the statement of a *desiderandum* rather than an analysis.)

---

[15] For a full defence of this account of the *Poetics*, see Ferrari (1999).

Instead of perusing in vain, then, those well-known passages in the dialogues where Socrates is intent on turning the poet's status as an imitator to
the poet's disadvantage, one would do better to look to a revealing comparison with art that crops up in a context where Socrates is discussing
something quite different, in Book 5 of the *Republic* (472d). Defending his
proposal for the ideal city from the accusation that his plan is worthless until
proven feasible in just the form proposed, Socrates brings up the case of a
painter who paints a picture of the most beautiful human being imaginable,
a 'model of how the most beautiful human being would be' (*paradeigma
hoion an eiê ho kallistos anthrôpos*), but cannot prove that such a person
could exist. You would not think him a worse painter for that, says Socrates,
not so long as he was able to 'render every detail of his painting perfectly
well'—or, more literally, 'render everything into his painting perfectly well'
(*panta eis to gramma hikanôs apodous*). Here a painter is described as making a model, not following one; and the work of supplying detail to achieve
an adequate result, even though it must, of course, take into account how
actual human beings look, cannot ultimately be determined by anything
external to the painting, but only by the artist's conception of perfect human
beauty; for, *ex hypothesi*, no such external model exists.[16] Here, when he
is not pressing a social point against artists—as in Book 10, where their
mercenary enslavement to the tastes of the masses is one of the points at
issue—but instead is considering, in terms of the artistic task alone, what
makes an artist good, Socrates offers an expression of artistic freedom along
the lines that I have been urging. His words prove, at a minimum, that this
was a thought that Plato, no less than Aristotle, was able to entertain.[17]

So far I have described the philosopher's choices throughout life, his
story-telling, and his writing of philosophic fiction, as, all three of them,
'domains of freedom'—suggesting perhaps to the reader that Plato, on my
account, assigns the three domains an equal value. But that would be an
implausible claim. For one thing, the second and third domains of freedom
can only be sub-domains of the first; the decision to tell stories or to write

---

[16] Writing of portrait-painters, whose models do exist, Aristotle explains that a good
portraitist will not allow the aim of achieving likeness to prevent him from making an image
that is more beautiful than the original (*Poetics*, 1454b8–11). Even in this case, the artist asserts
his freedom.

[17] Note, however, that Socrates' remark in Book 5 is not incompatible with his account
of art in Book 10. The artist described in Book 5 could, for all we know, derive his sense of
human beauty from the vulgar, or at any rate be painting with a view to pleasing the masses.
As an artist, he would still have his freedom, at least theoretically; but he would be selling it
cheap.

fiction are just some among the many choices the philosopher makes in life, choices whose effects on his soul he must gauge. For another, the dialogues themselves, as we have seen, include explicit statements from Socrates as to the supreme importance of choosing for the health of one's soul (*Rep.* 591c–592a, 618b–619b), the inadequacies of myth (*Gorg.* 527a, *Phd.* 114d), and the unseriousness of writing (*Phdr.* 276e). These, to be sure, are statements of the fictional Socrates, contributions to a larger artistic whole, and not, therefore, to be taken directly for the thoughts of his author. But an interpretation that takes account of the artistic whole may qualify and inflect the views expressed by the character Socrates without turning them upside-down.[18] Holding fast to the point that the philosopher's choices for his soul's health must constitute the all-inclusive domain of freedom, I conclude that the kinship between the three domains lends, to the artistic activities, the allure of philosophic independence, and to the life-choices, the allure of art, of beautification (in this case, self-beautification). But it does not put them on a par.

There is one artist, however, who exercises his artistic freedom in the most important domain of all—not the whole of human life, but the Whole, *tout court*. Let us see what Plato makes of him.

4. DIVINE ARTISTRY

The cosmology presented in the *Timaeus* is at times called by its presenter, the philosopher and astronomer Timaeus, a *muthos*, yet also at times a *logos*.[19] Timaeus' situation is different, however, from Socrates' in the *Gorgias*. In calling his myth there a *logos*, Socrates, we saw, defiantly asserts his artistic freedom to explore, for its own sake and without external constraint, a realm whose existence he cannot prove. Timaeus, by contrast, unlike the narrator of a myth, is operating with more than just internal constraints. After all, he must make his cosmology fit the evidence of the senses and conform to how the cosmos appears actually to be. He must do so, because explaining the workings of the cosmos is his goal. (It is only natural, then, that he should call his cosmology a *logos*.) Conformity to the empirical is not

---

[18] In § I of Ferrari (2003), esp. §5, I have attempted to qualify the supremacy of the soul's health as a philosophic ideal in Plato. In that same book (ibid., 106–109, 118), and in Ferrari (2008), 28–29, I have assessed the role of Platonic writing in Platonic philosophy by contrasting the activity of the fictional Socrates.

[19] Cogent treatments of the shift in vocabulary that take earlier scholarship into account can be found in Morgan (2000), 271–281, and Johansen (2004), 62–68.

for him, as it would be for a composer of plots, merely an ingredient instrumental to maintaining plausibility, *en route* to achieving the desired poetic
effect on the audience.

Nevertheless, Timaeus does not simply give an account of the universe;
he tells a story. He presents his cosmology as a cosmogony, a tale of how
the universe was constructed by a Craftsman-God who sought to make it
as beautiful as his raw materials permitted. (Thus, it is equally natural that
he should call it a *muthos*.) The effect of his presentation is this: external
empirical constraints imposed by the world we inhabit become internal
constraints on the creative activity of an artistic God—constraints like those
with which a myth-teller or a writer of fictions would operate.

So, for example: observation of the fixed stars informs us that the cosmos
as a whole moves with a circular motion. Timaeus, as an astronomer, wants
his cosmology to conform to his observations. But he also, as a philosopher,
wants to understand the cosmos as an entity that is rationally ordered for
the best. One way to achieve this is to describe the circular motion of the
cosmos as the outcome of the creative thinking of an artist who operates
under no constraints external to the artistic problem he has set himself.
Timaeus enters imaginatively into the thoughts of the Craftsman-God at
a moment before the cosmos has any motion, circular or otherwise, and
comes up with such considerations as these (*Tim.* 33a–34b): the cosmos
must use all available materials, so that it can be complete, and because
materials left unincorporated result in disorder; the 'appropriate' (*prepon*)
shape for that which contains everything is that of a sphere; nor, therefore,
will it be necessary to supply the cosmos with sense-organs or with limbs by
which it could deal with the outside world, since there *is* no outside world;
and since the otiose has no place in what is to be beautifully made, the
cosmic sphere will have no such outgrowths on its smooth surface. Finally,
then, its motion should be that which is 'proper' (*oikeian*) to its spherical
shape: it will go round in a circle. The reasonings that explain the empirical
evidence—explain why the cosmos moves with a circular motion—are the
reasonings of a creative artist, engaged in making something beautiful.[20]

It may seem strange to assimilate the Craftsman-God's activity to the
freedom of the artist, when the *Timaeus* emphasizes the constraints under
which he operates. These constraints arise from the contingent nature of his
materials, which just happen to have the qualities and powers that they do.
The regularities of cause and effect among these materials are what Timaeus

---

[20] Cf. Taylor (1928), 72: 'God is a true artist ... The world is the supreme work of art'.

means by 'necessity' when he sums up the Craftsman's task as one in which 'reason persuades necessity' (48a).[21] This God does not create *ex nihilo*, then, but works with matter that exists independently.

Nevertheless, the 'necessity' introduced by matter does not in fact impinge on the Craftsman-God's freedom, any more than the inherited ingredients of the tragedian's art impinge on the tragedian's artistic freedom. Rather, they help set the God's task for him, the task of creating beauty where none was before, using precisely these found objects—materials which, left to themselves, have no beauty. The constraints imposed by these materials are, in that sense, internal to his artistic task.[22]

Equally internal to the Craftsman-God's artistic task is the requirement that he must model his cosmos on the eternal paradigm if he is to succeed in making it the most beautiful of created things (29a, 30c). While human craftsmen too are described as modelling their work on such paradigms—the carpenter who looks to the Form of the couch in Book X of the *Republic* (596b), the shuttle-maker who looks to the Form of the shuttle in the *Cratylus* (389b)—the Craftsman-God differs from them crucially in the following respect: he is not making a tool for use; he is making an organism. The cosmos is not a tool, it is a living being, an organic unity, a supremely happy and self-sufficient god (33b, 37a–b). It is the apotheosis—literally—of the organic unity at which writers are urged to aim in the *Phaedrus*. This makes the Craftsman-God more like a creative artist than a manual craftsman.[23]

---

[21] Morrow (1965), 428; Johansen (2004), 98.

[22] Cf. the explanation in Morrow (1965), 435 of Plato's use of the term 'persuasion' in the phrase 'reason persuades necessity': 'Plato's use of this term to describe the ordering activity of intelligence is an apt characterisation of the way in which a planned world, as he believes this to be, could be brought about through the works of necessity. It implies that the plan realised in the world process *is not one imposed from without, but one that is elicited from the materials involved.*' [emphasis mine]. Morrow compares this planning to the insight required for 'genuine craftsmanship,' where I would compare rather the insight of the creative artist, for reasons given in the next paragraph of the main text.

[23] It is appropriate enough that the God is called a 'craftsman,' *dêmiourgos*, rather than an artist, since what he fashions is not literally a work of art. So too, the metaphors used to describe his actions—collected in Brisson (1974), 35–50—evoke the context of manual craftsmanship rather than that of art. Only once is the God compared to an artist—a painter (55c). But if Plato were, in any case, to call the God an artist (that is, a practitioner of the fine arts), what, in Greek, would he call him? While the first term that will spring to most minds is undoubtedly *mimêtês* ('imitator'—see e.g. *Rep.* 373b), another could, in fact, be *dêmiourgos*. At any rate, Plato is happy to use the abstract noun *dêmiourgia* to describe the class to which both painting and poetry belong (*Rep.* 401a, 493d respectively). It is not, however, a term exclusive to practitioners of the fine arts: at *Gorg.* 503e, for example, painters are called *dêmiourgoi*, but are thereby placed in the same class as housebuilders and shipwrights.

Manual craftsmen must subordinate their artistry to the service that
their tool is intended to perform for others; the maker's art, as Book X of
the *Republic* puts it, is subordinate to the user's art (601c–d). What the
Craftsman-God makes for use, by contrast, is not the whole cosmos but its
parts; not the living creature but, as it were, its organs. And their function
is determined not by any external user but by the beautiful whole that,
together, they constitute. This is how an artist works, not how a manual
craftsman works—except that human mimetic artists, of course, are said to
look not to the eternal paradigms but only to human models. The closest
human analogue to the work of the Craftsman-God is rather that of the
philosopher-kings of the *Republic* when they design a constitution and a
civic culture from scratch, and are compared as a result to painters, but
painters capable of looking to eternal models (500d–501c).[24] The city is no
tool for human use, but is rather the whole that gives its human parts their
functionality. It is, to human beings, what the cosmos is to all that has body.
Still, there is an important disanalogy, also, between the Craftsman-God and
the philosopher-king: the latter will himself dwell in and be a functional
part of the 'cosmos' that he has created; the former will not. The God has
an artist's independence from his artwork.

Timaeus presents his cosmology as a cosmogony; but the form taken by
his presentation is not, within the fiction, his own choice. The scenario at the
opening of the dialogue gave Timaeus no alternative but to come up with a
cosmogony—to tell a story of how the world came to be rather than to give
a purely synchronic explanation of its workings. A story, after all, is what
Socrates challenges his guests to supply at the outset, albeit a story of the
exploits of his ideal citizens rather than the story of the cosmos (19b–c). It is
Critias who, in taking up the challenge, insists on capping it by arranging for
a history of the cosmos, from its beginnings down to the origins of mankind,
to precede his own narrative; and he prevails upon Timaeus to supply that
history (27a–b).

The person who actually chooses to present a cosmology as a cosmogony,
then, is Plato. That is, he writes a drama in which a philosopher who is also
an astronomer fully qualified to discourse on the workings of the cosmos
(27a) is placed in a situation which requires him to express his knowledge
by looking backwards in time and offering an account of how the cosmos
was made. Plato has, furthermore, given his character the belief that the

---

[24] Notice that, when engaged in this task, the philosopher is called a *dêmiourgos* of the
various social virtues (500d).

cosmos is the most beautiful of created things (29a); this makes it natural for Timaeus to frame his creation-story as a tale of an artistic god. These dramatic strokes can only be deliberate choices on Plato's part. As writer, he has a freedom of presentation that Timaeus, as houseguest and invited speaker (17a–b), conspicuously lacks. We cannot know in what format Timaeus, left to his own devices (not that, as a character in a fiction, he has any), might have chosen to speak of the cosmos; but we can know for sure that Plato believed a cosmology should be presented as a cosmogonic myth, starring a creative artist. What is more, his scenario should prompt us to ponder why he believed this. It should do so, because it brings to the fore the freedom of his choice, by contrast with that of his character Timaeus. Plato had his own, freely motivated reasons for choosing this manner of presentation. What were they?

By choosing to frame cosmology as cosmogonic myth, one thing that Plato achieves is to render unmistakeable his sense of the limitations of cosmology as a philosophic pursuit. It is all very well to have Timaeus preface his account by qualifying it as, in principle, merely 'likely' (29c); or to call the pursuit of empirical detail a pastime, albeit a sober and sensible one (59c); or to warn against allowing the empirical spirit to mislead us into the attempt to test and reproduce god's handiwork rather than just appreciating it (68d). (In all three cases Timaeus labels as *muthos* the limited manner of inquiry he is in the course of recommending—a label that, presumably, is prompted by those limitations.)[25] But these scattered caveats cannot compare, for salience, with the fact that the entire account is a speculation about the actions of a divine craftsman at the beginning of the universe— actions that none of us can know, however reasonable our speculations about them might be. Such an account bears its limitations on its face.

Furthermore, by framing cosmology not just as cosmogonic myth, but as a myth whose hero is an artist, Plato contrives to bestow the highest praise he fittingly may on the activity of those who create beauty—creators who include the mythteller Socrates and himself, the dialogue-writing Plato. For the supreme artist, he who has made the most beautiful creation of all, the cosmos, turns out also to be a supremely good and beneficent god. Conceiving of him in this way, at any rate, yields a satisfying explanation of his willingness to disseminate beauty by making this world the best it can be (29e). The artistic impulse, in this formulation, is made to seem fundamentally generous. (In humans, of course, its generosity would not be

---

[25] Cf. Johansen (2004), 62–64.

incorruptible.) To be sure, the formulation belongs to a myth, and the myth to a drama written by one who himself experienced the artistic impulse. But as when Socrates in the *Gorgias* earns through victory in dialectic the right to praise and take delight in his own values by exploring them in myth, so Plato in the *Timaeus*, provided he can produce an account of the natural world at least as likely as its competitors, has the right to praise and take delight in his values, among them the value of the artistic impulse, by casting that account as myth.

But Plato would have had a more important reason than either of these for framing cosmology as he does. Timaeus, we saw, simply asserts that the cosmos is the most beautiful of created things (29a); he takes it as given. This determines the kind of cosmogony he proceeds to develop: the origins of the cosmos should be traced to the work of an artistic god. But Timaeus need not and does not attempt to defend his belief that the cosmos is the most beautiful of created things.[26] When Plato, however, freely chooses to explain the workings of the cosmos by imagining, in a myth narrated by a fictional character, the thoughts of a beneficent Craftsman-God engaged in creating that cosmos, he achieves two things concurrently: he produces an explanation of cosmic order, and he provides a reason to believe the cosmos the most beautiful of things that have come into being. That is, if we shift our focus from Timaeus' argument to Plato's decisions as author, if we turn from what Timaeus is saying to what Plato is doing, we see that Plato is demonstrating to the reader that empirical facts about the cosmos we inhabit (e.g. the fact that it revolves) can successfully be explained as the outcome of a generous artistic act, directed toward maximal beauty. And if they *can* be so explained, then those who are inclined to see the world in the light that such an explanation sheds—to see the world as the most beautiful of created things—are given good reason to indulge their wish; for the explanation both responds to their desire, and is an explanation that works.

To be sure, what Plato does—as opposed to what Timaeus argues—cannot constitute an inference to the best explanation, since it is impossible, in the nature of the case, for alternatives to be considered and shown to be less satisfactory. Plato can write only the one dialogue he is writing at the time; either he chooses to deliver cosmology as a cosmogony starring an

---

[26] His argument for the claim that the world was created by a divine craftsman looking to an eternal paradigm takes the form, as Thomas Johansen puts it, of an inference to the best explanation. Timaeus takes it as given that the world is beautiful, and seeks the most satisfactory explanation of its beauty. See Johansen (2004), 75–76.

artist, or he chooses to do something different. Some may be stimulated to write the alternatives; others may rest content with Plato's act of imagination. If so, then as with the story that Socrates tells at the end of the *Republic*, they would be accepting a 'myth that may save us, if we believe it' (*Rep.* 621b–c).

5. THE DIVERSITY OF PLATONIC MYTH

In conclusion, let the diversity of Platonic myth receive its due acknowledgment. If I promised at the outset to say something about Platonic myth in general, that was not because I believe one can readily generalize about Platonic myth as such—even assuming that one could agree in the first place on what to include in the list of those myths. (Would it, for example, include the account of the after-effects of the Flood in Book 3 of the *Laws*?)

Even among the three eschatological myths—in *Gorgias, Phaedo* and *Republic*—there is considerable diversity. The *Phaedo* myth, for example, contains no story to speak of; it is, rather, at least until its final paragraph, an extended *ekphrasis*, a description of the underworld that folds Homeric motifs into a contemporary geology and emerges with an evocation of a world that, for all its glittering surface, is a boiling pit within. And neither the *Phaedo* myth nor the myth of Er in the *Republic* have the kind of form that was the focus of my analysis in section II; in neither is a story followed by an account of what is required for the story to make sense.

Once we broaden our perspective from the eschatological, the diversity of Platonic myth only increases. Now the myths show up during the course of the dialogue rather than at its conclusion (or in the case of the *Critias*, occupy almost the entire work). They are less likely to be grand summations, more likely to help the discussion along, and to limit themselves to a particular issue within the larger discussion. Some of these myths are transparently allegorical, e.g. the story that Socrates tells about the birth of Eros in the *Symposium*, while others take the established form of just-so stories (the *aition*-form), e.g. the story that Protagoras tells in the *Protagoras* of how justice originated among humans beings, in order to 'explain' why all must be competent in its exercise; or it may be both allegory and *aition*, as with Aristophanes' story of the circle-men in the *Symposium*.

None of this diversity affects my general contention, which applies to what the fictional Socrates and his actual creator are doing, not to what they are saying or writing. Even if Socrates does not draw out the implications of a myth, as he does in the *Gorgias*, his imaginative freedom to explore its fictional world remains apparent. No less apparent should be the imaginative freedom of the author who set him to roam there. Plato's authorial freedom, unlike Socrates', extends throughout the dialogue; as a result, I have claimed, the border between *logos* and *muthos* in the dialogues is, for Plato, a matter of form rather than substance. In particular, it does not divide what is philosophical in the dialogues from what is not philosophical. This is not, however, because the myths are somehow philosophical too; rather, it is because the dialectic is, so to speak, also mythical, in that it is part of a whole, and the whole is a fiction. To explain how this last can be so has been my main reason for detaining the reader with these pages.[27]

---

[27] Many thanks to Catherine Collobert for making possible and pleasurable the conference on *Platonic Myths* for which this paper was originally written. The spirited resistance that it encountered from some among its audience on that occasion has helped me clarify my position.

CHAPTER FIVE

THE PLATONIC ART OF MYTH-MAKING:
MYTH AS INFORMATIVE *PHANTASMA*

Catherine Collobert

The Platonic reception of poetry comprises on the one hand, a reflection on the literary practice and the literary object, and on the other hand, the conscious appropriation of literature for philosophical ends. This was attempted for the purpose of making philosophy a poetic philosophy, that is, of making a synthesis of poetry and philosophy. It is from that perspective that I understand the Platonic use of myths: Plato conceives of myth as a poetic device. However, the way Plato uses the device is at odds with the poets' way. The poets are doomed to failure because their mimetic art cannot get at truth. Plato rivals them by creating images of a different status, whereby he opens an avenue for a new type of image-maker.

I regard a Platonic myth as consisting of a verbal non-substantial image, which has as its main characteristic the fact of being grounded in knowledge. It implies that all Platonic verbal image has a philosophical original, which is also its model. I shall defend the thesis that the art of Platonic myth-making belongs to the category of *historikê mimesis* and, therefore, that a Platonic myth amounts to a *phantasma*. Defining Platonic myth as verbal image leads to set forth the conditions for visualizing intelligible objects, in other words, for a sensible grasping of the intelligible. The grasping brings us inevitably to a sense of illusion albeit with no delusion.

I shall in the first place elucidate the words *eikôn, eikasia, eidôlon* and *phantasma* by analysing their various Platonic uses and the specific notion of verbal image. In the second place, I shall consider the various arts of image making and delve into the nature of philosophical image. Thirdly, I shall set forth the reasons why we are entitled to define the Platonic art of myth-making as *historikê mimesis*, and finally, I will examine the reception of Platonic myths by addressing their heuristic, persuasive, and didactic properties.

1. Images and Verbal Images

Plato has recourse to images in one way or another in almost every dialogue. Because of its diversity the use calls for an elucidation of the very nature of what we term image, which I shall do by analysing its various occurrences and setting forth its Platonic definition. I shall in the second place question the iconic nature of language that leads us to regard myth as a verbal image.

1.1. *The Non-Substantiality of Images*

The notion of image is expressed by four main words: *eikôn, eikasia, eidôlon,* and *phantasma*. The first three words share the meaning of representation—*eikazô* means to represent, to compare, to draw. An image is thus primarily understood as a representation[1] and copy—*eidôlon* means also reproduction.[2] *Phantasma* often refers to something almost unreal, a mere appearance or vision (*Rep.* VI, 510a2). An image in general is a representation of an object insofar as it makes the object present, thus substituting for it. However, for the image to be such a substitute, it has to reproduce it, i.e., to copy it. This is why *eikôn* also means likeness, comparison, and similarity (see *Phd.* 87b3). The ideas of comparison and likeness are tied together and constitute the essential elements of the definition of an image.

What is, however, paradoxical in the nature of image is the following: the image stands for the object and thus gives us a visible access to it, that is, a grasp of it, but nonetheless it is also what the object is not. The relation between an image and its corresponding object is that of otherness and sameness. An image possesses an antinomic nature, which is the condition for an image to be a comparison. In fact, comparing X to Y is defining Y as different from X. However, for the comparison to be relevant and appropriate, that is, to illuminate X, there must be a relation of sameness of whatever sort between X and Y. The image is that which resembles the object and the object is that which is resembled (*Rep.* VI, 510a11).[3] As being that which is like something else, an image is something that is in relation to

---

[1] The idea of representation is, too, expressed by the word *mimesis*, which I do not consider here given that I focus on the nature of image.

[2] For an analysis of the meaning of *eidôlon, phantasma,* and *eikôn,* see e.g. Ambuel (2007), 71–73.

[3] Cordero translates *eikôn* as copy in his edition of the *Sophist* (1993). In *Theatetus, eidôla* is opposed to the true thing (τὸ ἀληθές, 150b1, 151c2) and to ψεῦδος (150e6). Note in passing the positive use of the word in the same dialogue: a memory of a thought is an *eidôlon*

something else. For instance, to capture the sense of what the body means for the soul, that is, its relationship to the soul, Plato brings in the image of a prison (*eikona*: *Crat.* 400c7). The image works here as a metaphor. The otherness between the body and a prison reinforces the sameness in a telling way in order to make the grasping of the soul-body relationship not only possible but also illuminating.

Qua copy an image thus elicits a specific relationship with reality. Plato defines an image as a representation that exists only in virtue of something else (*Tim.* 52c2). An image is thus something essentially relative. Cutting away the image from that which it represents would make the image simply disappear (*mêden to parapan autên einai*: *Tim.* 51c5). Existing for the sake of something else and thus not self-representing, an image is non-substantial; it therefore depends for its existence upon its original. This is why the main feature of an image consists of partially capturing the object and of isolating only some aspects of it. Otherwise it would merely double it, as Socrates argues in *Cratylus* (432a–d), for images are far 'from having the same features as the things of which they are images' (432d1–2). An image copies something that cannot be fully there. In this regard, it is necessarily an incomplete copy.

Take, for instance, Renoir's painting of a wave. What we see in the painting is not, strictly speaking, a wave, but a representation of it among other possible representations. A real wave possesses features that the image lacks. Yet the image refers to the object (the actual wave) in virtue of some shared features. In the case of Renoir's wave, there are enough features that are shared with the real wave so as to allow us to maintain that Renoir's image is an image of a wave. Notice that the image must have at least one feature in common with its object. The image is shaped out of similarity and dissimilarity with its object.

To sum up, a non-substantial image is referential, that is, it refers to an actual object, which works as its model. A non-substantial and referential image is thus defined as a copy, a reflection and likeness of an original. On the one hand, as a copy, an image is an imperfect mirroring or reflection of an actual object and thus impoverishes it; on the other hand, an image must be incomplete for otherwise it would no longer be an image but the object itself. Impoverishment, imperfection, and incompleteness are the hallmarks of images.

(191d9). In *Sophist*, *eidôlon* is a genre of which *eikôn/eikasia* and *phantasma* are the two species while in *Republic* VI, *eikôn* is the genre (510a1).

1.2. *The Iconicity of* Logos *and Verbal Images*

A non-referential image, that is, an image with no object, is an oxymoron for Plato. This is why language itself is an image, a likeness (*apeikasian*: *Crit.* 107b6), and a name a picture of a thing, an image (*eikôn*) (see *Crat.* 430e–432c, 439a1–3). The Platonic conception of language is iconic, which entails a mimetic relationship between language and reality.[4] In *Cratylus*, Plato alludes to the fact that a name is a sort of reproduction of the essence, that is, an image (*eikôn*: 431d). Being what is reflected in words (*Tht.* 206d1–2), a thought is compared to a vocal image (*dianoias en phônê ôsper eidôlon*: 208c5).

The family resemblance between image and *logos* rests first on their sharing the same type of relationship to reality. In fact, the view that a narrative consists of a sort of image is grounded in the idea that they both are a representation of some kind, that is, a copy and likeness of an actual object whatever the object. It is worth recalling that in his critique of the poets in *Republic* book X Plato relies on the analogy between the two mimetic arts, painting and poetry, where the idea of painting as a copy of a copy is without further elucidation applied to poetry. However, painting and poetic image should not be confused even if a painting, though by definition speechless, conveys a narrative due to its capacity to tell a story, which refers to its vividness.[5] According to Plato, a narrative or a *logos* is by definition an image. In fact, it is not only the mimetic nature of the two arts that entitles Plato to draw the analogy, but also their iconic nature. It is worth mentioning that the idea of iconicity is widespread and shared by the poets. Simonides notes the affinity between *logos* and image when he defines painting as a 'silent poetry' (Plutarch, *De Glor. Athen.* 346F, *Mor.* 17F) and regards poetry as 'an imitative art and faculty analogous to painting' (*Mor.* 17F–18A). That poetry claims to be a kind of mirror of reality, as Plato argues (*Rep.* X, 596c), is in fact already attested in Homer. In the *Odyssey* the poet Demodokos is introduced as an eyewitness of the events he narrates (8, 491). Yet, when poets note the iconicity of poetry, the observation does not stem from any philosophical duality between language and reality, as in Plato's case.

---

[4] See also Aristotle, *Rhet.* 1404a25.

[5] According to Pausanias (X, 25–31) this is the case with the works of Polygnotos, Ilioupe–ris and Nekya. When mythological scenes are described in paintings we sometimes do not know which came first, the painting or the poetry. I will elucidate the narrative's quality of vividness in the last section of this paper.

Poetry is iconic because of the iconicity of language, which is the reason why reality cannot but manifest itself in images. An image is not only the condition for the visibility of reality, but also the condition for its grasping. It is the inescapable *medium* through which reality is not only expressed, but also known. Speaking is nothing but speaking through images. The narrative's iconicity is then grounded in the first place on the iconicity of language, that is to say, on the ontological status of a narrative as an image and, in the second place, on its iconic property to visualize, that is, to elicit images in the audience's mind. It is on the basis of these two grounds that Platonic myth can be defined as a verbal image, which thus belongs to the category of *logoi* (*eidôla legomena*: *Soph.* 234c6). This brings me to examining the arts of image making and, in consequence, the relationship that an image, and especially a verbal image like Platonic myth, entertains with the actual object of which it is a copy.

2. How to Copy and What to Copy

Mastering the art of image-making is no easy task and requires on the part of the image-maker knowing not only *how* to create images, but also *about* the model after which he shapes his images. I shall in the first place examine two types of image making whose distinction rests on the kind of image they produce: *eikôn* and *phantasma*. In the second place, I shall investigate the kind of reality an image should be a copy of, according to Plato, that is, the model after which a philosopher shapes his images, which turns out to be different from that of a poet and sophist.[6] The model is in effect crucial because it defines the nature of an image, as Plato argues. What is at stake in understanding the art of image-making is ultimately the type of reality with which the myth-maker should deal.

2.1. Eikastikê *and* Phantastikê

The distinction that Plato draws between *eikastikê* and *phantastikê* rests first on the idea that the former produces images in accordance with the true proportions of their model while the latter does not. In this regard, an *eikôn* consists in a copy respectful of its model's true proportions, which is not the case of a *phantasma* whose very purpose is to create the illusion of the

---

[6] I take that the poet and the sophist belong to the same category of image-maker. See on this issue Notomi (2001), 122–133.

object's true proportions. The problem with which all image-making deals is the deficiency of perception, which makes a straight stick appear curved in water (*Rep.* X, 602c–e). The art of image-making has to compensate for the perceptual deficiency by making us see the stick straight and not curved. By the same token, a large object in the distance appears small and thus not as it really is. Distance produces confusion in proportions. The fallibility of perception is partly considered as an incapacity to grasp the object's true proportions from a distance. A *phantasma*, which does not respect the object's true proportions for the sake of perspective, copies reality in the way we *see* it. On the other hand, an *eikôn* does not produce an illusion of perspective: it is not a *trompe-l'oeil*. In *Cratylus*, the relationship between reality and image is understood as the latter being an access to the former with no regard for the viewer.[7]

It is worth mentioning that a painting with no perspective elicits a sense of deformity because it does not reproduce what we *see*. Everything would then get confused since a large object would appear in the distance as large as if seen up close—in fact all objects would preserve their true proportions. However, in the case of a perspectival image, getting closer to it makes us unable to grasp that which is small, which makes sense only as seen from a distance (*Tht.* 208e6–9). The problem with which any image-maker is then confronted is to reproduce objects as seen from a distance. Distance is in fact a byproduct of the art of image-making. With regard to verbal images, the distance is no longer spatial but epistemological and ontological: it is a distance from the truth and reality.[8]

There is, however, another problem related to that of distance, that is, picturing a large-scale picture. Plato is, of course, aware of the two related problems since what he says in the *Sophist* about the requirement of respecting true proportions is qualified in *Cratylus*. There too he first claims that an image is beautiful (*kalê*) when it reproduces the object properly, that is, when it does not add or neglect details which belong to the object

---

[7] The *eikôn* makes us understand the relationship between reality and its expression. In other words, the nature of language manifests itself in the concept of *eikôn*. The *Sophist*'s *eikastikê* may amount to a kind of *onomastikê* (see *Crat.* 424a). It may be the reason why the knowledgeable image-maker is claimed to be a *phantasmata*-maker, as I shall make plain in the two next sections of this paper. As Vasiliu (2008), 175 argues, an *eikôn* 'est l'expression vraisemblable du modèle'.

[8] See e.g. Nightingale (2002). Sophistic and poetic images are distant from the truth because according to Plato the sophist and the poet are themselves distant from it. I shall fully address this point in the next section.

(431d2–8).[9] However, he notes further that the quality of an image does not in fact depend on its capacity to reproduce properly what the object is (432b1–d2). What is proper in the case of an image is different from what is proper in the case of figures, for instance. Adding or neglecting details about what the object is is a necessary condition for the production of an image as an image. In consequence, the image-maker is entitled to picture additional features not directly related to the object insofar as the object's main characteristic is provided (*tupos*: 432e6). In other words, he does not necessarily have to respect the object's true proportions (*Crat.* 432c2, also *L.* II, 668d–e). In fact, respecting them is an impossible task for an image-maker to accomplish because in this case he perfectly duplicates the object. Now such a perfect duplication counters the definition of image *qua* copy, as Plato makes plain.

It seems to follow, first, from the qualification in *Cratylus* and the *Laws* and, second, from the definition of *phantastikê* as not respectful of the object's true proportions, that *phantastikê* is the proper art of image-making, be it visual or verbal. The conclusion appears at first sight rather improbable and counterintuitive in the context of Plato's philosophy. In fact, it is worth noting first that the word used in *Cratylus* and the *Laws* is *eikôn* and not *phantasma* and that Plato usually uses *phantasma* in a derogatory sense. However, by defining in *Cratylus* and the *Laws* an *eikôn* as an image that does not and cannot respect the true proportions of its object, Plato seemingly collapses the distinction set forth in *Sophist* between an *eikôn* and a *phantasma*.[10]

Let us recall, however, that at the very end of the *Sophist phantastikê* is divided into two species, one of which is *mimesis*—Plato remains silent about the other. *Mimesis* is itself divided in two: first, as a product of knowledge, second, as a product of ignorance (*agnôsias*). The latter is dubbed *doxomimetikê* because of its grounding in *doxa*; grounded in knowledge, the former is dubbed informed *mimesis* (*historikên mimesis*: 267e1). In consequence, a *phantasmata*-maker produces either images grounded in knowledge or images grounded in *doxa*. The two types of images amount to two categories of image-makers: one is knowledgeable while the other ignorant. Given that the sophist and the poet cannot belong to the former category, the question arises as to who does. As the only one who is knowledgeable, the philosopher seems to be a good candidate.

---

[9] Along the same lines, in the *Laws* a reproduction is said to be correct if it reproduces the object in its own proper quantity and quality (II, 668b6–8).

[10] In the *Laws*, poetry, music and painting are τέχναι εἰκαστικαί (II, 667d1).

In the *Laws* Plato makes clear that in order to distinguish good poetry
from bad, one needs to know what the original is and how the image represents the actual object (II, 668c). Moreover, the philosopher is introduced
as the one who knows the nature of things so that he could properly represent them and judge the reproduction of others (668d–e, 669a–b).[11] In this
regard, by knowing the truth the philosopher is able to check whether or not
the image is proper (*Crat.* 439b1–2, see also *L.* II, 668a4–5). The philosopher
must, moreover, be a master of image-making and from this perspective
meet the three following criteria: he has 'first, a knowledge of the nature
of the original; next, a knowledge of the correctness of the copy; and thirdly,
a knowledge of the excellence with which the copy is executed' (*L.* II, 669b1–
3). However, if the knowledgeable *phantasmata*-maker is the philosopher,
we may ask the question as to whether a Platonic myth consists of a *phantasma*, that is, a *trompe-l'oeil* or an illusion.[12] Yet how is it possible that the
philosopher deludes his audience by making mere illusions even though
they are grounded in knowledge? Plato would have made our life easier had
he maintained in the *Sophist* that the *eikôna*-maker is the knowledgeable
imitator.

2.2. Doxastic *and Informative* Phantasmata

For the problem to be solved we need to examine the model after which
Plato makes his images. If an improper image is 'unlike the thing it claims to
be like' (*Soph.* 236b6) a proper image would then be like the object it claims
to be like. We may then ask the question as to what Plato's images claim to
be like. I shall argue that the philosopher as a verbal image-maker demonstrates an ability to compensate for the weaknesses of images by exploiting
them as devices to exhibit, that is, to make visible what is intelligible, which
works as an original, that is, as a model for Platonic myths. It is worth noting
first that the iconicity of language, which Plato claims, forces such compensation upon him—language whatever its form is after all the most obvious
access to the intelligible—and second, the original is the yardstick of an
image, making the image well or poorly done, proper or not.

There are at least two ways of understanding what a poorly-grounded
image is. It is a poorly-grounded copy on account of its poor execution,
that is, its bearing no resemblance whatsoever to the model after which the

---

[11] In *Rep.* X, 598e, Plato argues that it is necessary for a good poet to be a knower of what
he makes.

[12] It may well be the case that a Platonic dialogue belongs to the same category. However,
addressing the issue would outrun the scope of my immediate concern.

image-maker intends to shape it. Second, it is a poorly conceived image, that is, an image designed after an improper model, for instance, sensible reality. In the former case, dissimilarity is the sole quality of the image, while in the latter case it is resemblance. In both cases, ignorance grounds them, that is, ignorance of the proper model and of the art. The *phantasma qua* product of *doxometikê*, which I call *doxastic phantasma*, belongs to the latter. What goes wrong with the poet's and sophist's art of image-making is twofold. On the one hand, the type of reality that is mirrored in their images is improper: the *doxastic phantasma* consists of a grasping of appearances.[13] On the other hand, their images are meant to give us a direct and unproblematic access to the real object. The poet and the sophist are committed to the idea that the image looks like the object represented so much so that the object represented *appears* as real, resembling the object so closely that almost no difference appears between them.

The poet's and sophist's art of image-making, which consists of mirroring the realm of *doxa*, leads to confusing the image with its object and thus taking the object represented for the actual object. Image and object become thus elided into one: the image *is* the object. Either the sophist and the poet are not aware of the gap or they ignore it. In the former case, they are themselves deluded by their *trompe-l'oeil* because out of ignorance they are not aware of their image making, thinking that they convey reality to us by using images as merely a *medium*. In other words, they are not aware that among the essential weaknesses of the *medium* the most important is the distortion that it produces. Their ignorance thus bears on, first, the epistemic and ontological status of the image and, second, the true reality.

On the other hand, a philosophical image, like a myth, consists in a well-grounded copy because it is conceived of as a device to exhibit philosophical content. In fact, it has as its foundation knowledge, which means, broadly speaking, a grasp of 'what is'. As Socrates claims, 'you must know the truth concerning everything you are speaking or writing about' (*Phdr.* 277b5–6). Whenever Plato provides us with an image or likeness of X rather than abstract reasoning about, say, its nature, he already has a conception of X of which he is able to give an account. In other words, he has a grasp of the original he intends to copy. Consider the myth of the charioteer in *Phaedrus*. It pictures the nature of the soul in a way that patterns the conceptual

---

[13] It is worth mentioning that the illusion produced by the sophist works because of the viewer's position toward truth (*Soph.* 234c–e). A viewer who is closer to the truth, like a philosopher, is not deluded by the sophist's illusion. He then does not take the image for the real.

definition which Plato offers in the *Republic* (see IV, 436a; IX, 580b). It is in fact quite reminiscent of it, although there are discrepancies between the two depictions.[14] The myth is introduced as a likeness of the *idea* of the soul (*eoiken*: 246a5, *eoiketô*: a6). Plato draws the picture of it after its model, which is the actual structure of the soul.[15] The myth then appears to be a copy of the soul's nature in the sense that it provides us with insight into its structure.[16]

A philosophical image is meant to capture some essential features of its original, its *tupos*, as *Cratylus* has it, or its *skhêma*.[17] Like any image, a philosophical image cannot exhaust all the features of its original. More importantly, the philosopher does not have this aim, contrary to the sophist and poet who in their large-scale pictures try unsuccessfully to exhaust all the features of the real object. By contrast, the philosopher shapes his image so as to point to the specific features of the original he intends to illuminate.[18] Let us dwell upon the image of the sun to clarify this idea. In

---

[14] Moreover, the context in the *Republic* is different from that of the *Phaedrus*. In the former, a detailed demonstration of what the soul is is crucial to the overall argument. In fact, Plato aims to get at a definition of justice as the harmony of the soul.

[15] Note that Plato is familiar with providing pictures of the soul. In *Phaedo*, the soul is likened to a harmony (85e–86d) and a cloak (87b–88b).

[16] The mention of the essence of the soul as immortality points to a knowledge of what the soul is even though Plato makes a distinction between its essence and its *idea*. There is a rhetorical device on Plato's part. He has Socrates state on the one hand that a divine art is necessary to tell the *idea* of the soul and the iconic way is shorter than the divine's, which is not the case insofar as the shorter way turns out to be a rather long way. On the other hand, what the image is about is the divine nature of the soul and its relation to the divine. We would assume that talking about the divine require a divine art. Many recurrent Platonic themes are present in the myth for instance the contemplation of the Forms and reminiscence. Finally, it is worth mentioning that as in the case of many other Platonic myths it is protreptic. The myth should turn Phaedrus to philosophy (257b). I address this point fully in the last section.

[17] See the next section.

[18] Let us first specify that I do not take the Good as ineffable and Socrates (needless to say Plato) as having no knowledge about the Good. If it is the case, we must admit that Socrates is not a philosopher since any philosopher is able to reach the Good through dialectic (533a–534c). Moreover, to know what justice is requires to know the relation between justice and the Good, therefore to know the Good. Having defined what justice is, Socrates must therefore know the Good (see also 505a–b). Plato has Socrates say not that he does not know what the Good is but rather that at the stage of their enquiry ('from the time being'), Socrates' interlocutors do not have enough *hormê*. Socrates is supposed to tell the whole story of the father later (506e6), for his interlocutors are not yet philosophers and for the time being they would not be able to understand what the Good is. Socrates stresses their incapacity to reach the Good several times, and, in consequence, the uselessness of telling them what it is. They would be like blind people knowing the truth with no understanding of it (506c6–8), and

order to give an account of what the Good is, Plato provides us with an image that he does not term at first *eikôn* but rather *analogon* (*Rep.* VI, 508c1). The *analogon* of the Good helps us understand what the Good is. Plato formulates the analogy in the following way: what the sun is in the visible realm with respect to vision and visible things is what the Good is in the intelligible realm with respect to the mind and the intelligible. Further, the sun is the image (*eikôna*: 509a9) and likeness of the Good (*omoiêtatos*: 506e4, *omoiêtata*: 509c6). The likeness is based upon function: the sun and the Good both make possible the performance of a capacity: on the one hand, the ability of the eyes to see and of the visible to be visible; on the other hand, the ability of the mind to understand the true reality and of the intelligible to be knowable. There is an analogy of function between the Good and the sun, which the image is meant to capture. The function is thus the essential and common feature that the image aims to illuminate.

The truth about what the object is constitutes the guiding principle of the making of philosophical images.[19] In this sense, a myth consists of an image *qua* likeness of a true account, which, therefore, it approximates. As Coulter puts it, a myth is not 'a direct rendering of it'.[20] Hence, if Socrates often affirms the truth-value of myths, it is because it captures the essential features of the original, and therefore, helps us to grasp it (e.g. *Phd.* 114d1–2). It is an approximation because the image is necessarily incomplete and impoverished, as we have seen. Some features of the image are true accounts of the object, that is, those which resemble its original, but not all of them. Unlike improper images, a philosophical image possesses articulated similarities and dissimilarities with its object.

To conclude, what distinguishes a philosophic *phantasma* from a poetic and sophistic *phantasma* is that the former is shaped out of knowledge and after a philosophical model, which is a representation of truth. A *doxastic*

---

they would not be able to follow Socrates any longer if he provided them not with the image of the Good but with the truth (533a1–3). Socrates then adopts a strategic retreat: he is not telling what the Good is, rather he provides an image of its offspring whereby we know the function of the Good. The Good is what gives 'truths to the things known and the power to know to the knower. And though it is the cause of knowledge and truth it is also an object of knowledge' (508e1–4, trans. Grube, rev. Reeve [2004]). However, for providing the function of something—even analogically—one must know the nature of the thing or at least some features of it. In this very context, Socrates' use of the iconic way is meant to be didactic (see the last section of the paper). See White (2006).

[19] This is not to say that Plato's philosophy consists of a doctrinal body, a consistent set of doctrines. Rather the various images are shaped after models that may be provisional and incomplete.

[20] Coulter (1976), 35.

phantasma is an image based on a fake object, an ersatz of knowledge and truth, an appearance of appearance. Contrary to the sophistic and poetic discourses, sensible reality and opinion do not constitute the working-model of Platonic myth. The sophist moulds his discourse with an image in thinking that he thus gets at the truth, while Plato moulds it with truth, thereby making an image that provides true insight. I have so far argued that a philosophical image is a well-grounded copy, that is, grounded in knowledge. Even though the definition accords with what a product of *historikê mimesis* is, which I have called informative *phantasma*, we need to go deeper into the epistemic and ontological nature of Platonic myths as *phantasmata legomena*.[21]

3. PLATONIC MYTH-MAKING AS *HISTORIKÊ MIMESIS*

Let us first recall that *phantastikê* is not merely a way of image making with no regard to the original of which the image is a copy since the model shapes the type of image made. Second, a *phantasma* is not a copy of a real object but a copy of a vision of the object, that is, of the way in which the object is grasped. A *phantasma* is therefore a representation of a *vision of an object*, be it perceptual, as in the case of a *doxastic phantasma*, or intellectual, as in the case of an informative *phantasma*. I will in the first place elucidate myth as a transfer of a *skhêma*[22] of truth, and in the second place, demonstrate that the transfer issues in a *trompe-l'oeil*.

3.1. *Myth as a Transfer of a* Skhêma *of Truth*

Let us first specify that myth differs from images like that of the sun in two ways: first, it is not a comparison in which the two terms, such as the sun and the Good, are explicitly related to one another; secondly, myth is a verbal image,[23] that is, a specific form of narrative. As a well-grounded image, a Platonic myth consists of a transfer of knowledge about what X is. Plato provides an explanation of what I mean by transferring when he speaks about how to make a good constitution: 'As they work, they'd look often in each direction, towards the natures of justice, beauty, moderation,

---

[21] This has been argued by Nightingale (2002) though my argument differs in many respects from hers.

[22] In *Cratylus*, *skhêma* is tantamount to *tupos* (432e5–7).

[23] See e.g. *Rep.* IX, 588b10 (Εἰκόνα πλάσαντες τῆς ψυχῆς λόγῳ).

and the like, on the one hand, and towards those they're trying to put into human beings on the other. And in this way they'd mix and blend the various ways of life in the city until they produced a human image based on what Homer too called 'the divine form and image' when it occurred among human beings' (trans. Grube, rev. Reeve [2004], *Rep.* VI, 501b1–7). The way the lawgiver gazes at the intelligible—like the Demiurge in the *Timaeus*—is similar to the method employed by the philosophical myth-maker, except that what is produced differs in each case: an image like a discourse is not real in the same sense as a constitution. In the latter case what is produced is the immediate result of what is gazed at, while in the former there is the mediation of language.

In consequence, a myth is not tantamount to the reproduction of the essence. As a narrative, it deals with words, that is, language, which has a specific relation of resemblance to the essence (*Crat.* 431d). A philosophic *phantasma* like a myth is an image of an image of truth, in other words, a grasp of a grasp. Note, however, that a myth is second removed from the truth not in the same way as poetry insofar as the latter deals with sensible reality and opinion of which it is a copy.[24] The knowledgeable *phantasmata*-maker, that is, the philosophical myth-maker, unlike the *doxastic* image-maker, is said to be able to shape his images after the *skhêma* of what justice and other virtues are (*Soph.* 267c1–3). It is worth mentioning that the product of gazing at the Forms of justice, beauty, moderation, and the like consists in the *skhêma* of a constitution (*Rep.* VI, 501a9).

Skhêma has the general meaning of shape and figure, such as of a square (*Tht.* 147e6, see also *Men.* 73e4) or body (*Soph.* 267a6). Something is said to be beautiful on account of its *skhêma* (*Phd.* 100d1). It is also a property of a thing along with its colour and sound (*Crat.* 423d4). A *skhêma* is what is seen but also what is known like a colour (*Tht.* 163b10). In *Politicus*, Socrates observes that the *skhêma* of the king is not yet palpable because the myth failed to properly reproduce his *skhêma* (277a6). Some elements of it are missing, which results in not getting at a whole picture of it. Furthermore, the *skhêma* of what justice is is not the Form of justice but a representation of it, which is a tangible vision of it. The *skhêma* of justice consists in the outline or sketch, which is based on the knowledge of justice. The *skhêma* works as a mediation between knowledge and the verbal image that myth is.

---

[24] See Collobert (2011).

From this perspective, myth consists of linking two types of reality: the visible/sensible and the intelligible/invisible. The link amounts to a transfer by which a sketch of the intelligible is transported into the world of experience. The myth allows us to experience in a specific way the intelligible, that is, to have a sensible access to a representation of the truth. Myth operates as a visible and perceptible expression of the intelligible *skhêma* insofar as the Form is visible in its *skhêma*.[25] In this respect, myth constitutes an epiphany of it. As a way of visualizing a sketch of the invisible/intelligible, that is, as a device to give abstraction concreteness, myth consists of a concretization of a *skhêma*. Consider the myth of Gyges. It is meant to be a thought experiment, which by concretizing a thought makes it a perceptual object (*aisthoimetha*) that could, therefore, be seen ('We can then follow both of them and see (*theômenoi*) where their desires would lead': *Rep.* II, 359c2).[26]

3.2. *Platonic Myths as* Trompe-l'Oeil

As I shall make plain, the transfer of the *skhêma* of truth issues in a *trompe-l'oeil* of a specific kind. A *trompe-l'oeil* consists by definition of showing an object from a given perspective. I maintain that in most of his *trompe-l'oeil*, Plato uses a temporal perspective to make us grasp a sketch of some truth. Note first that Platonic myth is composed of elements which do not belong to sensible actual reality, although they borrow elements from it and from the tradition. In fact, for an image to be vivid, which is one of the main features of a *trompe-l'oeil*,[27] a kind of familiarity is required, which Plato introduces by reworking and redesigning images which belong to various traditions (e.g. Orphic, Hesiodic, Homeric). The resultant pictures are amalgams of actual and unreal sensible reality and traditional stories. A myth often describes a peculiar experience, foreign to ordinary life, and accordingly, exceptional and unique, which belongs to the past or future. In fact, myth does not at first sight bear on reality here and now, but rather

---

[25] As R. Stewart (1989), 277 puts it, 'it bridges that gap between thinking within the realm of the physical to that of the intelligible'.

[26] 'We would see more clearly if we do this by thought' (*Rep.* II, 359b9–10). *Theasthai* has two main meanings in Plato: seeing with the mind's eyes and with the body's eyes (see III, 402d4, 480a). There may be a word play here because the myth itself is about the fact of seeing and being seen or not. As Laird (2001), 21 argues, 'the iconicity *in* the tale is bound up with the iconicity *of* the tale as an object of philosophical speculation and as a virtual spectacle'.

[27] See section four in this paper.

on a reality that lies beyond the here and now.[28] Some commentators are committed to the idea that the myth of Er does not deal in fact with the afterlife but rather with our present life.[29] I take it that the same holds for all Platonic eschatological myths.

The so-called eschatological myths are pictures of the realm of the invisible (Hades), which is, however, radically different from the traditional one. This is the case because the very meaning of the invisible differs in Plato and the poets. In *Phaedo* 68a, Socrates explicitly links the invisible with thought (*phronêsis*) where Hades is meant to be a metaphor of the truly invisible. Socrates welcomes his coming into Hades not with the purpose of seeing his relatives, as people imagine they will and as Homer describes it in the *Nekuia* (*Od.* 11, 51–332), but to meet with thought (*enteuxeithai phronêsei*: 68b4). There is a philosophical use of Hades on Plato's part whereby he appropriates the common view and gives it a different meaning (see *Phd.* 80d).[30] This is why when Plato pictures the afterlife he does not aim to inform us about what is to be expected after death.

What the myth of Er illuminates is that we have to choose a life that enables us to live justly, i.e., to philosophize, and therefore to protect ourselves from choosing the life of a tyrant, which epitomizes an immoral life that amounts to terrible sufferings. The image of the afterlife thus carries a protreptic message (cf. X, 619c). Plato transposes the injunction to philosophize here and now into a future that demonstrates the validity of the injunction, though not because of the existence of the afterlife. Rather the converse holds. The injunction is valid even though there is no afterlife or, to put it in Plato's words, despite the transience of the incarnated soul (*ephemeroi*, 617d10) and a lack of continuity in the numerous incarnations of the soul. The immortality of the soul does not impact the moral choice, which then is crucial because the individual does not have a second chance. There is no other way to be just than to philosophize here and now; this is the lesson that the image of the afterlife conveys.

The myth is thus not a description *per se* of the afterlife. The image is made as though it is such a description and this is precisely what a

---

[28] It is worth mentioning in passing that the crowd accuses the philosopher of not being concerned with the here and now but with the remote. However, Plato demonstrates through myth that the remote is in fact here and now, thus inverting the categories.

[29] For such a position, see in this volume Gonzalez's paper and Halliwell (2007), Ferrari (2009).

[30] As Edmonds III (2004), 160 rightly notes, Plato identifies 'the unseen noetic realm of the Forms with the traditional Hades'.

trompe-l'oeil is. 'Here is what the afterlife consists of', Socrates pretends, therefore making us see what is here and now in a temporal distance. The temporal perspective is thus instrumental to emphasizing differences and similarities between the image and its model. This is the case because the temporal perspective produces a distancing effect. Contrary to the Sophistic art of image-making, the Platonic art does not conceal the distance and thus the inherent limitedness of images.[31] In consequence, the deluded viewer is aware of the delusion in somewhat the same way as a contemporary reader reading a novel of Flaubert. He is aware that the reality couched in *Madame Bovary* is nothing but fictional. Yet the act of reading requires him to read the story as if it were a true story. The Platonic *trompe-l'oeil*, too, is known as such by the maker and the receiver who are both aware of what is at stake, that is, of dealing with an image that cannot but have as its model a *skhêma* of truth. Although Plato uses the *phantastic* way of picturing, he avoids the confusion between the object represented and the real by introducing markers which signal dissimilarities, such as the transience of the soul in the myth of Er.

To conclude, as a philosophical image, a Platonic myth consists of a *trompe-l'oeil*. However, the Platonic *trompe-l'oeil* mirrors a reality that has nothing to do with the poetic and sophistic. A *doxastic phantasma* is an image of a sensible object, which is shaped out of a belief about what the object is, that is, an appearance, while an informative *phantasma* is an image of an *intelligible* object that is shaped out of knowledge about what the object is, that is, a sketch of the truth. The art of *phantasmata*-making *qua historikê* properly articulates dissemblance and resemblance so as to produce a *trompe-l'oeil* known as such because dissimilarities are emphasized and not concealed.

While reading a Platonic myth we come to grips with a specific issue, experiencing a way of looking at the issue and having a tangible and visible grasp of what is by nature invisible and intangible. However, this could not be the whole point as to why myths substitute for philosophical arguments and propositional knowledge. What is the purpose of transposing for instance the actual and present life in a remote future? In other words, why picture, for instance, the afterlife to tell us that we should philosophize here and now?

---

[31] As Imbert (1999), 11 puts it, 'Le critère de la bonne image est d'être une épiphanie physique qui donne en même temps que son contenu les dimensions de son raisonnement'.

4. WHY THE MAKING OF PHILOSOPHICAL *PHANTASMA*: THE COGNITIVE POWER OF IMAGES

I shall argue in this section that the Platonic art of image-making, that is, *historikê mimesis*, consists of reducing the epistemological and ontological distance from the truth in the viewer, be he a philosopher or a non-philosopher.[32] The Platonic use of verbal images is motivated by Plato's conviction that verbal images have a strong cognitive power, which rests upon the mind's ability to draw associations, as well as telling and striking qualities which impact the soul.[33] In many cases conceptual discourse is more difficult to grasp than the representational kind, hence the didactic character of myth. However, because of the non-substantiality of the verbal image, a myth is a kind of puzzle whose meaning needs to be uncovered, hence its heuristic property. Moreover, as addressing both the emotions and the mind, a myth is also persuasive. Heuristic, didactic, and persuasive: these are the chief properties that make Plato have recourse to a *trompe-l'oeil* like myth. Note that a Platonic myth possesses these properties because it has the specific characteristic of pointing to. What it points to is the model after which the image is shaped.[34] I shall elucidate these properties, which do not, of course, exhaust the properties of Platonic myths.

4.1. *The Puzzling* Trompe-l' Oeil: *The Heuristic Property of Myth*

I shall argue that as a *trompe-l'oeil* is in need of interpretation, verbal images like myths invite us to think further. Like any *trompe-l'oeil*, a Platonic myth is based on vividness, so much so that a *trompe-l'oeil* with no vividness is an oxymoron.[35] A *trompe-l'oeil* is, in fact, an instantiation of vividness (*enargeia*). The vivid quality of a narrative is achieved through description.[36] A detailed description of a place is meant, on the one hand, to facilitate the

---

[32] As Rosen (1983), 171 argues, 'Yet, it is easy to think of circumstances in which the production of fantasms would serve a useful function with respect to the pursuit of truth. One has to recall that Socrates, in the *Republic*, recommended various noble or useful lies, which he classified under the rubric of medicines'.

[33] See on this issue, e.g. Pender (2003).

[34] According to Verdenius (1949), 17–21, 'pointing to' ideal Beauty should be the chief function of art. I take it that it is not Beauty, as he argues, but truth.

[35] Cf. Quintilian, *Inst. Or.* 6.2.32. The idea of *trompe-l'oeil* is linked to that of realism and to what Barthes labels 'the effect of the real'. *Contra*: Nightingale (2002). However, addressing fully the issue would outrun the scope of my immediate concern.

[36] Note that *descriptio* is the Latin equivalent of ἔκφρασις, see Zanker (1981), 301.

vision of it, that is, to provide the audience with an idea of what the place looks like, and, on the other hand, not to let him have a loose or free representation of the place if it is the case that the background plays an important role in the ideas that the narrative conveys.[37] In fact, a misrepresentation of the place leads to a misinterpretation.

Making the reader see exactly and accurately what needs to be seen is in this regard crucial. But the myth-maker may also want to provide his reader with a blurry image of a place, that is, he may not want him to clearly envision a place, circumstances, context, and the like because in some specific cases it impedes his purpose. A blurry image of the background of a scene helps us focus on the foreground, be it a course of action or a character whose depiction is crucial to make a point. Let us recall that in *Cratylus* the image-maker is asked, first, not to respect the object's true proportions and, second, to add or neglect some features of the object. That is what Plato does while shaping his myths. According to the point he wants to make or the ideas he means to convey, his narrative has a specific focus, be it on a landscape, a character, or a course of action. However, what is thus visualized is not meant to be taken *à la lettre*. In other words, the image should not be taken as substantial, which is a recurrent Platonic warning (e.g. *Rep.* V, 476c6–7) and which is in fact what the sight-lovers do.[38]

As I have already pointed out, the proper art of image-making arouses the receiver's awareness of the essential difference between image and object, thereby leading him to inquire about what is represented, in other words, about the model to which the image points. The problem with a *trompe-l'oeil*, and images in general lies in the fact that resemblances with, and differences from, the object are not straightforward. All image is equivocal and ambiguous. In effect, an image does not contain in itself that which allows us to grasp it, that is, it is not self-explanatory. This is why for the image to be illuminating it must be interpreted.

I take the art of *phantasmata*-making as implying a strong form of allegorism, as Long defines it,[39] which is the sole form Plato admits. Allegory, which he criticizes, is the weak form of it. Poetry does not have any hidden and cryptic meaning on account of the poet's ignorance. On the other hand, as purposively conveying a philosophical meaning, a temporal *trompe-l'oeil*

---

[37] As Pender demonstrates in the case of *Phaedo*'s myth. See her contribution in this volume.

[38] See e.g. Stokes (1992b).

[39] Long (1992), 60. As Halliwell (2007), 469 argues the myth of Er is 'an allegory of the life of the soul in *this* world'.

like a Platonic myth is meant to be puzzling. It is a kind of riddle that we need to decipher. This is why, as Inwood puts it, 'the doctrine of reincarnation is not very plausible'.[40] In transporting us to a remote past and to future worlds, Platonic myths impact our ways of looking at things in at least two ways. First, in some cases it is easier to see the reality here and now from a distance. Things become clearer because seeing from a distance produces a shift in cognition that enables us to see from a different angle, that is, a temporal angle. Second, and on the other hand, to see something from a distance calls for a closer look at it. The distance is an incentive to look carefully at the object in order to properly define it (*Phlb.* 38c5–d). It arouses a question in the receiver: 'What could that be that appears to stand near that rock under a tree' (38c13–d1–2, trans. D. Frede). Due to its temporal distance a myth poses us a question and hence calls for interpretation. The temporal distance thus has the effect of stimulating the receiver to retrieve the meaning, that is, to find the truth to which the myth points.

In this sense, we are not engaged in the same way with a dialectical reasoning as with a myth, which plays with various layers of meaning[41] that a good dialectician, that is, also a good hermeneutist, is able to uncover. The uncovering partly consists in discriminating differences and similarities. Plato asks us to infer from the sensible/visible to the intelligible/invisible, from the most familiar to the less familiar.[42] Seeing one perceptible object brings us a perception of something else (*Phd* 74a8–9), e.g., a lyre's lover evokes the lover (*Phd.* 73d5–6, *Phdr.* 250a1). However, for the pitfall of endless interpretations to be avoided, explanation is needed whereby resemblances and differences are brought to light and at least partially identified. This is all the more the case given the complexity and richness of Platonic myths. For the goal to be met, Plato often gives us various keys or

---

[40] Inwood (2009), 35. It may not seem plausible to Plato's intellectual audience, as Stalley (2009), 197 observes.

[41] As Halliwell (2007), 455 suggests, Platonic myths have various levels of significance 'that can accommodate elements of the literal, the metaphorical, the personificatory, the symbolic, the allegorical (i.e., systematically symbolic), the speculative, and, ultimately, the mystical'.

[42] As Gordon (2007), 216 argues, 'by using our senses—in this case sight—we can come to know something of things-in-themselves'. In the same vein, Stewart (1989), 266 argues that, 'In the case of myth, our stating point is the physical realm from which our thoughts are drawn to the intelligible'. Human beings are not pure intellect, which justifies a didactic recourse to images. Yet I do not mean to argue that myth is a device to recollecting the Forms, although it would be possible to infer it from a passage in *Phaedrus* (250a1–b1). Lebeck (1972), 290 alludes to the possibility. See also Tarrant (1998), Harte (2006), Speliotis (2007).

signals. Some occur before the telling of a myth: Socrates introduces it as
an illustration of what has been previously said. Some occur after its telling:
Socrates infers a lesson from it which broadly amounts to its propositional
content—myth is by definition non-propositional. Some occur during its
telling: Socrates breaks the story of Er to direct our attention to what has
been previously demonstrated. In the two latter cases Socrates lends himself
to a philosophical exegesis.[43] A myth like an eschatological myth is protreptic not only in the sense that it delivers the message that we should
philosophize, but also in the sense that it invites and provokes us to philosophize. Socrates shows us the way by providing us with a piece of exegesis
at the end of the myth or even during its telling.

The hermeneutic work to which Plato invites us helps us to free us from
the power of images by making us aware of the *trompe-l'oeil* and inciting us
to go beyond it to seize a grasp of the truth (*Phdr.* 265b).[44] This is the case
because it opens a gap between what is seen and what is to be seen, the
latter lurking behind the former.

4.2. *The Didactic and Persuasive Properties of Myth*

The didactic property of myth manifests itself in the following ways. First, it
may facilitate understanding by supplementing some aspects of theoretical
discourse that the listener is incapable of understanding: 'there are certain
perceptible likenesses which are there to be easily understood' (*Stat.* 285d9–
e1). In this regard, having recourse to images can be a safer way (*L.* X,
897e1–2). Second, it may speed up understanding when in the particular
context the conceptual and analytic grasping proves useless or too lengthy.
Plato often claims that an image is a shortcut, that is, it allows us to get
summarily at the truth (e.g. *Gorg.* 517d6). The alternative would be a long
and maybe tedious reasoning to get at the same point. Third, it is more easily
memorized than reasoning and therefore could be a way of memorizing the
reasoning that lies behind the image, even though, as Plato demonstrates,
myth can be more complex than dialectic reasoning.

---

[43] In *Phaedo*, Socrates maintains that the geography of the Underworld with which he just
provides us should not be taken as a factual description (114d), thus pointing to a non-literal
meaning.

[44] Along the same lines, the myth of the charioteer in the *Pheadrus* does not aim, strictly
speaking, to provide us with a definition of the *idea* of the soul but rather to give us an
incentive to philosophize (257b), that is, to save our soul here and now. The myth works
as a puzzle that we have to sort out to understand what the soul is. It thus calls for its
interpretation, in other words, for philosophizing.

Moreover, in contrast with a dry understanding of analytic reasoning, myth provides us with a sensible experience of what is to be understood. It produces a cognitive and emotional experience whereby the receiver is persuaded. In fact, myth is more persuasive than any argumentative discourse. Plato's use of myth is closely related to his conception of philosophy as carrying truths that are often not accepted. The non-philosophers and sometimes philosophers are not totally and fully persuaded by the truth of an argument. There is a kind of resistance that needs to be overcome. The resistance is due to the fact that truth does not possess the quality of persuasiveness solely by virtue of being couched in argument. Plato is aware of the missing quality. Consider Glaucon's case. He knows that the common belief about injustice is false since Thrasymachus has been validly refuted (see *Rep.* II, 342e and ff.), yet the refutation does not convince him. He wants Socrates to go deeper into the nature of justice and to praise it since it has never been praised as it should be (*Rep.* II, 358d). We need to be persuaded and convinced about a truth not only with our intellect (*nous*), but also with our emotions (*thumos*). As Simmias illustrates, even philosophers need incantations. A myth like the myth of Er is such an incantation; this is why it could save us. It validates the philosopher's choice and introduces the philosophical life as the most rewarding of any life in a highly vivid way.

Conclusion

A *logos* can be a tool for *doxa*, *dianoia*, and dialectic. Used by a poet, a sophist, a politician, and a philosopher, it can be true, false, persuasive, deceptive, and cryptic. Language, therefore, takes the qualities that the speaker imparts to it. Yet the true *logos* is the yardstick against which any discourse must be measured. As used by the philosopher, the true *logos* is an image which makes distinctions, divisions, and clarifications. It is useful for dismissing false *logoi* as pretences which reflect deceptive reality. Some realities call for more than a mere image from the philosopher, who must therefore be able to give and receive an account of them (e.g. *Symp.* 286a5). That does not imply that myths are inadequate to capture the greatest realities or that these realities cannot be put into images, as the image of the sun demonstrates. Rather, given that images are not tantamount to accounts of truth, Plato maintains that the dialectician should be able both to put them into images and to account for them (see e.g. *L.* X, 966b).

The fact that there is no ineffable entity, since even the Good can be spoken of, as Plato argues at *Rep.* VII, 533a–534c, does not contradict the idea that language is impoverished. Yet in order to overcome the poverty of language, the philosopher uses all of the capacities and richness that language has to offer: argument, comparison, example, metaphor, analogy, narrative, etc. They are all media for knowledge and truth. Platonic myths, which partake in philosophical discourse, like dialectic aim at truth, either by presenting it in myth as a likeness or by leading to it. It is meant to be an education of vision insofar as it makes us see differently. We no longer see through the sensible but rather a *skhêma* of the intelligible, so that our gaze is redirected towards the truth. The vision of the sensible that a myth offers is no longer an obstacle to the vision of the intelligible. It is a powerful device to have access to a grasp of it. However, because of its temporal distance, myth is also a pedagogic way of demonstrating the irretrievable gap between an image and its model, that is, the intelligible, and of being aware of it.[45] As a myth-maker, Plato could be compared to the demiurge in *Timaeus* in the strict sense that as a producer he has as his model the invisible. Plato gives images a proper and correct status and is therefore able, unlike the sophists and poets, to make a proper use of them, thereby showing himself to be a true manipulator of images.

---

[45] Cf. Vasiliu (2008), 151.

CHAPTER SIX

SPECTACLES FROM HADES.
ON PLATO'S MYTHS AND ALLEGORIES IN THE *REPUBLIC*

Pierre Destrée

Republic book 10's critique against poetry begins in a rather peculiar way:

> I will have to tell you, although a sort of reverential love I have had for Homer
> since childhood makes me hesitate to speak. You see, he seems to have been
> the first teacher and leader of all these fine tragedians. All the same, a man
> should not be honoured more than the truth.[1]　　　　　　　　(595b–c)

It is Socrates who says this to Glaucon, and indeed he, and Glaucon were
not educated in Kallipolis, but like all Greeks, under the guidance of Homer,
and it is no wonder therefore that he has such a reverential love for his first
teacher. But it is difficult not to hear here also the voice of Plato himself
who cites Homer in so many places in his dialogues. And one should thus,
perhaps, not wonder that much either why, at the end of his philosophical
inquiry about the true nature of Homer's poetry (as well as tragedy—and
also comedy—which are 'led' by Homer), he makes Socrates emphatically
say that:

> if the imitative poetry that aims at pleasure has any argument to show it
> should have a place in a well-governed city, we should gladly welcome it back,
> since we are well aware of being charmed by it ourselves, but also that it is not
> pious to betray what one believes to be true.[2]　　　　　　　(607c)

Socrates, and obviously Plato too, are fully committed to sticking to his
'pious' engagement vis à vis truth, but the great pleasure Homer gives must
be taken into account, as well as that reverential love they have for him from

---

[1] ῥητέον, ἦν δ' ἐγώ: καίτοι φιλία γέ τίς με καὶ αἰδὼς ἐκ παιδὸς ἔχουσα περὶ Ὁμήρου ἀποκωλύει
λέγειν. ἔοικε μὲν γὰρ τῶν καλῶν ἁπάντων τούτων τῶν τραγικῶν πρῶτος διδάσκαλός τε καὶ ἡγεμὼν
γενέσθαι. ἀλλ' οὐ γὰρ πρό γε τῆς ἀληθείας τιμητέος ἀνήρ ... I am quoting Reeve's translation
(2004), with (sometimes) slight modifications.

[2] ὅμως δὲ εἰρήσθω ὅτι ἡμεῖς γε, εἴ τινα ἔχοι λόγον εἰπεῖν ἡ πρὸς ἡδονὴν ποιητικὴ καὶ ἡ μίμησις,
ὡς χρὴ αὐτὴν εἶναι ἐν πόλει εὐνομουμένῃ, ἄσμενοι ἂν καταδεχοίμεθα, ὡς σύνισμέν γε ἡμῖν αὐτοῖς
κηλουμένοις ὑπ' αὐτῆς: ἀλλὰ γὰρ τὸ δοκοῦν ἀληθὲς οὐχ ὅσιον προδιδόναι.

childhood on. Hence the proposal to allow 'its defenders—the ones that are not poets themselves, but lovers of poetry (*philopoiêtai*)—to offer a defence in prose on her behalf, showing that she gives not only pleasure but also benefit (*ôphelimos*) both to constitutions and to human life' (607d).[3]

As some interpreters have suggested,[4] it is rather difficult not to see here an allusion to Plato's own myths, especially the myth of Er that follows which is explicitly presented as a sort of rewriting of Homeric poetry (614b), and is full of Homeric references, and reminiscences. And there too, it must be added, Plato also makes it very explicit that Glaucon is very keen on listening to it because of the great pleasure he will gain,—probably a pleasure somehow similar to the one he has gleaned from Homeric poetry from childhood on. So, if this suggestion has some plausibility, how should this benefice be understood?

This whole passage should be read, I suggest, as an echo of the end of the first critique of poetry in book 3, where Plato opposes mimetic Homeric (and tragic, and comic) poetry which is 'by far the most pleasant to the children,' but deleterious to 'our government' (397d–e), to the 'poet and storyteller (*muthologos*)' he advocates 'for the benefit (*ôphelia*)' of his future guardians, who must be 'more austere and less pleasurable' (398b). The poet advocated here is a lyric poet who will be asked by the philosophers to write, and recite (and make recite) 'hymns to the gods, and eulogies to good men' (607a). To be sure, in the case of the *muthoi* that these hymns and eulogies are supposed to relate, the benefit is quite straight: it is by way of our admiration towards those morally excellent persons (heroic citizens, or morally perfect gods), and their deeds that we should be encouraged to 'imitate' them. This lyric poetry has clearly a direct, educative purpose: to offer youth morally excellent role models to emulate, and to booster the moral motivation of adults.

The case of the Platonic *muthoi* is obviously different: they are addressed to an Athenian (or more generally Greek) audience of people living in a democratic city, who, like Socrates and Glaucon, have been educated under the guidance of Homer. Yet even if Plato's myths, or prose poetry, are not to

---

[3] δοῖμεν δέ γέ που ἂν καὶ τοῖς προστάταις αὐτῆς, ὅσοι μὴ ποιητικοί, φιλοποιηταὶ δέ, ἄνευ μέτρου λόγον ὑπὲρ αὐτῆς εἰπεῖν, ὡς οὐ μόνον ἡδεῖα ἀλλὰ καὶ ὠφελίμη πρὸς τὰς πολιτείας καὶ τὸν βίον τὸν ἀνθρώπινόν ἐστιν.

[4] See Babut (1983), 51; Rutherford (1995), 215. An alternative interpretation has been offered by Else (1972) who sees here a sort of invitation to the young Aristotle to defend poetry, which he eventually does in his *Poetics*, but, needless to say, this is pure speculation, and does not take the context into consideration.

be confused with these lyric hymns, and eulogies, their benefit might not be completely different. To be sure, these myths are not supposed to offer any kind of moral habituation, and they do not provide us with any sort of heroes to be emulated. Contrary to that morally good lyric poetry, they are not part of any moral, direct education to be given to the inhabitants (probably only the guardians) of Kallipolis, but part of a dialogue about Kallipolis. And even more than that: in the *Republic*, they are part of a description, that is the description, or 'foundation' of Kallipolis, which is explicitly called a *muthos* by Plato himself.[5] This is one reason why these myths (and more generally all of Plato's myths) are more and more interpreted nowadays as part and parcel of the philosophical inquiry itself, and ought not be opposed, or even firmly distinguished from the arguments given throughout the dialogue. And one might also refer to the no less famous 'images', which modern interpreters (following ancient readers such as Proclus) have labelled 'allegories', or 'analogies', such as the 'Analogy' of the Sun in book 7, or the image of the multi-headed monster in book 9: they obviously are also poetical devices which are inclusive ingredients of the whole philosophical enterprise of that dialogue.

Yet, I want to suggest, if I agree that Platonic myths are not in principle very different from these 'images,' or more precisely, if their respective function is similar,[6] it would be a mistake to consider them to be a sort of philosophical argument, or to limit their function to a purely intellectual tool.[7] As I will try to show, these myths, and images or allegories are also, and maybe primarily, aimed at emotionally touching their audience, and therefore, as interpreters have traditionally said, that myths, and images are primarily addressed to the irrational part of our soul. But contrary to

---

[5] See 376d, and 536c, as well as 540c where he compares his construction of Kallipolis to the work of a sculptor, and 500e where he compares himself to a painter. See on this theme, Murray (1999). One may also note that, more generally, 'socratic dialogues' which in a way the *Republic* still is, were conceived as *mimêseis* of conversations held by (either the historical or the fictional) Socrates with interlocutors (see Ford [2008], 32).

[6] I resist the idea that there should be strong, and clear-cut differences between these 'images' and Plato's myths, at least as regards their function, even though there might be some formal marks that would be characteristic of myths as such (see Glenn Most's contribution here). It is worth noticing that interpreters do not agree on the name one should give to these 'images', calling them either 'analogies' or 'allegories', and sometime also, do not hesitate presenting them, as is typically the case with the Cave, as both a myth and an analogy (from Stewart [1905], 16 to Nightingale [2002], 98). In other dialogues, Plato is not making this distinction clearly either, it seems to me: see *Gorgias* 493a–d where the *eikôn* (d5) of the leaky jars is explicitly taken to be part of a *muthologein* (d2).

[7] An explicit, and forceful representant of such a recent view is Rowe (2009).

most traditional interpretations that tend to oppose myths to arguments, I agree that myths are part and parcel of the whole argument that is also a sort of myth, because arguments are not intended solely for the sake of understanding. For the aim of Plato, as some interpreters have rightly noticed, is also, and maybe primarily protreptic.[8] When Adeimantus and Glaucon want to be convinced that it is true that the just person will always be happier than the unjust one, or (to put it in other words) that being just, or virtuous, makes the agent better off, they do not mean to be intellectually convinced, or not only. In the beginning of Book 2, it is worth noting that Glaucon adds that he would like to hear Socrates praising justice and blaming injustice (358d; 367c–d). But praising, or composing an *enkomion*, and blaming, or composing a *psogos*, are not arguments: they are poetical depictions designed to express admiration for heroes (like the ones Plato seems to be advocating in book 10, 607a), and disgust for anti-heroes. That is, these are the kind of *logos* (or *muthos*) aimed at motivating hearers, or readers, to emulate morally good patterns, or to keep their distance from immoral patterns. What Glaucon wants, therefore, is to be convinced in such a way that he will always be motivated to act virtuously and in a way conducive to happiness. He not only wants to understand why it is true that a virtuous person will be happier than a wretched one; he also, and perhaps primarily, wants to be motivated to act in a virtuous way, so that he can fulfil his desire for happiness.

Being part and parcel of such a protreptic enterprise, I therefore submit, Plato's myths, and also 'images', are to be conceived not only as intellectual tools in a purely intellectual argumentation, but as emotionally loaded, protreptical ways to motivate his audience, mainly through Glaucon, who is the main interlocutor of Socrates, to adopt a philosophical life, and also (but both things are the two faces of the same coin) to pursue a morally good life.

1. THE MYTH OF GYGES

Let's first briefly review the myth of Gyges, and try to figure out how exactly it might be 'beneficial' for the audience. The challenge Glaucon urges Socrates to solve was addressed by Thrasymachus in book 1: according to him, and in fact for ordinary people, injustice is the real good (meaning by this

---

[8] See Gallagher (2004), and Yunis (2007); and, on Plato's dialogues in general, Blank (1993).

the good, or the highest good for the soul, or the human being), since by being unjust, we can fulfil all our desires, and therefore be happy. Now as people usually do not have the power to commit injustice without negative repercussions of some sort, they have established laws that determine what is conventionally just, in order to avoid suffering injustice. Justice, according to this conception, is in no way a good for the soul by itself. Instead, it is a good that people love because of their inability to commit injustice without damage. But of course anyone who would be in the position to commit injustice without harm to himself, would do so, unless he be completely foolish, or mad. In other words, when they act justly, or virtuously, people in fact act 'unwillingly'; the only thing they would like to do 'willingly' is unjust actions, as they all want to be happy, and injustice, they all think, will bring them happiness (358e–359b). 'That is the nature of justice, Socrates, Glaucon concludes, and those are its natural origins, according to their argument (*hôs ho logos*)' (359b).[9]

It is at this very point that Glaucon introduces his tale:

> We couldn't best realize (*malist' an aisthoimetha*) that those who practice it do so unwillingly because they lack the power to do unjustice, than by composing this through our imagination (*toionde poiêsaimen th(i) dianoia(i)*).[10]
>
> (359b–c)

As Plato explicitly says here, Glaucon is here *composing* (*poein*) something, that is, composing a *muthos*, or more precisely re-composing a *muthos* by allegedly reporting what some (unnamed) *muthologoi* have said (359d).[11] To be sure, Homer is not meant here, but (most probably) only Herodotus. Yet, as sounds evident for every reader, the way Plato is here composing, or re-composing this tale is very poetical, much more poetical than Herodotus' way of narrating his version, with a lot of details that are reminiscent of Homeric poetry, which is designed to please, and enchant (note the use of *thaumazein*, and *thaumaston* in the passage: 359d5, 6; 360a2) exactly as Homeric poetry does; and also note that the myth is obviously meant to allude to the underworld, and the reign of death which will be at the core of the very poetical, grand finale of the whole work (which is explicitly

---

[9] ἡ μὲν οὖν δὴ φύσις δικαιοσύνης, ὦ Σώκρατες, αὕτη τε καὶ τοιαύτη, καὶ ἐξ ὧν πέφυκε τοιαῦτα, ὡς ὁ λόγος.

[10] ὡς δὲ καὶ οἱ ἐπιτηδεύοντες ἀδυναμίᾳ τοῦ ἀδικεῖν ἄκοντες αὐτὸ ἐπιτηδεύουσι, μάλιστ' ἂν αἰσθοίμεθα, εἰ τοιόνδε ποιήσαιμεν τῇ διανοίᾳ.

[11] To my knowledge, Laird (2001), 21 is the only interpreter to notice this point; astonishingly, no translation I have consulted takes this into consideration.

presented as a re-composition of Homer at 614b).[12] So after a fashion, this
is also a defence of poetry. But what is its 'benefit'? And how should we
interpret the relationship between what is called a *logos*, and the *muthos*
to be told? And how is its aim, expressed by a rather vague 'best realizing'
or 'best perceiving', to be exactly understood?

Interpreters usually claim that Glaucon is offering what we nowadays
call a 'thought-experiment' (as even some translators render the dativ *tê(i)*
dianoia(i)) destined to make Socrates, and their audience, 'best perceive',
that is understand in the clearest possible way what the theory, the *logos*,
he has been defending so far, amounts to. The myth of Gyges would then
be no less but no more than a transparent illustration of that argument.
And later, (361b) when applying this to the 'judgment' (*krisis*) his audience
must make between a wicked and a morally good person, Plato even uses
the same word *logos* for imagining a good person who has lived according to
justice. There seems therefore to be no discrepancy at all between Glaucon's
logos (or more exactly, Glaucon's report of Thrasymachos' *logos*), and this
whole thought-experiment.

I certainly do not want to deny that Plato is here (re)composing a *muthos*
that is fully embedded in the course of a philosophical argument, and that
the possible distinction between *muthos* and *logos* is here rather thin. Yet,
one may doubt that this *muthos* is meant to be only a thought-experiment
in the strict sense of the term, solely aimed at better understanding the
argument presented so far. It is striking that contrary to all other images
and myths presented in the *Republic*, this one is put into Glaucon's mouth
(as it is also not by mere chance, the other way round, that the allegory of the
cave, and the myth of Er are, as we will see, specifically addressed to him). As
the reader understands little by little in reading the *Republic*, Glaucon is not
only a very intellectually gifted interlocutor who perfectly suits Socrates' (or
Plato's) grand philosophical construction, but also a man with a very strong,
competitive spirit, and also some very strong epithumetic desires, who,
as his brother Adimantus recognizes, critically resembles the timocratic

---

[12] There are four evident allusions to Hades in our passage: the fact that Gyges gets down
(*katabênai*) into the hole made by the earth quake; the word '*chasma*' (used by Hesiod in
Theogony, 740 for the Tartarus, and also by Plato himself referring to Homer, at *Phaedo*,
111e–112a) which also designates the underworld in the myth of Er (614c); the mention of
the naked corpse; and the way the ring functions as making invisible, which is a frequent
(false) etymology made of the word Hades (accepted by Plato himself at *Phaedo*, 81c, but—for
rhetorical purposes—refused by him at *Cratylus*, 404b), and which is alluded to in book 10,
612b, when the ring of Gyges is compared to the helmet of Hades (612b), which is another
Homeric reminiscence (*Iliad*, 5. 844).

man who is to become little by little a tyrant (548d).[13] And, indeed, in addition to the intellectual skills needed for becoming a philosopher (that is, a perfectly happy man), one surely needs to be competitive since becoming virtuous, and therefore happy, is a major struggle (see esp. X, 608b); without such a competitiveness provided by the spirited part of the soul, a *psyche* (or a person) would not be able to victoriously manage such a struggle (which is mostly a fight against her epithumetic desires). But the spirited part also represents a big (and in fact, a constant) danger: competitiveness also includes the desire for power, which, were one to give it too much scope, would lead to tyranny. Glaucon, in other words, has a natural gift for philosophy, and a great potential for moral goodness, but he is also in real danger of becoming a tyrant.

Glaucon is thus both the perfect candidate for becoming a really happy person if properly educated (we may suppose by Socrates through this discussion), but also, at the very same time, in constant need of protreptic advice and admonition, as his strong epithumetic, and thumetic desires might lead him into tyranny. And it is for this reason, I would like to suggest, that he is the one who so wholeheartedly plays the role of the devil's advocate: by urging Socrates to defend his main thesis that justice makes people better off, against his own speech in favour of Thrasymachos, Glaucon shows that he is the one most in need of such a defence in order not to fall into tyranny because of his own irrational desires.

Read from this perspective, the way Glaucon invites his audience to make this 'thought-experiment' becomes much more poignant. What Socrates says about the way Glaucon presents both the morally good man, and the wicked one, might as well apply to his previously narrating the Gyges' ring: it is 'vigorously' (361d) narrated by the vivid Glaucon ('I am doing the best I can,' ibid.) as if he himself would be Gyges, and have the same sort of wishes, and behaviour. In saying that 'nobody would be so incorruptible (*adamantinos*) that he would stay on the path of justice ... when he could take whatever he wanted from the marketplace with impunity, or go into people's house and have sex with anyone he wished, or kill anyone he wished ...' (360b),[14] it is difficult not to see in these words the confession

---

[13] On Glaucon, and his ambiguous nature, see Blondell (2002), 199–228, and O'Connor (2007), 64–68.

[14] ... οὐδεὶς ἂν γένοιτο, ὡς δόξειεν, οὕτως ἀδαμάντινος, ὃς ἂν μείνειεν ἐν τῇ δικαιοσύνῃ (...) ἐξὸν αὐτῷ καὶ ἐκ τῆς ἀγορᾶς ἀδεῶς ὅτι βούλοιτο λαμβάνειν, καὶ εἰσιόντι εἰς τὰς οἰκίας συγγίγνεσθαι ὅτῳ βούλοιτο, καὶ ἀποκτεινύναι (...) οὕστινας βούλοιτο ...

that the narrator himself might not be able to resist such epithumetic, and thumoeidic temptations. Glaucon is without a doubt a (more or less) virtuous person (as in fact Gyges himself seems to be, before finding the ring), but precisely because of his strong irrational desires he might be easily led to follow such temptations.

Now Glaucon is, also, obviously a sort of representative of Plato's wider (aristocratic) Athenian audience, that is Plato's direct readership. So by making Glaucon recount this *muthos*, which also represents themselves in a way, Plato can emotionally touch this audience, and exercise a protreptic implication of the reader into this philosophical (*cum* ethical and political) research. In particular, we cannot but notice that Plato explicitly presents his *muthos* as a sort of spectacle to be seen, where we readers are invited to 'follow' the just and the unjust men, and 'see (*theâsthai*) where their appetites would lead each of them' (359c).[15] One can take this as proving the continuity between *muthos* and *logos* as if this spectacle were part of the philosophical theory,[16] but I think that there is much more than that. It is a spectacle that you cannot see, and contemplate without being emotionally moved in one way or in another. One certainly might take this as a rhetorical way of eliciting the reader's *benevolentia*, that is, his eagerness to read further as to how Socrates will answer this striking challenge. But it might have a much more shocking effect: by vividly imagining such a scene, the reader is led, through Glaucon, to imagining himself as potentially acting like Gyges, as if this imaginative spectacle would be the *mise en scène* of his own irrational, tyrannical desires. The ring which makes its possessor invisible is paradoxically the tool by which Gyges' own secret, and, perhaps, unconscious desires to become a tyrant are revealed to himself. Attending such a spectacle might therefore help him, and the audience, to see, and thus face such desires which, if eventually realized, end up in complete unhappiness. Far from being only an intellectual tool, the myth of Gyges is thus best seen, first of all, as the way to emotionally motivate the reader to face his own irrational, tyrannical desires.[17]

---

[15] ... εἶτ' ἐπακολουθήσαιμεν θεώμενοι ποῖ ἡ ἐπιθυμία ἑκάτερον ἄξει.

[16] See Laird (2001), 21.

[17] Notomi (2010), 46–47, interestingly suggests that even the name of Gyges might also be taken as the metaphorical designation of tyranny; for Archilochus, referred to by Herodotus, might well be the first Greek author to use the word '*tyrannos*' (which might even have a Lydian origin) in relationship to the Lydian king Gyges.

2. The Allegory of the Cave

The so-called 'allegory' of the Cave should be read, I want to contend, in a similar way. It is true that, contrary to the tale of Gyges, which is narrated as the report of an old *muthos* told by *muthologoi*, this most famous passage of the *Republic* is simply named an *eikôn* (515a4; 517a8, d2). It is thus tempting to read it as a simple comparison, as the word will mean from Aristotle on, destined to give us a better understanding of what the state of uneducation (*apaideusia*) amounts to, and how to remediate it. For us moderns, reading such a sophisticated narrative might require a huge amount of intellectually demanding research in order to decipher the meaning of its various minute details. Yet, one may, here again, very much doubt that such a purely intellectual game was Plato's actual first intention towards his immediate (Athenian) readers.

True, the so-called 'analogy' of the Sun is also named an *eikôn*. But here, the function of this 'image' is relatively clear. Even though Socrates insists that he has already quite often told us about the idea of the Good (505a), he famously says he will not be explaining what the Good in itself is because 'even reaching what I currently believe about it is beyond the present effort (*hormê*)'.[18] Socrates here implies that he himself has not reached the science of the Good, but only some sort of *doxa*. But I do not think this is the most important fact Plato wants to tell us. I do not take this sentence to mean that he would be incapable of giving his own 'current opinion' about the Form of the Good either because he has not himself reached full knowledge of it, or because it would be something too difficult (and 'ineffable') to state, but I take it to mean that his audience is not ready to hear it: its effort, or desire to hear it, is not yet up to the task. This is confirmed by the attitude of Glaucon (and we may guess, Plato's readers as well) who, at the end of Socrates' explanation of the comparison cannot prevent himself from laughing, and making a pun on the last words by which Socrates famously describes the Good as 'beyond reality, superior to it in majesty and power' (*dunamei huperechontos*), in describing this as a *daimonias hyperbolês*, which means both 'a divine superiority,' and 'an extraordinary exaggeration'—laughing at philosophers, or philosophical arguments being the typical mark of the *Polloi*. The function of the image thus seems to be this: it is an intellectual tool to put us smoothly on the path

---

[18] πλέον γάρ μοι φαίνεται ἢ κατὰ τὴν παροῦσαν ὁρμὴν ἐφικέσθαι τοῦ γε δοκοῦντος ἐμοὶ τὰ νῦν.

of understanding how central the Form of the Good is, and to give us food for thinking about how it should be conceived as the 'cause of knowledge and being' of good things.

The status of the so-called 'analogy' of the Line (which in fact Plato does not name in any particular way) is even more straightforward, even though its precise interpretation has not received any better sort of an agreement among modern scholars. Socrates is here inviting Glaucon to 'conceive' (*katanoein*, 510a), and to imaginatively draw (*lambanein, temnein*, 509d) a mathematical figure in order to understand (*manthanein*, 510b9, c1, 511b2, c3) the domains of reality, and it should be noted that, contrary to his reaction of laughter in the previous case, Glaucon reacts to this mathematical thought-experiment with a clear, triumphant: 'I understand!' (*manthanô*, e5).

It seems to me that nothing of this kind could be so straighforwardly said of the so-called 'allegory' of the Cave.[19] At first sight, Plato seems to be presenting this third *eikôn* as a comparison by using the verb *apeikazein* (514a1), which in certain contexts can mean making a comparison, or approximating something with something else. But it is to be noticed that the imperative *apeikason* is relayed by the imperative *ide* ('see', or 'watch'—a2), which seems to indicate that it should be taken rather *ad litteram* as meaning: to represent with an *eikôn*, or 'imagining' in the strict sense of the term. And the reader cannot help but be struck by how emphatically Plato repeats the verb 'see' in the imperative (*ide*: b5; *hora*: b9) in the following lines, obviously making Socrates urge Glaucon (and the audience) to place the scenery vividly before his eyes. And as the comparison (here, in the strict sense of the word) of the statues' carriers to puppeteers indicates, the whole scenery of the cave is obviously to be seen as a theatre where the prisoners are the watchers of a show (the same verb *horan* is repeated on their behalf at 515a6, b5, d1). Glaucon, Socrates' wider audience around him, and we readers are therefore urged to attend the spectacle of a spectacle, so to speak.

Here again, one might point out the continuity between this, and the final aim of the ascent which is to 'see,' or 'contemplate' the Form of the Good, as if this spectacle would make us better understand why we need to convert our 'view' (cf. 518d) from sensible things to the Forms, and finally to the Form of the Good.[20] But yet again, why take pains to write such a vivid,

---

[19] Compare Frutiger (1930) who goes as far as to say that the Cave is 'almost as schematical as a geometrical figure'!

[20] On this, see esp. Nightingale (2004), § 3: 'The fable of philosophy in Plato's *Republic*'.

and fascinating story which, to be sure, reminds Glaucon, and his ancient readers, of traditional underworld, poetical stories (the cave being another representation of Hades)?

Perhaps we should take stock of the reaction of Glaucon once he is eventually envisaging the scene: 'It is a strange image that you are describing, and strange prisoners (*Atopon ... legeis eikona kai desmôtas atopous*)' (515a4).[21] The repetition of the adjective *atopos* (which is further emphasized through the construction in chiasm) is probably designed to prepare the reader for the shock Socrates' immediate reply is intended to give him: 'They're like us!' (a5).[22] No, Glaucon, Socrates is saying here, this image or this spectacle you are now imaginatively watching is not out of place, and these prisoners are nothing unfamiliar; on the very contrary, these prisoners are nothing but our own images, and this whole spectacle is nothing but the spectacle we give of ourselves.[23] And by 'ourselves,' we should understand, I think, not the whole of humanity as it were, but primarily Glaucon himself, and the audience around him (and further, Plato's Athenian readership): it is thus Glaucon (and Plato's audience) who is urged to open his eyes, and almost forced to watch this theatre which is like a mirror of his own life. For, since the cave is probably first of all the image of Athens (or any other democratic city), and the carriers represent the poets who are believed to educate people, the world of which Glaucon is a prisoner is his own cultural, and political world.[24] But realizing this cannot possibly be just a pure intellectualist understanding that his life would be better off if only he decided to deliver himself, to get out of this prison. To be sure, this is also, as Jonathan Lear has aptly called it, a 'wake-up call':[25] since the cave is presented as a world like Hades, where nobody wants to live, urging Glaucon to 'see' this vividly as himself being part of it, must be also a way to motivate him, and the audience, to undertake on their own the difficult path to the philosophic understanding of the Forms, and the Form of the Good. Not to be willing to try to escape the cave would be foolish, and in fact contrary to a human

---

[21] ἄτοπον ... λέγεις εἰκόνα καὶ δεσμώτας ἀτόπους.

[22] ὁμοίους ἡμῖν.

[23] See also Rutherford (2002), 258, commenting on the word '*atopos*': 'The simile itself is a reflection of reality; the strangeness of the other world evoked leads on to contemplation of our own'. On the importance of this sentence, see Smith (1999).

[24] I have tried to defend this claim in some detail in Destrée (2010). See also Schofield (2007), who rightly claims that the conversion which is here at the crux of this story 'involves primarily the shock of disillusionment about the moral values in the world of the city as it is' (222).

[25] Lear (2006), 35.

being's natural desire for happiness. By being given this depiction of such an awful world, and the dreadful state of its inhabitants, Glaucon cannot but be motivated to try to liberate himself from it. Or more precisely, he cannot but follow Socrates, who is, as it were, the unnamed character who delivers the prisoner who makes the ascent (this is alluded to a little further on, where Plato says that the prisoners would kill the philosopher who would wish to help them escape from the cave).[26]

This picture of the cave is also a sort of ironic rewriting of tragedy:

> What about when he reminds himself of his first dwelling place, what passed for wisdom there, and his fellow prisoners? Don't you think he would count himself happy (*eudaimonizein*) for the change and pity (*eleein*) the others?[27]
>
> (516c)

Pity is considered by Plato as the tragic emotion to be avoided because it destroys the courage of the guardians. Yet here, in a sort of ironic remark, it is the appropriate emotion that the philosopher would experience against the tragic Homeric world of Athens!

3. The Myth of Er

It is paradoxically, I have suggested, the invisible world of Hades which makes an audience see things that it does usually not (and, perhaps, does not want to) see: in the myth of Gyges, it is by descending into Hades that Glaucon discovers how he himself might be easily led to tyranny; and in the allegory of the Cave, he is urged by Socrates to see himself among the prisoners of the wrong values transmitted by the poets of Athens. The distance of Hades, we might say more generally, which is typically called *ekei*, in the distant 'there' (for example in the myth of Er), corresponds to the *diêgesis* of these narrations, as the distance needed by the audience to look at themselves.[28]

---

[26] David Reeve has objected to me that this is in fact a clear sign that the prisoners are perfectly happy with their situation, and the cave is thus not to be seen as a dreadful world to be got rid off. This is certainly true from their perspective since they do not know anything else, as it may also be the case that Glaucon is happy with Athens and its way of educating people. But this why Plato needs here such a vivid 'allegory': to open Glaucon's eyes to his in fact dreadful situation, and to make him aware that he is the prisoner of Athens' traditional (Homeric) values.

[27] τί οὖν; ἀναμιμνῃσκόμενον αὐτὸν τῆς πρώτης οἰκήσεως καὶ τῆς ἐκεῖ σοφίας καὶ τῶν τότε συνδεσμωτῶν οὐκ ἂν οἴει αὐτὸν μὲν εὐδαιμονίζειν τῆς μεταβολῆς, τοὺς δὲ ἐλεεῖν.

[28] On this, see also Nightingale (2002) who very interestingly interprets Plato's myths as instantiations of the *mimesis phantastikê* described in the *Sophist*.

At first sight, the myth of Er is an afterlife tale, intended to make us look at what our journey after death might look like. But the very paradoxical expression put into the mouth of the priest of Lachesis, '*psuchai ephemeroi*', should warn that the souls Plato is referring to are in fact human beings who are indeed alive, like us his audience, and there is no surprise then that he does not hesitate in oscillating between speaking of *psuchai* (with participles in the feminine) and human beings (using the masculine) in the description that follows. Or at least, this oscillation seems to indicate that this whole fantastic scenery of souls or people choosing their new life should be contemplated as a mirror-like description of the usual way people choose their lives.[29]

The comments Socrates offers to the settings of the scene (I mean by this, the announcement made the priest of Lachesis, and the description of the lots, 617d–618b) maintain the suspense before the reader is told of the scene of the choices of life, as if Plato was indicating how Glaucon and we readers should attend the spectacle that Er is about to report:

> Here, it seems, my dear Glaucon, human beings face the greatest dangers of all, and because of that each and any of us must, to the neglect of all other subjects, take care above all else to be a seeker and student of that subject (*mathêma*) which will enable him to learn and discover who will give him the ability and the knowledge to distinguish a good life from a bad, so that he will be always and in any circumstances choose the better one among those that are possible.[30]   (618b–c)

The spectacle that will be reported, Socrates announces, is intended to make us realize how important philosophy is here: the only important thing, if one wants to fulfil one's desire for happiness is to take care of the only *mathêma* that really counts, that is the *mathêma* provided by philosophy (which culminates in the *megiston mathêma* of the Form of the Good) that only would allow 'to choose always and in every circumstances (*aei pantachou*) the better life among the possible lives'. It would be exaggerating to infer from this that Plato would be talking about every choice, or every action one has to choose on an every-day basis.[31] But Plato certainly has in mind,

---

[29] On this I completely agree with Halliwell (2007), 469 (also followed by Ferrari [2009], 126). See also Thayer (1988), 376 who already suggested a similar interpretation.

[30] ἔνθα δή, ὡς ἔοικεν, ὦ φίλε Γλαύκων, ὁ πᾶς κίνδυνος ἀνθρώπῳ, καὶ διὰ ταῦτα μάλιστα ἐπιμελητέον ὅπως ἕκαστος ἡμῶν τῶν ἄλλων μαθημάτων ἀμελήσας τούτου τοῦ μαθήματος καὶ ζητητὴς καὶ μαθητὴς ἔσται, ἐάν ποθεν οἷός τ' ᾖ μαθεῖν καὶ ἐξευρεῖν τίς αὐτὸν ποιήσει δυνατὸν καὶ ἐπιστήμονα, βίον καὶ χρηστὸν καὶ πονηρὸν διαγιγνώσκοντα, τὸν βελτίω ἐκ τῶν δυνατῶν ἀεὶ πανταχοῦ αἱρεῖσθαι.

[31] So Thayer (1988), 370.

first of all (if not only), the fact that it is here and now that we have to take
care about this only really important subject of study, philosophy, which
alone can allow us the best 'choice of life,' that is the best possible life that
can lead to happiness. Something he repeats a little further along in saying
that such a *mathêma* would allow us:

> to always know how to choose the life that lies in the right measure and avoid
> the extremes, both in this life so far as it is possible, and in the whole of the
> life to come. For this is how a human being becomes happiest.[32]   (619a–b)

It is by doing philosophy with the help of the true philosopher (Socrates,
and not Thrasymachos) that we will be enabled to make the right 'choice of
life'.

The second point worth noticing in these comments is that Socrates
specifically addresses himself to Glaucon,—Glaucon who was already urged
by Socrates to embrace the life of philosophy in making the ascent out
of the cave. And Er is emphatically named twice as a 'messenger' (614d2,
619b2: 'a messenger who delivers a message'),[33] who is given the order to
deliver a message from the underworld of Hades. So it is a message to
be delivered to Glaucon (and the audience) through Socrates, as it were:
the last message, or the 'last call' delivered by Plato to his audience in
this nightly conversation urging them to take the firm decision to eventually practice philosophy in order to fulfil their desire for happiness. And
in the last, quite emphatic, sentence that ends the whole conversation,
which is also a sort of conclusion drawn from his narrating of the myth,
Socrates insists that taking advice from it might help us to 'stick to the
path upwards, and use every means to practice justice with wisdom in
order that we may be at peace with ourselves and the gods, both during our stay in this world, and once we have carried off the prize of justice like celebrating victors; and so that, both in this world and in the
thousand-year journey we have described, we may be happy' (621c–d).[34]

---

[32] ἀλλὰ γνῷ τὸν μέσον ἀεὶ τῶν τοιούτων βίον αἱρεῖσθαι καὶ φεύγειν τὰ ὑπερβάλλοντα ἑκατέρωσε
καὶ ἐν τῷδε τῷ βίῳ κατὰ τὸ δυνατὸν καὶ ἐν παντὶ τῷ ἔπειτα· οὕτω γὰρ εὐδαιμονέστατος γίγνεται
ἄνθρωπος.

[33] I think that we could also take Er's first mention, in the genitive form *Êros*, as a pun
with the nominative *hêrôs*, this *aggelos* being like the 'hero' Odysseus having escaped Hades'
world. Or might Plato have suggested a reference to *Odyssey*, 6.303, where Alkinous is named
a 'hero' (in fact, here, the master, or king)?

[34] τῆς ἄνω ὁδοῦ ἀεὶ ἑξόμεθα καὶ δικαιοσύνην μετὰ φρονήσεως παντὶ τρόπῳ ἐπιτηδεύσομεν,
ἵνα καὶ ἡμῖν αὐτοῖς φίλοι ὦμεν καὶ τοῖς θεοῖς, αὐτοῦ τε μένοντες ἐνθάδε, καὶ ἐπειδὰν τὰ ἆθλα
αὐτῆς κομιζώμεθα, ὥσπερ οἱ νικηφόροι περιαγειρόμενοι, καὶ ἐνθάδε καὶ ἐν τῇ χιλιέτει πορείᾳ, ἣν
διεληλύθαμεν, εὖ πράττωμεν.

By repeating the adverb 'here,' Socrates clearly emphasizes the fact that taking advice from his myth should help Glaucon here and now. But how exactly?

As Plato explicitly presents it, the myth of Er is a sort of re-writing of Homer's famous description of Odysseus in the underworld of Hades:

> It is not an Alcinous-story (*Alkinou apologon*) I am going to tell you, but that of a brave (*alkimou andros*) man called Er.[35]   (614b)

Obviously Plato warns his reader that he is going to replace Homer's poetry. But also, with this pun where the poetical word *alkimos* is emphatically used (only here in Plato), he also makes clear that his own *muthos* will be poetry too.[36] And it is also explicitly presented as a sort of theatre play to which Glaucon, and we readers, are conveyed to imaginatively attend in our turn:

> It was a spectacle worth attending, Er reported, to see how every soul chose their lives: a piteous, ridiculous, and surprising spectacle to be seen![37]
>
> (619e–620a)

I suppose Plato's present-day readers cannot but make the link here to the famous statement made at the end of the *Symposium* where Socrates, it is said there,

> was forcing them to recognize that it is up to the same man to be able to compose comedy as well as tragedy, and that the one who has the art of composing a tragedy can also be a composer of comedy.[38]   (223d)

Socrates is here talking to Agathon and Aristophanes, and one way to understand this surprising statement (since tragedy writers were usually not comedy writers) is that Plato is here describing how his own philosophical theatre, so to speak, is to replace traditional comic and tragic theatre.

In our passage of the *Republic*, the theatre is the scene Er is attending to, and also the one Glaucon has put before his eyes, and as is the case in

---

[35] ἀλλ' οὐ μέντοι σοι, ἦν δ' ἐγώ, Ἀλκίνου γε ἀπόλογον ἐρῶ, ἀλλ' ἀλκίμου μὲν ἀνδρός.

[36] Reeve (2004), 319, n. 25, suggests that the genitive *alkinou* might be taken as a compound of *alkê*, 'strength,' + *nous*, and *alkimou* as a compound of *alkê* + *Mousa*, which would imply that Plato wanted to show the force of poetry instead of philosophical understanding. This is a very interesting suggestion (even though, perhaps, a little bit put too far?) which would also show how ironic Plato remains towards Homer of whom he earlier argued that he has no understanding at all of important matters (598c–601a).

[37] ταύτην γὰρ δὴ ἔφη τὴν θέαν ἀξίαν εἶναι ἰδεῖν, ὡς ἕκασται αἱ ψυχαὶ ᾑροῦντο τοὺς βίους· ἐλεινήν τε γὰρ ἰδεῖν εἶναι καὶ γελοίαν καὶ θαυμασίαν.

[38] ... προσαναγκάζειν τὸν Σωκράτη ὁμολογεῖν αὐτοὺς τοῦ αὐτοῦ ἀνδρὸς εἶναι κωμῳδίαν καὶ τραγῳδίαν ἐπίστασθαι ποιεῖν, καὶ τὸν τέχνῃ τραγῳδοποιὸν ὄντα <καὶ> κωμῳδοποιὸν εἶναι.

comic and tragic theatre, ridicule and pity are to be felt by the spectators. Now, there is a major difference here between this literary theatre, and traditional Greek theatre. In tragic and comic theatre, as Plato has described it in the first part of book 10, the pleasure felt by the spectator essentially consists in *sumpathein*: in the case of tragedy, I paradoxically take pleasure in participating in the painful state of mind of the hero fallen into misfortune, that is I weep, and cry, and loudly lament, with, say, an Achilles in realizing that he has definitely lost his beloved Patrocles. Here, it must be emphasized, Plato obviously takes pain to multiply signs of indirectness: this is a report of an experience, which is told by Socrates, with only a few direct speech sentences. It is, briefly put, a *diegesis* of the type Plato is advocating in book 3, where the chance of *mimeistHai*, that is participating in sufferings, is very limited. As in the case of the pitiful state of the prisoners in the Cave, we spectators are not induced to feel pity, or only so in a sort of distant, ironic way. This is the reason why Plato seems to consider this whole scene as both pitiable and comic at the very same time. And, we may suppose that the benefit here, although indirect, is here patent too: Glaucon (and Plato's audience) are induced to be motivated to reconsider his own life, and values, and stick to his decision to follow Socrates in the difficult path towards the knowledge of the Good, which is the *conditio sine qua non* for obtaining the *eudaimonia* he is seeking after.

PART II

APPROACHES TO PLATONIC MYTHS

CHAPTER SEVEN

THE PRAGMATICS OF "MYTH" IN PLATO'S DIALOGUES: THE STORY OF PROMETHEUS IN THE *PROTAGORAS**

Claude Calame

Apart from a plot that has been paired with a few proper names belonging to a tradition, there is nothing more unstable, nothing more variable than a Greek myth; and there is nothing more varied than the use that has been made of tales which, by their reference to a time when mortal heroes were still near to the gods, offer a strong pragmatic dimension; a strong poetic dimension, must one hasten to add, insofar as it is true that the heroic tale does not exist outside the poetic form which addresses it to a given audience and political community, and which assures its symbolic and social efficacy.[1]

1. THE MYTHOLOGICAL FREEDOM OF THE HOMERIC POEMS

From the *Iliad* on, in the vast domain of the unfolding of heroic fiction that is epic poetry, plots involving heroes not participating in the Trojan War are used to a persuasive end. Such is the case, for example, of the well-known use of the story of Meleager made by old Phoenix in an attempt to convince Achilles to return to the centre of the battlefield of Troy. In his *muthos*, which is understood as an argumentative discourse, the hero inserts as a conclusion the high deed (*ergon*) of the Aetolians in the defence of the city of Calydon when the Couretes tried to conquer it—a heroic action of time gone by (*palai*) and not of recent events (*neon*), the protagonist of which is Meleager, son of the king of Aetolian Calydon. All takes place as if the sage Phoenix were applying to the fictional time of the heroes the same distinction as would later be adopted by the first historiographers,

---

* Translated by John MacCormick. Many thanks to Maria Vamvouri Ruffy; her reading of a first version of the present study was very useful to me as was also stimulating my reading of her own paper (to be published).

[1] In dialogue with others, I have had several occasions to defend such a thesis, notably in Calame (1996), 12–50 and (2000), 11–69. See also Buxton (1994), 18–52.

Herodotus and then Thucydides: then it is the Trojan War itself which becomes a *palaion* or an *archaion*, while the Persian Wars belong to the order of the recent past (*neon*) or of the 'new' (*kainon*)². This heroic age corresponds to the time of the ancestors (*hoi proteroi*, etc.), just as Phoenix likewise places the fight over the Boar of Calydon among the 'glorious acts of the warrior heroes' (*klea andrôn hêrôôn*), men of old (*prosthen*). This is to say that Phoenix, in the logic of epic narration, refers to the same sort of past as that which encompassed, for the first Greek historiographers, the ancient history which is represented by the reign of Minos or the Trojan War. And this within a narrative enunciation which is founded upon memory (*memnêmai*), just as for Thucydides the saga of the Atridae rests upon 'memory' (*mnêmê*)³—or, as we would say, on oral tradition!

Reduced to a mythographical summary, we know the story: In her rage against Oeneus who neglected to sacrifice to her, Artemis incites the boar of Calydon, which ravages Oeneus' vineyards. Meleager kills the beast, and the Aetolians and the Couretes quarrel over its remains. Faced with the curses of his mother, whose brother he has killed, Meleager leaves the combat out of spite, in order to rest at the side of his wife, the beautiful Cleopatra. Rejecting the gifts which the elders successively offer him to persuade him to take up the fight again, Meleager finally cedes only to the supplications of his wife, threatened by the Couretes who have now penetrated within the walls of the city of Calydon. Taken up by Phoenix as he tries to convince Achilles in his turn to return to the battlefield, the tale founds and illustrates a double argument for the hero's benefit: he should return to battle, not only to assure the safety of the endangered Achaeans, but also in order that he may accept the presents offered by his peers to maintain his honour. Achilles refuses the offer: to the honours done him by men he prefers the glory reserved for him by his Zeus-accomplished destiny.⁴

The version of the Meleager story that is put in the mouth of Phoenix differs from other poetic versions on three essential points. The Iliadic version omits Meleager's mother's attempt to fulfil her curse by burning the brand attached to the destiny of her son; moreover, it is silent concerning the succeeding death of Meleager by the will of Apollo; finally, by introduc-

---

² I have attempted a semantic analysis of these terms in a 2006 study.

³ Thucydides I, 9, 1–3, where this epic memory is then associated with the name of Homer. On the epic memory of the protagonists in the *Iliad*, cf. Nagy (1996), 138–144 and 151–152, with reference to Martin (1987), 77–88, which also offers a good analysis of the pragmatic sense of *muthos* (12–18 and 22–32) as a 'discourse from authority'.

⁴ Homer, *Iliad*, IX, 513–605, and then 606–619. On the 'prize of honour,' cf. Scheid-Tissinier (1994), 196–203.

ing the figure of Cleopatra this Homeric version turns the ephebe Meleager into a married man.[5] The adult Meleager thus becomes, in his privileged relationship with Cleopatra, the homologue of Achilles in his intimate relationship with Patroclus. The stakes of this double relationship seem to be inscribed in the names of the two partners compared: by an interposed etymological play; in effect, independently of all morphologically or linguistically founded etymology, the homological denomination of Cleopatra and Patroclus inscribes the two heroic figures within the order of the '*kléos* of fathers,' that is, ancestral glory.[6] It is indeed heroic glory that is at stake in the tale recounted by Phoenix as well as in the epic narration of the wrath of Achilles itself.

It is thus within the scope of the bard's poetic liberty to orientate and to recreate a tale belonging to the tradition of the heroic past, not only in order to adapt it to a particular enunciative context, but also to confer upon it, in this particular situation, a singular argumentative efficacy, within a pragmatic situation of which the outcome remains naturally uncertain.

2. 'PLATO'S MYTHS': ENUNCIATIVE ASPECTS

Les mythes de Platon, the title of a recent collection in French of the tales inserted into Plato's dialogues is, all in all, misleading. Not only do these tales have content which does not correspond to our encyclopaedic definition of myth; but the Platonic narratives have different speakers: Glaucon in the *Republic* for the 'myth of the ring of Gyges' or Aristophanes in the *Symposium* for the 'myth of the *androgunoi*'. These protagonists speak in different contexts: for instance the 'myth of the reign of Cronus' is evoked by the Athenian Stranger before his Cretan and Spartan interlocutors during the enquiry about the best political constitution which punctuates the *Laws* or, by reference to the same age of Cronos, the 'myth of the judgement of souls' is attributed to Homer and is told by Socrates during his discussion with Callicles about the just life in the *Gorgias*; and they offer different enunciative stratifications and hierarchisations with their polyphonic effect: the story of the genealogy of Eros told by Diotima to Socrates who recounts it

---

   [5] See respectively Bacchylides, *Victory-Odes*, V, 136–154, Hesiod, *Catalogue*, fr. 25, 9–13 Merkelbach-West and Simonides, fr. 564 Page. More references can be found in Bremmer (1988), 39–47, who mentions the different hypotheses brought forward for the last century and a half to account for these divergences.

   [6] On this topic one may consult the etymologizing demonstration in Nagy (1990), 196–197 and 205, with reference to an earlier study. See also the fine analysis proposed by Edmunds (1993), 37–39 and 64–66.

to the guests of the *Symposium*, or the story of Atlantis told by the Egyptian priests to Solon, who recounts it to the Athenians; among them Critias the Elder, whom Critias, the protagonist of the *Timaeus*, heard recount it while very young, only to tell it in his turn to Socrates and Hermocrates while invoking, like a poet, the authority of Mnemosyne.[7]

These remarkable enunciative gaps engage us to read the stories that Plato puts in the mouths of the characters in his dialogues not only in their internal logic, of both a syntactic and semantic nature, or in the reorientations they present from these two points of view with respect to other versions of the same narrative plot; but it invites us also to follow the enunciative strategies which bring us back, from a pragmatic point of view, to the context of the speech of the character who puts it forward and, beyond that, to the argumentative and thematic context of the dialogue as a whole, if not to its exterior philosophical and social context. In such an approach, it is not a matter of judging only the effectiveness of the 'myth,' but also of evaluating its effects within a particularly rich network of semantic lines and cultural representations.

It is thus a proposal situated between discourse analysis and anthropological perspective that I would like to illustrate by Plato's treatment of the 'myth of Prometheus' in the *Protagoras*. In a way, the dialogue itself invites us to do so, since Protagoras, while introducing his stories, explicitly asks his interlocutors whether they prefer a demonstrative illustration by means of a *muthos* or an exposition in the mode of *logos*; since the majority of them leave the choice to him, the sophist decides to tell a story (*muthon legein*). The criterion of contrast between *muthos* and *logos* is solely of the order of the charm exercised by the former; it has nothing to do with any form of rationality.[8] In brief, the reading proposed here will successively adopt four points of view: internal narrative analysis will concern the semantic logic of the story; then a study of differential comparison with another version of the story will reveal its specificities; enunciative study in context will allow us to give an initial explanation of these narrative and semantic particularities; finally, broad contextual perspective will assure the passage from aetiology to pragmatics in the dramatic setting and argumentative unfolding of the dialogue.

---

[7] The collection is that of Pradeau (2004). One may refer to the useful clarification by Clay (2007).

[8] Plato, *Protagoras*, 320c. On the argumentative alternative between the mode of *muthos*-story and *logos*-exposition (also offered, for example, at *Gorgias*, 523a and *Timaeus*, 26e), see Brisson (1982), 139–142, as well as Calame (1996), 27–28 and 166–168. For the *Timaeus*, cf. Rowe (1998), 271–278. For the sense of *epídeixis*, cf. *infra*, n. 22.

3. THE PROMETHEUS STORY IN THE *PROTAGORAS*:
NARRATIVE AND SEMANTIC LOGIC

To begin with, let us follow the unravelling of the story in its narrative logic and semantic development.[9]

First, a spatio-temporal framework: 'long ago,' in the indeterminate past when only the gods lived, 'inside' a land which will correspond to the inhabited world, and by necessity; the gods are the sole first protagonists of the story. Then a first narrative step, marking a first change of state: the creation by the gods of mortal beings from a mix of fire and earth. It belongs to Epimetheus, the first character named, to equip these animals with distinctive qualities, according to a principle of compensatory distribution: so there is no natural selection for living beings which will be provided, according to a functional principle, with organs that permit them to respond in different ways to the threats of the environment (hooves, fur, thick skin, etc.).

But Epimetheus, whose name means 'afterthought,' does not have the wisdom of his brother Prometheus, whose name endows him etymologically with foresight. In his concern for distributive equilibrium, the not-so-*sophos* forgets human beings who, when they appear in the light of day, remain in a state of utter lack. So there comes in a second narrative phase, of which the principal actor is Prometheus. To save men from their hopeless situation, Prometheus steals artisanal know-how (*entekhnos sophia*; 321d) from Athena, and from her associate Hephaestus the art of fire without which other skills are nothing. Second change of state: in passing from *aporia* to *euporia*, man now possesses all the necessities of life: housing, shelter and food. Added to these is the interaction with the gods which is allowed to him by his share in the divine nature and his communication by articulate language.

Nevertheless, as much in their relationships with animals as in their dealings with one another, men remain entirely at a loss, being ignorant of all community life and incapable of applying their technical skills (*hê demiourgikê tekhnê*, 322b) to life in cities. It now falls to Zeus to perfect, in a third stage, the civilization of men. The king of the gods thus asks Hermes to bring mortals shame (*aidôs*, 322c2) and justice (*dikê*) which make up, no doubt, 'the social bond'. Contrary to the technical arts which are the

---

[9] Plato, *Protagoras*, 320c–322d. For the Neo-Platonic interpretations of this *muthos*, see the study of H. Tarrant in the present volume.

domain of a few specialists, reserve and justice will be distributed equally to all. The law of Zeus will then be that anyone who transgresses these two fundamental principles of life in society will be punished by death.

One notices that the version of the Prometheus story as it is taken up by Protagoras to support his position obeys neither the logic of a completed narrative plot, nor that of a genealogical tale; we find in it neither the narrative sanction which would be represented by the punishment of Prometheus with the return to narrative equilibrium expected from any 'myth' (man is always in danger of transgressing the two principles of restraint and justice), nor the establishment of a diversified order resulting from the application of the narrative figure of engenderment. But the story is animated by a cumulative logic which, by the artisanal crafts which provide the necessities of life and promote association with the gods, allows men to survive, deprived as they are, before Zeus grants them the two principles that found the art of politics and thus life in society, all while intending to punish those who fail to respect them.

It is, no doubt, as hopeless to look in this founding story for the three functions of Indo-European ideology as to attempt to reduce its semantic material to a chain of structural oppositions.[10] On the one hand, even if it is really possible to make the art of politics correspond to the function of sovereignty and to bring together the 'public crafts' and agriculture under the title of the function of production, the art of strategy is explicitly subordinated by Protagoras to the first function. On the other hand, if, adopting a structuralist perspective, political skill really does seem to be opposed to artisanal know-how, the human being is not structurally opposed to the gods since he 'shares in the divine condition'. What is more, if beside the ambivalent action of Epimetheus, Prometheus's theft of the techniques of craftsmanship for the sake of mankind really does contrast with the gift of political know-how by Zeus (via the passer-god Hermes), the one cannot be 'radically' opposed to the other: in fact, not only are the public crafts provided to men just as much as is the art of politics, in a general and universal manner, but the two values founding political know-how cannot in the end be assumed by all people despite their universal distribution. The fact is that, in the logic of its unfolding in three steps, the story undergoes three slides which keep it from acquiring a binary structure; on the one

---

[10] Reference is made to the attempt at a structural study of the 'myth of Protagoras' presented by Brisson (1975), 9–23, which states the difficulty of giving a reading of this story in terms of tri-functional ideology.

hand, though both handicraft and statecraft are first envisaged as *sophia* and *tekhnê* given to man at large in a universal repartition, they come to be distinguished from one another insofar as the techniques of craftsmanship, by passing from singular to plural, become the province of specialists only; on the other hand, the participation in restraint and justice, which found the social bond and are universally 'placed' among human beings, seems in the end to depend on man himself. Neither the know-how of the craftsman, nor the art of politics with its military corollary is definitively inscribed, by a divine act, in mortal man. We shall have occasion to return to these disconnects and inconsistencies in a narrative syntax of which the end, from a semantic point of view, seems to indicate a process of education.

On the other hand, what we shall retain from the beginning is the linguistic isotopy which runs through the story while assuring its coherence from a semantic point of view. In contrast to the different animal species which Epimetheus provides with capacities (*dunameis*), the human race, for its part, has the benefit not only of ritual relationships with the gods and of a language to communicate, but also, through the intervention of Prometheus and then of Hermes, of technical arts which come under the framework of know-how (*sophia*). These are arts which, from the blacksmith's trade to the art of politics by way of language itself, are all products of the artisanal intelligence that is *mêtis* (a term which, curiously, does not appear in the story recounted by Protagoras). If, by way of justice, social wisdom ultimately depends on Zeus, the other *tekhnai* are the province of the clever Athena, born from the head of her father Zeus, and of the lame Hephaestus, the master of the arts of fire and the forge. The mention of the collaboration of these two divinities helps implicitly to centre the story on Athens.[11] Moreover, the modes of action of the three divine figures who intervene as intermediaries between living beings and the gods in the three phases of the *muthos* are all inscribed in their turn in the order of *mêtis*: Epimetheus by his *sophia*, partial though it is, Prometheus by trickery and theft, Hermes by his role as communicator and ferryman. All three are gods who act by means of expedients, with the ambiguity that the Classical Greeks attributed to any action placed under the sign of ingenious artisanal intelligence.

But what are the stakes of this semantically coherent, but narratively shaky story?

---

[11] Both for the craftsman's know-how and for the collaboration of Athena and Hephaestus and the domain of handicraft, one may refer to the classic study of Detienne and Vernant (1974), 167–175 and 242–258.

4. Differential Comparison: The Prometheus of Aeschylus

From the staging of *Prometheus bound* as a tragic hero to a cliff in a distant desert region of frigid Scythia, we shall retain here only that which concerns the *tekhnai* invented for mortal men. As we know, everything in the text of the *Prometheus Bound* as it has come down to us is subject to controversy, from its attribution to Aeschylus to its place in the trilogy consecrated to the Titan's fate.[12] For the sake of comparison (contrastive and differential) with the tale of Protagoras in the dialogue that bears his name, we shall essentially focus on one scene; enchained before the chorus of the daughters of Ocean who are bewailing the fate of the unfortunate Titan, Prometheus lists the different arts he conceived to give to human beings in their primordial lack.[13]

From the very beginning, there is mention of the theft of the fire that is qualified as the foundation of all technique (*pántekhnos*); Prometheus must be punished, in accordance the 'tyrannical' power of Zeus. Stolen through excessive love for mortal men, fire shows itself to be—according to the very words recited by Prometheus—'the master of every art, a powerful expedient'.[14] The story that the hero recounts, while enchained by the will of Zeus (with the help of Power and Violence), of the gift to mortals of the arts he invented is divided into two moments. In a first state of their existence, men, though now endowed with sight and vision, were blind and deaf: like ants they lived deep in dark grottos, 'like the forms of dreams,' acting in the most total confusion, without discernment. It is precisely because they are presented as arts allowing men to distinguish one thing or property from another that the *tekhnai* offered by Prometheus contribute to the advent of a second state: that of civilization.

Founded in general on signs to be deciphered in the surrounding world, the Promethean *tekhnai* are semiotic, interpretative arts: the reading of the movement of the stars to anticipate the seasons and plan agricultural work, the hermeneutics of dreams to determine the future, the interpretation of

---

[12] Aeschylus, *Prometheus Bound*, 436–506. The work's authenticity has often been questioned; on this topic see Griffith (1983), 242–253, with an exhaustive bibliography on the subject of this controversy. For the equally controversial question of the trilogy—or tetralogy— to which the *Prometheus Bound* no doubt belonged, cf. Griffith (1983), 281–305.

[13] Aeschylus, *Prometheus Bound*, 436–506. On the semiotic distinction between the *tekhnai* invented and offered to men by Aeschylus' Prometheus, cf. Calame (forthcoming).

[14] Aeschylus, *Prometheus Bound*, 7–9 and 107–123. See also 251–254. Cf. Saïd (1985), 118–122 for a study of the technical values attributed to the Promethean fire, in contrast to the Hesiodic version.

the songs and behaviour of birds for the purposes of the mantic art, the reading of the signs presented by the entrails of the animal sacrificed to the gods and by the flames that consume their flesh as presages, but also more abstract signs, such as numbers, the combination of the letters of the alphabet that is the 'memory of all things, the artisan mother of the Muses' or the means of handicraft such as the harness and the yoke that serve to submit the animal to the practice of man, and finally the arts of metallurgy, 'bronze, iron, silver and gold'. These are artisanal expedients of the order of that ingenious, hermeneutical dexterity which man forever after shares with Prometheus.

These techniques, no doubt, are *ôphelêmata*; they are the source of a profit which corresponds to the philanthropy displayed by the Titan. But as such, the Promethean *tekhnai* expose human beings, civilised for ever after, to the implicit risk of overstepping in their turn the limits that are assigned to mortal man. Returning to his own fate, Prometheus affirms it explicitly at the end of his long tirade: above the power and will of Zeus, there is the power of Fate, to which the master of gods and men is himself submitted; in this respect, '*tekhnê* is much weaker than necessity'. The hierarchy in the action of mortal man is that of traditional theology, already widely represented in the *Iliad*: the action taken by man is submitted to the will of the gods, who themselves contribute to accomplishing *moira*, the lot fallen to everyone.

If the *Prometheus Bound* ends with the intervention of Zeus's thunder, intended to destroy the arrogant loquaciousness of a tragic hero who deplores yet again the injustice of which he is the victim, we know nothing of the end of the trilogy and thus of the plot as a whole. We can only suppose that the third tragedy ended in an aetiological mode, with the institution of the ritual of the *Promethia*. Celebrated in Athens, this torch-race began at the altar consecrated to the Titan hero at the Academy and it was accompanied by the choral chants of adolescents and adult men.[15]

Thus Aeschylus' attribution to Prometheus of the technical gifts to men is distinguished from the version rewritten by Plato on three essential points. Contrary to the Platonic version where deprived men benefit from the moment of civilization from the artisanal intelligence that has been introduced by Prometheus and without which they could not survive, in Aeschylus the human race knows a first stage of life as animals. Furthermore, even if

---

[15] Cf. Griffith (1983), 282–283 and 303–304, and for Prometheus' cult at Athens, Pisi (1990), 21–57.

the arts of Prometheus are imagined in both versions in terms of *tekhnai* and *sophia*, neither Athena nor Hephaestus is mentioned in the *mûthos* staged by Aeschylus for arts that unfold in a much wider spectrum than those focussed on the artisanal use of fire to acquire food and clothing. What is more, everything happens as if, for the many arts of divination and foresight put forward by Aeschylus' Prometheus, Plato in his dialogue substitutes, after a fashion, the divine lot fallen to man in contrast to other living beings. Finally, there is no word from Aeschylus' Prometheus of the art of politics and the two qualities of restraint and justice which are at its foundation, except in so far as his own conflict with Zeus, because of the act of theft, comes entirely within the order of *dikê*.

5. Enunciative Structure and Semantic Slides: The Immediate Context

Independently of the discursive genre in question (tragedy on one side, philosophical dialogue on the other), one of the fundamental traits which differentiate Aeschylus' story from Plato's is of an enunciative nature. From the point of view of spatio-temporal location, if the story told by the tragic Prometheus of the gift to man of different civilizing *tekhnai* refers us to a relatively near past and to a spatial framework that is valid for all men, Protagoras' narration of the same story situates the Titan's action in a 'mythical' past where only the gods exist and in a space explicitly oriented on Athens. But the important difference is concerned with the subject of the enunciation: a story in the first person in the Aeschylean dramatization, and a third-person account in the Platonic dialogue. It is with this secondary narrative effect, saturated with *I*-forms, the story of *Prometheus bound* is referred directly, by its speaker, to the present situation, whereas due to the almost mythographical form conferred on the story of a Prometheus who remains free, it belongs to Protagoras to return to the present time and place of his enunciation.[16]

Thus we are brought back to the immediate context of the 'mythological' narration. In Aeschylus it takes the form of a defence of an action of which the protagonist, in full clear-sightedness, himself analyses in tragic terms the threefold motivation his action is submitted to: the tyrannical will of Zeus,

---

[16] The story told by Prometheus goes no further than to attribute to tradition (*legetai*, 322a) some punishment for the theft, a punishment of which the origin is traced to Epimetheus, in a text where attempts have been made to delete this strange remark.

the force of Moira with the necessity she imposes and finally the fault fully assumed by the hero—'willingly, willingly, did I err'.[17] In Plato's dialogue, it belongs to Protagoras, by the intermediary of a renewed address to Socrates, to inscribe the story in an explicitly aetiological perspective.

And so it is at Athens, in the present situation, imagined and dramatized for the dialogue, that the plot unfolded in the story finds its phase of narrative sanction and consequently its reason: it is a matter of giving at once the origin and the cause (*aitia*, 323a) of a present state.[18] Thence comes the cumulative logic of the tale itself. By an aetiological device, the story is focussed at its conclusion not only on the time of the conversation with Protagoras, but also on Athens: 'It is thus and for these reasons that all men, and in particular the Athenians ...' (322d). The pragmatic effect of the story is made explicit: the story accounts for the present and at the same time legitimises it. As for virtue-*aretê*, it is fitting to distinguish between artisanal capacities in general, such as architecture, which are the province of specialists, and political virtue, in which all must participate in order that life in the *polis* become possible.

Paradoxically, such a conclusion corresponds to the hypothesis advanced by Socrates, using the Athenian people as an example, in the speech which precedes and provokes Protagoras' story. We can, no doubt, affirm that the Athenians like other Greek have access to knowledge: they are *sophoi* (319b4). Nonetheless, when they are brought together in the assembly, they do not hesitate to call upon specialists as soon as a question arises concerning an artisanal practice, that is a practice which is learned and taught; however, when it is a matter of the administration of the city, everyone thinks he may take place in the debate, independently of his standing and the craft he has learned. Conclusion: virtue (*aretê*, 319e) is not the object of teaching, neither in public affairs nor in private. Socrates illustrates his thesis with two examples: that of the two sons of Pericles entrusted to a tutor for everything but virtue, and that of Clinias, the younger brother of Alcibiades, declared hopeless by his tutor, the brother of Pericles! To the examples drawn from the present regarding the non-teachable character of virtue, Protagoras responds by a declamatory 'demonstration' (*epideixis*, 230b) which is constituted by, in the literal sense of the term, the narration of the Prometheus story.[19]

---

[17] Aeschylus, *Prometheus Bound*, 10–11, 103–105 and 266 (for the quotation). Cf. Saïd (1985), 284–291.

[18] For the various procedures of Greek aetiology, see Delattre (2009).

[19] For the sense of *epideixis*, cf. *infra*, n. 22.

Is this to say that the 'mythical' story is nothing but the simple confirmation of Socrates' thesis regarding the non-teachable character of virtue? At the end of the mythographical-style narration, the original distinction made by Socrates between artisanal know-how and *aretê* has transformed into a division between technical skill and *tekhnê politikê* (322b). Moreover, the basic values of this particular skill have been made precise: they are restraint (or shame) and justice. Finally these two values, as guarantees of the social bond, are placed under the lofty jurisdiction of Zeus. The hierarchical order that the myth establishes, from the viewpoint of both distributive and egalitarian justice, among Zeus, Hermes, Prometheus and Epimetheus is striking: this order of justice more nearly evokes the Zeus who is master of *dikê* in the cities as imagined by Hesiod in the *Works and Days* than it does the tyrannical Zeus, jealous of Prometheus' philanthropy, of Aeschylus' conception.

But in the etiological commentary of Protagoras, the 'political skill' distributed by Zeus to all men by the intermediary of Hermes becomes *politikê aretê* (323a); as to its fundamental values *dikê* and *aidôs*, they have become *dikaiosunê* and *sophrosunê*. Thus, at the bottom of the hierarchy, the apologue of the successive gifts of Epimetheus, Prometheus and Zeus can appear as a narrative illustration (*muthos*!) of Socrates' initial affirmation: 'As for me, Protagoras, if I look at these examples, I consider that virtue (*aretê*, 320b) cannot be taught.' By the intermediary of the first lexical and semantic slide indicated, Protagoras admits that it is fitting to make a distinction, from the point of view of instruction, between the skills depending on artisanal know-how (given by Prometheus in the story) and virtue as now restrained to political excellence (still *tekhnê* under the control of Zeus in the myth). On the other hand, at the bottom of the hierarchy and by the second slide mentioned, the definition in abstract terms of the two foundations of excellence prepares the exchange which concludes the first exchange regarding the unity of virtue and the relative character of the good.

6. The Pragmatics of *Aporia*: The Wider Context

The pragmatic articulation of the Protagoras' story about the Promethean arts with both the immediate before and after of its context of enunciation is an invitation to look in the dialogue as a whole for some of the threads woven together in its figurative narrative argumentation.

Several studies have at last recognized the importance of the stage-setting of a Platonic dialogue for both its argumentative and semantic unfolding.[20] These initial stage-settings, with their different enunciative dis-connects, assume a function analogous to the preludes of the great narrative poetry of the Homeric type: they serve both to define the declarative pos-ture of the author and to give an indication of the theme of the poetic tale: the implications of the anger of Achilles or the tribulations undergone by Odysseus, told by the divine voice through the inspired mouth of the singer in the case of the Homeric poems. In the introduction to the long prologue of the *Protagoras*, it is precisely on Homer that Socrates calls to confirm the effect of grace provoked by the tender beauty of young men like Alcibiades; this is a way to confer upon the quality of the sage (*to sophôtaton*, 309c), incarnated by Protagoras, the charm (*kharis*, 310a) exercised by the physical beauty of a young man. The question is then asked, what is a sophist? This will be the thematic function of what follows the prelude, the enunciative function of which is to subordinate to Socrates' meeting with a friend the entire story of the exchange with Protagoras; this declarative device makes Socrates the 'author' and the dramatizer of the dialogue as a whole![21] True to the tradition of symposiastic conversations and like in other dialogues, the proposed theme is a matter of definition: 'What is a sophist?'

The question of the definition of the *sophistês* leads to that concerning the content of the knowledge of the expert in 'wise things' (*ho tôn sophôn epistemôn*, 312c) and of the possibility of transmitting it: these *sopha*, are they *mathêmata* in the same sense as the arts of the painter or the carpenter? With this first juxtaposition of the knowledge of the sophist with the skills of the artisan, the answer is suspended until Protagoras, at the end of the prologue, himself begins to speak: the sophist then compares his art with that of the poets, of the masters of imitation, of the prophets or of the masters of music and gymnastics. The comparison tends to make fluid, once again, the distinction between the art of the sophist and the arts of the other *sophoi*. In effect, in their educational aim, the arts of Homer, of Hesiod or of Simonides, of Orpheus or of Musaeus, of Herodicus or of Agathocles are but 'masks' (*proskhêma*, 316d) of the *sophistikê tekhnê*! From content, we have passed insensibly to the question of the form and to that of the function. By anticipation, Socrates had already compared the charm exercised by

---

[20] See for instance the study by Desclos (2001), which makes reference to other studies on the stage-settings that introduce Plato's dialogues.

[21] Because of the substitution of the 'I' of Socrates for the 'I' of the author, Laks (2004), 107–117 speaks of the 'disegotisation' of Plato's dialogues. For the structure of the dialogue as a whole, I follow for convenience the working proposal made by Demont and Trédé (1993), 27–29.

Protagoras on his adepts to the bewitching effect (*kelôn*, 315b) of the voice of Orpheus. So it is no surprise to see that Protagoras, as Socrates recounts, at first prefers a narrative and illustrative *muthos* to an argued *logos*: to tell (*legein*) a 'myth' is much more pleasant (*khariesteron*, 320c)!

Thus we come to the introduction of the first 'round' of a conversation which contains three. After having presented himself as a sophist and educator of men, Protagoras defines the object of his teaching (*mathêma*, 318e) as the enlightened administration of household and public affairs, by words and by actions. Thus the function of the sophist's knowledge and its effect through teaching count for as much as its content. It is then that Socrates—as we have seen—has no difficulty in labelling the sophist's art as *politikê tekhnê* (319a), while still pretending that, being as it surely is concerned with virtue, this knowledge cannot be taught! Thence a version of the myth of Prometheus which, even though it is spoken by Protagoras, ends up bringing confirmation in some way to Socrates' antithetical hypothesis. The Titan divinity brought to men all the techniques of artisanal intelligence, but it belongs to Zeus to distribute to them the craft of politics; a *tekhnê* which becomes *aretê* even in Protagoras' own commentary. As is claimed by our hypothesis, everything takes place as if the reorientations that have been remarked in the conduct of Protagoras placed the story firmly in Socrates' perspective. In contrast to the other arts, all citizens have a share in (political) virtue which, from the point of view of the mythical tradition, is a gift of Zeus to the human race in general.

'To have a share in justice (*dikaiosunê*, 323c), belongs specifically to humanity,' concludes Protagoras, before proposing again that such a virtue can be the object of instruction! To defend this rather contradictory position, the sophist passes from the mode of *epideixis* to that of *apodeixis* (*apodeixai*, 323c; cf. 324c),[22] and to pass from declamatory illustration by means of a traditional story to demonstration that relies on arguments means in this particular case to rely on the opposition between the innate and the acquired. To defects such as ugliness, shortness or weakness, which are the effects of nature or of chance (*phusei ê tukhêi*, 323d) are opposed injustice and impiety, which bring about punishment and exhortation and which thus come within the scope of the exercise and the teaching of which *politikê aretê* (323e) is the object.

---

[22] The semantic distinction between *epideixis*, notably as a rhetorical display of specialist knowledge, and *apodeixis* as a public demonstration supported by proof was already made by Herodotus: cf. Thomas (2000), 221–269. The narrative itself may follow the model of sophistic *muthoi* in prose: see Manuwald (2003), 49–57.

The passage from the mode of *muthos* to that of *logos* then brings about, in the mouth of Protagoras, a semantic widening of political virtue to virtue in general; it now includes *dikaiosunê, sôphrosunê* as well as respect for the gods (*to hosion*, 325a). In a flight of oratory worthy of the plea in the *Republic* regarding the necessity of musical education, epic and lyric poets are called upon to educate the body and the mind (*dianoia*, 326b) of the young child, by means of rhythm and harmony, to speak and act out of respect for justice. In return, by implicit reference to the story of Prometheus and Zeus, no man is a stranger to *aretê*. Thus the distinction posited between the innate and the acquired is diluted; every man is susceptible of becoming better under the effect of education. *Muthos* and *logos* definitively lead to the same conclusion: 'Virtue can be taught, and such is the opinion of the Athenians'. It is no longer a personal conclusion, but one of which the declaration is widened to include the authority of the Athenians in order to make it a truth that is generally affirmed. It is significant that the final example chosen by Protagoras is no longer the one put forward by Socrates just before the narration of the story of Prometheus: no longer the two sons of the statesman Pericles, the *sophos* in *aretê* (320a), but that of the two sons of the sculptor Polyclitus, who, moreover, has already been mentioned by Socrates in the prelude scene as an example of an artisan and a salaried instructor, along with the physician Hippocrates of Cos (311b). The offspring of the famous sculptor are no more comparable to their father than are the children of the eminent politician. From the point of view of instruction, the difference between artisanal techniques, given to man by Prometheus, and virtue, distributed by Zeus to all men, has apparently been erased!

Faced with this convergence of mythical narration and argued discourse,[23] Socrates prudently prefers to leave the minefield of pedagogy in order to take up again, still as a matter of definition but according to the mode of dialectic, the question of the unity of virtue and its parts in their reciprocal relationships: *dikaiosunê, sôphrosunê, hosiotês* (329c); they were mentioned successively in the story and in the speech of Protagoras. Surely we remember the dialogue of lexical semantics that is engaged from that point on, in a very sophistic fashion, to lead to the question of the relationship between the good and the useful. In the respect, as a true sophist, Protagoras can only adopt a relativistic conclusion; illustrating his point by

---

[23] On this subject in detail, see Morgan (2000), 138–147.

the example of the different uses that can be made of oil, he says: 'The good (*to agathon*, 334b) is something so varied and diverse that, for man, what is good for the outside of the body is very harmful inside'.

To Conclude: *Pro-mêtheia*

So much for the first section of the dialogue, in which the story of Prometheus is integrated. One ought naturally to pursue the enquiry through the second 'round' which unfolds entirely in the dialectical mode. To support his argument, instead of the narration of a *muthos*, Socrates employs an exegesis of a celebrated lyric poem of Simonides. This will be a pretext for returning to the question of education and the good in, on the one hand, a new discussion of a linguistic nature concerning the semantic difference between 'being (good)' and 'becoming' it (*emmenai/einai* and *genesthai*, 340b), and, on the other hand, by the introduction of the role played by the will not only in the performance of a good action, but in the praise that the poet may make of any action that is not ugly.[24] We should notice that in the cutting-up of the lyric poem that Socrates performs in order to integrate its ethical arguments into his own demonstration, he avoids the heroic examples that would necessarily be included in a poem written in Aeolian metre and composed to be sung in performance.

And so in the third debate the question of the unity of virtue can be taken up again, particularly in relation to courage (*andreia*, which is added to *sôphrosunê* + *sophia*, *dikaisosunê* and *hosiotês*, 349b); Socrates ends up attributing to this virtue the status of knowledge (*epistêmê*), which implies that it can be taught. In one final *mise en abyme*, Socrates calls upon his own speech, which has arrived like a tragedy at its *exodos* (361a), to give it voice and invite it to send both its author and Protagoras away without deciding in favour of either: the former because in maintaining that virtue, along with its various parts, is a form of knowledge, he implies that it can be taught, in contradiction with his original affirmation; and the latter because he in his turn contradicts himself in denying that virtue is knowledge whereas at the beginning of the conversation he had maintained that it is teachable. Socrates has the last word: 'As for me, I prefer to Epimetheus (who neglected

---

[24] Simonides, fr. 542 Page. On this see the commentary by Most (1994), 142–147, on the poetics of praise and blame, and the one by Cossuta (2001), 134–142, on 'Socrates' hermeneutical pragmatics'.

us), the Prometheus of the story; by following his example, filled with foresight (*promêthoumenos*, 316d) in all the conduct of my life, I apply myself to these subjects'.[25]

So the last words of the dialogue are for the heroic figure and consequently for myth! And this even when in the commentary on the poem of Simonides, all mention of the paradigmatic time of the heroes had been avoided.

The question is now no longer the one concerning the teaching of a sort of knowledge, but that of practical conduct in one's own life, in a predictable return to the conclusion of the story of Prometheus in the version Protagoras has presented: it is, without doubt, a matter of taking part in restraint and justice to avoid being put to death, as a 'sickness of the city,' according to the civic law established by Zeus. In any case, around a narrative core and a few proper names of heroes inscribed within a tradition, the 'mythical' story as shown once again its syntactic plasticity and it semantic polyvalence, to the point that in the fictional context drawn by the dialogue, it was able to be twisted to the advantage of the most antithetical positions; if the version of the story of Prometheus staged in the dialogue written according to the model of sophistic *muthoi* in prose, it is not without the irony of the author himself, Plato.[26] The stories which we conceive of as myths are rich in this diversity of signification; by the pragmatic dimension of its narrative and discursive realisation, it is actualised in a polyphonic context which situates it in opposition to any pretension to a single meaning. It is, definitively, what arouses our own uses of Greek myth.

---

[25] Cf. Morgan (2000), 147–153, who concludes: 'In their individual realms, them, both Protagoras and Sokrates can claim to be Prometheus'. See also Desclos (1992), 118–126, and now Milliat-Pilot (2009), 288–295.

[26] In this respect the story reformulated by Plato unfolds its pragmatic context beyond the discourse-dialogue, into other dialogues. For this intertextual play, see Manuwald (2003) and the contribution of G. Van Riel in the present volume.

CHAPTER EIGHT

RELIGION AND MORALITY.
ELEMENTS OF PLATO'S ANTHROPOLOGY
IN THE MYTH OF PROMETHEUS
(*PROTAGORAS*, 320D–322D)

Gerd Van Riel

In 1975, Luc Brisson[1] opened a very interesting article on the myth of Prometheus in Plato's *Protagoras* with the statement that this myth has not been the subject of a thorough examination. Even though, more than thirty years later, a number of thoroughgoing contributions have been written on this text, one might still open a new paper by stating that the Prometheus myth does not receive the attention it would deserve.

The reasons for this relative neglect are still the same as indicated by Brisson: the *Protagoras* as a whole is seen as a marvellous piece of literature without, however, meeting the standard of philosophical interest which one finds met in other dialogues. Secondly, the success of the myth is hindered by the question of its authorship: is this Plato's work, or does Plato merely quote Protagoras himself? Furthermore, if it is Plato's work, how could it be reconciled with his philosophical doctrines in other dialogues? And if it is Protagoras', then how to reconcile the acceptance of the existence of gods and divine forethought we find expressed in the myth, with Protagoras' notorious agnosticism?

In this contribution, I cannot address all of those questions at length. I shall not deal extensively with the philosophical interest of the *Protagoras*, which I hope will reveal itself through the analysis I shall present. But I do want to argue that, no matter how much the myth is influenced by Protagoras' own teaching, the text as we have it is Plato's own work, and that it expresses a number of anthropological points which represent Plato's own doctrines. In other words, I shall read the myth as part of Platonic philosophy, and not just as a stunning example of sophistic argumentation with which Plato disagrees. I hope to make this clear by clarifying the

---

[1] Brisson (1975).

role of the myth within the *Protagoras*, and by pointing out a number of objective links between Plato's Prometheus story and other Platonic dialogues, namely the *Laws* and the *Politicus*.[2] Those objective links will concern Plato's attitude towards religion and his analysis of the political virtue to abide by the law. My point will be opposite to the one put forward by Luc Brisson, who recognizes the philosophical value of the myth, but who attributes the ethical and political views expressed in it solely to Protagoras, in radical opposition to Plato.[3] Of course, there is an opposition between Socrates and Protagoras in the dialogue, but this opposition, as I will argue, does not lie in the myth—even though the myth is part of Protagoras' speech. Rather, the opposition lies in the underlying definition of virtue and art (*aretê* and *tekhnê*) that makes Socrates and Protagoras interpret the same words and phenomena in a different direction.

1. The *Protagoras*: Can Virtue Be Taught?

In the hilarious opening scene of the *Protagoras*, Socrates is confronted with Hippocrates, who declares himself prepared to give up all his belongings in order to be instructed by the great sophist Protagoras. Immediately, Socrates starts to temper the enthusiasm, as it is not clear yet what kind of teaching Hippocrates may expect to get. A sophist, they agree while walking to the dwelling of Protagoras, is 'a kind of merchant who peddles provisions upon which the soul is nourished' (*Prot.* 313c4–6), and the soul is nourished by teachings (*mathêmata*, 313d5). Yet, as merchants do not always have knowledge about the things they sell, it is not clear in the case of the sophists, either, whether they are experts in what they pretend to teach. Actually, it is up to the pupil to recognize 'which products are beneficial, and which detrimental to the soul. Only a knowledgeable consumer can buy teachings safely from Protagoras or anyone else' (313e3–5). This

---

[2] These parallels have been pointed out already, e.g., by Friedländer (1954), 186–188, and Shorey (1901), 208–209, and (1933), 124, who also take them to be convincing arguments for the myth's being Platonic. See also Maguire (1977) who indicates that the parallels with other Platonic texts may not *necessarily* mean that the ideas expressed in the myth are 'Platonic material' (115), but that the story can be proven to be substantially Platonic anyways by the fact that the all-important introduction of δίκη and αἰδώς is Plato's own addition to the traditional narrative. Thus, according to Maguire (1977), 119–121, the story certainly is Platonic in its essential point.

[3] Brisson (1975), 8. The question of the theism expressed in the myth is dismissed by Brisson as a point of rhetorical invention from the part of Protagoras, which does not mean that he really engages in the beliefs he expresses in the myth.

immediately indicates a very important point: the teaching of the sophists (and we are not told yet what this is about) presupposes a basic capacity of recognizing the value or non value of the things taught.

After this discussion, followed by a funny intermezzo at the entrance door and in the corridors of Callias' house (where Protagoras is hosted), Socrates does what he had to do, namely, to introduce Hippocrates to him, upon which Protagoras presents his learning programme: under his direction, Hippocrates will learn 'sound deliberation, both in domestic matters—how best to manage one's household, and in public affairs—how to realize one's maximum potential for success in political debate and action', which is rendered explicit as 'the art of citizenship' (*politikê tekhnê*, 319a4). To which Socrates immediately replies: 'I have never thought that this could be taught' (319a10–b1).

Interrupting the story here, we should make a point that is of central importance to the rest of the discussion in the dialogue. Protagoras introduces the object of his teaching as the art of citizenship, i.e., a technical skill that allows people to function well in their household and in public affairs. It is the skill to be a politician, or to be a manager in private matters. It is Socrates who takes this up as *aretê* (319e–320c), which is not too amazing from his perspective: the 'political art' is a very broad notion that includes all possible instances of the capability to be a *politês*, a citizen. Thus, it concerns the essence of social ability, which means that it equals moral virtue. So, on Socrates' view, one can rightly say that the art of citizenship (*politikê tekhnê*) is identical with *aretê*. Protagoras accepts this reformulation, and continues the discussion on *politikê aretê*. Yet there is something going on with the terminology here.[4] The exclusive identification of *politikê tekhnê* and *aretê* reflects only Socrates' use of the words, whereas throughout the entire dialogue, Protagoras makes a much larger use of the word *aretê*. He confuses all instances of *tekhnê* with forms of *aretê*: according to him, *dêmiourgikê tekhnê* (322b3) equals *dêmiourgikê aretê* (322d8), just as sophistic *tekhnê* (316d) equals sophistic *aretê*, or *tektonikê tekhnê* equals *tektonikê aretê* (322d7). Thus, the very terminology reveals that Protagoras does not confine *aretê* to just moral virtue: just as Aristotle will do later on (repeating a more traditional view over against Plato's and Socrates' moral innovations), he links virtue to all kinds of excellence in performing a function or activity. Plato and Socrates, on the other hand, use the same definition

---

[4] This shift from an amoral to a moral conception of ἀρετή has also been highlighted by Maguire (1977), 105–110 and 122.

of *tekhnê*, but they limit the scope of *aretê* to only moral virtue. Nowhere in the *Protagoras* where Socrates uses the word *aretê*, does he see this as a relative term, applicable to all different skills. He only links it with *political skills*, taken as the virtue needed for social behaviour.[5] Thus, Socrates' use of the word *aretê* covers an entirely different field: not just an excellent performance of any activity, and not even just the art of statesmanship, but the strictly moral virtue that makes human beings function in a social context.[6] This is no mere play of words, as it will be revealed in the 'position switch' on which the dialogue ends (361a–c): if *aretê* is taken as the art of being a statesman, then of course, a sophist would claim that this can be taught, whereas Socrates would say that this entirely depends on inborn talents—thus, it does not come as a surprise that Socrates at first does not accept that *politikê tekhnê* is teachable. Yet, when Socrates reformulates the *politikê tekhnê* in terms of moral virtue, then it becomes clear that, virtue being knowledge, this must be teachable, whereas Protagoras would not reduce all instances of *aretê* to the same origin (i.e., knowledge), and thus, he would not accept that virtue is one. That is exactly the dilemma at the end of the dialogue. Hence, one can say that the real difference between Protagoras and Socrates is that between two different models of *aretê*: interiorized moral virtue (Socrates) over against political skills, revealed in external deeds. In my opinion, this implicit difference of opinion about the nature of virtue is the main cause of the ever recurring failure of the discussion between Socrates and Protagoras.

2. THE MYTH

Let us return to the dialogue, then, and to Socrates' reaction that he had never thought that virtue can be taught. This objection determines the subject matter of the discussion in the first part of the dialogue: does not the Sophists' programme come down to an impossible project? Socrates makes this point by a double argument (319b–320b): first of all, in the Athenian constitution, no specialized knowledge is needed to partake in governance—which implies that the Athenians do not see civic virtue as a matter that can be taught. Moreover, great politicians like Pericles can be

---

[5] See, e.g., *Prot.* 329c3–6: καὶ αὖ πολλαχοῦ ἐν τοῖς λόγοις ἐλέγετο ὑπὸ σοῦ ἡ δικαιοσύνη καὶ σωφροσύνη καὶ ὁσιότης καὶ πάντα ταῦτα ὡς ἕν τι εἴη συλλήβδην, ἀρετή.

[6] This is particularly clear in cases like *Prot.* 323a, where Socrates links ἀρετή to various skills, adding 'as you would have it', thus not assuming this identification as his own.

shown to be unable to impart their political virtue on their own children. Pericles' sons have not been able to acquire virtue, despite the close presence of a great moral authority (this reproach does not sound too friendly, especially since the sons of Pericles are present in the audience!).

In any case, with the argument that the Athenians do not believe that virtue can be taught, Socrates confronts Protagoras with a dilemma. Either he accepts the thesis, and then he jeopardizes his own profession, or he proves that virtue can be taught, and then he contradicts the Athenian democratic ideology that allows him to act as a teacher. Hence, Protagoras must invalidate the dilemma itself by showing that Socrates misrepresents the thesis that underlies Athenian democracy. The Athenians are not as opposed to the idea that virtue can be taught as Socrates affirms them to be.

In order to make this point, and to counter the first objection, Protagoras tells the myth of Prometheus on the origin of human life.

This myth can be analysed in five phases, all of which have a strikingly negative ending. The text is famous enough, but I shall recall its headlines. In the short first phase of the story, we learn that 'there was a time when the gods existed but mortal races did not'. The living beings are formed out of the earth, but are not yet brought to the light. They should first be equipped with the natural powers needed to warrant their survival.

In the second phase of the story, which occupies the larger part of the myth, the task of distributing these powers is handed over to the brother titans Prometheus and Epimetheus. The latter is the silly little brother, the family's stupid, who recklessly asks permission to accomplish the mission on his own. And he sets himself to work: to some animals he gives claws, to other wings, quick paws, and so on, all in order to secure the survival of the species. He gives them protection against mutual destruction and natural enemies [A], against the seasons [B], and against hunger and thirst [C]. Weak animals are given a high fertility, large animals receive strong skins, etc. Everything looks very harmonious, and Epimetheus is satisfied with his achievement, until, suddenly, he notices one species which he has completely overlooked. There is humankind: naked, barefoot, without claws, entirely deprived of natural defence. The problem is that time is urging: a solution must be found at once, since the day has come at which the animals must be brought to the light.

Prometheus now has to come and help (third phase). He hastily steals the divine fire from the working places of Hephaestus and Athena. Yet by this haste, Prometheus' action will be insufficient for the rescue of human kind. Fire and technical skills will be a partial remedy to the problem, namely by protecting human beings against climatologic circumstances [B] and against hunger and thirst [C]. The main problem, however, that of mutual slaughtering and of natural enemies [A], remains unsolved. In the mean time, we have learnt where the solution to that problem lies: it is political wisdom, which is in the keeping of Zeus. Why does not Prometheus get it there, and provide a final solution at once? The story says he did not have time to do so, and that he was afraid of the terrible guards that protect the citadel of Zeus. He then steals fire as an inadequate provisional solution, for which he is punished (as the myth mentions only in passing). Thus, the end of this phase is appalling: the rescuer of human kind is punished, and the final rescue is unattainable.

In the fourth phase, all consequences of the gift of Prometheus become clear. Thanks to fire, human beings are able to develop culture: religion, language, clothing, housing, and so on. In this fourth phase, the myth tells us how the members of human kind initially organised their life. Once more, however, it becomes clear that the technical skills can only remedy the problems caused by the seasons [B] and by the need of nourishment [C]. The worst problem is not yet solved: fire does not protect against mutual slaughtering. To protect themselves against this horrible threat, people try to live together, but because they lack social abilities (called *politikê tekhnê*, the art of being citizens), they are scattered again, and fall prey to wild animals.

Finally, in the fifth phase, the supreme god Zeus brings safety: he donates right, or justice (*dikê*) and respect, or shame (*aidôs*), which enable people to live together. Now at last mankind has the *politikê tekhnê*, based on the divine gifts of *dikê*, i.e., the laws and in general societal abilities, and *aidôs*, i.e., the *observantia* in a broad sense: respecting others and their tasks, and abiding by the laws. In a little dialogue that closes the myth, Hermes, who has to bring over the gifts, asks whether he ought to be selective, as was the case for the technical skills. 'No', says Zeus, and he immediately promulgates a law: everyone must partake of the divine gifts, and 'death to those who cannot partake of respect and justice, for they are a pestilence to the city' (*Prot.* 322d4–5).

This is not a very nice picture of the beginning of human life. Epimetheus' (After-thought) optimism of handling it alone was praise worthy, but his failure is dramatic. Prometheus (Fore-thought) brings a partial solution, but he does not have the time nor the occasion to solve the worst problem. In the mean time, human beings are perishing and suffering. And all this is taking place while Zeus is watching, high up his mountain, surrounded by terrifying guardians. Only when everything is going wrong, he comes into action: after pages of sorrow and failure, he needs only a few lines to bring the solution. As a despot, Zeus here rules by means of decrees, promulgated through his messenger Hermes. And even if his solution consists in a gift, it is accompanied by the threat of capital punishment to those who neglect the gift.

This myth does not tell us a euphoric story of human supremacy, it is not a shout of joy like Sophocles' 'many are the great things, and nothing is greater than man', but rather a story of bitter misery. Plato's version of the myth of Prometheus is much more negative than what one finds in many other versions of the story. In particular, the central role attributed to Epimetheus, who causes the problem, and who is held responsible for Prometheus' punishment, highlights the dramatic failure that characterizes the origin of human existence. Eventually, humankind is not saved by its supremacy, but rather conversely, it gains its supremacy as the effect of its salvation, and that makes an important difference.

Yet, the overall message of the story is not entirely pessimistic: in the end, human beings do acquire a supremacy over nature, which allows them to distinguish themselves from purely animal life, and to become moral actors in a community. Thus, they enter a sphere of life that is not strictly natural, but that provides additional qualities over the strictly biological conditions: art, skills, religion, language, and social abilities. For our purposes, it is of essential importance to see that this accession to a non-biologic order is accomplished in two phases. The difference between the two lies, in the first place, in the fact that they cure different troubles. But there is an important extra element that accounts for their difference. Once the first gift is handed over to humankind, we are offered (in the fourth phase) a description of *real* human life: the skills and craftsmanship, as well as religion and language, *are* actually practised. People are organising their lives and try to cope with practical problems—although they fail in their attempts to live together.

If this is so, we must infer that an important event has taken place in the story, without being explicitly mentioned: immediately after the theft of fire, which we know was very urgent, humankind has been brought to the light. The day has broken at which the animals are led from within the earth to their concrete life. And this takes place *before* the second gift: Zeus gives *dikê* and *aidôs* when he sees that the poor humans are craving, by their incapacity to live together. This implies that there is an important difference between the human beings' having fire and their social abilities, resulting from Zeus' gift. The first, fire, is actually branded into their existence, before they come to be. So, although neither of the gifts is strictly natural, fire and its results are more closely bound to human nature than is social ability, which was handed over after humankind has come to be.

This means, then, that the anthropological issues of religion and morality, which are represented by fire and the gift of Zeus, have a different status. This will be important to bear in mind when we turn to the Platonic contents of the myth, revealing some of Plato's central claims on morality as well as on religion.

3. The Anthropological Basis of Morality

Let us first handle the question of whether the myth represents a genuinely Platonic view on the possession of social virtue. This can be shown to be the case by pointing out the similarities between this myth and other Platonic texts. It goes without saying that the closing part of the myth in the *Politicus* is parallel with the myth of the *Protagoras*.[7] During the reign of Cronos, as we are told in the *Politicus*, God himself was the shepherd and leader who provided all necessary goods to his flock. There was no enmity between the animals, no war or mutual destruction; no politics, as the people did not need it; no shortness of food, as the earth brought forth the crops by itself; no lack of clothes or covering, as the seasons were mild and did not harm human beings (271d–272a). After the reign of Cronos, however, the universe stops its movement, and turns back in the reverse direction. In this period, which is called the reign of Zeus (272b), there are remainders of the good order that preceded, but gradually the state of disharmony is growing, until, eventually, God will again invert the movement. Under the reign of Zeus, human beings and all other animals have to secure their own life:

> Since we had been deprived of the god who possessed and pastured us, and since for their part the majority of animals—all those who had an aggressive nature—had gone wild, human beings, by themselves weak and defenceless, were preyed on by them, and in those first times were still without resources and without expertise of any sort; their spontaneous supply of food was no longer available to them, and they did not yet know how to provide for themselves, having had no shortage to force them to do so before. As a result of all this they were in great difficulties. This is why the gifts from the gods, of which we have ancient reports, have been given to us: fire from Prometheus, crafts from Hephaestus and his fellow craftsworker, seeds and plants from others. Everything that has helped to establish human life has come about from these things, once care from the gods, as has just been said, ceased to be available to human beings, and they had to live their lives through their own

---

[7] Cf. the general comparison between these two texts by Friedländer (1954), 186–188.

resources and take care for themselves, just like the cosmos as a whole, which we imitate and follow for all time, now living and growing in this way, now in the way we did then. As for the matter of our story, let it now be ended.[8]

(*Pol.* 274b5–e1, tr. C. Rowe)

This description inverts the positive account of the description of the reign of Cronus, and contains a number of striking similarities with the Prometheus myth in the *Protagoras*: apart from the explicit mention of Prometheus, Hephaestus and his 'fellow craftsworker,' there are clear reminiscences of the three sorts of problems (A. mutual slaughtering, B. the seasons, C. hunger and thirst) that dominated the descriptions in the *Protagoras* myth. Yet the end of the story is different: there is no reference here to a gift from Zeus, nor to a distribution of *dikê* and *aidôs*. This difference has been taken as a major argument to contrast the myth of the *Politicus* with the account in the *Protagoras*, or even to state that the *Politicus* is to be read as a 'contra-*Protagoras*'.[9] Hence, the inference is that in the *Protagoras*, Plato is merely expounding Protagoras's own doctrines, without assuming them as his own, particularly on the point of the universal participation in political virtue. In the *Politicus*, Plato does take over the analysis of the specific position of human kind in nature, but stops there where Protagoras would add another human quality that allows for all people's participation in virtue, and hence in politics.[10]

Looking at what meets the eye, this may indeed seem what is going on: by the time of the *Politicus* Plato seems to have done more reflection on the subject, and keeps from his earlier myth those things which he can reuse, while leaving out the elements that cannot be reconciled with his austere

---

[8] τῆς γὰρ τοῦ κεκτημένου καὶ νέμοντος ἡμᾶς δαίμονος ἀπερημωθέντες ἐπιμελείας, τῶν πολλῶν αὖ θηρίων, ὅσα χαλεπὰ τὰς φύσεις ἦν, ἀπαγριωθέντων, αὐτοὶ δὲ ἀσθενεῖς ἄνθρωποι καὶ ἀφύλακτοι γεγονότες διηρπάζοντο ὑπ' αὐτῶν, καὶ ἔτ' ἀμήχανοι καὶ ἄτεχνοι κατὰ τοὺς πρώτους ἦσαν χρόνους, ἅτε τῆς μὲν αὐτομάτης τροφῆς ἐπιλελοιπυίας, πορίζεσθαι δὲ οὐκ ἐπιστάμενοί πω διὰ τὸ μηδεμίαν αὐτοὺς χρείαν πρότερον ἀναγκάζειν. ἐκ τούτων πάντων ἐν μεγάλαις ἀπορίαις ἦσαν. ὅθεν δὴ τὰ πάλαι λεχθέντα παρὰ θεῶν δῶρα ἡμῖν δεδώρηται μετ' ἀναγκαίας διδαχῆς καὶ παιδεύσεως, πῦρ μὲν παρὰ Προμηθέως, τέχναι δὲ παρ' Ἡφαίστου καὶ τῆς συντέχνου, σπέρματα δὲ αὖ καὶ φυτὰ παρ' ἄλλων· καὶ πάνθ' ὁπόσα τὸν ἀνθρώπινον βίον συγκατεσκεύακεν ἐκ τούτων γέγονεν, ἐπειδὴ τὸ μὲν ἐκ θεῶν, ὅπερ ἐρρήθη νυνδή, τῆς ἐπιμελείας ἐπέλιπεν ἀνθρώπους, δι' ἑαυτῶν τε ἔδει τήν τε διαγωγὴν καὶ τὴν ἐπιμέλειαν αὐτοὺς αὑτῶν ἔχειν καθάπερ ὅλος ὁ κόσμος, ᾧ συμμιμούμενοι καὶ συνεπόμενοι τὸν ἀεὶ χρόνον νῦν μὲν οὕτως, τοτὲ δὲ ἐκείνως ζῶμέν τε καὶ φυόμεθα. καὶ τὸ μὲν δὴ τοῦ μύθου τέλος ἐχέτω.

[9] Narcy (1995), 227–230. See also Brisson (1975), 7–8.

[10] Cf. Brisson (1995), 362–363. Yet this does not have to mean that the *Protagoras* myth is Protagorean rather than Platonic, as Maguire (1977), 119–121, argues that the addition of δίκη and αἰδώς in the myth of the *Protagoras* is precisely Plato's own contribution.

view of the shepherd-king. Under the reign of the good statesman, all that people have to do is obey the orders. No laws are needed: the statesman guides all people on the basis of his knowledge and insight. From this perspective, then, the subjects of the state do not need any political virtue; they simply have to recognize the moral and intellectual capacities of the king, and accept his leadership.

Yet things are more complicated than that: in the *Politicus* the myth constitutes a turning point in the discussion. Immediately after telling the story, the Stranger concludes that they have made two mistakes, first, by defining the king as a divine shepherd—which is wrong because it can now be revealed as anachronistic: it attributes characteristics to the king that actually belong to another world period—the period, that is, in which god reigns, and in which human kind is like a flock, having no quarrels, no search for food, housing, clothing etc. In our world-period, however, which is the reign of Zeus, things are different. The figure of a divine shepherd is too austere to be applicable to our present condition. Moreover, and that is the second mistake, it was not yet made clear how the king could reign, and how he can be distinguished from other power claimers (*Pol.* 274e–276e).

Thus, in the *Politicus*, a number of important issues are addressed only after the myth: only after the myth does the idea come up that the statesman as defined earlier might be too remote an ideal to be realizable. In a first move, Plato does continue the analysis of the ideal statesman, who is above the law, and for whom the law can only be a stand-in when he is absent. The statesman is continuously compared to medics and sports trainers, who are free to decide whatever they deem necessary, and who do this preferably without any book or manual. Yet, at the same time, the emphasis is shifting. Progressively, the idea comes to the fore that this ideal statesman will not be found, or that this type of leaders is so scarce that most generations would have to do without them. Hence, the discussion comes to the question of which constitution would be second best. Without immediately deciding on the size of the leading class (whether it should be one single king, or a number of aristocrats—democracy, for one, is not an option), it is in any case clear that the state needs laws, made by experts, and by which all subjects must abide. Without spelling it out in as many words, this second best alternative does rely on a sensitivity of the subjects to obey laws and to act accordingly. See, for instance, what is inferred at *Pol.* 297d4–e5:

> Tell me: given that this constitution we have talked about is on our view the only correct one, do you recognize that the others ought to employ the written documents that belong to this one, and save themselves in that way, doing what is now praised, although it is not the most correct thing to do?—What

are you referring to?—The principle that no one in the city should dare to do anything contrary to the laws, and that the person who dares to do so should be punished by death and all the worst punishments. This is very correct and fine as a second choice, when one changes the principle we discussed just now, which is our first choice.[11]   (*Pol.* 297d4–e5; tr. C. Rowe)

A reign governed by laws is the best imitation of the ideal statesmanship—and this imitation threatens to be perverted, when the rulers take themselves to be the ideal statesmen, and place themselves above the law. As long as the ideal statesman does not emerge (and they do not emerge like the queens of bees, who immediately reveal themselves by their difference in shape and soul: *Pol.* 301d–e), the law must be obeyed by everyone, including the leaders (300e–301a).

This means that the ideal statesmanship, in which everything is led by knowledge, is nothing common, if it ever occurs at all. In the mean time, every citizen must abide by the law. The same idea returns when Plato finally discusses the weaving capacities of the leading monarch. His task is like the one of educators: they have to bring their pupils to a well formed character, and to cut out those that are not susceptible to that formation:

> In just this very way, it seems to me, the art of kingship—since it is this that itself possesses the capacity belonging to the directing art—will not permit the educators and tutors, who function according to law, to do anything in the exercise of their role that will not ultimately result in some disposition which is appropriate to its own mixing role. It calls on them to teach these things alone; and those of their pupils that are unable to share in a disposition that is courageous and moderate, and whatever else belongs to the sphere of virtue, but are thrust forcibly away by an evil nature into godlessness, excess and injustice, it throws out by killing them, sending them into exile, and punishing them with the most extreme forms of dishonour.[12]
>
> (*Pol.* 308e4–309a3; tr. C. Rowe)

On the basis of this selection, the art of statesmanship will bring all subjects to fulfilling their task in the whole of community.

---

[11] φέρε γάρ· ὀρθῆς ἡμῖν μόνης οὔσης ταύτης τῆς πολιτείας ἣν εἰρήκαμεν, οἶσθ' ὅτι τὰς ἄλλας δεῖ τοῖς ταύτης συγγράμμασι χρωμένας οὕτω σῴζεσθαι, δρώσας τὸ νῦν ἐπαινούμενον, καίπερ οὐκ ὀρθότατον ὄν;—Τὸ ποῖον;—Τὸ παρὰ τοὺς νόμους μηδὲν μηδένα τολμᾶν ποιεῖν τῶν ἐν τῇ πόλει, τὸν τολμῶντα δὲ θανάτῳ ζημιοῦσθαι καὶ πᾶσι τοῖς ἐσχάτοις. καὶ τοῦτ' ἔστιν ὀρθότατα καὶ κάλλιστ' ἔχον ὡς δεύτερον, ἐπειδὰν τὸ πρῶτόν τις μεταθῇ τὸ νυνδὴ ῥηθέν ...

[12] Ταὐτὸν δή μοι τοῦθ' ἡ βασιλικὴ φαίνεται πᾶσι τοῖς κατὰ νόμον παιδευταῖς καὶ τροφεῦσιν, τὴν τῆς ἐπιστατικῆς αὐτὴ δύναμιν ἔχουσα, οὐκ ἐπιτρέψειν ἀσκεῖν ὅτι μὴ τις πρὸς τὴν αὐτῆς σύγκρασιν ἀπεργαζόμενος ἦθός τι πρέπον ἀποτελεῖ, ταῦτα δὲ μόνα παρακελεύεσθαι παιδεύειν· καὶ τοὺς μὲν μὴ δυναμένους κοινωνεῖν ἤθους ἀνδρείου καὶ σώφρονος ὅσα τε ἄλλα ἐστὶ τείνοντα πρὸς ἀρετήν, ἀλλ' εἰς ἀθεότητα καὶ ὕβριν καὶ ἀδικίαν ὑπὸ κακῆς βίᾳ φύσεως ἀπωθουμένους, θανάτοις τε ἐκβάλλει καὶ φυγαῖς καὶ ταῖς μεγίσταις κολάζουσα ἀτιμίαις.

In this description, as in the one quoted earlier on (*Pol.* 297d–e), we find a wording that comes very close to the final admonition in the myth of the *Protagoras*: those who are not susceptible to the kind of training that is required as a basis for community life, are severely punished and removed from the city.

I think this parallel is not a coincidence. It means that, even though there is no reference to the distribution of *dikê* and *aidôs* in the myth of the *Politicus*, the idea is clearly expressed there that the rule of the law can only serve as the basis for a state if the citizens have the basic capacity to accept and respect the law.[13] The reason why Plato left this out from the myth may be that there was no need to refer to the rules of the law at this stage of the discussion. By the time of telling the myth, the discussion is still about the king-statesman who does not need any law. But as this was an erroneous description, the obedience to the laws must be taken into account after all as an important feature of our second-best constitution.

In this line, the law of Zeus we find in the *Protagoras* may even be seen as the institution of a law as a stand-in for the absent king: Zeus gives his commandment and then leaves the stage, leaving human kind to its own task—in that case, Zeus would be not so much of a despot, as we called him earlier on, but rather an example of that which in the *Politicus* will be called the good statesman. One should not fail to notice, by the way, that this world period is described as the reign of Zeus (*Pol.* 272b), thus establishing yet another parallel between the *Politicus* and the *Protagoras*.

Yet, at this stage of the enquiry, one must wonder whether this universal distribution of *dikê* and *aidôs* in the *Protagoras* must be seen as a mythical form of the statement that all people have political excellence, by which Protagoras would be justifying Athenian democracy (over against Plato's aristocratic view). Is this really the idea in the Protagoras? I actually think it is not. As I intimated already, this idea cannot easily be reconciled with Protagoras' ambitions as a teacher of virtue. He loses his job, if all his pupils can be shown to possess already what he promises to impart on them. This paradox can be avoided, however, if we take seriously what Protagoras himself says in the explanation of the myth.

---

[13] Those who are not capable of doing this, the vicious, are treated as incurable—even though people in general are never completely ignorant, or totally insusceptible to improvement. Cf. Bobonich (1995), 320–322. This means that a susceptibility to education (as the improvement towards virtue) is presupposed; if this susceptibility would remain absent nevertheless, then the individual is to be most severely punished. Cf. *Gorg.* 525c.

As we saw, Protagoras tells his story in the context of a discussion on the question of whether virtue can be taught. As can be expected from a teacher, Protagoras' own answer is that virtue can and must be taught. The myth is told in order to provide an argument for this thesis. But, strangely enough, the conclusion of the myth is that all people partake of *politikê aretê*, i.e., civic virtue. How is that possible? If all people have virtue already, how then can one maintain that it must be taught? Protagoras addresses this issue in the reply to Socrates' second objection. There he refers to the role of instruction and severe punishment of those who do not share in virtue (*Prot.* 324d–325c). The answer to the inability of some great moral actors to impart virtue on their sons lies in the fact that some people lack the susceptibility required to become virtuous persons, just like not every son of a craftsman or a musician shares in the talent of their fathers (325a–327e). Thus, a basic ability is needed, which, in the case of morality, is widespread. In order to explain this, Protagoras draws an analogy between teachers of virtue and teachers of our native speech:

> As it is, Socrates, you affect delicate sensibilities, because everyone here is a teacher of virtue, to the best of his ability, and you can't see a single one. You might as well look for a teacher of Greek; you wouldn't find a single one of those either. Nor would you be any more successful if you asked who could teach the sons of our craftsmen the very arts which they of course learned from their fathers, to the extent that their fathers were competent, and their friends in the trade. It would be difficult to produce someone who could continue their education, whereas it would be easy to find a teacher for the totally unskilled. It is the same with virtue and everything else. If there is someone who is the least bit more advanced in virtue than ourselves, he is to be cherished.[14]   (*Prot.* 327e1–328b1; tr. S. Lombardo – K. Bell)

A grammarian cannot do his job of teaching the grammatical rules of the native language without his pupil's knowing the language already. He needs the language to explain the language. So there is an interaction between the basic foreknowledge or the natural capacity of the pupil, and the teaching by

---

[14] νῦν δὲ τρυφᾷς, ὦ Σώκρατες, διότι πάντες διδάσκαλοί εἰσιν ἀρετῆς καθ' ὅσον δύνανται ἕκαστος, καὶ οὐδείς σοι φαίνεται· εἶθ', ὥσπερ ἂν εἰ ζητοῖς τίς ἂν διδάσκαλος τοῦ ἑλληνίζειν, οὐδ' ἂν εἷς φανείη, οὐδέ γ' ἂν οἶμαι εἰ ζητοῖς τίς ἂν ἡμῖν διδάξειεν τοὺς τῶν χειροτεχνῶν υἱεῖς αὐτὴν ταύτην τὴν τέχνην ἣν δὴ παρὰ τοῦ πατρὸς μεμαθήκασιν, καθ' ὅσον οἷός τ' ἦν ὁ πατὴρ καὶ οἱ τοῦ πατρὸς φίλοι ὄντες ὁμότεχνοι, τούτους ἔτι τίς ἂν διδάξειεν, οὐ ῥᾴδιον οἶμαι εἶναι, ὦ Σώκρατες, τούτων διδάσκαλον φανῆναι, τῶν δὲ ἀπείρων παντάπασι ῥᾴδιον, οὕτω δὲ ἀρετῆς καὶ τῶν ἄλλων πάντων· ἀλλὰ κἂν εἰ ὀλίγον ἔστιν τις ὅστις διαφέρει ἡμῶν προβιβάσαι εἰς ἀρετήν, ἀγαπητόν.

which this basic knowledge is extended. The same holds, then, for teachers of virtue: they presuppose an established general attitude of the pupil, an ability to learn, on which everything relies.

This analogy has important consequences for the interpretation of the myth. If it states that everyone partakes of virtue, it actually means that everyone has this basic capacity of acquiring and practicing virtue, just as everyone shares a basic capacity of learning and speaking a native tongue. The degree of eventual success of actually being virtuous or mastering a language depends on the quality of education, but the most important thing remains the basic capacity of the pupils themselves. I believe this is a genuinely Platonic idea, which one finds elsewhere in Plato.[15] This was also already inferred, by the way, in the very opening scene, where Socrates pointed out that the sophists' pupils should be able to recognize good and bad before they can join their teachers. And it will also be present in the doctrine that no one willingly errs (*Prot.* 358a–d), the universality of which implies that in principle, all people partake in the capacity to make moral choices, aiming at what they see as good.

Thus, in this respect, the myth does not refer to a specifically Protagorean doctrine which Plato does not accept, but rather establishes an anthropological point on which both participants in the discussion agree. This point will be the main reason for Socrates' agreement that virtue is teachable (*pepeismai*, 328e3), and for the famous position switch which Socrates states at the end of the dialogue, as we saw already. Eventually, the discussion of the *Protagoras* fails by this implicit misunderstanding: Protagoras considers moral virtue as only one instance of 'virtue' (taken to mean 'excellence in the performance of activities'; hence, specifically moral virtue is defined as the excellence in managing private as well as public affairs), which is treated as a skill alongside other instances of excellent practices or skills, whereas for Plato and Socrates, the only virtue is moral virtue (defined as an interiorised moral excellence). Yet, they both agree that moral virtue relies on a basic susceptibility to morality, which is to be perfected by moral education. Hence, all people have a capacity for virtue, even though they do not all develop it. And that is exactly what the myth tells us.

---

[15] This is expressed, e.g., under the name of ἦθος: a disposition that must be good by nature, and which has to be perfected by education: see *Rep.* VI, 491d–492a (and 496b) on the disposition of a truly philosophical nature; or *L.* X, 903d on the Divine checkers-player who moves the souls on the board, according to their ameliorating or deteriorating dispositions.

The disagreement, or the failure of the discussion, can then be further articulated by highlighting the assumptions that both parties make on the basis of this basic susceptibility. To Protagoras, the talent for politics can be brought to true virtue on the basis of his skilful teaching (and he is even prepared to let the students decide on the tuition fee, depending on how much they value the lessons: 328b), whereas according to Socrates, a teaching of another kind is required, one that will consist in a development of knowledge and wisdom by the method of dialectic. That is the issue at stake in the conflicting underlying definitions of virtue, which is not directly addressed in the *Protagoras*. What we find spelled out here is much more of an elaboration on the common ground shared by Socrates and the sophist Protagoras alike.

4. The Anthropological Foundation of Religion

We can now address the second point, the anthropological account of religion that can be drawn from the myth. Again, we must ask the question of how this fits with the doctrines Plato expounds elsewhere. At least, in this case, it is clear that the religiosity of the myth, if it is to be taken seriously, cannot be ascribed to Protagoras himself. The clue to the recognition that we are dealing with genuinely Platonic doctrine is to be found in the status Plato gives to religion within his elaboration of the state.

It is obvious that Plato wants the state to interfere in the smallest aspects of life. But when reading the *Republic* and the *Laws*, it is very striking that this interference does not concern religion. Of course, the lawgiver must organise and warrant religious practice, but Plato never treats religion in itself as something to be instituted by the state. Religion is not 'founded'. This picture emerges among others from Plato's descriptions of how elementary states grow organically out of conglomerations of individuals and families (*Rep.* II, 369b–374e and *L.* III, 677a–681c). In this context, nothing is said about a possible starting point of religion. If we follow what is said in this respect in the *Republic* (II, 369b–372d), we learn that people first came together for the exchange of goods that allowed them to meet their daily needs: food, housing, clothing, etc. The basic state is very much axed on economy and utility and all is done to facilitate the supply of products and services. But of course, this opens a dynamic that can hardly be stopped, and people start to look for better and more luxurious products; they foster new needs, and soon enough, this leads to conflicts and wars (II, 372d–374e). Hence the need of guardians to protect the state at the inside and outside, and those guardians must be properly educated to an outstanding level of moral life.

It is notorious that in the education of the guardians, particular attention is paid to the theology handed over by the poets (II, 377b–383c); Plato bans poetry from his state for several reasons, one of which is the immoral character of their accounts of the gods. So it is unquestionable that the state has to watch over the purity of religious beliefs. But it is another thing to say that the state would institute or found religion. That idea is explicitly rejected in *Republic*, IV, 427b–e, where Plato concludes a survey of the things that must be organised by law, in the following way:

> What is now left for us to deal with under the heading of legislation?—
> For us nothing, but for the Delphic Apollo it remains to enact the greatest,
> finest, and first of laws.—What laws are those?—Those having to do with
> the establishing of temples, sacrifices, and other forms of service to gods,
> daemons, and heroes, the burial of the dead, and the services that ensure
> their favour. We have no knowledge of these things, and in establishing our
> city, if we have any understanding, we won't be persuaded to trust them to
> anyone other than the ancestral guide. And this god, sitting upon the rock at
> the centre of the earth, is without a doubt the ancestral guide on these matters
> for all people.[16]   (*Rep.* IV, 427b1–c4; tr. G.M.A. Grube)

Thus, religion and religious practice fall out of the scope of constitutional arrangements, and rest upon ancestral traditions, guided by their own legislator, the Delphic Apollo.[17]

The same idea is expressed in the *Laws* (III, 677a–681c), where we find a similar description of the origins of community and lawgiving.[18] In the earliest times, people did not suffer any lack; there was no injustice or jealousy, and no religious dissidence:

> [T]hey accepted as the truth the doctrine they heard about gods and men,
> and lived their lives in accordance with it.[19]
>   (*Laws*, III, 679c6–7; tr. T.J. Saunders)

---

[16] Τί οὖν, ἔφη, ἔτι ἂν ἡμῖν λοιπὸν τῆς νομοθεσίας εἴη;—Καὶ ἐγὼ εἶπον ὅτι Ἡμῖν μὲν οὐδέν, τῷ μέντοι Ἀπόλλωνι τῷ ἐν Δελφοῖς τά γε μέγιστα καὶ κάλλιστα καὶ πρῶτα τῶν νομοθετημάτων.—Τὰ ποῖα; ἦ δ' ὅς.—Ἱερῶν τε ἱδρύσεις καὶ θυσίαι καὶ ἄλλαι θεῶν τε καὶ δαιμόνων καὶ ἡρώων θεραπεῖαι· τελευτησάντων τε αὖ θῆκαι καὶ ὅσα τοῖς ἐκεῖ δεῖ ὑπηρετοῦντας ἵλεως αὐτοὺς ἔχειν. τὰ γὰρ δὴ τοιαῦτα οὔτ' ἐπιστάμεθα ἡμεῖς οἰκίζοντές τε πόλιν οὐδενὶ ἄλλῳ πεισόμεθα, ἐὰν νοῦν ἔχωμεν, οὐδὲ χρησόμεθα ἐξηγητῇ ἀλλ' ἢ τῷ πατρίῳ· οὗτος γὰρ δήπου ὁ θεὸς περὶ τὰ τοιαῦτα πᾶσιν ἀνθρώποις πάτριος ἐξηγητὴς ἐν μέσῳ τῆς γῆς ἐπὶ τοῦ ὀμφαλοῦ καθήμενος ἐξηγεῖται.

[17] On the role of Apollo as lawgiver and warrant of legislation: see Morrow (1960), 402–411.

[18] On the parallels between this text and the myth in the *Protagoras*, see Shorey (1901), 208–209.

[19] ἀλλὰ περὶ θεῶν τε καὶ ἀνθρώπων τὰ λεγόμενα ἀληθῆ νομίζοντες ἔζων κατὰ ταῦτα.

Hence, they did not need (positive) law. Again, religion is said to be earlier, and more natural so to speak, than constitutions and laws. It is only when smaller communities start to conglomerate into a larger whole that the lawgiver must decide which set of traditional practices of which group must be taken over by all members of community (III, 681c). But in general, it is clearly stated that the lawgiver must not touch upon the existing gods, temples, rituals, ceremonies, etc.:

> It does not matter whether he is founding a new state from scratch or recon-structing an old one that has gone to ruin: in either case, if he has any sense, he will never dream of altering whatever instructions may have been received from Delphi or Dodona or Ammon about the gods and temples that ought to be founded by the various groups in the state, and the gods or daemons after whom the temples should be named. [...] The legislator must not tamper with any of this in the slightest detail.[20]

(Laws, V, 738b5–c3, c7–d1; tr. T.J. Saunders)

There are, of course, magistrates for the religious services, and above all supervisors of religious affairs, but they are administrators of cults that predated the establishment of the state. Even the appointment of priests in the state must be made by lot, for it must be left to god to decide (although of course the candidate is screened for capability and purity) (*Laws*, VI, 759a–760a). At any rate, religion is treated very carefully, with a clear concern not to shake the unshakeable,[21] or not to make the divine subject to human measure. For god is the measure of all things, and we must do as he pleases (*Laws*, IV, 716c4). The only, but by no means the least, task of the state is to supervise people's religiosity, and to condemn atheists. Thus, in general terms, we may state that Plato's lawgiving and constitution presupposes religious beliefs and practices, as a matter of ancestral traditions.

The myth of Prometheus in the *Protagoras* provides an interesting clue as to the reason of this state of affairs. On the basis of the chronological dis-tinction between the two gifts described in the myth (the theft of fire before mankind's being brought to the light, and the gift of social abilities after-wards), we can now conclude that this means that religion—an effect of the possession of fire—is more deeply rooted in human nature than social-ity. It is more fundamental, and more 'natural' than what is handed over in

---

[20] οὔτ᾽ ἂν καινὴν ἐξ ἀρχῆς τις ποιῇ οὔτ᾽ ἂν παλαιὰν διεφθαρμένην ἐπισκευάζηται, περὶ θεῶν γε καὶ ἱερῶν, ἄττα τε ἐν τῇ πόλει ἑκάστοις ἱδρῦσθαι δεῖ καὶ ὧντινων ἐπονομάζεσθαι θεῶν ἢ δαιμόνων, οὐδεὶς ἐπιχειρήσει κινεῖν νοῦν ἔχων ὅσα ἐκ Δελφῶν ἢ Δωδώνης ἢ παρ᾽ ᾽Άμμωνος ἤ τινες ἔπεισαν παλαιοὶ λόγοι ὁπῃδή τινας πείσαντες, φασμάτων γενομένων ἢ ἐπιπνοίας λεχθείσης θεῶν [...] τούτων νομοθέτῃ τὸ σμικρότατον ἁπάντων οὐδὲν κινητέον.

[21] μὴ κινεῖν τὰ ἀκίνητα: *L.* III, 684e1; VIII, 843a1; XI, 913b9.

the second gift. So a religious attitude precedes all kinds of social behaviour, and of community. That is why Plato refuses to let his lawgivers interfere in religious matters. Laws and constitutions belong to a different level than that of religion. Hence, the reason for the political abstinence from religion is an anthropological one: religion is more profoundly attached to human nature than sociality, and that is why the state—as an organisation of man's sociality—cannot act upon this deeper level.

5. The Function of the Myth in the *Protagoras*

Once the doctrines of the myth have been shown (or so I hope) to be Platonic, we can take on the question of how this myth functions in the dialogue. For the sake of clarity, I add that this detection of a thoroughly Platonic content of the myth does not *have to* preclude any possible connection with a text written (or ideas expressed) by the historical Protagoras. Plato may well have taken over Protagoras' text, or he may have imitated Protagoras' style, or turned a Protagorean prose text into a myth. What really matters is that Plato assumes this myth and its contents as his own, and that the ideas expressed in it return on several occasions in Plato's other works.

What, then, is the function of this myth? I believe it plays an important role in the discussion between Socrates and Protagoras, a discussion that constantly fails, and leads up to the final conclusion that they switched positions. One of the main reasons for this failure is, as I have argued, a deeply grounded failure to understand each other's view on the nature of virtue. As we saw, Protagoras has a very broad notion of *aretê*, covering the excellent performance of all sorts of activity, over against Socrates who limits *aretê* to an interiorized state of moral excellence. Despite this difference of opinion, there is no discussion on the points raised in the myth. Quite the contrary, the myth's main point, that human beings share a basic capacity to acquire virtue, is actually the point made by Socrates at the outset of the dialogue. At the very beginning he claimed that, in order to judge the quality of the education offered by the sophist, the pupil needs to have some foreknowledge of what he is going to be taught (313c–e). Moreover, the myth does not directly contradict Socrates' initial point that virtue cannot be taught. Again, it is quite the contrary: the final conclusion of the myth, that all people share in a basic moral capacity, is *prima facie* supportive of Socrates' denial of virtue's being teachable rather than of Protagoras' affirmation of it. In fact, both speakers can rely on the myth to make their point: Socrates stresses the fact that a weak basic capacity never leads to actual virtue (as in the case of Pericles' sons, 319e–320c), and that the Athenian democratic policy presupposes that all people have a share in morality (319b–d). Likewise, Protagoras will argue that the Athenians presuppose that all have a basic capacity that can be instructed and educated towards virtue (322d–325c), and that people like the sons of Pericles do not have a well-disposed capacity to learn how to become virtuous (325a–327e). In other words, Protagoras and Socrates both take for granted what is explained in the myth.

This feature allows us to point out the specific function of the myth in this dialogue: it establishes the common anthropological ground on which both discussants will rely to make their own case. This does not mean that the myth reveals a factual truth (as this never seems to be the case in Platonic myth). Rather, it represents an a priori agreement that is not submitted to a dialectical discussion, but taken for granted as a basic starting point.

In that respect, it does not really matter who was to tell the myth, Protagoras or Socrates, but the choice to present a myth—arbitrary as it may seem in the course of the dialogue (320c)—does make a difference in terms of the epistemological status of what is expounded. It is exempt from being challenged in a dialectical discussion, and makes claims that are not being put to the test. This entails that it cannot be proven to be true, but that it is not refuted either. It constitutes the pre-dialectic common ground that is presupposed in the discussion.

CONCLUSION

To conclude, then, we may say that in more than one respect, the myth of the *Protagoras* does not stand alone in Plato's works. It reflects Plato's views on the origins of morality and of religion, and provides the anthropological basis upon which those doctrines will be elaborated in other dialogues. Thus, the myth is not just an element in Protagoras' defence within the dialogue, but a starting point of the discussion, on which both partners agree. The dividing line between Socrates and Protagoras, and the eventual failure of their discussion, is due to other factors than the contents of the myth, namely, their failure to recognize a deep misunderstanding on the definition of 'virtue'.

This means, then, that the *Prometheus* myth plays a particular role in the discussion, one which may be added to the list of 'functions and usages of the Platonic myths': it establishes a common ground for the discussion, providing a starting point on which both discussants can rely. Their disagreement will subsequently reveal itself through their explanation of the myth, not through the contents of the myth itself. The explanation of the myth is presented as a dialectical discussion (initiated by Protagoras' *logos*), and hence will be the object of questioning and challenging each other's opinions. The myth, on the other hand, remains above this struggle, as if it were safely dwelling in the fortified palace of Zeus.

CHAPTER NINE

WHIP SCARS ON THE NAKED SOUL:
MYTH AND *ELENCHOS* IN PLATO'S *GORGIAS*

Radcliffe G. Edmonds III

Stripped of his regal robes and all the trappings of his worldly power, the soul of the Great King cowers naked before Rhadamanthys, who looks down upon the crippled wretch before him, disfigured like the basest slave by the marks of the whip and covered with festering sores. Many scholars have interpreted this horrific image of the judgement of the soul from Plato's *Gorgias* as a threat of hell-fire designed to convince the skeptical Callicles that justice pays 'in the end'. The myth at the end of the *Gorgias* has thus been seen as a failure of Plato's philosophy, one of those places which, in Zeller's condescending words, 'indicate the point at which it becomes evident that as yet [Plato] cannot be wholly a philosopher, because he is too much a poet'.[1] Scholars have been critical of what they see as an attempt by Plato to beg the premises of his argument for the philosophic life by appealing to the idea that justice always pays off 'in the end' because of some system of compensation in the hereafter. Even Annas, whose treatment of Plato's myths of judgement is among the most sensitive, sees the myth in the *Gorgias* as asserting a necessary premise without proof: 'The *Gorgias* myth is both the most religiously coloured and the starkest in the claim it makes that justice pays *in the end* .... In the *Gorgias*, Plato insists flatly that justice will bring rewards in the end, though without giving us any good reason to believe this'.[2] Without the moral optimism that

---

[1] Zeller (1888), 163. This idea that the myths betray the limits of Plato's philosophic ability goes back to Hegel.

[2] Annas (1982), 125, 138, here 125: 'The myth, then, is giving a consequentialist reason to be just. Whether we take it as really threatening future punishment for wrongdoing, or demythologize its message as the claim that being wicked brings the punishment of a scarred and deformed soul now, its message is still that justice pays 'in the end,' on a deeper level than we can now see'. I would point out, however, the crucial difference between 'in the end' and 'on a deeper level' of reality.

justice will prevail in the end, she asks, how could one not be as unconvinced as Callicles by these old wives' tales?[3]

I argue, to the contrary, that the details of the myth help clarify the ways in which Plato tries to prove that Socrates' way of life really is better than Callicles', not just 'in the end,' after the afterlife judgement, but right now, at any given moment. Specifically, I suggest that a proper understanding of the myth helps resolve another of the recurring problems in Platonic scholarship, the nature of the Socratic *elenchos*. Plato carefully manipulates the traditional mythic details in his tale of an afterlife judgement to provide an illustration, in vivid and graphic terms, of the workings of the Socratic *elenchos*. Not only does myth of the reform of the afterlife judgement illustrate through narrative the contrasts between Socrates' *elenchos* and the rhetorical arguments of his interlocutors, but the description of the judgement and punishment as the examination and healing of a soul scarred with wounds and disease illuminates the effects of the *elenchos* on the interlocutors. The image of the Great King's scarred and misshapen soul, stripped of all its coverings and supports and examined by the expert in justice, illustrates the way Socrates puts his interlocutors to the test, while the afterlife punishments prescribed for the wrong-doers depict the suffering that the shame of the *elenchos* inflicts. Moreover, Plato manipulates the traditional mythic punishment of the water carriers to depict the life of those who fail to be cured by the therapeutic punishment of the *elenchos*. The myth does not supplement a deficient argument for the philosophic life; rather, Plato makes use of the narrative and the traditional aspects of the myth to depict the examination of the unexamined life in the here and now.

1. THE *ELENCHOS*

The 'Socratic *elenchos*' is a term used in the scholarship for the method of argumentation that Socrates employs in all of the so-called 'early' dialogues, a process of question and answer by which Socrates shows his interlocutor that his statements involve an inconsistency.[4] While in other

---

[3] Cf. Saunders (1991), 205, 'Socrates' interlocutors, who are commonly sceptical of the need to cultivate the soul and to adhere to just conduct at any price, are confronted with edifying and powerful stories designed to appeal to their feelings and imagination, even if argument has failed to convince their intellect'.

[4] Vlastos (1983), 39, translates the procedure into the propositional logic of modern philosophers, although Brickhouse and Smith (1991), 135 ff., have emphasized that Socrates

dialogues Socrates employs his *elenchos* without much comment on its form or method, in the *Gorgias* the *elenchos* is not only employed, but discussed by the interlocutors.[5] The verb Socrates uses to describe this process of refutation or cross-examination is *elenchein*, which derives from the Homeric *to elenchos*, meaning shame or disgrace.[6] The implicit competition in this form of argument has been stressed in recent scholarship; the *elenchos* is a contest of speech between two parties—to win is to put your opponent to shame (*elenchein*), to lose is to be humiliated (*elenchesthai*).[7] Like any of the contests which were central to the Greek way of life, however, the *elenchos* must be played by the rules, and, in the *Gorgias*, Socrates carefully specifies the rules for his kind of *elenchos*, rules that differ in significant ways from the refutations practiced in the law courts and the assemblies. The basic process of refutation, pointing out a contradiction between accepted premises and consequences that follow from them, is not much

---

is testing not so much propositions as ways of life, cf. *La.* 187e6–188a2; *Ap.* 39c7. See also the critique of Vlastos' *elenchos* in Talisse (2002). Whether the so-called 'early' dialogues (Vlastos' list is *Apology, Charmides, Crito, Euthydemus, Euthyphro, Gorgias, Hippias Major* and *Minor, Ion, Laches, Lysis, Menexenus, Protagoras*, and the first book of the *Republic*) were in fact written earlier than Plato's other dialogues is irrelevant for my purposes. They may be conveniently grouped together because they exhibit a number of common characteristics, one of which is the prominent use of the *elenchos*.

[5] Brickhouse and Smith (1991), in their examination of Socrates' use of the *elenchos*, draw together from other dialogues many of Socrates' comments on the way the *elenchos* should be conducted, but the *Gorgias* is the only dialogue in which Socrates explicitly compares types of refutations.

[6] The Attic ὁ ἔλεγχος is generally used in the specific sense of a legal or rhetorical refutation, in contrast to the broader epic sense of shame, but the sense of failing a test or contest always underlies this refutation. To lose a contest or to fail a test, particularly in a public arena such as a lawcourt or even a street corner in front of a crowd, inevitably produces shame for the loser. While in other dialogues, the *elenchos* can become a friendly game played between friends, where the element of shame is minimized, in the *Gorgias*, the game is less friendly and the shame element is more prominent.

[7] See especially Lesher (2002), who traces the use of the word from its Homeric uses to its philosophic uses in Parmenides and up to Plato, Ausland (2002), who emphasizes the forensic context for the *elenchos*, and Dorion (1990), who emphasizes the agonistic nature of the *elenchos* and shows the ways in which Plato builds upon contemporary forensic procedure to create his own type of philosophic *elenchos*. Cf. Tarrant (2002), 68: 'The Greek verb was still correctly understood as involving the *exposure* of an opponent. In forensic speeches, where it was extremely common, it might involve the exposure of the *faults* (and hence the guilt) of the defendant, or the accuracy (and hence the reliability) of a witness. It was never a friendly process'. See ibid., n. 3: 'I count 181 uses of *elenchos* terminology in the speeches attributed to Antiphon, Andocides, Lysias, Isaeus, and Isocrates'. Adkins (1960), 30–60 rightly points to the connections between shame and failure to succeed at heroic action.

different when employed by Socrates from the process employed by eristic opponents like Dionysiodorus or indeed by opponents in the law courts.[8] Plato nevertheless has Socrates insist on differences in his mode of *elenchos*, and he further amplifies and illustrates those differences with the myth at the end of the dialogue.

2. JUDICIAL REFORM

In the *Gorgias*, Plato plays off his contemporaries' understanding of the way a normal Athenian legal contest worked to level a critique at the judicial system that condemned his teacher to death, contrasting the contest of litigation with his ideal of philosophic examination. Success in the Athenian lawcourts, it must be remembered, did not depend on fingerprints, bloodstains, and DNA evidence. Rather, the trial was a contest between two opponents, both of whom were subject to the scrutiny and judgement of the huge panel of *dikasts*. In the absence of high standards for material evidence, the dikasts' decision had to be made largely on the grounds of the character of the accuser and accused. A fragment of Euripides' *Phoenix* expresses the idea nicely: 'I've already been chosen to judge many disputes and have heard witnesses competing against each other with opposing accounts of the same event. And like any wise man I work out the truth by looking at a man's nature and the life he leads'.[9] Accordingly, both sides tried to present themselves in the most positive light, appealing to the standards and prejudices of the dikasts. Much of the preparation for an effective law court speech consisted in the creation of a portrait of the speaker that would appeal to the *dikasts*. In the courts, the witnesses served to establish the litigant's status in Athenian society and to affirm his good reputation within the networks

---

[8] As Tulin (2005), 304 comments, 'admittedly, Plato never tired of distinguishing *his* dialectic from the petty, logic-chopping sophistic which he terms eristic, antilogic, and the like: his seeks truth, theirs seeks only victory, *doxa*, and appearance. But, this said, the fact remains that there is no *formal* difference between the two, and that Plato retains (from first to last) a lively interest in the gymnastic, or purely logical aspect of the *elenchus*—developing by example many of the finer points of logic which Aristotle would later formalize as precept'. Cf. Ausland (2002), who compares the usage of the *elenchos* in forensic contexts and Platonic dialogues. Dorion (1990) argues that Plato draws on the ἐρώτησις procedure of the law courts in manipulating the *elenchos*.

[9] ἤδη δὲ πολλῶν λόγων κριτὴς καὶ πόλλ' ἁμιλληθέντα μαρτύρων ὑπὸ τάναντί' ἔγνων συμφορᾶς μιᾶς πέρι. κἀγὼ μὲν οὕτω χὤστις ἔστ' ἀνὴρ σοφὸς λογίζομαι τάληθές, εἰς ἀνδρὸς φύσιν σκοπῶν δίαιτάν θ' ἥντιν' ἡμερεύεται (fr. 812 Nauck—from Aeschines, *C. Timarch.* 152). See Humphreys (1985), 313–369, esp. 322 ff.

of family and local units of which he was a part, thus supplementing the positive self-presentation in his speeches.[10]

In the myth, this normal Athenian system of justice is in place before the reign of Zeus over the cosmos: the one about to die appears before a large mass of *dikasts* to defend the conduct of his life, and he sways his judges with his displays of character and status, bolstered not only by his trappings of wealth and power but by the witness of his friends.

> For now the cases are judged badly. For those being judged (he said) are judged with clothes on; for they are judged while they're still alive. And so many (he said) with base souls are covered in fine bodies and noble birth and riches; and when their judgement comes, many witnesses come to support them and to testify that they have lived justly. And so the judges are impressed by all this; and at the same time they judge with clothes on, obstructed by eyes and ears and their whole body in front of their soul. All these things, then, are in their way, both their own coverings and the defendants.[11]
>
> (*Gorg.* 523c2–d5)

To remedy the injustices this system produced, however, Zeus reforms the whole system of judgement. Not only will mortals be judged after death by other dead people, but they will be stripped of the foreknowledge of death, leaving them no time to prepare an elaborate defence. Moreover, they will be stripped at death not only of their bodies, but also of all their marks of status in life, all of the clothes and riches and supporting witnesses. The naked soul alone will face judgement, and not by a mass of ignorant citizens, but by a single expert judge: one of the sons of Zeus famed for his wisdom— Rhadamanthys, Aiakos, or Minos (*Gorg.* 523a1–524b1).[12]

---

[10] As scholars such as Todd and Humphreys stress, the primary function of a witness in the Athenian court was not, as in the modern courtroom, to present impartial factual evidence, but rather to support the status of the speaker. Witnesses represented, in Humphreys' terms, 'the social networks in which litigants were personally known. The support and good opinion of such social networks was very important for the litigant' (Humphreys [1985], 350). See Todd (1990), 23: 'Traditional interpretation of the Athenian law of evidence rests on the unstated assumption that Athenian witness had the same primary function as a modern witness: to tell the truth. But it is clear even on a cursory examination that Athenians did not use witnesses in the way that we do'.

[11] νῦν μὲν γὰρ κακῶς αἱ δίκαι δικάζονται. ἀμπεχόμενοι γάρ, ἔφη, οἱ κρινόμενοι κρίνονται· ζῶντες γὰρ κρίνονται. πολλοὶ οὖν, ἦ δ' ὅς, ψυχὰς πονηρὰς ἔχοντες ἠμφιεσμένοι εἰσὶ σώματά τε καλὰ καὶ γένη καὶ πλούτους, καί, ἐπειδὰν ἡ κρίσις ᾖ, ἔρχονται αὐτοῖς πολλοὶ μάρτυρες, μαρτυρήσοντες ὡς δικαίως βεβιώκασιν· οἱ οὖν δικασταὶ ὑπό τε τούτων ἐκπλήττονται, καὶ ἅμα καὶ αὐτοὶ ἀμπεχόμενοι δικάζουσι, πρὸ τῆς ψυχῆς τῆς αὑτῶν ὀφθαλμοὺς καὶ ὦτα καὶ ὅλον τὸ σῶμα προκεκαλυμμένοι. ταῦτα δὴ αὐτοῖς πάντα ἐπίπροσθεν γίγνεται, καὶ τὰ αὑτῶν ἀμφιέσματα καὶ τὰ τῶν κρινομένων.

[12] Citations from the *Gorgias* are from the text of Dodds (1959); I take all the translations of the *Gorgias* from Irwin (1979).

The reforms of the judicial process that Zeus imposes in the myth correspond to the differences that Socrates points out between his *elenchos* and
the lawcourt rhetoric of his interlocutors, particularly that of the impetuous Polus. Just as souls under the new regime cannot prepare an elaborate defence speech, so Socrates repeatedly prohibits his interlocutors from
making the long, oratorical speeches that would be appropriate in a lawcourt, requiring them to submit to the examination of the *elenchos* (*Gorg.*
449b48).[13]

Calling witnesses as if in an Athenian court is another mark of the rhetorical style of Polus' refutation which Socrates rejects. When Socrates refuses
to agree with him, Polus appeals to the crowd to support him. 'Don't you
think you are thoroughly refuted, Socrates, when you say things like this,
that not a single man would say? For look, ask one of these people here'
(*Gorg.* 473e4–5).[14] Socrates accuses Polus: 'You're trying to refute me rhetor-
ically, like those who think they're refuting people in the jury-courts' (471e2–
3).[15]

Socrates, by contrast, claims that his *elenchos* produces the one crucial
witness worth more than any number of other witnesses, the interlocutor
himself. 'For I know how to produce just one witness to whatever I say—
the man I am having a discussion with whoever he may be—but I forget
about the many. I know how to put the question to a vote to one man,

---

[13] Ἆρ' οὖν ἐθελήσαις ἄν, ὦ Γοργία, ὥσπερ νῦν διαλεγόμεθα, διατελέσαι τὸ μὲν ἐρωτῶν, τὸ δ'
ἀποκρινόμενος, τὸ δὲ μῆκος τῶν λόγων τοῦτο, οἷον καὶ Πῶλος ἤρξατο, εἰς αὖθις ἀποθέσθαι; ἀλλ'
ὅπερ ὑπισχνῇ, μὴ ψεύσῃ, ἀλλὰ ἐθέλησον κατὰ βραχὺ τὸ ἐρωτώμενον ἀποκρίνεσθαι. 'Then would
you be willing, Gorgias, to continue this present way of discussion, by alternate question and
answer, and defer to some other time that lengthy style of speech in which Polus made a
beginning? Come, be true to your promise, and consent to answer each question briefly'. See
also 462a1–4: ἀλλ' εἴ τι κήδῃ τοῦ λόγου τοῦ εἰρημένου καὶ ἐπανορθώσασθαι αὐτὸν βούλει, ὥσπερ
νυνδὴ ἔλεγον, ἀνθέμενος ὅτι σοι δοκεῖ, ἐν τῷ μέρει ἐρωτῶν τε καὶ ἐρωτώμενος, ὥσπερ ἐγώ τε καὶ
Γοργίας, ἔλεγχέ τε καὶ ἐλέγχου. 'No, if you have any concern for the argument that we have
carried on, and care to set it on its feet again, revoke whatever you please, as I suggested
just now; take your turn in questioning and being questioned, like me and Gorgias; and thus
either refute or be refuted'.

[14] Οὐκ οἴει ἐξεληλέγχθαι, ὦ Σώκρατες, ὅταν τοιαῦτα λέγῃς ἃ οὐδεὶς ἂν φήσειεν ἀνθρώπων; ἐπεὶ
ἐροῦ τινα τουτωνί. Socrates characterizes this law court refutation as 'worth nothing towards
the truth. For sometimes someone may actually be beaten by many false witnesses thought to
amount to something'. 471e7–472a2: οὗτος δὲ ὁ ἔλεγχος οὐδενὸς ἄξιός ἐστιν πρὸς τὴν ἀλήθειαν·
ἐνίοτε γὰρ ἂν καὶ καταψευδομαρτυρηθείη τις ὑπὸ πολλῶν καὶ δοκούντων εἶναί τι (Plato, unlike
the Lord Chancellor in *Iolanthe*, tends to 'assume that the witnesses summoned in force,|
in Exchequer, Queen's Bench, Common Pleas, and Divorce,| have perjured themselves as a
matter of course ...').

[15] ῥητορικῶς γάρ με ἐπιχειρεῖς ἐλέγχειν, ὥσπερ οἱ ἐν τοῖς δικαστηρίοις ἡγούμενοι ἐλέγχειν. See
Dorion (1990), 323–327, on the use of witnesses in the courts and Plato's critique.

but don't even have a dialogue with the many' (474a5–b1).[16] Socrates rejects the 'wisdom of the masses,' preferring to settle the question with a dialogic interchange between two individuals.[17]

Plato crafts his description of the reformed afterlife judgement to resemble the Socratic *elenchos*, tailoring the traditional mythic motifs to fit with the process. Like the Socratic *elenchos*, the afterlife judgement in Zeus' regime takes place between two individuals, an examiner and an examined. In both, the examined is the only admissible witness, and that one witness is sufficient for a judgement, even superior to a crowd of false witnesses— the body, the clothes, the friends and relatives of the deceased—who could obstruct the examiner in his inquiry.[18] The striking image of the naked soul, unprepared and trembling before the expert judge, depicts the interlocutor whose beliefs are being examined in the *elenchos*, bereft of appeals to popular opinion or the authority of his social status, and the chronological structure of the narrative in the myth highlights the logical contrast between types of refutations.

3. MEDICAL METAPHORS

Rather than the afterlife judge acting as a surrogate punisher for the wrongs committed against others, as the limited evidence for earlier myths of the afterlife suggests, in the *Gorgias* myth, the judge uses his expertise to

---

[16] ἐγὼ γὰρ ὧν ἂν λέγω ἕνα μὲν παρασχέσθαι μάρτυρα ἐπίσταμαι, αὐτὸν πρὸς ὃν ἄν μοι ὁ λόγος ᾖ, τοὺς δὲ πολλοὺς ἐῶ χαίρειν, καὶ ἕνα ἐπιψηφίζειν ἐπίσταμαι, τοῖς δὲ πολλοῖς οὐδὲ διαλέγομαι. After Socrates has made Polus concede that neither he nor anyone else could prefer to do injustice rather than suffer it, he once again draws the contrast between their two styles of *elenchos*. 'You see, then, Polus, that when this refutation is compared with that one it is not at all like it. You have everyone else agreeing with you except me, but I am quite satisfied with you just by yourself, agreeing and being my witness. I put the question for a vote to you alone, and let all the others go'. 475e7–476a2: Ὁρᾷς οὖν, ὦ Πῶλε, ὁ ἔλεγχος παρὰ τὸν ἔλεγχον παραβαλλόμενος ὅτι οὐδὲν ἔοικεν, ἀλλὰ σοὶ μὲν οἱ ἄλλοι πάντες ὁμολογοῦσιν πλὴν ἐμοῦ, ἐμοὶ δὲ σὺ ἐξαρκεῖς εἷς ὢν μόνος καὶ ὁμολογῶν καὶ μαρτυρῶν, καὶ ἐγὼ σὲ μόνον ἐπιψηφίζων τοὺς ἄλλους ἐῶ χαίρειν.

[17] Cf. Socrates' rejections of the common opinion in *Laches*, 184e and *Crito*, 46d–47d (a contrast to Xenophon's depiction of Socratic argument starting from common opinion in *Memorabilia*, 4.6.15). Moreover, if indeed Socrates' mention of his service on the Council is meant to recall the illegal trial of the Generals after Arginusae, Plato is attacking not just the idea of having a mass of *dikasts*, but also the idea of trying a group of defendants en masse. Another layer of imagery that may be in play is the idea of the private arbitration that could often substitute for the public trial, in which a single arbitrator (chosen by both parties out of respect for his fairness and insight) would render a judgement instead of the mass of *dikasts*.

[18] The examiner too relies not on the bodily senses that perceive these superficial attributes, but on the faculties of his soul.

evaluate the soul by the wrongs it has done to itself, the harm caused to the soul by its way of life, and then, like a doctor, to prescribe the appropriate corrective treatment.

3.1. *Diagnosis*

In the myth, the deceased mortal, stripped of body and marks of mortal status, faces the judge with a naked soul. Just as presenting a good appearance through one's rhetoric and witnesses is the key to winning in an Athenian court, so too in the afterlife the primary criterion on which Aiakos or Rhadamanthys evaluates the deceased is the appearance of his soul.

But what, for Plato, is a good-looking soul? Plato employs very physical terms to describe the soul in this dialogue, and a good-looking soul is described in terms appropriate to a good-looking body. A soul must present an appearance worthy of a free citizen, well developed from exercise in the gymnasium and without the whip scars that mark the disobedient slave or the festering sores that indicate poor health.[19] The soul coming to judgement bears only the marks of the conditioning of its soul, which are exposed to the expert knowledge of the judge who can diagnose the disease or deformity of the soul from its appearance and prescribe the fitting correction.[20] The expert examination of the judge in the myth thus serves

---

[19] As so often, especially in an aristocratic context, the aesthetic appearance carries a moral connotation—καλός is both beautiful and good, while αἰσχρός is ugly, base, and shameful. Only an appearance that is fine enough qualifies for honoured treatment. However, the afterlife judgement of naked souls may well also recall the examination of the athletes before a competition such as the Olympic games, in which the competitors had to strip down and be examined by judges who, on the basis of the athletes' physical development, would classify them as *paides* or ephebes, cf. Pausanias V, 24.10 (I owe this idea to Betsy Gebhard). Unfortunately no evidence remains that gives any detailed description of such a process of judgement before the competition. It may well be that the *Gorgias* contains more imagery resonant of this process, but the allusions are lost to the modern reader.

[20] Cf. 524c5–d7, where the marks on the soul are compared to marks on the body. The souls of the dead were frequently imagined as *eidola* of the deceased—insubstantial, but essentially like the deceased as he was remembered from life. The deceased was frequently represented as being like to the living person, but with the wounds that caused his death. Such an image appears not only in Homer (*Odyssey*, 9, 40–41), where Odysseus sees 'many fighting men killed in battle, stabbed with brazen spears, still carrying their bloody armour on them,' but on numerous vases, where the depiction of dead men with bandaged wounds was a recognized topos. Dodds *ad loc* (p. 379) points out the tradition of scarred souls following Plato: Lucian, *Cataplus*, 24ff.; Philo, *Spec. Leg.* i. 103; Plutarch, *Ser. num. vind.* 22, 564d; Epictetus 2.18.11; Tacitus, *Annals* 6.6.; Themistius, *Orat.* 20, 234a. The wounds that the body sustained were, moreover, thought to leave their mark on the soul after death, to the extent that those who feared the retribution of the angry dead might deliberately mutilate the

the same function as the examination in the *elenchos*, to determine the errors in the patient's way of life. By using Socrates' myth, Plato presents in graphic form the contradictions exposed by the Socratic *elenchos* as the scars and wounds that mar the soul which is laid bare to Aiakos or Rhadamanthys.[21]

3.2. *Prescriptions for Corrective Treatment*

While Plato uses the tale of Zeus' reform and the image of the naked soul to illustrate the contrasts between the rhetoric of the Athenian lawcourts and the Socratic *elenchos*, other aspects of the myth depict the effects of the *elenchos* itself. The metaphor of the diagnosis and healing of the soul underlies both the discussions of the *elenchos* in the dialogue and the myth at the end, providing a link between the two. The effect of the *elenchos* is described in medical terms throughout the dialogue, and the myth separates the diagnostic and curative functions of the process in its images of judgement and punishment.

Scholars of ancient philosophy have debated what the Socratic *elenchos* is supposed to achieve in the philosophic arguments of the Platonic dialogues.[22] Many suppose that the *elenchos* is purely negative, disproving the false ideas of Socrates' interlocutors, whereas Vlastos and others have argued that Plato intended the *elenchos* to do more, to prove the truth of the

---

corpse to prevent it from being able to wreak its revenge. The ritual of *machalismos*, which Clytemnestra is said by both Aeschylus and Sophocles to have performed on Agamemnon, involves chopping off the hands of the dead man and stringing them under his armpits, effectively disarming any attempt he might make at revenge from beyond the grave, cf. Aeschylus, *Choephoroi*, 439, Sophocles, *Electra*, 445. According to the scholiast on Sophocles' *Electra*, this gruesome operation was performed to deprive the deceased of the power of avenging the murder: ἵνα, φασιν, ἀσθενὴς γένοιτο πρὸς ἀντιτίασθαι τὸν φονέα.

[21] Nothing in the soul was healthy, but it was thoroughly whip-marked and full of scars from false oaths and injustice—all that each of his actions stained into the soul—and everything was crooked from lying and insolence, and nothing straight, from being brought up without truth; and he saw that from liberty and luxury and excess and incontinence in actions the soul was full of disproportion and shamefulness. 524e4–525a6: οὐδὲν ὑγιὲς ὂν τῆς ψυχῆς, ἀλλὰ διαμεμαστιγωμένην καὶ οὐλῶν μεστὴν ὑπὸ ἐπιορκιῶν καὶ ἀδικίας, ἃ ἑκάστῃ ἡ πρᾶξις αὐτοῦ ἐξωμόρξατο εἰς τὴν ψυχήν, καὶ πάντα σκολιὰ ὑπὸ ψεύδους καὶ ἀλαζονείας καὶ οὐδὲν εὐθὺ διὰ τὸ ἄνευ ἀληθείας τεθράφθαι· καὶ ὑπὸ ἐξουσίας καὶ τρυφῆς καὶ ὕβρεως καὶ ἀκρατίας τῶν πράξεων ἀσυμμετρίας τε καὶ αἰσχρότητος γέμουσαν τὴν ψυχὴν εἶδεν.

[22] For further views on the *elenchos*, see Vlastos (1983); Kraut (1983); Irwin (1979); Brickhouse and Smith (1984, 1991, and 1997); Kahn (1984 and 1996); May (1997), and Talisse (2002). Scott (2002) contains a number of essays that treat the *elenchos* from a variety of perspectives, mostly using Vlastos (1983) as a starting point.

opposing positions and thus to teach the interlocutors something.[23] I would argue that the medical metaphor is crucial to understanding the effect of the *elenchos* in the Platonic dialogues. Is the *elenchos* merely diagnostic, pointing out the interlocutors' errors or does it also serve a curative function, correcting the errors that it has diagnosed? Plato supplements his discussion of the workings of the *elenchos* in the dialogue with the description of the afterlife judgement in the myth, and this description of the process of judgement and punishment of the soul in the afterlife provides a clearer picture of the effects and limits of the Socratic *elenchos*.

In developing the medical metaphor of the health of the soul, Plato again makes use of a contrast between the Socratic *elenchos* and forensic rhetoric. The philosophic *elenchos*, in contrast to the oratory of the rhetoricians like Polus and Gorgias, is described throughout the dialogue as a kind of purgative medicine designed to aid the soul in achieving a good condition. Rhetoric is compared to an elaborate banquet, designed to give pleasure to the audience.[24] Both rhetoric and cookery are part of that practice of pandering to the pleasures of the audience without regard to its welfare that Socrates terms 'flattery', *kolakeia*. The *elenchos*, by contrast, is not merely a diet, a regimen, but actually bitter medicine, painful and unpleasant to swallow, unlike the pleasing periods of oratory. Although pain is not the essential feature of medical treatment, it is an unavoidable result of the change in state that the treatment effects—a correction or restraint of the disordered elements, *kolasis*. If, according to contemporary Greek theories of medicine, health is a proper balance of elements, and disease is an improper balance, then any medical treatment must alter the balance of elements in the body, a process which Plato sees as involving a certain amount of pain merely through the change.[25] Nevertheless, those who do

---

[23] While some scholars, e.g., Vlastos (1983) and Irwin (1979), argue that *elenchos* is intended to produce a positive result by proving the truth of some proposition, others, e.g. Benson (1987), claim that the *elenchos* is intended only to disprove propositions by showing inconsistency in the interlocutor's beliefs. Brickhouse and Smith (1991), 135 ff., point out the the target of the *elenchos* is more the way of life that follows on the proposition in question, cf. *La.* 187e6–188a2; *Ap.* 39c7. Talisse (2002) argues as well against the idea that the proposition is the target of the *elenchos*, although he sees the interlocutor's knowledge, rather than way of life, as the target of the attack.

[24] Socrates and Chaerophon, arriving too late for Gorgias' oration, are told that they have missed a feast (447a). In the *elenchos*, one must proceed in a moderate fashion, not snatching and grabbing at clever phrases or unfortunate definitions as though trying to stuff oneself with the dainties prepared by the chefs (454c).

[25] Of course, in Plato's time almost any medical procedure would have been painful and unpleasant, more in the manner of dentistry today, which remains uncomfortable despite

not understand the benefits try to avoid the painful corrections (*kolaseis*) of the doctor's medicine, preferring the pleasant confections (*kolakeia*) of the cook.[26]

3.3. *Avoiding Treatment*

Plato also applies this medical metaphor in Socrates' debate with Polus whether it is better to be punished for injustice or to escape punishment. Like the child who would avoid the doctor for fear of the painful treatment, the foolish prefer to escape punishment for injustice. As Socrates remarks: 'For these people have managed to do about the same thing, my friend, as if someone suffering from the most serious illnesses, managed not to pay justice for the faults in his body to the doctors and not to be treated—afraid like a child of the burning and cutting because it is painful' (479a5–b1).[27] Polus' hero, the tyrant who can avoid paying for any of his crimes, is reduced to the little child whimpering with fear at the prospect of a visit to the doctor that would cure his sickness.

In just this way, Socrates' interlocutors try to avoid the bitter medicine of the *elenchos*. Socrates rebukes both Polus and Callicles for trying to wriggle out of answering the questions that have trapped them into contradicting themselves, urging them to take their medicine: 'Don't shrink from answering, Polus—you won't be harmed at all; but present yourself nobly to the argument as to a doctor; answer (475d5–7)'.[28] Answering in the *elenchos* is

---

all the advances in anesthetics and modern technology. In the *Laws*, Plato explicitly talks about the pain involved in any kind of shift of mode of life or regimen. 'Take as an example the way the body gets used to all sorts of food and drink and exercise. At first they upset it, but then in the course of time it is this very regimen that is responsible for putting on flesh .... But imagine someone forced to change again, to one of the other recommended systems: initially, he's troubled by illnesses, and only slowly, by getting used to his new way of life, does he get back to normal' (*La.* 797d ff., Saunder's translation). Saunders (1991), 172 ff., sees this idea that pain is a necessary component of any change as a new element in the penal theory of the *Laws*, stemming from the physiology of the *Timaeus*, rather than an idea implicit in contemporary medical ideas that Plato applies to the reform of the soul from injustice as early as the *Gorgias*.

[26] Cf. again the image of the doctor prosecuted by a cook in front of a jury of children (521e, 464de).

[27] Σχεδὸν γάρ που οὗτοι, ὦ ἄριστε, τὸ αὐτὸ διαπεπραγμένοι εἰσὶν ὥσπερ ἂν εἴ τις τοῖς μεγίστοις νοσήμασιν συνισχόμενος διαπράξαιτο μὴ διδόναι δίκην τῶν περὶ τὸ σῶμα ἁμαρτημάτων τοῖς ἰατροῖς μηδὲ ἰατρεύεσθαι, φοβούμενος ὡσπερανεὶ παῖς τὸ κάεσθαι καὶ τὸ τέμνεσθαι, ὅτι ἀλγεινόν.

[28] μὴ ὄκνει ἀποκρίνασθαι, ὦ Πῶλε· οὐδὲν γὰρ βλαβήσῃ· ἀλλὰ γενναίως τῷ λόγῳ ὥσπερ ἰατρῷ παρέχων ἀποκρίνου.

also likened to facing the doctor's treatment in the argument with Callicles. The effect of the *elenchos* is to restrain or temper the one who undergoes it, to correct the imbalance in his soul and restore it to proper balance and harmony. Callicles, when he sees that he is about to be put to the shame of having to deny his thesis, tries to avoid completing the *elenchos*.

Socrates rebukes him: 'This man won't abide being helped and corrected (*kolazomenos*), and himself undergoing the very thing our discussion is about—being corrected' (505c3–4).[29] The treatment of the *elenchos* cannot be effective if the patient is able to avoid taking his medicine. Callicles indeed grumbles that he has only gone along with this argument so far at the request of Gorgias, who intervened earlier to make Callicles continue the discussion (497b5). Gorgias' role in making the patient take his philosophic medicine recalls his boast at the beginning of the dialogue that he often was able to persuade patients to take the medicines his brother the doctor was not able to get them to take (456b). As Socrates warns Callicles, if Callicles cannot refute the idea that it is better to suffer than to do injustice but continues to live by that idea, then: 'Callicles himself will not agree with you, Callicles, but he will be discordant with you in the whole of your life' (482b5–6).[30] The *elenchos*, then, is depicted throughout the dialogue as a kind of purgative medicine that produces a painful effect of *kolasis* upon the patient, providing a shock to his system that checks the elements of his soul that are out of balance, restores the harmony, and makes health possible.[31]

---

[29] Οὗτος ἀνὴρ οὐχ ὑπομένει ὠφελούμενος καὶ αὐτὸς τοῦτο πάσχων περὶ οὗ ὁ λόγος ἐστί, κυλαζόμενος.

[30] οὔ σοι ὁμολογήσει Καλλικλῆς, ὦ Καλλίκλεις, ἀλλὰ διαφωνήσει ἐν ἅπαντι τῷ βίῳ. Callicles is trapped between his idea that it is better not to suffer anything, even helpful restraint, and his desire to achieve the best. At the heart of Socrates' debate with Callicles is the question of whether it is better to rule or be ruled, to do or to suffer. Callicles' advocacy of extreme hedonism in the debate, as well as his political ambitions, stem from the assumption that, in every case, it is better to do actively than to suffer passively. Socrates' example of the *kinaidos* (494e), is fatal to Callicles' position, not because it is so disgusting that it makes even Callicles ashamed, but rather because the *kinaidos* presents the paradoxical case of one who actively desires to be passive. Callicles cannot handle such a contradiction of his ideal and tries to avoid the issue by claiming that such an example is too shameful for mention. On the *kinaidos*, see Winkler (1990).

[31] Cf. the description in *Sophist*, 230cd. For just as physicians who care for the body believe that the body cannot get benefit from any food offered to it until all obstructions are removed, so, my boy, those who purge the soul believe that the soul can receive no benefit from any teachings offered to it until someone by cross-questioning reduces him who is cross-questioned to an attitude of modesty, by removing the opinions that obstruct the teachings, and thus purges him and makes him think that he knows only what he knows, and no more: νομίζοντες γάρ, ὦ παῖ φίλε, οἱ καθαίροντες αὐτούς, ὥσπερ οἱ περὶ τὰ σώματα

The myth separates, in the chronological order of the narrative, the diagnostic and punitive effects of the *elenchos*. While the exposure of contradictions corresponds to the examination by the judge in the hereafter, the pain and shame (*to elenchos*) the interlocutor feels as he loses the argument and his way of life is turned on its head correspond to the punishments (*kolaseis*) the judged soul undergoes.[32] In the *Gorgias*, Plato does not go into a detailed description of the process of punishment in the underworld for the one whom the judge condemns (as he does, for example, in the *Phaedo*); he merely describes it as undergoing 'what it is fitting for it to undergo' (525a7). This punishment, however, this suffering, produces benefit for the punished soul, since it is corrected and made better by the treatment prescribed by the judge. 'Those who are benefited and pay justice at the hands of gods and men are those who are at fault with curable faults; but still their benefit comes to them through pain and sufferings both here and in Hades—for there is no other way to get rid of injustice' (525b6–c1).[33] Plato makes the punishment of the wrongdoer in the afterlife judgement correspond to the shaming effect of the *elenchos* in this life on someone who is defeated in an argument.[34] Like taking the doctor's medicine, these processes consist of suffering something unpleasant but beneficial. However, their helpful function does have its limits; only those who submit to treatment can be cured, and those who, like Callicles, avoid the treatment cannot get the benefits. Such

---

ἰατροὶ νενομίκασι μὴ πρότερον ἂν τῆς προσφερομένης τροφῆς ἀπολαύειν δύνασθαι σῶμα, πρὶν ἂν τὰ ἐμποδίζοντα ἐντός τις ἐκβάλῃ, ταὐτὸν καὶ περὶ ψυχῆς διενοήθησαν ἐκεῖνοι, μὴ πρότερον αὐτὴν ἕξειν τῶν προσφερομένων μαθημάτων [230δ] ὄνησιν, πρὶν ἂν ἐλέγχων τις τὸν ἐλεγχόμενον εἰς αἰσχύνην καταστήσας, τὰς τοῖς μαθήμασιν ἐμποδίους δόξας ἐξελών, καθαρὸν ἀποφήνῃ καὶ ταῦτα ἡγούμενον ἅπερ οἶδεν εἰδέναι μόνα, πλείω δὲ μή. As Renaud (2002), 194–195, comments: 'according to this description of the *elenchus*, then, the soul cannot receive any benefit from knowledge if it is not first refuted and humbled, indeed brought to shame. ... If philosophy begins in wonder, the *elenchus* provides the wonder through the *aporia*, the sufficient proof of one's ignorance and of the necessity of learning'.

[32] As Callicles protests: 'If you *are* in earnest and these things you're saying are really true, won't this human life of ours be turned upside down, and won't everything we do evidently be the opposite of what we should do?' (481c). For discussions of the role of shame in the dialogue, contrast the arguments of Kahn (1984) with those of McKim (1988), but it is important to remember that, whatever else Socrates' interlocutors may or may not feel shame about, they all feel shame at losing a contest—in contrast to Socrates, who proclaims that he would rather lose and be corrected than win and be wrong.

[33] ὅμως δὲ δι' ἀλγηδόνων καὶ ὀδυνῶν γίγνεται αὐτοῖς ἡ ὠφελία καὶ ἐνθάδε καὶ ἐν ῞Αιδου· οὐ γὰρ οἷόν τε ἄλλως ἀδικίας ἀπαλλάττεσθαι.

[34] Allen (2000), 60–61, points out the equivalence, between loss in a contest and punishment, 'punishment, like reward, was the outcome of a contest for honour, but a punishment was equivalent to a loss in a contest and a loss of honour'. This equivalence would be particularly felt by an aristocrat such as Callicles, whose life is focused on winning honour.

unpleasant but beneficial medicine, whether it be the *elenchos* administered by Socrates in the streets of Athens or a judgement rendered by Aiakos in the underworld, is the only way to cure the erring soul. Those who refuse the treatment must live out their existence forever unhealed, for there is no other remedy.

4. THE INCURABLES

The *Gorgias*, however, is notable as a dialogue in which Socrates utterly fails to convince his interlocutors, to the extent that he must even finish his *elenchos* of Callicles by speaking both parts, since Callicles refuses to continue the contest. In the *Gorgias*, Socrates and Callicles both regard each other as pathological cases, in need of radical treatment to correct the unhealthy way in which they spend their lives. While Callicles warns Socrates to give up his practice of skulking in the corners, playing at philosophy with a few young boys, and to take up the place of a man, using rhetoric to win contests in the assembly and the lawcourts, Socrates earnestly tries to convince Callicles to submit his life to philosophic scrutiny and to give up the life of the mob orator. Callicles' refusal to take his medicine, however, marks him as one of the incurables Socrates describes in the myth, who cannot benefit from the treatment they get in the afterlife judgement, but can only serve as an example to others. The *elenchos* cannot cure those who refuse to accept the treatment and to adapt their lives to the conclusions of the argument, but the spectacle of their suffering may nevertheless induce others reform themselves.

The role of the incurable offenders in the *Gorgias* has been much debated, for the very idea of punishing an incurable seems to fly in the face of the rehabilitative idea of punishment that appears in the Platonic dialogues from the *Gorgias* to the *Laws*.[35] While there can be no doubt that Plato takes the idea of the eternal punishment of certain exceptional figures like

---

[35] Mackenzie and Saunders see the punishment of the incurables as a survival into Plato's penal theory of the retributive element of Greek penology, the idea that the divine surrogates inflict retribution on those who did not pay the penalty in life (Mackenzie [1981], 225–239 and Saunders [1991], 198, 206, particularly his discussion of the idea of the surrogate, 52–61). While Mackenzie sees the retributive element as a flaw throughout Plato's penology, Saunders argues that Plato eliminates this aspect from his later works. Contrast now, however, Brickhouse and Smith (1997 and 2002), who argue that the passages that appear to advocate retributive punishments in fact make sense in terms of Socratic intellectualist theories of punishment helping the wrongdoer become virtuous.

Tantalus from a mythic tradition in which they have been used to represent retribution, Plato himself has a use for them that does not include the retributive element. The fate of the incurables in the afterlife illustrates, in this life, the life of the unphilosophic who are powerful enough to evade any kind of outside restraint (*kolasis*).[36] Their inconsistent and irrational lifestyle actually inflicts continuous suffering upon them, and their souls are so deformed from the way they have lived that they can only continue, in the afterlife, the kind of life they lived when alive. Although it does not cure them, this punishment has a deterrent effect, serving as a warning to those who are considering choosing the life of Callicles instead of the life of Socrates.[37] Even if Callicles refuses to change his life in consequence of his public humiliation in the refutation, the silent audience of the dialogue, the aspiring students of rhetoric who had come to hear Gorgias (and, of course, the readers of Plato's dialogue), may profit from the spectacle of his suffering.[38]

---

[36] Cf. *Tht.* 177a: οὗ δὴ τίνουσι δίκην ζῶντες τὸν εἰκότα βίον ᾧ ὁμοιοῦνται. 'The penalty they pay is the life they lead, answering to the pattern they resemble'.

[37] Their deterrent value is not, as some have supposed, only for souls who are about to be reborn into another mortal life, for the *Gorgias* makes no mention of the metempsychosis that plays such an important role in Plato's other eschatological myths. The incurables serve as a deterrent to anyone who pays heed to the myth that Socrates tells, for like all *nekyias*, it reveals the conditions of the underworld for ordinary mortals who have not, like Odysseus, Heracles, or Theseus, ventured into the unseen realm. See Guthrie (1975), IV, 306, who points out that revelations of the afterlife need not imply metempsychosis, as Friedländer (1969 [1954]), i. 185 had argued. Friedländer was supported by Dodds, who commented, 'The passage only makes sense on the assumption that the dead will one day return to earth: it presupposes the doctrine of rebirth, which Plato evidently already held when he wrote the *Gorgias* but did not choose to expound in this context' (Dodds [1959], 381). Such an assumption comes from the misguided attempt to find consistency between the myths of Plato, as though they all expressed Plato's own beliefs about the afterlife rather than being used by him to express particular ideas in the different dialogues. As Long, in the best treatment of metempsychosis in the Greek tradition, remarks, 'there is no trace of metempsychosis in the *Gorgias* any more than in the *Apology*' (Long [1948], 65). Annas argues that metempsychosis need not be implied for the punishment of the incurables to make sense: 'it is inappropriately literal-minded to press any further the question, what happens to these curables who are cured. There is no answer within the myth in the form and to the extent that Plato has developed it' (Annas [1982], 124).

[38] At the end of the dialogue, of course, Callicles shows every sign of disregarding the admissions he has made in *elenchos*, of remaining uncured and incurable because he refuses to take his medicine. Socrates, on the contrary, says that if he is defeated in the *elenchos* and agrees with Callicles, but is found living contrary to his admissions, then he should be considered a complete fool and worthy of nothing: καὶ ἐάν με λάβῃς νῦν μέν σοι ὁμολογήσαντα, ἐν δὲ τῷ ὑστέρῳ χρόνῳ μὴ ταὐτὰ πράττοντα ἅπερ ὡμολόγησα, πάνυ με ἡγοῦ βλᾶκα εἶναι καὶ μηκέτι ποτέ με νουθετήσῃς ὕστερον, ὡς μηδενὸς ἄξιον ὄντα (488a6–b1).

Plato uses the myth of the water-carriers, earlier in the dialogue, to illustrate the sort of perpetual suffering that Callicles inflicts upon himself by refusing to change his way of life, to show how Callicles' choice of life, far from being a life of action without restraint, is actually a life of suffering, both on a personal and political level. Socrates signals the application of the myth of afterlife to life in this world by his quotation of the famous Euripides' tag: 'Who knows if being alive is really being dead, and being dead being alive?' (492e10–11)[39] While, on the literal level, the story conveys the familiar traditional idea that those who are not initiated 'carry water to this leaky jar with another leaky thing, a sieve,' Socrates builds an interpretation into the tale (493b5–7).[40] According to the clever man from whom he heard the tale, the uninitiate (*amuetoi*) are the unintelligent (*anoetoi*), and the jar (*pithos*) is the persuadable (*pithanon*) and impressionable (*peistikon*) soul, which is leaky like the sieve.[41] 'In the foolish men that of the soul with appetites, the foolish, intemperate, and insatiable in it, was a leaking jar, because it couldn't be filled' (493a6–b3).[42] Socrates goes on to develop this idea of the soul as a jar which the intemperate man spends his whole life trying to fill in vain, deriving pleasure from the process of filling but pain from the endless emptying. On this level, the image obviously applies to Callicles' ideal of suffering no restraints on one's appetite, but Plato also

---

[39] τίς δ' οἶδεν, εἰ τὸ ζῆν μέν ἐστι κατθανεῖν, τὸ κατθανεῖν δὲ ζῆν, cf. Euripides' *Phrixus*, fr. 833. The tag is attributed either to the *Phrixus* or the *Polyidos*. Sextus Empiricus attributes the same idea to Heraclitus (*Pyrrh. Hyp.* 3.230, see Heraclitus, fr. 62, 88). Cf. Dodds' treatment of the passage in the *Gorgias, ad loc.* Aristophanes repeatedly uses the line to great effect in the *Frogs* (1082, 1477), finally turning it against Euripides when Dionysos abandons him in the underworld and brings up Aeschylus instead.

[40] φοροῖεν εἰς τὸν τετρημένον πίθον ὕδωρ ἑτέρῳ τοιούτῳ τετρημένῳ κοσκίνῳ.

[41] Irwin translates πιθανόν as 'persuadable' and πειστικὸν as 'impressionable,' but, as Dodds points out, both adjectives should have an active sense. If both are derived from πειθω, the meaning would be some sense of 'persuasive'. A similar phrase occurs just above, attributed to some 'wise man,' τῆς δὲ ψυχῆς τοῦτο ἐν ᾧ ἐπιθυμίαι εἰσὶ τυγχάνει ὂν οἷον ἀναπείθεσθαι καὶ μεταπίπτειν ἄνω κάτω. 'That of our soul with appetites is liable to be persuaded and to sway up and down'. Ἀναπείθεσθαι, however, is unequivocally passive in sense. Blank (1991), 26–27 points out that the confusion between the active and passive senses, persuadable and persuasive, reflects the confusion of Callicles about the role of the orator, whether he is the persuader of the masses or is constantly persuaded by the masses to different things. One might speculate whether the words in question also carried the sense of πείσεσθαι derived from πάσχω, to suffer, playing on the pun between πίθος, πειθω, and πάθος. If the words carried the resonance of suffering, as well as persuadable and persuasive, the connection between Callicles' confusion and the fate he will suffer, both in life and in the myth, would be neatly drawn. But perhaps this word play would be too much, even for a κομψὸς ἀνήρ.

[42] παράγων τῷ ὀνόματι διὰ τὸ πιθανόν τε καὶ πειστικὸν ὠνόμασε πίθον, τοὺς δὲ ἀνοήτους ἀμυήτους, τῶν δ' ἀνοήτων τοῦτο τῆς ψυχῆς οὗ αἱ ἐπιθυμίαι εἰσί, τὸ ἀκόλαστον αὐτοῦ καὶ οὐ στεγανόν, ὡς τετρημένος εἴη πίθος, διὰ τὴν ἀπληστίαν ἀπεικάσας.

uses the image to describe the life of the orator trying to gratify the ever-changing and unsatisfiable appetites of the persuadable masses, a task as vain and tormenting as the labors of the water-carriers.[43]

The power to persuade the masses, Gorgias has claimed, 'is responsible for freedom for a man himself, and at the same time for rule over others in his own city' (452d6–8).[44] Callicles urges Socrates to a life of public speaking because learning how to please the crowd will enable him to save his life, but Socrates objects that to be able to have power in a city requires one to accommodate oneself to the rulers.[45] For Plato, who could not accept the idea of the 'wisdom of the masses,' the policy of an orator trying to express the will of the people is nothing more than pandering, *kolakeia*. Like the cook who strives to delight the palates of his diners regardless of the effect on their health, the orator who stays popular by telling the people what they want to hear is merely gratifying irrational appetites, a task that is ultimately as fruitless as trying to fill a leaky *pithos*, for the masses will

---

[43] Socrates opens his attack on both the personal and political position of Callicles with his observation that Callicles is in love with two beloveds, Demos, son of Pyrilampes and the Athenian *demos* (481c ff.). The choice of the homoerotic metaphor allows Socrates to point out the confusion of the active and passive, ruler and ruled in Callicles' ideal. Although the adult male *erastes* like Callicles is the active pursuer, and the younger *eromenos* or *paidika* like Demos is the more passive, pursued person in the ideology of this kind of Athenian aristocratic homoerotic relationship, the beloved was also able to exercise a fair amount of control over the lover, who would go to great lengths to win his beloved's favour. Socrates notes that however absurd the things their beloveds say may be, both he and Callicles are helpless to contradict them (481d–482b). Although they are, in theory, the active partners in the relationships, guiding the youths into manhood, they are both, in fact, helplessly subject to their beloveds, the ruled instead of the rulers. The familiar paradox of the homoerotic romance allows Plato to bring out the ambiguity of Callicles' relation to the masses he desires to dominate.

[44] αἴτιον ἅμα μὲν ἐλευθερίας αὐτοῖς τοῖς ἀνθρώποις, ἅμα δὲ τοῦ ἄλλων ἄρχειν ἐν τῇ αὑτοῦ πόλει ἑκάστῳ.

[45] 486b–c, 521a–d, 510a–e. Callicles here expresses the ideology found in Demosthenes and other orators, that the orator reflects the ideas of the masses whom he is leading. Ober (1989), 167 summarizes this ideology: 'the worthy orator prefers the same things as the many, and therefore, when speaking in public, he simply vocalizes the desires of the majority of his listeners. Because the wisdom of the group is superior to that of the individual, the desires of the majority are right desires, and the orator who voices these desires is therefore advocating the right decision ... The presumption that to agree with the masses was to be in the right easily led to the implication that one's opponent must be regarded as a traitor. The savage tenor of Athenian political invective must be seen in the light of this progression'. Demosthenes 18.20 is the most concise expression of this idea in the extant speeches: 'but it is not the speech of a rhetor, Aeschines, or the power of his voice which are his worth, but it lies rather in his preference for the same things as the many and in his hating and loving the same things as his homeland. Having such a disposition, everything a man says will be patriotic'.

never be satisfied.[46] What Callicles thinks is ruling, both gratifying one's own appetites and gratifying the masses as an orator, is in fact being ruled, being enslaved to the never-ceasing, ever-changing demands of an irrational, contradictory mass. Callicles' chosen mode of life, which he refuses to reject even after his encounter with Socrates, this life amounts, in short, to nothing more than the fate of the uninitiate in the underworld, the eternal vain carrying of water in a sieve in the attempt to fill a leaky jar.

5. THE ADVANTAGES OF MYTH

The myth of the water-carriers, like the myth of judgement at the end, serves to amplify and clarify the arguments in the dialogue, not to present ideas ungraspable by reason or to supplement a deficient argument with threats of hell-fire hereafter. In the *Gorgias*, as in other of his dialogues, Plato takes advantage of the nature of myth as a traditional tale by utilizing both the traditional and narrative aspects. His myth plays with a variety of ideas and motifs familiar from the mythic tradition, elements that would evoke for his audience many other tales. The resonance of these traditional elements permits Plato to convey complex ideas in compact form, without a large amount of tedious explanation, since he need merely mention the name, for example, of Aiakos to conjure up the associations of just behaviour, judging disputes between the gods, and a special function in the realm of the dead.[47] Not only does the general familiarity of these elements lend credibility to Plato's often radical ideas, but Plato sometimes invokes a specific myth from the tradition that carries special authoritative force. He situates his narrative of a shift from the judicial system of Kronos to that of Zeus with

---

[46] When ill health results from the diet of flattering oratory, the city will blame the orators who are currently dishing it up, not those who accustomed them to Sicilian banquets instead of healthy regimens. Cf. Socrates' warning to Callicles and prophecy (*post eventum* for Plato) about the catastrophe of Alcibiades (519ab). The connection between Sicilian banquets and the Sicilian disaster of 415 should not be overlooked.

[47] Aiakos, as Pindar (*Isthmian*, 8.21) tells us, settled disputes among the gods, καί δαιμό-νεσσι δίκας ἐπείραινε. No tale of such judging survives, but Aiakos plays a privileged part in interactions between the gods and men in a number of other stories, and later tradition gives him the role of the doorkeeper of Hades. In many manuscripts of Aristophanes' *Frogs*, the doorkeeper is labelled Aiakos, but there is no evidence that Aristophanes' audience would have thought of him as such. Lucian (*DMor.* 6) and Apollodorus (3.12.6) make him the holder of the keys to Hades. Isokrates relates that he was made a special servant of Hades and Perse-phone as a reward for his virtue, just as Rhadamanthys becomes the servant of Kronos on the Isles of the Blest in Pindar. (Isokrates 9.14; Pindar, *Olympian* II, 83 and *Pythian* II, 73, Cratinus, *Cheirones*, 231 [i: 83 K], Plato, *L.* 948b, Plut. *Theseus*, 16b.)

a reference to Homer's tale of the division of the cosmos when Zeus took power from Kronos (523a3–5). He also calls upon Homer to confirm his assertion that only the most powerful will be punished eternally in the afterlife (525d6–e2). Even his assignment of the expert in justice, Minos, as judge in the afterlife, is backed up by a direct quotation from Homer (526c7–d2). The support of the most authoritative voice in the tradition, whose tellings are familiar to nearly all of Plato's intended audience, shows that Plato's ideas fit within the framework of Greek culture, making them more acceptable and persuasive to his audience even as he engages in shifting their values and ideals.[48]

Plato also makes use of the features of myth as narrative to augment the force of his ideas in the dialogue by employing the temporal sequence of the narrative to bring out the relations between ideas. As scholars of myth as far back as Plotinus have noted, one advantage of a mythic narrative is that it can illustrate through chronological sequence the logical relations of ideas.[49] Plato depicts the relation between the Athenian lawcourt system and the philosophical judgement of Socrates in terms of the shift from the system of judgement in Kronos' time to the system in Zeus's time. By separating them in time and portraying the system he prefers as the reform of the other system, Plato builds his evaluation of the two systems into his presentation of them and shows how the advantages of the later system specifically compensate for the problems of the former system. The contrast between the systems can be represented more clearly in narrative than in a discussion because of the temporal sequencing of the narrative.

Plato also uses this feature of narrative to illustrate more clearly several different aspects of the Socratic *elenchos*. In the myth, the stripping of the soul so that it appears before the judge without any witnesses occurs before the judge examines the soul of the deceased and before the deceased

---

[48] Allen (2000), 267 suggests that Plato's reshaping of the traditional story serves as a philosophic medicine for the audience (within and outside the dialogue). 'Both the stories about punishment and the decisions about punishment "cure" injustice in the soul by making a statement about the proper way to think about desert and by teaching the wrongdoer the "right" system of value. The storyteller who effects a resignification of a symbol that encapsulates principles of authority and desert has the power to effect a cultural paradigm shift and to change "the present order of things". This is Hippocrates' definition of what a *pharmakon* does (*Top. And.* 45), and stories are medicine in this way'.

[49] Δεῖ δὲ τοὺς μύθους, εἴπερ τοῦτο ἔσονται, καὶ μερίζειν χρόνοις ἃ λέγουσι, καὶ διαιρεῖν ἀπ' ἀλλήλων πολλὰ τῶν ὄντων ὁμοῦ μὲν ὄντα, τάξει δὲ ἢ δυνάμεσι διεστῶτα (*Ennead* III, 5.24–27). 'Myths, if they are really going to be myths, must divide out in time the things they relate and separate from one another many realities which are together, but which stand apart in rank or powers' (text and translation from the Loeb edition).

suffers the corrective punishments. Each of these incidents, however, reflects an aspect of the *elenchos*. The lack of witnesses corresponds to the
elenctic examination of a single person's ideas, without the recourse to
the opinions of others or to long oratorical speeches. The examination of
the naked soul by the judge corresponds to the analysis of the person's
ideas and the pointing out of the inconsistencies. The suffering in the
afterlife corresponds to the shame of the *elenchos*, the effect of the defeat
in this philosophic contest which provokes the one who has undergone the
elenchos to change his life. Although Plato illustrates the process of *elenchos*
in many of his dialogues by depicting the interlocutors engaged in *elenchos*,
the myth in the *Gorgias* separates out these different aspects of the *elenchos*
from one another, giving the reader a better understanding of the different
effects of the Socratic *elenchos*.

6. PLATO'S *ELENCHOS*

The *elenchos*, then, does not merely point out the inconsistency in an interlocutor's argument, diagnosing his problem. Rather, as the parallels with the
judgement and punishment in the myth suggest, the shameful defeat in the
elenchos also serves as a bitter purgative medicine that can transform the life
of the interlocutor, checking the inharmonious elements and correcting the
deformities of his soul. The Socratic *elenchos* humiliates its victim by showing him to be a fool who does not know what he is talking about or how he
should live, but the pain of this experience can serve a positive function if
he abandons his former ideas and way of living. The *elenchos* has its limits, however. Just as correction of injustice in this life can only be effective
if the guilty one is not able to escape punishment, the curative treatment
of the *elenchos* can only work if the victim takes his medicine and engages
in dialogue. If like Callicles he sulks and refuses to admit that he has been
defeated in the *elenchos*, then he will continue to inflict the sufferings of
the unphilosophic life upon himself. The spectacle of his humiliation and
sufferings, nevertheless, can serve to educate those who see it, just as the
punishment of the incurables in the afterlife acts as a deterrent to others.
Plato makes use of the narrative logic of the myth to clarify the presentation
of the philosophic mode of self-examination, supplementing the discussion
of the *elenchos* with the illustration in the myth.

The vivid images of the myth are perhaps the most memorable parts
of the whole dialogue. The picture of the naked soul of the Great King,

covered with the festering sores of his unchecked injustices, who is facing the stern judgement of Rhadamanthys, encapsulates a number of ideas in a compact and memorable form. In this one image are crystallized the ideas of the self made witness against itself, the damage that injustice does to the wrongdoer, and the need for an expert in justice to replace the reliance on the 'wisdom of the masses'. In the *Gorgias*, Plato makes use of the mythic tradition to condense his philosophic ideas into evocative images—whip scars on the naked soul.

CHAPTER TEN

THE STATUS OF THE MYTH OF THE *GORGIAS*, OR:
TAKING PLATO SERIOUSLY

Christopher Rowe

The following short paper is, in effect, an extended commentary on a single sentence in the *Gorgias*: the single sentence with which he introduces the concluding myth:

> 'Give ear, then,' as people say, to a very fine account (*logos*)[1]—one that you, for your part, I imagine, will consider a story (*muthos*), but that I consider an account; because the things I'm going to tell you I'll tell as being true.[2]
>
> (*Gorg.* 523a1–3)

The 'account,' or *logos*, will be an account of something very specific:

> ... But if I met my end for lack of ingratiatory[3] rhetoric, I'm certain you'd observe me bearing death with equanimity. For no one fears dying as such, if he isn't wholly irrational and unmanly—what a man *does* fear is doing injustice; because for his soul to arrive in Hades brimming with injustices is the ultimate evil of all. If you want, I'm happy to give you an account of how this is so.[4]
>
> (*Gorg.* 522d7–e6)

But how exactly, as any reader is bound to ask, and as Plato no doubt intended us to ask, can Socrates consider what he says in the following 'account,' which we inevitably describe as the 'myth,' as 'true'? He says that

---

[1] 'Give ear, then' is borrowed from Dodds (1959), 376; 'as people say' substitutes for Dodds's 'as story-tellers say'—and it is plainly story-tellers that Socrates is referring to (only, of course, half to deny that that's what he is going to be).

[2] Ἄκουε δή, φασί, μάλα καλοῦ λόγου, ὃν σὺ μὲν ἡγήσῃ μῦθον, ὡς ἐγὼ οἶμαι, ἐγὼ δὲ λόγον· ὡς ἀληθῆ γὰρ ὄντα σοι λέξω ἃ μέλλω λέγειν.

[3] I borrow this translation of *kolakikos* from Sedley (2009), in preference to the traditional 'flattering'. As Sedley (2009), 51, n. 2 remarks, 'while in Plato's usage the term [*kolakeia*] certainly indicates currying favour, this is not necessarily achieved by praise of one's auditors, as "flattery" would imply'.

[4] εἰ δὲ κολακικῆς ῥητορικῆς ἐνδείᾳ τελευτῴην ἔγωγε, εὖ οἶδα ὅτι ῥᾳδίως ἴδοις ἄν με φέροντα τὸν θάνατον. αὐτὸ μὲν γὰρ τὸ ἀποθνῄσκειν οὐδεὶς φοβεῖται, ὅστις μὴ παντάπασιν ἀλόγιστός τε καὶ ἄνανδρός ἐστιν, τὸ δὲ ἀδικεῖν φοβεῖται· πολλῶν γὰρ ἀδικημάτων γέμοντα τὴν ψυχὴν εἰς "Αιδου ἀφικέσθαι πάντων ἔσχατον κακῶν ἐστιν. εἰ δὲ βούλει, σοὶ ἐγώ, ὡς τοῦτο οὕτως ἔχει, ἐθέλω λόγον λέξαι.

Callicles will regard it as a myth, or 'story' (*muthos*); but wouldn't anyone? Even if Socrates actually believed in the reality of the sort of post-mortem punishment in Hades he includes in his 'account',[5] his description includes some elements that are plainly his own invention: for example, the change of policy instituted by Zeus on the trials of the dead or soon-to-be dead, so that the judged have to appear naked before their judges (a passage to which I shall recur shortly). Thus he evidently cannot intend a claim to believe that the account is *literally* true. What, then, does he intend to claim?

One standard type of interpretation is represented by E.R. Dodds: 'the *Gorgias* myth is called a *logos* because it expresses in imaginative terms "a truth of religion"'.[6] Terry Irwin, meanwhile, seems to opt for a secular version of the same reading: '[by saying he takes the story as a *logos*] he probably means that (a) it is true ...; and (b) it is rationally defensible'.[7]

What I propose to do in the present paper is to offer an alternative interpretation, connected to a larger thesis about Plato's relationship with his readers.[8] In brief, this larger thesis is as follows. The argument of Plato's dialogues frequently operates on more than one level, using, or appearing to use, premises—or more broadly, ways of seeing things—that will have seemed fairly standard to Plato's contemporaries and his Socrates' interlocutors (and indeed to us, his readers), while it *also, and simultaneously, operates with premises and perspectives that belong to a different mindset.* These premises and perspectives collectively form a distinctive, connected set of ideas about which Plato and his main speaker, Socrates, stand convinced, which they do not fully reveal on every occasion, and which they mean to introduce to, and urge upon, their addressees, whether readers or interlocutors. The interlocutors sometimes catch on, or at least partly catch on. As for Plato's readers, whether ancient or modern, my general claim (see my subtitle) is that they—we[9]—tend radically to underestimate the

---

[5] With Homer as his only named witness (525d).

[6] Dodds (1959), 377. I treat this is a representing—or resembling—a 'standard' way of treating Platonic myth generally, as a substitute for argument where argument has failed. See, e.g., Partenie (2009a), 8: 'Myth represents a sort of back-up: if one fails to be persuaded by arguments to change one's life, one may still be persuaded by a good myth' (though Partenie does not, of course, regard this as the only function of Platonic myth). Cf. also Mackenzie (1981), 236: 'The *Gorgias* myth is presented to complete (*perainein*, 522e7) the argument that wrongdoing is the supreme evil ...'. (But *perainein* is ultimately Callicles' word, not Socrates'.)

[7] Irwin (1979), *ad loc.*

[8] The core of the argument of the paper is to be found in Rowe (2007a), esp. § 4. *Gorgias*, 523a is discussed there in a single paragraph (151–152); I now wish to build on and refine the interpretation offered so briefly there.

[9] For the record, I acknowledge here the inclusion of a previous, and not so distant, self of my own.

distance between Plato and his contemporaries, and between Plato and us. As a result we too quickly assume that he shares our own assumptions, and, missing the assumptions with which he is in fact, or simultaneously, working, too quickly accuse him of mere opportunism, or just general incompetence in the business of argument. The thesis of the present paper is that in *Gorgias* 523a Socrates is allowed briefly to acknowledge this two-level strategy: built into the story he is about to tell there is a genuine *logos* which he regards as saying what is straightforwardly true, overlapping with but separable from other elements that are purely mythical. If this gives the 'myth' something of the appearance of an allegory, it is also something rather more subtle than that.[10]

I begin with a series of observations made by David Sedley about the description, in *Gorgias* 523a–524a, of the changes to the divine judicial system brought in by Zeus. (a) The passage is 'a parable of political *progress*, [which] trades on Socrates' conviction, made explicit throughout the *Gorgias*,[11] that the sole criterion of a good politician is his success in making the citizens better people'. (b) The system under Cronus, which Zeus replaced, mirrored the actual Athenian system, especially insofar as it allowed judges to be swayed by external factors like birth and wealth instead of the qualities of defendants' souls, and gave weight to the wrong kinds of witnesses. (c) Zeus' new system makes good both these failings, by having defendants and judges face each other naked, i.e., stripped of bodies and their accoutrements—and so after death, since death is the separation of soul from body (524a);[12] the defendant also appears to have no witnesses other than himself.

---

[10] Dodds (1959), 376 denies that the myth is philosophical allegory: '[Plato's] eschatological myths describe a world which he admits to be beyond ordinary human knowledge [Dodds compares 527a]; they are the imaginative expression of an insight which could not be expressed save in symbolic terms'. My reasons for rejecting this judgement—specifically in relation to the *Gorgias* myth—will, I hope, emerge in the course of the following pages; but meanwhile see Mackenzie (1981), 236–237 for reasons why we should look for allegory in Plato's eschatological myths generally.

[11] Most explicit, in fact, only a couple of Stephanus pages earlier, when Socrates claimed that he himself was—perhaps—the only contemporary Athenian to practice true *politikê* (521d–522a).

[12] The bizarre idea that under Cronus defendants were tried on the day of, and before, their death (because only then will their external, bodily advantages be visible) is thus there merely because of the requirements of the story. It is a feature of the passage that clearly provokes us to treat it *as* a story, undercutting Socrates' original claim that he actually believes it—and, implicitly, that we should.

The soul will ... be its own witness. And if we are to take seriously Socrates' notion of a dialectical witness, we must bear in mind the likelihood that the way in which each soul acts as its own witness is itself dialectical: its moral state is exposed by dialectical questioning. The technique of dialectically examining people ... will then be inseparable from the technique of discovering those people's moral state ... That this conflation is one we are being encouraged to make is suggested by the fact that the foregoing examination of Callicles has very evidently combined both of these functions—so much so that in the closing words of the dialogue Socrates feels able to warn Callicles of the horrific danger his soul faces after death. One is reminded too of Nicias' remark in the *Laches* that whatever subject Socrates starts questioning you about, you will end up giving an account of yourself and your life, and probably learn ways to improve them both (187e–188b).

Sedley concludes:

It is, I hope, already becoming plausible that the regime of Zeus, with its advances over the Cronus regime, symbolizes a method of examining and improving souls which we are being asked to recognize as superior to the current Athenian political and judicial system. And that method is, in spirit, both Socratic and dialectical.[13]

Thus, if Sedley is right, two things are going on in 523a–524a (the passage about Zeus' innovations): (1) an older divine system of judgement is being contrasted with a newer one that is more adapted to achieving the desired ends;[14] and (2) the Athenian judicial system is being contrast with a new and radical kind of judgement and 'trial,' i.e., by means of Socratic questioning—of the very sort that the Socrates of the *Gorgias* has been deploying against Gorgias himself, against Polus, and against Callicles. Once the myth is seen from this perspective, it is no longer clear whether the 'myth' is really about Hades, or about this world, especially when (1) is self-evidently more fictional, and more transparently fictional.[15] But that already begins to illustrate how the mythical and the non-mythical combine in Socrates' story, and how exactly we need to understand his suggestion that while Callicles will see it (just) as a story, he himself regards it as a *logos*, a true account

---

[13] Sedley (2009), 57–58.

[14] Sedley (2009), 56 asks how the use of the contrast between Cronus and Zeus and their regimes in the *Gorgias* compares with its use in the *Politicus* and the *Laws*. But I suspect that it may also be useful, in the context of the *Gorgias*, to remember the other connotation of 'Cronian' (*Kronikos*), i.e., obsolete, outdated: as Cronus was forced to give way to Zeus, so old has to cede to new.

[15] See n. 12 above. On the other hand, (1) cannot just be thrown away; the lessons of the 'myth' must ultimately be at least partly about what happens to us after death, because of the way it is both introduced (i.e. in 522d–e, quoted on p. 187 above) and rounded off (527c–e).

or report. It is not that Callicles and he will see the same things differently (except insofar as they are hearing, and interpreting, the same collection of words); rather it is that they will see different things *in* the same story. Callicles will just not understand what Socrates has in mind. He will grasp the text, which he'll treat as a mere story,[16] but he will miss the all-important sub-text—even as we are told, in 523a1–3, that we should not. (But all the same, Callicles should have been persuaded—or so Socrates implicitly claims—by what he *has* understood of the argument. It is not Socrates' fault that he has long since given up on it.)

The *Gorgias* as a whole represents a particularly clear example of this layered, two-level approach of Plato's;[17] and especially in relation to the way the idea of *punishment* is used.[18] Thus the whole dialogue appears, on the surface, to be operating with a perfectly normal, everyday notion of punishment. But this appearance is at least in part deceptive. Yes, the argument as a whole—the version of it that Socrates' interlocutors actually hear—does indeed talk in terms of imprisonment, flogging, death, and so on; but there is good reason to believe, or so I claim, that *that* kind of punishment is of no great interest or use to Socrates or Plato in their great project of saving souls. For what drives human beings, according to the Socrates of the *Gorgias*[19] and of at least a swathe of other dialogues, including the *Symposium*,[20] is their beliefs—their desires being universally for the good and the useful, that is, the *real*, not merely the apparent, good; what we *really* desire is what is *really* good for us (whatever that may be), and not just what is apparently so. In which case, despite appearances, and despite what we ourselves (we human beings, or most of us) are likely to claim, we do not actually desire what's bad for us, and it is not our

---

[16] 'An old woman's tale,' 527a5.

[17] The approach in question is by no means restricted to the myth. The myth simply exhibits a particular kind of layering; or else, perhaps, to the extent that the surface text of the remainder of the dialogue relies on premises and notions to which Socrates and his author are less than fully committed, we may say (tentatively) that this surface text approximates more or less closely to the condition of the surface of the myth.

[18] See Rowe (2007a), § 4, esp. 147–152. The chapter in question builds on three previous papers, the most relevant of which is Rowe (2007b); the others are Rowe (2005) and (2007c). The first of these papers was presented in its original form at the *XII Congreso Nacional de Filosofía*, held in Guadalajara, Mexico, in November 2003. Mackenzie (1981), the classic treatment of Plato on punishment, has relatively little to say about the *Gorgias*, but identifies with particular clarity the difficulties that arise on a standard reading of the treatment of punishment in the dialogue (see esp. 179–188, 226, 230–239).

[19] See Rowe (2007c).

[20] See esp. Penner and Rowe (2005), and—for the *Symposium*—Rowe (2006).

desires that take us towards such bad things at all—it's rather our mistaken thinking about what is in fact good for us. But then the question arises: how will punishment, in the ordinary sense, help us to think better, and get our beliefs straight? Imprisonment, flogging, fines, exile might sometimes be a sort of encouragement to think differently, and not to act in the way that has presently brought us to the attention of the authorities; but it might equally be an encouragement to be cleverer in future about covering our tracks.[21] The only surefire way of changing people's beliefs is to *reason with them*.

And that, I have proposed, and propose again now, is the preferred view of punishment of the Socrates of the *Gorgias*[22]—as is shown both by occasional hints (as e.g. at 505c, a passage to which I shall return),[23] and, e.g., by the fact that it is also the only view that will make sense of one of the sub-themes of the dialogue, namely that it will be better for the criminal himself to take steps to ensure that he is punished immediately rather than getting away with his crimes.[24] If by 'punishment' here Socrates really intends flogging, imprisonment, fines, exile or execution, what kind of

---

[21] This is the point, of course, of the story of the ring of invisibility as Glaucon introduces it in *Republic*, II.

[22] Sedley (2009)—an essay whose origins go back as far as 2001—reaches what is essentially the same conclusion about Socratic 'punishment' in the *Gorgias* (cf. also Cholbi (2002), cited by Sedley). However there are differences between Sedley's ('S.'s') overall approach and my own: (1) S. tends to think of the Socratic redefinition of punishment as restricted to the *Gorgias* (even while acknowledging that 'it is not hard to recognize in [the] implied correspondence [between 'eradicating false moral beliefs' and 'ridding someone of ignorance'] a quintessentially Socratic equation of virtue with knowledge and vice with ignorance' (Sodley (2009), 61); (2) S. does not recognize in the Socratic redefinition of punishment, as I do, an instance of a general feature of Platonic writing (i.e., a general tendency to redefine, or transform, common-or-garden notions of things); (3) he focuses particularly on the larger, political consequences of this redefinition; (4) he sees the *Gorgias* as only partly committed to the sort of intellectualist position suggested by the 'implied correspondence' referred to in (1) above, whereas—for reasons given in Rowe (2007c)—I understand the dialogue as committed to it through and through; so that (5), importantly, he sees the redefinition of punishment as less central than I do to the argument of the *Gorgias* as a whole. In particular, S. takes Socrates' talk, e.g. in 506c–508b, about 'appetite control' at face value, and seems to find him accepting some complementary role for conventional punishment. On my view, by contrast, Socratic 'punishment' is intended—in the *Gorgias*—to *replace* its conventional counterpart.

[23] Callicles here suggests to Socrates that he find someone else to question, to which Socrates replies: 'this fellow won't put with being benefited and with his undergoing the very thing the discussion's about, being punished (*kolazesthai*)'. As Sedley (2009), 60 comments: 'just as dialectical *interrogation* is the superior counterpart of judicial *trial*, so too are their respective outcomes related: dialectical *refutation* is the superior counterpart of judicial *punishment*.'

[24] See, e.g., 480b–d.

sense could that possibly make? It would be a *merely* paradoxical, and what is more a *merely* provocative claim, insofar as neither Socrates nor anyone else has any reason to believe—even on standard assumptions—that such forms of treatment will reliably improve anybody. And part of my overall argument is that we should not be satisfied with leaving Plato's Socrates in the position of a mere *provocateur*; we need to take him seriously.[25]

In any case, my proposal is just this: that the Plato of the *Gorgias* is actually working with two separate notions of punishment, one his own and one not his own. What he is doing is to have Socrates talk to, and try to persuade, his interlocutors in terms they can understand, while at the same time *also* introducing different terms, different perspectives.[26] And in the context of the *Gorgias* myth, which is of course the particular concern of the present paper, my proposal will have immediate benefits. For example, the myth refers to the usual horrible punishments for criminals once they have died and moved off, or their souls have moved off, to Hades.[27] Or, in case anyone should object that our aesthetic sensibilities are a poor basis for criticising Plato's argument, one need only point to the fact that, as commentators have acknowledged, the myth itself fails at least in one respect to work even in its own terms: for, given that there is no hint that souls in Hades will be born again in new bodies, the supposed deterrent effect of the eternal punishment of 'incurables' will actually have no subjects to work on.[28] Equally (another problem frequently raised), even if the 'incurables' could be properly identified, what kind of justice, exactly, would be involved in punishing them *for ever*[29] for crimes that they once committed, or indeed committed any number—but a definite number—of times in the context of a lifetime? But if Socrates is not himself endorsing such conventional Greek ideas of post-mortem punishment, then the problems

---

[25] That is, rather than—for example—treating him as saying things that are actually, or literally false, just in order to make us think.

[26] As a matter of fact, I believe that the case for this, in relation to punishment (and trial) is already firmly established by Sedley (2009). It seems nevertheless useful to repeat some of my own arguments, insofar as these are slightly different from, and come from a somewhat different perspective from, Sedley's.

[27] See 525c–e.

[28] 'As for those who have committed the worst injustices, such as to make them incurable, examples are made of them. They are beyond being benefited themselves, being incurable, but others are benefited, when they see them' (525c1–5). But if there is no rebirth, it will be too late even for those who 'see' the sufferings of the incurables to be improved by seeing them.

[29] 525e1, on Homer's testimony (with reference to Tantalus, Sisyphus, and Tityus).

in question melt away, as does at least part of the problem of how exactly we are supposed to interpret the idea of the punishment of disembodied souls, which is portrayed, insofar as it is portrayed at all, exclusively in quasi-physical terms.[30]

But then: if Socrates is not committed to the standard ideas of punishment, whether in the context of the myth or in the *Gorgias* at large, quite what is he doing bringing them in, in the first place? My answer is as before; he is responding to Callicles in terms that Callicles can understand, even if he would utterly reject the ideas Plato has Socrates use those terms to express. In short, Socrates portrays the souls of criminals being subjected, in a Homeric-style Hades, to punishments of the sort that Homer and others talk about—only with the difference that *Homer*'s 'souls' have a kind of enduring corporeal aspect, which Socrates' explicitly do not.[31] These punishments are meted out to them, Socrates specifies, either by gods or by men (525b5–6), as a kind of 'vengeance'[32] or 'retribution/compensation':[33] a rather strange kind of 'vengeance' or 'retribution,' which either will lead to the benefit, i.e. the reform or 'cure,' of those criminal souls that are curable (525b1–c1), or at any rate, in the case of those 'incurables,' help others to become better people. But this is the only sort of 'vengeance' or 'retribution,' the only kind of 'payback,' that Socrates himself will allow as appropriate:

> It is appropriate *for everyone* who is subject to vengeance, if vengeance is being taken on him by another in the correct way, either to benefit by becoming better or to become an example to others, so that when others observe him suffering whatever he is suffering they may take fright and become better themselves.[34]   (*Gorg.* 525b1–4)

---

[30] See below for a brief speculation on what Socrates' notion of post-mortem punishment for 'naked' souls might be like. Those 'incurables' Socrates mentions are, I propose, another part of what Plato appropriates from his audience, not part of what he himself wishes to endorse—for after all, Socrates is not willing to give up even on Callicles himself (527c–e). The argument will be just that *if* there is anyone who is incurable, then he will serve as an example to others; just as Callicles wanted to use really top-rank criminals like Archelaus as examples for his side of the case—if anything, Socrates will claim, Archelaus and his kind count in favour of my argument, not yours.

[31] 524b again.

[32] I.e., *timôria*, 525c1; cf. 472d8, e6.

[33] I.e., *tisis*, 523b3.

[34] προσήκει δὲ παντὶ τῷ ἐν τιμωρίᾳ ὄντι, ὑπ' ἄλλου ὀρθῶς τιμωρουμένῳ, ἢ βελτίονι γίγνεσθαι καὶ ὀνίνασθαι ἢ παραδείγματι τοῖς ἄλλοις γίγνεσθαι, ἵνα ἄλλοι ὁρῶντες πάσχοντα ἃ ἂν πάσχῃ φοβούμενοι βελτίους γίγνωνται.

It is, then, a special kind of 'retributive justice' that Socrates has in mind for criminal souls;[35] and it will be meted out through *either* divine *or* human agency.[36] In the latter case, evidently, the agent will be a philosopher like Socrates, or perhaps even better than Socrates, who will 'punish' a Callicles, or the criminals he purports to admire, by subjecting them to the power of argument—however long the process of reform might take. Socratic 'punishment,' as I have argued,[37] *is* Socratic dialectic: as Socrates himself puts it at 505c3–4, 'This fellow [Callicles] won't put with being benefited and with his undergoing the very thing the discussion's about, being punished (*kolazesthai*)'.[38] And in the *Apology* he imagines himself continuing to examine others even in Hades (41b). However the key players there are presumably the judges of the dead themselves: *they*, apparently, will examine the unjust in Hades, and find them wanting. But then what kind of sentence will they mete out? Here, I suspect, the machinery of the myth begins to fail, except as a story plain and simple.

---

[35] In effect, Socrates here quietly transforms the notion of vengeance, in conformity with his redefinition of punishment: if all punishment is a matter of making people better, and wiser, then vengeance must be the same—and not something that takes place 'for the sake of the person punishing' (I take the phrase from Sedley (2009), n. 16). Contrast Mackenzie (1981), 233: '[C]onsider the myth of the *Gorgias* in which the official theory of reform is preceded by a story of retribution,' with Sedley (2009), n. 16: 'I have suggested that the evidence of the *Gorgias* is the weakest for retributivism. However, the myths as a whole offer a strong retributive account, thus strengthening the *Gorgias* presentation where, alone of all these passages, reform and retribution appear together, thus provoking the problems of conflict'. My own view is that 'retribution' occurs as a theme in the myth for several reasons: (a) because it is something Callicles understands (or thinks he understands), (b) because Socrates wants to hint at a payback for Callicles, or his prize exhibits like the appalling Archelaus (n.b. the rather more explicit language of 527a3–4, when Socrates imagines Callicles appearing before Aeacus: in Sedley's translation, 'and perhaps someone will inflict on you the indignity of a smack on the jaw too, and heap all kinds of abuse on you'); (c) in recognition of the fact that, as the story stands—and so long as it is really about the dead in Hades—it is actually too late for anything except retributive justice (see above; note, however, that if the story also contains a subtext about *this* life, then the rule announced in 525b, against punishment that does not somehow improve people, can be taken at face value). But the most important reason, perhaps, for the role of 'retribution' in the myth is that on Socrates' assumptions there is an *automatic* payback for those who have committed injustice, independent of any 'punishment' that a Socrates, or an Aeacus, might hand out. See below.

[36] 'The ones who are benefited by being punished, *whether by gods or by men*, are those who have committed errors that are curable; all the same, the benefit comes about by way of pain and anguish, whether here or in Hades, because it is not possible to get rid of injustice by any other route' (525b4–c1).

[37] And as has David Sedley, at greater length.

[38] In the Hackett translation, slightly modified.

Or does it? After all, Socrates' position is that people who go wrong are damaged *by and in doing so*, and the more seriously they go wrong, the greater the damage. This is made explicit in the myth itself:

> If someone was a scoundrel who earned the lash, and in life had the marks of his whippings, wounds on his body caused either by lashing or other injuries, when he is dead too his body can be seen to bear these. Or if someone's limbs were broken and deformed [sc. on the rack?] when he was alive, the same things are visible when he is dead too ... This same principle seems to me to apply to the soul too, Callicles. Everything is visible in the soul once it has been stripped of its body—the various aspects of its nature, and the things that befell it, which the person had in his soul because of the way he performed each activity. So when they come to their judge—Rhadamanthus for the ones from Asia—Rhadamanthus stops them and examines each one's soul. He doesn't know whose soul it is, and often he has seized the King of Persia or some other king or potentate and seen that there was nothing healthy in his soul, but that it was covered in lashings and filled with injuries thanks to its oath-violations and injustices ... [39] When he saw, he sent this soul off in disgrace, straight to the prison where it was to go and face the sufferings that were its due.[40]   (*Gorg.* 524c5–525a1, 525a6–7, in Sedley's translation)

In short, the unjust will already have punished themselves; if Rhadamanthus and the other judges add anything, it will be the realization by the 'defendants' of their own condition, and of the damage they have already done to themselves.[41] All that remains will be for them to be sent off to reflect on their history, and suffer accordingly.

And this, I propose, we need to take quite seriously—not just as provocative, provisional, *ad hominem*, or otherwise *temporary and substitutable*, but rather as building blocks of a larger, and quite distinctive, structure of

---

[39] *These* 'injuries,' to the soul, will evidently not be the result of actual, conventional punishments (actual flogging, etc.); according to what Socrates says, they are the direct result of 'oath-violations and injustices'.

[40] μαστιγίας αὖ εἴ τις ἦν καὶ ἴχνη εἶχε τῶν πληγῶν οὐλὰς ἐν τῷ σώματι ἢ ὑπὸ μαστίγων ἢ ἄλλων τραυμάτων ζῶν, καὶ τεθνεῶτος τὸ σῶμα ἔστιν ἰδεῖν ταῦτα ἔχον· ἢ κατεαγότα εἴ του ἦν μέλη ἢ διεστραμμένα ζῶντος, καὶ τεθνεῶτος ταὐτὰ ταῦτα ἔνδηλα. ἑνὶ δὲ λόγῳ, οἷος εἶναι παρεσκεύαστο τὸ σῶμα ζῶν, ἔνδηλα ταῦτα καὶ τελευτήσαντος ἢ πάντα ἢ τὰ πολλὰ ἐπί τινα χρόνον. ταὐτὸν δή μοι δοκεῖ τοῦτ' ἄρα καὶ περὶ τὴν ψυχὴν εἶναι, ὦ Καλλίκλεις· ἔνδηλα πάντα ἐστὶν ἐν τῇ ψυχῇ, ἐπειδὰν γυμνωθῇ τοῦ σώματος, τά τε τῆς φύσεως καὶ τὰ παθήματα ἃ διὰ τὴν ἐπιτήδευσιν ἑκάστου πράγματος ἔσχεν ἐν τῇ ψυχῇ ὁ ἄνθρωπος. ἐπειδὰν οὖν ἀφίκωνται παρὰ τὸν δικαστήν, οἱ μὲν ἐκ τῆς Ἀσίας παρὰ τὸν Ῥαδάμανθυν, ὁ Ῥαδάμανθυς ἐκείνους ἐπιστήσας θεᾶται ἑκάστου τὴν ψυχήν, οὐκ εἰδὼς ὅτου ἐστίν, ἀλλὰ πολλάκις τοῦ μεγάλου βασιλέως ἐπιλαβόμενος ἢ ἄλλου ὁτουοῦν βασιλέως ἢ δυνάστου κατεῖδεν οὐδὲν ὑγιὲς ὂν τῆς ψυχῆς, ἀλλὰ διαμεμαστιγωμένην καὶ οὐλῶν μεστὴν ὑπὸ ἐπιορκιῶν καὶ ἀδικίας [...] ἰδὼν δὲ ἀτίμως ταύτην ἀπέπεμψεν εὐθὺ τῆς φρουρᾶς, οἷ μέλλει ἐλθοῦσα ἀνατλῆναι τὰ προσήκοντα πάθη.

[41] In the terms of the story, they will of course be able to see the damage more easily with their souls 'naked'.

ideas. Another part of this distinctive structure, closely connected to, indeed essential to his position on punishment, is Socrates' idea of what it is to be harmed (and to be benefited). This idea surfaces not just in the myth, but also and especially in two complementary claims that Socrates makes in the dialogue: first, that orators and tyrants—praised by all three interlocutors in succession for their ability to commit injustice on the greatest scale and get away with it—in fact do what they want less than anyone else in the world;[42] and second, that doing injustice is worse for the person who does it than his or having injustice done to him.[43] Injustice *in itself* damages the person who commits it, even as justice is beneficial *in itself*: that fundamental thesis of the *Republic*. Of course few think the argument of the *Republic* successful, and probably the majority of readers of Plato will continue to suppose that the theses of the *Gorgias* about tyrants and orators, about the preferability of suffering over doing injustice, and about the damage done by injustice to one's own soul, are nothing much more than try-ons, and recognized by Plato as such.[44] But this is a mistake. Not only the Socrates of the *Gorgias* but (I suppose) his author and controller are deadly serious about the claims in question; and that, I suggest, is directly confirmed by that passage from which I began. Socrates claims that the myth, for him, is a *logos*, because it says what is true. And what it says, above all, is that the unjust suffer, are damaged, *harmed*, and go on being harmed, by the very fact that they commit injustice. Socrates does sometimes suggest that injustice is damaging because making the wrong choices lessens one's chance of making the right choices in the future (so in effect decreasing one's share of that most vital commodity, wisdom).[45] But plainly, tyrants like Archelaus are supposed already to have plumbed the depths of bad judgement and ignorance. What makes *their* lives so bad is just the distance that separates them from the good and wise life. They simply live the worst lives imaginable for human beings—worse even than the lives of those who suffer from their cruelties, who will be protected from the degree of misery suffered by the perpetrators by their lack of power,[46] and—if they happen to be just— by the very fact of their justice. The just cannot be harmed by the unjust,[47]

---

[42] First introduced at 466b–e; see Penner (1991).

[43] 469b, 474c ff.; see Rowe (2005).

[44] Even if not by Socrates, that alleged master of paradox (and falsehood).

[45] See, e.g., *Rep.* IV, 443c–e.

[46] *Gorg.* 525d–526a.

[47] *Ap.* 30d.

because by being just they are, *ipso facto*, happy and fortunate; they have what they need for the good life (especially: wisdom), and that cannot be taken away from them by any mere tyrant or orator.

Callicles does not grasp much, if any of this, and even if he had done he would have scorned it even more, perhaps, than the old wives' tale he'll take Socrates to be telling, there at the end of their conversation. And if modern readers fully grasp what Socrates really wants to say in that 'story,' most of them will probably react, if not with the scorn he expects from Callicles, at least with disbelief. But what Socrates wants to say, he wants to say, he tells us as well as Callicles, 'as being true'.

CHAPTER ELEVEN

THE RIVERS OF TARTARUS:
PLATO'S GEOGRAPHY OF DYING AND COMING-BACK-TO-LIFE*

Elizabeth Pender

In *Phaedo* Plato offers various arguments for the immortality of soul and completes the discussion with a myth of the afterlife. The purpose of the myth is to alert the audience to the urgent need to philosophize in the here-and-now in order to seize this brief chance to escape from the horrors of eternal re-incarnation. The myth takes the form of a geographical account of the regions of the afterlife and the journeys of the souls within those regions. While much progress has been made in interpreting the contribution of the *Phaedo* myth,[1] Plato's geography of the true earth remains intriguing. The following reappraisal of the great rivers of Tartarus will offer solutions to particular interpretative errors and puzzles on the relationship between souls and bodies in this vision of the afterlife, why souls in the underworld do not practise philosophy, and how the ideas on reincarnation in *Phaedo* are consistent with its myth of final judgement. My answers to questions raised by Annas (1982), Edmonds (2004), Rowe (2007a) and Inwood (2009) follow from my view that the myth presents five distinct regions of the true earth, where the different terrains and climates match the moral condition and cognitive capacities of the souls dwelling there. I shall show how the myth is placed carefully within the composition of the dialogue as a whole (part 1), explain the ethical message of the geography of Tartarus (part 2), and explore the ontological and epistemological aspects of this extraordinary landscape (part 3). Overall, I shall argue that, through the topography of the myth, the rivers of Tartarus support the teleology of *Phaedo*.

---

* For valuable discussion and comment on this paper I thank Professor M.F. Heath and Dr J.B. Kennedy. I am grateful for criticism from participants at the 'Platonic Myths/Les Mythes Platoniciens' conference at the University of Ottawa 2008, from the editors of the volume, and from seminar audiences at the Universities of Cambridge, Oxford and Newcastle.
    [1] Particularly influential on my reading of the myth are: Burnet (1911); Hackforth (1955); Sedley (1989 and 1990); Morgan (2000); and Rowe (1993 and 2007a).

1. The Place of the Myth in *Phaedo*

On the simplest analysis *Phaedo* has a dual structure: a question and response, as Echecrates asks Phaedo how Socrates died and Phaedo recounts his final conversations and death. Phaedo's account of Socrates' death can then be divided into various main sections consisting of narration of action and interludes, the central arguments, and the myth. The structure is highly ordered:[2]

57a1–59c7	Echecrates asks Phaedo 'How did Socrates die?'
59c8–69e4	Phaedo tells Echecrates of going to the prison and Socrates explaining to his friends the correct attitude to death
69e5–84b7	Socrates begins the case for immortality: argument 1, from cyclical processes; argument 2, from recollection; argument 3, from affinity
84c1–85e2	First interlude: Socrates responds to the disquiet of Simmias and Cebes
85e3–88b8	Simmias and Cebes express their objections to the case for immortality
88c1–91c6	Second interlude: Phaedo tells Echecrates how Socrates sought to reassure him
91c7–102a3	Socrates' replies to Simmias and Cebes
102a4–a10	Third interlude: Echecrates approves Simmias and Cebes' agreement with Socrates
102a11–107b10	Argument 4, from opposites
107c1–115a9	Socrates' myth of the afterlife
115b1–118a17	The death of Socrates.

1.1. *Life and Death before the Myth*

The myth of *Phaedo* completes Socrates' conversation with his friends and is built upon key concepts agreed by the interlocutors. In order to understand the functions of the Tartarus rivers, it is necessary to identify a particular network of ideas connecting the myth closely with the earlier discussion of life and death.[3] This network involves: journeying; impurity; imprisonment; assimilation; and balanced opposition.

---

[2] My scheme draws on the sections and headings used by Rowe (1993) and Gallop (1993), xxix.

[3] Kingsley's insights on the myth as Orphic in origin are highly illuminating but I reject his final view on Plato's contribution (Kingsley [1995], 109): 'However, there is no evidence whatever that he contributed to the creation—or even the arrangement—of the mythical material in any significant way'. While Plato does adapt earlier material, he offers a radically new telling, blending elements of his own thought and shaping the new myth precisely to fit its dramatic and discursive context.

Early in the dialogue Socrates identifies death as the separation of soul from body (64c). The key Greek term is *apallagê* which can be translated as either 'departure' or 'release', leading to the motifs of the journeys and bonds of the soul, used throughout this text.[4] The idea that the soul at birth enters the body and at death departs to another place permeates the discussion (e.g. 58e6, 61b1, 63b6, 67b8, 68a1, 69c6, 77b8). The journey motif is also consistent with Socrates' references to death as an *apodêmia* ('a going or being away from home', 61e2, 67c1). The second element in this network of ideas is the language of pure and impure souls, which runs throughout the debate on immortality (e.g. 66a2; 67a, 67c, 69c, 79d). The interlocutors agree that contact with the body contaminates the soul while philosophy provides its *only* means of purification (e.g. 66e–67c).

In terms of bonds and imprisonment, birth is the tying or binding of soul in body while death frees and separates it (see 67d).[5] The full image of the prison is introduced in an important passage where Socrates explains that the while the body imprisons the soul, philosophy can set it free 82d9–83a5:

> Lovers of knowledge recognize that when philosophy takes their soul in hand, it has been veritably bound (*diadedemenên*) and glued to the body, and is forced to view things as if through a prison (*hôsper dia heirgmou*), rather than alone by itself; and that it is wallowing in utter ignorance. Now philosophy discerns the cunning of the prison (*heirgmou*), sees how it is effected through desire, so that the captive (*dedemenos*) himself may co-operate most of all in his imprisonment (*tou dedesthai*). As I say, then, lovers of knowledge recognize that their soul is in that state when philosophy takes it in hand, gently reassures it and tries to release (*luein*) it, by showing that inquiry through the eyes is full of deceit, and deceitful too is inquiry through the ears and other senses.[6]   (tr. Gallop)

Philosophy tries to 'free' the soul from the harmful influence of the body by fostering the insight that bodily senses cannot be relied upon to provide knowledge of the truth. Freedom lies in the soul's choice to reason independently, while imprisonment lies in its choice to work in close conjunction with the bodily senses, allowing physical desires to reinforce these bonds (82e6).

---

[4] See Pender (2000), 150–155 and 165–170 for more detailed discussion of the metaphors of journeys and bonds.

[5] 67d1: δεσμῶν; 67d4–5: λύσις καὶ χωρισμὸς ψυχῆς ἀπὸ σώματος; 81e2: ἐνδεθῶσιν; 83d1: καταδεῖται; 92a1: ἐνδεθῆναι.

[6] Translations of the text are from Gallop (1993), unless otherwise specified. The text used is that of Duke, Hicken, Nicoll, Robinson and Strachan (1995).

As the discussion on soul develops, various changes in its condition are explained through the principle of assimilation. Put simply, the soul becomes like that with which it associates, adapting its characteristics to fit its various companions and environments. The argument from affinity explains how the soul can become constant and unvarying as a result of its contact 'with things of a similar kind' (79d). Conversely, a soul too attached to the human body finds itself at death unable to leave behind its companion and so haunts the graveyard (81d). The story of the animal incarnations at 81e–82a presents assimilation also as a key factor in reincarnation: men who have lived like donkeys and wolves during their human life actually become donkeys or wolves in their next incarnation.

The final element in this network is balanced opposition. Pairs of opposites feature throughout the interlocutors' discussion on death and the dialogue at large. While the central oppositions are those of life and death, including living/being dead, dying/coming-back-to-life, and generation/destruction (e.g. 62a; 71c; 89b; 95d; 105d), many other opposites are used as elements of the discussion or aspects of the narrative.[7] At the very start of the narrative, as Phaedo and the others enter his prison-cell, Socrates' first philosophical observation is on how the opposites of pleasure and pain appear as if 'joined by a single head' (60c). This unity of opposites sets the scene for the cyclic argument, where life and death are shown to be opposite but balancing processes. A key term repeated in this argument is *antapodidômi* 'to give back, repay in turn, assign as a balance' (71e8 and 72a12). In the conclusion of this argument Socrates maintains that generation is a process of 'perpetual reciprocity' (Gallop's translation) and likens it to a circular course (72b1).

All of these individual ideas—journeying; impurity; imprisonment; assimilation and balanced opposition—are essential elements in the myth of soul and provide important points of contact between the myth and the previous arguments on immortality. Indeed, Plato's story of the geography of dying and coming-back-to-life would not make sense without the prior, and gradual, introduction of this complex network of ideas in the course of the main discussion.

---

[7] As elements within the discussion, e.g.: pleasure/pain, 59a; contaminated/pure, 66a–b; increase/decrease, separating/combining, cooling/heating, 71b; being awake/sleeping, waking up/going to sleep, 71c; equality/inequality, 74b; recollection/forgetting, 75d–e; composite/incomposite, constant/inconstant, invariable/variable, 78c; good/evil, 81d; imprisonment/release, 81d–e; intelligence/stupidity, goodness/evil, 93b–c; union/division, 97a; contraction/relaxation, 98d; hot/cold, 103c; odd/even, 104b. As aspects of the narrative, e.g.: movement up/down, 61c–d; daybreak/sunset, 59d/61e.

1.2. *The Myth as Second Conclusion*

The myth of the afterlife functions as part of the extended conclusion of the dialogue. Phaedo's response to Echecrates' opening question—how did Socrates die?—is shaped into a moving narrative with three climaxes: the final argument, the afterlife myth, and the account of Socrates' actual death. In this section I shall show how Plato carefully marks the transitions into and out of the myth in order to identify the myth as a detour from the preceding arguments and from the death scene (1.2.1). The transition into the myth shows that Socrates is aware that the myth will not outweigh dialectic as a means of dispelling doubt. Rather, in the face of Simmias' remaining concerns, he now simply takes a different approach (1.2.2). The transition out of the myth re-focuses attention away from eternity and back to the immediate hour of Socrates' death (1.2.3). With these transitions Plato delineates his separate conclusions—the dialectical analysis, the imaginative fiction, and the eye-witness report of historical events—so that each can achieve its individual purpose within the composition.

1.2.1. *'Nothing Further': A Detour*

The final argument, and with it the dialectical defence of immortality, is formally concluded when Socrates says to Cebes (106e8–107a):

> Beyond all doubt, then, Cebes, soul is immortal and imperishable, and our souls really will exist in Hades.[8]   (tr. Gallop)

The emphatic *pantos mallon* (lit: 'more than everything') and *tôi onti* ('really') stress the concluding nature of the admirably succinct philosophical proposition *psychê athanaton kai anôlethron* ('soul immortal and indestructible'). But also illuminating is the switch from singular abstract soul to plural and personal ones: *hêmôn hai psychai* ('our souls'). As Socrates pulls the argument into the personal realm, considering Cebes' soul and, more particularly on this day, his own, he uses the traditional poetic and religious language of existence in Hades. In this single sentence therefore can be seen in miniature the project of *Phaedo* at large—to provide abstract argument, based on the best that the current dialectical approach can achieve, but also to present this argument in a form that can engage the emotional responses of the audiences, both inner and outer, and so provide consolation and reassurance. By 107a the final argument is concluded but while

---

[8] Παντὸς μᾶλλον ἄρα, ἔφη, ὦ Κέβης, ψυχὴ ἀθάνατον καὶ ἀνώλεθρον, καὶ τῷ ὄντι ἔσονται ἡμῶν αἱ ψυχαὶ ἐν Ἅιδου.

Cebes now accepts the proposition 'soul immortal and indestructible', he remains aware that his friend Simmias may still not be satisfied and invites him to voice any further objections. At this point it is Simmias who puts the four arguments of the text into the broader, human perspective. In answer to Cebes' invitation and comment that there will be no future occasions for such discussion, Simmias replies (107a8–b3):

> Well no [...] nor have I any further ground for doubt myself, as far as the arguments go (*oud' autos echô eti hôpêi apistô ek ge tôn legomenôn*); though in view of the size of the subject under discussion, and having a low regard for human weakness (*tên anthrôpinên astheneian atimazôn*), I'm bound to retain some doubt in my mind (*anagkazomai apistian eti echein*) about what's been said.
>   (tr. Gallop)

Simmias is persuaded by the arguments, that is, persuaded *at least as far as* they go, with the limiting *ge* here very expressive and suggesting that they can indeed go only so far. In short, in relation to this vast subject of death Simmias' doubt (*apistô, apistian*) is human. And so, however compelling these arguments are, he is 'forced' (*anagkazomai*) to have some reservations. Socrates' response to him here is to agree, to recommend that the 'initial hypotheses' should indeed 'be examined more clearly', but also to express his own belief (*hôs egôimai*) that following the argument 'to the furthest point to which a human being can follow it up' (*kath' hoson dynaton malist' anthrôpôi epakolouthêsai*) will lead to satisfaction for Simmias: 'you'll seek for nothing further' (*ouden zêtêsete peraiterô*, 107b9).

An older view of myth in Plato was that it was a device that helped to overcome the limitations of argument.[9] Yet Socrates has here reassured Simmias that argument *can* lead to answers and satisfaction—albeit if pursued as far as possible. Indeed Socrates' 'human' language at 107b8 seems a pointed rejoinder to Simmias, i.e. that there is no need to 'despise' human limits as a 'weakness' because actually arguments can lead the human mind quite far, to the point at which even Simmias will be satisfied. When Simmias agrees with Socrates (*Alêthê, ephê, legeis*, 107b10), he is not accepting the truth of the arguments so far but accepting the view that the search for knowledge can lead to a definitive end, where the seeker seeks no further (*ouden [...] peraiterô*). At this concluding remark, Socrates explicitly shifts

---

[9] On J.A. Stewart's views on 'transcendental feeling' in Platonic myth and why seeing these myths as 'mystical' is unhelpful, see Pender (2000), 78–86. See also Edmonds' rejection of this as a valid approach (Edmonds [2004], 164) within his useful summary of recent scholarly approaches to Plato's myths, ibid., 161–171.

the direction of discourse. For he turns away from the case for immortality and the question of how to determine its truth-status, and moves on to a new theme: the need to care for the the soul.

1.2.2. 'Into Hades': Transition into the Myth

At 107c–d Socrates argues that we must look after our souls because our treatment of them now has consequences for eternity. Socrates seems very careful in his language relating to the case for immortality just concluded, as he says that 'if' (*eiper*) soul is immortal, then it is going to need care forever (107c2–4). It seems to me that the 'if' here shows that Socrates is sensitive to Simmias' remaining doubts and does not wish simply to override them. This seems confirmed at 107c5–6 in the similarly careful choice of language as he proposes a supporting argument on the need to care for soul, namely that '*if* death *were*' a release from everything, then this '*would*' be a 'godsend' for the wicked who would face no consequences for their wickedness in life (*ei men gar ên* [...], *an ên*, 107c5–6). This argument for immortality rests on the unspoken premise that this state of affairs would not be consistent with a just universe, but instead of saying this explicitly Socrates simply reasserts his previous conclusion that soul is immortal and allows this to support his rejection of the idea that death could provide a 'refuge from evil'. So does he at this point brush aside Simmias' doubts? Again the statement in Greek seems careful (107c8–d1): *nyn d'epeidê athanatos phainetai ousa, oudemia an eiê autêi allê apophygê kakôn.* Gallop's translation 'but since, in fact, it is evidently immortal' keeps the force of *epeidê* ('since') and translates the verb *phainetai ousa* as 'evidently is'. But does this apparently emphatic Greek allow any remaining concession from Socrates to Simmias' doubts? The *epeidê* is solid enough but what about *phainetai ousa*? Does the verb show Socrates dismissing Simmias' doubts and simply asserting that his arguments have settled the issue? Or is the 'evidently' emerging from *phainomai* a concession to the need to further analyse these arguments (as stated at 107b), a concession further evident in the potential optative of *an eiê* in the following clause: 'since soul is evidently immortal, there *would* be no other refuge from ills'?

Perhaps the matter is decided by the shift to the indicative in the next sentence, which seems at first to sound a more certain note (107d2–3): 'For the soul enters Hades taking with it nothing else but its education and nurture'. But the fact that the content of the indicative phrase is 'soul enters Hades' (*eis Haidou hê psychê erchetai*) means that this phrase too can be seen as a less than direct overriding of Simmias' doubts. For in the philosophical transformation of Hades worked in this dialogue the familiar Greek name for the place of death is applied to what is 'unseen' as distinct from what is visible and material (the new relationship is explained at 80d5–7).[10] This dual use of Hades allows Plato/Socrates to switch instantaneously between the religious and philosophical uses of the term in order to maximise the rhetorical effect of either the philosophical arguments or the various emotional reassurances that are at any time being given or enacted. At this particular point of the text (107d3), Socrates' use of Hades seems perfectly poised between these two different senses. But as the text goes on, linguistic markers are used which change the emphasis and evoke the traditional Homeric conception: first the verb *legetai* ('it is said') and second the adverb *ekeise* ('to there') in the phrase 'at the beginning of its journey there'. The resonance of the adverb is rendered effectively by Gallop's 'yonder', which suggests a mysterious 'realm of the beyond'. Socrates then makes his definitive transition into myth when he begins his new theme—the afterlife journey—by repeating at the opening of the next sentence the key marker *legetai* (107d5) and by alluding to an account of the underworld journey as told by 'Aeschylus' Telephus' (107e5)—an explicit reference to the tales of tragic poetry.

So it seems that Simmias' doubts are not being roughly dismissed but gently set aside, just for the moment, by the gradual transition into mythological discourse. I therefore contend that however supportive to the previous arguments the myth turns out to be, Simmias himself would still understand perfectly that the myth is nonetheless a detour from the previous mode of argument. The myth is presented, then, as an alternative way of speaking, not as confirming or superseding the arguments but as simply taking a different approach to the subject of death and the afterlife.

1.2.3. 'Time to Turn': Transition out of the Myth

Plato marks the movement out of the myth and into the final conclusion of Socrates' death scene with similar precision. This transition occurs at 115a where Socrates raises the emotional tone from mytho-poetic to tragic. For at the close of the myth Socrates recalls himself to his present circumstances by comparing himself to a tragic hero, using the tones of tragic verse (note the suitably poetic delay in word order, 115a5–6): *eme de nyn êdê kalei, phaiê an anêr tragikos, hê heimarmenê* ('but now she calls me, as a tragic hero might say, [...] Destiny').[11] With the mood apparently becoming solemn and

---

[10] Rowe (2007a), § 'The Myth: Two Kinds of Hades', 97–109.
[11] My translation.

prophetic, and building to a poetic climax for the work, the tragic tone, which balances the reference to Aeschylus at the opening of the myth (107e), is soon summarily dismissed and Socrates' pose as 'tragic hero' turns out to be ironic. The irony is evident as Socrates completes his poetic reference by highlighting his next step on his 'tragic' course, where again the key word is saved in the Greek until last: *kai schedon ti moi hôra trapesthai pros to loutron* (115a6, 'and it's just about time I made for [...] the bath').[12] The abrupt refocusing of attention from the lofty to the everyday is achieved not just by the noun 'bath' in final position but also by the very phrase that itself enacts and announces the transition: *hôra trapesthai* ('time to turn').

This reference to time (lit. 'hour') pinpoints the different perspectives on time in this dialogue, i.e. the 'here-and-now' of Socrates and his friends in the prison as against the respective eternities that they are living through, if the arguments for immortality stand. The myth of the afterlife opens an eternal perspective while the historic event of Socrates' death brings the prospect of eternity clashing into the everyday. But this potentially disturbing divergence is resolved by Socrates' quiet acceptance of the need to bathe. I take the verb *trapesthai* as the precise point of transition out of the myth, indicating that Socrates is for the moment leaving behind his vision of eternity to attend to the practical necessities of his physical situation. When Socrates adds 'it really seems better to take a bath before drinking the poison, and not to give the women the trouble of washing a dead body' (115a7–9), the reference to his 'dead body' again captures the tension between Socrates as eternally-living soul and Socrates as corpse (see 115d where Socrates spells it out).[13] The reference to 'washing' may retain a spiritual significance, following the religious language of 'purification' as at 69c: *katharsis*.[14] But even so the dominant tone at the close of the myth is that of everyday life and thus Plato marks the movement into the third and final conclusion of the dialogue: Phaedo's report of the actions and words of Socrates at the moment of death. I see this transition as also supported by the mention of 'women' at 115a8, since it grounds the fact of Socrates' death in the physical and social world. The language in the closing part of the text is simple and unadorned, reflecting its concerns with family and friends,

---

[12] My translation.

[13] A tension palpable also in the dramatic situation of Phaedo's narrative.

[14] Stewart (1972), 256: 'Thus, Socrates' bath [...] is meant as a parody of Orphic ritual cleansing'. Edmonds (2004), 181–182: 'Rather than rituals that need to be performed *after* death, Plato emphasizes solutions to the potential problems of the transition that must be performed *before* death'.

those who are preparing to mourn and are fixed on Socrates' physical experiences of taking the poison (esp. 117e–118a). So Phaedo completes his narration (118a15–16): 'Such was the end (*teleutê*), Echecrates, of our friend'.

2. The Geography of the Afterlife

The myth is organised into four distinct sections where the narrative of the soul's afterlife experiences frames an inner account of the geography of the earth, revealing the true nature of the unseen world. Section 1 (107d–108c) presents the story of the soul's journey to Hades. Section 2 (108c–111c) turns to the geography of the earth, its hollows and its upper surface. Section 3 (111c–113c) delves into the earth's lower regions: Tartarus and the rivers of the underworld. Finally, section 4 (113d–114c) returns to the story of the soul's afterlife experiences, focussing on its judgement and subsequent journeys. My exposition of the regions of the earth and the Tartarus rivers will show how the different environments correspond to the natures of the souls living there and so serve a moral purpose within the myth.

2.1. *To Hades and Back (107d–108c)*

At the opening of the myth Socrates explains that the dead are guided to a place of judgement from where they travel onwards to Hades. The 'spirit' (*daimôn*, 107d6) they were allotted for their human lifetime escorts them to the place of judgement whereupon the guides of Hades take over. A first guide (*hêgemôn*) conducts 'those here to there' (107e2) and, once the souls have experienced in Hades 'whatever they must', and for the time 'required' (e2–3), a second guide (*hêgemôn*) brings them 'back here again' (e3–4). This return journey between the worlds of the living and dead, consistent with the cyclical argument (69e–72d), is described as taking place 'over many long cycles (*periodois*) of time' (107e4). The need for guides is attributed to the nature of the road (*hodos*, 108a4) which is complicated with many forks and branches (*schiseis te kai triodous*). This introductory passage summarizes the key proposition of the myth: that each soul after judgement will travel to its 'appropriate' dwelling place (*prepousan oikêsin*, 108c2; *topon prosêkonta*, 108c5).

2.2. *The Geography of the Earth (108c–111c)*

The account of the road to Hades opens up to reveal a much fuller geography of the earth and its many 'wondrous' regions (108c6), a geography that

Socrates has been 'convinced of' by another. This Platonic account will blend with its original vision familiar features of traditional afterlife myths.[15] Socrates is careful at the outset to insist that, although he is able to relate these views of the earth, to 'prove them true' is probably beyond him and is certainly precluded by the short time of human life he has left. Therefore what follows will be an account of what the earth 'is like'.[16] First Socrates explains the shape of the earth as *peripherês* ('rounded, spherical', 108e5)[17] and its position as in the centre of the universe, held there by its equilibrium (*isorropian*, 109a4). Next he identifies the earth's vast size and our own modest dwelling places located within the 'hollows' (*koila*) that penetrate its surface (109c). These 'hollows' inhabited by humans are places where water, mist and air have 'flowed together' (*synerryêkenai*). In contrast to these misty hollows the 'earth itself' (*autên de tên gên*) is 'pure' and is located in 'heaven' (*tôi ouranôi*) alongside the stars—a correspondingly pure place (*katharan en katharôi*, 109b7–8) which has been named 'ether'. By setting up an analogical ratio between the areas underneath the sea, on land and in the air,[18] Socrates points to the existence of a further region, one beyond the summit of the air. He tells that if someone were able to gain access to that higher region, 'he would realize that that is the true heaven (*ho alêthôs ouranos*) and the true light (*to alêthinon phôs*) and the true earth (*hê hôs alêthôs gê*)' (109e7–110a1). In this section of the myth, then, 'heaven' is relocated: starting out as the region of the stars (109b8), as normally understood in Greek popular thought or as called 'ether' by more specialist thinkers, it is shifted to a higher and more remote region, *beyond* the upper surface of the air. This purest region is identified, therefore, as both 'the true heaven' and 'the true earth', an identification which collapses the usual distinction, linguistic and geographical, between heaven and earth.[19] The geography of

---

[15] Edmonds (2004), esp. 159–220, provides a very sharp account of how Plato 'co-opts the mythic tradition' (169) of underworld journeys.

[16] The same careful distinction between what something is and what it is *like* is used at 114d2–3 (ἢ ταῦτ' ἐστὶν ἢ τοιαῦτ' ἄττα). The formulation at *Phaedo* 108d–e is similar to *Phaedrus* 246a4–7 on telling the nature of soul. Both passages contrast human with divine skill; point to the restrictions of time; and present a 'likeness' as a second-best option.

[17] For the round *versus* spherical earth debate, see Morrison (1959) and Sedley (1989). I take it as spherical.

[18] The analogical ratio: 'under the sea : above the sea/on land :: above the sea/on land : above the earth/in the air'.

[19] Kingsley's interpretation is correct ([1995], 106–107): 'the *Phaedo* myth describes two earths, not one. The original earth is our earth [...] And then, [...] we are also presented with another, 'true' earth [...] an aitherial, celestial world inhabited by divine beings. [...] This juxtaposition of earths has, understandably, caused confusion; but when we stop trying to choose between the one level and the other and accept the existence of them both, we are

the earth is set out so far on a model of higher and lower regions: travelling upwards from the depths of the misty hollows, one reaches this highest and purest part of the earth.[20]

The myth then describes the appearance of the true earth 'if viewed from above' (110b6). If anyone could go beyond the limit of the earth, they would see its surface revealed as a patchwork of marvellous colours.[21] The true earth's splendours include many beauties and a perfect climate; it is a place of proportion in nature (*ana logon*, 110d3) and bliss for men (*eudaimonia*, 111c2) as they live alongside gods, enjoying face-to-face communion (110b5–111c3).[22]

2.3. *Tartarus and the Rivers (111c–113c)*

The tour of the earth goes on to reveal further regions hidden beneath the hollows: Tartarus and the underworld rivers. These are places where much water flows (*poly men hydôr*, 111d4)—a vast underground network of rivers, lakes and waterways. The rivers are of 'unimaginable size' with hot and cold waters. There are great rivers of fire (*poly de pyr*, 111d7) and many of liquid mud (*pollous de hygrou pêlou*, 111d8). Socrates notes that while some of these muddy rivers are purer (*katharôterou*, 111d8), others are more miry (*borborôdesterou*). These streams are compared to those 'in Sicily' (111e1)— with the muddy streams like those which precede the lava flow and the fiery streams like the lava flow itself (*rhyax*).

The next section of the myth explains what is responsible for all the movements of the rivers (111e4–6):

> All of this is kept moving back and forth by a kind of pulsation going on within the earth and the nature of this pulsation is something like this: [...] [23]
>
> (tr. Gallop)

---

in a position to start appreciating the real density and complexity of the myth at the end of the *Phaedo*'.

[20] The language of this section speaks of areas 'higher' and 'lower' than others, see e.g. ὑποστάθμην (109c2); ἄνω (109c4); πυθμένι (109c5); ἐπάνω (109d6). Note also the ἀνα- prefix in ἀνακύψας (109d2, e3, e4) and ἀνάπτοιτο (109e3).

[21] The primary point of the leather ball comparison (110b) is to illustrate the idea of an unbroken, multi-coloured surface but the image also suggests to me that the earth is being presented as spherical.

[22] As Friedländer (1958 [1954]), 264 notes, 'All these features are derived from the image of the Isle of the Blessed or Paradise' (Friedländer (1958 [1954]), § 'Plato as Geographer', 261–285). For the Isles of the Blessed in Homer and Hesiod, see *Odyssey* 4.563ff. and *Works and Days* 171.

[23] Ταῦτα δὲ πάντα κινεῖν ἄνω καὶ κάτω ὥσπερ αἰώραν τινὰ ἐνοῦσαν ἐν τῇ γῇ· ἔστι δὲ ἄρα αὕτη ἡ αἰώρα διὰ φύσιν τοιάνδε τινά.

This *aiôra* (pulsation) is then traced to a particular location (111e6–112a5):

> One of the openings in the earth happens to be especially large, and perfo-
> rated right through the earth; it is this that Homer spoke of as: 'A great way
> off, where lies the deepest pit beneath earth;' and it is this that he and many
> other poets have elsewhere called Tartarus.[24]   (tr. Gallop)

Thus the pit of Tartarus, a familiar feature of the underworld from Greek
epic, is given a new identity as a huge chasm piercing right through the
earth.[25] All the rivers of the earth are said to flow into and out of this chasm
and a note is added on how the region through which each river flows affects
its nature (112a7–b1). But the chasm of Tartarus is not simply a place or space
since it also serves as the pumping mechanism of the earth's rivers (112b1–3):

> The reason why all the streams flow out there, and flow in, is that this liquid
> has neither bottom nor resting place.[26]   (tr. Gallop)

Since Tartarus provides no resting place for their waters, all the rivers flow in
and out in ceaseless motion with no place to gather, however temporarily.

To help the audience grasp this remarkable geophysical phenomenon,
the myth provides further detail on how the mechanism operates and uses
a simile of breathing (112b3–9):

> So it pulsates and surges back and forth, and the air and the breath enveloping
> it do the same; because they follow it, when it rushes towards those areas
> of the earth and again when it returns to these; and just as in breathing the
> current of breath is continuously exhaled and inhaled, so there the breath
> pulsating together with the liquid causes terrible and unimaginable winds, as
> it passes in and out.[27]   (tr. Gallop)

The reference to the movement of air and breath (b4) prepares for the simile but also introduces the 'terrible and unimaginable' winds (b8–9) caused
by the surging water. This terrifying vision combines a regular mechanical pulsation with irregular turbulence, a combination supported by the

---

[24] ἕν τι τῶν χασμάτων τῆς γῆς ἄλλως τε μέγιστον τυγχάνει ὂν καὶ διαμπερὲς τετρημένον δι' ὅλης
τῆς γῆς, τοῦτο ὅπερ Ὅμηρος εἶπε, λέγων αὐτό 'τῆλε μάλ', ἧχι βάθιστον ὑπὸ χθονός ἐστι βέρεθρον·'
ὃ καὶ ἄλλοθι καὶ ἐκεῖνος καὶ ἄλλοι πολλοὶ τῶν ποιητῶν Τάρταρον κεκλήκασιν.

[25] For Tartarus in Homer, see *Iliad* VIII, 13 ff., and in Hesiod, see *Theogony*, 119.

[26] ἡ δὲ αἰτία ἐστὶν τοῦ ἐκρεῖν τε ἐντεῦθεν καὶ εἰσρεῖν πάντα τὰ ῥεύματα, ὅτι πυθμένα οὐκ ἔχει
οὐδὲ βάσιν τὸ ὑγρὸν τοῦτο.

[27] αἰωρεῖται δὴ καὶ κυμαίνει ἄνω καὶ κάτω, καὶ ὁ ἀὴρ καὶ τὸ πνεῦμα τὸ περὶ αὐτὸ ταὐτὸν ποιεῖ·
συνέπεται γὰρ αὐτῷ καὶ ὅταν εἰς τὸ ἐπ' ἐκεῖνα τῆς γῆς ὁρμήσῃ καὶ ὅταν εἰς τὸ ἐπὶ τάδε, καὶ ὥσπερ
τῶν ἀναπνεόντων ἀεὶ ἐκπνεῖ τε καὶ ἀναπνεῖ ῥέον τὸ πνεῦμα, οὕτω καὶ ἐκεῖ συναιωρούμενον τῷ ὑγρῷ
τὸ πνεῦμα δεινούς τινας ἀνέμους καὶ ἀμηχάνους παρέχεται καὶ εἰσιὸν καὶ ἐξιόν.

ambiguity of the Greek phrase *anô kai katô*, which means 'up and down' but is also used to denote disorderly motion.[28] The inclusion of air in this description at 112b also completes the list of the four elements shown as involved in the mechanism of Tartarus, with water appearing at 111d4, fire at 111d7, and earth in the form of mud at 111d8.

Socrates next describes how the rivers fill the subterranean channels and in turn recede, rushing one way and then the other (112c). In this way 'seas and lakes and rivers and springs' (112c7–8) are formed but in time all the waters will return to Tartarus. While the returning rivers will discharge into Tartarus at different points, all will flow in again beneath their point of outflow. On the return to the chasm, Socrates further explains (112d8–e3): 'It is possible to descend [...] as far as the middle but no further; because the part on either side slopes uphill for both sets of streams' (tr. Gallop). In response to Aristotle's criticism of this description as presenting the 'proverbial impossibility of rivers flowing uphill',[29] commentators have shown that—since Tartarus is located at the centre point of the spherical earth—confusion can be avoided if the normal usage of 'up' and 'down' is replaced with that of movement 'away from' or 'towards' the centre.[30]

Tartarus, then, is a channel at the centre of the earth that acts for the earth's rivers as a water-pump in a system of irrigation (112c3). The key Greek term for the mechanism is *aiôra*, introduced first as a simile (111e5). LSJ gives the primary sense as 'swing, hammock, chariot on springs', as used at *Laws* 789d, and a secondary sense as 'oscillatory movement, see-saw, pulsation', as used here. Archer-Hind's note is helpful:

> *aiôra* properly signifies a seesaw movement, like that of a pair of scales equally balanced. It is the name given to a kind of gymnastic machine like a swing. By the force of this *aiôra* the volume of air and fluid in Tartaros is perpetually swaying to and fro like a pendulum.[31]

Burnet further clarifies (135): '*aiôra* meant a "swing" or "hammock". [...] The whole description shows that a sort of pulsation, like the systole and diastole of the heart, is intended'. Thus the *aiôra* simile is used to demonstrate the rhythmic reciprocity of the influx and outflux of waters. The 'swing' or pulsation of the waters takes place within the Tartarus channel, the

---

[28] See Pender (1999), 98, n. 74.

[29] Arist. *Meteorologica*, 356a15–20 [tr. H.D.P. Lee].

[30] See Archer-Hind (1894 [1883]), 134–135 and Burnet (1911), 135–139, who observes that when Plato is speaking of 'down', he 'really means nearer the centre of the earth' (137). Plato acknowledges the terminological point at 112c2 ('the so-called "downward" region').

[31] Archer-Hind (1894 [1883]), 131–132.

most central point of the physical earth. The mechanism drives the waters outwards towards the surface of the earth and when the force changes its direction, the waters recede again to the centre.[32]

With the mechanism of the rivers identified and given its poetic name of 'Tartarus' (*Tartaron keklêkasin*, 112a5), the description of the underworld— or better 'innerworld'[33]—geography turns at 112e to introduce its four great rivers.[34] These rivers are dependent on Tartarus for their movement and so in this sense play a supporting role in the narrative. But in this next section of the story the rivers take centre stage, first since the detailed focus now switches to their individual identities, features and activities, and second since they, like Tartarus, are carefully named. The first river identified is the largest; it flows outermost and in a circle. This is the river 'called Oceanus': *ho kaloumenos Ôkeanos* (112e7). Next, and in balanced opposition with Oceanus, is Acheron. Flowing in the opposite direction (*toutou de katantikry kai enantiôs rheôn*), Acheron runs through deserted regions into the Acherusian Lake (112e8–113a2). The third river is the fiery river, boiling with water and mud. Like Oceanus this flows in a circle and after 'coiling around within the earth' (113b1) comes near to the Acherusian Lake but does not mingle with it (*ou summeignumenos*, 113b3). After further 'repeated coiling underground' (113b3–4), it pours into Tartarus. This is the river that 'men call Pyriphlegethon' (*eponomazousin Pyriphlegethonta*, 113b5) and it is from this that the streams of lava 'blast fragments up' to the earth.

As with the pairing of Oceanus and Acheron, Pyriphlegethon's partner, the fourth river, is again opposite to it (*au katantikry*, 113b7). It flows into a terrible and wild region which has a gloomy colour all over, black or deep blue,[35] and creates the Stygian Lake. The fourth river, like the third,

---

[32] Burnet (1911), 135 136: 'We must keep in mind throughout this passage that everything falls to the earth's centre. The impetus (ὁρμή) of the water takes it past the centre every time, but it falls back again, and so on indefinitely'. Friedländer (1958 [1954]), 266: 'The water content of these subterranean channels depends upon whether the "balance" (αἰώρα) of this mass of water tilts in one direction or another from the center of the earth'.

[33] The switch to the terminology of 'inner' and 'outer' occurs at 112e7 in the use of ἐξωτάτω, 'outermost'.

[34] For Oceanus in Homer, see *Il.* I, 423; XIV, 245–246, and *Od.* IV, 568; V, 275; X, 139, 508; XI, 13, 21, 158, 639; XII, 1; XIX, 434; XX, 65; XXII, 197; XXIII, 244, 347; XXIV, 11. For Oceanus in Hesiod, see e.g. *WD* 171. For Oceanus with Acheron, Pyriphlegethon and Cocytus, see *Od.* X, 511–514.

[35] The colour is described as 'like *kyanos*'. Burnet (1911) notes that while it is not certain which substance is intended, it is possibly *lapis lazuli*. He is alert to Plato's balancing of colour (140): 'In any case, we are to think of a bluish grey, steely colour, in strong contrast to the fiery plain of Pyriphlegethon'.

'coils around' under the earth (113c4) and, as with the first pairing, flows opposite to its partner: 'it proceeds in the opposite direction (*enantios*) to Pyriphlegethon'. It also flows near the Acherusian Lake but from the 'opposite' side (*ex enantias*). Like Pyriphlegethon, this river does not mingle with any other (*oude* [...] *oudeni meignutai*, 113c6). The name of this fourth river is introduced with the longest rhetorical flourish. As its description ends, and saving the actual name until the final position, the river is formally presented (113c8–9): *onoma de toutôi estin, hôs hoi poiêtai legousin, Kôkytos*—'and the name of this river, as the poets say, is Cocytus'.[36]

So the four rivers have their own names and distinctive identities. Further, the point is made twice (113b3 and 113c6) that although Acheron, Pyriphlegethon and Cocytus run very close to one another in the vicinity of the Acherusian Lake, their waters do not mingle. In this way the rivers retain their individuality and separate identities. In addition, the rivers become distinctive figures in the narrative as a result of their force and energy. A few of the verbs used of them in this passage illustrate the point: *ekballei* (113a6); *ekpiptei* (113a7); *emballei* (113b4); *anaphysôsin* (113b6). In this part of the myth, then, a particularly active landscape is being brought to the fore.

2.4. *The Judgement and Transit of Souls (113d–114c)*

In this final section of the myth the narrative of the soul's judgement, suspended at 108c to allow the revelation of the earth's true geography, is resumed. With this panoramic view in place, Plato can now combine with it the story of the afterlife journey, showing the soul's subsequent fortunes in their fuller context.

The souls of the dead, conveyed by their spirit, arrive at the underworld/innerworld region (113d1–2). On arrival they are judged (*diedikasanto*) and sorted into categories: those who have lived 'middlingly' (*mesôs bebiôkenai*, 113d4); the incurably evil; the curably evil; and, finally, the exceptionally good and holy. Following judgement their different journeys begin. First, the 'middlingly' or 'mediocre' go to the river Acheron and are ferried onwards to the Acherusian Lake. Second, those who are incurably evil are 'hurled by the appropriate destiny' directly into Tartarus, from where they will emerge 'nevermore' (*oupote* 113e6).[37] Thirdly, the curable souls must also fall into Tartarus but, after they have stayed there for one year, the current

---

[36] My translation.

[37] Burnet (1911), 141: 'οὔποτε, "nevermore," is more solemn than the everyday οὐδέποτε, "never"'.

or surge (*to kyma*, 114a4) casts them out and they are further discriminated into two new sub-classes—with the homicides sent on to gloomy Cocytus, and those who have assaulted parents on to fiery Pyriphlegethon (114a5–6). These curably evil souls are given the brief opportunity to call out to their victims dwelling on the Acherusian Lake and plead for release (114a6–b1).

The judgement of souls is concluded with those judged to have lived 'exceptionally holy lives' (114b6–7). Once identified and separated from the others, the exceptionally good souls are afforded immediate transit out of the Tartarus region. These souls travel upwards (*anô*, 114c1) to live on the surface of the earth, the beautiful place above our hollows. But the final part of the myth reveals that some of the exceptionally good souls living in this pure region are able to reach places even more beautiful (114c2–6):

> And among their number, those who have been adequately purified by philosophy live bodiless for the whole of time to come, and attain to dwelling places fairer even than those, which it is not easy to reveal, nor is the time sufficient at present.[38]

Thus the geography of the myth spans from Tartarus at its innermost core to the outermost limits of the surface of the earth, and points to even more remote regions beyond.

In the first part of the myth Socrates asserted that each soul 'inhabits the region that befits' it (108c) and in this final part he delivers the detail of the correspondences. The myth maps six dwelling places which, on a linear perspective, run from 'highest' to 'lowest'. First, beyond the spherical earth lie the mysterious 'still fairer' dwelling places (*oikêseis eti toutôn kallious*) for the philosophical souls—the purest souls awarded with the most beautiful environments of all. Second, in the fairest environment of the *physical* earth, its outer surface,[39] live the other holy souls, second in blessedness. This place, marvellous for its beauty, bright colours, climate and proportion (110b5–111c3), provides for these pure souls a pure home (*katharan oikêsin*, 114c1). Continuing inwards, the third location is the misty world of the hollows, a corrupted environment where the 'sediment' or 'dregs' of the upper world have settled (109b–110a). This is the familiar human world where

---

[38] τούτων δὲ αὐτῶν οἱ φιλοσοφίᾳ ἱκανῶς καθηράμενοι ἄνευ τε σωμάτων ζῶσι τὸ παράπαν εἰς τὸν ἔπειτα χρόνον, καὶ εἰς οἰκήσεις ἔτι τούτων καλλίους ἀφικνοῦνται, ἃς οὔτε ῥᾴδιον δηλῶσαι οὔτε ὁ χρόνος ἱκανὸς ἐν τῷ παρόντι.

[39] In the terms of the passage at 109c–e, this surface, as its highest or furthest point, is its ἄκρα (109d1–e2).

embodied souls face the life of moral struggle described so vividly in the earlier discussions of the dialogue. But the earthly hollows nevertheless provide a mixed environment for souls, since despite the 'mud and mire' (110a5–6), there exist also 'beauties in our world' (*ta par' hêmin kallê*, 110a6–7). Inside the earth lies the world of the unpurified dead, a turbulent environment dominated by the vast mechanical flux of Tartarus. This region has various dwelling places for souls within its intricate waterways. The outermost river is Oceanus and inside its circuit flow the three great rivers of purgation: Acheron, Pyriphlegethon and Cocytus.[40] The fourth region is Acheron and its lake, the destination for souls judged as of 'middling' or 'mediocre' moral quality. These souls 'undergo purgation by paying the penalty for their wrongdoings, if any has committed any wrong' (*kathairomenoi tôn te adikêmatôn didontes dikas apolyontai, ei tis ti êdikêken*, 113d7–8), while those who have managed some good deeds are rewarded with honours, 'each according to what they deserve' (*kata tên axian hekastos*, 113e1). The inferiority of the Acherusian Lake to the earthly hollows is evident in its lack of any beauty. Souls here use 'vessels' (*ochêmata*, 113d5–6) and the waters are calmer than elsewhere in the underworld[41] but due to the over-riding influence of the Tartarus tides, this environment is still precarious for souls. The fifth region includes both Pyriphlegethon and Cocytus, destination of wicked but curable souls. The specific environment for these souls is the actual waters of the rivers, since part of their punishment is to be pitched into them. The punishments provided by both are suggested by their depictions as, respectively, 'fiery' and 'gloomy'. That the experiences of souls here are unpleasant is made explicit when they are described as 'woes' (*tôn kakôn*, 114b2). The sixth and lowest position in the hierarchy belongs to the chasm of Tartarus, at the earth's innermost core. This is the final destination for the most wicked souls, whose punishments are left to the imagination. The swinging pulsation of Tartarus is the most turbulent place in the underworld region and so corresponds to the disturbed and corrupted nature of the lost souls.

The different regions are therefore presented as places of reward or punishment, with the outermost or 'higher' entailing always a better experience

---

[40] Oceanus is not used as a destination for the impure souls after judgement. This may reflect its traditional role as the boundary between the worlds of living and dead, a boundary marked in this myth by a series of roads to the underworld (108a).

[41] Socrates' comment at 111d8–e1, that some of the underworld rivers are 'purer' or 'more miry' than others (καθαρωτέρου καὶ βορβορωδεστέρου), is consistent with the differentiation of environments in the Tartarus region.

for souls then the innermost or 'lower'. Thus the geography of the earth presents a hierarchy of places where the pure and impure environments match the moral condition of the souls living within them.[42]

3. AN UNSTEADY CORE

The rivers of Tartarus are a means of punishment for unpurified souls and represent the soul's inferior moral conditions, as curably or incurably corrupt. Since different consequences for good and evil behaviour are necessary in Plato's presentation of a just universe, this is the first teleological role of the rivers. In this next stage of my argument I shall show how the rivers serve further teleological purposes since their ethical role relates to both their ontological status and epistemological implications. Socrates and his interlocutors have agreed that a soul cannot reason properly or gain knowledge in the flux of human life with all the disturbances caused by the human body (e.g. 79c, 82e–83c). The myth now reinforces that argument by depicting how the greater ontological turbulence of the Tartarus region will render a soul more helpless in its cognitive capacities and remove it further from abstract truth. As a whole the myth echoes and supports the affinity argument (78b–84b) by further applying the principle of assimilation to souls in their afterlife environments.[43] The most significant outcome of this further application is the identification of Tartarus as a place where the soul cannot philosophize. This section will therefore show how the different locations of soul in the myth are depicted as intensifying the positive and negative aspects of their natures.

3.1. *Tartarus and the Affinity Argument*

According to the affinity argument whenever the soul contemplates abstract essences it 'departs yonder (*ekeise*) towards that which is pure' (79d1–2) and so strengthens its 'kinship' with what is immortal and unvarying (79d3). Thus the philosophical soul assimilates itself to reality, as shown in their parallel descriptions: *auto kath' hauto* (78d6) and *autê kath' hautên* (79d4). The soul can grasp (*ephaptomenê*) reality and so become like it when

---

[42] Friedländer (1958 [1954]), 267: 'The important thing is that we realize that all these features are invented and described in order to prepare, and make possible, the destiny of the different categories of souls'.

[43] The note at 112a7–b1, that the regions of the underworld affect the natures of the rivers flowing through them, is a further instance of the myth's use of the principle of assimilation.

it is—in spatial terms—'about' the abstract essences: *peri ekeina*, 79d5.[44]
But when soul 'consorts and keeps company with' the body, it becomes
'interspersed with the bodily element' (81c4–6).[45] Thus the soul's nature
changes according to the company it keeps. The soul is further assimilated
to the body when it is so convinced by the strength of the body's experiences
that it makes errors about what is actually real (83d6–7). Socrates believes
that through such sharing of wrong opinions (*homodoxein*), each pleasure
and pain makes the soul 'corporeal' (*sômatoeidê*) and forces it to become 'of
like character and nurture' (*homotropos te kai homotrophos*) to body. The
result is that such a corrupted soul cannot 'enter Hades in purity' (83d7–
10) and can have no part of 'communion' (*sunousias*) with the divine, pure
and uniform (83e2–3). The conclusion of the affinity argument presents the
corresponding fate of the pure soul (84a7–b3):

> Rather, securing rest (*galênên*) from those feelings, by following reasoning
> and being ever within it (*en toutôi*), and by beholding what is true and divine
> and not the object of opinion, and being nurtured (*trephomenê*) by it, it
> believes that [...] when it has died, it will enter that which is akin and of like
> nature to itself (*eis to suggenes kai eis to toiouton aphikomenê*), and be rid of
> human ills.   (tr. Gallop)

The noun *galênê* means literally the 'stillness of the sea'[46] and the metaphor
is used for the peace gained by the philosophical soul from the disturbance of pleasures and pains that afflicts the soul assimilated to body. When
Socrates completes the argument from affinity, he notices that his companions remain troubled. Therefore in the first 'interlude' (84c1–85e2) he
compares himself to the swans of Apollo (84e–85b) who sing not through

---

[44] The passage on animal reincarnations further connects locations and conditions, as the
'direction' taken by souls is said to be 'according to the affinities of their training': ἴοι κατὰ τὰς
αὐτῶν ὁμοιότητας τῆς μελέτης, 82a8–9.

[45] For other contamination vocabulary, see 66b5, συμπεφυρμένη, and 81b1, μεμιασμένη.

[46] The further sailing metaphor in 'embarking on a raft' and 'risking the dangers of the
voyage through life' (85d1–2) also establishes the motif of water ahead of the myth. A
further passing use of the motif comes in Socrates' allusion to the myth of Heracles and
the Lenaean Hydra, a water serpent (89c5–10). While in *Republic* (588b–589c) the Hydra
signifies the growing multiplicity of desires in the tripartite soul, the proliferation here lies
in the mounting objections of Simmias and Cebes. For extensive sea and water references
in the myth, in addition to the Tartarus rivers, see 109b–110a with the Phasis river, marsh
simile and various marine comparisons used to make epistemological points. I am indebted
to Christopher Green's MA thesis (Leeds 2010) for illumination on how the motif of Theseus'
ship sailing to Delos sets up various water and journey metaphors in the text. See also Dorter
(1969–1970), 565–570.

distress but in joy (*gegêthotes*, 85a2; *terpontai*, 85b3) at their approaching deaths. They are joyful because as servants of Apollo, they are about to depart into the god's very presence (85a) and so they realise 'the blessings of Hades' (*ta en Haidou agatha*, 85b2).[47] What is being established through the use of *galênê* and the delight of the swans is that the true unseen is a place of joy and calm.

Given the insistence of the affinity argument that soul is harmed by being kept within the human body, it is logical that when the philosophical souls in the myth are rewarded for their goodness, they are allotted lives 'without bodies' (*aneu te sômatôn*) for the whole of their subsequent eternity (114c). When Plato points to these *non-physical* dwelling places he marks them off from *all* the other regions of the earth. Through this central ontological distinction the myth of *Phaedo* presents the physical world as stretching above the misty hollows not only to the bright surface of the earth but also to the dark regions of Tartarus. The earth's surface—the 'true' earth— is explicitly identified as a physical region in various ways. It is a place of 'true light' (*alêthinon phôs*, 109e7) with a landscape notable for its bright colours (110c–d). Things grow here—trees, flowers and fruit (110d), and there are mountains, rocks and precious metals (110d–e), which are 'plainly visible' (*ekphanê*, 111a). Any remaining ambiguity is removed when the true earth's surface is shown as home to embodied creatures. In this golden-age existence where ether takes the place of air (111b1–2), the fairer climate allows people to live 'free from sickness' (*anosous*, 111b3) and a far longer time (*chronon* [...] *polu pleiô*, 111b3) than we do in the misty hollows of familiar human life. Further, these people 'surpass us in sight and hearing' (*opsei kai akoêi*) as well as in wisdom and other faculties (111b4–5). Therefore these golden-age people, the purified souls, still have physical bodies subject to old-age, decay and death, albeit over a much longer life-span. Tartarus is equally marked as a physical realm. First, its landscape features water (111d4), fire (111d7), earth (111d8) and air (112b). Second, the rivers of the underworld are explicitly shown to be the same rivers that flow up into the hollows and create the familiar waterways of our world (112c4–8).[48] Thus Plato's version of 'Hades' as place-of-the-dead is distinct from his idea

---

[47] The pun in Ἀιδου/ᾄδουσι provides a further play on the name 'Hades'.

[48] I take the directions (here/there) in this passage (ἐντεῦθεν, 112b1, ἐκεῖθεν, δεῦρο, ἐνθάδε, 112c4) to refer, as they do throughout the dialogue, to the world of the living and the world of the dead (e.g. 61e; 64a; 70c7, 107d5). On this reading, the 'so-called downward region' (112c1–2) is Tartarus or the underworld, and not, as Burnet (1911), 136 reads, the antipodes.

of the 'true Hades' which is both invisible and divine (80d5–7). For in the geography of the myth only the regions on the surface of the earth or beyond qualify as places of purity consistent with divine nature.

Given that Tartarus is a physical realm, the first puzzle I would like to solve is the relationship between soul and body in this region. Corrupted souls have left the individual bodies they inhabited during life in the hollows but have not been rewarded with better golden-age ones. Since freedom from embodiment is a privilege reserved for only the philosophical souls, the corrupted souls must still be subject to physical nature. But by what means? On my reading of the myth, the unique purpose of the region of Tartarus is to convey this specific condition of soul, i.e. separated from its individual human body but still trapped in physical nature. Plato's radical transformation of Tartarus presents its central mechanism as the very engine of physical generation and the whole region as a 'super-body' for the corrupted souls.

3.2. Tartarus as 'Super-Body'

The crucial role of the Tartarus region in the myth is to show how the corrupted souls in the afterlife experience a more intensive assimilation to corporeal nature. Tartarus presents the raw nature of physics. With its nightmare vision of punishments, this landscape magnifies the distorting limitations of the body and warns against the soul's over-attachment to it.

First, Tartarus can be seen as central to the world of generation. It shares with the rest of the earth a nature based on the four roots but also— consistent with the cyclical argument that living people are born from the dead (69e–72d)—it is the place of transit for impure souls in their endless cycle of coming-to-be and passing-away (107d–e, 113a). Second, an analogy is suggested between Tartarus and the human body. When the pulsation of Tartarus is introduced, a breathing simile is used to illustrate the influx and outflux of its waters (112b6–7). The breathing simile suggests that Tartarus functions like the human body[49] and the analogy is further supported when the prison simile used of the body in the earlier discussion is extended.[50] When the exceptionally holy souls are judged, they are transported directly from the place of judgement to the purest dwelling places (114b7–c1):

---

[49] Burnet (1911), 135–136 adds his own physiological illustration of the 'systole and diastole of the heart' and notes how Stewart ([1905], 103) sees Plato speaking of 'waters circulating in channels through the Earth, like blood through the veins of the body'.
[50] See Edmonds (2004), 177.

it is they who are freed and delivered from those regions within the earth, as
from prisons.[51]   (tr. Gallop)

In contrast, the impure souls have shed the human body only to find themselves imprisoned in a much larger and more powerful physical frame: the
Tartarus region, presented as a sort of gigantic body. By presenting Tartarus as both a physical system and a prison, Plato can use the analogy with
the human body to prompt a reassessment of our physical bodies on earth:
human bodies are prisons but they at least allow more freedom for the soul
than during the time of afterlife punishment, when they are encased in a
body writ-large, over which they have no control whatsoever.

The affinity argument stresses the inconstant nature of the body (e.g.
80b5) and Tartarus is shown in turn to share this lack of stability. The influx
and outflux of the underworld rivers is attributed to a mechanical cause: the
open channel of Tartarus provides 'neither bottom nor resting place' *puth-
mena ouk ekhei oude basin* (112b2)[52] for the waters that rush into it. When
the waters fill the channel, they are simply pushed out again and the primary purpose in mentioning this absence of a base is to explain how the
force driving this interchange is purely physical. But the language of the
gaping chasm with no ultimate foundation also has ontological connota-
tions, and Plato uses the gap of Tartarus, alongside its ceaseless flux, as a
powerful symbol for the sheer unsteadiness of the physical world. A particular verbal repetition in the description of Tartarus further indicates that
physical matter has no ultimate or independent security. At 111e the pulsation of Tartarus going on within the earth is described as movement *anô kai
katô* ('back and forth'). After the lack of resting place is noted, the mechanism is again described at 112b3: *aiôreitai dê kai kymainei anô kai katô* ('so
it pulsates and surges back and forth'). The phrase *anô kai katô* as noted
above (2. 3.) can be used to convey disorderly motion, and in various dialogues Plato uses it as a metaphor for unreliable opinion.[53] The repetition
of *anô kai katô* at 111e5 and 112b3 is suggestive and the epistemological reference emerges clearly when it is set beside a passage from the second
'interlude' of the dialogue (88c1–91c6), where Socrates criticises those who

---

[51] οὗτοί εἰσιν οἱ τῶνδε μὲν τῶν τόπων τῶν ἐν τῇ γῇ ἐλευθερούμενοί τε καὶ ἀπαλλαττόμενοι ὥσπερ
δεσμωτηρίων.

[52] Kingsley's detailed argument that this line is of Orphic origin is persuasive. See Kingsley
(1995), 127–130 for his careful explanation of how Plato's phrase is a direct allusion to *OF* fr. 66:
μέγα χάσμα πελώριον [...] οὐδέ τι πεῖραρ ὑπῆν, οὐ πυθμήν, οὐδέ τις ἕδρα.

[53] E.g. *Protagoras* 356d, *Gorgias* 481e, *Hippias Minor* 376c, and *Theaetetus* 195c.

are devoted to contradictory arguments. These people, he says, believe they are most wise (*sophôtatoi*), since they alone have realised that (90c3–6):

> There's nothing sound or secure whatever, either in things or arguments; but that all realities are carried up and down, just like things fluctuating in the Euripus, and never remain at rest for any time.[54]   (tr. Gallop)

This attack on the relativists uses the simile of realities turned 'upside down' just like objects 'in the Euripus'. LSJ explains the noun *euripos* as 'a place where the flux and reflux is strong, esp. the strait which separates Euboea from Boeotia, where the current was said to change seven times a day'.

Thus the repetition of the phrase 'up and down' at 111e/112b is used to create a parallel between the fluctuations of Euripus and Tartarus, where both carry ontological and epistemological implications. At 90c the people who cannot find anything 'stable' or 'at rest' in reality are themselves unsteady in that they have lost any secure reference points for their thought.[55] For Plato these people, detached from fixed truths, become increasingly vulnerable to the influence of the unsteady physical world around them. The later vision of Tartarus then adds a new dimension: such unsteady souls in the afterlife become subject to the far greater and more relentless physical flux of turbulent rivers with no foundation at all.

In ontological terms the region of Tartarus is even more physical, more unstable and therefore less real than the earthly hollows of the familiar phenomenal world. Following the principle of assimilation, the souls here become increasingly unsteady themselves. Carried on the underworld rivers, the impure souls are depicted as subject to the tides of Tartarus relative to their level of immorality. The best of them embark on 'boats' (113d5–6) for their passage to the Acherusian Lake. Protected from the waters, these 'middling' souls experience the steadiest journey available in this region, suggesting that they maintain a slightly higher degree of autonomy. But since all the waterways of the underworld are subject to the fluctuating tides to some extent, entirely calm waters are not available even for them. The evil souls are all cast directly into the surging waters of Pyriphlegethon and Cocytus but the curable souls fare better. Hurled into the Tartarus

---

[54] οὔτε τῶν πραγμάτων οὐδενὸς οὐδὲν ὑγιὲς οὐδὲ βέβαιον οὔτε τῶν λόγων, ἀλλὰ πάντα τὰ ὄντα ἀτεχνῶς ὥσπερ ἐν Εὐρίπῳ ἄνω κάτω στρέφεται καὶ χρόνον οὐδένα ἐν οὐδενὶ μένει.

[55] The same idea is used of the Heracliteans at *Tht.* 179d–180a. Edmonds (2004), 213 also sees the connection between 90c and 112b: 'The fate of the punished soul in Tartarus is thus like the lot of an unphilosophic person who distrusts all arguments and relies only on his senses'.

mechanism, they receive an annual opportunity to persuade their victims to pity them. While success would bring release into the calmer waters of the Lake of Acheron, to receive further purification there, failure brings a return to Tartarus. Finally, the incurably evil souls simply face an eternity subsumed in the turbulent flux in and out of the chasm. It is hard to differentiate these souls from the surging tides and, far from having any remaining control over themselves, they seem to have reached the limit of their assimilation to physical nature. Therefore the myth illustrates that the impure souls on the underworld rivers are denied the 'stillness' (*galênê*) enjoyed elsewhere by the philosophical souls.

The epistemological consequences of this unsteadiness are evident. During human life it is possible for soul to learn to separate itself from body through contemplation and so make contact with truth (65c–66a). But if rational enquiry is neglected and too much energy is devoted to the body's concerns, souls are contaminated with the corporeal and so liable, in the afterlife, to a whole new level of physical pressure and distortion. For after judgement the corrupted souls will travel to a region where direct contemplation of abstract truth and reality is impossible.

Thus the Tartarus region shows how afterlife punishment imprisons the soul more deeply within the realm of generation, effecting an ever-closer assimilation of soul to corporeal nature. The turbulent and automatic flux of the rivers parallels the nature of souls who, as the result of over-attachment to the body, have no knowledge of truth and so no fixed point of reference for their judgements and moral choices. In the afterlife these lost souls become more like their much-loved but unstable bodies, to the point at which they lose their identity and become absorbed in the merely mechanical churnings of a vast 'super-body' with no head. Tartarus and the rivers are therefore the means of punishment for ethical weakness and a warning against epistemological error.

3.3. The Judges and Universal Order

For all their horrors, the regions of Tartarus are nevertheless part of a just and ordered universe. As places of punishment, they are still regulated by rational powers: the intelligent design of the universe at large but more specifically also the underworld judges.

In contrast to Tartarus and the rivers, the personified arbiters of justice remain unnamed and their influence more oblique. The first reference to afterlife judgement in the myth occurs in the opening passage as Socrates explains how the souls are escorted to a 'certain place' where those gathered are judged (*diadikasamenous*) before their journey to Hades (107d7–e1). After the lengthy description of the earth, the second reference is part of the resumption of the narrative of the souls' journey as the point is repeated that, when the dead arrive in the afterlife, their first experience is to be judged (*prôton men diedikasanto*, 113d1–4). The third reference to judgement is indirect as the souls sent to the Acherusian Lake spend some of their time receiving rewards and some 'undergoing purgation by paying the penalty for their wrongdoings' (*kathairomenoi tôn te adikêmatôn didontes dikas*, 113d7–8). Here the role of the judges is left implicit and the text speaks simply of how the souls 'appear' or 'have been considered' (*doxôsin*, 113e2 and e7).[56] Judges are not mentioned explicitly until the fourth reference. At 114b5–7 the souls of violent criminals are said to be forced to suffer until they win a particular form of release—'for that is the penalty imposed on them by their judges' (*hautê gar hê dikê hypo tôn dikastôn autois etachthê*). Therefore the only use of the noun for 'judges' in the myth is at 114b, in the genitive as part of a passive construction.

But, despite their low profile,[57] judges are present in this vision of the underworld and their power is evident. First, although the places of the afterlife provide the rewards and punishments for souls in the form of the lives that can be lived there, the decisions on which souls go where rest firmly with the judges. No souls travel onwards to either the underworld rivers or the surface of the earth until they have received their judgement (107d8). Second, the myth suggests that the onward punishments in the underworld remain under the supervision of these judges in respect of time. For their intervention can be seen in the setting of a limit (of one year) on the curably evil souls' time in Tartarus (114a4), and in the determination of the length of stay of the souls on the Acherusian Lake (*tinas heimarmenous chronous*, 113a).

Also apparent in the Tartarus region is the presence of a universal order. Despite its corrupted physical nature, the element of chance (*tychêi*, 111e3), and its turbulence (112b3), the central mechanism with its rivers still obeys certain physical laws. The 'swing' (*aiôra*) of Tartarus follows the regular

---

[56] The same formulation is used for the souls found to be exceptionally holy 114b6: δόξωσι.

[57] Edmonds (2004), 197–198: 'The lack of description of the place of judgement stands in stark contrast to the abundance of description of the various realms to which the soul goes as a result of its judgement. Since the focus is on the location of the soul after judgement rather than on the process, the judges are likewise anonymous'. I am grateful to Malcolm Heath for the further observation that the fleeting appearance of these judges in the myth stands in contrast to the prominence of the Athenian judicial system elsewhere in the dialogue (e.g. 58a–c, 59e).

rhythm of outflux and influx (*ekrein/eisrein*, 112b1) and, although it provides no base for its waters, it has fixed spatial limits: the rivers can descend into Tartarus 'as far as the middle but no further' (*mechri tou mesou/pera d'ou*, 112e1). The four rivers of the underworld are symmetrically arranged. Oceanus and Pyriphlegethon circle in one direction and Acheron and Cocytus in the other, with their positions fixed as opposites (*katantikry kai enantiôs*, 112e8; *katantikry* [...] *enantios/ex enantias*, 113b7–c5). As attention turns to punishment, a different counterpoise balances the fires of Pyriphlegethon with the gloom of Cocytus (113a7–8 / 113b8–c1). Further, despite their 'unimaginable size' (111d6) and 'terrible powers' (113c3), the rivers do not follow their own random courses. Oceanus runs at the outer edge of the innerworld and the three rivers of punishment are kept apart. These rivers are not permitted to mingle with one another, since each must remain distinct as part of its task of providing the appropriate experiences for the particular class of souls it carries around (113d–114b). In effect, then, the rivers provide different penalties which must not become confused, since such a lack of discrimination would be inconsistent with the justice of the universe. Thus even this region displays the balanced opposition evident elsewhere in the myth, e.g. the proportion in nature of the true earth (*ana logon*, 110d3), and in the discussion at large, e.g. the unity of opposites at 60b6–c1, the perpetual reciprocity in the cyclical argument (*antapodidômi*, 71e8, 72a12), and the entire argument from opposites, *ta enantia*, 102a11–107b10.

3.4. *The Absence of Philosophy in Tartarus*

The topography of the *Phaedo* myth, as Rowe rightly observes, allows it to 'provide efficiently for the reward and punishment of the good and bad after their "death"'.[58] In this context he further notes how one of the myth's 'strangest aspects' is that the mediocre souls on the Acherusian Lake are allowed to decide the length of the punishment of the evil souls circling on Cocytus or Pyriphlegethon. As he says, 'Apparently everything would depend on the whim of souls with somewhat less than perfect judgement', which 'hardly seems consistent with the kind of rational justice Socrates calls for in the *Apology*'.[59] He further points out that the condition of the middling souls on the Acherusian Lake seems puzzling:

---

[58] Rowe (2007a), 102.
[59] Ibid., 103.

> How, we may reasonably ask, will the uninitiated be purified in Hades by 'paying penalties' [...] if the cause of their 'impurity' was their lack of philosophy? Shouldn't they be getting some philosophy instead?[60]

To the question 'why does Plato have Socrates introduce so flawed a system for delivering justice in a supposedly just cosmos?', he offers a solution from two observations. The first is that 'the parts of the mythical penal system in question exhibit aspects of *ordinary* Athenian practice'.[61] The second is that Socrates in *Phaedo* (80d5–8) has introduced 'two different kinds of Hades'.[62] Rowe's resolution of the puzzle posed by the picture of justice at the Acherusian Lake is that:

> The myth [...] is *both* an account [...] of what awaits us after death, *and* an allegory of life as we live it now. Those middling souls are at their Acherusian lake even now, in life, punishing and rewarding each other [...] in the only way they know how, just as their philosophical counterparts are already in their heaven.[63]

I accept Rowe's reading of this scene and my interpretation of the Tartarus region as a bodily prison writ-large supports the point of this allegory. The innerworld rivers portray the nature of the confused and corrupt soul in the here-and-now. But I disagree with Rowe's conclusion that if the allegorical reading is right, 'the myth will after all have introduced rather little of substance, on the subject of our fate after death, that is not also contained or implied in the *Apology*'.[64] For it seems important to me that the myth illustrates not only the condition of the unenlightened soul in the here-and-now but also the *consequences* of this condition in the afterlife.

The discussion of *Phaedo* stresses that the unpurified souls of the dead remain in the physical sphere before returning to life on earth. Thus to the cyclical argument's conclusion (72d8–10)—'there really is such a thing as coming-to-life again, living people *are* born from the dead, and the souls of the dead exist'—the myth can specify exactly *which* souls of the dead are reborn and *where* in Hades they exist. It is made clear that the only souls reborn to the earthly hollows are the 'middling' souls. For their dwelling on the Acherusian Lake is described as the place (113a2–6):

> where the souls of most of those who have died arrive, and where, after they have stayed for certain appointed periods, some longer, some shorter, they are sent forth again into the generation of living things.   (tr. Gallop)

---

[60] Ibid., 104.
[61] Ibid., 105.
[62] Ibid., 106.
[63] Ibid., 107.
[64] Ibid., 108.

More importantly, the myth goes beyond the *Apology* in presenting how the journeys of souls in the afterlife *intensify* their human experiences. To Rowe's question about the souls on the Acherusian Lake—'Shouldn't they be getting some philosophy instead?', my answer is that they cannot philosophize here because this is part of the penalty for their failure to do so when they had the chance, in human life. On my reading, the different regions of 'Hades' in the geography of the myth represent the soul's level of attainment of abstract truth and, conversely, its assimilation and subjection to the physical. The various locations of the earth offer different physical environments and different opportunities for philosophy. By far the best *physical* place to seek knowledge is on the surface of the earth, where the soul's more perfect physical body does not degenerate at the same speed as its earthly one and is generally less harmful to it. This golden-age experience for the holy souls is both the reward for goodness and a further opportunity for philosophical purification. The second-best physical place to philosophize is in the earth's hollows, where the human philosophers seek to overcome their bodily limitations. But once one has missed the chance in the hollows of seeking the truth and living well, there remains only punishment in the underworld. There is an absence of philosophy in Tartarus because the lives available here offer no chance to gain knowledge through direct contemplation of truth. This afterlife existence is therefore inferior to life in a human body and so can be presented as a larger 'prison' of generation, where souls are subject to hitherto unimaginable physical pressures and distortions. In contrast to *all* of these earthly lives, the reward for being 'sufficiently' (*hikanôs*, 114c3) purified by philosophy is to escape physical incarnation altogether.

On this reading, the soul's chances of philosophizing are made better or worse as a *consequence* of its previous life which leads directly to its current location in the earth's regions. And this point is more than an allegory for life in the here-and-now, since it also makes clear that access to abstract truth through contemplation is not equally available in all regions and lives. On this perspective, it is important that the middling souls on Acheron cannot do philosophy—for this is precisely part of their punishment.

Inwood's interpretation of the souls' periods spent in the underworld fails to take into account that its nature here is compromised even further than it is in human life. Considering the question of what the soul remembers in its different stages of life, he observes:

> The most important parts of my career will be the periods I spend in the underworld, for they are much longer than my earthly lives and also contain more vivid and enduring memories than I have in my lives. My earthly lives

will be related to my periods in the underworld rather in the way that my
dreams are related to my waking experience in this life.[65]

Inwood goes on to imagine the underworld as offering a soul the chance
'to contemplate these diverse lives in one's interludes of disembodiment'.[66]
But on my reading this is exactly the sort of situation that Plato rules out
in the myth of *Phaedo*, where the length of time in the underworld is not
a break from incarnation, during which one might contemplate earthly life
at leisure, but rather a deeper and more corrosive experience of physical
limitations which dulls the soul's powers still further. As Sedley has pointed
out, the different 'zones' in the myth of *Phaedo*, those 'both below and
above our level', are places 'to which souls pass at the appropriate stages
of their purification, until they are finally altogether purged of their bodily
leanings'.[67] Thus it is more appropriate to see a hierarchy of experiences,
where all of the regions of the earth are places of purification, from the
Tartarus rivers as the worst to the outer surface of the earth as the best, and
where the types of purification and cognitive activity are correspondingly
relative.

To assess what types of cognitive activities or thoughts are possible for the
impure souls in the Tartarus region, let us follow Plato's scale. The philosophers are the highest class of souls. Already purified by philosophy they
are transported to the purest regions beyond the physical earth—a fully
abstract realm that will delight the rational soul. The earth's surface is a
blessed region for the seeker of truth, since it provides ultimate answers on
the nature of the world. In this pure environment of truth (*ho alêthôs ouranos kai to alêthinon phôs kai hê hôs alêthôs gê*, 109e7–110a1) the human beings
'surpass us in wisdom' (*phronêsei*, 111b4), they see the sun, moon and stars
'as they really are' (111c1–2), and they have 'awareness' of and direct 'communion' with very gods (*aisthêseis, sunousias*, 111b8–9). Finally, even in the
misty hollows there is enough truth to allow philosophy. But, moving down-
wards to the underworld, what picture is given of the cognitive capacities
of souls judged to be impure? The middling souls on the Acherusian Lake
undergo purification for their injustice but also receive 'honours' for their
good deeds, reflecting, as Rowe astutely notes, their '"demotic", unphilosophical excellence'.[68] These souls can differentiate between good and evil
and their purgation must, presumably, involve some level of reflection on

[65] Inwood (2009), 34.
[66] Ibid., 38.
[67] Sedley (1995), 9.
[68] Rowe (2007a), 104.

the mistakes of their former lives and their current consequences. But there is no suggestion that their analysis is secure or that they are able to connect properly with truth. Subject to the instability of Tartarus the souls on the Acherusian Lake are, even in the best-case scenario, simply spending time paying their penalty, waiting however long it takes to return to their more meaningful lives above. The curably evil souls experience greater turmoil cast into the rivers of punishment but their once-a-year opportunity, as they pass near the Acherusian Lake, to seek clemency from their victims shows that each has sufficient cognitive capacity still to make an appeal and, potentially, to merit rehabilitation through purgation with the others on the Lake.[69] But the depiction of the incurably evil souls shows no rational or purposeful activity whatsoever: completely subject to the overwhelming force of the Tartarus tides, they are merely washed back and forth, passive for eternity. Their story, for me, allows no exercise of cognitive faculties beyond the very minimum level of awareness needed to make suffering possible.

The myth, then, presents a vision where the chance to philosophize is *itself* the reward for goodness and is available only in special circumstances. The corrupted souls in the afterlife, cut off from their all-too-brief chances to exercise their reason properly, become increasingly blunted in their perceptions and awarenesses as a result of their relative experiences of the distorting effects of the ontologically unstable region of Tartarus. In this way Plato's myth is uncompromising: certain souls are so assimilated to the physical and so detached from abstract truth that they lose their ability to reason, the core of their identity.

3.5. *Tartarus and Reincarnation*

In Annas' view the myth of *Phaedo* is 'confused and confusing'.[70] The main problem she identifies is that reincarnation (introduced at 81d–82a) has not been 'successfully combined' with afterlife judgement. She concludes: 'No way is offered, in the *Phaedo*, to reconcile these different sets of ideas'.[71] I reject Annas' interpretation and will explain how it arises from a misunderstanding of the Tartarus region.

---

[69] Rowe (2007a), 103 is right to be concerned that allocating a role in actual judgement to the victims on the Acherusian Lake would raise questions of their judicial competence and the relation of their verdicts to those of the underworld judges. But perhaps the purpose of the appeal is to suggest how the *hope* of a possible 'transfer' would provide the curable soul with an opportunity for self-reflection and so represent how the process of internal reform might begin.

[70] Annas (1982), 125.

[71] Ibid., 127.

Annas rightly notes that in this dialogue there is a 'repeated insistence that the best fate for a soul is permanent escape from the body, and that being returned to a body is appropriate as a punishment'.[72] She then observes that the myth's identification of a way *back* from Hades to earth (107d5–e4) 'leads us to expect that reward and punishment after death will consist in appropriate reincarnations'. This may be a reasonable expectation but this story is not the one Plato chooses to tell. Annas then explains how the idea of reincarnation 'has not been grafted successfully on to the basic judgement myth':

> We begin with souls going to Hades and returning after appropriate treatment, in a context that strongly suggests that the punishment is the reincarnation attaching soul to a new body. But then we move on to the cosmologically transposed version of the judgement myth, and find quite a different set of ideas: now the souls are judged and then rewarded or punished not in another life here but in the afterlife there, not by appropriate reincarnation but more traditionally, by torture in hell or bliss in heaven.[73]

She sees the 'lack of fit' as showing up 'sharply' at 114c2–6. Noting that the good souls are rewarded here with a life 'in a heaven', while those purified by philosophy will be released from their bodies, she regards the philosopher as 'aiming at escape from reincarnation'.[74] The difficulty she sees is that 'this presupposes that those less perfect are rewarded, but are still not free from being reincarnated'. The problem is explained in more detail:

> If the philosophers' reward is final disembodiment, then the Isles of the Blessed, the second-best reward of the non-philosophical good, will have to represent some kind of embodiment. Yet this has been put forward as a repulsive punishment, whereas the Isles of the Blessed must symbolize some afterlife reward.[75]

Edmonds gets into similar difficulties:

> The best interpretation seems to be that the idea of reincarnation and the idea of endless disembodiment in torment or bliss are meant to be considered separately rather than as parts of a coherent system.[76]

These interpretations overlook the subtlety of the myth's portrayal of embodiment and reincarnation and involve various errors.

---

[72] Ibid.
[73] Ibid.
[74] Ibid., 127–128.
[75] Ibid., 128.
[76] Edmonds (2004), 218, n. 179.

Annas regards the judgement in Hades as 'final' and cites as problematic a claim that is not actually made in the text:

> The final morally rectifying judgement is still there, together with vivid pictures of the afterlife; and they are unreconciled with the idea that the only appropriate punishment for bad souls is rebirth into another body.[77]

First, the judgements in Hades are not uniformly 'final'. Plato's story, in addition to the cyclic argument, sets out that some souls of the dead travel both to and from Hades. On each return to the afterlife a soul will therefore need to be judged anew, to take account of its recent life and in order to determine its onward journey. So while some, *exceptional* souls—namely the wholly purified and the incurably evil—will receive a *final* judgement after a particular life, most souls of the dead will continue to receive ongoing judgements as they go around the cycle of life and death. Second, the claim is never made in *Phaedo* that the 'only' appropriate penalty for bad souls is rebirth. To respond to Edmonds, the souls in torment in Tartarus, just as those in bliss on the surface of the earth, are not disembodied, since that privilege is reserved for the philosophical souls alone. While the text is silent on whether these purified souls would ever face reincarnation (although it would seem unlikely), it does rule out the incurable souls returning to human life, since these souls will 'nevermore' leave Tartarus (113e6). But these two minorities at the extremes of good and evil do not affect the continuing reincarnations of the majority of 'middling' souls.[78] In addition, the golden-age bodies of the holy souls are merely 'longer-lived' than ours, not immortal, which suggests that at some point even these souls will be judged again in Hades, leading either to appropriate reincarnation or full release.

What Annas and Edmonds both miss is that the myth presents a *scale* of punishments and rewards, on which embodiment features at different levels, in contexts of both punishment *and* reward. The human beings living on the surface of the earth are embodied—but with bodies far superior to those in the misty hollows. Nevertheless, this embodied golden-age life remains an inferior experience to the final disembodied state where the limitations of physical incarnation are overcome completely. Thus the Isles

---

[77] Annas (1982), 127.

[78] Since 'most of those who have died' arrive at the Acherusian Lake (113a2–3) and since the only souls here are the 'middling' ones (113d4), it is clear that the majority of the souls of the dead is made up of those neither good nor bad. This point is fully consistent with Socrates' explicit statement at 89e–90a: 'one would surely have recognized the truth, that extremely good and bad people are both very few in number, and the majority lie in between' (tr. Gallop).

of the Blessed are simultaneously a place of embodiment and reward. In the same way, life on the Acherusian Lake is better than life on Pyriphlegethon or Cocytus but—since still dominated by the physics of Tartarus—worse than human life in the hollows, where philosophy can free the soul from physical influence. Thus, *contra* Annas, I contend that the geography of the true earth, with its *scale* of experiences of embodiment, is precisely the way that Plato reconciles afterlife judgement and reincarnation.[79]

CONCLUSION

The myth of *Phaedo* reveals inside the earth a place the poets intuited as grim. Plato transforms the Hades of traditional Greek myth and explains exactly why, in his terms, the place is to be feared. Tartarus, once simply a pit in the depths of the earth, becomes the central feature of a terrifying landscape: a ceaseless, mechanical swing causing the turbulent tides of the mighty underworld rivers. Following the verdict of underworld judges, impure souls are punished by imprisonment in this gigantic bodily system, where moral and cognitive weakness binds them ever more deeply into an unstable world devoid of reason. For these souls philosophy is impossible, since this region allows no direct contemplation of true reality. The failure during human life to exercise and develop rational capacities brings in the afterlife an intensification of physical disturbance and corruption, further alienating the soul from its true rational nature. On the principle of assimilation if a soul loses contact with abstract truth, the ground of all ontological security, it will itself become deeply unstable. But there is also hope and reassurance: if a soul lives an exceptionally holy life, it can gain access, after death, to more blessed lives and, if sufficiently purified by philosophy, can win release altogether from the instability of incarnation. As an alternative to the ongoing circle of earthly life and death, in successive physical realms of change and decay, Plato's map of the earth traces a single linear route to freedom from generation: an escape to bliss through abstract enquiry and attainment of truth. The topography of the myth provides not only an allegory for the condition of soul as it experiences various lives but

---

[79] Annas' final objection to the myth (128) is that the idea of 'some place "still better" leaves us looking in vain for some place to put [the philosophers] within what we have been told is the *whole* universe described to us so far'. But we have not been told that this is the whole 'universe': Socrates' myth presents rather the true nature of the 'whole *earth*' (ὅλην [...] τὴν γῆν, 111c4)—something quite different.

also a vision of afterlife punishments and rewards as direct consequences of a soul's earlier incarnation. Therefore the story of Tartarus, with its complex ethical, ontological and epistemological layers, plays an important teleological role in supporting Plato's arguments for a rationally-ordered and just universe.

CHAPTER TWELVE

CHOICE OF LIFE AND
SELF-TRANSFORMATION IN THE MYTH OF ER

Annie Larivée

Of all the questions that the myth of Er raises, the question concerning its relation to the rest of the *Republic* is one of the most pressing. The aim of the interpretation that I propose here is to demonstrate the continuity of Socrates' investigations throughout the *Republic*, including the myth of Er, by taking the theme of the choice of life as the guiding thread. Indeed, Socrates' principal goal in relating the myth of Er is the same as in all of the complex philosophical argumentation deployed up to that point: to demonstrate that the choice of a certain *bios* is of crucial importance for the becoming of the soul.[1] However, in spite of this continuity, the difference in the orientation of the questioning in the myth of Er and the rest of the dialogue is, at first glance, striking. Indeed, whereas the challenge put to Socrates by Glaucon and Adeimantus at the beginning of book II is to demonstrate that the just and virtuous life is intrinsically superior when it comes to securing happiness, the myth of Er is centred rather on the impact of physical, social and material conditions on the becoming of the soul— here described as being immortal and bound to a cycle of reincarnation. It is the nature of this complex thematic unity that I aim to clarify in this article.[2] My analysis will proceed in three stages. First, I will discuss the peculiar and apparently incongruous character of the question of choice of life in the myth of Er in relation to Socrates' famous exhortation to care primarily for the soul. To resolve the apparent paradox that results from this comparison,

---

[1] Socrates' challenge consists in presenting a 'defence of justice' proving that *the most desirable life, the happiest existence* is that of the just man rather than that of the vicious man who has secured wealth, fame and political power by only appearing to be honest. It is for the sake of evaluating the relative worth of these two opposed *bioi* that Socrates endeavours to reveal, with the aid of an analogy between the individual soul and the *polis*, the intrinsically desirable quality of justice. On *way of life* as the stakes central to Socrates' argumentation, see *Rep*. I, 344e1–2, 347e4–5, 352d3–4, II 360e1 ff. and 578c7–8.

[2] Thayer (1988) emphasizes the unity but misses the tension that I want to investigate here.

I will then endeavour to clarify, by relying on two crucial passages from books IV and VIII, the nature of the causal relationship between the choice of life conditions, actions and virtuous disposition of the soul. Finally, in light of the preceding analysis, the last part of this text will be dedicated to the protreptic function of the myth and to its possible use as a tool of self-transformation.

1. That Which Is
the Object of Choice According to the Myth

From a thematic perspective, the myth of Er can be divided into five main parts:

1. What happened to Er after his 'death,' presentation of his initiatory journey (614b–615a)
2. What was taught to Er about the judgement of souls: the punishments and retributions (615a–616b)
3. Er's vision of what supports the cosmic order (616b–617d)
4. Explanations concerning the responsibility of souls in the choice of their next incarnation, and Socrates' general reflections on the mixing of the diverse components of a life (617d–621a)
5. Conclusion of the story, where the journey of the souls towards incarnation is described (621a–621d).

While parts 1, 2, 3, and 5 are essentially narrative, the fourth part, which concerns the choice of a life by souls preparing to be reincarnated, has clear philosophical implications. Rather than being content with the mere reporting of Er's discourse, Socrates speaks in his own name, explaining why the choice of a model or pattern of life is of primary importance for human beings.[3] The fact that Socrates speaks directly here in order to draw out lessons justifies paying special attention to this passage and this is why my analysis will focus on this fourth part. It is true that Socrates introduces the myth of Er in order to evoke the rewards and punishments that await the soul in the afterlife, which seems to indicate that the second part of the myth is the most essential. However, the altogether summary character

---

[3] I thus disagree with Druet (1998), 28, when he claims that 'Socrate accorde tout crédit à Er; il se contente, ici et là, d'émonder un récit rendu touffu par l'abondance des détails'. Between 618b6 and 619b1, Socrates addresses himself to Glaucon and brings out the myth's philosophical lesson. Strictly speaking, this section does not thus constitute a 'niveau de récit,' a 'level of narrative'.

of the description of these retributions—that primarily dwells, as Karel Thein notes, on the duration rather than on the qualitative nature of those punishments and rewards[4]—suggests on the contrary that this element occupies a secondary place in the *Republic* (in opposition to the treatment of the eschatological myth in the *Gorgias*, for example, where the principal theme is that of judgement and retributions).[5]

In fact, the most remarkable and singular idea expressed in the myth is, without a doubt, the responsibility that each soul has concerning the choice of its next earthly incarnation. At first glance, we may think that Plato is attempting to provide a mythical answer to the philosophical problem of moral responsibility—a problem which will later be discussed by Aristotle in Chapter Five of Book III of the *Nicomachean Ethics*.[6] The man who acts under the impulse of anger or the influence of alcohol does not act in a fully conscious or voluntary manner. Nevertheless, his actions were caused by certain dispositions of his soul: the fact that he was violent while in a state of drunkenness having been indirectly caused by intemperance for example. And should this person not be held responsible for his character, the dispositions of his soul, for the fact of being, for instance, a quick-tempered person, intemperate or negligent? In other words, is he not responsible for what he *is*? Aristotle's answer is both simple and subtle. This man is certainly not—*now*—making the deliberate choice to be as he is (alcoholic, intemperate, and negligent). In fact, it may no longer be in his power to modify his mode of being.[7] But he nevertheless remains responsible for having *become* the way he is.[8] We are thus responsible not only for our actions, but also for

---

[4] Thein (2001), 104.

[5] As Ferrari (2009), 126 explains: 'Of all Plato's eschatological myths, the myth of Er is the most rooted in the problems of mortal life. Socrates' story deals hardly at all with the rewards of justice in the afterlife. Instead, both the moral and the narrative weight of Socrates' story is carried by its account of how each soul is caught in a cycle of reincarnation and is compelled to choose its next embodied life'. For a comparative analysis on the theme of retribution in the *Gorgias*, the *Phaedo* and the *Republic*, see Annas (1982).

[6] See Dixsaut (2000), 115 ff.

[7] 'If someone does, not in ignorance, the things that will result in his being unjust, he will be unjust voluntarily—and yet, he will not stop being unjust, and be just, merely if he wishes it. For no more will the sick person be healthy merely for wishing it; [...] Previously, then, he had the option not to be ill, but once he has let himself go, he no longer has it' (*Nicomachean Ethics* (= *EN*) III, 5, 1114a12–21, Broadie & Rowe [2002] translation). See also *EN* III, 5, 1113b30–1114a10.

[8] 'But perhaps the agent is the kind of person not to take care? But we are ourselves responsible for having become this sort of person, by living slackly [...]for it is the sort of activity we display in each kind of thing that gives us the corresponding character' (*EN*, III, 5, 1114a5–10).

what we have become, for our acquired dispositions. With the myth of Er, is Plato attempting to establish, in the garb of myth, the same type of responsibility? According to the story of Er, we are completely responsible for our life, having chosen the components of our present existence ourselves. We chose ourselves, so to speak, and we thus owe it to ourselves to be who we are. Furthermore, if we have been negligent while making our choice, not having taken the time to properly examine all the elements included in the life which was the object of our preference, we are nevertheless responsible for having been negligent.[9] The famous formula 'an unexamined life is not liveable for a human being' thus takes on a particular meaning here.[10] However, to adequately grasp Plato's intention, one must be attentive to what is designated, exactly, in the myth of Er, when the choice of a life is at issue. Indeed, the problem raised here is somewhat different from what we find in Book III of the *Nicomachean Ethics*.

First, we find two instances of the claim that we do not choose a life which is, in itself, virtuous or vicious. Virtue does not figure in the choice which concerns us here.[11] This aspect contrasts with Socrates' investigation in the rest of the *Republic* because, as we know, the examination is aimed at demonstrating the superiority of the just person's way of life over that of the unjust person when it comes to attaining *eudaimonia*.[12] The choice was thus about leading a virtuous life or not. Neither is it really, in the myth of Er, a question of the choice of a life as a form of activity as is the case in the *Philebus* or in the *Nicomachean Ethics* where the respective merits of a life devoted to pleasure, a life devoted to exercise of intelligence, etc. are examined. Here, the choice bizarrely involves all those characteristics which we generally believe are precisely *not* subject to choice or which, in any case, are partially subject to chance and often belong to the domain

---

[9] The importance of attention, of care, is highlighted many times in the myth of Er; it is indeed appropriate to make a choice on the basis of philosophical examination and not merely on habit. See 618c1, 619a, 619c–d, and the allusion to the plain of *Lethe* and to the River of Forgetfulness at 621a–b, the theme of which is the subject of Vernant's (1965) text.

[10] The sentence which opens the most philosophical part of the passage I examine (ἔνθα δή [...]ὁ πᾶς κίνδυνος ἀνθρώπῳ, 618b7) recalls not only the 'noble risk' of the *Phaedo* ('καλὸς γὰρ ὁ κίνδυνος ...,' 114d6), but also the 'ὁ δὲ ἀνεξέταστος βίος οὐ βιωτὸς ἀνθρώπῳ' of the *Apology* (38a5–6). The link with the *Phaedo* has been underlined by Morgan (2000), 207–208.

[11] See *Rep.* X, 617e3–4 and *Rep.* X, 618b3–4. At 618c, the soul's dispositions are mentioned, but only insofar as the good or bad effects of adding a particular characteristic (poverty or wealth for example) to a particular disposition of the soul (τινὸς ψυχῆς ἕξεως) must be calculated. I will comment on these passages in the second part.

[12] See the textual references mentioned in n. 1.

of the uncontrollable.[13] We touch upon an aspect of ethical reflection in ancient thought to which Bernard Williams and Martha Nussbaum have accorded special attention in their works on the link between moral life and luck.[14] In fact, to be precise, what is chosen is not a way of life, but a 'model,' a 'pattern' of life (literally a paradigm of life, *biou paradeigma*). In other words, the object of choice refers to a set of components forming a sort of 'package deal'. Here are, in order, the characteristics enumerated at 618a–b and at 618c–d:

618a–b:

- belonging to humankind/to an animal species
- having a specific social function (e.g.: tyrant)[15]
- having a life with a happy/unhappy end (life ending in poverty, exile, beggary)
- having a reputation for physical strength, aptitude for competitions, ascendancy and the quality of ancestors/absence of reputation in the same domains
- being male/female
- the mixture of these diverse characteristics with the following conditions: wealth, poverty, sickness, good health, mean between the extremes

618c–d:

- beauty
- poverty/wealth
- high/low births

---

[13] Inwood (2009), 45: '… what a soul chooses in the underworld is precisely what it does not choose in life. What it chooses in the underworld is the 'facticity' of its life, the unchosen setting in which its choices are made'. Ferrari (2009), 129 is astounded that the philosophic life is not 'on display'. There is, however, nothing shocking in that because philosophy is an activity and not a life condition. It is rendered possible or improbable by certain life conditions.

[14] It is in fact unfortunate that Nussbaum (1986) does not offer an analysis of the myth of Er in *The Fragility of Goodness*, a book she dedicated to the issue of chance and the uncontrollable aspects which affect human life. Her work was inspired by Williams' seminal texts in *Moral Luck* (1981). See also his *Shame and Necessity* (1993).

[15] It is surprising that Plato does not mention here the possibility of being born a slave. It is true that this situation (that no-one would freely choose) threatens the plausibility of his myth. On the radical change of identity that results from emancipation in Antiquity—'the most complete metamorphosis one can imagine'—see Williams (1993), 108.

- leading a private existence/assuming a position of leadership
- possession/lack of physical strength
- facility/difficulty in learning
- 'all the things that are either naturally part of the soul or can be acquired by it, when they are mixed with one another (*sugkerannumena*)'

It is surprising to realize that the choice involves not only the conditions which we generally consider as being the outcome of chance (sex, physical characteristics, intelligence, social origin, certain external events)—aspects to which I will return in the third part—, but equally elements that are generally held in contempt in the Platonic (or Socratic) hierarchy of care, a hierarchy in which bodily goods and external goods usually come last. This hierarchy, central to the *Alcibiades*, is well-known: one must care first and foremost for the virtue of the soul since this is what caring for the self means.[16] As for what most people desire and pursue (positions of leadership, reputation, bodily strength or pleasures, wealth), these must not be cared for, or, at least not in any privileged way.[17] Far from being a theme specific to the *Apology*, the *Alcibiades* and other Socratic dialogues, this idea can equally be found in the *Republic*. Now, strangely enough, in the myth of Er, the object of choice seems to be what Socrates invited one and all *not to* care about (or at least not primarily)! Indeed, in the myth, Socrates emphatically claims that each person must take care (*epimeleteon*) to acquire the knowledge allowing for the best possible choice concerning these life conditions while neglecting (*amelêsas*) all other subjects of study.[18] How may we resolve this apparent contradiction then?

2. On the Complex Relation between Life Conditions, Actions, and Disposition of the Soul

I will now concentrate my analysis on two crucial passages that conclude Socrates' arguments in books IV and VIII. We will see that the kind of relationship that Socrates establishes between life conditions, actions, and

---

[16] See *Alc.* 129b1–130c1.

[17] See *Ap.* 36b5–d1.

[18] 'Here [...] a human being faces the greatest danger of all, and because of that each must, to the neglect of all other subjects, take care above all else to be a seeker and student of that subject which will enable him to learn and discover who will give him the ability and the knowledge to distinguish a good life from a bad ...' (*Rep.* X, 618c1–3). I will return to this crucial passage in the third part.

the virtuous or vicious disposition of the soul will allow us to elucidate the apparent contradiction that emerges in the myth of Er. Let us begin with the passage at the end of book IV. Having arrived at the definition of justice, which he describes as an internal unification and harmonization of the different functions of the soul, Socrates concludes his account with a depiction of the just man's attitude towards external and bodily goods:

> Then and only then [once he is 'harmonized'] should he turn to action, whether it is to do something concerning the acquisition of wealth or concerning the care of his body, or even something political, or concerning private contracts. In all these areas, he considers and calls just and fine the action that preserves this inner harmony and helps achieve it, and wisdom the knowledge that oversees such action; and he considers and calls unjust any action that destroys this harmony, and ignorance the belief that oversees it.[19]   (*Rep.* IV, 443e2–444a1)

I now turn to the second passage, situated at the end of book VIII. To put the finishing touch on his praise of justice—after having described the soul as a composite creature—Socrates evokes once again the necessity for the just man to subordinate the other objects of care to the care of the soul. He begins by explaining that 'he won't make health his aim nor give precedence to the ways of becoming strong or healthy or beautiful, unless he is also going to become temperate as a result of them. On the contrary, it is clear that he will always be tuning the harmony of his body for the sake of the concord of his soul' (591c7–d3). He then further explains that such a man will 'also keep order and concord in his acquisition of money' (591d6), and will 'guard against disturbing anything there either with too much money or with too little. Captaining himself in that way, he will increase and spend his wealth, as far as possibly by reference to it' (591e1–4). The same holds for honours. Indeed, 'he will willingly share in and taste those he believes will make him better,' explains Socrates, 'but those that might overthrow the established condition of his soul, he will avoid, both in private and in public' (592a1–592a4).

The primary lessons imparted in these two passages are, it seems to me, similar. Socrates does not say that we should neglect those things that do not directly concern virtue and the care of the soul. Nevertheless, our actions

---

[19] οὕτω δὴ πράττειν ἤδη, ἐάν τι πράττῃ ἢ περὶ χρημάτων κτῆσιν ἢ περὶ σώματος θεραπείαν ἢ καὶ πολιτικόν τι ἢ περὶ τὰ ἴδια συμβόλαια, ἐν πᾶσι τούτοις ἡγούμενον καὶ ὀνομάζοντα δικαίαν μὲν καὶ καλὴν πρᾶξιν ἣ ἂν ταύτην τὴν ἕξιν σῴζῃ τε καὶ συναπεργάζηται, σοφίαν δὲ τὴν ἐπιστατοῦσαν ταύτῃ τῇ πράξει ἐπιστήμην, ἄδικον δὲ πρᾶξιν ἣ ἂν ἀεὶ ταύτην λύῃ, ἀμαθίαν δὲ τὴν ταύτῃ αὖ ἐπιστατοῦσαν δόξαν. I am using Reeve's (2004) translation of the *Republic*. For all other dialogues, I will use those translations included in Cooper and Hutchinson (1997).

and our life conditions (material, bodily, social) have nothing other than a subordinate value. They are important only insofar as they can promote and preserve the good state of the soul and we may only evaluate them in terms of their impact on the *psuchê*. Furthermore, the second passage stresses the potentially deleterious effects that certain life conditions could have on the soul; it seems that Socrates is more concerned with their disruptive influence than with any positive role that they could play. This insistence on the disruptive aspect of life conditions echoes the passage on the corruption of the philosophic nature where we find that, far from becoming better, the soul becomes corrupted by its own talents and by those conditions that seem most favourable (nobility, beauty, wealth).[20] Life conditions—even those that seem favourable—are an important factor in the degradation of the soul's *taxis*; they enable certain actions that affect, in turn, the soul that performs them.[21] This crucial role that life conditions play in the becoming of the soul is equally well illustrated in the distinction that Socrates makes in book IX between the individual with a tyrannical disposition who remains a private citizen and the one who, having inherited political power, has the 'misfortune' of obtaining the life conditions of a true tyrant.[22] Those seemingly favourable life conditions open the door to actions that will ultimately ruin this soul entirely.[23]

We now return to the myth of Er to see if the teachings of Socrates in this myth differ in any fundamental way from the position he maintained earlier in the *Republic* when he declared that those actions undertaken out of consideration for life conditions should first be subject to the consideration for their (possibly damaging) effect on the soul. First, let us consider the

---

[20] See *Rep.* VI, 491c1–3: 'The most surprising thing of all to hear is that each one of the things we praised in that nature tends to corrupt the soul that has it and drag it away from philosophy. [...] Furthermore, in addition to those, all so-called good things also corrupt it and drag it away—beauty, wealth, physical strength, powerful family connections in the city, and all that goes along with these'.

[21] On the deleterious effect of life conditions, we could equally refer to the passage from book VIII where Socrates explains how the family milieu (in the context of certain constitutions) causes the degeneration of character that finally results in a tyrannical soul 547c ff.

[22] IX, 577e5–579d7. The most miserable man is 'the tyrannical man who does not live out his life as a private individual, but is unlucky, in that some misfortunes gives him the opportunity of becoming an actual tyrant' (578c1–3). See Inwood (2009), 29–31.

[23] '... we said that he is inevitably envious, untrustworthy, unjust, friendless, impious, and a host and nurse to every kind of vice; that ruling makes him even more so than before ...', *Rep.* IX, 580a1–3. Inwood (2009), 29 goes still further when he writes: 'A wrong act is not only or even primarily something that is caused by one's vice, but something that causes one's soul to be bad or vicious'.

absence of virtue among the elements that the souls can choose. This absence is explicitly underlined when the hierophant announces: 'Virtue has no master: as he honours or dishonours it, so shall each of you have more or less of it' (617e3–4). At first glance, this declaration seems to refute the pessimism of the interpreters who insist on the fatalism of the myth of Er: regardless of one's material or bodily condition, the soul nevertheless reserves the ability to determine its own course and to cultivate virtue.[24] Er's remarks as related by Socrates, however, differ somewhat from the hierophant's account. He asserts (here it becomes difficult to distinguish the voice of Er and that of Socrates)[25] that the *taxis* of the soul is not part of the package deal chosen by the individual preparing to be reincarnated, not because it would be possible for the soul to honour virtue regardless of the circumstances, but rather because in being incarnated, the soul preserves its precedent *taxis* which in turn will be affected by its new life conditions: 'the order (*taxis*) of the soul was not included, because with the choice of a different life it would inevitably become different'.[26] In being incarnated, the soul is thus thrown into a process of becoming that is conducive to affecting its disposition.

---

[24] I distinguish here between prospective fatalism and retrospective fatalism. For the former see Annas (1983), 134 who declares that all of the elements of the life to come are predetermined by the selection of a life-pattern in the afterlife: 'the foolish soul has chosen not just what kind of person he will be but absolutely everything that will happen to him'. This deterministic interpretation seems to me erroneous. Even though certain outstanding events are mentioned as constituting a part in the chosen pattern of life (the tyrant destined to eat his children in 619c1) this does not imply that all the events in a future life are predetermined by the choice of certain conditions of existence. Rather what we have is the basic framework for the life and a few outstanding external events. Despite certain circumstantial pressures, it is always possible to act in a virtuous manner (note that the text does not tell us whether the tyrant of 619c will eat his children willingly). I thus concur with Inwood (2009), 29 when he says, on the topic of 'powerful politicians' who share the fate of the incurables in Tartarus: 'This is not to say that a king or a tyrant inevitably does wrong; they can resist the temptations that offer themselves, but most of them do not'. As regards retrospective fatalism, it is well exemplified by Dixsaut (2000), 114, who writes: 'Celui qui choisit qui il sera fait ce choix en fonction de qui il était. Avant le choix, donc, un autre choix, et ainsi de suite à l'infini, si bien que le moment d'un premier choix, d'un choix qui ne serait pas déjà prédéterminé par un autre, est proprement inassignable'. Cf. Annas (1982), 132 f. As I will demonstrate in the third section, I believe for my part that this kind of pessimism is countered by what Inwood (2009), 29–30 calls 'the libertarian spirit of the myth'. That a choice has been preceded by others does not diminish its own importance as Socrates emphasizes at 618b7.

[25] As Halliwell (2007), 450 notes, the narrative is 'filtered, as it were, through Socrates' own poetic-authorial voice'.

[26] *Rep.* X, 618b2–4, translation slightly modified.

I open a parenthesis here to emphasize that this phase of transformation contrasts with the experience of the soul in the afterlife in that the latter seems to be characterized by a curious lack of progress. Indeed, insofar as the retributive sojourn lasts one thousand years, be it in the celestial or the subterranean region, we might expect that in this time the soul would evolve considerably, that it would learn (not only by 'digesting' the events of its past life but also by gaining from the experiences acquired in this milieu). This, however, does not appear to be the case given that the souls, on the point of making their choices after a thousand years of recompense or punishment, follow the tendencies and tastes that were developed in their prior existence.[27] Not only have these souls kept their identities from their previous incarnations, but the orientation of their desires also remains determined by their earthly experience from a millennium ago.[28] The souls apparently have not changed much at all. Indeed, the punished souls have learned to make their choice more cautiously.[29] It is clear, however, that the privileged occasion for the transformation of the soul and the shaping of the self remains its incarnate life. This is because incarnation appears to be simultaneously a test and a unique opportunity to work upon the self in a context where it is susceptible to change, as Socrates emphasizes. The crucial period for the becoming of the soul is the one where it finds itself embodied.[30] And the *taxis* is not a component of the chosen life-pattern since it is rather one of those rare components of the soul that is transmitted from one incarnation to the next, endures trials and is transformed by its new incarnation.

I close the parenthesis now and turn back to the initial question: that of the coherence or the contradiction between the Socratic exhortation to privilege the soul's virtue, and the fact that this element seems to be absent from the 'package deal' selected by the soul in the myth of Er. Is there a paradox here? Socrates' account of the finality of the choice of

---

[27] 620a2–3: 'For the most part, their choice reflected the character of their former life'.

[28] On the persistence of their desires, see Moors (1988), 58–59. The carrying on of their earthly identities is attested to by the fact that some of those souls recognize one another and greet one another upon their arrival to the meadow, returning from the subterranean or celestial realm, see 614e3–4.

[29] *Rep.* X, 619d3–5: 'The majority of those from the earth, on the other hand, because they had suffered themselves and had seen others doing so, were in no rush to make their choices'.

[30] I do not agree with Inwood's interpretation, which suggests that we conceive of the soul's time on earth as a dream from which it wakes upon dying. Imagining the soul's time on earth in this way neglects its importance for the becoming of the soul. See Inwood (2009), 34.

physical, material and social conditions clearly indicates that there is not. Indeed, according to his advice, the crucial element that should guide this decision is the way in which these 'external' elements risk affecting the soul by transforming its *taxis*. The 'package deal' must be chosen in light of its capacity to better the soul: 'on the basis of all that', explains Socrates, 'he [the one who makes his choice] will be able, by considering the nature of the soul,[31] to reason out which life is better and which worse and choose accordingly, calling worse the one that will lead the soul to become more unjust, and better the one that leads it to become more just' (*Rep.* X, 618d5–e2).[32] This part of the myth brings to light the way in which the soul can act indirectly on its *taxis* and shape itself through the choice of its life conditions. It makes clear that even if virtue is not directly included in the 'package deal' chosen by the soul, *aretê* remains the final objective of this choice after all. Thus the life pattern should be evaluated in accordance with a single criterion: its capacity to promote and preserve virtue.

Thus we conclude on this point by remarking that, according to the myth of Er, it turns out that the care of the soul is always the first priority but that its mode of operation is *indirect*. This is what distinguishes the lesson of the myth: it is here a question of the soul affecting itself, not directly and internally, but rather *through the device of the body and all of the facticity that accompanies incarnation*.[33] The myth awakens the soul's capacity for self-shaping and self-transformation by bringing the resources offered by the body, sex, social role, and life conditions into sharp relief.[34] The *psuchê*—and more precisely, its intelligence—retains its decisive role in that, according to the myth, it can assess in advance the impact of the diverse social, physical and material circumstances to which it will submit itself.[35] Yet another distinctive trait of the myth appears. The insistence on

---

[31] ... πρὸς τὴν τῆς ψυχῆς φύσιν ἀποβλέποντα, 618d6–7.

[32] See also 618c6–7 where it is written that one should 'calculate the effect of all the things we have mentioned [...] on the virtue of a life (ἀρετὴν βίου)'. The responsibility to mix life conditions in order to create virtue recalls the task Plato attributes to the legislator in the *Laws* for example, see Larivée (2003).

[33] I borrow this Sartre-inspired expression ('facticity') from Inwood (2009), 45.

[34] I use the term 'shaping' to echo the recurrent use of the verb *'plattein'* at 377a–c which evokes the manner in which the myth acts on the soul: 'We will persuade nurses and mothers to tell the acceptable ones to their children, and to spend far more time shaping their souls with these stories (καὶ πλάττειν τὰς ψυχὰς αὐτῶν τοῖς μύθοις) than they do shaping their bodies by handling them' (*Rep.* II, 377c3–4).

[35] The nature and role of this art of decision-making will be discussed in the third section.

the necessity of developing an art for choosing life-patterns emphasizes the positive capacity for exerting an influence on ourselves by paradoxically employing the apparatus of facticity, rather than insisting almost exclusively on the vulnerability of the soul in the face of conditions that threaten to corrupt it. This exhortation to develop a skill of decision-making, which lies at the heart of the myth of Er, reveals its protreptic nature. This brings me now to the intended effect of the myth of Er and the use that we may make of it.

3. THE POSSIBLE USES OF THE MYTH OF ER

Up until now, my aim has consisted in clarifying the reconcilable and complementary character of the philosophic part of the myth of Er and the position expressed by Socrates elsewhere in the *Republic* on the subordination of all objects of care to the care of the soul. My interpretation has therefore been centred on the semantic aspect (what it says) rather than on its function as a 'speech-act', its performative aspect.[36] Let us pose here the question of the desired effect of the myth of Er and of its possible uses, a question raised by Socrates in the text. Indeed, Socrates' final remark that this myth might 'save us' clearly indicates that the reader is not only invited to understand the story but to put it to active use. Before undertaking this task, we must raise a crucial hermeneutic question: should we interpret the myth of Er in a literal or allegorical fashion?

3.1. *Preliminary Hermeneutic Remarks: Literal or Allegorical Interpretation?*

To phrase it differently, the question that arises is the following: is Plato, through Socrates, asking us to truly believe in the transmigration of the soul and in the account of Er concerning the process of choice in the afterlife? Or rather, should we interpret the content of the myth simply as a symbolic way of calling to mind the life choices that we make here and now? The reincarnation of the soul, then, would simply represent through allegory the succession of our diverse 'selves' as they result from the choices that we make in the course of our immediate existence. This suggestion seems perfectly plausible if we recall the passage from the *Symposium* where

---

[36] I borrow the expression 'speech-act' from Morgan to describe the effect of the myth, Morgan (2000), 17.

Diotima explains that we are never the same in body or in soul,[37]—a passage which may be seen as a distant ancestor of contemporary philosophic debates on the question of personal identity that have arisen in the wake of Parfit's famous work.[38] As Halliwell has stressed, the allegoric interpretation has the advantage of resolving numerous problems of interpretation raised by the question of human souls being reincarnated in animal bodies and vice versa.[39] So, which do we choose: the literal or the allegorical reading? How to decide?

First, it seems that the simple recurrence of eschatological myths in Plato's works makes the allegorical interpretation unlikely. How can we explain these myths if their role is strictly instrumental? Must we believe that Plato employed these eschatological myths to realize an essentially political aim by acting on the fears of those individuals who would have no time or ability for philosophic arguments?[40] While we need not rule this possibility out, by no means should we take it to be the sole function of these myths. If this really were the case, Plato would not have felt the necessity to develop sophisticated philosophical arguments in favour of the immortality of the soul, arguments that are laid out in book X of the *Republic* (608d–612a) as well as in the *Phaedo*. These arguments indicate that Plato took this belief very seriously.[41] Furthermore, in book VI of the *Republic* we find a brief passage that proleptically alludes to the transmigration of the soul,

---

[37] 'Even while each living thing is said to be alive and to be the same–as a person is said to be the same from childhood till he turns into an old man—even then he never consists of the same things, though he is called the same, but he is always being renewed and in other respects passing away, in his hair and flesh and bone and blood and his entire body. And it's not just his body, but in his soul, too, for none of his manners, customs, opinions, desires, pleasures, pains, or fears ever remains the same, but some are coming to be in him while others are passing away' (*Symp.* 207d2–e5).

[38] Parfit (1984). It would be an interesting project to interpret the myth of Er in light of the components that Parfit regarded as more decisive for what matters in survival than personal identity; that is, psychological connectedness and continuity. Halliwell (2007), 462–463 offers certain reflections that could lead to undertaking such an analysis.

[39] What would become of a human's rational capacities once it is reincarnated as an animal? How would an animal understand the hierophant's instruction in the afterlife and go about making a decision? These questions are troubling for the reader who wishes to give the myth of Er a literal translation, as Halliwell (2007), 468 notes. On this problem, see also Inwood (2009), 37.

[40] In which case these myths would just be a form of the 'noble lie' ... Opinion expressed by Couturat as reported by Frutiger (1930), 15.

[41] As Morgan (2000), 209 puts it, 'the Myth of Er is the culmination of tendencies at work in the *Gorgias* and *Phaedo*. These final myths are constructed on the basis of reasoned argument and express a meta-logical intuition about the nature of the soul'.

later evoked in the myth of Er; a passage whose own brevity precludes the possibility of an allegorical interpretation.[42]

In fact, Plato's attitude towards eschatological stories is expressed in clear terms by Socrates in the *Phaedo*, and as such we should allow this description to guide our method of interpreting these myths. Inasmuch as it seems impossible to answer these questions with any great certainty despite the philosophic arguments in favour of the immortality of the soul, Socrates maintains that the best attitude consists in accepting this belief as a 'noble risk'.[43] In this way, if the soul really transmigrates, as suggested in the story of Er, we shall be ready. And if nothing of the sort occurs, well then, at least we will have lived in the best possible way (the important thing being not to live but to live well as Socrates makes clear in the *Crito*).[44] Indeed, we lead better lives if we believe in the immortality of the soul in that, according to Socrates, it increases our care of it.[45] This idea from the *Phaedo* (that the belief in the immortality of the soul could have benefits for our present life), is also evoked by Socrates at the end of the myth of Er. Indeed, when he declares that belief in this myth can, in a sense, 'save' us or 'protect' us,[46] he makes sure to emphasize that the adherence to this belief is beneficial not only in the hereafter, but also in the context of *this life*.[47]

In light of all this, my hermeneutic stance thus consists in a literal interpretation of the eschatological narrative in the myth of Er, but in the spirit of the *Phaedo*'s noble risk. That is to say, I propose a literal reading that pays special attention to the benefits that a belief in these myths grants for this incarnated life. The belief in the immortality and the transmigration of the soul accomplishes these benefits regardless of whether or not they are

---

[42] After Adeimantus expressed his worries over the negative reactions that Socrates' praise of true philosophers could possibly stir, especially from Thrasymachus, Socrates replies by saying: 'Please do not try to raise a quarrel between me and Thrasymachus just as we have become friends—not that we were enemies before. You see, we won't relax our efforts until we convince him and the other—or at least do something that may benefit them in a later incarnation when, reborn, they happen upon these arguments again' (*Rep.* VI, 498c9–d4).

[43] I have already pointed out (see note 10) how the sentence which begins the developments at 618b ('Here [...] a human being faces the greatest danger of all ...') echoes the *Phaedo*.

[44] See *Cr.* 48b5.

[45] *Phd.* 107c1–d5, 115b6–10.

[46] ἡμᾶς ἂν σώσειεν, ἂν πειθώμεθα αὐτῷ (*Rep.* X, 621b9).

[47] See 621c6–8: if we believe in the myth, 'we will be friends to ourselves and to the gods, both while we remain here (ἐνθάδε) on Earth and when we receive the rewards of justice'. See also 618e3–4 where it is said that this choice is as crucial for the living as it is for the dead.

founded (which remains unverifiable).[48] With these qualifications in mind, let us now pass on to the possible effects and uses of the myth of Er.

3.2. *The Protreptic Aim*

As suggested earlier, the most obvious practical effect that the philosophic part of the myth of Er aims for seems to be a protreptic effect.[49] Indeed, Socrates exhorts us, in order to prepare us to make the crucial choice of life, to develop a certain capacity. What exactly does this capacity consist in? One thing is certain: to make a good choice of life a good character grounded in good habits alone is not sufficient. The myth indeed insists on the wavering and fragile character of all 'virtue' which would depend merely on habit. At 619c6–8, Er explains that the one whose fate it was to choose first opted for a tyranny which ended in tragedy: this soul 'had come down from heaven, having lived his previous life in an orderly constitution, sharing in virtue through habit but without philosophy'. It seems then that the capacity that enables one to choose well can be described as *philosophy*. But the question then emerges: what exactly is designated by philosophy here? In fact, a little further on Socrates uncovers the nature of the capacity that he urges us to cultivate, which can be described as an art of discerning as well as an art of decision-making with regards to the choice of a life. The following passage is decisive; as such I will cite it in its entirety:

> Here it seems, my dear Glaucon, a human being faces the greatest danger of all, and because of that each must, to the neglect of all other subject, take care above all else to be a seeker and student of that subject which will enable him to learn and discover who will give him the ability and the knowledge to distinguish a good life from a bad, so that he will always and in any circumstances choose the better one from among those that are possible. He must calculate the effect of all the things we have mentioned just now, both jointly and severally, on the virtue of a life, so as to know what the good and bad effects of beauty are when it is mixed with wealth or poverty and this or that state of the soul; what the effects are of high and low birth, private lives and ruling offices, physical strength and weaknesses, ease and difficulties in learning, and all the things that are either naturally part of the soul or can be

---

[48] Therefore, the tension that Halliwell (2007), 469–472 perceives between the literal interpretation and the 'this-wordly' interpretation seems to me to be exaggerated.

[49] That is to say, a way of inviting one to practice a certain activity, here, philosophy, as an art of choosing one's way of life. On the ancient genre of the protreptic, see Jordan (1986), Slings (1995), Van der Merren (2002). According to Lieb (1963), 283, the purpose of the myth is to stabilize 'the order they [Socrates' interlocutors] have come to in the course of the dialogue'. This approach, I think, is compatible with a protreptic interpretation.

acquired by it, when they are mixed with one another. On the basis of all that he will be able, by considering the nature of the soul, to reason out which life is better and which worse and choose accordingly, calling worse the one that will lead the soul to become more unjust, and better the one that leads it to become more just. Everything else he will ignore. For we have seen that this is the best way to choose, whether in life or death.[50]   (*Rep.* X, 618b6–e4)

Let us attempt to analyze the various components of the capacity that Socrates invites us to cultivate. First, the competence in question implies a general knowledge of the 'nature of the soul'[51] and of its virtue (Socrates provides us with a brilliant picture of just this sort of knowledge in the rest of the *Republic*). It must also be accompanied by knowledge of the ways that various external conditions may affect the soul. And the competence in question here seems to be all the more complex because the mixing of various conditions produces different results. At 618c8 Socrates explains that in order to make the right choice, one must know what results from the addition of different conditions (such as beauty and poverty for example).[52] Knowing how to mix these life conditions, however, does not suffice. This is because the art of decision-making with which we are concerned here not only implies a familiarity with the nature of souls in general but it also implies a familiarity with the individual soul that will be affected by the choice of life. Indeed, Socrates specifies that one must also know what results from the combination and mixture of these conditions with specific dispositions of the soul.[53] Thus, it is not enough to master the art of combining life conditions or to possess a general knowledge about the

---

[50] ἔνθα δή, ὡς ἔοικεν, ὦ φίλε Γλαύκων, ὁ πᾶς κίνδυνος ἀνθρώπῳ, καὶ διὰ ταῦτα μάλιστα ἐπιμελη- τέον ὅπως ἕκαστος ἡμῶν τῶν ἄλλων μαθημάτων ἀμελήσας τούτου τοῦ μαθήματος καὶ ζητητὴς καὶ μαθητὴς ἔσται, ἐάν ποθεν οἷός τ' ᾖ μαθεῖν καὶ ἐξευρεῖν τίς αὐτὸν ποιήσει δυνατὸν καὶ ἐπιστήμονα, βίον καὶ χρηστὸν καὶ πονηρὸν διαγιγνώσκοντα, τὸν βελτίω ἐκ τῶν δυνατῶν ἀεὶ πανταχοῦ αἱρεῖσθαι· ἀναλογιζόμενον πάντα τὰ νυνδὴ ῥηθέντα καὶ συντιθέμενα ἀλλήλοις καὶ διαιρούμενα πρὸς ἀρετὴν βίου πῶς ἔχει, εἰδέναι τί κάλλος πενίᾳ ἢ πλούτῳ κραθὲν καὶ μετὰ ποίας τινὸς ψυχῆς ἕξεως κακὸν ἢ ἀγαθὸν ἐργάζεται, καὶ τί εὐγένειαι καὶ δυσγένειαι καὶ ἰδιωτεῖαι καὶ ἀρχαὶ καὶ ἰσχύες καὶ ἀσθένειαι καὶ εὐμαθίαι καὶ δυσμαθίαι καὶ πάντα τὰ τοιαῦτα τῶν φύσει περὶ ψυχὴν ὄντων καὶ τῶν ἐπικτήτων τί συγκεραννύμενα πρὸς ἄλληλα ἐργάζεται, ὥστε ἐξ ἁπάντων αὐτῶν δυνατὸν εἶναι συλλογισάμε- νον αἱρεῖσθαι, πρὸς τὴν τῆς ψυχῆς φύσιν ἀποβλέποντα, τόν τε χείρω καὶ τὸν ἀμείνω βίον, χείρω μὲν καλοῦντα ὃς αὐτὴν ἐκεῖσε ἄξει, εἰς τὸ ἀδικωτέραν γίγνεσθαι, ἀμείνω δὲ ὅστις εἰς τὸ δικαιοτέραν. τὰ δὲ ἄλλα πάντα χαίρειν ἐάσει· ἑωράκαμεν γὰρ ὅτι ζῶντί τε καὶ τελευτήσαντι αὕτη κρατίστη αἵρεσις.

[51] ... πρὸς τὴν τῆς ψυχῆς φύσιν ἀποβλέποντα ... 618d8.

[52] Here, Socrates is probably thinking of the conditions that may lead one into prostitu- tion.

[53] μετὰ ποίας τινὸς ψυχῆς ἕξεως, 618d1.

nature of the soul to make a good choice. One must also know how to apply it to a particular soul with specific dispositions. This is so because not all souls react to poverty in the same way, or to the mix of poverty and other conditions, like beauty, for example. Knowledge of the specific dispositions of the soul concerned is thus necessary to foresee the effect that certain life conditions will have on it.[54] In that regard, Socrates' account of the conditions that are liable to corrupt the philosophic nature in book VI are once again illuminating: they indicate the complexities involved where even seemingly favourable conditions may prove fatal for certain natures.

This, then, is the kind of 'philosophy' that everyone should cultivate in order to make a good choice of life according to Socrates' account in the myth of Er.[55] It is true that the question of how to develop this complex art remains wholly unanswered. But this is precisely one of the characteristics of protreptic discourse: it seeks to 'turn' the interlocutors (or the readers) towards philosophy without necessarily providing them with a detailed account of the nature of this activity.[56] Furthermore, we must bear in mind an aspect of Socrates' advice that some translations of this complex passage completely obscure: Socrates does not advise us to develop such an art of decision-making ourselves. Rather he invites us to go out in search of *the one who* (*hoios ... tis*, 618c3) has such a knowledge at his disposal and who proves to be competent in this sort of evaluating and decision-making.[57] The question of whether Socrates is urging us to seek out and find this expert so that he will train us in his art or rather to simply ask for his services as a life counsellor remains obscure here. This said, one thing remains certain: in other dialogues Plato depicts Socrates as a master not only in the art of determining the correct mixture that constitutes the good life (in the *Philebus*),[58] or as an excellent counselor of choices of life whose services are solicited (in the *Laches*), but also in the art of making important life

---

[54] These considerations recall the passage in the *Phaedrus* where Socrates compares the good orator to the good doctor who knows which specific treatments to apply to a given individual, 270c–271d.

[55] One of the traits that characterize philosophic protreptic consists in presenting philosophy from the point of view of its finality, as a condition of happiness. See Van der Merren (2002), 599.

[56] This is a 'trait fondamental' according to Van der Merren (2002), 621: 'ils [les discours protreptiques] sont en attente d'autre chose, et, par là, posent généralement le problème de la détermination effective de l'objet de la philosophie particulière à laquelle ils exhortent'.

[57] This element is evident in the translations of Chambry (1932), Lee (2003 [1955]), Robin (1955), Shorey (1961), Leroux (2002), Reeve (2004), but obscured in the translations by Grube in Cooper & Hutchinson (1997) and Pachet (1993) for example.

[58] See Larivée (2011).

decisions of his own (as the *Crito* eloquently attests to).[59] It is, then, entirely possible that vis-à-vis its first audience, the myth of Er had a protreptic aim in the way that K. Gaiser understood it. That is to say, to convert young men to philosophy and to attract students to the Academy by using the prestige of the figure of Socrates.[60] This said, the protreptic aim of the myth of Er is original in that Socrates is not so much attempting to provoke a particular choice of life in us (the philosophic life), as he is trying to persuade us to turn to philosophy (as an expertise in evaluating life-patterns) in making our choice of life. Thus we have brought the unique protreptic effect of the myth of Er to light. This is not, of course, the myth's sole effect. I would now like to explore the following idea: that the myth of Er can serve as the basis of a *thought experiment* which the reader is invited to perform.

3.3. *The Myth of Er as a Retrospective Thought Experiment*

My hypothesis here is that the myth of Er—as well as the myth of Gyges for that matter—can be used as an instrument of self-diagnosis and self-transformation. This more 'active' and self-oriented reading of the myth is far from being arbitrary. As mentioned above, Socrates' final remarks that belief in the myth can 'save' us, justifies that we attempt to apply the lessons of the myth to our own situations. We also find an invitation to apply myth in a similar way in the passage of the *Phaedrus* where Socrates explicitly invites us to use myths as a tool of self-knowledge and of care of the self. He is not, he says, at leisure to occupy himself with the allegorical interpretation of myths in light of the fact that his primary concern is to know himself. Thus, if mythological characters are of interest to him, he explains, it is only insofar as they can contribute to this self-knowledge:

> I have no time for such things [trying to give a rational account of the stories told in traditional mythology]; and the reason, my friend, is this. I am still unable, as the Delphic inscription orders, to know myself; and it really seems to me ridiculous to look into other things before I have understood that. This is why I do not concern myself with them. I accept what is generally believed, and as I was just saying, I look not into them but into my own self: Am I a beast more complicated and savage than Typhon, or am I a tamer, simpler animal with a share in a divine and gentle nature?[61]   (*Phdr.* 230a)

---

[59] Thayer suggest that this art of decision-making can be learned by studying Plato's *Republic*, which he sees as 'one of the first in a line of Enchiridions, a handbook to illuminate and guide one in living the good life,' Thayer (1988), 371.

[60] Gaiser (1959). Both Gallagher's (2004) and Yunis' text (2007), dedicated to the protreptic aims and function of the *Republic*, do not examine the myth of Er.

[61] Translation by Nehamas and Woodruff. ἐμοὶ δὲ πρὸς αὐτὰ οὐδαμῶς ἐστι σχολή· τὸ δὲ

By undertaking to demonstrate how the myth of Er can be used as a tool of self-knowledge and of care of the self, we thereby remain true to the way that Socrates himself made use of myths.[62]

3.4. *On Having Chosen One's Life: Facticity and Self-Transformation*

Up until now, my protreptic interpretation of the myth has been centred on the present and the future. Socrates urges us, *now*, to go find a philosopher who is skilled in the art of decision-making in matters that concern the choice of life. And the training or counsel that this philosopher could provide would impact the *future* of our soul once it comes time to make our next choice of incarnation in the afterlife. However, the myth also invites us to conduct a thought experiment, the object of which is the *past*. Construed in the simplest possible manner, this thought experiment consists in seeing our present life conditions as the result of a past choice.[63] But what is the objective of such an exercise? What virtue could there be in the consideration of our present *bios* as being the object of a past decision? The myth attempts to make us responsible for all these life conditions which we generally consider to be purely contingent and completely (or partially) beyond our control. Our sex, our social origin, the type of body we possess, our intellectual capacities, inherited richness or poverty—the myth invites us to consider all of these as the outcome of a past choice. But why? What use could there be to think that everything in one's life that *does not depend on us*—following the distinction which became classic in Stoicism—in fact does depend on us (or rather depended on us)? And how can considering ourselves as the agents of such a past choice affect our way of life in the here and now?

αἴτιον, ὦ φίλε, τούτου τόδε. οὐ δύναμαί πω κατὰ τὸ Δελφικὸν γράμμα γνῶναι ἐμαυτόν· γελοῖον δή μοι φαίνεται τοῦτο ἔτι ἀγνοοῦντα τὰ ἀλλότρια σκοπεῖν. ὅθεν δὴ χαίρειν ἐάσας ταῦτα, πειθόμενος δὲ τῷ νομιζομένῳ περὶ αὐτῶν, ὃ νυνδὴ ἔλεγον, σκοπῶ οὐ ταῦτα ἀλλ' ἐμαυτόν, εἴτε τι θηρίον ὃν τυγχάνω Τυφῶνος πολυπλοκώτερον καὶ μᾶλλον ἐπιτεθυμμένον, εἴτε ἡμερώτερόν τε καὶ ἁπλούστερον ζῷον, θείας τινὸς καὶ ἀτύφου μοίρας φύσει μετέχον.

[62] I subscribe to Yunis' thesis regarding Plato's aim: 'Plato's purpose as a philosophical writer was not merely to present compelling arguments about how one should live, but to present them in such a ways that the reader would be most likely to be compelled by them to choose to live in a particular way' (Yunis [2007], 1). Indirect support for this active reading also appears in the famous passage where Socrates suggests (at 592b2–5) that the whole of his discourse on the ideal *politeia* constitutes a paradigm that each person may use for self-governance (ἑαυτὸν κατοικίζειν), a method of heautocracy. Plato thus explicitly invites us to use the *Republic* as the basis for a practice of knowledge and care of the self.

[63] In what follows, I take up, in a revised form, the thesis put forward in Larivée (2009).

We might think that this aspect of the myth of Er represents an attempt at ideological manipulation aiming to bring about that all—and particularly those who seem not to have been favoured by chance—docilely accept their life conditions and social position without striving to modify them. It is true that such an ideological goal seems to agree somewhat with the declared intention that informs the 'noble lie' behind the myth of the metals.[64] Although such a possibility cannot be ruled out, there is nothing in the myth to indicate that this would be its only or even its main objective. We should note, first, that this thought experiment, conducted by considering our present life conditions as the results of a past choice, has different meanings for the philosopher and for the non-philosopher. For the non-philosopher who is dissatisfied with his lot in life, the myth teaches him that he must attribute the shortcomings of his present situation to some past negligence—since he is responsible for this choice of life—and that the only way to avoid such an error in the future is to become a philosopher or to solicit the guidance of a philosopher, who knows how to choose a life-pattern well. The desired effect then, is essentially protreptic. As regards one who is already a philosopher in her present life, what can she attribute the conditions of her life to, if not to a past choice that she made in full knowledge of the facts? And what other goal could the philosopher have had in making her choice than to act positively on the disposition of her soul through life conditions carefully evaluated? If this is the case, then the thought experiment of imagining present circumstances as the result of a past decision can also benefit the philosopher. In effect, this thought experiment leads the philosopher to become more attentive to the way that the present life conditions, particularly the apparently disadvantageous ones (for example: being poor, ugly, of modest birth, and finally being condemned to death by one's fellow citizens—the lot of Socrates!), can contribute to the betterment of his soul. This idea finds concrete textual confirmation in the passage from book VI, already cited above, where Socrates explains that some apparently unfavourable conditions (exile, low birth, physical weakness) are in fact the very conditions that can save the philosophic nature from corruption, whereas some apparently advantageous conditions (intelligence, wealth, noble birth, beauty, for example) may be its ruin. He evokes the example of Theages, whose physical weakness

---

[64] In that these accounts attempt to justify the present situation by basing it on an unverifiable mythic past. That said, the element of choice is absent from the myth of the metals and the myth of Er does not allude to political life.

unexpectedly proved to be his salvation, when it prevented him from becoming involved in politics leading him instead into philosophy.[65] According to the myth of Er, the philosopher can therefore consider these apparent obstacles (that currently escape his will) as an occasion, deliberately chosen (in the past) to contribute to his own betterment. This thought experiment therefore permits us to consider the apparently detrimental aspects of our present lives as occasions, chosen beforehand, to work towards the transformation (and/or the preservation) of our souls.

We should however note that this type of thought experiment was probably more pertinent in Antiquity. This is because the life conditions relevant to the myth of Er were much more constraining and difficult to modify in that period than they are today. Having been born male or female, rich or poor, beautiful or ugly, with a disability or without, an aristocrat or a craftsman obviously implied a form of constraint much more serious and rigid in Ancient Greece than today. In fact, social mobility, and medical progress now even allow for the modification of conditions which seemed, not so long ago, completely out of our control. Sex—one of the truly unalterable traits for the Greeks, as Williams notes—being an example of one such condition.[66] Clearly, we can only rejoice about this increased flexibility. Today, we work mostly to modify our material and physical conditions to adapt them to the needs and desires of our 'soul,' and not the contrary. However, and this is what the myth makes evident, it is not impossible that this malleability makes us forget the transformative virtues of facing a certain 'external' resistance regarding our spontaneous desire for 'advantageous' life conditions. Let us attempt to discern this difference of approach between the myth of Er and contemporary practices of self-transformation more exactly.

---

[65] 'Then there remains, Adeimantus, only a very small group who associate with philosophy in a way that is worthy of her: a noble and well brought-up character, perhaps, kept down by exile, who stays true to his nature and remains with philosophy because there is no one to corrupt him; or a great soul living in a small city, who disdains the city's affairs and looks beyond them. [...]. And some might be held back by the bridle that restrains our friend Theages—you see, he meets all the other conditions needed to make him fall away from philosophy, but his physical illness keeps him out of politics and prevents it' (*Rep.* VI, 496a11–c3).

[66] In his comparative analysis of two elements seen as the result of a bad 'chance,' *tuchê* (being born a female, and being born a slave), Williams (1993), 122, holds the position that sex constituted, for the Greeks, what he calls 'a necessary identity': 'Being a woman really was a necessary identity; being a slave or a free man, despite Aristotle's desperate efforts to the contrary, was not. That is why as I put it before, his attempt can be seen as an attempt to assimilate the condition of a slave to that of a woman'.

Recently, diverse practices of self-transformation have caught the attention of several feminist philosophers, such as Susan Bordo and Cressida
Heyes. As Susan Bordo has suggested, it is indeed the case that Platonic dualism, which postulates a division between an inner and an outer inessential
self,[67] is in fact implicitly presupposed by what we could call the contemporary ethics of authenticity, which encourages the discovery and expression of the genuine, authentic self.[68] The contemporary practices of bodily
transformation such as plastic surgery, transsexuality, and dieting, explored
by Cressida Heyes, rest on such a dualist distinction between a real inner
self and an (supposedly inauthentic) exterior which should be modified to
accord with the nature of the interior. However, in spite of this persistence
of Platonism in the contemporary understanding of the self, the dynamic
of self-transformation presented by Plato in the myth of Er reveals itself to
be something altogether different. Indeed, the myth of Er brings to light the
way in which *the self (or, in Platonic terms, the soul) is affected, shaped and
transformed through the body, sex, life conditions, and social roles.* The myth
of Er rightly acknowledges and places value on the transformative potential
of these elements which are construed as 'external' or 'heterogeneous' to
the (real) self (i.e., the soul). And it is precisely because these external conditions have the power to transform us that we must, as much as possible,
attempt to carefully choose them. In other words, whereas the contemporary culture of authenticity encourages us to engage in transformative
practices that will allow us to express our real, inner, hidden self (namely
by modifying our body and life conditions), the myth of Er invites us rather
to see how we could transform the self with the help of those life conditions
over which we have, in many cases, little or no control. Despite the persistence of soul/body dualism, we are thus faced with two contrary methods
of self-transformation.[69]

Let us proceed to clarify, in closing, that the absence of belief in the reincarnation of the soul does not fundamentally affect the virtues of the transformative approach promoted by the myth of Er, where external adverse

---

[67] *Alc.* 128d1–131c5.

[68] On the survival of the platonic dualism of body and soul into the contemporary
world, see Bordo's famous text: 'Anorexia Nervosa. Psychopathology as the Crystallization of
Culture,' in Bordo (1993), 144–145. On the opposition of inner and outer see Heyes (2007), 20–
28. Unfortunately, I cannot here examine the question of whether the philosophical version
of this 'popular' ethics proposed by C. Taylor (1991) in his *Ethics of Authenticity* implies such
a division.

[69] This said, in the conclusion to her book, where she evokes the possibility of a counter-
attack founded on a form of 'somaesthetics,' Heyes (2007), 123–132 seems to approach Plato's
privileged strategy in the myth of Er.

conditions are seen as opportunities to work upon the self. Indeed, for those who would not accept a literal interpretation, such as Thayer, it is nevertheless possible to put forward a metaphoric interpretation of this crucial aspect of the myth of Er. In that case, the myth of Er simply calls attention to the opportunity we have, here and now, of making decisions that will induce a transformation of ourselves: changing one's life conditions to change oneself.[70] For certain philosophers, this type of transformative strategy takes extreme forms. Consider, for example, the French philosopher Simone Weil who, in the 40s, chose to abandon her teaching career in order to work as a farmhand and then as a worker in an automobile factory in extremely harsh conditions.[71] Immersing oneself into completely different living conditions does not leave the self intact. One could equally consider the fascinating life experience of Thoreau who retreated into the woods to live in a self-sufficient manner and which he recounts in *Walden*. In both these cases, the decision to act upon oneself by the voluntary adoption of certain singular and difficult living conditions has aspects both drastic and spectacular.[72] However, even the most ordinary human life implies a similar experience. The choices we make on a daily basis concerning the framework and conditions of our lives expose us to influences which have the power to transform us. The case of choosing where we live, of choosing a profession, of choosing mentors or friends for example—an aspect on which Plato insists in many places—is a good example of this.[73] We choose our friends and friendship thus implies, in the beginning, a decision which makes this type of relation voluntary. However, once this choice is made, we expose ourselves to an influence which on many occasions, will put up a resistance to our own spontaneous tendencies and which will transform us to our great benefit.[74] The method of transforming the self depicted in the myth of Er reminds us of the virtues of such a resistance.

---

[70] See Thayer (1988), 377. This is also the position that Halliwell (2007), 469, seems to be inclined towards: 'Every choice [...] brings with it its own "afterlife". Every choice makes us what we are'.

[71] She recounts this transformative experience in her 'Expérience de la vie d'usine' (Weil [1941]).

[72] Not to say masochistic in Simone Weil's case as Sontag (1966), 48–51 suggested.

[73] On the importance of finding the individual who can make us better, see, for ex. *Men.* 96d7–e1, *Phd.* 62d8–e4, *L.* XII, 951b4–c4.

[74] Friedman (1993) insists on this characteristic. See especially § 8, 'Friendship, Choice, and Change,' 207–230.

CHAPTER THIRTEEN

COMBATING OBLIVION:
THE MYTH OF ER AS BOTH PHILOSOPHY'S
CHALLENGE AND INSPIRATION

Francisco J. Gonzalez

That the *Republic* should end with any myth must surprise anyone who has followed the dialogue's critique of poetry and its generally hostile attitude towards traditional myths. But what should be much more surprising is the particular myth that is chosen. For the Myth of Er is a strange myth. Unlike other Platonic myths, what it directly describes are not the heavenly joys awaiting the virtuous nor the punishments awaiting the vicious; Er's access to these is confined to the recollections of the souls he encounters.[1] What the myth directly describes, and what Er *sees*, is an ambiguous transitional state between lives where all is given over to free choice, chance, careless-ness, and oblivion. Far from being morally edifying, this spectacle is, in the words of the myth itself, pitiful, comic and bewildering. Why, then, end with such a myth a dialogue whose argument has insisted on the absolute rule of reason both within the soul and within the city? The aim of the present paper is to show that what the *Republic* leaves us with is an irresolvable tension between what the philosopher demands and the tragicomedy of human life depicted in the myth: a tension which is key to understanding the dialogue as whole. To characterize the myth as only an illustration or dramatization of the dialogue's philosophical argument,[2] or indeed as 'un *hymne à la rationalité*',[3] is completely to miss this tension. My approach in what follows will be to highlight some of the key aspects of our human fate and nature as recounted by the myth that appear to render problematic the dialogue's argument up to this point. I will then consider why a myth is cho-sen to accomplish this task as well as what this might tell us about Plato's use of myths in general.

---

[1] Specifically, Er can only hear from the souls descended from heaven their recollections (ἀναμιμνῃσκκομένας) of the extraordinarily beautiful sights (θέας ἀμηχάνους τὸ καλλος) they saw there.
[2] Thayer (1988), 380.
[3] Droz (1992), 146.

1. A Worldly Myth

The myth takes the form of Socrates' narration of Er's narration of what he saw in, according to the Grube/Reeve translation, 'the world beyond,' according to the Leroux translation, 'là-bas,' according to the Vretska translation 'im Jenseits,' but according to the Greek, simply 'over there' (*ekei*, 614b7). Indeed, a fundamental ambiguity of the myth is the location of the place Er is describing. This place is neither in the heavens nor beneath the earth since the souls are described as coming to it *from* the heavens or *from* beneath the earth. As Proclus already saw, the description of this place as a *daimonios topos* (614c1) suggests a place *between* the heavenly realm of the gods and the earthly realm of mortals.[4] But can this 'in between' be precisely located? And can it be sharply distinguished from *this world* and our present condition, itself in between the heavens and the place beneath the earth? Whether or not these questions can be answered, they at least point to what is arguably the myth's most peculiar and striking feature: its emphatically this-worldly description of the world beyond. In a number of ways to be considered next, the myth seems almost systematically to blur dichotomies that have come to define 'Platonism'.

The first such dichotomy to be blurred is that between the soul and the body.[5] One would expect a myth of a world beyond to describe the souls there as completely lacking any attachment to the body and even to personhood in the fullest sense. But the contrary is the case here. As Halliwell has noted, the myth of Er depicts the souls as 'embodied, spatio-temporally enduring entities' and thus as persons (459, 461–462).[6] For example, they are described as travelling to different places, wearing their verdicts around their necks, having their hands, feet and necks shackled, and, perhaps most interestingly, using language. These souls indeed seem indistinguishable from their embodied counterparts in this world. This is not to deny that the myth

---

[4] Proclus, appealing to the characterization of *daimones* in the *Symposium* (*Procli Diadochi in Platonis Rem Publicam* Commentarii, ed. W. Kroll [Leipzig: B.G. Teubner, 1901], 133.24–27]), locates the daimonic place between the heavens, where the gods live, and the earth, where mortals have their dwelling (135.12–14 & 136.10–12).

[5] A recent study by Jean Derrida (2010) focuses precisely on this blurring of body and soul in the Myth of Er and sees it as the intersection at which myth and philosophy both meet and oppose each other: 'Le discours philosophique et le mythe ne se lient pas ici autrement que par une affirmation qui les oppose: celle de l'autre genre d'âme, divisible et prenant part au temps et à l'étendue dans des "affections terribles"' (18). Derrida examines how the Neoplatonists deal with this 'problem'.

[6] Halliwell (2007).

sometimes makes a distinction, as when we hear of 'the soul that was once that of Orpheus' (620a3–4).[7] But then this distinction is immediately blurred when this soul is described as acting and behaving just as Orpheus would. This would explain something that has puzzled many readers and scholars: that Lachesis should address the souls as *psychai ephêmeroi* (617d7). This is puzzling because it would seem that according to Plato souls are themselves immortal while only their embodiments are ephemeral. If the myth can characterize the souls themselves existing in the world beyond as 'ephemeral', this is only because it does not make the kind of sharp separation between soul and body we have come to associate with Platonism.

But there is an even more striking way in which the myth's description of the world beyond appears to affirm embodiment and this world. Proclus already drew attention to the surprising fact that not only the souls arriving from punishment in Hades, but even the souls descending from heaven *rejoice* (*hasmenas*, 614e2) when they arrive at the field which will represent for them a return to the cycle of generation. As Proclus notes, this means that even the souls that have experienced the delights of heaven continue to desire generation and participation in the material life here below.[8] But how can this be? How could separation from the joys of heaven be anything but a catastrophe and cause of lamentation for a soul? What could the soul which has known such joys possibly find desirable and rewarding in generation and material life? Proclus himself suggests an extraordinary answer with momentous implications: that heaven satisfies only one part of the soul and, by therefore leaving the rest of the soul without activity, in the end produces weariness and fatigue in the soul as a whole (160.4–11). In other words, the soul is bored by heaven after a thousand years because it cannot fully exercise its powers there. The implication is that some of the powers intrinsic to the soul and needing to be exercised if the soul is to be fulfilled are inseparably tied to generation and bodily life. If this is the message of the myth, then it makes body and soul inseparable indeed. But whether or not one accepts Proclus' suggestion, it is hard to deny that the myth, with the festival atmosphere it describes (*hoion en panêgyrei*, 614e3) among the souls waiting to enter a new life, *celebrates* generation and embodiment.

---

[7] Thayer (1988), 372 points to the significance of this passage.

[8] 'If the plain is indeed the source of generation, and if they feel joy upon entering the plain, it is clear that they all greatly desire generation and want to participate in the material life here below; this is because there are in this life many occasions for action' (159.23–26). Leroux (2002), 725, n. 64, rightly contrasts this with the unwillingness of the philosopher kings to descend back into the Cave.

Another significant and related feature of the myth is the emphasis on *choice*: souls are not simply sent into a particular form of embodiment and a particular form of life, but are allowed to choose. The past (Lachesis)[9] does not determine which type of life a soul will enter, but rather provides a number of possible lives among which it can choose (617d4–5).[10] This is particularly striking in contrast to the rest of the dialogue which can hardly be said to have emphasized the centrality of choice in the kind of life one leads. Indeed, the clearest parallel to the choice of lives described in the myth is the description in Book 8 of the democratic soul as containing within itself many models of different lives (*paradeigmata ... tropôn*, 561e6) and choosing now one and now another (561c6–d8), just as the democratic city is a colourful marketplace of different characters and different constitutions (557d2–8). Yet this kind of freedom is there condemned while here in the myth something at least analogous is made a central feature of the soul's journey. That the myth's emphasis on choice is by no means necessary is clear if one considers that souls could have been described as simply assigned specific lives according to their character and conduct in previous lives. We indeed have such a contrasting description in the *Phaedo* where Socrates, describing different reincarnations for different souls, asserts that their 'destination ... will conform to the way in which they have behaved' (82a8–9; Grube trans.). In the Myth of Er, a soul's previous life along with other factors will, as we will see, play a role in the choice it makes, but without at all determining this choice.

Yet there are indeed two key ways in which the choice is limited. First, as the role of the 'lot' indicates, the range of possible lives among which a soul must choose is limited and not in its control. One's choice is restricted, in other words, to a determinate number of possible lives (*biôn paradeigmata*)

---

[9] The presence in the myth of the three dimensions of time working together is itself highly significant though beyond the scope of this paper. This significance is confirmed rather than denied by Proclus' need to dismiss as ridiculous any involvement of real time in what the myth recounts (250.5–10) and his insistence that time is here only a symbolic expression, adapted to human perception, of what is in fact atemporal (250.29–30, 253.14–17, 257.12–18).

[10] See Adam's remark: 'It is appropriate that Lachesis should be the only Fate involved in the act of choice; for the Future is the child of the Past ...' (Adam [1902], II, 461). Barbarić (1999), 71, notes: 'Hier ist also nicht die Vergangenheit unverändert und unumkehrbar, wie es sonst üblich ist zu meinen, sondern eben die Zukunft, während die Vergangenheit immer offen und reich an angebotenen Möglichkeiten ist'. Droz (1992), 144, characterizes the lots as '*proposés comme des possibilités d'existence et non imposés comme des existences obligées*'. But Droz, with little support from the text, also insists that choice continues to play a central role in determining the goodness of one's life even after one's lot is chosen.

according to one's 'lot' (*klêroi*).[11] Secondly, necessity figures prominently in the myth[12] and in the end is the ruling power in the world the myth describes. Once a type of life is chosen, it is made fixed and inescapable.[13] Both of these limitations raise important problems and questions to be addressed in what follows. But the question that the second limitation in particular most immediately forces to our attention is the following: Does free choice exist only prior to this life and not at all during it? Is our future determined once we have chosen one of the possible lives offered by our past? Is free choice something that exists in the world beyond and not at all in this world?

But a prior question must be addressed first: *what* exactly is being chosen here? What we are told is *not* chosen is the internal order (*taxis*) of the soul. This order is *not* included in the models of lives since it is altered (*alloian gignesthai*) according to which model of life is freely chosen (618b3–4). This claim makes the soul's internal constitution distinct from the life it chooses but at the same time completely vulnerable to being affected by it. The infamous case, to be discussed further in what follows, of the virtuous man who chooses the life of a tyrant is a striking illustration of this: in this case the man's virtue did not guarantee the choice of a virtuous life[14] and the tyrant's life he has chosen will presumably destroy whatever virtue he currently has within his soul.[15] What needs to be inferred from

---

[11] Thus Proclus identifies the lot with the total sum of types of existence proposed for each soul (263.17–21, 265.7–9, 281.8–10, 282.10–12), with earlier lots containing all the lives contained in later lots and more (320.27–321.3). And for Proclus there is no real chance or fortune involved here since each is given the lot it merits (279.27–29); the principle of distribution is therefore justice and not fortune. However, Proclus assigns fortune a role in the accidental circumstances that attend the life chosen (299.20–25).

[12] Halliwell (2007), 457, sees in the instrumentality of the spindle an indication that what Ananke embodies is 'a principle of cosmic purposiveness, rather than a materialist, Anaxagorean conception of necessity …'.

[13] Though defending the existence of free will, Proclus must grant that according to the myth 'the action of the spheres' takes precedence (262.4–6); see also 266.6–8; 275.14–19.

[14] As Proclus writes, commenting on this passage, 'For nothing prevents the better [soul] from preferring a worse life, nor accordingly the worse from choosing and aiming at a better type of life' (284.25–27).

[15] Though Proclus maintains the existence of free will even here: 'For we can maintain ourselves in either good or bad dispositions, we can act with piety no matter what the form of life, and we can prepare for ourselves something better than the type of life we presently have' (266.23–26). Here Proclus has to perform a careful balancing act: while granting that it is impossible to live another type of life after the choice of life has been made (275.14–16), he insists that 'the necessity inherent in the kinds of lives as a result of the choices made has not deprived us of participation in virtue' (277.5–7) and that 'in no type of existence is

both this example and the general claim at 618b3–4 is that a virtuous soul
does not simply choose a life of being virtuous, which would be to choose
a certain type of soul and to render irrelevant the external and accidental
characteristics of a life. Instead, the soul chooses a life largely defined by
external and accidental characteristics and thereby risks losing whatever
virtue it currently has within itself. This means that according to the myth,
the order of the soul is by no means independent of, or immune to, the
externals of life. Proclus is therefore forced by the myth to conclude that for
Plato external goods (*echtos*), though not part of the definition of the good
in itself, do not thereby contribute any less to the happiness of souls (303.13–
17). The distinction between the good of the soul and external goods is
indeed another one of those 'Platonic' distinctions that the myth thoroughly
and radically blurs.

This is precisely why the choice of lives is described by Socrates as representing *the greatest risk and danger* for a human being (618b7–8). As
the infamous case already alluded to shows, even a soul that has spent a
thousands years in heaven contemplating the sights there *hazards itself* in
making this choice. Socrates indeed goes on to claim that our only way of
countering the danger (618d6–e3) is for our choice to be guided by a knowledge of what is good for the soul and what makes it just. But the myth, in
depicting the character of each life as determined by a wide variety of different factors and thereby suggesting the importance of finding the right
mixture and right mean (616d4, 619a5), makes the knowledge required here
extremely complex and anything but purely ideal or abstract. Socrates himself outlines as follows the things a soul must know if it is to succeed in its
choice (618c7 c3): 1) it must know the good and bad effects of beauty when
it is mixed with wealth, poverty, and a particular state of the soul; 2) with
regard to qualities either natural to the soul or acquired (good birth/bad
birth, strength/weakness, learning ability/inability to learn), it must know
both what effects each produces and what effects they produce when combined with each other in different groupings and different proportions; 3) it
must know the nature of the soul and what justice or injustice is within it.
This third type of knowledge is seemingly the only type that it is has been
the goal of the argument of the *Republic* to provide. And has not this argument at least implied such knowledge to be sufficient for happiness? What

---

the possibility excluded of honouring virtue in some way and, if one honours it more, of
participating in it in a larger measure' (279.4–6). Yet I see neither how these latter claims are
consistent with the inalterability of the life chosen nor what support they find in the text.

of the other two types of knowledge which Socrates now, in commenting on the myth, claims to be indispensable? Where in the dialogue are we taught what good and bad effects beauty has when it is mixed with poverty? Where are we told what would be the right mixture of beauty and poverty or ugliness and wealth? Where are we even told how we might go about figuring this out? If faced with a choice between a life in which we are nobly born but sickly and a life in which we are meanly born but healthy, how do we decide? How do we determine, and by what knowledge, whether or not this life would 'alter' our soul for the best?

The problem here is that what the soul is required to choose between is not virtue and vice, but between lives defined by accidental agglomerations of goods external to and independent of the soul's own constitution. This leads Proclus to speak of a 'lot' posterior to one's choice, by which he means the sum total of accidental elements made the consequence of this or that type of life (263.8–9). In other words, one is 'allotted' not only a determinate and finite set of lives between which to choose, but also, once a particular life is chosen, one is 'allotted' a number of accidents that accompany such a life. Let's take again the most striking example offered by the myth: the man who chooses the life of a tyrant is choosing a life of great power and *not* choosing to eat his own children: the latter horror just happens to accompany this life in this case (if one grants, as one apparently must, that it would be possible to be a tyrant without eating one's children). Of course, one could insist, as apparently Socrates does, on the need to examine the life so carefully as to spot all of its particulars and be able to judge whether the particular mixture of goods and evils it contains is most conducive to producing virtue in the soul. But could the most careful attention really reveal *all* of the particulars? And even if it could, what would enable one to make a good choice here, given that, to repeat, what is chosen is not a particular type of soul but rather a particular type of life defined by accidents and external goods of great diversity which, though beyond our control once the life is chosen, will still affect our souls? In short, the myth so complicates what is chosen, so multiplies the relevant factors and the possibilities while at the same time requiring the utmost specificity (how much poverty in relation to how much beauty, for example), as to render the risk not only great but seemingly irremovable.

As already noted, virtue is therefore *not* enough for making the right choice, as it presumably would be if the choice were simply one between virtue and vice. Many of those coming down from heaven, we are told, will make the *wrong* choice, exchanging a good life for a bad one (619d1–7). It is in this context that the case already noted of a man descended from heaven choosing the life of a tyrant becomes especially significant. Possessing virtue as a result of having lived under a well-ordered constitution (like the ideal republic, perhaps?) could not save this man from a horrible fate (619c7–d1).[16] This case has shocked many readers and rightly so: a shock, and even repugnance, that only increases when one recognizes that according to the myth this case is by no means unique or even unusual. Halliwell, for example, comments on the case of this tragic soul as follows: 'Not only does its previous existence count for nothing; the same is true for its millennium of beatitude in the presence of a transcendent beauty' (451). Halliwell even goes so far as to suggest that 'the soul's choice of tyranny in the myth appears to introduce an element of failure into the cosmic apparatus of justice' (452).[17] There does indeed seem to be something terribly amiss in a system in which those who have lived lives sufficiently virtuous to merit and be able to enjoy for a thousand years the indescribable reality of heaven should still be vulnerable to making a choice that plunges them immediately into the worst evil imaginable.[18] Indeed, one cannot speak of a 'system' at all where there is this possibility of rupture, discontinuity, and sudden reversal.

What is threatened here, however, is not only the system of justice but the very justice of this system. This is something that bothered Proclus in particular who asked how the offering of such a terrible life to someone who has done nothing to deserve it is compatible with divine justice (292.19–22). And the only possible response to such a question is to assert what the myth itself never even suggests: that the soul of the man in question was in reality given to vice. Thus Proclus argues that the fate of eating his own children was just punishment for someone who, through lack of reflection, was still ruled by insatiable desire and gluttony (294.25–27); he also cannot resist suggesting the possibility, without committing himself to it, that before the well-ordered life that earned him heaven, this man had lived a disordered life for which he still must pay (295.16–21). That Proclus should need to make such claims to find in the myth a just cosmic order shows just how much the myth endangers such an order. And even Proclus is not satisfied with

---

[16] F. de Luise (2007), 337, 360–361, sees here an acknowledgement of the unbridgeable gap between the justice of the philosopher king and the justice of the citizen in the *kallipolis*, between absolute virtue and political virtue.

[17] As Roochnik (2003), 124 emphasizes, this is an absolutely disastrous decision since tyrants in the myth are classified as incurables never to be allowed another chance (615d3–616a3; see also Halliwell [2007], 452). But it is probably going too far to conclude that 'all who are not philosophers will end up in hell' (Roochnik [2003], 125).

[18] Ferrari (2009), 128 rightly observes that 'the pessimism of the unending exchange of lives is more devastating than anything directly expressed earlier in the *Republic*'.

his own moralizing since he still must find it baffling that those descending from heaven should be, on the myth's account, the ones most intent on choosing a tyrannical life. If Proclus' explanation were the true and whole story, then the case in question would be unique and rare rather than, as the myth suggests, one case out of many cases of people from heaven choosing a bad life. Proclus is therefore led to offer another explanation that is terrifying in its implications: that their vision of the celestial powers that govern creation formed in these heaven-descended souls themselves a desire to command (301.18–22). This suggestion would leave us with a very strange cosmic apparatus of justice indeed since it would make the soul's desire to imitate what it saw in the light of heaven the cause of its being plunged into the darkness furthest removed from this light. Such a cosmic system is of course no less strange for being more familiar to us today in the guise of Lucifer.

At this point one will object that however one explains the case of the heaven-descended souls which choose bad lives, the *philosopher* need not worry at all. The man who chooses the life of the tyrant is explicitly said to have been virtuous *without philosophy* (619c8–d1). Does this not imply that philosophy is excluded from the ambiguity and fallibility which the myth emphasizes? Philosophy alone can save us by guaranteeing that we make the right choice. But, alas, the myth seriously undermines this claim in two ways. First, many of those coming from beneath the earth make the right choice in carefully choosing a good life, not because they have practiced philosophy, but because they have themselves experienced or witnessed the suffering that a bad life can bring (619d3–6).[19] Philosophy is therefore not according to the myth a *necessary* condition for choosing a good life. Secondly, even someone who philosophizes will still also need the luck (*tên tou klêrou tychên*, 619d7)[20] of not being the last one to choose (619e1–2). And

---

[19] Given that the myth describes many of those who have previously lived a life of virtue as choosing a life of vice and many of those who have previously lived a life of vice as choosing a life of virtue, it seems simply wrong to assert, as does Leroux (2002), 729, n. 82, that 'Cette conception assujettit donc la liberté du choix au déterminisme qui découle de l'existence antérieure: plus une âme s'est enfoncée dans le vice, plus il lui sera difficile de choisir autre chose qu'une existence dans le mal. Inversement, plus quelqu'un sera vertueux, plus l'existence qu'il choisira sera vertueuse'.

[20] Against the attempt of scholars to emend the text here to exclude the role of τυχή Adam (1902), II, 459 writes: 'In point of fact, however, Plato nowhere denies that the fortune of the lot affects the issue'. See also Leroux (2002), 731, n. 91: 'Cet élément de hasard fait partie de l'eschatologie platonicienne'. Halliwell (2007), 465–468, too emphasizes the role of chance or luck here. It should be noted that if in the rest of the dialogue τυχή is glimpsed 'only in the margins,' as Halliwell (*id.*, 470, n. 37) puts it, it is still granted an important role: whether a

even then it is only likely (*kinduneuei*, 619e2) that he will find happiness and the straight path to heaven. Philosophy is therefore not even a *sufficient* condition for choosing a good life.[21]

This last claim needs some defence since it is indeed said at 619b3–6 that even the person who chooses last can win a pleasing life (*agapêtos*) if he chooses with *nous*.[22] This claim is at least in tension with the passage just cited in which *not* being among the last to choose is explicitly listed as a condition along with philosophy. One way of trying to resolve the tension would be to say that while the luck of the draw can not prevent you from finding a life that is *pleasing and not bad*, it *can* keep you from the happiest life and the direct path to heaven. This solution would itself grant luck a very important role in achieving happiness. But the myth appears to go further: in another passage, Er gives the 'luck of the lot' as a cause of many souls finding themselves exchanging a good life *for a bad life* and vice versa (619d5–7). Furthermore, the claim that even the last person to choose can with *nous* find a pleasing life appears to refer back to an earlier claim that virtue knows no master (*aretê adespoton*, 617e3). How then could that bald claim possibly be made consistent with the claim that luck too is needed?

If there is an irresolvable contradiction here, that may be because the two claims are not made by the same person: the first claim, along with the later claim that the last person to choose can still choose well (619b3–6), is made by a priest or *prophêtês*, while the second claim that mentions luck as a necessary condition is made by Socrates. Halliwell thus notes that 'while the priest implies that [ethical] understanding [*nous*, 619b] can always prevail over the external or material conditions of a life [because 'virtue has no master,' 617e], Socrates implies that even philosophical wisdom cannot sustain itself independently of external circumstances' (466). It is hard not

---

philosophical nature finds the appropriate instruction or is corrupted by an inappropriate environment is up to τυχή (492a1–5); whether or not someone with a tyrannical nature becomes an actual tyrant is a matter of τυχή (579c7); the just man will want to rule in the ideal city but not in his own city, if not for some divine τυχή (592a8).

[21] Ferrari (2009), 129 makes the important observation that a philosophical life does not even figure among the types of lives that can be chosen. This is presumably for the same reason that a virtuous or vicious life is not chosen: the lives between which the souls are to choose are defined by those factors of life that transcend the soul's character and disposition. Ferrari (2009), 132 himself suggests an alternative or perhaps additional reason: that 'to choose a human life is already to have put limits on one's love of wisdom ...'.

[22] Droz (1992), 145 gives great emphasis to this passage and it is essential to her characterization of the myth as an 'hymn to rationality'.

to see the irony of putting the so-called 'hymn to rationality' in the mouth of a priest while having Socrates, the true defender of reason, express himself more skeptically. This tension between the two voices—another important feature of the myth or of its retelling—will be discussed further in what follows. The point to stress here is that the priest's exhortation is at odds with what the myth shows us and what Socrates himself is forced to infer from it. Even philosophy cannot defeat bad luck.[23]

But in addition to the role of luck, one must also ask how exactly philosophy enables one to choose the best life given Socrates' earlier account of what such a choice requires. If philosophy is understood as a knowledge of the Forms, how can such knowledge determine the positive and negative effects of poverty, wealth, strength, weakness, health, sickness, beauty and ugliness, both in themselves and in different combinations and proportions? Can what the philosopher has contemplated outside of the Cave really have much application in the murky, shadowy Hades described by Er? Not only luck, but the extreme diversity and concrete determinacy of the factors that contribute to a human life being good or bad appear to set a limit to what philosophy can achieve.

The choice of lives is therefore exactly what the myth not only shows it to be but also explicitly describes it as: a pitiful, funny, and surpassingly strange sight (620a1–2). It is in this context that we are told, as an explanation of this description, that a person's choice for the most part depends on that person's character in the previous life (*kata synêtheian tou proterou biou*, 620a2–3). This is a strange claim, both because it severely curtails the role of knowledge Socrates has wanted to emphasize and because we have already seen that one's character in no way determines one's choice while one's choice can radically transform one's character. What makes for the tragicomic spectacle is indeed the extraordinary complexity of the factors that influence a choice of life and the extent to which these factors are beyond a person's control. Also an element in the comedy is the way in which the souls described simply choose the opposite of what they have been in the past, thus going from one extreme to the other and thereby missing entirely the 'mean' recommended by Socrates. But perhaps the most telling feature of this comedy is the spectacle of great heroes choosing to be reincarnated as animals (620a3–b5). Proclus finds this so shocking

---

[23] As Ferrari (2009), 130–131 puts the point, 'to face reincarnation is to face a struggle attended by real risk; and it is this rather than the philosopher's happiness that Socrates chooses to emphasize in the myth of Er'.

and simply blasphemous that he must conclude that Plato's own thoughts are not here in agreement with the myth (312.10–16), though he also offers the charitable interpretation that the names of heroes are here only code for certain types of lives that imitate these heroes without truly being like them (313.7–15 & 314.11–14). Proclus' shock, if not his interpretation, is just as it should be since we do have here a collapse of the distinction between the heroic and the base, between the semi-divine and the bestial. The passing description in this context of animals choosing a human life also appears seriously to undermine the distinction between animals and humans (620a7–8).[24] This undermining of hierarchies is precisely the kind of thing that makes the myth comical rather than morally edifying. And the question is whether the philosopher can truly transcend this pitiful comedy.

With this question, which the details of the myth have repeatedly forced upon us, we should turn to perhaps the most significant and surprising feature of the story, and the one not anticipated by anything said earlier in the *Republic*. I am referring here to the account of how the souls, after the lives they have chosen have been assigned, confirmed and rendered inalterable by past (Lachesis), present (Clotho), and future (Atropos), respectively, must travel to the plain of *Lêthê*, which is described as the absolute antithesis of *physis* i.e., a place in which nothing grows, nothing emerges into the light (621a3–4). Here the souls must drink from the river of Carelessness (*Amelês*, 621a6–7), also referred to as the river of *Lêthê* (621c1–2), before entering suddenly into their new lives. Most significantly with regard to our question, the difference between those said to possess *phronesis* (philosophers?) and those lacking it is not that the former do not drink of the water, the difference is instead that the latter drink more than they should while the former presumably drink the proper measure (621b6–b1). The implication is that even philosophers must ingest a certain degree of oblivion and carelessness. But why and how is this a necessary condition for entering upon a new life?

---

[24] This aspect of the myth thus leads Plotinus to distinguish between what is human and the soul, seeing in the latter the continuity of all life and in the former that act of reasoning that is only a heightened and more explicit version of that desire for the One that characterizes all life: for a detailed discussion with references, see Derrida (2010), 61–90. The result, according to Derrida (2010), 73, is that 'l'humain est un acte ou un projet avant d'être un genre ou une espèce, et comme *vie rationelle*, il est peut-être condamné à rester un problème, un paradoxe et même un oxymore. Il ne nous est donc pas donné comme quelque chose de tout fait, et ce n'est pas comme cela que nous devons le chercher'.

Others have seen in *to tês Lêthês pedion* an antithesis to *to alêtheias pedion* referred to in the *Phaedrus* myth (248b6).[25] But it would be more correct to see the one as complimenting and presupposing the other. There is no contradiction between the claim of the *Phaedrus* that the soul must have seen the truth in order to become human and the claim in the myth of Er that every soul must imbibe oblivion and carelessness before being embodied. The fate of humans is an entanglement of truth with oblivion, care with carelessness. The best that can be achieved is a certain balance between the two.[26] Note that the virtuous person's disastrous choice of a tyrannical life is attributed to *aphrosynê* (619b8) as a result of which what the chosen life really contained was hidden to him (*auton lathein*, 619c1). If not so much will be hidden to the philosopher who has *phronesis*, the implication of the myth is that still much will. If in the proper measure, the philosopher has still imbibed carelessness and oblivion.

Here it is important to note that if Er's story is saved (*muthos esôthê*, 621b8) for our salvation, this is not because he is a philosopher. Instead, he is given the special dispensation of becoming a messenger (*angelon*, 614d–2) to humans of what he both sees and hears in the *daimonios topos*. This literally requires him to be more than human and thus a kind of *daimon*, as shown by his escaping death (his body remains uncorrupted for days; 614b5) and his ability to return to this life without having drunk the water of *Lêthê* (621b5).[27] Not only in its content, but also in the circumstance of its preservation and telling, the myth shows that philosophy is not enough

---

[25] See Adam (1902), II, 461, and Leroux (2002), 733, n. 101, who both attribute this contrast to Proclus. Proclus notes that while the plain of Λήθη is barren and infertile, the plain of truth is described as nourishing the soul; he also locates the plain of truth in the highest region and the plain of Λήθη in the lowest region (346.20–26).

[26] 'Every man who measures out upon the earth the journey pregnant with death [die todesträchtige Fahrt] is on the earth and in the midst of beings in such a way that on account of this drink a concealing and withdrawing of beings holds sway [eine Verbergung und ein Entzug des Seienden waltet], so that beings are only to the extent that at the same time and counter to this concealing and withdrawing [entgegen dieser Verbergung und dieser Entgängnis] an unconcealment [Unverborgenheit] holds sway [waltet], in which the unconcealed [das Unverborgene] remains capable of being held and is held [behaltbar und behalten]' (Heidegger [1992], 178). Heidegger thus finds in the myth a conception of truth and untruth as unconcealment and concealment, respectively, and thus as inseparable one from the other. For an analysis and assessment of Heidegger's interpretation, see Gonzalez (2009), § V. If the Plain of Truth is beyond the heavens, where is the Plain of Oblivion? Adam (1902), II, 462 takes the word ἄνω at 621b10 as showing that the souls are under the earth prior to their embodiment. Leroux (2002), 733, n. 102, in contrast, denies any such implication. It is probably appropriate that the location of the Plain of Λήθη is left completely indeterminate.

[27] That Er is not Greek might also be significant in this context. Halliwell (2007), 448, n. 6, detects in 'Pamphylian,' which means 'of the whole race,' a possible hint of universalism.

to combat the oblivion and carelessness that normally rule over us. Even becoming fully aware of our human-all-too-human condition requires a superhuman perception.

The description of what takes place in the plain of *Lêthê* is the key to bringing together the diverse elements of the myth discussed so far: for what generally characterizes human life according to the myth is a fundamental *opacity*. Philosophical reasoning seeks to make the choice between good and bad clear and in our control, but the myth thematises everything that such reasoning cannot penetrate and master, everything that stubbornly remains dark and irrational: embodiment, chance, character, carelessness, and forgetfulness, as well as the inherent complexity and diversity of the factors that define a life and that must be balanced in order to achieve a good life. Rather than merely dramatizing the dialogue's philosophical argument or offering an 'hymn to rationality', the myth describes everything in human life that resists and opposes what this argument recommends.

Something else that is recalcitrant and opaque to philosophical reasoning here is the transition from the plain of *Lêthê* to the start of a new life. This transition is described by the word *exaiphnês* (*exapinês*): 'all of a sudden' (621b3, 621b6). The suddenness of this change is emphasized by the lightening and the clap of thunder that accompany it (621b2–3). Indeed, this sudden transformation cannot be strictly characterized as a change at all: it is not a process taking place in time nor therefore measurable by time; the 'being-carried' into *genesis* (621b4) cannot itself be *genesis*. As characterized in the *Parmenides*, the *exaiphnês* is therefore this strange nature (*physis atopos*) that exists in between motion and rest and therefore *in no time* (156d6–c1).

But the important thing to stress here is that what interrupts and ruptures the flow of the narrative in the *exaiphnês* is precisely the indefinable and imperceptible boundary between the soul and its embodiment, as well as between the world beyond and this world. Proclus, who also draws the parallel with the characterization of the *exaiphnês* in the *Parmenides*, notes the result 'that the separation between life out of the body and life in the body is imperceptible [*anepaisthêton*]' (352.27–353.1); this is perhaps the significance of having the transformation occur in the middle of the night (621b2).[28] While the myth recounts the soul's journeys in the other world, between these journeys and the soul's life here in this world no journey takes

---

[28] Said by Proclus to represent 'the extreme of obscurity in life' (351.1–2).

place.[29] While Er can recount what he saw in the other world, he cannot recount how he came to reawaken on the funeral pyre; as we are explicitly told, Er does not know how he came to enter the body (621b6).

The imperceptibility and indescribability of the boundary and transition between the other world and this world makes it quite possible to follow Halliwell's suggestion of reading the myth as 'an allegory of the life of the soul in *this* world' (469). Then the factors we have mentioned would affect not only an initial choice prior to this life that would fix once and for all the course of this life, but rather this life itself and all the choices made throughout it.[30] The myth would in this case describe not what happened to us in some past but rather what characterizes our condition now. Whether or not one adopts this suggestion, the important point is that the myth *can* be read in this way. One reason is that what it describes seems, in the ways enumerated above, particularly this-worldly: souls as whole persons rejoicing in generation; choices both finite and genuinely free; luck both limiting one's choices and dictating the unforeseen consequences of one's choices; the continual struggle against the universal power of carelessness and oblivion; the unexpected reversals between good and bad; and the collapse of hierarchies. But the other reason is what Proclus characterizes as the imperceptibility of the separation between the life beyond and this life. And indeed, given the impossibility of any perceptible transition between the two, is there a great difference between the tragicomedy of human life which Er witnessed on that battlefield littered with corpses and the tragicomedy of human life he witnessed 'over there' and saw conclude on a

---

[29] As Derrida (2010), 101, well expresses the point, 'L'instantanéité de ce passage le rend paradoxal: c'est un passage sans passage; il marque l'impossibilité de toute transition entre la durée du mythe et celle de la vie ordinaire, entre ce qui anticipe le corps et la vie corporelle'. According to Derrida (ibid., 104–111), Proclus and Damascius find in this instantaneous passage without passage the very being of the soul!

[30] Ferrari (2009), 126, observes that of all of Plato's myths, the myth of Er is 'the most rooted in the problems of mortal life'. Thayer (1988), 376, defends a non-literal reading of the myth, insisting that 'The full moral force of the story is concentrated in this present moment which will continue to be repeated endlessly in an eternal series of 'nows''. Thayer (ibid., 372) argues that if we were to take the myth literally, it would bring into question 'the very possibility of the Platonic and Socratic endeavour of education and changing human life' since 'if we were living out an inexorable pattern no amount of Socratic questioning or prodding can change our ways'. Such a 'this-worldly' reading of the myth would correspond to J.-F. Mattéi's characterization of myth in general as presenting in time and genealogically what in fact transcends time and genealogy (Mattéi [2002], 16–17). Yet like Ferrari I think we should resist the conclusion that 'the function of a Platonic myth in general is to represent in narrative form claims made more directly elsewhere ...' (Ferrari [2009], 128). If the myth uses a story of the afterlife to express a truth about this life, it does not follow that this truth could be expressed more directly through an argument.

plain bereft of tress and of all that grows? The ambiguity is enough to render the myth philosophically problematic.

2. MYTH AND PHILOSOPHICAL DISCOURSE

What exactly, then, turns out to be the relation between the myth and philosophical discourse of the kind that takes up most of the dialogue? In answering this question we must note that this relation is already at issue in the telling of the myth itself in the form of a tension between the story attributed to Er and the philosophical interpretations with which Socrates at various points interrupts the story. This tension is already apparent in what Halliwell describes as 'the strangely obsessive' use of indirect speech in the narration of the myth (450) versus the direct speech in which Socrates offers his comments. Socrates' first interruption is at 618b7–619b1 where, as we have already noted, he insists that knowledge is more important than anything else in guaranteeing our happiness in the face of the great danger of choosing a life. Yet, as we have also already noted, such knowledge is rendered problematic and at least seriously limited in its efficacy by what the myth shows regarding the complexity, diversity and specificity of the attributes that characterize each life and that must therefore be taken into account in making one's choice. Furthermore, if the myth is taken literally, the knowledge Socrates recommends appears to be relevant only prior to entering a particular life, after which this life appears ethically determined (that is, there is no chance of the life of the tyrant who eats his own children becoming a good one, no matter how much a philosopher might instruct him). But even if the myth is not taken literally but interpreted as describing the choices we make at every moment of this life, the implication is still that our choices can have unforeseen and irreversible consequences beyond what we explicitly choose and that these consequences are capable of altering for the worse the constitution of our souls. Halliwell (2007) therefore rightly speaks of 'an instability between the mythic narrative and [Socrates'] commentary on it' (464) and even claims that 'the myth threatens the entire vision of how individuals can be morally formed in the course of their passage through the educational, social, and political settings of their lives' (465),[31] which is to say, of course, that the myth threatens the entire project of the *Republic*.

---

[31] Even Droz, who arguably overemphasizes the role of reason and choice in the myth, comments: 'On sent le malaise de Platon, déchiré entre destin et liberté, entre une tradition

Socrates' next intervention in the myth's narrative occurs at 619d7–e5. Yet this intervention is in form significantly different from the first in being less of an interruption and much better integrated into the narrative. In Halliwell's words, Socrates' comment here 'is interposed unobtrusively into the flow of Er's account' (Halliwell [2007], 465). It is as if the two voices were momentarily coming together. And it is indeed here that Socrates, as we have seen, qualifies his insistence that the philosopher is the one who will move between this world and the next along the smooth heavenly path by granting luck to be an indispensable condition. It has also been seen that Socrates in granting this condition is responding to what the myth shows while no more taking at face value the attempts of the priest within the myth to deny the significance of luck than a modern philosopher would take at face value the exhortations within a religious sermon.

Finally, in concluding with reflections on the practical significance of the myth Socrates sharply and strikingly demarcates his own voice and authority from the story that has just been told. If we are persuaded by the myth (*an peithômetha autôi*), then we will achieve a successful crossing of the river of *Lêthê* and preserve the soul unpolluted (621c1–2). But in order to believe that the soul is immortal and able to endure any good and any evil, in order to believe that we should practice justice with *phronesis* in every way possible (621c3–6), we must be persuaded not by the myth, but *by Socrates* (*all' an emoi peithômetha*, 621c3). The reason for this change in voice should by now be clear. We have seen that far from persuading us of the soul's immortality, the myth describes souls as embodied and ephemeral persons. The myth is furthermore so far from persuading us that the soul is able to endure any good or evil that it instead emphasizes the ease and frequency with which a soul exchanges good for bad and vice versa as well as suggesting that the internal order of the soul can be altered by the many external and accidental goods and evils that come with the life it chooses. Finally, instead of emphasizing the virtue of *phronesis*, the myth emphasizes the universality and inescapability of its opposite: forgetfulness and carelessness. For these reasons, Socrates' concluding words do not recap the myth or draw out its implications, but rather *defy* it. This defiance,

---

fataliste du tout-est-écrit, et une aspiration novelle à faire de l'homme un être qui réponde de sa vie, c'est-à-dire au sens propre, un être responsable' (Droz [1992], 145). Proclus in contrast sees the mixture of moral counsel with the fiction of the narrative as simply showing the character Plato's myths have of being both political and educational (285.25–28). He also sees here an imitation of the fragmentation in which alone our souls can perceive what is unified in the intellect of the gods (288.16–22).

however, is not a repudiation of the myth or a rejection of its truth. On the contrary, this defiance is an acknowledgement of the myth's power and the power of what it describes. Faced with the tragicomic spectacle of the human condition as described by the myth, the philosopher can only exhort us to care for virtue and knowledge and pursue them to the utmost degree and in every way possible.

What does all of this tell us about the relation between myth and philosophical argument, at least in this dialogue? Clearly, that the myth is in no way subordinate to the philosophical argument of the dialogue, if one can even characterize as an argument what is a philosophical drama no less 'mythical' than the myth itself.[32] Er's story is not an illustration or application of some preceding philosophical argument nor a more vivid and popular packaging of this argument's content. What the myth describes is rather what lies outside the boundary of philosophy, limiting its scope and continually threatening its project.[33] Not only the incredibly beautiful objects

---

[32] Halliwell (2007), 452–455 rightly stresses how fluid the boundary is here between myth and philosophical argument. See also Mattéi (2002), 3–4. It is important to stress that in contrasting the philosophical argument and the myth we are abstracting the former from a rich dramatic context that, as many have noted, already significantly situates and qualifies the argument narrowly conceived. Since Socrates at one point describes the ideal city itself as a μῦθος they have offered in speech (ἡ πολιτεία ἣν μυθολογοῦμεν λόγῳ, 501e3), it is perhaps more accurate to speak here of a contrast between one myth and another: between the myth of a city whose model is in the heavens and the myth of an underworld reality resistant to this model.

[33] One of the characteristics Brisson attributes to myth is that it is 'invérifiable' because 'son référent se situe soit à un niveau de réalité inaccessible aussi bien à l'intellect qu'aux sens, soit au niveau des choses sensibles, mais dans un passé dont celui qui tient ce discours ne peut faire l'expérience directement ou indirectement' (Brisson (1994 [1982]), 127–128). But then he argues that if a myth is considered true this is only on account of its agreement with philosophical discourse (ibid., 136–137, 158 [and on this page he asserts explicitly that for Plato 'la vérité ne se manifeste réellement que dans le discours philosophique ...']; which is why he sees the myth as being of use only on the ethical or political plain [ibid., 143–145, 171]). Yet Brisson appears to alter his view significantly in making additions to the second edition. Specifically, he adds a passage on the myth in the *Phaedo* in which he asserts that the myth enables Socrates to believe firmly in that immortality and indestructibility of the soul 'que la méthode déductive s'est révélée impuissante à démontrer' (ibid., 219). Furthermore, in the *Postface* he describes as his current project showing to what extent Plato is aware that 'la raison humaine en tout cas, ne peut s'émanciper du mythe qui lui fournit les présupposés à partir desquels elle déduit rigoureusement les propositions qui présentent pour elle le plus d'importance' (ibid., 222). Proclus appears to defend a similar view when he suggests that myths can teach without probable arguments and demonstrations because they correspond to the innate ideas we have of things prior to reasoning about them (355.2–7). Yet to characterize myth as only furnishing the presuppositions from which philosophical argument takes its start is still to subordinate myth entirely to philosophical argument.

in the place beyond the heavens, but also the chance, oblivion, carelessness and even free choice that arguably characterize our condition in this
world are inaccessible to philosophical discourse and therefore require the
different kind of discourse called 'myth'.[34] Myths are needed to express not
only the supersensible but also the nonsensical,[35] not only the divine place
beyond the heavens but also the inbetween-place or non-place of human
embodied life, not only the plain of truth but also the desolate plain of utter
oblivion.[36] But if the myth thereby shows the limits of philosophy, pointing
to everything that evades its grasp, it does so not in order to undermine its
validity but rather in order to heighten its urgency. The relation between
myth and philosophy is, in short, like the relation between Er's narrative
and Socrates' interventions, a dialectical one.[37]

It will be useful, I hope, to conclude with some more specific indication
of what significance the Myth of Er might have for our understanding of
the *Republic* as a whole. Such an indication can be had in contrasting the
lottery described in the myth with the lottery which the rulers of the ideal
city are described as setting up in Book Five. The goal of that lottery required
by the ideal city is to ensure the best offspring and to prevent different
classes of citizens with different natures from 'mixing' with one another.
Here the individual is given no choice in defining his life. Furthermore, the
lottery is rigged so that the losers will blame *tuchê* rather than their rulers
(460a8–10). In reality, of course, the outcome owes nothing to *tuchê* and
everything to the wisdom of the rulers. Yet we find out later, at the beginning
of Book 8, that this is precisely where the wisdom of the rulers will fail them.
Despite being wise, their ignorance of 'the geometrical number' will lead

---

[34] And when Critias characterizes Socrates' description of the ideal city as itself a 'myth'
which to achieve truth needs to be given a historical referent (*Tim.* 26c7–d3), is not the
suggestion that Socrates' philosophical discourse itself has no accessible referent? (Something Brisson (1994 [1982]), 164 himself appears to recognize). It is possible that the tension
between philosophy and myth is a tension within philosophy itself.

[35] See Monique Dixsaut's paper in this collection.

[36] A detailed comparison between the Myth of Er and the other eschatological myths,
especially those of the *Gorgias* and the *Phaedo*, is of course not possible here, but one contrast
suggested by De Luise deserves to be highlighted: while the other myths offer a kind of escape
from this world to another world in which philosophy and justice finally triumph, the Myth
of Er follows an account of justice and philosophy triumphing in this world in the form of the
kallipolis (see 333). One can therefore expect, I would suggest, that the aim of the Myth of Er
is the opposite of that of the other two myths: i.e., to illustrate everything in this world that
opposes the realization of the philosophical ideal. If the other myths offer the philosopher a
form of escapism, the Myth of Er is his nightmare.

[37] Halliwell (2007), 455 speaks here of a 'shadow dialectic'.

them to join brides and grooms at the wrong time (*para kairon*, 546d2) and thus to produce offspring who have neither good natures nor are fortunate (*eutucheis*, 546d2). This, then, is what ultimately brings about the dissolution of the ideal city (assuming it could ever be brought into being in the first place).

What therefore evades the wisdom of the philosopher king and thus threatens the city is the appropriate time and good luck which, along with free choice, are arguably incalculable and beyond the control of reason. But are not these recalcitrant and opaque elements of mortal life that threaten the ideal city precisely what the concluding myth attempts to bring into view? From the perspective of the myth of Er, the project of the *Republic* is thus revealed to be a utopian ideal, i.e., only an *exhortation* to care for what continually sinks into carelessness, to bring to knowledge what continually retreats into oblivion. The model set in heaven of a human community governed entirely by reason can be inspiring rather than dangerously self-delusional only as long as we preserve the insight into the human condition to be had only on the war-ravaged battlefield and at the very boundary between life and death. If reason demands that we banish myth, our ephemeral and embodied souls require that we preserve it. If justice can be for us only an exhortation and never a fully realized state, we must save not only the Myth of Er but myth itself in order to be saved.

CHAPTER FOURTEEN

THE MYTH OF THEUTH IN THE *PHAEDRUS*[*]

Christopher Moore

Plato's *Phaedrus* depicts Socrates in a conversation with Phaedrus, a young acquaintance in thrall to the power of composed speeches. Socrates, aware of this zeal, worries about Phaedrus' indiscriminate appreciation of composed speeches and his hopes for his own future in speech-composition. Harnessing Phaedrus' eagerness for talk, Socrates aims to bring Phaedrus to gain some critical facility as both a listener and a writer. This involves trying to help him become a better *conversationalist* (one who engages in *dialegesthai*, 'thorough talking' (269b6)).

It is in the context of Socrates' hope that Phaedrus will come to talk well with others that he tells him what we now call the Myth of Theuth (274c5–275b2). In this story, near the end of the dialogue, the Egyptian god is said to have brought seven discoveries to the god-king Thamos for his dissemination to the Egyptian people. The last of these discoveries is *grammata*, what we might call scripts, prepared compositions, or writings. Theuth lauds this discovery as a boon to wisdom and memory. Thamos disagrees. He predicts that this discovery will instead generate the mere pretence of wisdom, cause the dereliction of memory, and make people difficult to associate with. *Grammata* may at best help people remember what they already know. Finished with the story, Socrates soon extends its criticism, and concludes that, were a knowledgeable person to choose to write, he would do so only playfully, storing up a treasury of reminders for forgetful old age and for those following his track, providing himself with alternatives to sympotic or related amusements (276d1–8).

Though it is the most direct discussion of composition, the Myth of Theuth is only one of many in the dialogue. The topic of writing's value arose explicitly first when, in his first remark after Socrates' great charioteer speech, Phaedrus observed that his idol Lysias had been harangued as being

---

[*] I thank Elizabeth Belfiore, Christopher C. Raymond, and the editors for their comments.

a 'speech-writer' (*logographon*: 257c6), and that, accordingly, he had been worrying that writing speeches might always be shameful (d6), earning one the name sophist (d8). Socrates dissuades Phaedrus from this view: by reminding him of the pride public people have in composing long-lasting documents (i.e., laws), Socrates gets Phaedrus to accept that only some, not all, instances of speech-writing (*to graphein logous*) are considered shameful (258d1–2). This partial amnesty allows them to discuss what might make (written) speeches good and acceptable. They inquire specifically into what might make them beneficial to the city, persuasive, and properly technical. By the time Socrates says that they are now to turn to the topic of writing's appropriateness (*euprepeias ... graphês*: 274b6)—or, as Socrates rephrases it, what is most gratifying to the god with respect to making or talking about speeches (*logon peri prattôn ê legôn*: b9)—the topic of speech-writing has already been long discussed.

Yet the Theuth story does not simply put a vibrant literary twist on the previous criticisms. What's new about Thamos' judgment is its shift from assessing the quality of a speech and the success of its speaker to considering how to prepare to speak. This is a surprising shift, from what one says to how one becomes able to say it. Why Socrates needs this novel criticism and voices it as a story is the key question of this paper. The trouble with compositions, we come to see, comes not so much from the practices of reading, writing, and memorizing themselves but from the assumption that those suffice one to teach and learn, to give and receive advice. That writing allows one to prepare in advance does not exhaust the kinds of preparation one needs to be good. One needs the preparation necessary for good conversation: befriending one's interlocutors, coming up with pertinent questions, and practicing giving sincere and precise answers. Phaedrus' taste for composition risks ignoring the role of conversation and these other kinds of preparation.

Across the extant writings about Socrates, Socrates shows that reading is vindicated only in conversation.[1] Telling the myth of Theuth is part of Socrates' strategy in the *Phaedrus*. To show this I start by discussing Phaedrus' character and the aims of Socrates' conversation with him. This gives some context for a closer reading of the Myth of Theuth. Assessing its claims about 'memory' and 'wisdom' shows why Socrates presents the Myth to his friend.

---

[1] Cf. most explicitly at Xen. *Mem.* IV.ii.

1. The Grammatophilic Phaedrus

The *Phaedrus* opens with a discussion of Phaedrus' script-immersed morning. Phaedrus had been trying to memorize Lysias' laboriously-prepared (228a1), refined (227c7), and paradoxical (c8) speech. He was doing this by listening repeatedly to Lysias reciting it, reading to himself the scroll (*biblion*) on which it was written, and practicing reciting it (228a8–b6). When Socrates guesses correctly that this is what he had been doing—a guess surely based on his familiarity with Phaedrus' preexisting passion for written speeches—Phaedrus denies knowing Lysias' speech verbatim (*ta ge rhêmata ouk exemathon*: 228d2, cf. *exepistamenos*: b8), and so asks to summarize the script. Socrates refuses, requesting that Phaedrus read from the text itself instead (*ton logon auton*: d7–8). Why Socrates wants to hear the speech straight through is hard to say. He may want to remind Phaedrus that complete memorization of the script is just like reciting the script, his memorization adding nothing but the false appearance of spontaneity (243c2). Or he may want Phaedrus, able to reread and rehear the script, to remain a spectator of it, so that Socrates may later draw his attention to his uncritical reactions (234c6–d9). Or he may want a composed speech to talk about later (262d8–264e6). Whichever it is, it is clear that Phaedrus takes pride in this prepared document, and Socrates wants to draw Phaedrus' attention to his fancy.

These early clues about Phaedrus' deep interest in Lysias' prepared speech are corroborated by his sensitivity to the charges of *logographia* already cited (257c8–d2). He notes that many people seem ashamed to write speeches and to leave compositions behind (*suggramma*: d6–7, cf. e7–8). (Phaedrus may have already acknowledged this shame when he hides the book in his cloak and goes outside the city walls to practice.) But because proposed laws are a kind of composition, as Phaedrus acknowledges, and people are not ashamed to propose laws—in fact they hope for immortality through adopted laws—then not all composition can be shameful. Consistent with his emphasis on compositions and speech-writing in this passage (a6, 8, 9, b4, 4, c2, 5, 8, d2), Socrates makes clear that it is not the fact of a composition's durability that matters (though that quality was used as part of his argument: c2), but its having been composed. This is clear from his indiscriminate mention of 'speaking and writing' (258d4–5, 259e2) and 'speaking' in place of 'writing' (259e4–6).

A third symptom of Phaedrus' interest in the composition of speeches is his having read lots of rhetorical handbooks (*technai*: 266d5, cf. 271c1). Such books, which Socrates has also read and is glad Phaedrus has reminded them to talk about (*hupemnêsas*: 266d7), are about the technical production of speeches, which Socrates glosses as 'refinement' (*kompsa*: 266d9, cf. 227c7). Rhetorical handbooks are written, read, and memorized to allow future writing, reading, and memorizing, the activities of rhetorical practice, just as medical handbooks allow future medical practice.

Given this evidence that Phaedrus loves composition, we can speculate about what exactly Socrates judges Phaedrus really eager for. Technical handbooks identify and systematize language's resources. Writing—spending time on drafts—allows one to pack in and deploy the most resources—rhetorical devices—into a speech.[2] Socrates identifies the contrast to technical preparation when he says that he himself gives only casually improvised speeches (*idiôtês autoschediazôn*: 236d5; Phaedrus calls this being 'possessed by fluency,' *euroia tis se eilêphen*: 238c7–8). Language has its mysterious and powerful effects on people, in its most exceptional cases like a doctor's drug, acting on a passive audience.[3] Like the distiller of naturally-occurring plants into elixirs, the speech-writer culls speech's most active elements. Phaedrus is amazed by the conversion of writerly work into spectatorial spellbinding.

This equation of composition with the marshalling of language's affective resources gets support from the best explanation of the politician's skepticism about Lysias' speech-writing. It would be natural for someone—especially a civic-minded public figure—to worry about the concentration of language's manipulative powers in prepared speeches. Everyday talk of course cannot avoid using such powers, but it does so diffusely or haphazardly. It might be thought that talking, especially in the formal decision-making settings—the courts and the assemblies with which the politician has the most familiarity—should present itself transparently as a vehicle for facts and beliefs for rational consideration. Speechifying need not be expected to be psychologically inert, but one might find suspect those who think first about a speech's effect rather than its rightness.[4]

---

[2] The amount of time composition takes comes up not just in Lysias' case (228a1) but in Socrates' fourth remark, his quotation of Pindar's *Isthmian I*, to the effect that composing poems uses up all one's free time (227a9–11).

[3] Cf. *Chrm.* 156a1, where Charmides hears that Socrates has a charm to heal his headache, and wants to write it down; more generally Laín-Entralgo (1970), de Romilly (1975).

[4] Cf. Ferrari (1987).

2. Socrates' Conversation with Phaedrus

For Phaedrus, writing, reading, and memorizing are just different moments in composed speech. Writing composes by setting down thoughts, reading verbalizes a composition, and memorizing conceals the fact that writing and reading have ever occurred. Memorizers wish to preempt two kinds of suspicion. The first is that someone else composed one's speech. This might be a particular person (e.g., Lysias) or nobody in particular (e.g., 'earlier people' or 'the wise'). Since in order to memorize one relies on (repeated) imitation rather than comprehension, there's the chance that one could be articulating well what one knows nothing about. The second suspicion is that one's (possibly self-composed) speech is not responsive to its particular audience. Memorization orients one's speech backwards or inward, to the script or original production, rather than forward or outward, to the listeners and a future good. Since one can address speeches to listeners blind to their needs or desires one might be saying something pointless or inappropriate.

At the end of his Charioteer speech, Socrates prays that Phaedrus direct his life toward love accompanied by philosophical talk (257b6). Given that Phaedrus seems most notable for his zest for prepared speech, I take it that Socrates means 'love accompanied by philosophical talk' to be an improvement to that. (What 'love accompanied by philosophical talk' precisely means, I cannot say here, but it seems at least something that advances the cause of love as depicted in the Charioteer speech). Thus we could see the dozens of turns in the *Phaedrus* conversation as Socrates' cumulative attempts to bring Phaedrus, by harnessing his desire for speech, to perceive, want to modify, and have the ability to modify his desire for prepared speech. A full appreciation of the dialogue, from this perspective, would take showing how each piece of conversation partially contributes to this three-fold goal. We would see Socrates showing Phaedrus how a speech could fail to benefit the city and its people (227d1–2), in particular out of ignorance (260b1–d2); be too long (241e7), especially by recycling its meagre ingredients (235a4–8); try to persuade people about what well-born and gentle people know to be false (243c1–d1) or what's simple-minded and even impious (242d7); persuade unreliably (262c1–3); obscure its precise topic (263d7–e4); have its parts in disarray (264c2–5); be vague and inconsistent (265d6–7); ignore the nature of the audience (268a8–272b4); depend mistakenly on probabilities rather than knowledge (273d2–e4); or aim to gratify one's fellow slaves rather than one's good and well-born masters, the gods (273e9–274a2). What we can see from this list is that

Socrates had not yet broached with Phaedrus the issues with using prepared scripts, the hazards of depending on reading for learning, and the
narrowness of treating speech too pathetically or aesthetically. None of
these criteria for shameful speech address the critic of speechwriting as
such or, more importantly, isolate and cure Phaedrus' desire for *scripted*
speeches.

3. THE MYTH OF THEUTH

Socrates starts his story by saying that the ibis-related Egyptian god, Theuth,
has just discovered number and calculation, geometry and astronomy,
draughts and dice, and, to top it off, *grammata*.[5] There's also the god-king
Thamos; Socrates reminds Phaedrus of the Greek versions of both his name
and his territory ('Ammon'; 'Egyptian Thebes'). Theuth, he says, brought the
seven skills (*technas*) he discovered to Thamos. Thamos asks about their
respective benefits (*ôphelian*), and as Theuth goes through them, he praises
and censures what he's thought Theuth has said well and poorly (*hoti kalôs
ê mê kalôs dokoi legein*). The details for the first six Socrates says he's not
going to go through,[6] but for the seventh Socrates turns to direct quotation. Theuth, the story goes, says that *this* study (*mathêma*) will make the
Egyptians wiser and be better with memory (*mnêmonikôterous*); his jingle
is that this will be a 'drug' (*pharmakon*) for wisdom and memory. Thamos,
in response, addressing Theuth as 'most skillful' (*technikôtate*), claims that
it is for some people to beget skills but for others to judge what degree
of harm and benefit will come to those intending to use those skills. As
father of *grammata*, Thamos says, your favour toward them has led you to
attribute powers quite opposite to their real ones. For the students (*math-
ontôn*) of *grammata* will come to have forgetfulness (*lêthê*) in their souls,
having neglected their memory (*mnênês ameletêsiai*); and in depending on
(*dia pistin*) writing they are reminding themselves from the outside, by
foreign impressions, rather than from the inside, by themselves. The drug
Theuth has discovered is not for memory, so it seems, but for remembering. Students of writing will merely seem wise, not truly (*alêtheian*) be wise.
Having absorbed much, without being taught, they may come to seem very
worldly (*polugnômones*) but be, for the most part, the opposite; and this
false appearance of wisdom will make them difficult to get along with.

---

[5] Cf. *Gorg.* 450d6, where many of these skills are taken to be special for not being manual.
[6] MS T omits this acknowledgement; I will not depend on it for my interpretation.

How Socrates narrates this story presents a number of puzzles worth much future reflection. Both gods get strangely verbose introductions;[7] Theuth cannot bring his discoveries directly to the people;[8] Thamos evaluates not Theuth's inventions but his presentation of them;[9] Thamos does not support his claim about the division of labor about discoveries;[10] and Greek mythology generally attributed the invention of letters to Prometheus or Palamedes rather than to Theuth.

How Socrates leads into and follows this story presents further puzzles. In both his prefatory and defensive remarks he treats the story as a distinctly traditional tale.[11] He does this here more explicitly than he does with any of the dialogue's other myths. Socrates prefixes his story by saying that he's heard it from the 'earlier' ones (*tôn proterôn*), and emphasizes that only they (*autoi*) know the truth about it. This is nearly the most general and neutral way possible of indicating this story's status as traditional,[12] believed solely because others believed it and had their reasons to retell it. Socrates underlines this meagre epistemic warrant by suggesting that were Phaedrus and he, however, to discover for themselves the truth of the matter (*de ... heurimen autoi*), they would hardly concern themselves about what other men—presumably these 'earlier' ones—might've believed. So the earlier people believed the story, for whatever reasons, and thought to pass it on, and we can thank them for doing so—and indeed they vouch in some way for its moral value—but our attitude toward the story cannot simply be that it happened or did not. The Myth is about something we very well may be able to find the truth about for ourselves. Since Socrates nevertheless

---

[7] For instance, Theuth is introduced through repeated deferrals: he's (1) one of the ancient gods, (2) associated with the bird, (3) the sacred, (4) the one indeed they call the ibis, (5) the name of this very divinity, (6) being 'Theuth'.

[8] This is contrast to Prometheus, who apparently does (Aeschylus, *Prometheus Bound*, 7–8).

[9] This is the same thing Socrates claims to be doing—appraising speeches as good or bad (ἐν λόγοις τισὶ τὰ μὲν ψέγοντα ὡς αἰσχρά, τὰ δ' ἐπαινοῦντα ὡς καλά)—when he says his alter-ego checked whether he had grounds for his assessments (*Hip.Ma.* 286c).

[10] Socrates makes a similar claim at *Tht.* 150c, drawing the analogy to *maieusis*; and cf. *Prot.* 320e1–3.

[11] Socrates' opening word is that he's 'heard' the following; this is the third and not last time 'hearing' is mentioned (*êkousa*: 274c5, cf. c1, c4, 275b9). The movement from *dramatis personae*, to situation, to selective summary, and then to direct quotation pulls the attention to the antithetical punch-line (*'grammata* will make people seem but not actually be wise'), which is itself triply repeated. The compression, quippiness, and echo throughout the story further betray its constructedness.

[12] Perhaps even more general is his sourcing of the Boreas myth: 'it is said' (*legetai*: 229b5) and 'it is believed' (*nomizomenôi*: 230a2).

retells it, he must have some firm reason to do so besides claiming that this interaction that supposedly happened in Egypt really happened in this way. What Phaedrus is to listen for, think about, and talk through, must be something else.

The exchange between Phaedrus and Socrates at the end of the story reinforces this sense. Phaedrus exclaims that Socrates easily makes up stories (*logous poieis*), not just ones supposedly from Egypt but from anywhere he wishes. How Socrates responds to this—that the source hardly matters—suggests again that Socrates has some tendentious purpose in telling the story. But before we can make sense of Socrates' response—where he adds the myth of the Grove at Dodona—we must consider why Phaedrus even challenges Socrates' claim. After all, challenges from Phaedrus are rare; it is only the second time Phaedrus has definitely resisted something Socrates has said.[13]

That Socrates attributed an invention to Theuth that Greek myth often talked about as the gift of Prometheus should not itself have proved Socrates' fabrication. Not only did the Greeks sometimes attribute the introduction of *grammata* to Palamedes or Orpheus instead;[14] there's evidence the Egyptians did in fact attribute literacy—or at least the differentiation of languages—to Theuth.[15] Nor does Phaedrus seem exactly justified in charging Socrates with pervasive and geographically-disparate myth-invention. Phaedrus did not earlier challenge Socrates' source in the myths of the charioteer or of the cicadas, and neither of them have any special foreign location.[16] Phaedrus must accept that there are untold stocks of myth in circulation, one perhaps for most occasions. But perhaps not for every occasion. To take a myth as invented on the spot, it must, it seems, appear too manifestly apt for the present occasion, too pointedly allegorical for the specific audience, to be drawn simply from the vast cultural memory of myths.[17] And so, in acknowledging Socrates' ability to make up stories from anyplace, Phaedrus acknowledges, if tetchily, the use of stories for ad hominem purposes.

---

[13] The first time is in his response to Socrates' initial judgment of Lysias' speech (234e1).

[14] Steiner (1994), 195.

[15] Spence (1990), 106–108, and Černý (1948).

[16] About the former, Phaedrus is simply awed at how much finer that speech was than either of the preceding (257c2); its believability does not even come up until Socrates brings it up, in his remarks about its usefulness (265b6–8, c8–9). About the latter, Phaedrus says he has not heard it before (259b3), but accepts the moral Socrates draws from it (259d9).

[17] Aristotle, at *Rhetoric* II, 20. 1394a2, says that didactic or persuasive stories are relatively easy to invent.

Socrates responds to Phaedrus' incredulity—and implicitly acknowledges having tailor-made the myth—by presenting Phaedrus yet another incredible story (275b5–c2). In the olden days, Socrates says, people even listened to an oak, and happily so, were its message true. How this response is at all relevant, we should admit, is hard to say: those listeners at the grove of Zeus of Dodona believed the oak's words to be divine, and they would be unable to test the prophecy's truth except by waiting for its realization. And the details of this myth are hard to account for.[18] But what's important is that Socrates pretty easily succeeds at getting Phaedrus to accept that the source of a story should not matter, that only the truth of the story's claims should, and that the words of that story should be as closely interpreted as 'mantic utterances', a most closely-read and pointed genre of speech.[19]

When Phaedrus admits that Socrates was right to rebuke him (*epeplêxas*: 275c3) for his outburst, he seems to be admitting he wrongly took Socrates as being unfair in his pointedness. If this is so, Phaedrus may have come to have been able to see this story as something to think about in ways other than as a source of fact about the past. We may, of course, doubt the depth of Phaedrus' allegorical reading; he simply goes on to say that he takes what Thamos says to be true, without substantiating his agreement, testing the view, or giving the tale any closer reading. (In Phaedrus' defence, Socrates does not much elicit anything else.) But Phaedrus is making advances if he at least entertains the idea that *grammata* could lack the virtues Theuth attributed to it and that he implicitly assumed for it; and Phaedrus is making further advances if he at least partially revises the way he reacts to mythic stories, from dismissal on grounds of artifice or fictionality to appreciation of allegorical potential or moral resonance. Near the dialogue's beginning, Phaedrus had queried Socrates about whether he was persuaded that the mythic story (*muthologêma*) of Boreas was true, by which, on evidence of the way Socrates responded and Phaedrus' earlier question about its purported location, Phaedrus meant whether it actually happened (229b5–d2). Socrates there prompted Phaedrus to a different kind of question about myths. He now he quells Phaedrus' curiosity about the historical facts about

---

[18] In particular, it's hard to know whether birds in the tree or the tree itself gave the oracle; for example, Sophocles' *Trachiniae* is ambiguous in its first mention (171–172) but seems to specify the tree on the second (1168); see Rowe (1986) *ad loc.* for further discussion. Whoever speaks, as we see in the *Trachiniae*, it's hard to discern the meaning.

[19] At *Charm.* 164e8, Socrates says the *mantis* speaks enigmatically, and one must give some complex interpretations to make sense of it; see also *Apol.* 21b4. Cf. Steiner (1994), 82–83, Bowden (2005), 21, 33, 47.

literacy's birth, encouraging him instead to have a view about the value of literacy. Myths occasion a different kind of question to be asked.

Thus Socrates' briefing and debriefing recommends to Phaedrus treating this story—which is short enough to be memorable and reflected on in the future—with some care. That it includes indirect and direct speech might seem to make it, like other points in the conversation, similar to a dialogue and thus particularly worth studying.[20] It is among the most fantastical of these depicted conversations, telling about the cusp of prehistory, mimicking not mundane exchange but epic aetiology. Even more, it's not even a proper aetiology: Thamos' pessimism about *grammata* put no stop to its proliferation; the myth tells only an incomplete story about the birth of literacy. All this makes hearing the story like enough to eavesdropping or watching a conversation to excite one's attention but arresting enough to encourage reflection.

4. Reading the Myth Seriously

Phaedrus, we observe, takes these devices, initially, just to reveal Socrates as the overly-clever author of this story, and then, and only after some brusque encouragement, to highlight the basic message he thinks he's to take from it. Yet the richness and complexity of the story would be wasted on only these two bulky goals. The story abides, and would seem to claim, further attention. Socrates might not be unwarranted in hoping Phaedrus might return to this story. In the first place, the story is not hard to remember, and Socrates' recapitulation repeats many of its phrases.[21] In the second place, Phaedrus has not elsewhere hesitated to ask to hear interesting things repeated (228a8, 277b4).[22] Given the friendliness of his departure

---

[20] The introduction to *Tht.* (143a–c) and remarks early in *Symp.* (172c–173c) about recording everything Socrates says seem to show a familiarity with writings in the dialogue form; see Sharp (2006). The Myth of Theuth would not be special in the *Phaedrus* for depicting conversation; Socrates recounts or mentions imaginary conversations between a well-bred man and the censors of love (243c1–d1); a donkey-marketer and someone who needs a horse (260b1–c1); some unnamed arguments and the science of speech (260d4–261a5); an autodidact with Eryximachus or Acumenus, or with Sophocles or Euripides, or with some musician (268a8–269a3); Pericles and Adrastus with Phaedrus and Socrates (269b4–c5); a writer and the rhetoricians (271c10–272b4); and Tisias also with our friends (273d2–274a5).

[21] E.g., genealogical talk with *tekein* (274e8) and *patêr* (275a1) picked up by *patros* (275e4) and *adelphon gnêsion* (276a1); the games invented by Theuth (274d1) by reference to play (276b5, d2, 6); reminders (275a5) with the same (276d3).

[22] Compare Critias at *Tim.* 26b.

with Socrates (279c6)—and what appears to be a pretty leisured life—it seems reasonable to expect he would talk with Socrates again, giving him a chance to hear the story again. Either way, upon turning his mind back to the Myth, he might ponder some of the following difficulties. (Another way of putting this, for those who doubt Phaedrus' resolve, is to think that Plato would hope his audience—to the extent we, like Phaedrus, do not understand everything at once—might return to this story and ponder some of the following difficulties.) In any event, all the things Socrates has said before, during, and after the Myth—that we can find the truth for ourselves, that we need to understand why someone says what he does, and that we might treat such stories as ours like superficially inscrutable mantic utterances—speak to working through what one reads.

I leave aside for expedience the puzzles I've noted above (about the introduction of the gods, etc.) to talk mainly about the discussion of memory and its connection to wisdom. Together Theuth and Thamos make seven claims about *grammata*, which I will address in order:

1. the *mathêma* of *grammata* will make people *mnêmonikôterous*
2. it is a *pharmakon* of *mnêmês*
3. no; it will bring *lêthên* to people's *psuchais*
4. this corruption will happen through *mnêmês ameletêsiai*
5. it is a reliance on external alien remarks rather than oneself by oneself
6. it is a *pharmakon* not of *mnêmês* but of *hupomnêseôs*
7. it will make people difficult to be around

4.1. *The Improvement in Memory*

Theuth praises *grammata* with a surprising explanation, that it would improve people's memory and their wisdom. These are not the obvious benefits of *grammata*. It would seem more natural to say they allow for the stability of worked-out thought, or for its finer arrangement, more convenient dissemination, or handy reference. Or, if *grammata* were to benefit people and not just their ideas, then why not say *grammata* would bring greater familiarity with diverse ideas, greater persuasiveness, or the chance for polymathy? It is odd, at least initially, to think of composition as something principally to modify a person's cognitive faculties.[23] To see the

---

[23] In saying this I'm not saying that upon reflection or experience such a change would be unexpected; not only do theorists about the change to literate culture marshal plenty of reasons to think there would be cognitive change, as suggested in Havelock (1962) and following.

plausibility in Theuth's claim we need to make clearer what he could mean by 'memory', and why he would speak of it as a pair with 'wisdom'. I will consider a couple of possibilities.

Might *grammata* directly improve people's memory-abilities? It is doubtful that this is Theuth's boast. Nobody would yearn for *grammata* to teach mnemonic devices, something obviously already taught orally. Nor does the sheer availability of scripts give a person appreciably more material on which to practice memorizing; a society's treasure of oral stories provides plenty (229e1). More likely *grammata* could increase the quantity of things in one's memory, the content available to be recalled. *Grammata* could certainly make learning more efficient. Books always have the leisure to teach us, whenever there's someone to read them aloud or silently (cf. 275d9–e3), and their compression or dilation may promote effective uptake. So a person or a culture that reads could have better memory in the sense of having more beliefs readily discursively accessible. This is not the same as having a better faculty of memory—speed or reliability of recall, storage, or maintenance—but seems part of good memory nevertheless. And having better memory would accompany 'being wiser' if wisdom meant 'having much knowledge'. All the same, it does not seem Socrates would attribute this meaning to Theuth, for two reasons. First, having knowledge, while perhaps the same as having lots in one's memory, seems something separate from having better memory,[24] and if becoming more knowledgeable were a benefit of *grammata* (which it probably is), then Theuth could easily have said so. Second, and more relevant to the dialogue itself, is that neither Socrates nor Phaedrus have yet brought up the power of *libraries* to expand their readers' knowledge or improve their memories. Despite asking Socrates about the truth of the Boreas story (229b4–9), Phaedrus seems no zealous collector of knowledge. Socrates would have no reason to voice, through Theuth, a hope for composition's contribution to capacious learning, and through Thamos, a curt rejection of it.

A distinct through apparently similar idea is that *grammata* could help one function *as though* one had excellent memory, as though one were a fast learner, a reliable repository, and a quick recollector. The existence

---

[24] In the *Clouds*, Socrates wants to learn Strepsiades' 'turn' (*tropon*) of mind, to find out how susceptible he is to learning. His first question is about whether Strepsiades has good memory (*mnêmonikos*); Strepsiades responds that he tends to remember his credits and to forget his debts (478–485). In the *Statesman*, the Eleatic visitor lauds Socrates' memory (*mnêmonikôs*) for mathematics when Socrates applies the concept of proportion (257b).

of texts would aid one in doing, but more reliably and on a larger scale, what memory has traditionally been for. Facts and quotations and passages, ideas and theories and systems, any record useful for living well, would be always at hand. A person with *grammata* nearby would seem to have great memory and, to the extent wisdom means something like 'having much resource for living well,' would be wiser. Since recall from memory takes time anyway, even quite protracted time, there seems no disadvantage, and no difference, to having what we might now call external storage.[25] It seems indisputable that, all else being equal, the person with a library will have a better chance to live well than the person without one. But, again, such a hope for *grammata* does not seem reflective of Phaedrus' hopes or responsive to his desires. He does not talk about developing a copious reservoir of written-down thought from which he might draw. Nor has he dismissed the usual networks of advisors, craftsmen, and theoreticians as sufficient for his reference needs. A further criticism of this reconstruction is that on it, *grammata* would be, in a certain respect, exactly the opposite of memory, not something to make one's memory *better* but to *replace* a poor memory. For Thamos' critique to be apt, Thamos needs to think that Theuth believes that *grammata* would actually improve memory, not just simulate or replace it. Of course, even if Theuth did think *grammata* could improve memory by replacing it, and augment wisdom by adding knowledge, Thamos' criticism would be responsive to the view that memory is nothing but memories, wisdom nothing but facts. That response is addressed below.

Given how Phaedrus has treated composition and memorization, I think a simpler reading of Theuth's hopes for *grammata* makes the best sense. With the existence of scripts one would be more able to memorize any particular speech. This is what Phaedrus exhibits with Lysias' *biblion*, what the *logographoi* are chastised for doing, and what the context for the description of 'true rhetoric'—namely, making and giving individual speeches—suggests. *Grammata* free one from having to pester the creator of a speech to repeat it or from having to invent one's speech at the same time as proclaiming it.[26] One can compose at leisure, and then memorize at an appropriate time. The connection to wisdom is in what such preparation allows. Composition allows careful assessment of an issue; memorization presents such

---

[25] This view is argued, in general terms, by Clark (2003) and (2008). Against it, see recently Fodor (2009).

[26] In the *Theatetus*, Eucleides does verify his record of the conversation between Theaetetus and Theodorus from Socrates (143a1–4), but then does not need Socrates' help.

assessment as 'natural, spontaneous, and vivid'.[27] Those who speak smartly spontaneously—those who are good at memory—seem wise. The Egyptians, Theuth supposes, would be wiser if they could prepare in advance and then remember what they were going to say. It is such a claim that Thamos responds to. Rather than *being* wise, Thamos says, they may merely *seem* wise. They will seem wise because they'll seem to be speaking spontaneously about what seems well-considered; but such appearance does not ensure the actuality. Thamos never explicitly commits himself to the impossibility of someone using *grammata* actually being wise. What he is committed to is the fact that the invention of *grammata* can by itself bring someone from not seeming wise to seeming wise. But more on Thamos' criticism below.

4.2. *The Drug of Memory*

Socrates has Theuth call his *grammata* a *pharmakon*—a drug, elixir, or potion—of memory. Calling it this does not reveal anything new about the discovery or its value, so it's not obvious why Socrates has Theuth deploy what appears basically a catchy slogan. Any explanation would, I think, have to respond somehow to Phaedrus' expectations for composition.

The most familiar observation about this slogan is that the term *pharmakon*, just like any of its English translations, does not unfailingly refer to curatives, balms, and other salutary treatments; a *pharmakon*, if overused or misused or used on the wrong person, can harm its patient. A poison is just too much of a drug. Phaedrus seems particularly interested and well-informed about medicine (227a5, 268a9, 270c7), and so would presumably know this. More relevantly, only a few pages earlier Socrates had wondered about a person who claimed to know medicine simply from having heard about medical drugs (*pharmakiois iatros*) by reading books (*bibliou*): would this be enough to practice medicine? Of course not, Phaedrus said; without knowing how to diagnose a patient or prescribe the proper dosage, such claim to practical skill would be absurd (268a9–c4). Phaedrus would thus be in a position to see that *grammata* could be a *pharmakon* insofar as its value depended not just on itself but on the wisdom of its application: when, why, and how to read or otherwise use them.

What's remarkable about this term *pharmakon* is not just its aptness in the context but the way understanding it instantiates its lesson about compositions. Phaedrus is able to understand it not by being familiar with the

---

[27] Notopoulos (1938), 478.

word but because he brings to its interpretation that about which he already knows: for example, that drugs are prescribed only in the context of a larger health-promoting practice. When Socrates has Theuth call reading a *pharmakon*, that is, something whose benefit is assured only when used within a larger wisdom-promoting practice, he is giving Phaedrus an opportunity to prove that attribution correct. (If Phaedrus does, he'll know it's from himself; since Thamos never plays on the term's bad sense—instead of saying that *grammata* is a 'poison' of memory, he says that it's a *pharmakon* of 'remembering rather than memory'—recovery of its ambivalence would come not from the Myth but from the reader himself.)

Theuth's reference to *pharmakon* could, of course, have additional resonances.[28] His excitement about *grammata* may encourage him to emphasize how easy and effective the study really is. Compared to the rigors of learning geometry or astronomy, and the uncertain benefits of them, literacy may seem relatively easy to acquire (basically everyone who tries does), and the resultant wisdom almost gratuitous. Oppositely, to the extent *pharmakon* signifies 'bad-tasting decoction' (cf. *Gorg.* 456b3), the idea might be that acquiring literacy may be painful and even shameful—studying may seem quite unmanly—but the outcome worth it. But against the importance of substantiating either suggestion—that *pharmaka* are especially easy and effective or especially painful but effective—is Thamos' retort, that *grammata* are *pharmaka* for remembering rather than for memory, a claim that depends on neither idea for its sense. It depends only on the idea that drugs can have different effects depending on their use.

4.3. *Forgetfulness in the Soul*

Phaedrus attributes this mythic exchange's lesson entirely to Thamos (273c3–4, cf. c9). But he does not make specific what he takes to have learned from Thamos, only that what the Theban has said about *grammata* seems to him to be the case. (It is Socrates who recapitulates the lesson, that *grammata* are reminders about what a person already knows (d1), and who extends it, that nothing 'clear or certain' comes from *grammata* (c6); Phaedrus assents to this.) So it's worth looking a little more closely at what Phaedrus could be taking himself to accept.

---

[28] All of these explanations are consistent with Rutherford (1990)'s thought that the jingle might have been suggested to Plato from earlier literature about the invention of language, particularly μνήμης ὄργανον (Gorgias, *Defence of Palamedes*, 30) and τὰ τῆς ... λήθης φάρμακα (Eur. fr. 578, 1).

Thamos' first charge against *grammata* is that studying *grammata* will put forgetfulness 'in their soul' (*en psuchais*). Why does Thamos locate it in this way? The most obvious reason is to emphasize the internality of memory, in reaction to a thesis about '*grammata* as external memory storage'.[29] No doubt *grammata* will preserve all kinds of information outside oneself. But if the imagery of 'forgetfulness' or 'concealment' being *in* the soul suggests an incapacitation of the soul, then Thamos can say that reliance on *grammata* by themselves could cause an inability to do whatever would be necessary to take advantage of those external resources.[30] Socrates' return to this formulation, some pages after the Myth, encourages this reading. He suggests that the best speaker will try to sow knowledge in the learner's soul (276e6) by means of deliberate conversational practice (*têi dialektikêi technêi*: e5–6). It does not seem Socrates would need to specify 'conversation' if he thought teaching involved the gradual conveyance only of 'content,' thoughts that could just as well be preserved in *grammata*. Thought-out conversational instruction would seem specially suited, even necessary, for inculcating the various cognitive competences: the ability to support an argument, to explain the value of a lesson, to teach someone else, and to use one's newfound good reasons for living happily. Forgetfulness in the soul, then, would seem to mean not simply failure of access to memories or other vehicles of content, but failure of access to the kinds of thought-processes constitutive of wisdom. And this is not inconsistent with the observation that the 'writing on one's inner tablet' locution is common in Greek poetry. It generally means 'taking to heart' something deeply enough that it may play a role in difficult decisions.[31] What one character is telling the other is not some mere fact they've overlooked but something meant to marshal their prior commitments and values. Socrates seems to acknowledge or depend on this view of inner writing (or failure of writing) to emphasize the systemic or comprehensive nature of Thamos' complaint.

4.4. *The Neglect of Memory*

The cause of this forgetfulness or broader psychic incapacity is, Thamos claims, the neglect of memory. This sounds like a common disparagement of technology—of calculators, search engines, and anything else that frees a person from ratiocinative, investigative, or reflective exercises. But Thamos

---

[29] Because 'souls' is plural, I do not think this formulation rules out attention to 'cultural forgetting'.

[30] See Cherubin (2009) on a rich conception of *lêthê* and *alêtheia* compatible with this.

[31] De Vries (1969), *ad* 276e6, and Steiner (1994), 25–27, 100–105.

does not say what aspect of memory one will be 'failing to care for' (*amele-têi*).[32] There's hardly any reason to think he refers to mere uptake, since the topic of mnemonic devices is absent in this dialogue, and the theme of memorizing as a skill a rather minor one.[33] Nor can he mean that *grammata* would make one neglect the *content* of memory; it seems that with *grammata* one would either treat the content the same or add to it. Memory must, then, it seems, be equivalent to something broader: say, understanding. Presumably it is more than a bromide that we remember best, or longest, what we understand. To neglect our memory is not just to eliminate 'memorizing' from our life—though with dependence on books we may indeed eliminate such memorization. It is instead, it seems, to eliminate trying to understand things—how medicine works, how talking works—on the assumption that one can always read about them when the occasion demands. Indeed, we'd be wrong to think that most of the things we need to memorize to live successfully, wisely, are strings of words or instructions to follow. What we are to memorize—what we are to learn, take up from culture, assimilate ourselves into, appreciate the reasons for, determine our distinctiveness by—are abilities. It is the rare activity fully constituted by knowing a script.[34] (What are we to do with the script? On what occasion?) *Grammata* may give some rules, or some facts, or some ideas, but they cannot themselves cause us to understand anything. Acquiring abilities requires having a teacher or other interlocutor with whom to interact, to ask questions of, and to have to identify errors.

4.5. *Alien Marks*

Thamos gives what looks like a causal explanation, at least the sketch of one, for *grammata*'s bad effects. People who trust writing remind themselves by external alien marks (*exôthen hup' allotriôn tupôn ... autous ... anamimnêiskomenous*) rather than by themselves (*huph' hautôn*). Such dependence is what puts forgetfulness into the soul, what causes the neglect of memory. It is clear that Thamos' criticism does not mean that one should trust

---

[32] Cf. *Symp.* 208a: *meletê* is how we keep from *lêthê* as the exodus of *epistêmês*; it 'preserves memory.'

[33] This absence is noticeable since other dialogues do involve such topics: see *H. Ma.* 285e8, on mnemonic devices, and *Rep.* 468d, 494d, 535c, for explicit remarks about the benefits of having a good memory.

[34] Even Ion, the rhapsode who seems mainly to memorize the Homeric compositions, acknowledges the centrality of discerning Homer's thoughts: *Ion,* 530cd.

what's inside more than what's outside. After all, we are often wrong or ignorant; something being our own belief does not make it trustworthy. Nor are the beliefs inside our mind necessarily more stable; that we forget things we thought we knew is itself one of the encouragements for writing. Since one's reading-independent beliefs could be wrong or evanescent, Thamos cannot be saying that *grammata* are problematic because they are external; the location does not seem important. Bringing those alien marks within does not solve any problem; it just repeats it.[35] The problem must be instead that the marks used for reminding are 'someone else's'.

What is it to remind 'oneself *by* oneself'? This locution is not uncommon. Earlier in the dialogue, Lysias' speech included the observation that lovers think they're envied by others just as they're envied by themselves (*autous huph' hautôn*: 232a1–2). In other conversations, Socrates presents an argument that the gods change neither on some external basis or by themselves (*Rep.* 380e1). Aristotle says that completely unified things cannot act upon themselves by themselves (*Met.* 1046a25). Such everyday uses are found even more often outside of philosophy; Euripides' Phaedra says the tongue brings plenty of harm onto itself by its own doing (*Hipp.* 397); Plutarch's Alcibiades told the barbarians simply to let the Hellenes destroy themselves (*Alc.* 26.7), and Polybius, reporting more self-destruction, says the Aetolians trampled themselves to death (4.58.8). So speaking of 'oneself *by* oneself' has no necessary technical, 'theory of Forms' or 'theory of Soul' aspect.[36] It means simply to emphasize the absence of the usual external force.

But what is it to be the internal force of one's reminding? We have already seen that it cannot be simply having internalized a composition. In the case of playing a song, or reciting a speech, then, knowing it cannot simply be remembering what notes or what words follow the ones currently being played or recited. For this is what scripts do: they tell you what comes next. A contrast with this is playing or reciting what's next because one knows it *ought to* come next. It is on the basis of understanding the concept of the score or of understanding the purpose of the speech and its context that

---

[35] Cf. *Charm.* 161b5–162e1. At the beginning of the *Protagoras* Socrates warns Hippocrates of incorporating sophistic views into his own outlook without analysing them (313a1–314b5); he cannot mean 'don't listen to them,' since he accompanies him to Protagoras anyway; he means 'examine what one hears'.

[36] Broackes (2009), 55, who argues for the technicality of *auto kath' auto* in the *Clouds*, observes that most *auto* + prep. + *hauto* constructions are mundane; he does not appeal to *hupo* constructions for his technicality thesis.

one continues. Of course there has been memorization early on, to become familiar with the notes or the phrases; but it is not this memorization which propels the performances. The music and the speech become one's own once their intentions, their meanings, their lemmas and theses, become one's own. The musical or linguistic phrasings were another's, but now, because they express one's own reasoning and commitments, they are one's own.

On this view, reminding oneself means depending on one's understanding of the composition. Such understanding does not require any particular independence from others. Coming to understand something 'oneself by oneself,' therefore, does not imply studying in utter privacy. Indeed, coming to understanding something for oneself may take rather more community with others than being able to mimic what other people have to say or than being able to come up with merely wise-appearing documents. Being asked a question, or hearing someone give his view, or wondering aloud with another, can each prompt the process of understanding. Coming to understand may not always require another person, but for those of us without perfect self-mastery, our quests for self-knowledge surely benefit from others' aid. A questioner can help make sure you're appealing to your own discoveries rather than simply reporting what you've heard from others or what sounds catchy at the moment. A conversational partner can appeal to a large range of the listener's existing norms—of sincerity, of curiosity, of skepticism—to ensure he relies not on mere memory but on reflection. Such help seems to explain much of Socrates' action throughout his conversation with Phaedrus (e.g., just from the dialogue's middle, 257c6–258c10, 259d7, 260a5–7, b6). So conversation is not merely to bring two heads together, to give multiple viewpoints, but to make sure we each give at least our *own* viewpoint—reveal our own self-knowledge—not someone else's or no viewpoint at all.

4.6. *A Drug for Being Reminded*

Thamos' retort, that the discovery of *grammata* is the discovery of a drug not for memory but for reminding, is not just a glib reversal of Theuth's jingle. It helpfully reminds those hearing or reading the Myth that talking about memory in gross is too vague. Memory, as we've had to distinguish above, refers to being able to stow things, to having lots of things stowed, to being able to recall what's been stowed, and, perhaps most importantly, to being able to come to do all the activities one was born capable but not ready to do.

Saying that *grammata* do serve well to remind a person about what he already knows is consistent with the thesis of this paper, that Phaedrus needs to see compositions as, narrowly, recording instruments, and that recording or playing back is not itself the leading part of speaking well. Being able to prepare a speech or recall it later is a legitimate ability; the durability of what's good is, all else equal, good. But a remembered speech is only as good as the speech itself; the only things worth preserving are those things worth having come by or been written in the first place. Thus Socrates glosses Thamos as saying *grammata* are for reminding those who already know. *Grammata* would also remind those who were mistaken of that about which they were mistaken, but then a script's durability would not be valuable.

4.7. *Wisdom and Apparent Wisdom*

Grammata's relation to memory has throughout the Myth, and the dialogue, been paired with its relation to wisdom. Indeed, a closer reading of the Myth has shown that Socrates must mean by memory something rather similar to wisdom.[37] Theuth's claim that reliance on memorized *grammata* could make one seem wise without actually being wise reinforces what we've discovered above. Memorizing could make someone appear wise, either to others or to oneself, when what one memorized itself seemed wise. Speaking on the basis of memorization itself—spontaneous talking— produces no particular impression except for spontaneity. So it's not the memorization of *grammata*—which could sound stupid, or garbled, or irrelevant—that would lead to the false appearance of wisdom; therefore the appearance of wisdom is not a consequence simply of *memorization*. It is the consequence of repeating things someone else or you said that sound wise in the new context. For such things to sound wise in the new context, they must seem appropriate to the new context. Such portability requires that the string of words seem divorceable from its original context; it must seem responsive to more than a single interlocutor on more than a single occasion. But seeming wise is not the same as being so. On the one hand, the first use of some speech might have been wise, but on subsequent uses, at new times and for new people, the same speech would not have been wise. On the other hand, in an effort to make a speech seem wise to potentially many people, the writer may have paid attention only to what many people

---

[37] The Charioteer myth seems to use the language of memory and remembering universals to describe wisdom.

might come to believe, not to what is really wise and true (cf. 260a1–4).[38] No doubt it can be helpful to stock up on excellently phrased advice or persuasive arguments or beautiful and memorable descriptions; there is no argument against having or memorizing a commonplace book.[39] But being able to *reproduce* things that seem wise does not suffice for being wise, just as having an excellent pharmacopoeia on hand does not suffice for being a good doctor.

Just as being able to reproduce wise-sounding speeches does not make one wise, producing them does not suffice either. There is surely much skill in producing wise-sounding things, including facility with, say, expansion or compression (267b2), laconisms and the use of argument form, using what people believe, and so forth. But this skill is not wisdom. Composition does not obligate one to use these superficial devices, but when writing in the absence of an immediate audience, one may be encouraged to focus not on one's ethical obligations to one's friends or fellow deliberators, but instead on gathering up one's rhetorical devices. Since composing takes a long time, one may be enticed into writing something rather general, once-and-for-all, useful for any range of audiences, and thus not wholly responsive to any particular person. And, it is possible that, in the excitement of assembling a speech, one will neglect certain virtues—truth, audience, pedagogy, etc.— in favour of, say, 'invention' or 'arrangement'.

4.8. Being Difficult to Be With

Thamos' final charge is that dependence on *grammata* will make people difficult to be with. The verb for he uses for association, *suneinai*, though it can refer to intimate relations, refers more broadly to the time spent with one's companions, generally in diverse conversation, or even in large groups.[40] Thamos must include this reference to the moral dimension to show that his argument against *grammata* does not depend purely on matters of self-interest. You may not care about your own memory or wisdom, but you've got to care about your effect on other people. This effect may be minor, as when we confront know-it-alls at parties, or the effect may be grave, as when we confront in formal political settings conceited people who mistake their ability to advise their peers. Indeed, Plato's dialogues seem almost universally an indictment of those highly-placed individuals

---

[38] And cf. *Rep.* 601a.
[39] Hence Aristotle's *Topics* and *Rhetoric*.
[40] Cf. Ford (2009).

whose confidence in their leadership or powers of advice far exceeds their ability to substantiate that confidence.[41] We know little about Phaedrus' potential for public influence, but his friendship with the very influential Lysias, his vigorous involvement in speech-production (242b1), and the way Phaedrus and Socrates joke about his pushiness (236d1–7, 242b2) suggest that his zeal could be a risk to himself and to others. A reliance on *grammata* can cause a lack of self-knowledge, and this ignorance of oneself, coupled with an incomplete discovery of wisdom, can lead to a failure of justice.

4.9. *Summary*

Reliance on *grammata* without accompanying reliance on one's own faculties of reflection and discussion leads to three problems: (i) the failure of memory and cognitive ability, which is to say, understanding; (ii) the failure of self-knowledge, knowing what one is committing oneself to; and (iii) failure of justice or virtue, which is what being difficult to be around amounts to. There is no claim, much less an argument, about avoiding *grammata*. But any value from *grammata* will come not from their introduction, but from something else. We might call it 'serious writing' or 'serious consideration' or 'serious reading' (*spoudê*: 276e5), depending on which moment of memorization is at issue. This seriousness presumably comes from something people already could know how to do: dealing with the hazards of life. And we might suspect that just as Plato depicts the kind of conversations Socrates' arguments seem to urge people into, Socrates depicts in Thamos' assessment the kind of reading, assessment, or judgment his criticism of *grammata* urges. Deliberate conversation depends not only on advanced methods of distinction (266b3–c1, 265d3–6), though this may be a way of speaking about the conversational ideal of clarity and consistency (d7). It seems to involve, as well, speaking in all the ways Socrates does, and, perhaps most importantly, speaking *on and on* (258e6–259d8, 227b9–11).[42]

---

[41] Hippias is perhaps the most notable example, a man who lauds his speeches meant to educate the youth about how to live finely solely on the basis of their formal properties (*H. Ma.* 286a).

[42] For the range of everyday uses of the term *dialegesthai* across the Socratic dialogues, see Dixsaut (2001).

5. EXPLANATIONS FOR THE USE OF (THIS) MYTH

Going back through the Myth of Theuth would bring the good reader to see that memory, considered in its breadth, is being spoken of as something hardly different from wisdom. Because it is absurd to think that one becomes wise—lives well or helps others live well—simply by saying things others have once said about living well or by coming up with things that may sound wise, it is absurd to think that memorizing what people have written will by itself augment wisdom.[43] It is reasonable, however, to think that composition can be helpful, especially for organizing the thoughts one has had, for oneself or others. Planting crops in a line may not increase their yield, but it does simplify their harvest. Part of self-knowledge, and thus of wisdom, may be knowing what thoughts tend most readily to be forgotten but tend as well to be of most value, and thus which ones, and in which ways, should be recorded.

Socrates' lesson in the Myth is apt; Phaedrus must remember that cultivating his ideas must follow understanding them and those people, including himself, on whom he ought to use them. The relevance and value of the lesson, however, does not itself explain why Socrates tells it as a myth, or as this myth in particular.

Asking why Socrates uses myth or the Myth of Theuth specifically contributes not just to a survey of Socrates' pedagogical panoply. In this Phaedrean case there is the suspicion that a critique of composition has special resonance in its coming in the form of a story rather than through continued discussion or question-and-answer exchange. We might be wary about a lesson about how to read well put in the form of something which needs to be read well. For what if Phaedrus were to read this story badly? Might he simply dismiss it on the basis of its dubious provenance, as Socrates denounces the sophisticated rationalizers for dismissing the other strange stories of Greek mythology with their rustic wisdom (229e)? Might Phaedrus find the absence of explicit reasons given for Theuth's position instantly prejudicial to that position? Might he even think that one just has to try even harder to memorize clandestinely? In other words, why would Socrates risk having Phaedrus interpret a story when he already believes Phaedrus is not inclined to interpret well? Why not keep leading Phaedrus through the analysis of composed speeches, as he did elsewhere? Is not the best practice for good conversation further good conversation? Accounting for Socrates'

---

[43] This is the theme of Nightingale (1995), § 4, and Ferrari (1987).

reasoning will be at best speculative, but I think we can find a plausible enough reason to have confidence Socrates would intend to use a story like this one.

The main reason is that Socrates seems to take Phaedrus as particularly drawn to myths. Phaedrus asks about the Myth of Boreas, and Socrates describes his apathy toward assessing it by appealing to a whole load of other myths he might anticipate Phaedrus wanting to ask about. Then as a sort of reason for giving the palinode Socrates cites Stesichorus' improbable report of his poem about Helen (243a5–b7). Then he gives the long and profound Myth of the Charioteer, which Phaedrus adores (257c2), and of the Cicadas, to which Phaedrus seems also to respond well (259d9). We may not be able to explain what exactly draws Phaedrus to myths; it could be their imagery, their cultural currency and resonance and estimation, their handiness, or their popularity in good examples of public speech (e.g., *Prot.* 320c1–7). But on the assumption that Socrates speaks in a way optimally persuasive to his interlocutor (cf. 272a1–3), Socrates' use of numerous myths suggests something about Phaedrus' character.[44] What this is, I am not sure. Perhaps it is Phaedrus' sensuality, perhaps his slacking attention to question-and-answer conversation, perhaps his lack of promise in following Socrates' analytic manoeuvres. (I do not know whether the text provides compelling evidence for any of these suggestions; perhaps Plato relied on his reader's extratextual knowledge of Phaedrus.)

By giving Phaedrus what he finds appealing (but not just pandering to him), Socrates may hope Phaedrus will pay close attention, remember, and wish to return his thoughts to it.[45] If Socrates helps Phaedrus adopt improved reading techniques, Phaedrus may preferentially return to the myths of the conversation; after all, they're both more memorable and his attitude toward them more in need of work. Since myths are basically unsubstantiated and are, in most respects, implausible on their literal reading, any initial acceptance, on the basis of their traditionality, will call out to be revisited.

It is perhaps harder to say why Socrates uses *this* myth. Writing had been spoken of often as a mythic invention, in particular by Thoth (Egypt might have been thought to have had a distinctive relationship with writing). By thinking about the introduction of some technique, one can reflect on how human life may have been before that introduction. In this case, we see that a most significant aspect of wisdom, judging something's benefits and

---

[44] Cf. Werner (2005).
[45] Cf. Asmis (1986).

harms, preceded literacy, and is of superior importance. Less significant might be the fact that in querying how writing gratifies the god (275b9), we might consider some gods talking about it. Or to encourage reflecting on whatever one hears, it might be productive for Socrates to show even a god getting something wrong (cf. 260a5–6 on testing what even the wise say). Lastly, besides being drawn to myths Phaedrus seems drawn to depictions of conversations.

To explain why Socrates would use this myth suffices to explain why Plato would depict Socrates using this myth, if it's true that Plato wants generally to depict Socrates speaking to people in ways that will capture their attention and have a chance of getting them to shift their motivation to caring for virtue. But of course there's the question about why Plato would depict Socrates talking to people with such particular susceptibilities, in this case to mythology. It seems likely that Plato thought that plenty of his readers, or plenty of their friends, shared such susceptibilities to a strong enough degree that he would want to help those readers and friends to think through and talk about their zeal for composition in a way possible for them.

CHAPTER FIFTEEN

MYTH AND TRUTH IN PLATO'S *PHAEDRUS*

Franco Trabattoni

1. Myth and Truth: The Case of the *Phaedrus*

Among all Plato's dialogues the *Phaedrus* is perhaps the one where the
presence of myth is most apparent and most important. Indeed, not only is
much of Socrates' second discourse taken up with myth, but one also finds
scattered in the texts many passages where myth plays a more or less central
role. To quote, for example, the myth of Boreas and Oreithyia, which we
read at the beginning of the dialogue, the myth of the cicadas (258e–259d),
the myth of Helen (which Socrates hints at with reference to Stesichorus'
'palinode'), and finally the 'Platonic' myth of Thamous and Theuth. But
that is not all. Indeed, the text also contains a number of references to
characters or to mythological tales, such as the River Achelous (230c, 263d),
the Cypselids (236b), the Muses (237a, 245a, 259b), the gods Eros (242d, 257a,
265c), Pan, Hermes (263d), Apollo (265b), Dionysius (265b), as well as the
priests of Zeus at Dodona (244b, 275b).

This being so, one of the most stimulating exegetical problems posed
by the *Phaedrus* is to establish 'comment doit-on comprendre l'emploi du
mythe par la philosophie?', not only in relation to Socrates' second discourse
(as is the case with Léon Robin, from whom we have borrowed the sentence
just quoted),[1] but also and above all in relation to the *Phaedrus* as a whole,
and finally in relation to the philosophy of Plato as such. Indeed, it is
precisely the heavy use of myth in this dialogue that bids us to seek in the
Phaedrus a kind of benchmark for an overall review of the issue surrounding
the relationship between myth and logos, and of the philosophical worth of
myth in Plato.

Let us begin with one very simple, even hackneyed, observation: among
all the myths mentioned in one way or another in the *Phaedrus*, some

---

[1] Robin (1985), cxxvii.

are quite simply drawn from traditional mythology (for example, the myth of Boreas and that of Helen), while others are the product of Platonic invention. This second category famously comprises both the great myth of the winged chariot and the final myth of Theuth and Thamous. As regards the first, its nature as a literary creation is expressly stated by Plato himself, who has Socrates say:

> The region above the heavens has never yet been celebrated as it deserves by any earthly poet, nor will it ever be. But it is like this, for one must be bold enough to say what is true, especially when speaking about truth (*peri alêtheias legonta*).[2]   (247c3–6)

But the same applies, albeit in a more elaborate literary fashion, to the myth of Thamous and Theuth. Just as Socrates has completed his story, Phaedrus claims to have well understood that his interlocutor has made it up, and then gently mocks him and his great imagination (throughout the whole dialogue Socrates demonstrates considerable eloquence, which is said to rely heavily on exceptional divine inspiration):

> Socrates, you easily make up stories from Egypt or from anywhere else you like.[3]   (275b3–4)

However, we must pay attention to Socrates' reply:

> Well, my friend, those at the sanctuary of Zeus of Dodona said that words of an oak were the first prophetic utterances. So the men of those days, because they were not wise like you young folks, were content in their simplicity to listen to oak and rock, provided only that they said what was true: but for you, Phaedrus, perhaps it makes a difference who the speaker is and where he comes from: you don't just consider whether what he says is right or not.[4]
> (275b5–c2)

The reply clearly smacks of a certain degree of irony, especially when Socrates refers to men who would be as 'wise' as the young folks like Phaedrus. It may well be that here Plato hints at the youth corrupted by sophistry or even by excessively indulging in dialectics,[5] which is why they believe

---

[2] Τὸν δὲ ὑπερουράνιον τόπον οὔτε τις ὕμνησέ πω τῶν τῇδε ποιητὴς οὔτε ποτὲ ὑμνήσει κατ' ἀξίαν. ἔχει δὲ ὧδε—τολμητέον γὰρ οὖν τό γε ἀληθὲς εἰπεῖν, ἄλλως τε καὶ περὶ ἀληθείας λέγοντα. Here, as well as in the following quotations of the *Phaedrus*, we quote Rowe's translation (1986), sometimes with slight modifications.

[3] Ὦ Σώκρατες, ῥᾳδίως σὺ Αἰγυπτίους καὶ ὁποδαποὺς ἂν ἐθέλῃς λόγους ποιεῖς.

[4] Οἱ δέ γ', ὦ φίλε, ἐν τῷ τοῦ Διὸς τοῦ Δωδωναίου ἱερῷ δρυὸς λόγους ἔφησαν μαντικοὺς πρώτους γενέσθαι. τοῖς μὲν οὖν τότε, ἅτε οὐκ οὖσι σοφοῖς ὥσπερ ὑμεῖς οἱ νέοι, ἀπέχρη δρυὸς καὶ πέτρας ἀκούειν ὑπ' εὐηθείας, εἰ μόνον ἀληθῆ λέγοιεν· σοὶ δ' ἴσως διαφέρει τίς ὁ λέγων καὶ ποδαπός. οὐ γὰρ ἐκεῖνο μόνον σκοπεῖς, εἴτε οὕτως εἴτε ἄλλως ἔχει.

[5] See *Rep.* III, 339b–d.

themselves to be *kompsoteroi* (to use a word not included in this passage, but which might be fitting to the subject) compared with the *euêtheia* of the ancients. But we shall return to this point later. For now it is more important to note that the two passages just cited contain a reference to the notion of truth (*alêtheia*). As regards the second passage, the meaning of this reference is clear. Since Phaedrus is well aware that Socrates told a myth born from his own imagination, and which therefore cannot rely on divine tradition or consecrated prophesies, he raises the question of its truthfulness. Socrates replies that the principle of authority should not carry any weight in this matter, and to prove this he quotes the case of the priests of Dodona, which were *euêtheis* to the point of even heeding the words coming from an oak. After all, the word *euêtheia* (made up of *eû* + *êthos*) does not just have the pejorative connotation of 'naivety', but also means 'good character', thus justifying the definition of an attitude that is utterly good and rightful, precisely by reason of its simplicity, its lack of sophistication and cunning.

Furthermore, it is essential to note that this fair disposition does not follow from a pious attitude towards the gods (possibly in opposition to the hollow character of a rationalism which claims to be subtle, but is in fact deceptive and destructive)[6] but from reverence for the truth. The reason the priests of Dodona pay attention to the words of the oak is not simply that they are certain it is the spokesman of Zeus. But they listen to its words 'provided only that they said what was true' (*ei monon alêthê legousin*). What follows from this is that the only condition capable of lending authority to a *logos* is the truthfulness of the content it expresses. Consequently, if it is fairly possible that words coming from an oak be heeded, providing they speak the truth, it must also be possible to ignore words coming from a god, as long as he is stating falsehoods. As we know, for Plato this can never be, since the gods cannot lie. So if it seems that a divine word is untruthful, one must necessarily infer that its origin is false, namely, not divine at all. In any case, however, it is obvious to Plato that every word or speech must be examined in the light of reason, for reason only, and not authority, can establish whether a word or speech is truthful (or divine) or not.[7]

The outcome of this reasoning is that truth may dwell anywhere, even in myth and in the fabulous tales of great poets. It may be useful in this context to recall what the Athenian says in Book III of the *Laws*:

---

[6] See *L.* X, 888e, 890a.
[7] On this subject the main text is, of course, the *Euthyphro*.

> For poets are also a divine race, inspired when they sing, and with the aid of the Graces and Muses, instantly grasp the truth of events that really happened.[8] (682a3–5)

This song of praise for poets reminds us of the *Phaedrus* (as we know, the *Phaedrus* is almost certainly subsequent to the *Republic*), and of the kind of rehabilitation of poetry and poet that this dialogue seems to present (but we will come back to this).

In the other passage, the one introducing the description of the other-worldly dimension, the context is somewhat different. Here it is not a matter of showing that, though artificially created and without the backing of honoured tradition, the myth can still embrace the truth. The aim of Socrates here is to show that there is a kind of truth that only the myth is entitled to expound. Socrates is well aware that this task requires courage (*tolmê-teon*), but this courage is made indispensable by the very nature of the object being sought, namely, truth or truthfulness. Just as Socrates explains that no poet has had this courage, he admits at the same time that, by accepting the burdensome task of describing the supra-celestial world, philosophy must somehow be on a par with poetry and myth, though exceeding by far the level of truth hitherto attained by the latter. In fact, one may easily perceive that in this case Plato's agenda is not to replace the myth and poetry with the *logos*, as seems to be the case in the early dialogues up until the *Republic*, but to devise a new brand of poetry and mythology that is far more courageous and true than current poetry and mythology appear to be. The speech uttered by Plato to describe true reality does not, in fact, take after either dialectics or *epistêmê*, but relies upon myth and poetry instead.

At a first glance, we seem to be faced with a serious inconsistency here. Yet, a more careful analysis shows that such an inconsistency is soon dispelled. For sure, there is a consistent line of thought that runs throughout Socrates' approach to myth in the *Phaedrus*. The basis for this line of thought is to demonstrate how the assumption whereby a myth ought to be heeded merely on the grounds that it gives voice to gods, and hence must embody some kind of truth, is simply false. The validity of this hypothesis is demonstrated by the following considerations:

1) Socrates has no qualms in refusing to put forward an interpretation of a traditional myth such as that of Boreas and Oreithyia. He gives reason for his refusal by invoking the main task of the philosopher, namely that of

---

[8] θεῖον γὰρ οὖν δὴ καὶ τὸ ποιητικὸν ἐνθεαστικὸν ὂν γένος ὑμνῳδοῦν, πολλῶν τῶν κατ' ἀλήθειαν γιγνομένων σύν τισιν Χάρισιν καὶ Μούσαις ἐφάπτεται ἑκάστοτε.

self-knowledge. This means that there is no necessary implication between myth and philosophy: in other words, Socrates believes the myth has no intrinsic philosophical interest *qua* myth. And his unwillingness to explain a traditional myth coupled with the complementary urgency of doing philosophy proves this assumption to be right.

2) The same point is brought up, conversely, in the two myths of the winged chariot and of Theuth and Thamous. The first myth is noteworthy not because it discloses some kind of divine revelation but because it is connected with truth (247c3–6).

3) As for Thamous and Theuth, the situation is slightly more intricate, but the outcome is the same. Phaedrus, who is clearly committed to a traditional use and interpretation of myth, comes across as rather skeptical of a myth made up by Socrates (hence, not born of a god). To that, Socrates replies with the example of Dodona's priests, who claim not to care about the source of the myth, being willing even to accept one uttered by oaks and rocks, 'provided only they spoke the truth'.

4) In sum, a myth could have philosophical interest if and only if it is connected with truth. So the philosophically more fruitful myths are for the most part those created by philosophers, indeed like the winged chariot myth and that of Thamous and Theuth. This does not rule out the possibility that traditional myths might also bear some truth; nonetheless, the worth of such a myth should only be measured against the degree of truth therein, rather than the authority of the source. And one can easily infer that, in Plato's view, the task of detecting that truth falls upon the philosopher.

The point is that, on the one side there is no strict connection between any kind of myth (or myth in general) and philosophy, while on the other side this does not stop myth from actually being relevant to philosophy. The problem we have to deal with now, then, is to set the guidelines whereby myth can become useful, if not necessary, to the philosopher.

2. The Wrong Way: Myth as an Alternative to Philosophy

If our observations are sound, we can say that the *Phaedrus* might be helpful in drawing a link between myth and truth. But what is the means by which the truth of the myth can become clear? In the first part of the *Phaedrus*, when Socrates and Phaedrus are wondering about the meaning of the myth of Boreas and Oreithyia, we find a good example of a bad approach. Upon reaching the Ilissus stream, Phaedrus reminds Socrates of the legend of Oreithyia's abduction by Boreas, and immediately asks him if he deems the fable (*mutholoğêma*) true (229b–c). Socrates' reply is both quite complex and somewhat allusive. He never actually says whether or not he believes the tale to be true. At first, he merely states that even if he does not believe it, his stance does not necessarily hinge on his 'strangeness' (*atopia*). I think we can understand the meaning of such a cautious remark if set in connection with the trial of 399 and the charge of impiety: according to his accusers, not only does Socrates not believe in the gods of the city, but he introduced new ones, and that is exactly what reveals his 'otherness' with regards to the city, its laws and its customs. Hence, Socrates prefers not to take a position, while remarking that his hypothetical disbelief does not stem from his bizarre originality, but is fairly common among would-be wise men. Furthermore, it is also clear that while Socrates does not say he believes in the truth of myth, he neither counts himself amongst these wise men. Had he wanted to rank among them, he could well have given an allegorical interpretation of the myth, saying that Oreithyia's abduction by Boreas is the mythological representation of Oreithyia's fall from the cliff to the rocks below, swept by the Boreal wind. Socrates here clearly refers to a practice of allegorical interpretation, fairly widespread in the fifth century, mainly among the sophists (especially Prodikos, although older examples are found in Herodotus and even in Homer). It is also common knowledge that Plato did not appreciate this method at all, as can easily be inferred from this same passage,[9] where Socrates mockingly remarks on this alleged *sophia* using the adjective *agroikos*, and finally leads us to believe it would all amount to a pointless waste of time.

So Socrates gives no real answer to Phaedrus' question. Moreover, though, he seems to take no interest in seeking out the truth in the interpretation of myths:

> For myself, in no way do I have leisure for these things, and the reason for it, my friends, is this. I am not yet capable, in accordance with the Delphic inscription, of "knowing myself"; it therefore seems absurd to me that while I am still ignorant of this subject I should inquire into things which do not belong to me. So then saying goodbye to these things, and believing what is commonly thought about them, I inquire—and said just now—not into these

---

[9] But see also *Tim.* 40d–e.

but into myself, to see whether I am actually a beast more complex and more violent than Typhon, or both a tamer and a simpler creature, sharing some divine and un-Typhonic portion by nature.[10]   (229e3–230a6)

It is clear that respect for the tradition Socrates speaks of here does not in any way mean he really believes in the truth of myths, let alone refuses to discuss them precisely for this reason. On the contrary, his respect is of a purely formal nature, and is but a feeble dissimulation of his lack of interest in the subject. But what is more interesting for us is the reason for which Socrates justifies this lack of interest: he must dedicate all his time to self-knowledge, and he would therefore be foolish to apply himself to something peripheral while this goal has not yet been reached. It is as if this knowledge of oneself was the main goal—or, better still, the only goal—of philosophical practice (as confirmed by the importance that the Platonic Socrates generally attributes to it), whereas the interpretation of myths, far from being considered in its specificity, is but one of the many activities that have little bearing on this goal. Indeed, there is no particular opposition between self-knowledge and the interpretation of myths, but only a general disagreement between what is philosophy and what is not. What follows, then, is that the interpretation of the myths is of no interest to philosophy.

3. The Metaphysical Meaning of Truth: The 'True' Reality

Yet at least to some degree this outcome is downright astonishing. Commenting on passage 275b, we have indeed seen that the myth may well be the vehicle of a true word. But that is not all. When in our passage Socrates speaks of self-knowledge, his main issue is to learn whether human nature is marked by a passionate irrationality, unyielding to reason, or if it is restful and party to a divine destiny. Still, in the course of the dialogue Socrates will actually provide an answer to this question. Rather surprisingly, though, he will do so through a myth: the myth, of course, is that of the winged chariot, where we discover that human nature is a mixture of opposing forces, divine reason and disorderly passion that clash all too often.[11]

---

[10] ἐμοὶ δὲ πρὸς αὐτὰ οὐδαμῶς ἐστι σχολή· τὸ δὲ αἴτιον, ὦ φίλε, τούτου τόδε. οὐ δύναμαί πω κατὰ τὸ Δελφικὸν γράμμα γνῶναι ἐμαυτόν· γελοῖον δή μοι φαίνεται τοῦτο ἔτι ἀγνοοῦντα τὰ ἀλλότρια σκοπεῖν. ὅθεν δὴ χαίρειν ἐάσας ταῦτα, πειθόμενος δὲ τῷ νομιζομένῳ περὶ αὐτῶν, ὃ νυνδὴ ἔλεγον, σκοπῶ οὐ ταῦτα ἀλλ' ἐμαυτόν, εἴτε τι θηρίον ὂν τυγχάνω Τυφῶνος πολυπλοκώτερον καὶ μᾶλλον ἐπιτεθυμμένον, εἴτε ἡμερώτερόν τε καὶ ἁπλούστερον ζῷον, θείας τινὸς καὶ ἀτύφου μοίρας φύσει μετέχον.

[11] This point is stressed also by Ferrari (1987), 11: 'That mythological monsters should

Firstly, one might point out that there is a difference between the myths
drawn from tradition, such as the myth of Boreas and Oreithyia, and myths
made up by the philosopher, such as the myth of the winged chariot: since
the philosopher is the one who has the right and the power to interpret
myths in order to glean any truth they may hide, it is clear that the philosophical myth is somehow crafted via the channel of the truth itself. But this
answer, in turn, poses a fresh problem. As Robin pointed out, in Book IV of
the *Republic*, when Plato reveals the nature of the self, i.e. of the soul, by ultimately putting forward a tripartition roughly similar to the one expounded
in the myth of the Phaedrus, he does not come to this result by way of a
mythical image; on the contrary, it emerges 'd'une analyse dont le carac-
tère est principalement logique'. So then, 'pourquoi dans le *Phèdre* Platon
procède-t-il autrement?'[12]

To answer this question we shall follow the suggestions put forward by
Robin himself—albeit developing them in a different direction—based on
the assumption whereby 'l'emploi du mythe s'imposait à Platon par des
nécessités internes et qui dérivent de la nature même de ce dont il parle'.[13]
But what does the myth speak about? Not just about the soul, clearly. The
bottom line of the story is that two worlds exist: one is the world here on
earth, the world of our experience and our practice, the world of illusions
and ghosts; the other one lies above us, and its realities are true, being purely
intelligible and logical while remaining real.[14]

In my view, the decisive point of this observation is the word 'truth'. From
Socrates' words we can infer that Plato is forced to draw on the myth here, as
only the myth is capable of telling the 'truth'. If one understands the phrase
'telling the truth' in the sense of 'constructing true propositions', then what
I have just said is clearly false and not Platonic at all: indeed, for Plato the
duty of constructing true propositions rests with the *logos* and not the myth.
But if 'telling the truth' means, as in the abovementioned passage (247c),
'speaking about truth' (*peri alêtheias legonta*), i.e. somehow describing the

continue to stalk Socrates' phraseology even after he has "said goodbye" to myth (230a1–2) ...
anticipates and exhibits a situation of epistemological significance': a significance that will
become quite clear when, in attempting to describe 'the human and especially philosophic
soul (that is, when he delivers the psychological analysis here promised), Socrates finds
himself incapable of describing it "as it is", and compelled to resort to the simile of a chariot
with winged horses and charioteer (246a3–7)—a simile which grows into a full mythical
allegory as the chariot plies its way among the Olympian gods (246e4–249d3)'. See also Rowe
(1986), 139.
    [12] Robin (1985), cxxviii.
    [13] Ibid., cxxix.
    [14] Ibid.

world above us, and whose realities are true,[15] then the hierarchy between myth and *logos* must be reversed, and this time the myth is set to gain the upper hand.

So, what urges Plato to make use of the myth (the counter-example of the *Republic* shows that Plato could avail himself of dialectics to achieve the same purpose) is not the psychological theory outlined above but the transcendence of the object he seeks to talk about, as well as the fundamentally metaphysical nature of the link which necessarily exists between said object and the human soul. In fact, the key point of the myth, which at the same time represents Plato's real response to the Delphic behest to know oneself, is to be found where Socrates draws attention to this link:

> For a soul which has never seen the truth will not enter this shape [*i.e.* the human form]. A man must comprehend what is said in accordance with the form, made up by binding into one through reason (*logismôi*) many sensations; and this is a recollection (*touto d'estin anamnêsis*) of those things which our soul once saw when it travelled in company with a god and, treating with contempt those things we now say are, rose up into real being (*to on ontôs*).[16]   (249b5–c4)

At first glance at least, this passage is rather strange. We find in the first part a highly abridged description of dialectics, or rather the 'synagogical' process, leading from the multiplicity of perception to the intellective unity of the form; in the second part this dialectical process is immediately identified with recollection (*touto d'estin anamnêsis*), which in turn is made possible by the 'mythical' vision of forms accomplished by the soul when travelling in the supra-celestial realm in the wake of the gods. In reality, this connection may seem bizarre to contemporary scholars only, who maintain there is a fundamental incompatibility between the doctrine of recollection and dialectics: it is commonly held that at first Plato based his epistemology on the mythical theory of *anamnêsis*, but later abandoned this naive and fanciful doctrine in favour of a far more scientific process, represented by dialectics. In this perspective, a diachronic history charting the development of platonic thought would set forth before us the makeover from muddled philosopher—mainly devoting himself to telling legendary tales

---

[15] Cf. Rowe (1986), 179: 'Socrates will be talking about truth because he will be talking about Forms'.

[16] οὐ γὰρ ἥ γε μήποτε ἰδοῦσα τὴν ἀλήθειαν εἰς τόδε ἥξει τὸ σχῆμα. δεῖ γὰρ ἄνθρωπον συνιέναι κατ' εἶδος λεγόμενον, ἐκ πολλῶν ἰὸν αἰσθήσεων εἰς ἓν λογισμῷ συναιρούμενον· τοῦτο δ' ἐστὶν ἀνάμνησις ἐκείνων ἅ ποτ' εἶδεν ἡμῶν ἡ ψυχὴ συμπορευθεῖσα θεῷ καὶ ὑπεριδοῦσα ἃ νῦν εἶναί φαμεν, καὶ ἀνακύψασα εἰς τὸ ὂν ὄντως.

and framing metaphysical theories as far-fetched as they are childish—
to contemporary analytical philosopher who is both mature and reasonable.[17]

Yet it would suffice to read the passage just quoted to debunk this idea:
the two aspects of Plato's philosophy—the calm, systematic exercise of
dialectics alongside the relatively mythical construction of a metaphysics
that is strongly marked by ontological dualism—always go together and it
can neither be said that they are in contradiction with one another, nor that
at some point Plato has traded one for the other.

That said, we cannot even speak of dialectics and the myth as performing
exactly the same task. In actual fact, it is more a question of two complementary aspects of the same theory. At first, dialectics manifests itself as the
unifying approach that leads from the multiplicity of perception to the unity
of the idea—where it turns out that the idea towards which research leads
can only be a transcendent reality, qualitatively unlike perceptive things.
Once that goal is achieved, dialectics ceases to concern itself with the actual
metaphysical nature of ideas (as the *Phaedo* suggests, no full and perfect
knowledge of them is accessible to the soul when detached from the body)[18]
and focuses on the partial data of ideas truly knowable by man, through the
inherently inexhaustible method of placing each idea in relation with others.[19] But the guarantee that such an undertaking can be accomplished is
afforded by the existence of ideas as unitary metaphysical objects, which
the synagogical process has already established beforehand.

And that is precisely why, in the passage quoted above, Socrates says that
dialectics *is* reminiscence. In fact, dialectics can only supply partial and relative knowledge of ideas in the form of *anamnêsis*, i.e. the exercise through
which the soul recalls what it saw when travelling in the *hyperouranios topos*
in the wake of the gods. The condition for realizing the unifying/dividing
process that constitutes dialectics is in fact fulfilled by the existence at a
metaphysical level of absolute units represented by forms. And if the ideas
did not exist, or if the human soul had never managed to contemplate them
in their fullness and perfection before its fall into the body, man would now
be unable to practice dialectics, for he would find not a thread in his mind
to guide him in his tasks of analysis and synthesis on a quest for truth.

---

[17] This point is stressed in Trabattoni (2006) and Trabattoni (2010).

[18] See *Phd.* 66b–67b.

[19] Such a method is expounded, though in different ways, in the *corpus* of the dialectical
dialogues (*Pamenides, Sophist, Philebus, Politicus*). See the 'coherentist' model of knowledge
rightly ascribed to Plato's epistemology by Fine (2003).

4. MYTH AS A PROSECUTION OF *LOGOS*
BEYOND THE BOUNDARIES OF DIALECTICS

Until now, we have talked about dialectics and the metaphysical conditions that make it possible. As for the metaphysical doctrine proper, i.e. the doctrine that strives to understand ideas precisely in their metaphysical otherness from the world of perception, neither the *logos*, nor reason, nor dialectics have the power to concern themselves with it. And if philosophy seeks to advance human knowledge past the world of perception and beyond the unifying work that man is in a position to perform upon that world, then it must indeed turn to myth.

The approach we have described tallies fairly well with the development of Socrates' second speech in the *Phaedrus*. Let us set aside for the moment the first part of the discourse, in which Socrates sets forth to rehabilitate the irrational (we will come back to it a little later). After this section, Socrates crafts a gripping, painstakingly well-reasoned demonstration of the soul's immortality (so much that this exposition is widely held to be Plato's best on the subject). Only when the demonstration is completed does Socrates begin to expound the myth. So then, just as with the pattern we suggested above, we have a first dialectical step. This, in turn, results in a wholly metaphysical kind of reality, in the sense that it is unlike and far above any perceptive reality. In this case, then, it is not the idea but the soul. However, if the soul is truly immortal, it means that it can exist all by itself, bereft of a body, in a dimension that clearly cannot be that of the senses. Thus, with proof of the immortality of the soul, one has at the same time laid down the existence of a 'region above the heavens' (*hyperouranios topos*).

Having reached this point, philosophy's next step should of course afford us some knowledge of this field. And that is precisely what Plato readies himself to do, though not by means of dialectics, which henceforth comes to an end. It is now time for myth, as it now falls upon the latter, and no longer dialectics, to describe this supra-celestial place, whose existence had been established by dialectics itself.[20]

---

[20] As previously seen (n. 11), Ferrari (1987), 122 too thinks that Socrates' choice in favour of myth stems from a sort of constraint. But I cannot agree with his (rather complicated) explanation for such a constraint. He believes the soul to be the heart of the problem: since inquiring into the soul is at the same time tantamount to looking into our soul, it follows that 'to *learn* about the soul can also be ... to *learn* a way of life'. Then, 'Socrates in his mythic hymn examines not only the nature of the soul but also ... what happens to philosophers when they look into the soul; for he wants to stress the subjective effects of the investigation on the investigators, as well as its objective results'. And it is precisely

Hence, one can easily understand what constitutes apportioning the work between the *logos* and myth. The point of contact between the two is the existence of a metaphysical dimension, which, albeit in a different and almost opposite manner, represents a condition for possibility of one and the other. Dialectics meets the metaphysical dimension as the furthermost boundary of any perceptive, human reality, which lends this reality its existence as well as its recognizable features.[21] But dialectics is unable to make any progress in the direction of metaphysics. The myth, for its part, takes up its work right where dialectics left off, deep in the heart of metaphysical reality, with the aim of somehow representing its true nature.[22]

5. WHAT DOES 'METAPHYSICAL REALITY' MEANS?

To avoid dangerous misunderstandings, I think it behooves me to explain how the adjective 'metaphysical' is used in this paper. The word 'metaphys-

---

for this reason that 'here mythic allegory takes up its proper place'. In fact, 'an allegory does not present the soul as it is, but says what it is like. It is a way—not the only way, perhaps, but an excellent way—of both acknowledging and putting into effect the twofold perspective of our enquiry: how we are looking into the soul in general, and our own (and our lovers') souls in particular; and how we are thus not only scrutinizing our target from a distance, but changing its nature, creating it anew'. I am not going so far as to say the topics emphasized by Ferrari are pointless if we are to understand Socrates' second speech in the *Phaedrus*. But I do not think that they provide us with sound answers to the problem at stake here, namely why Socrates opted for a mythical tale. Actually, the myth is concerned not only with the soul, but also with the ὑπερουράνιος τόπος. If it is true that, as Heitsch (1997) 100 claims, 'anders als die Seele ist die Welt nicht eigentlich Thema der Darstellung,' it is also true that 'sie bildet ... den Raum, in dem die unsterblichen Seelen bewegen'; and the description of the soul deserves a mythical treatment precisely because it is depicted during its body-free condition. As we saw above, when there is no such qualification, Plato shows no qualms in adopting the path of dialectics. More in general, it happens quite often that an underestimation of the real nature of Plato's metaphysics—eventually influenced by its seemingly scant philosophical appeal in our times—leads to unconvincing (or not fully convincing) interpretations.

    [21] See what Plato says in the *Republic* about the idea of Good, 509b.

    [22] According to Morgan (1990), 178, 'the *Phaedrus* myth ... provides a psychological ground for the possibility of learning and hence a noncognitive foundation for philosophical inquiry'. I cannot agree with this definition. As I have attempted to show, the aim of the *Phaedrus* myth is not psychological but metaphysical. Moreover, the problem with which the myth is concerned is not the foundation of philosophical inquiry. Such a foundation, in fact, is provided by the recollection theory. And if it is true that recollection is obviously implied in the myth, the myth itself is not entrusted with accomplishing the same task assigned to it: the recollection theory aims at showing the *existence* of the metaphysical realm (see *Phd.* 72e–77b), while the *Phaedrus* myth is looking for a way to *describe* it somehow.

ical' refers primarily to any kind of reality that does not belong to the world of corporeal and movable things; secondly, to any kind of condition other than the present time, wherein men traditionally dwell. Under this definition, metaphysical knowledge coincides with that kind of knowledge that deems itself capable of uttering positive assertions about the classes of reality or situation I have just specified. Given these assumptions, there is little gainsaying that the primary tool of metaphysical knowledge in Plato is the myth itself. This is clearly true for the myths of an eschatological strain, such as those found in *Gorgias*, *Phaedo*, *Republic* and *Phaedrus*. The same, however, can be said about the myth of the cave. Also possessing a metaphysical nature are those myths that seek to recreate an idyllic primeval age of mankind, which not only predates historical time but is also qualitatively separated from it. Such are e.g. the Atlantis myth, the races myth in the *Republic*, and the myths of the age of Cronos as outlined in the *Statesman* and the *Laws*. Yet even the *Phaedrus* myth of Thamous and Theuth belongs to the same category, for Plato cannot be thought to truly believe in the historicity of what is told therein. In summary, what binds myths thus construed is that they claim to have something good to say about reality or situations that are beyond the ken of man in his physical, temporal, and worldly state.

That said, one might ask whether Plato credited myth alone with the ability to make 'metaphysical' utterances of this kind, or whether he deemed it possible to use other means (e.g. dialectics) instead. My argument, which I shall put forward neither absolutely nor dogmatically, is that Plato generally keeps the two forms of knowledge apart. In the case of the soul, which is clearly a metaphysical reality, Plato truly deems it ever-moving and immortal. But neither of these qualities amounts to a positive description of a metaphysical event or thing. That the soul is ever-moving draws from the empirical finding that only living things can move. The metaphysical claim consists in assuming there is a non-corporeal substance capable of moving by itself (and for evermore), but the arguments merely prove the existence of a substance of that kind, while nothing positive is said about it. Indeed, the task of positively establishing the nature of the soul falls upon the myth (ref. the image of the winged chariot in *Phaedrus*). The same goes for immortality. The claim that the soul is immortal merely reverses the seeable and manifest mortality of everything our senses perceive, whereas the immortality of the soul is neither seeable nor manifest. Likewise, a substance that is not mortal, but immaterial and immobile is neither seeable nor manifest, and neither can it be described through words (unlike mortal, material and mobile substances).

318 FRANCO TRABATTONI

A like reasoning applies to ideas. Forsooth, ideas are described as self-same, eternal, unchanging, the subject of reminiscence, etc. But none of these determinants are positive claims. Plato had good reason to believe that immobile substances exist alongside moving substances. But saying a substance 'is immobile' by no means bestows upon it a positive quality. We say only that this substance is 'not moving'. Thus far dialectics can go. But it cannot go further, i.e. it may not reach beyond this negative determination nor classify immobile substances with positive attributes, unlike moving substance (which for example are also coloured, heavy, shock-resistant, etc.). As Francisco Gonzalez noted, Plato never truly answers the question 'what kind of entities are ideas'; and this, in his opinion, is one of the reasons why we cannot speak of a 'doctrine of ideas by Plato'.[23] My guess is that this theory does not exist for the very reason that Plato did not deem the human logos mighty enough to make positive claims about metaphysical entities (in the sense set out above), wherein ideas are foremost. I do not mean that Plato duly entrusted myth with this task, for his chosen strategy is mostly silence, but wherever silence is withheld, myth generally sets in.

Interestingly, this state of affairs is mirrored exactly in the criticism that Aristotle has levelled against Plato. With regard to some crucial metaphysical issues (e.g. participation) Aristotle accuses him time and again of being unclear, of speaking emptily (i.e. without a real appraisal of the content), of failing to outline anything other than poetic metaphors. Aristotle had clearly noted, then, that when it comes to making positively metaphysical claims, the *logos* in Plato is still; and should the word perchance dare cross this boundary,[24] then the word is no longer that of the *logos* but that of myth and poetic metaphor.[25]

---

[23] Gonzalez (2003), in particular 34–35, 39–41.

[24] At the end of the *Phaedo*, all that has be proven is the immortality of the soul. But Socrates want to add something about the places where the souls are going after their detachment from the body. So, the myth comes into play. But Socrates warns that the truth of the myth is by no means as powerful as the truth provided by logos: 'Well, Simmias, I don't think the skill of Glaucus is needed to relate what they [i.e. the regions of the earth] are; although to prove them (ὡς μέντοι ἀληθῆ) does seem to me too hard for the skill of Glaucus—I probably couldn't do it myself, and besides, even if I knew how to, I think the life left me, Simmias, doesn't suffice for the length of the argument. Still, nothing prevents me from telling of what I've been convinced the earth is like in shape, and of its regions' (108d–e, tr. Gallop). The myth, in other words, is neither simply true nor simply false (in that case, the philosophers should refrain from it). As it is used by the philosopher, it consists in the merely likely words that *nothing prevent him from uttering*, once provided that they are grounded on some truth already showed by dialectic and reason (in that case, the immortality of the soul).

[25] Let me quote a passage from McCoy (2008), 164–165, where exactly the same point is stressed. According to her, Plato's Socrates 'does not reject the possibility of metaphysics ...

6. Dialectics as a Condition of
Possibility of Philosophical Myth

There is one last question which we must necessarily seek to answer. Even if one takes into account the crucial difference between myth handed down by tradition and myth constructed by the philosopher, how could we be assured that the philosophical myth really tells the truth? Ultimately, in fact, Plato believes that the right to establish whether a word, mythical or not, contains a kernel of truth always returns to the *logos* itself. Hence, by what means can one rule on the truth of a word whose outspoken aim is to overreach the *logos*, establishing itself beyond it?

To solve this problem it is useful to return to the rehabilitation of the *mania*, in its four different forms, that we find at the start of Socrates' second discourse (244b–245c). This passage has often astonished critics, who have sometimes regarded it as a kind of odd exception within the strict rationalism that is thought to permeate Plato's philosophy, and especially his epistemology. Like Martha Nussbaum, one even might have believed that the *Phaedrus* represented a kind of palinode on Plato's part, akin to the one attributed by the text to the poet Stesichorus.[26] In this respect and, more strictly, on the subject of myth we are now dealing with, the difference between the *Phaedrus* and the *Republic* has been repeatedly noted with regard to poetry: the strongly negative opinions one finds in the greater dialogue are transformed here into a largely positive assessment. Moreover, the theme of the poet's divine inspiration appears to reconcile the *Phaedrus*, over and beyond the *Republic*, with an early dialogue such as the *Ion*.

First of all, let us note that the similarities between the *Ion* and the *Phaedrus* regarding the poet's inspiration are only apparent. In the *Ion*, in fact, Plato summons inspiration as a countermark to the poet's ignorance and to poetic culture in general which, even when producing good results, only succeeds notwithstanding a total absence of the *logos* and its control. This is already enough, in Plato's eyes, to maintain that poetry, poets and their interpreters have no claim to a governing role in the city and in society. The use of inspiration in this context has therefore no other aim than that

---

However, his understanding of human nature and especially the need for acknowledging the limits of human knowledge make the possibility of a complete metaphysics unlikely. When Socrates speaks of the forms, *he uses imagery and metaphor* [italic mine]—as in the *Republic*, which admits to describing only a 'child' of the good and not the god itself—or he engages in criticism of metaphysical issues—as in the *Parmenides*, which does not resolve the problems it sets out'. As far as Aristotle is concerned, see Trabattoni (2007).

[26] Nussbaum (1986), 200–233. On this topic, see Trabattoni (2008).

of highlighting the inferiority and subordination of mythical and poetic speech vis-à-vis the *logos*.[27] It is quite a different story in the *Phaedrus*. The practice of *logos*, which from a general point of view is undoubtedly superior to the use of the mythical and poetic word, has therefore exposed a metaphysical reality that the *logos* itself has neither the power to describe nor to shed light on. So, unless we completely refrain from using words to cross over the boundaries of the physical universe (which therefore means retaining the most rigorous silence on realities such as *hyperoûranios topos*), we must give a second chance to the irrational, namely, to myth and poetry. In other words, since for Plato there is a kind of truth not expressible through *logos* (as it is available only in a pre-discursive way, with reference to the anamnesis-theory), both myth and poetry, though far weaker than logos, could be possibly philosophical useful as substitutes of strictly dialectical arguments.

But how can we be sure that this mythical discourse, which obviously cannot be controlled by the *logos*, is really true? First of all, let us answer that nowhere in Plato do we find assurance that man has ultimately lodged himself within the realms of truth—not even through dialectics. This is for the simple reason that fully achieved knowledge of the truth of being, as inferred also from the myth under present examination, is the exclusive concern of the soul when detached from the body. Secondly, it must be said that the approach undertaken by the philosophical myth, while fabulous as such, draws its thrust from the existence of a metaphysical reality (the immortal soul, eternal ideas, the *hyperoûranios topos*) that was established not by the myth itself but by the *logos*.

Clearly, *logos* has only succeeded in establishing this existence within the limits of its capabilities; yet these are also the limits of all discourse and all human knowledge regarding the truth. As for the philosophical myth, if on the one hand it is unrealistic to accord it a degree of certainty that is not granted to *logos* itself, and if we must settle for something less instead, then on the other hand we can assert that its link to the truth is therefore real, and consequently can never be utterly severed. This conclusion reminds us of what Socrates himself notes immediately after completing the narrative of the eschatological myth of the *Phaedo*:

> After all, it would not be fitting for a man of sense (*noûn andri echonti*) to maintain that all this is just as I have described it. But still this or something like it is true concerning our souls and their abodes, at least that the soul is

[27] This is maintained in Trabattoni (1985–1986), Trabattoni (2000) and Trabattoni (2004).

shown to be immortal, hence I think he may properly and worthily venture to run the risk, which is worth while when one believes (*oiomenôi*) in this immortality.[28]   (114d1–d6)

In this passage, providing one has the wisdom not to take all the specific elements literally, the truth of the myth is linked to the truth of the dialectic demonstration whence the myth draws its thrust, it being understood that this very truth is not completely beyond doubt. Perhaps, these necessarily limited and partial 'truths' do not seem much to some. But to Plato this represents the whole truth, part dialectic and part mythical, that man can have at his disposal in his mortal state.

---

[28] Τὸ μὲν οὖν ταῦτα διισχυρίσασθαι οὕτως ἔχειν ὡς ἐγὼ διελήλυθα, οὐ πρέπει νοῦν ἔχοντι ἀνδρί· ὅτι μέντοι ἢ ταῦτ' ἐστὶν ἢ τοιαῦτ' ἄττα περὶ τὰς ψυχὰς ἡμῶν καὶ τὰς οἰκήσεις, ἐπείπερ ἀθάνατόν γε ἡ ψυχὴ φαίνεται οὖσα, τοῦτο καὶ πρέπειν μοι δοκεῖ καὶ ἄξιον κινδυνεῦσαι οἰομένῳ οὕτως ἔχειν.

CHAPTER SIXTEEN

THERIOMORPHISM AND THE COMPOSITE SOUL IN PLATO[*]

Kathryn Morgan

The question of how we conceive and picture the soul is one to which several essays in this volume return, central as it is to Plato's deployment of myth in his dialogues. My contribution here, rather than focusing on myths of post-mortem judgment of the soul, will examine an aspect of mythological presentation that offers resonant narrative trajectories: images of the composite soul that include animal elements. These images, clustered in the *Republic* and *Phaedrus*, have the merit of bringing to the fore a central methodological issue, namely, the extent to which it is possible for human language to represent the soul and the consequences of doing so. I shall argue that attempts to picture the soul bring an attentive audience to the realization of the incapacity of even metaphorical language accurately to express its nature.[1] The job of theriomorphic images of the soul is to make this point obvious. Second, I shall stress that the image of the soul as a composite with one or more animal parts is intimately connected with the problem of embodiment. Although the soul and its constituent parts may be immaterial, we can only conceive of them from the perspective of human beings, souls encased in bodies, and this perspective inevitably colours our image construction. I will not, then, be concerned with technical questions of psychic structure[2]—how Plato thought the various aspects of the soul interact—but with questions of representation and its heuristic function. My essay will begin with a consideration of one configuration of the relationship between the human soul and animals, the metempsychosis of souls into animal bodies. Next it will examine the group of passages in the *Republic* and *Phaedrus* that connect the soul with composite mythological monsters, moving from there to focus on the image of the psychic chariot in the *Phaedrus* and *Timaeus*. It will conclude by reflecting on the implications of

[*] Thanks are due to David Blank, Andrea Nightingale, and Mario Telò for valuable comments on this paper; also to Kristin Mann for help with editing.
[1] See also Morgan (2000).
[2] For a recent treatment of psychic partition along these lines, see Lorenz (2006).

the famous passage of the *Phaedrus* that compares a speech to a living animal (264c): to what extent is the *Phaedrus* itself a monstrous compound?

1. MEN AND BEASTS

That there was ethical purchase in the comparison of men and animals was made obvious by the fable tradition. Most famously represented by Aesop, fable was made possible by a perceived fundamental similarity between animals and human beings, though it also perhaps played on the notion that important distances separated, or should separate, the world of animals from that of humans.[3] Plato's *Phaedo* develops yet also transforms the notion of the Aesopic fable.[4] At the start of the dialogue, Socrates is shown versifying Aesop's fables as part of his response to the divine command to 'make music' (*Phd.* 60c9–e7). This adumbration of the genre of fable is taken up at 81c8–82b8 in one of Socrates' initial accounts of the fate of the soul after death: the souls of the wicked wander until their desire for the corporeal (*sômatoeidous*, 81e1) unites them again with a body. Gluttons are reincarnated as, e.g., donkeys; the lawless and violent become wolves and hawks and kites; decent people without knowledge of philosophy become bees, wasps, or ants. The notion that an unphilosophical soul might be reincarnated into an animal body may be regarded as the most basic Platonic expression of the affinity between animals and certain aspects of the human soul. There is no thought in the *Phaedo* that the soul is itself a compound some of whose parts are animalistic; thus the expression of similarity between the soul and animals must be cast diachronically: a human soul is reincarnated in an animal body.[5]

Even so, certain aspects of the *Phaedo*'s description of the fate of the soul after death are resonant for present purposes. We note that souls who have been too influenced by the body in life cannot shake it off and are trapped by their desire for the corporeal, 'that which has the form of a body'

---

[3] On fable and the complex relationship between humans and animals, see Clayton (2008), especially 189–191 on Aristotle's conception of the place of humans in the animal world and his observation that the untrained soul of a child 'has practically no difference from that of wild animals' (*HA* 588a–588b).

[4] Morgan (2000), 192–196. Kurke (2006) sees the popular Aesopic tradition as an important and elided precursor for Plato's mimetic prose. She too draws attention to Socrates' Aesopic activities at the beginning of the *Phaedo* (13–15), but does not connect this with the dialogue's narrative of metempsychosis.

[5] As Robinson (1970), 25–33 points out, the main division of the *Phaedo* is between body and soul.

(*sômatoeidous*, 81e1). Since the soul has been sullied by life in the body it cannot depart into the underworld 'pure' (*eilikrinê*, 81c2). The contamination of the soul by the corporeal is the explanation for ghostly apparitions.[6] Interestingly, then, even Plato's non-tripartite souls can lose their original unmixed nature and become compounds of a sort. The combination of soul and body is itself a compound and soul-animal compounding takes place diachronically, as we have seen. Moreover, even the immaterial soul can be 'weighed down and ... earthlike and visible' (*Phd.* 81c8–9).[7] The soul becomes 'visible' to us when it is admixed with the material world. The body infects our soul and its thought processes. To be sure, the *Phaedo* is talking in the first instance about shadowy apparitions as an extreme version of corporeal contamination, but I would like to take from this passage the important idea that the soul is made visible to us by compounding, both at the physical level and also, perhaps, conceptually.

The idea that the soul's affinity with animalistic properties can cause reincarnation into an animal body occurs even in dialogues where the soul is presented as a composite entity. The *Phaedrus* presents a complicated picture of reincarnation based on conduct during a previous life. At 248c5–e3 we are presented with a hierarchy of possible lives available for reincarnated souls. This list includes only human ones, with the 'musical' or 'erotic' souls that love wisdom or beauty at the top and the tyrant at the bottom. Yet it is also clear that souls may choose to be reborn in the bodies of animals, and may transfer from animal lives back into human ones (as long as they had originally seen the Truth in the place beyond the heavens) (249b1–6). Similarly in *Republic* X (620a2–c3) at the choice of lives some souls choose to be reborn as animals: thus Orpheus chooses to be a swan and Ajax a lion. The progression is put on a pseudo-scientific basis in the *Timaeus*, where it seems that all mortal souls start out as men, and then are demoted into women if they do not live a life of virtue, and thence (42b3–d2) continually into the nature of a beast (*thêreion phusin*) until they reform. In all these scenarios we see a concern to make bodily nature express the character of the soul. The intuition that the soul can operate like an animal is stretched

---

6 For a more detailed examination of how Plato appropriates cultural traditions about the restless dead, see Edmonds (2004), 177–195 (in particular 192–193 for an acute analysis of how the difference between phenomenal and non-phenomenal is presented in the dialogue in terms of a contrast between the multiple and the simple). Robinson (1970), 32–33 comments usefully on the physicality of the soul in this passage, even describing it (30) as a kind of 'ectoplasm'.

7 Ἐμβριθὲς ... καὶ γεῶδες καὶ ὁρατόν.

out on a diachronic axis over a series of lives, until the soul shall, one hopes, regain its primal purity. Yet Plato evidently also felt the urge to illustrate this intuition from a synchronic perspective, projecting the animal into composite pictures of the soul at a single moment. It is to these pictures that we now turn.

2. Mythological Monsters

We can conveniently start with the *Phaedrus* and Socrates' famous dismissal of rationalizing treatments of mythology. At 229c4–230a6 Socrates is asked whether he accepts the story of Boreas' rape of Oreithyia. He refuses to be drawn into such a discussion because he would then be obliged to address the reality of monsters such as centaurs, the Chimaera, Pegasuses and Gorgons. But he still has not yet learned to 'know himself,' whether he is a 'more complex beast than Typhon and more inflamed, or a more gentle and simpler creature, sharing naturally in a divine and un-Typhonic portion' (*Phdr.* 230a3–6).[8] As G.R.F. Ferrari has pointed out, Socrates here reinstates a kind of myth even as he dismisses certain types of analysis: in his second speech with the myth of the charioteer he will return, as we shall, to the vision of the soul as a composite mythological monster. The emphasis, both in the case of Typhon and the charioteer, is on the use of myth as a heuristic device for psychic analysis rather than as an object of historical research.[9] The use of Typhon is resonant both because of the way the monster has been described by Hesiod and through its narrative trajectory. The Hesiodic Typhoeus was distinguished by one hundred snaky heads, which had the ability to mimic all kinds of sounds (*Theogony*, 823–835). Andrea Nightingale[10] notes the essential plurivocality of the typhonic soul and connects this characteristic with the problem of alien and authentic voices in the soul.[11] I want to come at this plurivocality from a related direction, stressing that it results from Typhon's nature as a composite creature; a composite, moreover, that contains physically both animal and anthropomorphic elements. The animal elements produce sounds that the gods can comprehend, but also the noises of animals. When Socrates wonders how similar he is to Typhon,

---

[8] εἴτε τι θηρίον ὂν τυγχάνω Τυφῶνος πολυπλοκώτερον καὶ μᾶλλον ἐπιτεθυμμένον, εἴτε ἡμερώτερόν τε καὶ ἁπλούστερον ζῷον, θείας τινὸς καὶ ἀτύφου μοίρας φύσει μετέχον.

[9] Ferrari (1987), 11–12.

[10] Nightingale (1995), 134–135.

[11] Both Ferrari and Nightingale realize the significance of the composite theme, but do slightly different things with it.

therefore, he is using the image heuristically, asking a question about psychic complexity and its implications. Is he more complex, more inflamed, simpler, or gentler?

At this stage in the dialogue there has, of course, been no formal analysis of psychic structure such as we are given in Socrates' second speech. Yet just as pregnant for the dialogue's thematic development as Typhon's multiple voices is his (related) nature as a physical composite of animal and non-animal elements, which foreshadows the charioteer/chariot-team complex later in the dialogue and has connections to the image of the appetitive part of the soul in the *Republic*, to which we shall shortly return. This compound nature makes him a useful device for considering something as difficult and mysterious as the soul; yet also useful is the narrative that goes along with him. In the *Theogony* Typhon, a final child of earth, rebels against the will of Zeus and is forcibly defeated, subdued by his lightening. Blasted into submission, he is thrown into Tartarus by Zeus, who descends from Olympus. Zeus' lightening is what makes Typhon *epitethummenon*, inflamed and smoking—the perfect passive of *epituphomai*.[12] Yet the participle may also recall the verb *epithumeo* and its noun *epithumia*, desire. This verb does not exist in the perfect passive, but its projected form would be very close to this. Later in the dialogue the black horse of the soul will be the most irrationally inflamed at the sight of beauty and the most rebellious to the charioteer; it is the part of the soul most easily associated with, though perhaps not identical to, appetitive desire. Typhon, then, is a passionate rebel against the gods who is cast down to earth and even below it. Socrates, or indeed any human, needs to measure himself against this trajectory and place his passions correctly: more or less complex, tamer or wilder than a many-headed animal composite? Deploying the Typhon comparison immediately brings up the problem of fit between tenor and vehicle, and this is only reinforced by the diffident comparatives.

Once we allow the Typhon comparison its full resonance, it is tempting also to take a closer look at the other composite creatures Socrates mentions: centaurs, the Chimaera, Pegasuses and Gorgons. Centaurs had long been a mythological paradigm of bestial lust and all kinds of incontinence gone wild, with centauromachies adorning the Temple of Zeus at Olympia

---

[12] LSJ *s.v.* We might also understand the verb as meaning that he has been puffed up by his own stormy winds of passion. Rowe (1986), 141 notes in addition that Greek *tuphos* can mean 'delusion' or 'craziness,' a connotation which 'in light of the theme of the later speeches on love (love as *madness*) ... is also likely to be relevant'.

as well as the Parthenon at Athens. If, moreover, we follow the account of Pindar in *Pythian* 2. 33–48, the centaurs were created as a consequence of Ixion's attempted rape of Hera. Instead of achieving his goal he lay with a cloud, an illusion, and produced the monstrous Kentauros, which then coupled with horses on Mt. Pelion and produced the race of centaurs. The name of Ixion's monstrous child is a pun on *kentron* (a prick or goad), and *aura*, the breeze, an etymological coupling that represents the useless and unfulfilling coupling of Ixion with the cloud. It also evokes the horse goad with which a rider or charioteer will attempt to control his horses (*Phdr.* 253e4–254a4), and in the *Phaedrus* the goads of desire which madden the lover (251e3–5, 253e6–254a1). The resonances are, then, over-determined: the pricks of desire which torment the lover and tempted Ixion; the pricks that discipline the wayward horse; Ixion's loss of his favoured status with the gods on Olympus (his punishment is to be transformed into a living love-charm, a *iugx* wheel); the production of monstrous composite creatures due to a lack of control—the same monstrous composites of man and horse that are regularly overpowered by passion in heroic myths. It is difficult to be certain that all these nuances are active, but they are certainly possible, and even if only the most coarse-grained of them is in operation (licentious man-horse composites), this still makes an interesting juxtaposition for the later chariot image.

The Chimaera, Pegasus and the Gorgons are linked in mythological narrative. The hero Perseus (wearing winged sandals and flying) kills the Gorgon Medusa (another terrifying snaky composite), and from her blood springs the winged horse Pegasus. In a later generation the hero Bellerophon will mount Pegasus in his quest to kill the Chimaera (head of a lion, tail of a snake, with a goat head added on in the midsection for good measure: a three-part composite). Bellerophon's tale comes to a bad end when he attempts to ride Pegasus to Olympus. He is cast down to earth, but Pegasus remains in Zeus' stables (Pindar *O.* 13.92). Both the Gorgon and the Chimaera, then, are composite creatures whose defeat is a measure of human and heroic achievement. They are defeated by heroes who either have wings themselves (Perseus) or are mounted on a winged steed (Bellerophon). In the case of Bellerophon, the winged horse can raise him towards the heavens, but since he tries to attain them in a spirit of rebellion, he is cast down. None of these episodes is, of course, a direct match for the myth of the charioteer later in the *Phaedrus*, but they do give a sense that composite monsters exist, for the most part, to be defeated. Taken together, the centaurs and Pegasus provide almost all the elements that will be important in the later speech: passion, barely or not at all under control, and the power of the wing, under the right circumstances, to bring us closer to the gods.[13] The combination of man and horse is particularly suggestive; while composites of several animals are frightening, the real interest arises from the combination of man with another animal.

This brings us to the fascinating image of the soul in *Republic* IX. Socrates has decided to construct an image of the soul in speech:

> One of the sort of ancient natures that are said in myths to have existed: the Chimaera and Scylla and Cerberus, and many other creatures that are said to have been produced with many forms in one body ... So shape one form of a complex and many-headed beast, one that has in a circle the heads of beasts both wild and tame and is capable of changing and growing all these out of itself.[14]   (*Rep.* IX 588c2–10)

Apart from this complicated beast, which is also the largest in size, we are also to imagine a lion and a man. These three beings are to be joined together into one, so that they grow together (*sumpephukenai*, 588d7–8). The final stage is to put the image of one of the parts, that of the man, over the outside, so that an onlooker who could not see the inside would think it was one animal, a man (588d10–e1). This passage piles complexity upon complexity. The many-headed beast is the appetitive part of the soul, the *epithumêtikon*, which, as we learned at 580d11–e4, is the largest and strongest part of the soul and is characterized by its many forms (*polueidian*). This beast is like a mythological monster, and it will be the job of the rational part of the soul to tame the wild parts of it and encourage the gentle parts (589a6–b6). As others before me have observed, this image of the appetitive part of soul as a many-headed monster is connected to the picture of the soul as a typhonic being at the opening of the *Phaedrus*.[15] In light of this passage, one of the things Socrates is wondering at the beginning of the *Phaedrus* is whether or not he is to be identified with this appetitive aspect of the soul.

---

[13] Cf. de Romilly (1982), 100.

[14] Τῶν τοιούτων τινά, ἦν δ' ἐγώ, οἷαι μυθολογοῦνται παλαιαὶ γενέσθαι φύσεις, ἥ τε Χιμαίρας καὶ ἡ Σκύλλης καὶ Κερβέρου, καὶ ἄλλαι τινὲς συχναὶ λέγονται συμπεφυκυῖαι ἰδέαι πολλαὶ εἰς ἓν γενέσθαι ... Πλάττε τοίνυν μίαν μὲν ἰδέαν θηρίου ποικίλου καὶ πολυκεφάλου, ἡμέρων δὲ θηρίων ἔχοντος κεφαλὰς κύκλῳ καὶ ἀγρίων, καὶ δυνατοῦ μεταβάλλειν καὶ φύειν ἐξ αὐτοῦ πάντα ταῦτα. For an analysis of this image in terms of human-animal hierarchy, see Pender (2000), 213–219. Cf. also *Rep.* 487e–488a, where Socrates compares his image-making to painters who paint 'goat-stags.' When the concept is difficult to illustrate one must 'compound [the image] from many sources.'

[15] Adam (1902), II, 363; Rowe (1986), 140; Nightingale (1995), 144. Robinson (1970), 117 connects the many-headed beast with the black horse of the *Phaedrus*.

The process of 'composition' here is twofold, and its ordered presentation is deliberate. The construction of the many-headed beast comes first; this is the part whose creation is obtrusively labeled as mythological (*mutholo-gountai*, 588c2).[16] Then in a second round of composition the lion and man are encased, together with the mythological beast, in an anthropomorphic coating. The appetitive part of the soul is thus seen as most truly composite and glossed as the most appropriate counterpart of composite mythological monsters—another indication that the conception of the soul as a quasi-mythological compound is tied to the imaginations of the flesh. Yet the whole soul is clearly also a composite, though of a peculiarly philosophical type. Whereas mythological beasts terrify at first sight, the composite soul has a misleading external impression of normalcy. It *looks* like a man, and it is only the philosophical mind that can penetrate the disguise and recognize it for the strange creature it is. In a further step, the well-intentioned philosopher can use the image as a way to educate the partisans of injustice (588e2–589a4). Philosophical mythologizing, then, goes beyond that of its ancient predecessors in complexity and subtlety.

We shall shortly return to this issue with a consideration of the image of the sea god Glaucus towards the end of the *Republic*, but before we do it will be useful to take a brief detour into the *Cratylus* for another example of a mythological composite, this time one closely connected with the problems of speech. As Socrates completes his discussion of the names of gods, he remarks (408b7–8) how reasonable it is that Pan is the 'two-natured' son of Hermes, the god most closely connected with speech. Speech signifies everything (*to pan sēmainei*) and is double, both true and false (408c2–3). So, then, in his 'true' upper part Pan is smooth and divine and lives with the gods, while in his 'false' lower part he is rough and goatish (*tragikon*, 408c5–7). In a further pun on the word *tragikos*, 'goatish' or 'tragic', Socrates observes that 'myths and falsities' are very numerous in that part of life that is *tragikos* (408c7–9). Although this passage is not analysing the human soul, it does have close affinities with the other passages we have been studying. It conceives a human-animal composite whose lower part is connected with the mortal as opposed to the divine, but in this case the composite represents speech in human life. False speech is connected with mythology

---

[16] We may contrast the presentation of the appetitive part of the soul at *Timaeus* 70e3–5. It is placed in the belly near the 'manger': 'they bound it there like a wild animal (*thremma agrion*), but one that had to be nourished once it had been joined to the whole, if there was ever going to be the race of mortals'. Again we see a forcible compounding of what goes into the human soul where one part is a beast, but there is no interest in developing a mythological analogy, nor in elaborating the appetitive portion soul as itself a composite.

and also with the genre of tragic poetry, and for those familiar with Socrates' critique of tragedy in the *Republic*, it is a simple matter to conclude that the tragic, animal life has affinities with the lowest (appetitive) part of the soul. The double nature of speech in the *Cratylus* is inextricably connected with the problems of human life; how could one possibly separate one nature from the other?[17] We realize that (as will be the case with Glaucus) we are very much dealing with a god of mythology, whose appearance and conception outside the human realm is almost unfathomable.[18]

The issue of the extent to which embodiment affects our conception and understanding of the nature of the soul comes to the fore especially in the case of the comparison of the soul to Glaucus in *Republic* X (611b9–612a6). Commentators have differed over whether to interpret this passage as saying that the soul unaffected by embodiment may in fact not be divided into parts, or that even the disembodied soul is divided into parts:

> ... as for how it [the soul] truly is, we must not look at it mutilated by its association with the body and other evils, as we observe it now, but how it is when it's pure ... but we have been looking at it just like those who see the sea god Glaucus; they no longer can see easily his original nature, because some of the ancient parts of his body have broken off, others have been worn away and totally maimed by the waves, and others have been added: barnacles and seaweed and rocks, so that in every way he looks more like a wild animal than he is by nature. Just so, we observe the soul affected by countless evils.[19]
>
> (*Rep.* X, 611b10–612d7)

For, e.g., Adam, the comparison implies that the lower parts of the soul are 'incidental to its association with the body and consequently perishable',[20]

---

[17] Halliwell (2002), 104–105 speaks of the 'harshly material humanness' that characterizes the 'tragic' view of life in this passage.

[18] Pan's double nature of goat and man—thus satyr-like—reminds us of course of Alcibiades' famous description of Socrates and his words as a *silenos* on the outside but with a divine and golden interior containing representations of gods (*Symp.* 221d1–222a6). Upper and lower (in Pan) have transposed into inner and outer (in Socrates). Moreover, this disjunction between inner and outer also inverts the image of the homunculus in the *Republic*, where a normal exterior is belied by its composite and problematic interior. On similarities between Socrates, satyrs (as mediators between the human and divine) and the black horse of the *Phaedrus*, see further Belfiore (2006), 199–203.

[19] οἷον δ' ἐστὶν τῇ ἀληθείᾳ, οὐ λελωβημένον δεῖ αὐτὸ θεάσασθαι ὑπό τε τῆς τοῦ σώματος κοινωνίας καὶ ἄλλων κακῶν, ὥσπερ νῦν ἡμεῖς θεώμεθα, ἀλλ' οἷόν ἐστιν καθαρὸν γιγνόμενον ... τεθεάμεθα μέντοι διακείμενον αὐτό, ὥσπερ οἱ τὸν θαλάττιον Γλαῦκον ὁρῶντες οὐκ ἂν ἔτι ῥᾳδίως αὐτοῦ ἴδοιεν τὴν ἀρχαίαν φύσιν, ὑπὸ τοῦ τά τε παλαιὰ τοῦ σώματος μέρη τὰ μὲν ἐκκεκλάσθαι, τὰ δὲ συντετρῖφθαι καὶ πάντως λελωβῆσθαι ὑπὸ τῶν κυμάτων, ἄλλα δὲ προσπεφυκέναι, ὄστρεά τε καὶ φυκία καὶ πέτρας, ὥστε παντὶ μᾶλλον θηρίῳ ἐοικέναι ἢ οἷος ἦν φύσει, οὕτω καὶ τὴν ψυχὴν ἡμεῖς θεώμεθα διακειμένην ὑπὸ μυρίων κακῶν.

[20] Adam (1902), II, 426–427. Bobonich (2002), 255 also suggests that this passage 'at least

whereas Frutiger argues energetically for the opposite.[21] One point at issue is whether the barnacles and other sea garbage should be thought to represent the lower parts of the soul.[22] It does seem clear that they are to be connected with embodiment; just as in the *Phaedo*, there is a strong emphasis on the effects of incarnation on the soul. Equally, however, it is unlikely that the many-headed beast is to be regarded as equivalent to a barnacle. One potential answer to this set of problems might be found in the figure of the god Glaucus himself. He is, unfortunately, very seldom represented in ancient art, and the tradition concerning his origins is not uniform, so it is impossible to state with any certainty what resonances would have been evoked by his mention here. But we do know that he featured in Pindar and Aeschylus as a mortal fisherman who ate a magic herb and became immortal and a sea god (Paus. 9.22.7). In Ovid's *Metamorphoses* he appears as the suitor of Scylla, rejected because his body is part anthropomorphic, part fish (13.904–965).[23] In later traditions, then, Glaucus was a composite creature like a Triton, with an upper body like that of a man and a fishy lower one, not unlike the kind of composite that Pan is in the *Cratylus* passage just considered. If this tradition reaches back to the Classical period, and there is no reason to believe it does not, Plato would be using another mythological composite to conceive the soul. The addition of barnacles and seaweed could then rightly be associated with the perversions caused by the body, but this would not affect the underlying reality of the soul as a composite entity. Such an understanding of the allusion keeps intact the notion of psychic partition while maintaining the crucial point that embodiment affects both our understanding of psychic structure and even, to an extent, the way that structure manifests itself. The very elusiveness of the mythological tradition—the move from mortality to immortality and the uncertainties over representation—reflects the central issues of Plato's presentation here. The monstrous mythological composite again emerges as an ideal analogue not just for the complexities of the soul but for how we choose to talk about them.

---

broaches the possibility of a significant revision in the Book 4 account of the soul. On the Book 4 account, the soul or person is identical with a compound of the three parts. In Book 10, Plato seems to suggest that once the soul is no longer embodied, the Reasoning part loses the other two parts'.

[21] Frutiger (1930), 90–95.
[22] Frutiger (1930), 92; Robinson (1970), 51–52.
[23] Jentel (1988), 271–273.

3. The Chariot Team

Typhon, the many-headed beast, Pan, and Glaucus—these mythical figures are either familiar already or have been constructed according to familiar principles in order to focus on the problem of psychic representation. They are useful partly because their mythological status keeps the issue of metaphorical fit firmly in view. This problem recurs in the famous image of the soul as chariot team and driver in Socrates' second speech in the *Phaedrus*, to which we now turn. The image is introduced with familiar hedging over the status of the account:

> This is the way we must speak about its [the soul's] form: what it *is* is the subject of an absolutely and in every way divine narrative; what it's *like* is the subject of a lesser and human one. Let us therefore speak in this way. Let it be likened to the innate force of a winged team and driver.[24] (*Phdr.* 246a3–7)

The account is thus an image (*eikôn*) and the myth that is based on it is, in a literal sense, an *eikôs muthos*, a likely account. The soul is likened to the force of a winged team of horses and charioteer. This force is innate; the parts are engendered together. We might at first be tempted to conceive this composite in similar terms to the mythological creatures we have already examined, but this would be too hasty. When we think of Pegasi and centaurs and Gorgons, we envision a composite nature united in one body. Even the alarming composite of man, lion, and many-headed beast is enclosed in a covering that imposes a (deceptive) appearance of unity. The chariot team and driver is different. First because we are instructed to think in terms of a 'force' rather than a body; we have moved further into the realm of metaphor. Second because any attempt to conceive the pair and driver as an innate (*sumphutos*), naturally occurring composite is, to say the least, difficult. We may be able to imagine a creature with a human torso and the lower parts of a horse, but it is well-nigh impossible to conceive a unified compound of two horses and driver, and possibly even more impossible for a Greek to do so. The image as first presented has certain interesting omissions that render its interpretation problematic, and it is difficult to tell whether the various parts of the image exist at the same ontological level. Thus the charioteer is identified as the one who holds the reins (*hêniochos*, 246a7), but in a team of horses and driver, the reins are distinguished by not being alive at all: they are technological enhancements designed to enable

---

[24] περὶ δὲ τῆς ἰδέας αὐτῆς ὧδε λεκτέον. οἷον μέν ἐστι, πάντῃ πάντως θείας εἶναι καὶ μακρᾶς διηγήσεως, ᾧ δὲ ἔοικεν, ἀνθρωπίνης τε καὶ ἐλάττονος· ταύτῃ οὖν λέγωμεν. ἐοικέτω δὴ συμφύτῳ δυνάμει ὑποπτέρου ζεύγους τε καὶ ἡνιόχου.

direction of the team. In the physical world a chariot team is made up of parts that are both animate and inanimate, but the initial presentation of the image in the *Phaedrus* mentions only the animate parts.[25]

What of the chariot itself? That this is a real issue and that the effort to specify its role is not misplaced is suggested both by pedagogical experience and by neoplatonic interpretation. When one teaches the dialogue, one is often confronted by students who expend considerable energy in trying to work out what the chariot represents. Moreover, neoplatonist critics found a role for the chariot that, although it seems puzzling to us, shows a perceived need to have it play a part in interpretation. For such critics, as Finamore puts it, '[t]he vehicle is intended to join together two diametrically opposed entities: the incorporeal soul and the corporeal body. It is, therefore, neither material nor immaterial, but a mean between these two extremes'.[26] Even if we do not accept this interpretation, it shows that the notion of the chariot was felt to be connected to the problem of materiality and focuses our attention on the place of the body. The soul is, of course, incorporeal when considered in itself, but the presence of the chariot forces the issue of materiality.

Nor does the text give us any real help. Although we receive some good clues about the two horses and the charioteer that enable the conventional associations (the charioteer as reason, the black horse as appetite and the white horse as the spirited part of the soul—all familiar from the *Republic*), the chariot is more difficult to track down. We hear at 247a8–b2 that the chariots of the gods (*ochêmata*) are equally balanced and obedient to the rein and that they have, therefore, no trouble in making the arduous trip to the place beyond the heavens. Yet although Socrates speaks of vehicles, it is clearly the horses who are well-balanced and obedient, rather than the chariot.[27] In our world, the charioteer is conveyed in a chariot from which he directs the horses. But in the symbolic world of the myth, where we are talking of a disembodied soul, there simply is nothing for the chariot to represent. Like the reins it is a piece of technology, but whereas the inanimate reins at least serve the function of direction, the charioteer has no substance

---

[25] Griswold (1986), 93 considers briefly (but rightly dismisses) the possibility that it is the chariot that unifies the different parts of the soul.

[26] Finamore (1985), 1. The term 'vehicle' translates the concept ὄχημα-πνεῦμα: 'it houses the rational soul in its descent from the noetic realm to the realm of generation; it acts as the organ of sense perception and imagination; and, through theurgic rites, it can be purified and lifted above, a vehicle for the rational soul's return through the cosmos to the gods' (Finamore [1985], 1).

[27] Cf. Griswold (1986), 262, n. 28.

that needs to be conveyed. Indeed, if we ask ourselves what that thing is that is moved by the power and direction of soul, we would have to answer, the body. There is, however, no body for the soul at this point in the myth.[28]

One wonders, then, how far the details of the image are meant to be pressed. One response would be to retreat and concede that the details of any match between image and reality will never be one to one. Thus in his analysis of psychic tripartition in the *Republic*, Moline remarks that the image of a man taming the many-headed beast and a lion is 'a simile ... not a piece of psychological theorizing'.[29] He further stresses the dangers of 'likening anything whatever to a human being'; if we carry anthropomorphism too far we risk raising at a new level the questions that the image was designed to illuminate.[30] This is a legitimate danger, and Socrates does, after all, stress when he introduces the chariot image that it is only a likeness. The net result of this image is tripartition with one superior directive part and two inferior more animalistic parts.[31] A conservative reading would thus be to entertain the notion of a psychic composite but to suspend that rationalizing impulse that Socrates dislikes so much. I would like to resist this program, reasonable though it is, for two reasons. First, because my concern here is precisely with the possible philosophical implications of mythological images, so it seems worthwhile to see where pushing the evidence leads us. Second, because two details in Socrates' second speech bring the issue to the surface. At 247e2–6, we are told that the divine teams, after having looked at the place beyond the heavens, return to the stables where the charioteer sets the horses next to the manger and feeds them nectar and ambrosia. This seems to be an unproblematic picture, but how could it possibly work if the parts of the soul really are engendered together and are a natural composite? Does the image not imply that the horses are separable? It may be true to comment here that allegory alternates with full-blown myth, but why?[32]

---

[28] Cf. the similar problem that arises for Buccioni (2002), 339 in her consideration of the meaning of the psychic horses in the *Phaedrus*. Her aim is somewhat different from mine—to argue against mapping the tripartite psyche of the *Phaedrus* onto the three parts of the soul in the *Republic*—but the corporeality returns. How can we identify the black horse of the soul with appetite when appetite is usually associated with bodies and we do not know how it would function in a discarnate state?

[29] Moline (1978), 13. See further Pender (2000), 225–226 on the implications and risks of anthropomorphic imagery.

[30] Moline (1978), 23.

[31] For a useful summary of scholarly approaches to psychic partition in the *Phaedrus* see Ferrari (1987), 125–126.

[32] Ferrari (1987), 130–131.

Even more to the point are Socrates' strictures on our faulty faculty of religious imagination at 246c2–d3. Here we learn that the non-divine souls, if they lose their wings, fall to earth and take on an earthly body that seems to move itself through its own power.

> The entire compound constructed of body and soul is called a living creature, and has the name 'mortal'. We use the term 'immortal' on the basis of no reasoned argument, but neither having seen nor sufficiently understood god, we form an immortal living creature that has a soul and a body engendered together for all time. But let this be and be spoken of as is dear to god.[33]
>
> (*Phdr.* 246c5–d3)

Here Socrates comments first on the kind of compounding that characterizes our mortal existence: body and soul joined together. We create our notions of the unseen, in this case, our notions of the gods, on the basis of our own experience, and this imaginative process can also be conceived as a process of creating a composite. On the basis of the human composite (soul plus separable and destructible body), we create the divine composite (soul plus non-separable and indestructible body), which is a natural and eternal composite. The word used to describe the divine composite, *sumpephukota* (translated as 'engendered together' above), is cognate with *sumphutos* (the word I have been translating as 'innate'), and connects this mistaken vision of the divine with the image of the chariot team that introduced the myth (the 'innate force'). Interesting conclusions follow from this. Our mortal problem is that we have done the compounding across different realms, the sensible and the intelligible, when we should have, presumably on the basis of philosophical argument, kept the realms separate. Our imagination has committed a category mistake, conceiving immortally embodied gods with a spurious impression of naturalness. This passage shows that Plato's myth-making Socrates is alive to the problem of inaccurate compounding. It is therefore unlikely that Plato expects the difficulties of the chariot simile to go unnoticed. It carries with it a particular physical charge and we are meant to recognize this.[34] The creation of mythological composites is an exercise in putting together the familiar to express new ideas. In the case of the chariot image we have the projection onto the soul of a pre-existent

---

[33] ζῷον τὸ σύμπαν ἐκλήθη, ψυχὴ καὶ σῶμα παγέν, θνητόν τ' ἔσχεν ἐπωνυμίαν· ἀθάνατον δὲ οὐδ' ἐξ ἑνὸς λόγου λελογισμένου, ἀλλὰ πλάττομεν οὔτε ἰδόντες οὔτε ἱκανῶς νοήσαντες θεόν, ἀθάνατόν τι ζῷον, ἔχον μὲν ψυχήν, ἔχον δὲ σῶμα, τὸν ἀεὶ δὲ χρόνον ταῦτα συμπεφυκότα. ἀλλὰ ταῦτα μὲν δή, ὅπῃ τῷ θεῷ φίλον, ταύτῃ ἐχέτω τε καὶ λεγέσθω.

[34] Ferrari (1987), 126–130 suggests that the divine horses are to be associated with the divine concern for the material (corresponding to the sensuous human appetites modelled in the human team).

and non-natural composite comprised not only of animal and human elements, but inanimate technological parts (bit, bridle, chariot). It is thus a much more complex entity than a centaur or the many-headed beast, and calls attention to its own complexity: a linguistic construct that uses as its vehicle something that is not a unity in the sensible world even in our imagination. This is a new departure in Plato's figuration of the soul, and deserves to be signalled as such.

I have been arguing that the lack of fit between the chariot image and the soul becomes obtrusive when we press the details, and that this lack of fit is precisely the point, designed to focus attention on the problems of imaginative compounding that can have its basis only in the world of sense experience. Yet the chariot ensemble as an artificial compound not only calls attention to its own constructedness (a phenomenon concerned with the methodology of myth) but also carries with it a concept of central importance for the soul, the idea of an *agôn*. A chariot team and charioteer evoke a narrative trajectory, that of the chariot race (without, as was the case with Typhon and many-headed beasts, setting up the specific narrative expectation that the composite must be defeated). It is, however, a chariot race with a difference. We are told at 247a4–7 that human souls can follow the gods as the latter range around the cosmos doing their work. The only requirement is the desire and the capacity to follow, 'for envy (*phthonos*) is outside the divine *choros*'. The gods then, unlike their counterparts in archaic and classical poetry, are not jealous gods, and they welcome human emulators. Their movement is like a dance, an orderly and beautiful motion.[35] Human psychic motion is of course different, especially when it is a question of getting to the banquet, to the place beyond the heavens. Now it is a question of 'toil and the utmost *agôn* for the soul' (247b5). The ascent to the place beyond the heavens involves trampling, laming, broken bodies and a kind of competition that is certainly non-cooperative. A chariot accident, in fact. Even though there is no envy among the psychic chariots of the gods, non-divine souls enjoy no such concord, and their fate is portrayed in very resonant contemporary terms (we might think here of the fictional chariot race of Sophocles' *Electra* 698–760, where Orestes is said to have died).[36]

---

[35] Belfiore (2006), 204–211 draws out the implications of the dancing of the gods, stressing that a successful performance by the mortal chariot teams is a means of psychic integration whereby the teams endeavour to rejoin the divine 'dance'.

[36] The struggle between the charioteer and his horses also underlies Socrates' account of the taming of the black horse, as de Romilly (1982), 108–112 has observed.

If the fall of the soul is portrayed in terms of a chariot accident, success-ful ascent will take on a flavouring of athletic victory. The motif of what we might call the psychic Olympics is not unfamiliar in Plato. As the myth of the charioteer draws to a close, Socrates predicts that philosophic lovers have a happy fate after death, 'having won one of the three truly Olympic wrestling bouts' (*Phdr.* 256b4–5), the aim being to regain one's wings in three suc-cessive philosophical incarnations. The close of the *Republic* also speaks of going to receive one's post-mortem rewards 'as the victors go around and collect their prizes' (*Rep.* X, 621c7–d1).[37] Athletic contest offers a rich ana-logue for the philosophical life. Certain events such as wrestling required a series of victories, while the number of contests and possible victories also evoked the idea of progression—the philosophical victor must be a *periodonikês*, one who wins the prize in all the major panhellenic contests. The advantages of the chariot image, then, are multiple. It enables Plato to access the tradition of metaphorical chariot journeys, ranging from the poetic chariot of song to the chariot ride of Parmenides' narrator to a place of philosophical revelation.[38] It foregrounds the idea of directed motion (par-ticularly important in a dialogue where immortality is analysed in terms of self-motion).[39] It encapsulates the idea of psychic life as a contest in very vivid and immediate terms. Finally, as argued above, it presents a complex figuration of the soul that keeps alive the issue of correspondence between image and reality and the process by which we visualize the unseen and non-physical. Constructing metaphors for the soul is a kind of mythologiz-ing.

Interestingly, the combination of gods, chariots, divine dance and force-ful compounding recur in the *Timaeus*, which might (depending on one's view of the problematic chronology of this dialogue) have its origins at a time not too far removed from the *Phaedrus*. There, the production of the world soul on the part of the Demiurge is represented as a difficult opera-tion, chiefly because he is trying to push together the same and the different. What the Demiurge puts together is 'hard to mix'; he has to fit the elements together 'by force' (35a6–8). Once he has created soul, he goes about the formation of the physical universe and creates the planets in order to help us measure time. These are engendered as 'living creatures, bodies bound with ensouled bonds' (38e5–6). The number of the gods is made up by the creation of the fixed stars (plus provision for traditional gods); the creation

---

[37] Cf. also *L.* V, 729d5–e1.
[38] See most recently Slaveva-Grifin (2003).
[39] Griswold (1986), 93.

of birds, sea creatures and land creatures will come later. What is significant for our present purposes is the speech made by the Demiurge when the first act of physical creation has been completed. He addresses the gods, states that he has crafted them, and then assesses their status as compound entities:

> ... since you have come into being through me you are indissoluble unless I wish it. Now, everything that has been bound can be dissolved, but wishing to take apart what has been well-fitted together and is in a good condition is the act of an evil person. So then, since you have come into existence, you are not immortal nor totally indissoluble, but you will not be dissolved, nor will you obtain the fate of death, since you have been allotted a still greater and more authoritative bond than those with which you were bound when you came into existence, namely, my will. (41a7–b6)

When read next to the *Phaedrus* this creation story provides a different and valuable perspective on some of the problems considered here.[40] In this case we are presented with some instances of eternally embodied gods (precisely what was denied in the *Phaedrus*), but the scandal is decreased because they are not the prime and original divine forces. The divine soul is still immaterial, but still a compound, put together from the difficult-to-mix elements of Being, the Same, and the Different. The soul compound is then further compounded when it is tied to bodies by 'ensouled bonds'. This final compound is conditionally eternal; it could be dissolved, but shall not be, since the will of the Demiurgic creator is stronger than any other bond. Indeed, the presence of a creator figure makes the entire notion of compounding and complexity easier to comprehend. We have, as it were, a subject for the verb *symphuo*, 'make to grow together'. The *Timaeus* also helps us see how the issue of compounding is directed towards the issue of embodiment. Soul is created with a view to the material cosmos, and is bonded to it. While this does not solve the problem of psychically compound yet disembodied gods in the *Phaedrus*, it suggestively reinforces the notion that the human souls there are described in terms of their eventual embodiment.

The *Timaeus* also features the divine dance and the chariot image. At 40c3–d3 Timaeus talks about the dances (*choreias*) of the planets, impossible to demonstrate without a model, whereby they overtake and come into conjunction with each other. The fixed stars, on the other hand, are

---

[40] For the difficulties of reconciling a compound entity with immortality, see also *Rep.* X, 611b5–7.

associated with human souls, since the number of non-divine souls is equal
to the number of the stars (41d8–e1). When the Demiurge had created the
divine part of the soul, 'he distributed each soul to each star, and having
mounted them as in a vehicle (*ochêma*), showed them the nature of the
whole and told to them the laws of destiny' (41e1–3). Timaeus is not speaking
here of the whole mortal soul, since the lesser divinities have not yet created
the body and the lesser parts of the soul associated with it, but what the
Demiurge calls 'the divine and hegemonic part'. Thus the part of the soul
that leads and guides, the part that is divine, is placed in a metaphorical
chariot, and one is hard-pressed not to think of the Phaedran charioteer
here. There are, of course, no horses now; there is no need of them when the
star is forever fixed and characterized only by the motion of revolution on
the spot. Once this part of the soul is embodied, it must leave the chariot and
live a life aimed at conquering the passions. If it succeeds, it is rewarded by a
return to the 'dwelling of its corresponding star', where it enjoys a happy life
(42b3–5). We may note that in this habitation it would be carried around by
the revolution of the star, without moving itself, not unlike the divine soul
of the *Phaedrus* that obtains bliss when it stands on the back of heaven and
is carried around in a circular motion.

The object of these comparisons is not to argue that the picture of
the soul we get in the *Phaedrus* can be reconciled with the *Timaeus*, a
task first undertaken by the Neoplatonists with mixed results.[41] Rather, I
want to emphasize that both dialogues are concerned with the problems
that occur when we deal with psychic compounds and the compounding
that goes on when the soul is joined to the body. How contingent are the
bonds that bind the compound soul together? What guarantees them and
how might they be loosed? What happens when we try to express the
compound in an image? The movement of the soul has been compared to
the ordered movement of the dance and the agonistic movement of the
chariot race. But basic is the intuition that our accounts of what happens
to the soul are always governed by our conceiving it in terms of the body
and embodiment even though in terms of importance and dignity the soul
is prior to the body. This is not a question of Plato's metaphors breaking
down under the weight of the philosophical analysis they need to express.[42]

---

[41] Finamore (1985), 107–108.

[42] See Pender (2000), 226–229 for a sensible discussion of how the interaction between
the various parts of the soul is described in anthropomorphic terms because the abstract
language to describe this interaction does not exist.

Plato is far too canny and conscious an artist to trap himself in this way. Rather, he constructs his images and his 'likely stories' (that is, *muthoi* that are likenesses) to raise methodological questions about the process of philosophical (and indeed, human) conception. When Socrates calls the myth of the charioteer a human narrative (*Phdr.* 246a5), he speaks true. It is human because it is impossible, from our perspective, to give an account of the soul that is uncorrupted by the flesh and this is intimately tied to the problem of compounding. We exist as soul-body composites. Our souls may or may not be compound themselves. The compound soul may or may not be indissoluble. Most fundamentally, the appetitive aspect of the soul is the home of compounding, the origin of animal impulses that lead to the creation of hybrid mythological monsters as analogues for the soul.

The flesh in which we live seems to bias us towards animal imagery. The task of the philosopher, as early as the *Phaedo*, is to use all the resources of his intellect and imagination to correct this bias. He must think away the flesh, and mythologizing plays an important role in helping him to do so. It provides a group of stories and creatures that can be used to create resonant and clarifying images for a soul that seems to the earth-bound philosopher to be compound. The animal nature of mythological hybrids provides a particularly good analogue for the lower parts of the soul. Lastly, if hybridity is a function par excellence of the lowest part of the soul, we are faced with the possibility that such models might be misleading (as the examples of Glaucus and the chariot remind us). If this is so, mythologized images of the soul prove their worth because of their obtrusively mythological status (we *know* that they cannot be the whole truth).

Conclusion

As we have seen throughout the course of this analysis, the question of how to conceive the soul is a rhetorical as well as a philosophical issue. Just as the soul exists in mortal life encased in the distorting medium of the body, so speech about the soul is expressed in language that is influenced by mortal existence, language that uses metaphor, that mingles the true and the false. If human discourse, as represented by the biform and goatish Pan of the *Cratylus*, is a composite, false (metaphorical?) speech maps onto the animalistic part of the soul. This, in turn, may shed light on the *Phaedrus'* famous comparison of discourse to a living creature (*zôon*) at 264c2–5, and on the implications this passage has for the dialogue as a whole. Scholarship on the *Phaedrus* has been alive to the strangeness of the dialogue as a composite entity. Thus Nightingale observes that the plurality of generic voices in the dialogue lends a 'typhonic' aspect to the text, and Rowe has connected the complex and variegated nature of the soul with the Typhon passage at the beginning of the dialogue (and also with the 'variegated' democratic individual of the *Republic*).[43] What I want to stress here is that the *Phaedrus* only presents in a more obtrusive form an issue that underlies most discourse, even Plato's own as he presents the struggle to discover and express accurately the nature of reality. It is not just that his text comprehends a multiplicity of generic voices (although it does), nor that the complexity of the text matches the complexity of the soul (also true). The paradigm of composite theriomorphic bodies renders interestingly problematic Socrates' common-sense notion that 'every speech must be composed like a living creature, having its own body, so that it is without neither head nor feet, but has a middle and extremities appropriate to each other and written with a view to the whole' (264c2–5). The imagination is, as we have seen, populated by many strange creatures, and the attempt to interpret a text means that we must identify not just its head and feet, but whether those feet are those of a fish, goat, or man. We must ask ourselves which parts do, or do not, belong in philosophical (or indeed, any) discourse, a problem as old as Socrates' criticism of the goatish tragedians in the *Republic*. Plato's satiric Socrates, unsurprisingly, embodies the problem.

---

[43] Nightingale (1995), 135; Rowe (1986), 212–213, with Rowe (2009), 142–143 (Rowe now links Plato's textual variegation (*poikilia*) with Plato's 'own practice of constructing texts which talk to people who do not share his view of the world, while also making that view available to them'. Thus his text is *poikilos* because it changes its colour depending on the position of the observer).

CHAPTER SEVENTEEN

MYTH, IMAGE AND LIKENESS IN PLATO'S *TIMAEUS*[*]

Elsa Grasso

'It is mostly around the *Timaeus* that the issue of the value of Platonic myth is raised'.[1] The claim, crude as it may appear, does at least highlight the importance of the dialogue's cosmological questions: are we talking about myth in the sense of 'fiction'? If so, an extreme interpretation, by and large denying the Platonic myth any truly philosophical value, would result in the bewildering conclusion that the explanation of the universe in the *Timaeus* is by no means Platonic *per se*, while more moderate and recent readings should eventually succeed in unravelling what is metaphoric and what is not, or even in 'reading through the metaphor'.[2] Are we dealing with a discourse that is chiefly narrative, albeit not fictional, and that should mostly be interpreted literally? In that case the divine craftsman's fashioning of a world 'born' or 'become' would be part and parcel of Plato's philosophy; but then one knotty task would still remain to be addressed: reducing those apparent inconsistencies[3] in the text that are pointed out by the advocates of the opposite interpretation. Our purpose in this paper is not to re-open the whole thorny case, but to examine the *Timaeus'* muthos from two different angles, both revealing its singularity: first, what makes it stand out among other Platonic myths, i.e. the well-known *eikôs muthos* qualification; next, because it relates to the world as *mimêma*, it is of all other Platonic myths the one most directly and overtly dedicated to an image,[4] an '*eikôn*'

---

[*] Translated from French by Jean-Charles Khalifa.

[1] Brochard (1974), 49.

[2] See respectively Brochard (ibid., 48) criticizing the abovementioned radical interpretation, and Brisson (1998 [1974]), 105.

[3] Mainly concerning: chaos (obviously predating the ordering by the Demiurge, but 'visible' and which therefore should be 'become' as any sensible being); time (produced with the world, but can this production take place elsewhere than in a pre-existing time?); soul (how can its self-movingness be reconciled with its being constituted from the outside by the Demiurge?). Cf. Vlastos (1965ab); *contra*: Cherniss (1944), Tarán (1971).

[4] The Allegory of the Cave might arguably be said to be also dedicated to image; however: 1) Plato does not call it *muthos*, but only *eikôn* (515a4, 517a8, 517d1); and, as most scholars rightly assume, it is best qualified as allegory rather than myth; 2) moreover, it does not *relate*

promoted to 'sensible God' status (92c7); the cross-examination of both angles leading us to discuss the relationship of *eikôs muthos* to the issue of likeness and *mimesis*.

1. EIKÔN, EIKOS, MUTHOS

Admittedly, the dialogue gives the myth a 'head' (69b1–2), but it also veils it; indeed, the interpretation difficulties concerning the status of cosmology are to be analysed within a broader context where the *logos-muthos* boundaries are remarkably blurred. For the *Timaeus*, even as it provides hermeneutics with an enigmatic, savoury meta-discursive richness, embeds the myth—or rather a series of myths—in a *mise en abyme* and specular game.[5] The former (partly presented as embedded true *logoi*, not *muthoi*) is quite obvious: Critias' narrative to Socrates at the beginning of the dialogue is presented as an extended version of his earlier[6] 'narrative' (*logos*, 20d1), in which he recounted Solon's '*logos*' (as told by Critias the Elder), which 'though strange (*atopos*), is entirely true'. (20d7–8)[7] However, over and above the *mise en abyme* expressing the myth's irrational ingredient as well as its sacredness and immemorialness, there appears a specular game in which the embedded discourses endlessly reflect the mythhood itself.

Indeed, within Critias' narrative, the myth category applies first to (a) what the Greeks consider their 'most venerable' stories, e.g. the first man and the Deluge, told by Solon to the Egyptian priests (22a4–b3), one of whom derides them as children's myths (23b5).[8] The allegedly historical knowledge is dissolved in myth because of the Greeks' childish lack of memory of their own origins. Here, '*muthos*', as is the case of Phaethon's chariot in 22c7–d1, stands in sharp contrast to 'truth'. Which is definitely not the case of (b) the atopic story of the origins of Athens and its war against Atlantis, indeed presented by Critias as an 'entirely true' *logos* (20d7–8), and after him by Socrates as 'genuine history' (*alêthinon logon*) as opposed to 'fabricated'

---

to an image (nor to the constitution of an image) but rather uses the theme and vocabulary of image to represent an object that is first and foremost the philosopher's own path.

[5] More generally speaking, a relation between myth and game can famously be read in *Tim.* 59c5–d2.

[6] The previous day (20c6–d1; 26a7–b2); and in the morning (26c3–7).

[7] Cornford's translation (1952 [1937]) hereafter, and except when explicitly noted my reference translation of *Timaeus*.

[8] παίδων (...) μύθων.

fiction (*muthon*, 26e4–5),[9] when actually it can hardly be regarded as anything but myth in the eyes of Plato himself. In short, it is under the authority of a myth (which had been brought back from Egypt) that the (Greek) knowledge of origins takes on the trappings of myth; through myth, it is amnesia that is uncovered, in what is merely another instance of a familiar 'derealizing' function which, being psychagogic, is properly philosophical. The function is obvious in the Allegory of the Cave, pregnant in the myth of fall in *Phaedrus*, and is a subversion of the relation of ordinary reality and atopicity. But the truth asserted by Critias, which anchors the exemplary value of the early Athenians not only in discourse but more crucially in history, also leads to reducing to *muthos* the very philosophical *logos*, i.e. the just city's description given by Socrates the day before (26c7–d1). Lastly, the story of the early Athens in turn frames (c) the cosmological *muthos*, which it precedes in sketchy form and subsequently prolongs. As it receives from Timaeus 'the men born of his speech',[10] and from Socrates those of them who stand out through their education (27a7–b1), it is entirely to save the ethical and political discourse from the (Socratic) myth, thus building it on two pillars: first the story of the origins of Athens that has every appearance of a legend, but which Critias recounts as non-mythical; then a cosmological statement, which we would unhesitatingly take to be a 'scientific' doctrine of Plato's were it not called '*muthos*'.

It is in 29d2, in the *prooimion*,[11] that the word is first applied to Timaeus' speech. The *prooimion* begins by making a distinction between what always is and remains identical and what is always becoming. After stating that Becoming necessarily proceeds from some cause, Timaeus goes on to distinguish, on the basis of the two terms, two possible productions: one that is brought into being from an unchangeable pattern, and one that follows the pattern of Becoming. The world, however (which, being sensible, has necessarily become), can only have been produced on the former pattern, since it is fair and its artificer is good. As the end-product of a process thus framed 'on the model of that which is comprehensible by rational discourse and understanding and is always in the same state' (29a6–b1),[12] it is as an '*eikôn* of something' (29b2) that Timaeus thinks it should be conceived. The notion thus only appears, as a counterpart to *paradeigma*, after its

---

9 μὴ πλασθέντα μῦθον ἀλλ' ἀληθινὸν λόγον.
10 My translation.
11 *Tim.* 27d5–29d3 (see 29d5).
12 πρὸς τὸ λόγῳ καὶ φρονήσει περιληπτὸν καὶ κατὰ ταὐτὰ ἔχον δεδημιούργηται.

conformity to the intelligible is evidenced. And Timaeus overtly ('Concerning a likeness, then, and its model we must make this distinction [...]') takes it as the groundwork to the purely epistemological passage that follows: the distinction to be made between *eikôs logos*—or *eikôs muthos*— and irrefutable discourse is indeed entirely based on the relation between the physical copy and the original:

> accounts (*logous*) are akin (*sungeneis*) to those things of which they are interprets (*exêgêtai*). On the one hand, (accounts that interpret) that which is permanent and stable and manifest to reason, are themselves permanent and unchangeable; to the extent that it is possible and fitting for accounts to be irrefutable and invincible, there ought to be no falling short of this; on the other hand, (accounts that interpret) that which is made to be like (*apeikasthentos*) the latter, and that is a copy (*eikonos*), are *eikôs* and proportionate to the former (accounts). As Being is to Becoming, so is truth to belief.[13]

(29b4–c3)

The second and third occurrences of *eikôs*, and the first of *eikôs muthos*, are to be found in the next few lines, where Timaeus asks for indulgence: the audience will have amid the many opinions about 'the gods and the generation of the universe' to make do with the accounts (*logoi*) he will deliver, if those, even though they be neither truly exact or consistent, are no less *eikôs* than any other, 'remembering that I who speak and you my judges are only human, and consequently it is fitting that we should, in these matters, accept the *eikôs muthos* and look for nothing further' (29c8–d3). As Socrates approves and leaves him the floor for good, Timaeus proceeds with a speech that is considered as *logos* as well as *muthos*, and whose defining feature is *eikôs*[14] (used thirteen times to qualify *logos*[15] and three times to qualify *muthos*: 29d2, 59c6, 68d2; see also the occurrence of *muthos* in 69b1). How is this defining character, which is obviously so crucial to the status of the *muthos* under consideration, to be understood?

---

[13] (...) τοὺς λόγους, ὧνπέρ εἰσιν ἐξηγηταί, τούτων αὐτῶν καὶ συγγενεῖς ὄντας· τοῦ μὲν οὖν μονίμου καὶ βεβαίου καὶ μετὰ νοῦ καταφανοῦς μονίμους καὶ ἀμεταπτώτους—καθ' ὅσον οἷόν τε καὶ ἀνελέγκτοις προσήκει λόγοις εἶναι καὶ ἀνικήτοις, τούτου δεῖ μηδὲν ἐλλείπειν—τοὺς δὲ τοῦ πρὸς μὲν ἐκεῖνο ἀπεικασθέντος, ὄντος δὲ εἰκόνος εἰκότας ἀνὰ λόγον τε ἐκείνων ὄντας· ὅτιπερ πρὸς γένεσιν οὐσία, τοῦτο πρὸς πίστιν ἀλήθεια. I am here mostly, though not entirely, following Burnyeat's translation (2009), 171; see below.

[14] On the meaning of *eikôs logos* and/or *muthos* in the *Timaeus*, see in particular: Berti (1997), Donini (1988), Hadot (1983), Howald (1922), Mesch (2002), Meyer-Abich (1973), Racionero (1998), Robinson (1993), Santa Cruz (1997), Smith (1985), Turrini (1979), Witte (1964).

[15] 29c2, 29c8, 30b7, 48d2, 48d3, 53d5, 55d5, 56a1, 56b4, 57d6, 59d1, 68b7, 90e8. Εἰκός is also used in: 44d1, 48d6, 53b3, 56d1, 59d3, 67d1,72d7, 87c2; εἰκότως in: 48c1, 49b6, 55d4, 62a4; see Morgan (2000), 272.

In 29b4–c3, I am following most of the points made by M.F. Burnyeat,[16] who highlights the importance of the word *exêgêtai* in a prelude that closes by calling the following speech *muthos*. Translating this as 'ayant une parenté avec les objets mêmes *qu'ils expliquent*', or 'akin in character to that which *they expound*'[17] (which overlooks the primary meaning and the fact that it is normally used only for human being), is an impoverishment of the original. For the accounts in question by no means consist in just any statement on the physical world: 'they are very special accounts personified as the exegetes who expound or explain the unobvious significance of an object like a dream, ritual or oracle which does not bear its meaning on its surface, because it comes from, or has some important connection with, the divine'.[18]

Burnyeat then argues that *eikos*-hood, far from being a necessary and immediate consequence of the fact that it is the sensible world we are talking about, is rather what such an account *must* reach for (cf. *dei* in 29b8, on such *logoi* as deal with what is permanent). Indeed, just because a speech is about the intelligible does not make it irrefutable and invincible, or more generally true; those are qualities it can and should strive to obtain. If this is correct, then likewise the discourse on the world can and should *aim at eikos*. And those accounts being in a position to achieve either irrefutability and invincibility (in the case of such *logoi* as relate to the original) or *eikos* (in the case of such *logoi* as relate to the copy) are those that *succeed* in speaking fittingly of their objects, i.e. those that succeed in becoming their interpreters.

Moreover, contrary to what ordinary readings suggest, the *prooimion* does not only profess the accounts of Becoming to be inferior to those on the unchangeable. Timaeus indeed hints at a limitation of the latter when he claims: 'to the extent that it is possible and fitting for accounts to be irrefutable and invincible, there ought to be no falling short of this';[19] but in so doing, he also expresses the *exigency* for the accounts of Being to raise themselves to certainty as far as possible. It follows that, in the same way, *eikos* will arguably be considered as the criterion to which all accounts of Becoming do not necessarily, but *can and should* comply with. Thus, in

---

[16] Burnyeat (2009), 171.

[17] Trans. Rivaud (1925) and Taylor (1928), 74 (italics mine).

[18] Burnyeat (2009), 173.

[19] That reservation echoes the limitation first posited by Critias: 'All that is said by any of us' is 'imitation and representation' (*Crit.* 107b5–7; Jowett's translation [1892], hereafter my reference translation of *Critias*).

48d1–e1, Timaeus repeats that he is striving to produce a speech that is no less—and if anything more—*eikôs* than any other, and calls again upon the Gods to lead him towards a doctrine pertaining to that quality. In 67d1–2, he claims (about colours) that it is the highest possible degree of *eikos* that he is aiming at. In 72d4–e1 he argues that even though a God only could confirm that his accounts of the soul are true, one may nevertheless 'venture to assert' that they have been *eikôs*, and thereafter use the same method; which not only shows that the latter quality is inferior in value to the former, but indeed that it does not necessarily belong to accounts of Becoming; achieving it is far from certain, and any such achievement will license continuation along the same principles.

M.F. Burnyeat's abovementioned reading helps do justice to such passages, as well as explain away the anomalies that will inevitably obscure analyses if *eikôs* is translated, as it usually is, as 'likely,' 'probable,'[20] thus implying an epistemological devaluation indifferently affecting physics or cosmology in any form; and that debasement would then be taken up and even radicalised by the most cautious of readings in the characterization of Timaeus' speech as myth, in the sense of fiction (following a strict opposition between *muthos* and *alêthes* used for instance by the Egyptian priest in 22c7–d1, when he contrasts the myth of Phaethon, son of Helios, with its astronomical 'truth').[21]

Plato repeatedly and unambiguously criticizes *eikos*. The *Euthydemus* associates it with *euprepeia*, likelihood as opposed to truth (305d7–306a1). More detailed analyses set it in contrast with demonstration or proof: accounts that, without any demonstration (*apodeixis*), rest 'on probable and plausible grounds'[22] (*meta eikotos tinos kai euprepeias*) are in fact a case of 'charlatanism' (*Phd.* 92c11–d6); in the *Theaetetus* (162d5–163a1) there appears an opposition between *eikos*, as associated with plausibility, and demonstration (*apodeixis*) and rational necessity as used by geometers. Lastly, it is well-known that the *Phaedrus* takes it as the foundation of oratory art. If likelihood only is liable to please the crowds, then 'always in discourse, one should aim at *eikos*, and bid truth good-bye' (272e4–5). For the

---

[20] Taylor's interpretation (1928), 74 looks quite anachronistic, as nothing whatsoever in the *Timaeus* can possibly bear out the reading of *eikôs* as some 'provisionality' of the discourse of physics, which should constantly take its own improvement into account.

[21] A similar opposition of *muthos* and (historical, and no longer astronomical) 'truth' is to be found in 26e4–5, as Socrates repeats Critias' claim.

[22] Jowett's translation (1892).

sole concern will be 'persuasiveness' (*tou pithanou*), and persuasiveness 'is likelihood (*to eikos*, 272e1)';[23] and the only example given thereof is a case of using falsehood (*pseudesthai*, 273c3).

What about the *Timaeus*? There, the word is never indeed associated with falsehood. The prelude links it with belief, which is opposed to *alêtheia*; the latter to be understood first and foremost as *certain* truth, which characterizes *logoi* that are as irrefutable and invincible as accounts can and must be. In 72d4–8, as mentioned above, *alêthes* is again distinguished from *eikôs*. Yet there is a sharp contrast between the way the latter is condemned in the abovementioned dialogues and the treatment it gets in the *Timaeus*, where epistemological devaluation is very largely backgrounded: *eikôs logos/muthos* appears, in Witte's words, as 'a precisely defined type' of discourse (see 48d2: 'the virtue of *eikotes* accounts'; 59c6–7: 'the kind of *eikotes muthoi*')[24] that is repeatedly associated with truth and 'straight' discourse. Among the most significant examples:

- 48a5–7: 'if a person will truly tell'[25] how the world was born, he (or she) must call upon the 'Errant Cause'; Witte argues that Timaeus 'follows this prescription himself in the remainder of his analysis, so much so that—even though it is *eikôs logos*—it is sufficient for the truth exigency that had been initially posited';
- in 49b2–7, regarding the elements, Timaeus combines an *eikotôs*-oriented account with the use of a *logos* at once convincing and stable (*bebaios*), which quality had been related specifically to the accounts of Being in the prelude;
- more explicitly, he says in 53d4–e4 that he will now follow 'the account which combines *eikôs* with necessity' (53d5–6)[26] and goes on to claim: 'if we can hit upon the answer to this [i.e. the properties of the most beautiful solid bodies], we have the truth (*echomen tên alêtheian*)';
- in 56b4, the phrase *kata ton orthon logon kai kata ton eikota*, equating *eikôs* and 'straight reason' or 'straight discourse' does not refer to irrationality of some kind, but rather to some gnoseological value of *eikôs*;
- lastly, the obviously ironical claim that one must believe those theogonies relating to 'the other divinities' (i.e. Gaia, Ouranos and their

---

[23] My translation.
[24] Witte (1964), 1–2 (cf. 48d2: τὴν τῶν εἰκότων λόγων δύναμιν; 59c6–7: τὴν τῶν εἰκότων μύθων ἰδέαν [my translation]).
[25] My translation.
[26] κατὰ τὸν μετ' ἀνάγκης εἰκότα λόγον.

offspring) is clearly echoed by a critique of those tales, which are, to say the least, dubious in so far as they lack *eikôs* and rational necessity: 'though they speak *without* eikôs *or necessary proofs*',[27] 'when they profess to report their family history, we must follow established usage and accept what they say' (40e1–3).

Within that epistemological but not moral critique of what now appears to be a worthless myth, *eikôs*, far from being opposed to demonstrative necessity, is linked to it as a criterion by virtue of which an account will be acceptable (as in 53d5–6). That passage shows that the abovementioned invocations to the God do not imply that any discourse on *genesis* will display some degree or other of that quality: what Timaeus is showing is that some of them may lack it, thus associating it to some form of demonstration (contrary to the passages from the *Phaedo* and *Theaetetus*). By presenting it as an exigency which some accounts of the Gods fail to comply with, he highlights by contrast the positive value of his own speech and the myth he recounts.

Now how should *eikôs* be translated in the prelude, where it is used twice to qualify *logos* (29c2, 29c8) and once *muthos* (29d2)? Burnyeat prefers 'reasonable' or even 'rational' to the traditional[28] 'likely' or 'probable'; he goes on to argue that this results in the seemingly jarring phrase 'rational myth', since in his view it is indeed a myth that Timaeus presents (as opposed to a mere narrative). He adduces two main arguments in support of his claim: as *muthos* was consistently used before the prelude in the narrow sense of 'myth' or 'fiction'[29] (and not simply 'narrative'), there is no indication whatsoever that it should be understood otherwise when applied to Timaeus' speech;[30] but, more importantly, his cosmogony is also a theogony, since the world whose birth he describes is also a God. It must depict how the Demiurge had to cope with the resistance of his materials in order to achieve the highest degree of resemblance with the model. Burnyeat further argues that the passages under consideration should be read as a most accurate reconstitution, from the sole knowledge of the completed work, of the reasoning and decisions of a practical divine intelligence who has chosen the best

---

[27] ἄνευ τε εἰκότων καὶ ἀναγκαίων ἀποδείξεων.

[28] Brisson/Patillon (1999 [1992]) being in that respect one of the exceptions (for 29c2 and 29c8).

[29] Cf. 22c7, 23b5, 26c8, 26e4.

[30] *Contra* Vlastos (1965a), 382, of course, who claims that the phrase *eikota muthon* should not be read 'as though the emphasis were on *muthon* instead of *eikota*. (...) *Eikos* is the important word'.

of several options. Given this, and on a 'second reading', the most reasonable speeches will also be the most probable ones. The significance of *eikôs muthos* is not that of an account that is merely plausible because it deals with the sensible, but one that meets the exigency of probability because, dealing with a divine *genesis*, it is the most reasonable or rational, and thus the most fitting to the rationality that must characterize the Demiurge.

2. THE MYTH'S OBJECT AND MODEL

If *eikos* is indeed an exigency, and if, on 'the second reading,' the meaning 'probable' is to be assigned to it, in legitimate contrast to a 'stable', 'irrefutable' truth, i.e. certainty, the meaning that in my own view springs to mind 'on the first reading' is not necessarily 'reasonable', but a more basic sense. The term is the (attic morphology) participle form of *eoika*: 'look like, be similar' (and in impersonal form 'it befits'). Its uses are found to be the same as those of *epieikes*: 'likely', 'probable', but also 'reasonable' or 'equitable'.[31] However, occurrences of the term are found in Plato's works in connection with *eikôn* (as is the case in the *prooimion*), for which none of those meanings is suitable, and where the only possible translation is 'alike', not in the sense of 'look-alike', 'similar only in appearance', but indeed of 'conform'. This use refers in turn to the basic idea contained in the theme **weik-*, the common root of *eoika* or *eikôn*, *eikotôs*, *eikastikos*, etc., which 'indicates adequacy or agreement'.[32] Words belonging to this group, unlike *eidôlon* or *phantasma*, 'refer to the image's positive reality, its granted latitude of letting the imitated object's reality loom behind it without distorting its intimate structure'.[33]

Nowhere in the *Dialogues* does the translation of *eikos* as 'alike' seem more self-evident than in a passage from the *Sophist*. *Eikastikê*, the first of the two kinds of imitation, 'consists in creating a copy that conforms to the proportions of the original in length and breadth and depth and giving

[31] See Chantraine (1968), s.v. *epieikes*, 354–355.

[32] Saïd (1987), 310.

[33] Turrini (1979), 302 and n. 10. Saïd (1987), 321 notes that Homeric uses of *eoikos, eikelos* or *ikelos* conjure up images that cannot be reduced to a mere reproduction of visible appearance (contrary to *eidôlon*, deriving from the theme **weid-* relating to vision): 'when Patrocles as he speeds through the front ranks is described as "swift as a hawk", (...) the similarity (...) does not lie in his appearance, but is linked to the presence of the same quality in both image and model. Patroclus does not look like a hawk, but displays, at least when he starts running, one of the defining and permanent properties of the bird.'

moreover the proper colour to every part' (235d6–e2).[34] After contrasting the work thus produced to *phantasma*, the Stranger asks: 'The first kind of image, then, being like (*eikos*) the original, may fairly be called a likeness (*eikôn*)?' (236a8–9)[35] *Eikos*, here used *without a complement* (as in *Timaeus'* prelude) can only mean 'alike'; more precisely, it refers to a conformity that should mainly be taken as mathematical, one that, far from being deceptive, may be measured and rationally verified. Its value is further highlighted through the contrast with the non-*adæquatus*-hood of *phantasma*, whose makers 'give up the truth' (i.e. the 'true' or 'real' 'proportions')[36] by giving up the proportions of the model in favour of those that (since they correct the optical distortion resulting from the remote position of the spectator) 'will appear beautiful' (235e5–236a6). *Eikos* thus refers to real likeness as opposed to that 'fantastic' similarity that 'is not (really) like' (cf. 236b7: *eoike de ou*).[37] Unlike the hierarchical perspective in e.g. *Republic* X, the species of image is not entirely marked by dissemblance, but only by alterity or non-identity: the *eidôlon* may be an *eikôn*, which is not its model, but stands in actual conformity to it.

In the *Cratylus*, 439a1–4, the term '*eikôn*' is also restricted to specific images, those onomastic *mimêmata* that do have *eikos*-hood: *those nouns that are 'well-made'* are 'alike' (*eoikota*) and are 'copies (*eikones*) of the things' that they name.[38]

Lastly, *eikos* is articulated with *apeikasia* in the *Critias*, whose prelude closely echoes that of the *Timaeus*: 'epistemological' considerations that justify a call to forbearance, followed by Socrates' assent—together with a call for the invocation of the God—, the whole thing being meant as an introduction to what we must indeed consider as a myth. So, not only should *eikos* in this context be read as 'alike', but it should also be acknowledged as a touchstone for our own discourses, which Critias (107b5–7) claims boil down to *mimesis* and *apeikasia* ('imitation and representation'; the prefix in *apeikasia* emphasizing the fact that the image is made from a model). Critias also distinguishes between two kinds of models, this time not Being *vs*. Becoming but Divine *vs*. Human. The value of our accounts, like that of paintings, is assessed in terms of faithfulness of imitation, 'render(ing) every point of similarity' (107d4–5) being indeed tantamount to perfection.

---

[34] Cornford's modified translation (1935).

[35] Cornford's translation (1935), hereafter and except when expressly noted my reference translation of the *Sophist*: Τὸ μὲν ἄρα ἕτερον οὐ δίκαιον, εἰκός γε ὄν, εἰκόνα καλεῖν.

[36] *Soph.* 235e6–7: τὴν ἀληθινὴν συμμετρίαν; 236a5: τὰς οὔσας συμμετρίας.

[37] My translation.

[38] My translation.

We may be harsh judges regarding representations of human models, which are easy to perceive, but, even as we have to make do with an approximate painting (i.e. a *skiagraphia*) when we are distant from a landscape, 'we may observe the same thing to happen in discourse; we are satisfied with a picture of divine and heavenly things *which has very little likeness* (*smikrôs eikota*) *to them*' (107d6–7).[39] In this case, *eikos* can of course be read as 'alike,' for not only has Critias set up an analogy between discourse and painting (an analogy that would only acknowledge the latter to be mimetic), he has also more properly marked out 'all that is said by any of us' as imitation and representation, thus laying the groundwork for a possible assessment of discourses themselves in terms of likeness. *Eikos* does not then refer to some shortcoming pertaining to any account of divine and heavenly things, but rather to an objective that allows different degrees of achievement, and which may be wrongly felt to have been produced by the speaker: it cannot be reduced to likelihood, which is indeed the effect produced in the hearer's mind—which is what is expressed by the idea of 'satisfaction'—, even though discourse admittedly has no value nor conformity to its object.

In the *Timaeus*'s prelude, *eikôn* has been shown to have a central function: from its relation with a model, the distinction between two sorts of accounts is first grounded and *eikos*-hood introduced, followed, after a reference to our 'human nature,' by the idea of *muthos*. And indeed, it is only when the relevant meaning of *eikôs*, as used by Plato when directly associating the term with *eikôn*, is taken into account, that the analogy posited in 29c3 can be clearly related to the previous lines, whereas the sole 'likely,' 'probable' (or 'reasonable') meaning cannot possibly bring out any immediate connection between the utterance of it ('As Being is to Becoming, so is truth to belief') and the preceding lines, especially those in which the *eikôn-eikôs* relationship is put into place (29c1–2).

Those commentators who favour the translation 'likely' tend to take the passage as a mere 'pun';[40] but in point of fact, if the term is taken to mean 'alike,' with the sense of conforming and befitting, as in the *Sophist*, 236a8 or *Cratylus*, 439a2, what we have is more fundamentally and strictly a reminder that *eikôs* is the proper quality of *eikôn*, which justifies its name. What does the analogy in 29c3 really say? It posits that as Being is to Becoming, so is truth to belief. Now 1) what has just been established about

---

[39] Italics mine; τὰ μὲν οὐράνια καὶ θεῖα ἀγαπῶμεν καὶ σμικρῶς εἰκότα λεγόμενα.
[40] *Inter alios*, Meyer-Abich (1973), 34 & 36.

the relationship of Being to Becoming is that it boils down to a relationship
of model (paradeigma) to copy (eikôn);[41] and 2) an analogy sets up an *identity*
between relations that are respectively at work within two (or more) sets
of terms. Therefore the aforesaid analogy shows that the relationship of
truth to belief should be of the same kind, the latter being the *eikôn* of the
former; which means that accounts of Becoming should be *eikôs* or 'alike'
accounts of Being.[42] Accordingly, we may then translate: '(accounts that
interpret) that which is made to be like the latter, and that is a copy, are
alike and proportionate to the former (accounts). As Being is to Becoming,
so is truth to belief' (29c1–3). The likeness of 'exegetic' accounts of Becoming
will here consist in standing as close as possible to the truth contained in
'exegetic' accounts of Being, just as the world stands as close as possible to
the perfection of its unchangeable model.

However, what the text establishes is a cross- or trans-relation of likeness,
since the *logoi*'s 'kinship' or similarity (cf. *sungeneis*, 29b5) with their objects
involves both the permanency of the former accounts and the latter's being
eikôn, or *alike images*; being akin to—or of the same kind as—their objects,
some will be permanent and stable (like Being), others *eikôs*, endowed with
likeness (like Becoming, which is an *eikôn*). *Eikôs* in the latter accounts
should then be understood as a dual likeness: 1) to 'exegetic' accounts of
Being, which play the role of *paradeigma* for them, and which they look like
as attempts at an explanation,[43] albeit only to a degree that endows them
with a lower epistemological value; and also 2) likeness (through 'generic
kinship') to their objects, to the world as a copy.[44]

Now the copy's defining characteristic is to be *really* alike, *eikôs* in the
sense of *Sophist*, 236a8; it is not only presented as *mimêma*,[45] a term that may
refer to any product of imitation. By calling it *eikôn*, never *eidôlon* or *phantasma* (both of those referring, in the Dialogues, to images whose likeness
may be haphazard or low),[46] Plato highlights its faithfulness to the model.
Moreover, more than once does he highlight that degree of conformity that

---

[41] See in particular Witte (1964), 3 and Ashbaugh (1988), 25.

[42] It is quite obviously that sense of *eikos* which is chosen in 29c2 in Brisson/Patillon's
translation (1999 [1992]).

[43] On this point, I am here following Ashbaugh (1988), 25.

[44] In the *Timaeus*, *eikôn* always refers (29b2, 29b3, 29c2, 37d5, 37d7, 52c2, 92c7) to the
sensible world or to the phenomena therein (with the exception of 29b3, where the term,
on top of that meaning, may also have a more general sense, i.e. any sort of image).

[45] *E.g.* in 48e6–49a1: the second class of Being is a '*mimêma*' of the model.

[46] In the dialogue, even though they never take on the value of conformity to a beautiful
model, they apply to such images as received by the liver (71a5–6, 71b5, 71c3), those of dreams
(*phantasma*) and optical reflections (*eidôlopoiia*) (46a2–3).

should be as high as possible—especially through the definition of time itself as that '*eikôn*' (37d5–7) brought about by the Demiurge's will to make the world's likeness more perfect still.[47] The maximality of what likeness pertains to the sensible is also borne by the oneness of the world as an image, but also by the fact that permanency itself, restricted to the intelligible in the prelude, is indeed granted to sensible copies: phenomena (e.g. a perceptible fire) may well endlessly become something else (e.g. air, water, earth, i.e. images of models that are forever different), but it cannot be the case of that which does not change in the sensible world, that is the 'such' (*toiouton*) or 'the similar principle circulating in each and all of them' (49e5–6).[48] That characteristic (which imitates eternal realities: 51b6), found to be identical in all phenomena we call e.g. 'fire', may legitimately, and unlike the latter, be called 'this,' being indeed sustained across all fleeting phenomena.[49] Therefore, the initial claim of a mimetic relationship between the sensible and the intelligible is deployed along the principle of maximum likeness, incorporating, in spite of all the change and alteration characteristic of Becoming, a 'hard core' of stable identity that ensures maximum conformity.

Under the analogy in 29c3, the accounts of Becoming to be delivered by Timaeus will likewise be as similar to true accounts as possible, thus as conform as possible with their objects. And, as the sensible copy is unable to match in perfection the intelligible model, which it can only transpose onto a different level, likewise the likeness that characterizes *eikôs* accounts is only proportional: they can only resemble or befit their objects to the extent allowed by their inferiority to paradigmatic accounts of the immovable. As they share through 'kinship' with the world the abovementioned maximum likeness to the model, yet short of complete faithfulness, they resemble their objects, but not to the extent of certain conformity. Those accounts, to use M.F. Burnyeat's phrase when associating 'probable' to 'reasonable'

---

[47] The Demiurge 'desired that all things should come as near as possible to being like himself' (29e3). Time is fostered by his will to make the world 'yet more like (μᾶλλον ὅμοιον) its pattern' (37c8). Between these two passages, the determination of the model fluctuates between the Demiurge and the intelligible being (which might be adduced as an argument in favour of an interpretation of Timaeus' speech as myth in the sense of fiction).

[48] Jowett's translation (1892).

[49] See Brisson (1998 [1974]), 194: 'sensible things present themselves as a phenomenon that is ruled by Becoming, and whose intermediate phases escape any form of knowledge or denomination, but one that displays, as a global process, recurring distinct and identical characteristics that allows for a common denomination together with some kind of knowledge.' Without that recurrence, 'the phenomenon will disaggregate into a dust of phenomenal phases, thus annihilating the possibility of any discourse on the sensible'.

in his translation, may be said, on 'a second reading',[50] to be probable because they are alike but cannot possibly approach absolute conformity: they fit, as much as possible, the idea we may shape of a divine intelligence's ordaining activity through our human representations and models. Because they are alike and befit—albeit only from our human viewpoint—whatever that activity might have been, they are for us fitting or worth *approving*, 'probable' in the etymological sense of *probare* in Latin. As G. Turrini notes, Timaeus' speech highlights *eikos*'s 'semantic ambiguity'; it 'is both *alike and appropriate*'.[51] As stability is necessarily lacking from *eikôs* exegetic accounts, since it is also lacking (almost completely, as has been noted above) from Becoming, which they are 'akin' to, they can only stand as close as possible to the epistemological value of discourses on Being, thus constituting the most probable exposition of what the demiurgic process might have been, since they are for us the most similar to it. Therefore, they meet that exigency which is neither met by the theogonies criticized by Timaeus (40d6–e3), nor by the 'deceitful myths' (*Rep.* II, 377d5–e3), in which 'an erroneous representation is made (*hotan eikazê tis kakôs* ...) of the nature of gods and heroes—as when a painter paints a portrait not having the shadow of a likeness (*mêden eoikota graphôn*) to the original.'[52] If *muthos* is never absolutely false, if it can incorporate *alêthes* (*Rep.* II, 377a5–6), the latter characteristic does indeed consist in likeness/conformity to that which is being depicted.

Timaeus' exposition, both as myth and discourse that resembles its object, can thus get as close as possible to achieving the task indirectly delineated at the end of the *Sophist*: to implement that 'force of persuasion' (*peithous anankaias*, 265d7) which is required for all of those who attribute physical reality to 'some spontaneous cause that generates without intelligence', and therefore refuse to believe that the world is born from divine demiurgy (cf. *theou dêmiourgountos*) and by a 'reason' which 'proceeds from divinity' (*Soph.* 265c1–d8). As it meets that wish, the *Timaeus*, which displays that rationality present in the universe with which the conduct of human

---

[50] Burnyeat (2009), 185 (Timaeus' *eikôs* speech, he argues, should be understood as 'reasonable'; however, because the wisest of men cannot possibly claim to be able to reconstitute with any degree of certainty what the Demiurge's thoughts might have been in the course of his ordaining action, therefore that speech should also be understood, 'at a second reading,' as 'probable').

[51] Turrini (1977), 551, n. 41.

[52] Jowett's translation (1892).

life should conform through ethical imitation,[53] does seem to deploy, as
P. Hadot suggests, a type of philosophical rhetoric akin to that presented in
the *Phaedrus*, where the account of soul must be submitted to a psychagogy
that takes nature and the Whole into account.[54] That approach is expressed
in the *Timaeus* in terms of 'direction', or *paidagôgia* (89d7), and imitation:
in the same way as the 'secondary' gods must imitate the fashioning and
ordering action of the Demiurge (41c5–6, 42e8, 69c5), we as products of their
fashioning should, in an intellective contemplation that re-establishes our
soul's conformity to 'its pristine nature', make ourselves like[55] those products of divine imitation, the cosmos' regular movements (90c7–d7; 47c2–3)
and *summetria*.[56] What is at stake is our becoming (again) the suitable image
of a (cosmic) image, under the *eikôn* principle of the *Sophist*, which correctly
reproduces the proportions or internal structure of its beautiful model. It
is thus that Man will crown—through his likeness to a model that is itself
shaped on the most beautiful *paradeigma*—the likeness and inner homo-
geneity of the Whole; it is well-known that the latter has that spherical shape
that is 'fitting' and 'akin' (*sungenes*) to it, i.e. 'the most perfect and the most
like itself of all figures'. Therefore, Man is to be submitted to the founding
principle posited by the Demiurge, who 'considered that the like (*homoion*)
is infinitely fairer than the unlike' (*Tim.* 33b1–7).[57]

What then is the nature of the discourse that goads us into making
ourselves as much as possible in the likeness of an image?

3. *Logos, Muthos, Mimesis*

Are we then to apply that psychagogical aspect to cosmology as a whole,
thus positing no difference between *eikôs logos* and *eikôs muthos*? Or should
we restrict it to the latter, then considered as meeting the epistemological
limitation and the affective dimension proper to our 'human nature' (in
the prelude, the word *muthos* is introduced only after the mention of it;

---

[53] *Tim.* 90b6–d7; the likeness (90d4–5) is here associated, as it is in the prelude, to 'kinship'
(cf. *sungeneis*, 90c8). Likewise in *Republic* III kinship is linked to imitation, works of art being
said to be 'sisters' (401a7–8) and *mimêmata* of moral characters.

[54] Hadot (1983), 127 (his reading is a continuation of Witte's in this respect [1964]. See also
Racionero [1998] for a very similar approach). Cf. *Phdr.* 269e4–270c2.

[55] Cf. *exomoiôsai, homoiôsanta* (*Tim.* 90d4–5).

[56] God having established proportions (*summetrias*, 69b4) for each object, there must be
movements in our souls that are proportionate (*summetrous*, 90a2) to one another. See also
80b6–8, on that '*mimesis* of divine harmony' achieved by sounds.

[57] Jowett's translation (1892).

29c8–d1)? Should we even differentiate between both types of exposition by positing two different objects for them, then arguing that *eikôs muthos* deals with 'the gods and the generation (*genesis*) of the universe' (29c4–5), whereas *eikôs logos* refers to 'quantitative' and mathematical physics? We might then go so far as to suggest that some passages of the dialogue belong to the latter discourse, as quantitative knowledge of nature, and some to the former as qualitative description.[58] A related parallel distinction may be made between the former, as non-verifiable discourse on the divine shaping of the universe and the latter as discourse on the present, perceptible state of the world, which as such, even though it also lacks irrefutability, is yet verifiable.[59] By and large, those interpretations are predicated on a primary distinction that would have to be acknowledged in the *Timaeus*: that between cosmogony and physics.[60]

Nevertheless, no clear distinction between quantitative physics and qualitative description—or verifiable physics and unverifiable cosmogony—may be established on the basis of the occurrences of both phrases. Nothing in the prelude indicates that the putative object of *eikôs logos* is only the present physical reality, and not its prior shaping by the Demiurge, or even physical reality as separate from divinity; indeed, when Timaeus claims that he will be giving *eikôs* expositions about 'the gods and the generation of the universe,' the term qualifies *logoi* (29c4–8). Further down, thoughts concerning the shaping of the world by the Demiurge or anterior/posterior stages of the perceptible state of sensible things, are at several points called *eikôs logos*: see in particular 30b7 (the world was born truly endowed by God with soul and intelligence), 55d5 (the world was born unique), 90e8 (some men are reincarnated as women).

W. Mesch puts forward a different interpretation, based on the issue of image. This approach is justified by the fact that, in the prelude, the notions of *eikôs logos* and *eikôs muthos* are introduced and put into place on the basis of the mimetic relation. An account of image may adopt two different angles: that of its structural relation to the model, in which case it is the dual character of likeness and non-identity to the latter that has to be thought; but also that of its production, i.e. issues regarding its cause or origin. On that point, Mesh refers his readers to the *Sophist*: in the determination of image

---

[58] Meyer-Abich (1973), 41–42.

[59] Brisson (1994 [1982]), 163.

[60] See Frutiger (1930), 199: 'The *Timaeus* in truth contains two completely different, albeit intertwined things': 'a cosmogony' and 'a physics, i.e. a theory of the sensible world'; Frutiger considers 'both,' however, as 'undoubtedly mythical,' and only differentiates between 'genetic myth' and 'parascientific myth'.

as 'another such thing fashioned in the likeness of the true one' (240a8),[61] the former angle is provided by the phrase 'another such thing' (and, further down, *eoikos*; 240b2, 240b7), the latter by *'fashioned* in the likeness of'. Unlike the 'causal aspect,' the 'structural' aspect of mimesis does not involve any reference to time or the issue of origin.[62] In this dual approach, accounts of the world may be analysed as incorporating on the one hand *eikôs logos*, where it is the former aspect that is activated, under a treatment that may be mathematical, but which mainly consists in establishing how the image can be both similar to its model and other, and on the other hand *eikôs muthos*, where what emerges is the 'causal aspect' of image production. Is this interpretation borne out by the various occurrences? Mesh argues that the three uses of *eikôs muthos* all refer to the *birth* or *shaping* of the world taken as a whole (29d2), or of phenomena like metals (59c6) and colours (68d2).[63] On the other hand, the structural dimension of the image-model relationship would be pregnant in the uses of *eikôs logos*: in 30b7, where the emphasis is not so much on the fact that the world was born than on 'what as which' it was born; in 48d2 and 53d5–6, where *eikôs logos* is associated with refusal of the issue of origins; in 56a1, 56b4, 57d6, the structural aspect would be emphasized in the mathematical determination of the elements, and in 55d5, in the emphasis laid on the oneness of the world; in 68b7 the image-model structural relationship would be at stake in the issue of proportions (in the mingling of colours); lastly, in the difficult occurrence in 90e8 itself, where it refers to the 'second birth' of men who have turned into women, structural reasons for the change in form would come into play.

However, let us repeat that this reading cannot possibly be predicated on the prelude, where *logos* is used about the birth of the world and gods. In 53d5–6 it is also difficult not to take into account the issue of origin, when what is under discussion is indeed *eikôs logos* (cf. 53e3–4: it will help us know 'the truth concerning the generation of earth and fire [...]'). The use of *eikôs muthos* in 59c6, which might be said to refer to the genetic dimension in the constitution of metals, is followed with no significant context change by an occurrence of *eikôs* that now qualifies *logos* (59d1). Even though W. Mesch insists that it is the dual perspective that matters, more so than the specific use of the phrases under consideration, it must be conceded that no clear distinction whatsoever emerges from the sole review of occurrences.

---

[61] τὸ πρὸς τἀληθινὸν ἀφωμοιωμένον ἕτερον τοιοῦτον (my translation).
[62] Mesch (2002), esp. 199–200.
[63] Ibid., 212.

Yet the two aspects emphasized are clearly present in the *Timaeus*, which expands as much on the image-to-model relationship (conformity/alterity) as on the issue of image creation. Overt mentions of processes linked to image or comparison,[64] anthropomorphism, artisan-oriented metaphors coming with e.g. the mention—which is difficult to read as anything else but an image—of the cup in which the Demiurge mingles elements (41d4), all concur to facilitate the understanding of the second aspect, the creation of the copy, as being *treated* in the form of a myth. The mythical treatment does indeed add to a mathematics-based physics the dimension of '*poiesis*' and '*muthologia*'. 'Poets' and 'mythologers' are known to deliver 'a narration of events, either past, present, or to come', through the use of 'simple narration (*diegesis*)', or narration that uses 'imitation' (*dia mimêseôs*), i.e. that represents, in the *drama* mode, first-person accounts (a much more restrictive definition than in *Republic* X, where all poetry is said to be imitative), or else by 'a union of the two' (*Rep.* III, 392d2–6).[65] Timaeus does use narrative—but also *mimesis* in the narrow sense of *Republic* III— as he reports, 'as if he were'[66] the Demiurge, what the latter said to the lesser gods.[67] As for *mimesis* itself, it is here duplicated as both form and content of the discourse: the Demiurge calls on the gods to 'imitate', as they fashion the living beings, the crafting power shown by himself in creating them (41c5–6; cf. 69c5). Timaeus, who is called a 'poet' by Socrates (*Crit.* 108b5), and thus uses the third type of poetic and mythological *lexis* as defined in *Republic* III—the one combining mere narrative exposition with mimetic exposition—, causes a god to be born again in words (*Crit.* 106a4).

At this stage, the conclusion should not be that the very idea of demiurgy necessarily pertains to the realm of fiction; the *Dialogues* famously contain other mentions of it. Even if the *Statesman* inscribes it in a mythical frame (cf. in particular 273b1–2, with the same 'father' and 'maker' of the world as in *Tim.* 28c3–4), this is nevertheless neither the case in the *Philebus* (which seems to refer to a demiurgic work, with the wisdom and intelligence of that cause that 'orders and arranges' the Universe), nor above all in the *Sophist*.[68] The *Timaeus* however deploys something totally different:

---

[64] E.g. 50d2–3, 68c7–d2 (where the mention of *muthos* is linked to that of assimilation or comparison).

[65] Jowett's translation (1892).

[66] Cf. *Rep.* III, 393c1.

[67] *Tim.* 41a7–d3.

[68] *Phlb.* 30c5–7, 27b1 (*to dêmiourgoun*); *Soph.* 265b8–e6 (esp. 265c4: *theos dêmiourgôn*).

the *representation*—through myth—of the content and process of such demiurgy, difficult though it may be (as much so as its author) to understand and express (cf. 28c3–5).

As he gives them the same name ('artificer' or 'maker' and 'father'),[69] Plato presents the mythmaker as a counterpart to the Demiurge; what the Demiurge produces is a *mimêma*, so how about the mythmaker? Critias claims that to say is to imitate, for 'all that is said by any of us' is *mimesis* (and the question here is how is the 'us' to be understood, there being no obvious reason to analyse it as referring to poets only). Taking a narrower perspective, we may at least argue that since he is a poet (*Phd.* 61b4–5; *Rep.* II, 379a2–3), since—as Socrates points out by equating 'the poetic clan' with 'the tribe of imitators' (*Tim.* 19d5–6)[70]—the poet's trade is *mimesis* in the broader sense of *Republic* X,[71] then the mythmaker is indeed an imitator (his mimetic act being supplemented by that secondary imitation achieved through the incantatory, persuasive effect of his words, where the hearer becomes similar to what is being expressed). What he delivers is an image, e.g. when he describes in the *Phaedrus* what the soul 'is alike to' (*hô* [...] *eoiken*, 246a5).[72] Therefore, Timaeus is an imitator, and what he imitates is an imitation process, or the making of an image.

Even though Critias may appear to be extending mimeticism to all forms of speech (and not only to poetry), a stance also apparently espoused by Socrates in *Phaedo* (99d4–e6), where he compares *logoi* (in that case, the philosophical accounts themselves) to copies (*eikones*), at no point does Plato explain in detail how such a view of discourse in general as image or imitation should be understood. However, mythical discourse clearly deserves to be called 'mimetic' in so far as it is a poetic discourse.[73] And Timaeus' *muthos* in particular may be understood, more precisely, as pertaining to image and imitation in two main senses.

(1) From an elementary point of view, it is a *reproduction*, in and through discourse, of a creation process; i.e. a *representation*—in the etymological sense of doubling—of a reality (which is external to discourse) thus made accessible to mind in a new dimension as it offers itself to intelligence as well

---

[69] *Phd.* 61b4–5; *Tht.* 164e2–3; *Tim.* 28c3, 37c7; *Pol.* 273b1–2.

[70] My translation.

[71] Especially *Rep.* X, 600e4–6.

[72] The puppets *muthos* (*L.* I, 645b1) is also called *eikôn* (644c1); however, its stativity and non-narrativity, in particular, make it more akin to analogy than to myth.

[73] The references were *Phd.* 61b4–5 and *Rep.* II, 379a2–3; see also *e.g. Rep.* II, 373b5–7, 377b11–e3, *Rep.* X, 600e4–5.

as imagination. Myth does pertain to image in that it may be said to *unwind*, as *before our very eyes*, the world's *genesis*, which (being outside our grasp because it belongs to a 'time' that antedates that of our possible experience, or more controversially time in itself, and because any knowledge of it would imply our accomplished knowledge of the precise nature of a divine action and thought) becomes representable for us in myth, by unwinding itself at once chronologically, along narrative principles, and 'visually', in the mental images which discourse elicits in the reader.

At bottom, the image does not boil down, in this case, to analogy. The latter does include a 'literary,' descriptive dimension, one that may be loaded with sensible details, which makes the hearer's understanding easier; hence the frequent implementation of its pedagogic virtue by Socrates in the *Dialogues*. The 'sensible', imaginative side, however, may be reduced to a minimum without the analogy dissolving as such: what remains essential is indeed the identity of logical relations between the various terms involved, which constitutes analogy *per se*, and which as such can be intellectually apprehended in a satisfactory way, virtually free from the wanderings of imagination (e.g., to quote well-known texts: (A) in the case of the identical relationship between, on the one hand, the actual uselessness of a really competent pilot kept idle on a ship and the ignorance of the seamen who refuse to call on his craft, and, on the other hand, the actual uselessness of philosophers in the city and the ignorance of citizens who refuse to entrust them with political leadership; or (B) in the case of the identical relationship that must be acknowledged between some arts, some 'routines', and the good, whether it be real or only apparent, of the body on the one hand, and the soul on the other hand).[74]

Timaeus' mythical images do not really belong to the long list of *eikones*-analogies used by Socrates and other alleged Plato spokesmen, as their prime aim is not the straight accuracy of this process, which is first and foremost a logical one, and as they exceed the *ratio* (relationship and calculation) dimension, while being able to elicit a rather boundless wealth of representations in the reader's mind.

(2) More generally and under a second aspect, the mythical image is rather to be viewed as pertaining to what is usually called metaphor. A craftsman-demiurge giving instructions to his subordinates, a nurse-earth, secondary

---

[74] *Rep.* VI, 487e4–489b1 (see in particular 489a4–b1, where Socrates overtly underlines the accuracy and reliability of such correlations as are established by his analogy); *Gorg.* 465b6–c3.

gods fashioning the human body, those are by no means contents that Plato hoped would win over a philosopher reader who would take them 'literally'. At least in this sense, the self-assumed fictional part is undeniable in Timaeus's *muthos*, which does not purport to be a *logos* that is 'historical,' or thoroughly adequate to its object. However, as metaphor—that 'rhetorical process,' as P. Ricoeur writes, 'through which discourse frees the power some forms of fiction have of redescribing reality', it can gain access to a form of 'metaphorical truth,' 'in a *tensional* (...) sense of the word *truth*'.[75] In Platonician terms, it can on the one hand, as Socrates notes about *muthos* in general (*Rep.* II, 377a5–6), not be false but still contain some *alêthes*; and, on the other hand, legitimately appeal to belief, aim at *pistis* or the confidence the philosopher may have in what is largely expressed metaphorically, i.e. through transfer from literal to figurative sense. That a god should have empirically worked on some material with the help of tools and secondary divinities, that he should have mixed in a crater the elements of the World-Soul, Plato no doubt does not expect his reader to understand otherwise than as 'poetic' fiction. Neither does he urge us, through an overt parallelism of two sets of terms, to consider the relationship of that creation—depicted in terms of craftsmanship—and its product to be the strict and accurate *analogue* of the relationship between divine action as actually deployed and the world we behold. That mythical, poetic fiction, however, by *transferring* a fundamental thought content and meaning from one order (physicometaphysical and religious) to another (pertaining to a largely anthropomorphic and artisanal model, a concrete one maybe for ordinary men), does call through metaphor to a belief that the philosopher can reasonably consider.

The mythical image is here distinguished not only from straight analogy, but also from simple allegory. In allegory, two sets of terms, which make up the proper sense on the one hand (e.g. being locked up in a cave, and visible things outside the cave) and the figurative sense on the other hand (e.g. the lack of philosophical culture, and intelligible realities) are clearly and instantaneously identified as distinct (especially when Socrates highlights the distinctiveness of the two registers as he explains *how* the cave's *eikôn should* be *understood*, i.e. how to get from the proper to the figurative).[76] Neither analogy nor allegory maintain any indetermination or confusion between the object they purport to represent and the image they convey of it; in contrast, Timaeus' *muthos* does not draw a sharp line

---

[75] Ricoeur (1975), 11.
[76] *Rep.* VII, 517a8–e2; 532a1–d1.

between the actual object to be understood and the representation given of it. More importantly, neither as such aim at eliciting *belief* (the former rather emphasizing some sort of pedagogic clarity, of imaginative ease for the representation, e.g. the allegory of the cave; the latter, for pedagogic or heuristic reasons, aiming at a form of accuracy that is ideally transferable in the mathematical terms of proportion or identical relationships, e.g. in the case of the analogy between arts and the routines meant for body or soul in the *Gorgias*). In contrast, myth, through the metaphors deployed, which feed a religious and metaphysical—call it spiritual if you like—content, purports to elicit belief, and what is more, belief of the highest order: in this case, the existence of a good, divine rationality that explains the glorious, intelligibility-laced ordaining of our world.

Because the deep nature and precise mode of action of the divine rationality are outside the reach of human intelligence, any discourse taking them as its object and interpreting them (to use the same terms as the *prooimion*) cannot possibly aim at certain truth, a truth that can produce certainty in the mind, i.e. a mind-state that is entirely constrained by a strictly rational necessity, demonstrative in kind, or pertaining to immediate intellectual evidence. The content of the belief called forth by myth can only be viewed as the most satisfactory representation for thought, as regards axiologically major issues: the meaning conveyed by *muthos* through its images will be as similar as possible, on a largely sensible, anthropomorphic mode, to what a divine intelligence's action may be. It is through that befitting similarity to an object that by rights escapes us, or at least mostly so, that it can elicit adhesion of mind, confidence or a *pistis* that is aware of its lack of demonstrative foundation. Philosophers may reasonably believe in what appears to them as most probable, by which we mean worth approving, because it resembles and befits what they can conceive of as divine action. They can believe in an intelligent, rational constitution of the Whole, through which the world by no means is the product of some blind contingency (like the one appearing at the end of the *Sophist*, 265c8–10), but does at bottom carry sense (i.e. meaning and intentionality of the God who chose and picked the best *paradeigma*), or through which, in other words that are both common and strictly Platonic, the world *looks like something* (i.e. something intelligible) rather than nothing (nothing but itself, or else nothing at all …).

That *pistis*, the possible adhesion of the mind to a thought content not perceived as necessarily self-imposing, but rather, on account of its meaning and the added intelligibility and value it provides, as confidence worthy, does indeed have lower epistemological value than the *prooimion*'s *alêtheia*, just as the line's *pistis* is epistemologically lower than intellection, i.e. the state of the soul endowed with the highest degree of *saphêneia*, clarity or certainty (*Rep.* VI, 511e2–3). However, much as *alêtheia*'s epistemological superiority in Timaeus' preamble can be compared to the superiority of the line's *noêsis*, the comparison of the two texts is notoriously thorny: indeed, *alêtheia* in the description of the line is not the highest epistemological quality a *logos* or a soul's *pathêma* may be endowed with, but the criterion (the ontological counterpart of *saphêneia*, which is an epistemological one) that makes it possible to hierarchize the *objects* of the four states of the soul (those concerned with, respectively, objects whose 'truth'—in the sense of true reality—is more or less weighty). As regards the line's *pistis*, unlike that of the *Timaeus*, it involves illusion insomuch as it may be understood, at least largely so, as the viewing of the sensible 'originals,' which we can perceive, as the only existing realities (however, it is noteworthy that it cannot be *reduced* to pure illusion, for it may also refer to the certainty of— or belief in—the existence of a sensible object we perceive, which in Plato's view is not in itself tantamount to delusion).

There still remain common points in both texts: the fact that *pistis*, confidence or belief, has lower 'scientific' value than truth-certainty (*alêtheia* in the *Timaeus*; or, in the line passage, the highest *saphêneia* characterizing *noêsis*); and in both cases, it lies outside the scope of the reasoning on purely noetic objects. In the case of the line, however, *pistis* concerns immediately empirical objects, whereas in Timaeus' preamble, it concerns precisely what falls short of our sensible perception as such, yet does not pertain to noetic apprehension: the *'manufacturing'* of the image that is the world, or the ordering of the Whole, and the presence therein of a divine intelligence which is represented by the myth largely in metaphoric terms.

Now, regarding the treatment of the cosmic image presented in the *Timaeus*, what about the aspect described above as 'structural,' i.e. which does not concern the image's *manufacturing*, but only its relation to its model? Since it does not require any narrative or temporal dimension, only a descriptive one, it might be taken to pertain to descriptive and argumentative *logos*, and not to *muthos*. Furthermore, it might also be argued that a cosmogony, here to be considered as poetry, can only be mythical: indeed, as poetry, and thus as imitation, it is more precisely about imitating through discourse (cf. *Crit.* 106a4, 105b5–7) a model that is arguably absent, in the sense of ungraspable, for the world's fashioning or birth is no object for our senses or intellect to grasp. Then again, representing a model we cannot know for sure fits the image one has of it boils down to producing *muthos*: it is in accordance with this principle that Critias, who professes that all we say is *mimesis*, calls (as noted above) Socrates' ethical and political speech a myth (cf. too in *Rep.* II, 376d9–10, the link Socrates establishes between his words and *muthos*; also in *Rep.* V, 472d4–7, his analogy between his words and the painted representation of a *paradeigma* which we cannot be sure exists in actual fact). On the other hand, when the representation (whether poetic or not) is that of a perceptible or knowable object, it would then not pertain to myth, and indeed it would therefore seem to be the case for Timaeus' non-cosmogonic physics. However, his physical description of the world is that of a *divine* copy, not only because it is produced by a god, but also because it *is* a god: Timaeus' last words depict the world at once as an '*eikôn*' and a 'sensible god' (92c7). In its very non-genetic dimension, his discourse pertains to myth: as an account purporting to represent a divine object, the description of the world is not to be restricted to a form of physics by rights independent from all theology, but stands inseparable from an axiological, exegetical perspective that is to trigger the emergence within the sensible itself of what the sensible owes to its model, to wit that god's greatness, excellence, beauty and perfection (92c7–9).[77]

The subject matter of cosmology does indeed pertain to those models both 'divine' and 'heavenly' which Critias declares to be easy to represent through discourses that satisfy their hearers, even though they may bear very little likeness (*Crit.* 107d6–7). Timaeus had already answered him when he asserted the likeness and fittingness of his *muthos*, that 'mythical hymn' of sorts, chanted 'in meet and pious strain',[78] to quote Socrates on his speech about Eros (*Phdr.* 265c1). On that day of sacrifice to the goddess (*Tim.* 26e3) who imparted to the early Athenians the best political order and arrangement (*diakosmêsis* and *suntaxis*), tribute is also paid to the Demiurge, who endowed the cosmic image with the most beautiful possible order (*taxis*);[79] thus, it is in an equally similar and likely *muthos* that the likeness (to the most perfect of models) of an image that is 'the fairest of creations' (29a5) should be represented.

It is also, however, an account that should provide a representation of a relationship that stands on the very verge of representability; the *Dialogues* do assert the existence of such a relationship, but do not describe its enigmatic process, through which the intelligible reproduces itself (should we say: as such?) in its image. We may of course admit that the mimetic relationship between the sensible and the intelligible is no fiction, but 'the

---

[77] These terms being in the superlative: μέγιστος καὶ ἄριστος κάλλιστός τε καὶ τελεώτατος.
[78] My translation.
[79] *Tim.* 23c4–6, 24c4, 30a5.

cardinal doctrine of Platonism';[80] we must, however, note that it is through images that the 'cardinal doctrine' of images is expressed in the *Dialogues*: the symbol of the Line, the Allegory[81] of the Cave, or the passage in the *Phaedrus* (250a6 ff.) that is a continuation of the preceding myth. The mimetic relationship is not only a doctrinal content, it is also the only possible principle of (discursive) representation of the said (metaphysical) content. Timaeus' *muthos* does have a psychagogical, even rhetorical, function since it is supposed to persuade us of the suitability of the discourse that asserts the rationality at work in the Universe which we ought to imitate. But it is also the myth that, because it describes along with the divine world a contradictory relation between two orders that are radically different and yet linked—so much so that one duplicates itself in the other, its 'another such'—builds up a blind spot at the very heart of Platonism.

---

[80] Cornford (1952 [1937]), 28.
[81] Also *'eikôn'* (*Rep.* VII, 515a4, 517a8, 517d1).

CHAPTER EIGHTEEN

WHY IS THE *TIMAEUS* CALLED
AN *EIKÔS MUTHOS* AND AN *EIKÔS LOGOS*?[*]

Luc Brisson

Proceeding as he had done in his introduction to the *Theaetetus*,[1] M. Burnyeat proposes two readings of the expression *eikôs muthos*[2] in the *Timaeus*.
His first reading is based on the prelude, and insists on the religious dimension of the *Timaeus*, in which Timaeus describes for us the divine plan that
will lead to the fashioning the world, which is a likeness of an eternal rational order.[3] So, according to that interpretation, the best translation of *eikôs*
would be 'reasonable', 'rational'. A second reading proposes a non standard
interpretation of the adjective *eikôs*.[4] Since the demiurge's plan for fashioning the sensible world depends on practical knowledge,[5] it cannot achieve
perfect rigor, and hence truth. The demiurge does not reveal the truth, but
limits himself to making the best order in the sensible world true, that is,
real.[6] As the main interlocutor of the dialogue, Timaeus tries to describe
the divine plan presiding over the fashioning of the sensible world, but this
task is beyond him as a man. In this context, *eikôs* may be translated 'likely',
'probable'.[7] And Burnyeat concludes by producing a synthesis of these two

---

[*] Translated from French by Michael Chase.

[1] Burnyeat (1990).

[2] 'To sum up by combining my first and my second readings. In *Timaeus*' physics,
the more appropriate or reasonable the account of some phenomenon, the greater the
probability of this being true, precisely because the one unchallengeable proposition about
the cosmos that we must hold true, on pain of impiety, is that the Maker made it the best
possible the materials allow. A far cry from the empiricist philosophies of science which
so many scholars have projected anachronistically back into the *Timaeus*, where what is
probable is our best extrapolation, from what we already know of the cosmos, to what is
true of it in some part or aspect hitherto unexplored' (Burnyeat [2005], 163).

[3] 'I conclude the exegesis Timaeus will offer is precisely an exegesis, explanation, exposition, or revelation of the rationality embodied by the Maker in the cosmos he produced'
(Burnyeat [2005], 156).

[4] Burnyeat (2005), 143 n. 1 and 2.

[5] On the meaning of this expression, Burnyeat (2005), 159–160.

[6] Burnyeat (2005), 157. See also the example of 75b–c.

[7] Burnyeat (2005), 162.

translations: 'Remember that Timaeus is trying to engage us in the almost ungraspable thought experiment of imagining what it would be like to craft *everything*. A potter or architect does not and cannot craft their product by rigorous reasoning. The Divine Craftsman is in the same situation but on a vastly larger scale. That, I submit, is why Plato tells us to read the *Timaeus* as an *eikôs muthos*. Practical wisdom cannot aspire to the same standards of rigour as theoretical wisdom can, so if we are learning to be connoisseurs of a product of practical wisdom we should not ask our teacher to be more than an *eulogos exêgêtês*, a reasonable exegete of the reasonable order or things.'[8]

The interpretation proposed by M. Burnyeat is brilliant, and it has the advantage of resituating the *Timaeus* within a tradition that inquires into the origin of the universe and goes back to Hesiod;[9] it thus recognizes, as I myself have tried to do, the dialogue's 'mythical' character. It allows us to focus on the role of the main interlocutor. Yet it has the disadvantage of trying at all costs to shunt aside Platonic doctrine on two essential points that contemporary philosophers find hard to accept. 1) For Plato in the *Timaeus*, all sensible things are merely images of a genuine separate reality that plays the art of model, and 2) the status of a discourse with regard to truth depends on the ontological status of its object. The interpretation Burnyeat proposes introduces a distinction found not in Plato, but in Aristotle, between practical wisdom and theoretical wisdom.[10] Above all, it comes close to the interpretation of the *Timaeus* maintained by the Middle Platonist such as Alcinoos, for whom the Forms that serve the god as models for fashioning the world are his thoughts,[11] and the reader of the *Timaeus* has the task of rediscovering the divine plan, the traces of which subsist in this world.

In this paper, I will try to show in what sense the *Timaeus* can be qualified as a myth, and especially how *eikôs*, qualifying *muthos* as well as *logos*, assumes his full meaning, that does not really vary, only in the context of an opposition Plato introduces between levels of reality in ontology, epistemology, and linguistics. Here, I will first limit myself to recalling my position on *muthos* in Plato's works, before returning to the interpretation of *eikôs*. As usual, I will quote and discuss the relevant passages,[12] in order to avoid pure speculation.

---

[8] Burnyeat (2005), 163–164.
[9] See now Boys-Stones and Haubold (2010).
[10] *De motu animalium* 7, 710a16–17. See Brisson (2004).
[11] *Didaskalikos* XII, 166, 39–168, 7; see also 163, 11–164, 6.
[12] The translation of the *Timaeus* is Cornford's (1952 [1937]), modified.

1. *EIKÔS MUTHOS*

To understand the phrase *eikôs muthos*,[13] one must first read 28b2–29d3 in its totality,[14] and not only 29b1–d3, the omission of 28b2–29d1 making it possible to conceal the ontological and epistemological opposition between sensible and intelligible, and to avoid mentioning the causal role of the Demiurge:

> So concerning the whole heaven or world—let us call it by whatsoever name may be most acceptable to it—we must ask the question which, it is agreed, must be asked at the outset of inquiry concerning anything: Has it always been, without any source of becoming; or has it come to be, starting from some origin? It has come to be; for it can be seen and touched and it has body, and all such things are sensible; and, as we saw, sensible things, that are to be apprehended by belief which involves sensation, are things that become and can be generated.

> But again, that which becomes, we say, must necessarily become by the agency of some cause. The maker and father of this universe it is a hard task to find, and having found him it would be impossible to declare him to all mankind. Be that as it may, we must go back to this question about the world: After which of the two models did its builder frame it—after that which is always in the same unchanging state, or after that which has come to be? Now if this world is beautiful and its maker is good, clearly he looked to the eternal; on the contrary supposition (which cannot be spoken without blasphemy), to that which has come to be. Everyone, then, must see that he looked to the eternal; for the world is the most beautiful of things that have become, and his maker is the best of causes. Having come to be, then, in this way, the world has been fashioned on the model of that which is comprehensible by reason and understanding and is always in the same state.

> Again, these things being so, our world must necessarily be a likeness of something (*eikona tinos*). Now in every matter it is of great moment to start at the right point in accordance with the nature of the subject. Concerning a likeness (*peri eikonos*), then, and its model (*peri tou paradeigmatos autês*),

---

[13] The expression *eikôs muthos* occurs three times in the *Timaeus* (29d2, 59c6, 68d2). On seven occasions in the *Timaeus* (30b7, 48d2, 53d5–6, 55d5, 56a1, 57d6, 90e8) Plato calls Timaeus' discourse on the constitution of the sensible world an *eikôs logos*. In addition, *eikôs, eikotôs* etc, occur in seven other passages from the *Timaeus* (34c3, 44d1, 48c1, 49b6, 55d4, 62a4, 72d7) in a similar context and with similar meaning. On the significance of all this, see Brisson (1999 [1982]), 161–163.

[14] It is interesting to note that M. Burnyeat begins his quotation and therefore his transla- tion of the text at 29b1 (and not c4, as indicated), and ends it at d3. He thus avoids mentioning the opposition between sensible and intelligible, on which the opposition between image and model in based. This is why he should not call this passage 'A much misread passage of the *Timaeus*' (Burnyeat [2005], 147), alluding to a famous article by Cherniss (1977 [1954]) on a truly difficult passage of the *Timaeus* (49c7–50b5).

we must make this distinction: accounts (*logous*)[15] are of the same family as the things which they set forth (*exêgêtai*)[16]—an account of that which is abiding and stable and transparent to intellect must (*dei*)[17] itself be abiding and unchangeable (so far as it is possible and it lies in the nature of an account (*logois*) to be incontrovertible and irrefutable, there must be no falling short of that); while an account of what is made in the image (*apeikasthentos*) of that other, but is only a likeness (*ontos de eikonos*), will itself be but likely (*eikotas*), standing to accounts of the former kind in a proportion: as reality is to becoming, so is truth to belief.

If then, Socrates, in many respects concerning many things—the gods and the generation of the universe—we prove unable to render an account at all points entirely consistent with itself and exact, you must not be surprised. If we can furnish accounts no less likely (*eikotas*) than any other, we must be content, remembering that I who speak and you my judges are only human, and consequently it is fitting that we should, in these matters, accept the likely myth (*ton eikota muthon*) and look for nothing further.[18]

(*Timaeus*, 28b2–29d3)

---

[15] That is any *logos*. Burnyeat over-interprets the passage: 'Thus the accounts (*logoi*) we are talking about are not any old statements, or discourses about the physical world. They are very special accounts personified as the exegetes who expound or explain the unobvious significance of an object like a dream, ritual or oracle which does not bear its meaning on its surface, because it comes from, or has some important connection with, the divine.' (Burnyeat [2005], 149).

[16] On *exêgêtês*, see *infra*.

[17] I do not interpret the *deî* like Burnyeat (2005), 150: 'Note the "ought". Stability and irrefutability are not automatic consequences of the accounts having a stable unchanging subject matter. Rather, they are standards the accounts are expected to live up to. The point is not that you cannot go wrong when expounding a stable unchanging subject matter, e.g. that you cannot make mistakes in mathematics (like the slave in the *Meno*) or when you talking about the Forms (like Socrates in the *Parmenides*). Of course you can. But you ought not to. If you do, you are falling short of the standards require for successful exegesis *of such things*'. The question is not whether a human being may be mistaken when doing mathematics or recollecting Forms, but what sort of truth may be reached by science and opinion according to their respective objects. On this point, see *infra*.

[18] ὁ δὴ πᾶς οὐρανὸς—ἢ κόσμος ἢ καὶ ἄλλο ὅτι ποτὲ ὀνομαζόμενος μάλιστ' ἂν δέχοιτο, τοῦθ' ἡμῖν ὠνομάσθω—σκεπτέον δ' οὖν περὶ αὐτοῦ πρῶτον, ὅπερ ὑπόκειται περὶ παντὸς ἐν ἀρχῇ δεῖν σκοπεῖν, πότερον ἦν ἀεί, γενέσεως ἀρχὴν ἔχων οὐδεμίαν, ἢ γέγονεν, ἀπ' ἀρχῆς τινος ἀρξάμενος. γέγονεν· ὁρατὸς γὰρ ἁπτός τέ ἐστιν καὶ σῶμα ἔχων, πάντα δὲ τὰ τοιαῦτα αἰσθητά, τὰ δ' αἰσθητά, δόξῃ περιληπτὰ μετ' αἰσθήσεως, γιγνόμενα καὶ γεννητὰ ἐφάνη. τῷ δ' αὖ γενομένῳ φαμὲν ὑπ' αἰτίου τινὸς ἀνάγκην εἶναι γενέσθαι. τὸν μὲν οὖν ποιητὴν καὶ πατέρα τοῦδε τοῦ παντὸς εὑρεῖν τε ἔργον καὶ εὑρόντα εἰς πάντας ἀδύνατον λέγειν· τόδε δ' οὖν πάλιν ἐπισκεπτέον περὶ αὐτοῦ, πρὸς πότερον τῶν παραδειγμάτων ὁ τεκταινόμενος αὐτὸν ἀπηργάζετο, πότερον πρὸς τὸ κατὰ ταὐτὰ καὶ ὡσαύτως ἔχον ἢ πρὸς τὸ γεγονός. εἰ μὲν δὴ καλός ἐστιν ὅδε ὁ κόσμος ὅ τε δημιουργὸς ἀγαθός, δῆλον ὡς πρὸς τὸ ἀίδιον ἔβλεπεν· εἰ δὲ ὃ μηδ' εἰπεῖν τινι θέμις, πρὸς γεγονός. παντὶ δὴ σαφὲς ὅτι πρὸς τὸ ἀίδιον· ὁ μὲν γὰρ κάλλιστος τῶν γεγονότων, ὁ δ' ἄριστος τῶν αἰτίων. οὕτω δὴ γεγενημένος πρὸς τὸ λόγῳ καὶ φρονήσει περιληπτὸν καὶ κατὰ ταὐτὰ ἔχον δεδημιούργηται· τούτων δὲ ὑπαρχόντων

In the first paragraph of this passage omitted by Burnyeat, the question raised is whether or not the world is generated. The answer appears as follows. The world is visible, and therefore has a body. But since it has a body, it has been generated, and can be destroyed. And because it has been generated, we must wonder who has generated it, and after which model it has. In the second paragraph, we learn that the world was framed by the demiurge, after a model that is not sensible. The demiurge who framed the world is the best of causes, and he is good. He has therefore taken his model not in what is becoming, but in what is eternal and is apprehended by reason and thought. In the third paragraph, the consequences deriving from the use of an explanation based on the opposition between model and image are stated. In the first instance, the consequences are metaphysical: the forms are immutable, and, as models, they differ from the demiurge who is but a fashioner, and are thus superior to him. As images, sensible things are both different from and similar to their model. Hence these cosmological consequences: as we shall learn further on, the difference of sensible things from their model is explained by the existence of *khôra* in which sensible things are located, from which they are made, and which explains why they are distinct from one another, while the similarity of sensible things with their model is explained by the demiurge, who introduces mathematics into the sensible world: all of astronomy depends upon three mathematical relationships, and the world of bodies is made up of only four elements, which correspond to four regular polyhedra. It is thus mathematics that introduce enough regularity and permanence into the sensible world for us to be able to perceive it, speak about it, and act within it. Hence, finally, these epistemological consequences: intelligible forms are known by the intellect and are objects of science, whereas sensible things are perceived by sensation and are the objects of opinion. And since the status of a discourse depends on the status of the object with which it deals, the discourses that deal with the intelligible achieve truth, and are stable, unshakable, and

---

αὖ πᾶσα ἀνάγκη τόνδε τὸν κόσμον εἰκόνα τινὸς εἶναι. μέγιστον δὴ παντὸς ἄρξασθαι κατὰ φύσιν ἀρχήν. ὧδε οὖν περί τε εἰκόνος καὶ περὶ τοῦ παραδείγματος αὐτῆς διοριστέον, ὡς ἄρα τοὺς λόγους, ὧνπέρ εἰσιν ἐξηγηταί, τούτων αὐτῶν καὶ συγγενεῖς ὄντας· τοῦ μὲν οὖν μονίμου καὶ βεβαίου καὶ μετὰ νοῦ καταφανοῦς μονίμους καὶ ἀμεταπτώτους—καθ' ὅσον οἷόν τε καὶ ἀνελέγκτοις προσήκει λόγοις εἶναι καὶ ἀνικήτοις, τούτου δεῖ μηδὲν ἐλλείπειν—τοὺς δὲ τοῦ πρὸς μὲν ἐκεῖνο ἀπεικασθέντος, ὄντος δὲ εἰκόνος εἰκότας ἀνὰ λόγον τε ἐκείνων ὄντας· ὅτιπερ πρὸς γένεσιν οὐσία, τοῦτο πρὸς πίστιν ἀλήθεια. ἐὰν οὖν, ὦ Σώκρατες, πολλὰ πολλῶν πέρι, θεῶν καὶ τῆς τοῦ παντὸς γενέσεως, μὴ δυνατοὶ γιγνώμεθα πάντη πάντως αὐτοὺς ἑαυτοῖς ὁμολογουμένους λόγους καὶ ἀπηκριβωμένους ἀποδοῦναι, μὴ θαυμάσῃς· ἀλλ' ἐὰν ἄρα μηδενὸς ἧττον παρεχώμεθα εἰκότας, ἀγαπᾶν χρή, μεμνημένους ὡς ὁ λέγων ἐγὼ ὑμεῖς τε οἱ κριταὶ φύσιν ἀνθρωπίνην ἔχομεν, ὥστε περὶ τούτων τὸν εἰκότα μῦθον ἀποδεχομένους πρέπει τούτου μηδὲν ἔτι πέρα ζητεῖν.

invincible, whereas the discourses that deal with the sensible can only be likely, because they are not irrefutable. Finally, when one speaks of the gods and of the generation of the universe, the discourse one holds is equivalent to a likely myth (*eikôs muthos*). To understand this phrase, one must explain its two component parts: *muthos* et *eikôs*.

2. *MUTHOS*

As M. Burnyeat recalls,[19] and as I did in my translation of the *Timaeus*,[20] *muthos* should be translated by 'myth,' for the following reasons,[21] some of which are accepted by Burnyeat, others not.

1) A description of the generation of the sensible world demands the use of a tale, that is a narrative. Yet as Burnyeat rightly notes,[22] one cannot, like G. Vlastos,[23] followed by C. Rowe,[24] maintain that *muthos* means nothing but a 'narrative tale,' for in that case one would remain on the level of language alone, where the distinction between *logos* in the broad sense of discourse, and *muthos* would tend to be erased.

2) In fact, this tale in which the *Timaeus* consists is situated in the lineage of Hesiod's *Theogony*,[25] for it deals with the generation of the gods, with the world itself being a god.[26] We note that the demiurge is qualified as the 'fashioner and father of the universe,' but since the image of the fashioner will prevail over that of the father, the *Timaeus* thus dissociates itself from Hesiod's *Theogony*, which accounts for the appearance of the gods by using

---

[19] Burnyeat (2005), 144–145.

[20] Brisson (1992).

[21] Brisson (1999 [1982]).

[22] 'So, it is argued, especially by Vlastos, *muthos* must just mean a narrative story. It does not stand in contrast to *logos* as it did when the *peri phuseos* tradition set itself up in opposition to Hesiod' (Burnyeat [2005], 145).

[23] Vlastos (1965a), 380–383. The words *eikôs muthos* appear only thrice in the *Timaeus*, while *eikôs logos* recurs sixteen times: 30b, 34c, 44d, 48c, 48d (bis), 49b, 53d, 55d, 56a, 56d, 57d, 59c, 62a, 72d, 90e.

[24] Rowe (2003), 21, n. 1. Not a demonstration or rigorous argument that would take us more in the direction of the *logos*, as we will see a bit later.

[25] As Burnyeat (2005), 144–145 once again rightly saw.

[26] This allows us to understand this passage: 'If then, Socrates, in many respects concerning many things—the gods and the generation of the universe—we prove unable to render an account at all points entirely consistent with itself and exact, you must not be surprised' (*Tim.* 29c4–7).

as images exclusively those paternal relations that imply sexual relations and conflictual relationships between father and son.

3) The *Timaeus* describes[27] the deeds of a god, the demiurge, who works like an artisan, has feelings, reasons, and calculates while he fashions the sensible world. The fact that the demiurge works,[28] and thus must begin his work at a given moment and stop at another, the fact that he is limited by his model and by the material he uses, is the source of many critiques by Aristotle.[29] Since the demiurge is a god, and should therefore be sufficient unto himself, this demand is incompatible with work in general, which is always the consequence of a need or a lack.

4) However, that which, in my view, constitutes the essential point when Plato comes to calling the *Timaeus* as *muthos* derives from the epistemological status of the dialogue. Since it makes no reference to the intelligible, the discourse of the *Timaeus* cannot be qualified as 'science,' and cannot even be ranged as such alongside opinion, which accompanies sensation. Indeed, who could be our informer for the description of the generation of the world, and then of man, when neither world nor man yet existed? Like discourse on the gods, and especially on the origin of the gods, the *Timaeus*, as a whole, is a myth situated upstream of error and of truth, because nobody was there at time.

5) Hence there derives another characteristic of myth which is not minor, as one might think. Myth cannot produce certainty in man, and remains on the side of belief. This being the case, however, whence does the efficacy of myth derive? Myth touches the lowest part of human soul, which corresponds to spirit (*thumos*) and desire (*epithumia*), dealing respectively with fear and temerity, pleasure and pain. Hence its efficacy, for it thus addresses all human beings from their earliest youth, not only the small group of those who have been trained to use their intellect in the best possible way; the *Timaeus* should make everyone[30] share in the opinion that our world is the best possible.

---

[27] Brisson (1974), chap. 1.

[28] Hoffmann (2003).

[29] Two examples. If the world had been framed by a demiurge, how could it be indestructible (*De Caelo*, I, 10, 280a30)? How could it be self-sufficient (*Nicomachean Ethics*, X, 6, 1178b20–23), as a god should be?

[30] See *infra*.

6) As well any other myth,[31] the *Timaeus* is likened to a living being that must not wander without a head,[32] and that must, without perishing, arrive safely at a friendly port.[33] These two proverbial expressions enact an important rule concerning the narration of a myth; when a myth is told, one must go to the end of the tale. Moreover this explains why, as we can observe particularly in the *Gorgias*, the *Phaedo*, the *Phaedrus*, the *Symposium*, and the *Republic*, when a myth begins, the dialogue stops; the story cannot be interrupted or even questioned. The *Timaeus* is, moreover, a monologue much more than a dialogue.

What has just being said is confirmed by the three occurrences of the expression *eikôs muthos* in Plato's *Timaeus*.

There is an occurrence of 'myth' qualifying the *Timaeus* at the beginning of the dialogue's third section, devoted to the cooperation of intellect with necessity, which refers to one of these proverbial expressions. We thus find ourselves here in a similar context as in 28b2–29d3:

> Now that the materials for our building lie ready sorted to our hand, namely the kinds of causes we have distinguished, which are to be combined in the fabric of our remaining discourse, let us in brief return to our starting-point and rapidly trace the steps that led us to the point from which we have now reached the same position once more; and then attempt to crown our myth (*kephalên tôi muthôi epitheinai*) with a head fitting all that has gone before.[34]
>
> (*Timaeus*, 69a6–b2)

The *Timaeus* describes the birth of one god, the world, from another, the demiurge, as in Hesiod's *Theogony*, and it does so in a religious context, for the dialogue begins with a prayer requesting the help of the gods and goddesses (*Tim.* 27c1–d4), and it ends with an hymn (*Tim.* 92c4–9) in honour of the god known as the world. So such a myth can be assimilated to a (divine) living being.

Another occurrence evokes the pleasure provided by myth. After explaining how the four elements—fire, air, water, and earth—are to be associated with four regular polyhedra—icosahedron, octahedron, dodecahedron, and cube—Plato tries to show that all other varieties of body can be reduced to these four elements, associated with a geometrical form. While discussing

---

[31] See Brisson (1999 [1982]), 59–61.
[32] *Gorg.* 505c10–d3, *L.* VI, 752a2–4, *Phdr.* 264c2–5; see also *Stat.* 274e1, 277b7, *L.* VII, 812a1–3.
[33] *Rep.* X, 621b8–c1, *Phlb.* 14a3–5, *Tht.* 164d8–10, *L.* I, 645b1–2.
[34] Ὅτ᾽ οὖν δὴ τὰ νῦν οἷα τέκτοσιν ἡμῖν ὕλη παράκειται τὰ τῶν αἰτίων γένη διυλισμένα, ἐξ ὧν τὸν ἐπίλοιπον λόγον δεῖ συνυφανθῆναι, πάλιν ἐπ᾽ ἀρχὴν ἐπανέλθωμεν διὰ βραχέων, ταχύ

metals—which, according to him, are nothing but varieties of water, since metals melt like water when heated—Plato, who is about to move on to other varieties of water, ends his exposition by the following statement:

> It would be no intricate task to enumerate the other varieties (of water), following the method of a likely myth (*tên ton eikotôn muthôn idean*).[35] When a man, for the sake of recreation, lays aside discourse about eternal things and gains an innocent pleasure from the consideration of such plausible accounts of becoming, he will add to his life a sober and sensible pastime.[36] So now we will give it rein and go on to set forth the likenesses that come next (*peri ta exês eikota*)[37] in this subject as follows.[38]   (*Timaeus*, 59c5–d3)

Since there is no limit to the transmutation of metals into one another, because they are varieties of water, this exposition could be continued indefinitely. But it will be purely and simply as a game, and for pleasure; these are two features that characterize myth.[39] The rest of the discourse will remain in on the level of the likely, but will assume another appearance.

The last occurrence of the formula is the most interesting, for it parallels the human being's effort to account for the origin of colours in their diversity with the work performed by the demiurge. Since he is only a man, Timaeus must be content with an explanatory model, which he cannot submit to experimental verification, that is a local, controlled and repeatable experiment showing the proposed explanation should be preferred to any other:[40]

> From these examples it will be sufficiently clear by what combinations the remaining colours should be represented so as to save (*diasôizoi*)[41] our likely myth (*ton eikota muthon*). But any attempt to put these matters to a practical

---

τε εἰς ταὐτὸν πορευθῶμεν ὅθεν δεῦρο ἀφικόμεθα, καὶ τελευτὴν ἤδη κεφαλήν τε τῷ μύθῳ πειρώμεθα ἁρμόττουσαν ἐπιθεῖναι τοῖς πρόσθεν.

[35] On this expression, cf. Brisson (1999 [1982]), 160–162. I do not agree with Burnyeat (2005), 158–159, n. 32; the pleasure provided by the myth is here the most important thing to be considered.

[36] On the relation between myth and games that provide pleasure, cf. Brisson (1999 [1982]).

[37] That is, the other varieties of water, and thus of sensible things.

[38] τἆλλα δὲ τῶν τοιούτων οὐδὲν ποικίλον ἔτι διαλογίσασθαι τὴν τῶν εἰκότων μύθων μεταδιώκοντα ἰδέαν· ἣν ὅταν τις ἀναπαύσεως ἕνεκα τοὺς περὶ τῶν ὄντων ἀεὶ καταθέμενος λόγους, τοὺς γενέσεως πέρι διαθεώμενος εἰκότας ἀμεταμέλητον ἡδονὴν κτᾶται, μέτριον ἂν ἐν τῷ βίῳ παιδιὰν καὶ φρόνιμον ποιοῖτο. ταύτῃ δὴ καὶ τὰ νῦν ἐφέντες τὸ μετὰ τοῦτο τῶν αὐτῶν πέρι τὰ ἑξῆς εἰκότα δίιμεν τῇδε.

[39] Cf. Brisson (1999 [1982]).

[40] Cf. Brisson (2006b), esp. 229–230.

[41] See the proverbial expression, *supra*.

test (*basanon*) would argue ignorance of the difference between human nature and divine (*anthrôpinês kai theias phuseôs*), namely that divinity has knowledge and power sufficient to blend the many into one and to resolve the one in to many,[42] but no man is now, or ever will be, equal to either task.[43]

(*Timaeus*, 68c7–d7)

For Plato, experimental verification is first assimilated to torture (*basanon*), an image that pertains to juridical vocabulary.[44] At Athens, the testimony of slaves was always presented as having been obtained under torture.[45] This may have been the case at one time or another, but the 5th and 4th centuries, that is, the period of the great orators and Plato, it was a juridical fiction that allowed the court to take into consideration the testimony of someone who theoretically had no right to testify. To treat the world, which is a god, like a slave, is unacceptable, just as it is also unacceptable for a man to take the place of a god, the demiurge. In this passage, we find most of the features that characterize a myth (*muthos*): 1) the *Timaeus* describes the fashioning of one god by another god, a god which man cannot equal; 2) since it deals with origins, the story cannot be declared either true or false, insofar as there was no witness at the time; 3) what is more, unlike the modern science, no experimental verification enables a choice between the model proposed and another. That is why, since this myth deals with the images (*eikones*) constituted by sensible things, it can only be likely (*eikôs*).

To sum up, like M. Burnyeat,[46] I think the meaning of *muthos* cannot be reduced to that of a tale, as is the view of G. Vlastos[47] and C. Rowe,[48] or to see

---

[42] This phrase recalls the *Philebus* (15c–d).

[43] τὰ δὲ ἄλλα ἀπὸ τούτων σχεδὸν δῆλα αἷς ἂν ἀφομοιούμενα μείξεσιν διασῴζοι τὸν εἰκότα μῦθον. εἰ δέ τις τούτων ἔργῳ σκοπούμενος βάσανον λαμβάνοι, τὸ τῆς ἀνθρωπίνης καὶ θείας φύσεως ἠγνοηκὼς ἂν εἴη διάφορον, ὅτι θεὸς μὲν τὰ πολλὰ εἰς ἓν συγκεραννύναι καὶ πάλιν ἐξ ἑνὸς εἰς πολλὰ διαλύειν ἱκανῶς ἐπιστάμενος ἅμα καὶ δυνατός, ἀνθρώπων δὲ οὐδεὶς οὐδέτερα τούτων ἱκανὸς οὔτε ἔστι νῦν οὔτε εἰς αὖθίς ποτε ἔσται.

[44] Brisson (2006a).

[45] Gagarin (1996).

[46] Burnyeat (2005), 145: 'It is not that *muthos* is equivalent to, and no different from *logos*, but that an *eikos muthos* is a *logos* as well as a myth. Timaeus' myth, unlike Hesiod's, is as well reasoned as any of the Presocratic cosmogonies in the *peri physeôs* tradition. But unlike your typical Presocratic, whom Plato tends to regard as an atheistic materialist (*Laws*, X), Timaeus' cosmogony will be a theogony too'.

[47] Vlastos (1965a).

[48] Rowe (2003), 27: 'I propose however, that the real explanation of the appearance of *muthos* in 29d (and its two subsequent appearances) is rather more prosaic. My positive thesis can be stated very briefly and simply: it is (a) that the emphasis in the phrase *eikôs muthos* at *Timaeus* 29d2 falls on the work *eikôs*, not on *muthos*; and (b) that *muthos* is used here only, or primarily, as an alternative to or substitute for *logos*, and does not operate in this typical opposition to that term. But (c) finally, and more speculatively, I propose that a

in it an admission of the limitation of discourse, like Morgan.[49] But I oppose Burnyeat with regard to the meaning to be given to *eikôs*.

3. *EIKÔS*

Burnyeat is right not to accept the meaning of *eikôs* proposed by A.E. Taylor, because it is anachronistic: 'To begin with, it is too suggestive of the cautious atmosphere of modern empiricist philosophy of science, according to which a scientific hypothesis is (to quote A.E. Taylor's Whitehead-inspired gloss on *eikôs muthos*) always 'provisional,' because held subject to revision as we learn more and more about the physical world.'[50] As we have seen *supra*,[51] Timaeus does not believe it is possible to submit the model of physical explanation he proposes to experimental verification. It follows that any evolution in the area of physical explanation is impossible.

But I oppose M. Burnyeat in his critique of Cornford: 'Alternatively, the standard translation encourages the thought that the reason why readers of the *Timaeus* are offered a *likely* story—or only a likely story as it is sometimes (but illegitimately) put—is that no statement about the world of becoming be certain. Any number of scholars will tell you that the subject matter of physics precludes anything better than probability, because physics deals with the changeable realm of becoming. But this is not in fact—I repeat *not*—the reason we are given why we should be content with an *eikôs muthos*.'[52] And in a footnote Burnyeat is very explicit: 'So Cornford (1952), 28–29, just after translating 29c2 as follows: 'an account of what is *only* a likeness will itself be *but* likely,' where the words I have italicized

---

very particular sense is to be attributed to the idea, expressed by Timaeus at 29b3–c3, that his account is merely *eikôs* because it is a merely *eikôs* account of its immediate object, the phenomenal world, the world of "becoming"'.

[49] I quote Rowe (2003) who quotes Morgan (2000), 275: 'Luc Brisson attempts to account for the phenomena by suggesting that (I quote Morgan's summary): "*eikôs muthos* signifies a myth that bears upon the copies of intelligible forms (i.e. the sensible), while *eikôs logos* signifies a discourse bearing upon these same objects. Only the actual state of sensible objects can be perceived by the senses and described by a verifiable discourse (*eikôs logos*); the state of these objects before and during their creation cannot be perceived by the sense and cannot therefore be verified. *Eikôs muthos* thus signifies a non-verifiable discourse relative to sensible objects before and during their constitution"'.

[50] In his first note, Burnyeat refers to Taylor (1928), 59–61. He then adds: 'Compare the same author's (1926), 440–441. A note in Whitehead (1929), ix, suggests that the influence was mutual'.

[51] See, p. 378.

[52] Burnyeat (2005), 143.

have no correlate in the Greek'.[53] Translation is no mechanical operation, but consists in understanding an ancient text, then making it understandable to the readers of this modern translation. But since this proposition, introduced by a *de*, which deals with discourse relative to sensible things, considered as inferior to discourse relative to the intelligible forms mentioned in a proposition introduced by a *men*, we can admit that the nuance indicated by *but ... only* is not alien to Plato's text. Some translators emphasize this; others (like me) do not, but the former cannot therefore be condemned for having over-translated. In fact, Burnyeat reproaches Cornford for insisting on a doctrinal point that he does not accept, viz. that the truth value of a discourse depends not only on its adequacy with the object on which it bears, but also and primarily on the ontological status of this object.

The presupposition on which M. Burnyeat bases his argument is that 29c2 does not refer to any kind of discourse about the sensible world: 'Thus the accounts (*logoi*) we are talking about are not any old statements, arguments, or discourses about the physical world. They are very special accounts personified as the exegetes who expound or explain the unobvious significance of an object like a dream, ritual or oracle which does not bear its meaning on its surface, because it comes from, or has some important connection with, the divine'.[54] Several objections can be raised against this interpretation. 1) At 29b4–5, Timaeus speaks, in general, of every kind of discourse, both those dealing with intelligible forms and with sensible realities. In other words, the *logoi* cannot be reduced to the discourses that will be held in the *Timaeus*. 2) Although it is true that in Plato the noun *exêgêtes* is used to denote magistrates having to do with religion, the noun *exêgêsis* and the verb *exêgeisthai* also have uses that are completely secular.[55] 3) Finally, we must consider 29b3–c3 as an axiom implying an opposition that goes from levels that are ontological (model—image), to epistemological (truth-belief), and linguistic (true discourse—likely discourse). This is the axiom

---

[53] Burnyeat (2005), 143, n. 2. And Burnyeat goes on saying: 'Cornford presumably follows Taylor (1929): "discourses concerning that which is ... but a likeness, [are] themselves but likely". I say "presumably" on the grounds that Cornford's translation has the merit of plundering at will from Taylor's splendidly elevated imitation of Plato's *Timaeus* style.' I have to say that I do not particularly appreciate the insinuation that Cornford plagiarized Taylor. I admire Taylor, but I think Cornford did not really need to plagiarize him.

[54] Burnyeat (2005), 149.

[55] It is true that the *exêgêtai* are religious magistrates in the *Laws* and in the *Republic*. Yet *exêgêsis* can have a non-religious meaning (*L.* I, 632a2), as the verb *exêgeisthai* (*Crat.* 407b1; *Rep.* V, 474c6; *L.* VII, 816c2, XII, 959a2).

that M. Burnyeat rejects. Refusing a translation of *eikôs* by 'what is like what is true,' he proposes to understand this adjective as follows: 'what is like what ought to be what you or the situation need and require.'[56] This subtle specification does not suffice to abolish the great Platonic oppositions that have just been mentioned. We should recall, as an item of evidence, this passage from the *Timaeus*:

> My own verdict, then, is this. If intellect (*nous*) and true opinion (*doxa alêthês*) are two different kinds, then these things—Forms that we cannot perceive by our senses but only by our intellect—certainly exist in themselves; but if, as some hold, true opinion in no way differs from intellect, than all the things we perceive through the bodily senses must be taken as the most certain reality (*bebaiotata*). Now we must affirm that they are two different things, for they are distinct in origin and unlike in nature. The one is produced in us by instruction (*dia didakhês*), the other by persuasion (*hupo peithous*); the one can always give a true account of itself (*to men met' alêthous logou*), the other can give none (*to de alogon*); the one cannot be shaken by persuasion (*akinêton peithoi*), whereas the other can be won over (*metapeiston*); and true opinion, we must allow, is shared by all mankind, intellect only by the gods and a small number of men.[57]   (*Timaeus*, 51d3–e6)

So far, I have interpreted the epithet *eikôs* in a double sense ([a discourse] about an image of reality, and [so not true but] likely), corresponding, it seems to me, to what Plato indicates in the passage cited at the very beginning, and to his practice in other dialogues. A discourse, be it a myth or an explanation, is qualified on an epistemological level as a function of the ontological status of its object. A discourse that deals with a sensible object, which is a mere image (*eikôn*) of the genuine reality which is akin to the intelligible, cannot attain the truth (*alêthês*) in the full sense of the word, and must therefore be qualified as likely (*eikôs*). In fact, there is an ambiguity in the use of the word truth in Plato. When it is used in a weak sense, the word indicates the adequation of discourse with the thing or event on which it bears; this, moreover, is why we may speak of true opinion. Yet this true discourse can be declared to be true in the strong sense if, once

---

[56] Burnyeat (2005), 146.
[57] ὧδε οὖν τήν γ' ἐμὴν αὐτὸς τίθεμαι ψῆφον. εἰ μὲν νοῦς καὶ δόξα ἀληθής ἐστον δύο γένη, παντάπασιν εἶναι καθ' αὑτὰ ταῦτα, ἀναίσθητα ὑφ' ἡμῶν εἴδη, νοούμενα μόνον· εἰ δ', ὥς τισιν φαίνεται, δόξα ἀληθὴς νοῦ διαφέρει τὸ μηδέν, πάνθ' ὁπόσ' αὖ διὰ τοῦ σώματος αἰσθανόμεθα θετέον βεβαιότατα. δύο δὴ λεκτέον ἐκείνω, διότι χωρὶς γεγόνατον ἀνομοίως τε ἔχετον. τὸ μὲν γὰρ αὐτῶν διὰ διδαχῆς, τὸ δ' ὑπὸ πειθοῦς ἡμῖν ἐγγίγνεται· καὶ τὸ μὲν ἀεὶ μετ' ἀληθοῦς λόγου, τὸ δὲ ἄλογον· καὶ τὸ μὲν ἀκίνητον πειθοῖ, τὸ δὲ μεταπειστόν· καὶ τοῦ μὲν πάντα ἄνδρα μετέχειν φατέον, νοῦ δὲ θεούς, ἀνθρώπων δὲ γένος βραχύ τι.

it is established, it is irrefutable. If it can be doubted, then it will be declared
to be merely likely. In the first case one will speak of 'science,' and in the
latter of 'opinion'. This second meaning, the strong meaning, thus depends
on the ontological status of the object on which the discourse bears. Such
a criterion, which involves a metaphysical position, cannot be accepted by
scholars interested in contemporary linguistics and epistemology. However,
this criterion was accepted by Plato.[58]

Such is the standard interpretation, defended in particular by Cornford[59]
and to which D. Sedley seems to return in a recent book.[60] From this axiom,
attached for more than two millennia and a half to the name of Plato, a
double consequence derives: thought and the discourse that expresses it
are qualified as a function of its object. The truth pertains to the genuine
reality grasped by the intellect, whereas the likely concerns opinion, which
results from a sensation having a sensible thing as its object. The discourse
held in the *Timaeus*, be it a *muthos* or a *logos*, is likely (*eikôs*) simply because
its object is the sensible, which is a mere image (*eikôn*) of the intelligible. In
fact, the passage cited makes it apparent that the truth attained in the case
of true reality is definitive and stable, whereas that which concerns sensible
things is provisional and changing. It is in this sense that opinion, even if it
may achieve the truth, must be called likely (*eikôs*).

4. *EIKÔS LOGOS*

To verify whether or not this interpretation is well-founded, I intend to
examine all seven occurrences of *eikôs logos* in the *Timaeus*. In all these
occurrences, *eikôs logos* designates a reasoning, an explanation (*logos*) or
an account, backed up by arguments, but only probable, because dealing
with the world in which we live.

In the first instance, the use of *eikôs logos* may simply indicate a reasoning
of the following type:

---

[58] Because, for Plato, ethics and politics were not kept separate from epistemology and
physics. See Cherniss (1977 [1936]).
[59] Cornford (1952 [1937]), 28–29.
[60] Sedley (2007), 110 with note 40: 'It is in this context that we can also make the best sense
of Timaeus's methodological reservations about cosmology (29b1–c3). Because the world is a
mere "likeness" (*eikon*) of an eternal model, the kind of discourse appropriate for it to aspire
is, he says, a "likely" (*eikos*) one, as distinct from the entirely stable discourse that is possible
when the unchangeable model itself is at issue. Why so? He might have been thought to mean
that a mere likeness of X can never give you a completely secure knowledge'.

Let us, then, state for what reason becoming and this universe were framed by him who framed them. He was good, and in the good no jealousy[61] in any matter can ever arise. So, being without jealousy, he desired that all things should come as near as possible[62] to being like himself. That this is the supremely valid principle of becoming and of the order of the world, we shall most surely be right to accept from men of understanding. Desiring, then, that all things should be good and, so far as might be, nothing imperfect, the god took over all that is visible—not at rest, but in discordant and unordered motion[63]—and brought it from disorder into order, since he judged that order was in every way the better.

Now it was not, nor can it ever be, permitted that the work of the supremely good should be anything but that which is best. Taking thought, therefore, he found that, among things that are by nature visible, no work that is without intellect will ever be better than one that has intellect, when each is taken as whole, and moreover that intellect cannot be present in anything apart from soul.[64] In virtue of this reasoning, when he framed the universe, he fashioned reason within soul and soul within body, to the end that he work he accomplished might be by nature as excellent and perfect as possible. This, then, is how we must say, according to the likely account (*kata logon ton eikota*), that this world came to be, by the god's forethought,[65] in very truth (*têi alêtheiâi*) a living creature with soul and reason.[66]

(*Timaeus*, 29d7–30c1)

---

[61] The demiurge is a god, and a god, according to the *Republic* (II, 379b), must be good. This is why he cannot be jealous (*Phdr.* 247a). On this feeling, cf. Brisson (1989), reprinted in Brisson (2000).

[62] This restriction returns like a *leitmotiv* throughout the *Timaeus*. Here are a few examples: 30a, 32b, 37d, 38c, 42e, 53b, 65c, 71d, 89d.

[63] For a more detailed description of this world prior to the demiurge's intervention, cf. *infra*, 53a–b.

[64] On this postulate, cf. *Soph.* 249a.

[65] This is how I translate *pronoia*, to avoid using the term 'providence'; cf. *supra*, 44c, 45b.

[66] Λέγωμεν δὴ δι' ἥντινα αἰτίαν γένεσιν καὶ τὸ πᾶν τόδε ὁ συνιστὰς συνέστησεν. ἀγαθὸς ἦν, ἀγαθῷ δὲ οὐδεὶς περὶ οὐδενὸς οὐδέποτε ἐγγίγνεται φθόνος· τούτου δ' ἐκτὸς ὢν πάντα ὅτι μάλιστα ἐβουλήθη γενέσθαι παραπλήσια ἑαυτῷ. ταύτην δὴ γενέσεως καὶ κόσμου μάλιστ' ἄν τις ἀρχὴν κυριωτάτην παρ' ἀνδρῶν φρονίμων ἀποδεχόμενος ὀρθότατα ἀποδέχοιτ' ἄν. βουληθεὶς γὰρ ὁ θεὸς ἀγαθὰ μὲν πάντα, φλαῦρον δὲ μηδὲν εἶναι κατὰ δύναμιν, οὕτω δὴ πᾶν ὅσον ἦν ὁρατὸν παραλαβὼν οὐχ ἡσυχίαν ἄγον ἀλλὰ κινούμενον πλημμελῶς καὶ ἀτάκτως, εἰς τάξιν αὐτὸ ἤγαγεν ἐκ τῆς ἀταξίας, ἡγησάμενος ἐκεῖνο τούτου πάντως ἄμεινον. θέμις δ' οὔτ' ἦν οὔτ' ἔστιν τῷ ἀρίστῳ δρᾶν ἄλλο πλὴν τὸ κάλλιστον· λογισάμενος οὖν ηὕρισκεν ἐκ τῶν κατὰ φύσιν ὁρατῶν οὐδὲν ἀνόητον τοῦ νοῦν ἔχοντος ὅλον ὅλου κάλλιον ἔσεσθαί ποτε ἔργον, νοῦν δ' αὖ χωρὶς ψυχῆς ἀδύνατον παραγενέσθαι τῳ. διὰ δὴ τὸν λογισμὸν τόνδε νοῦν μὲν ἐν ψυχῇ, ψυχὴν δ' ἐν σώματι συνιστὰς τὸ πᾶν συνετεκταίνετο, ὅπως ὅτι κάλλιστον εἴη κατὰ φύσιν ἄριστόν τε ἔργον ἀπειργασμένος. οὕτως οὖν δὴ κατὰ λόγον τὸν εἰκότα δεῖ λέγειν τόνδε τὸν κόσμον ζῷον ἔμψυχον ἔννουν τε τῇ ἀληθείᾳ διὰ τὴν τοῦ θεοῦ γενέσθαι πρόνοιαν.

This passage simply resumes what has been said, but instead of evoking the tale of origin of the world, which is a likely myth (*eikôs muthos*), it develops the following explanation to give a likely account (*eikôs logos*) of the same thing: 1) the god known as the demiurge is good, and therefore devoid of jealousy; 2) he wishes to fashion a beautiful object, as similar as possible to himself; 3) beauty is indissociable from order, which can be found in a visible body; for 4) order requires the presence of an intellect; which 5) itself can only be found in a soul. Hence this conclusion: 'this world came to be, by the gods, in very truth a living creature with soul and reason'. This account, or *logos*, is true (*alêthès*), but cannot be considered scientific (*epistêmê*), for it deals with that image (*eikôn*) of true reality known as the sensible world. This is why it is merely likely (*eikôs*). Its truth is provisional, because its object is the world that was born, is always changing and can be destroyed.[67] According to the situation, the explanation proposed can be criticized and even replaced.

With this initial reasoning, we must associate another one concerning not the origin of the sensible world, but its unity.

> Now if anyone, taking all these things into account, should raise the pertinent question, whether the number of worlds should be called indefinite or limited, he would judge that to call them indefinite is the opinion of one who is indeed indefinite about matters on which he ought to be definitely informed.[68] But whether it is proper to speak of them as being really one or five, he might, if the stopped short there, more reasonably feel a doubt. Our own verdict, indeed, declares the world to be by nature a single[69] god,[70] according to the probable account (*kata ton eikota logon*);[71] but another, looking to other considerations, will judge differently. He, however, may be dismissed.[72]
> (*Timaeus*, 55c7–d6)

---

[67] Although it will not in fact be destroyed, for the demiurge, who is good, cannot destroy the beautiful object he himself has fashioned (41a–c).

[68] A pun on *apeiros* (in unlimited number), *empeiros* (expert), and *apeiros* (inexperienced). Another example of this play on words is found at *Phlb.* 17e, and perhaps at *Tht.* 183b.

[69] Cf. *supra*, 31a–b.

[70] The Greek text is highly controversial. The key to the problem is to decide whether we must read *theos*, which then becomes the subject of *mênuei*, or *theon*, which must be interpreted as the direct object of the same verb. It is hard to believe that in the context of the *Timaeus*, a god should indicate to a human being all about the geometrical constitution of the elements. Nevertheless, retaining the reading *theon* raises formidable problems, this time of a grammatical nature, for we must make *to men oun de par'hemon*, which has as its counterweight *allos de*, the subject of *menuei*.

[71] The expression is found a few lines previously, cf. 53d5–6, and a few lines further on (56a1, b6).

[72] Ἃ δή τις εἰ πάντα λογιζόμενος ἐμμελῶς ἀπορεῖ πότερον ἀπείρους χρὴ κόσμους εἶναι λέγειν ἢ πέρας ἔχοντας, τὸ μὲν ἀπείρους ἡγήσαιτ' ἂν ὄντως ἀπείρου τινὸς εἶναι δόγμα ὧν ἔμπειρον χρεὼν

Neither the interpretation by Keyt[73] who concludes the argument is not valid, nor that by Burnyeat,[74] who criticizes Keyt and considers Timaeus' conclusion is reasonable, hold water, it seems to me. The unity of the world is deduced from the uniqueness of the total living being, but as the world is just an image of its model, the truth of this deduction is limited by the fact that in an image unity is less evident than in its model.

The four other occurrences of *eikôs logos* concerns the link established by Timaeus between mathematics and physics. Because physics deals with sensible things, this link can be questioned and is but likely. This is what we can observe when, after setting forth what reason has done (*Tim.* 29d–47e), Timaeus undertakes to explain all about necessity, that is, the disorderly movement of the sensible world (*Tim.* 47e–69a).

> We must, in fact, consider in itself the nature of fire and water, air and earth, before the generation of the heaven, and their condition before the heaven was. For to this day no one has explained their generation,[75] but we speak as if men knew what fire and each of the others is, positing them as original principles,[76] elements (as it were letters)[77] of the universe; whereas one who has ever so little intelligence should not rank them in this analogy even so low as syllables.[78] On this occasion, however, our contribution is to be limited as follows. We are not now to speak of the first principle or principles—or whatever name men chose to employ—of all things, if only on account of the difficulty of explaining what we think by our present method or

---

εἶναι, πότερον δὲ ἕνα ἢ πέντε αὐτοὺς ἀληθείᾳ πεφυκότας λέγειν ποτὲ προσήκει, μᾶλλον ἂν ταύτῃ στὰς εἰκότως διαπορήσαι. τὸ μὲν οὖν δὴ παρ' ἡμῶν ἕνα αὐτὸν κατὰ τὸν εἰκότα λόγον πεφυκότα μηνύει θεόν, ἄλλος δὲ εἰς ἄλλα πῃ βλέψας ἕτερα δοξάσει. καὶ τοῦτον μὲν μεθετέον ...

[73] Keyt (1971).

[74] Explaining *hina oun*, Burnyeat (2005), 160–161 comments: 'The question we have to ask as judges of Timaeus' cosmic discourse is not "Does that follow?", but "Was that a reasonable choice, was it for the best?"'.

[75] Timaeus thus considers himself the first to try to describe the generation of the elements. He thereby shows himself to be aware of the originality of the explanation he is proposing, which reduces the structure of the entire physical world to two right-angled triangles, isosceles and scalene.

[76] The ancient Greek reads only *arkhas*. Cornford adds 'original' to remind the reader that these principles here are the four elements: fire, air, water, earth.

[77] We find *stoikheia* in the text, a term which, in ancient Greek, can designate a letter of the alphabet or a physical element (cf. *Tht.* 201e). Probably a criticism of Democritus.

[78] Probably an allusion to the explanations of Leucippus and Democritus (DK 67 A 6), who compared the atoms to the letters that make up words. In the doctrine of the *Timaeus* (*infra*, 53c ff.), the four traditional elements distinguished by Empedocles (DK 31 A 37) correspond to solids, limited by surfaces which themselves break down into triangles. These triangles are assimilated to letters (54d, 55b); the surfaces they constitute correspond to syllables, and the elementary solids to words.

exposition.[79] You, then, must not demand the explanation of me; nor could I persuade myself that I should be right in taking upon myself so great a task; but holding fast to what I said at the outset—the worth of a probable account (*tên tôn eikotôn dunamin*)—I will try to give an explanation of all these matters in detail, no less probable than another (*mêdenos hêtton eikota*), but more so, starting from the beginning in the same manner as before.[80] So now once again at the outset of our discourse let us call upon a protecting deity[81] to grant us safe passage[82] through a strange and unfamiliar exposition to the conclusion that probability dictates (*pros to tôn eikotôn dogma diasôizein*); and so let us begin once more.[83]

(*Timaeus*, 48b3–e1)

Timaeus refuses to expatiate on the state in which the elements were found before the intervention of the demiurge, but tries to move from the tale to an explanation describing the mathematical constitution of the regular polyhedra associated with the four elements. The four elements of which our universe consists are earth, water, air, and fire. Plato accepts this postulate, which goes back at least to Empedocles, but he is aware of displaying the greatest originality by giving it a mathematical interpretation.

The link established between physical elements and mathematical figures is not a matter of pure intuition, but a deduction from whose structure is as follows:

In the first place, then, it is of course obvious to anyone that fire, earth, water, and air are bodies; and all body have depth. Depth, moreover, must

---

[79] The repetition *dokei ... dokounta* is completely relevant. The method of exposition adopted by Timaeus is not appropriate for communicating opinions, even if it does not forbid such communication. In fact, Timaeus here recalls the status of the explanation he will propose; it is a 'likely explanation'.

[80] As Timaeus will say later, the 'likely explanation' he proposes is not the only one, or even necessarily the best. These limits do not prevent him from attributing some value to it.

[81] On the need for directing a prayer to the gods before undertaking anything, cf. *supra*, 27c–d; cf. also *Phlb.* 25b, *L.* X, 887c, *Ep.* 980c. Note the repetition *ap'arkhes ... ep'arkhei*.

[82] We find this kind of expression elsewhere in the Platonic corpus (*Rep.* X, 621b–c, *Tht.* 164d, *Phlb.* 14a, *L.* I, 645b). For an attempt at an explanation, cf. Brisson (1999 [1982]), 73–75.

[83] τὴν δὴ πρὸ τῆς οὐρανοῦ γενέσεως πυρὸς ὕδατός τε καὶ ἀέρος καὶ γῆς φύσιν θεατέον αὐτὴν καὶ τὰ πρὸ τούτου πάθη· νῦν γὰρ οὐδείς πω γένεσιν αὐτῶν μεμήνυκεν, ἀλλ' ὡς εἰδόσιν πῦρ ὅτι ποτέ ἐστιν καὶ ἕκαστον αὐτῶν λέγομεν ἀρχὰς αὐτὰ τιθέμενοι στοιχεῖα τοῦ παντός, προσῆκον αὐτοῖς οὐδ' ἂν ὡς ἐν συλλαβῆς εἴδεσιν μόνον εἰκότως ὑπὸ τοῦ καὶ βραχὺ φρονοῦντος ἀπεικασθῆναι. νῦν δὲ οὖν τό γε παρ' ἡμῶν ὧδε ἐχέτω· τὴν μὲν περὶ ἁπάντων εἴτε ἀρχὴν εἴτε ἀρχὰς εἴτε ὅπη δοκεῖ τούτων πέρι τὸ νῦν οὐ ῥητέον, δι' ἄλλο μὲν οὐδέν, διὰ δὲ τὸ χαλεπὸν εἶναι κατὰ τὸν παρόντα τρόπον τῆς διεξόδου δηλῶσαι τὰ δοκοῦντα, μήτ' οὖν ὑμεῖς οἴεσθε δεῖν ἐμὲ λέγειν, οὔτ' αὐτὸς αὖ πείθειν ἐμαυτὸν εἴην ἂν δυνατὸς ὡς ὀρθῶς ἐγχειροῖμ' ἂν τοσοῦτον ἐπιβαλλόμενος ἔργον· τὸ δὲ κατ' ἀρχὰς ῥηθὲν διαφυλάττων, τὴν τῶν εἰκότων λόγων δύναμιν, πειράσομαι μηδενὸς ἧττον εἰκότα, μᾶλλον δέ, καὶ ἔμπροσθεν ἀπ' ἀρχῆς περὶ ἑκάστων καὶ συμπάντων λέγειν. θεὸν δὴ καὶ νῦν ἐπ' ἀρχῇ τῶν λεγομένων σωτῆρα ἐξ ἀτόπου καὶ ἀήθους διηγήσεως πρὸς τὸ τῶν εἰκότων δόγμα διασῴζειν ἡμᾶς ἐπικαλεσάμενοι πάλιν ἀρχώμεθα λέγειν.

be bounded by surface;[84] and every surface that is rectilinear is composed of triangles. Now all triangles are derived from two, each having one right angle and the other angles acute. Of these triangles, one has on either side the half of a right angle, the division of which is determined by equal sides (the right-angled isosceles); the other has unequal parts of a right angle allotted to unequal sides (the right-angled scalene).[85] This we assume as the first beginning of fire and of the other bodies, following the account which combines likelihood with necessity (*kata ton met' anagkês eikota logon*);[86] the principles yet more remote than these are known to heaven and to such men as heaven favours.[87]

(*Timaeus*, 53c4–d7)

This reasoning, dealing with bodies which are mere images of genuine realities, is relatively simple: bodies are solid, and a solid has surfaces as its faces, which can themselves be broken down into triangles. One could go further and speak of the line and the point, but Plato refuses to do so, for practical reasons. We can therefore understand why it is the term *logos*, not *muthos*, that is used here: it is an explanation, not a tale; it does not tell a story, but gives a mathematical description. And this is a 'likely explanation' (*ton eikota logon*), since it deals with sensible things; in other words, it is not. In a way, this explanation is related to necessity, which has just been defined as *khora*, and bears traces of the four elements (cf. *supra*, 52d–53c). The demiurge will transform this necessity and these first drafts of elements into regular geometrical figures.

---

[84] I read *hê orthê* (*phusis*) *tês* ..., and I understand this as a reference to the plane, a surface whose sides are two straight lines.

[85] Isosceles and scalene right-angled triangles respectively.

[86] It combines likehood, because it is about bodies (primary bodies), and necessity, because the polyhedral are mathematical construction.

[87] Πρῶτον μὲν δὴ πῦρ καὶ γῆ καὶ ὕδωρ καὶ ἀὴρ ὅτι σώματά ἐστι, δῆλόν που καὶ παντί· τὸ δὲ τοῦ σώματος εἶδος πᾶν καὶ βάθος ἔχει. τὸ δὲ βάθος αὖ πᾶσα ἀνάγκη τὴν ἐπίπεδον περιειληφέναι φύσιν· ἡ δὲ ὀρθὴ τῆς ἐπιπέδου βάσεως ἐκ τριγώνων συνέστηκεν. τὰ δὲ τρίγωνα πάντα ἐκ δυοῖν ἄρχεται τριγώνοιν, μίαν μὲν ὀρθὴν ἔχοντος ἑκατέρου γωνίαν, τὰς δὲ ὀξείας· ὧν τὸ μὲν ἕτερον ἑκατέρωθεν ἔχει μέρος γωνίας ὀρθῆς πλευραῖς ἴσαις διῃρημένης, τὸ δ' ἕτερον ἀνίσοις ἄνισα μέρη νενεμημένης. ταύτην δὴ πυρὸς ἀρχὴν καὶ τῶν ἄλλων σωμάτων ὑποτιθέμεθα κατὰ τὸν μετ' ἀνάγκης εἰκότα λόγον πορευόμενοι· τὰς δ' ἔτι τούτων ἀρχὰς ἄνωθεν θεὸς οἶδεν καὶ ἀνδρῶν ὃς ἂν ἐκείνῳ φίλος ᾖ. This passage has been invoked in support of the existence of an unwritten doctrine reserved for initiates. Yet this hypothesis is not necessary. We may simply suppose that by this remark, Timaeus limits himself to indicating that the difficulty it presents reserves the explanation he will propose to a tiny number of human beings, the philosophers (cf. *Phdr.* 278d). We recall the distinction that has just been made with regard to the intelligible and intellection, between the large number and the small number of those who can imitate the gods, up to a certain point (cf. *supra*, 51e5).

Plato goes still further. He links the physical properties of the four elements with the mathematical structure of the polyhedra associated with
them:

> Let us next distribute the figures whose formation we have now described,
> among fire, earth, water and air. To earth let us assign the cubical figure;
> for of the four kinds earth is the most immobile and the most plastic of
> bodies. The figure whose bases are the most stable[88] must best answer that
> description; and as a base, if we take the triangles we assumed at the outset,[89]
> the face of the triangle with equal sides[90] is by nature more stable than that
> of the triangle whose sides are unequal;[91] and further, of the two equilateral
> surfaces respectively composed of the two triangles, the square is necessarily
> a more stable base than the triangle, both in his parts and as a whole.[92]
> Accordingly we shall preserve the probability of our account (*ton eikota logon
> diasôizomen*), if we assign this figure to earth; and of the remainder the least
> mobile to water, the most mobile to fire, and the intermediate figure to air.
> Again, we shall assign the smallest body to fire, the largest to water, and the
> intermediate to air; and again the body with the sharpest angles to fire, the
> next to air, the third to water.[93]   (*Timaeus*, 55d6–56a6)[94]

By means of this account (*logos*) that deals with the image (*eikôs*) constituted by the body, we end up with a complete mathematization of physics.

But physics deal with bodies which are mere images of true realities; so its
links with mathematics can be shaken by criticism. That is why this account
(*logos*) is but likely (*eikôs*).

---

[88] In ancient Greek, the term *basis* indicates that a line is considered as a starting geometrical element of a plane figure, and a plane figure is considered as a starting geometrical
element of a figure in space.

[89] Cf. *supra*, 53c–55c.

[90] That is, as we shall soon see, the square and the equilateral triangle, all of whose sides
are equal.

[91] Isosceles and scalene right-angled triangles, respectively.

[92] Because it is a square (whole), made up of four right-angled isosceles triangles (parts).

[93] All this must be expressed in terms of triangles.

[94] καὶ τοῦτον μὲν μεθετέον, τὰ δὲ γεγονότα νῦν τῷ λόγῳ γένη διανείμωμεν εἰς πῦρ καὶ γῆν
καὶ ὕδωρ καὶ ἀέρα. γῇ μὲν δὴ τὸ κυβικὸν εἶδος δῶμεν· ἀκινητοτάτη γὰρ τῶν τεττάρων γενῶν γῆ
καὶ τῶν σωμάτων πλαστικωτάτη, μάλιστα δὲ ἀνάγκη γεγονέναι τοιοῦτον τὸ τὰς βάσεις ἀσφα-
λεστάτας ἔχον· βάσις δὲ ἥ τε τῶν κατ' ἀρχὰς τριγώνων ὑποτεθέντων ἀσφαλεστέρα κατὰ φύσιν
ἡ τῶν ἴσων πλευρῶν τῆς τῶν ἀνίσων, τό τε ἐξ ἑκατέρου συντεθὲν ἐπίπεδον ἰσόπλευρον ἰσοπλεύ-
ρου τετράγωνον τριγώνου κατά τε μέρη καὶ καθ' ὅλον στασιμωτέρως ἐξ ἀνάγκης βέβηκεν. διὸ γῇ
μὲν τοῦτο ἀπονέμοντες τὸν εἰκότα λόγον διασῴζομεν, ὕδατι δ' αὖ τῶν λοιπῶν τὸ δυσκινητότατον
εἶδος, τὸ δ' εὐκινητότατον πυρί, τὸ δὲ μέσον ἀέρι· καὶ τὸ μὲν σμικρότατον σῶμα πυρί, τὸ δ' αὖ
μέγιστον ὕδατι, τὸ δὲ μέσον ἀέρι· καὶ τὸ μὲν ὀξύτατον αὖ πυρί, τὸ δὲ δεύτερον ἀέρι, τὸ δὲ τρίτον
ὕδατι.

This mathematization of physics is taken to the point where the plurality of dimensions of the elementary triangles is supposed to explain the variety of the elements:

> In this way, then, the formation of all the uncompounded and primary bodies is accounted for.[95] The reason why there are several varieties within their kinds lies in the construction[96] of each of the two elements: the construction in each case originally produced its triangle,[97] not of one size only[98] but some smaller, some larger, the number of these differences being the same as that of the varieties in the kinds. Hence,[99] when they are mixed with themselves or with one another, there is an endless diversity, which must be studied by one who is to put forward a probable account of nature (*peri phuseôs eikoti logôi khrêsesthai*).[100]
> (*Timaeus*, 57c7–d6)

Such an hypothesis, however, weakens the strength of the explanation proposed. If the length of the hypotenuse of the elementary triangles can vary, the extreme economy to which a mathematical construction based on a one single length led is thus reduced. Such may well be the price to be paid for an easy account of the variety of the elements. Nevertheless, the mathematical account of nature can be saved, even if is but likely, because it concerns bodies and therefore can compete with another account.

The remaining occurrence of *eikôs logos* concerns not mathematics, but biology, and is found at the end of the *Timaeus*, where the topic of discussion is the origin of animals.

---

[95] The causes pertaining to necessity.

[96] This postulate allows the mathematical explanation formulated above to be applied to the diversity of sensible bodies. Like F.M. Cornford, I take *sustasis* not in the passive sense of 'structure,' but in the active sense of 'union,' or 'composition,' which meaning corresponds to the action evoked by the verb *sunistanai* (89c, 54e, 55a, 89a; cf. also *L.* VI, 782a).

[97] Obviously, the scalene and isosceles right-angled triangle, respectively.

[98] In fact, the right-angled isosceles and scalene triangles have as their hypotenuse a, which, according to what has just been said, may be of variable dimension. This explanation accounts for the existence of a variety of elements, but seems to contradict what was said above (56b) about the relative weight of each element. For if the elementary triangles that make up the elements are of different dimensions, their number cannot suffice to evaluate the weight of an element. One must also take into account the dimension of the hypotenuse of the isosceles or scalene right-angled triangle that serves as a base.

[99] As will be seen *infra*, 58c–60b.

[100] Ὅσα μὲν οὖν ἄκρατα καὶ πρῶτα σώματα διὰ τοιούτων αἰτιῶν γέγονεν· τὸ δ' ἐν τοῖς εἴδεσιν αὐτῶν ἕτερα ἐμπεφυκέναι γένη τὴν ἑκατέρου τῶν στοιχείων αἰτιατέον σύστασιν, μὴ μόνον ἐν ἑκατέραν μέγεθος ἔχον τὸ τρίγωνον φυτεῦσαι κατ' ἀρχάς, ἀλλ' ἐλάττω τε καὶ μείζω, τὸν ἀριθμὸν δὲ ἔχοντα τοσοῦτον ὅσαπερ ἂν ᾖ τὰ ἐν τοῖς εἴδεσι γένη. διὸ δὴ συμμειγνύμενα αὐτά τε πρὸς αὑτὰ καὶ πρὸς ἄλληλα τὴν ποικιλίαν ἐστὶν ἄπειρα· ἧς δὴ δεῖ θεωροὺς γίγνεσθαι τοὺς μέλλοντας περὶ φύσεως εἰκότι λόγῳ χρήσεσθαι.

And now, it would seem, we have fairly accomplished the task laid upon us at the outset: to tell the story of the universe so far as to the generation of man.[101] For the manner in which the other living creatures have come into being, brief mention shall be enough, where there is no need to speak at length; so shall we, in our own judgment, rather preserve due measure in our account of them. Let this matter, then, be set forth as follows. Of those who were born as men,[102] all that were cowardly and spent their life in wrongdoing were, according to the probable account (*kata logon ton eikota*) transformed at the second birth[103] into women ... [104]   (*Timaeus*, 90e1–91a1)

For Plato, metensomatosis is not a matter of pure belief (that is a *muthos*), but of an account (*logos*) depending on what has been said. The notion of an immortal soul that existed before entering such-and-such a body, and will continue to exist after leaving it, may be considered to pertain to myth, insofar as it is a tale concerning the adventures of one of the groups of personages who play a role in the myths are the souls of the dead.[105] But what is under discussion here are not the adventures of such-and-such a soul, but the reasons that can explain why a soul comes to inhabit such a body as a function of the quality of its previous existence. And because that account refers to the lives of soul animating bodies, it can only be likely.

Because it appears in the form of a story that describes the making of a god, the world, by another god, the demiurge, the *Timaeus* is akin to a myth (*muthos*) like the one told by Hesiod in the *Theogony*. Yet it also wants to be an explanation (*logos*), backed up by arguments, of the origin of the world in which we live. The major difficulty to be faced by the interpreter of the *Timaeus* resides in the fact that Plato adopts both viewpoints, without really choosing between them. Since, in both cases, we have to do with discourse, the question arises of the status of such discourse. The answer is the same in both cases. Since Timaeus is talking about the sensible world, which is a mere image of genuine reality, intelligible reality, his myth and

---

[101] Cf. *supra*, 27a.

[102] The Greek texts reads *tôn genomenôn andrôn*. There can therefore be no doubt that Timaeus is speaking of 'male,' even though human beings at their very first birth are bereft of gender.

[103] Cf. *supra*, 42b.

[104] Καὶ δὴ καὶ τὰ νῦν ἡμῖν ἐξ ἀρχῆς παραγγελθέντα διεξελθεῖν περὶ τοῦ παντὸς μέχρι γενέσεως ἀνθρωπίνης σχεδὸν ἔοικε τέλος ἔχειν. τὰ γὰρ ἄλλα ζῷα ᾗ γέγονεν αὖ, διὰ βραχέων ἐπιμνηστέον, ὃ μή τις ἀνάγκη μηκύνειν· οὕτω γὰρ ἐμμετρότερός τις ἂν αὑτῷ δόξειεν περὶ τοὺς τούτων λόγους εἶναι. τῇδ' οὖν τὸ τοιοῦτον ἔστω λεγόμενον. τῶν γενομένων ἀνδρῶν ὅσοι δειλοὶ καὶ τὸν βίον ἀδίκως διῆλθον, κατὰ λόγον τὸν εἰκότα γυναῖκες μετεφύοντο ἐν τῇ δευτέρᾳ γενέσει ...

[105] See Brisson (1999 [1982]).

his explanation cannot achieve a stable truth, whose object is reality, and they must be content with the likeness (*eikôs*), whose truth can be shaken by persuasion.

In this article I have subjected to a critical analysis, M. Burnyeat gives a reading of the *Timaeus* that tries to extract the dialogue from the totality of Plato's work, and propose an interpretation of it that does not take into account the existence of separate intelligible realities of which sensible things are mere images, with the relation of model to image serving, moreover, as a criterion to determine the truth-value of thought and of discourse. For Burnyeat, Timaeus provides his auditors, who will give judgment on what he says, a 'reasonable myth' (*eikôs muthos*), that is, a myth describing the work of reason (that of the demiurge) involved in world-making, which is therefore practical, not theoretical. We thus end up with an interpretation of the *Timaeus* that is akin to the one proposed by the Middle Platonists, who made the intelligible models the thoughts of god, that is, of the demiurge. For my part, I have tried to show in this paper that an attentive reading of the *Timaeus* in its historical context could not help but make the intelligible forms realities separated from the Demiurge, whatever may be the idea we have of these separate realities.

CHAPTER NINETEEN

WHY TWO EPOCHS OF HUMAN HISTORY?
ON THE MYTH OF THE *STATESMAN**

Christoph Horn

Plato's *Statesman* presents formidable interpretative problems with regard to its form, its method and its doctrinal content. And the myth of the *Statesman* (268d–274e) which I will analyze in what follows turns out to be a particularly difficult challenge to its interpreters. In the context of the dialogue it has the function of explaining why the first attempt to define the essence of a statesman—i.e. to characterize him as a shepherd of herds of men (267a8–c4)—is no longer appropriate in present times. A first paraphrase of the content of the myth can be spelled out in this way: in a previous epoch the cosmos was directly controlled by a god. Yet in the meantime, he seems to have withdrawn from caring for the world (without disappearing completely), and this fact has grave implications. The main consequence is a reversal of the direction of the cosmos' rotation. Let us call it the *cosmological* consequence. It is depicted as an event with far-reaching further effects. One of the secondary consequences is the superseding of the Golden Age, traditionally described as that of Cronos, which existed until then, by the non-ideal epoch of Zeus. Let us call this effect the *theological* consequence (although nothing is said about the question whether the names of Cronos and Zeus are more than labels for two periods of time). Moreover, the course of human biographies turned into its opposite: whereas during the period of Cronos, people were born at very high age from the earth and dissolved, as it were, as infants, now, during the period of Zeus, people originate via sexual reproduction and live through the stages of their lives in the way familiar to us. We may thus also talk of an *anthropological* consequence. While the people living during the previous epoch lead an unproblematic and peaceful life under the custodial care of gods and daemons, the people living during the epoch of Zeus were

---

* This article is a revised version of Horn (2002). I would like to thank Manfred Weltecke for his translations and suggestions.

forced to look after themselves and thus had to fall back on the use of crafts and technical devices as a further consequence of the reversed direction of rotation of the cosmos. In this context it also has to be mentioned that in the present time, in contrast to the past, people exercise power over their own kind. During the epoch of Zeus political rule has become the dominion of equals over equals, namely humans over humans. For Plato, the problem of this type of governance is usually practiced by completely unqualified rulers who cannot be compared with shepherds. The consequence of the myth is that a definition of the statesman has to be given which takes into account the new cosmological, theological, anthropological, as well as historico-cultural and political situation.

It would be impossible to get all scholars working on the *Statesman* to agree even on as little as this summary of its content. Indeed, the myth displays a confusing plethora of nuances and details which makes its inter-pretation a precarious task. In what follows I will concentrate on three prob-lems:

(1) How is it possible that in the course of the dialogue an author as rational-ist as Plato corrects the results of a methodical procedure via, of all things, a myth, and such a long and complicated narrative at that? What is the func-tion of the myth? In my view, the mythological passage does not contain a narrative, but rather a series of philosophical claims as well as the *exegesis* of a myth.

(2) What exactly is narrated in the mythological passage: a sequence of two epochs (as the traditional reading assumes) or of three stages (as L. Brisson and Ch. Rowe maintain)?[1] In my contribution, I will support the traditional interpretation, as I think it has clear advantages over the reading of Brisson and Rowe.

And (3): What is the importance of the myth for the political philosophy developed in the *Statesman*? It seems to me that Plato intends to paint an idealized picture of the perfect guidance of human life by a governing God.

---

[1] Brisson (1994 [1974]), 478–496 and 1995 as well as Rowe (1995a), 13 and 188 ff. See also Rowe (2002).

1. WHICH COGNITIVE FUNCTION DOES PLATO ASCRIBE TO MYTHS?

What is the philosophical import of the many narrative passages Plato has woven into his dialogues? How seriously does he take his own myths? Do they merely have a ludic and literary function or do they impart genuine knowledge? If the first assumption were correct they would lack philosophical significance, in which case their value would be similarly modest as that of the many playful accounts of or ironic allusions to contemporaries. However, if the later were true one would have to distinguish further between a substantial and an instrumental epistemic function: either Plato believes that myths can be used to portray genuine philosophical insights or at least intuitions (in which case it would even be possible that he regards them as a means of exposition which transcends the rational form of presentation and which is suitable for the mediation of higher truths, as it were); or he believes instead that philosophical insights can only be gained via the exchange of arguments. For these mythical passages there would then remain a number of subsidiary functions. Thus they might serve to illustrate a philosophical insight or provide a link to the traditionally shared Greek view of the world.

Let us look in turn at these possible views as they relate to our narrative. Despite its initial characterization as a game (*paidia*: 268d–e) we can surely rule out that the sole function of the *Statesman* myth is a purely ludic one. As a piece of literature, the myth seems quite poor and unattractive. Furthermore, it marks an objective turning point in the dialogue and, finally, its declared purpose is to increase the dialectic abilities of the interlocutors.[2] Consequently, it has to contain some philosophically relevant aspect. Let us therefore assume that Plato allocates to it the task of mediating a substantial insight. As far as I can see, there are three possible ways in which the myth can be read.

[i] One might think, e.g., that Plato puts forward a specific narrative form of cognitive access. According to this view the telling of stories would have to be a unique and irreducible form of mediating knowledge. Now, it may be true that certain insights can be mediated solely by oral and literary forms of narration, for example if we are dealing with empathy for subjective states of mood, for human experiences or with the understanding of individual biographies. However, Plato's philosophical interests do not seem to be directed towards insights of this type. His most important themes lie in the

---

[2] This is claimed in *Pol.* 285d7 and 287a3.

areas of moral philosophy, epistemology, philosophy of language and ontology. In our context, the story is about political philosophy and the philosophy of history. Moreover, what speaks against such a reading of the myth
are reasons which have to do with Plato's concept of knowledge, his philosophical methodology as well as his poetics. The first thing to note is that he
develops (especially in his early and middle epistemology) a highly demanding concept of knowledge. His conception of *technê* as well as his juxtaposition of *epistêmê* and *doxa* set up unusually strict standards for genuine
knowledge which he consequently reserves for the philosophers.[3] In the
Statesman this conception of knowledge is still present, more specifically in
the concept of a *basilikê* or *politikê technê*, which is portrayed as cognitively
demanding and extremely elitist.[4] It is impossible to see how such a level
of knowledge could be achieved by telling stories. Furthermore, we need to
observe that for Plato knowledge can only be gained via a methodological
procedure. Central key terms representing this approach are the methodological concepts *elenchos*, *hypothesis*, *dialektikê*, and *dihairesis*. These procedures do considerably differ from each other, yet what is common to all
of them is that they proceed via small argumentative steps and consist in
conceptual and argumentative investigations. In the *Gorgias*, e.g., Plato's
rejection of the rhetorical *makrologia* and the corresponding praise of the
philosophical *brachulogia* leave little room for accepting the idea of a genuinely narrative form of knowledge. And finally, the criticism of poets and
myths in *Republic* II, III, and X also results in a poetics according to which
myths merely have an extrinsic illustrating character for which Plato uses
the term *mimêsis*. According to this, myths work on the soul only with
a non-cognitive suggestive force. Philosophically inferior myths thus have
a disastrous effect on their recipients: they deprave their characters. But
even philosophically acceptable myths have a non-rational, suggestive and
manipulative effect, as is evidenced by the example of the 'noble lie' of the
myth of metals.[5] In this dialogue we also find a strictly evaluative contrast
between the *muthologia* intended for the masses and the wider populace
and a philosophical doctrine (*didachê*) (*Pol.* 304d1–2).

---

[3] Accordingly only the unchangeable ideas can be objects of true knowledge.

[4] Compare the description of the *basilikê* or *politikê epistêmê* in *Pol.* 292b ff. and 305e.
Under the description 'the exact itself' (*auto takribes*: 284d) an object of knowledge is picked
out which, comparable to the idea of the good in the *Republic*, is supposed to mark the end
point of an arduous path to knowledge. Moreover, the *Statesman* mentions a 'double art of
measurement' (285b f.) one of which is concerned with mathematical content whereas the
object of the other is what is appropriate, proper, and necessary.

[5] *gennaion pseudos*: *Rep.* III, 414c–415d.

[ii] Furthermore, it seems possible that in his myths Plato is practicing a free exercise of fantasy and imagination in which he does not feel bound by the duty to make use of precise concepts, to offer strict proofs and to put forward considered arguments. Viewed in this way his myths would be thought experiments without a strict truth claim, i.e. collections of intuitions. They form an imaginative preliminary stage for the theoretical grasp of the truth, which might perhaps be regarded as indispensable. The purely theoretical grasp of the truth would then be something for which an argument has to be made in a second step. I think that this interpretation of the *Statesman* myth can be ruled out because if it were accepted the narrative could not have any value of its own as part of the argument of the *Statesman*. Besides, I will try to show in this essay that the myth is brimming with arguments and theories. If I am right about this the myth cannot possibly be read as an experimental imaginative game or a precursor to the development of philosophical claims.

[iii] As a further option, one could read an intuitive and transrational epistemic function into the *Statesman* myth. Occasionally Plato sympathizes explicitly with non-cognitive forms of insight of this type, as is especially evidenced in *Phaedrus* and the *Symposium* with regard to madness (*mania*) and love (*erôs*) respectively.[6] In order to be able to interpret our myth in this sense, its emphasis would have to be such that with the help of mythical elements true (or at least persuasive) claims, thoughts and intuitions are presented, without it being either possible or necessary to give reasons for them. Yet the *Statesman* myth at no stage claims to derive from a special form of insight, e.g. from divine inspiration. Anyway, it would be a general misunderstanding to assume that in the cases mentioned Plato recognized an intrinsic value *sui generis* of irrational inspiration. The full value of intuitive insights seems for him only to result from a rational reconstruction of the mythical content.[7]

As far as the three interpretative options we have considered are concerned we may rule out a substantial epistemic function of the *Statesman* myth. Thus we are left with the other side of the alternative, i.e. with the

---

[6] *Phdr.* 243e ff. Further examples for the same phenomenon are Plato's praise of poetic inspiration, his respect for traditional stories, religious oracles or also for dreams. Some of Plato's myths are undoubtedly characterized by such an archaizing tendency or a religious aura.

[7] Compare the analysis of Janaway (1995), § 7.

possibility that Plato has in mind an instrumental epistemic function. As far as I can see this reading may be spelled out in four different ways (in the following referred to as [iv]-[vii]).

[iv] One might assume that the dialogue contains an instrumental mediation of knowledge, if it was possible to give the *Statesman* myth an allegorical reading, i.e. if one could take from it some cryptic or enigmatic messages. For in that case, while the mythical form would be an important medium of presentation, the allegorically presented content would nevertheless be won by argumentative means. Such an interpretation has a certain historical credibility, insofar as it was pursued by the Neo-Platonists between Iamblichus and Proclus.[8] However, it seems to me that an allegorical reading is hardly suitable in the case of the *Statesman* myth, as its narrative content is too complex to be deciphered without a sizeable opaque remainder. We must ask: with respect to which unitary phenomenon should it be possible to interpret the many details related in the myth? According to a Neo-Platonist reading the two epochs of Cronos and Zeus have to be referred to the contrast between the intelligible and sensible world. Yet by adopting this interpretation one would eliminate all historical aspects of the myth, and in general it does not seem to be the case, as the reflection on myth in the *Phaedrus* shows, that Plato sympathized with a rationalist and allegorical interpretation.[9]

[v] Furthermore one might attribute an instrumental cognitive value to the *Statesman* myth if one were to maintain that it mediates in an aesthetic and suggestive form knowledge gained by way of an argument. For this to be a tenable reading the myth would have to be structured in such a way that it captivates by its literary quality or that it emanates a desired suggestive or manipulative effect on the conversation partner or reader. In this case the truth content of the text would derive from philosophical considerations which remain unmentioned in the text itself. However, the text certainly does not captivate by its aesthetic attractiveness, as I already pointed out. On the contrary, it seems cumbersome and theory-laden. The myth contains the brief remark that it is narrated in order to help us 'see

---

[8] Compare the contributions of Dillon (1995) and Schicker (1995) in Rowe (1995b).

[9] Cf. *Phdr.* 229c–230a. A further reference in point is *Rep.* II, 378d6f., where Plato distances himself from the 'ulterior motives' (*huponoiai*) which are supposedly characteristic for myths.

more clearly' (*enargesteron idoimen*: 275b4) the one to whom the idea of a herdsman alone applies. This seems to refer to the illustrative function of the text. Nevertheless, it cannot be composed primarily with its suggestive effect in mind, for as we learn in a reflection following it (274e–275b), the myth serves the purpose to create a certain insight in the first place, that is the insight that the concept of a herdsman only applies to the God and not to the king and that the *dihairesis* accomplished up to this point is mistaken. In a further reflection (277a–c) the Eleatic stranger even criticizes the illustrative breadth and elaborateness of the myth. However, he distinguishes it from the art of painting in so far as it is more adequate for people with strong powers of comprehension. Both these passages imply that the myth, even though it may have turned out to be somewhat rambling and florid, is not intended to be merely illustrative but rather to have argumentative content.

[vi] The myth would have an instrumental epistemological function also, if it had to fulfil a pedagogical task relative to the addressees—according to the dictum of the *Phaedrus* about the psychagogical force of a correctly used speech (*Phdr.* 271c10 ff.). Viewed in this way the story told here would have the purpose of being the vehicle or medium of transport for a cognitive content which had been presented in a narrative form due to the limited powers of comprehension of the young interlocutor. In actual fact the Eleatic stranger refers to the circumstance that a myth turns out to be the suitable form of presentation for the young Socrates who up until recently has been listening to childrens' stories (268e). Yet the Eleatic stranger does not go as far as to say that he believes Socrates capable only of this narrative form of argument, to which he does indeed not limit himself in the course of the whole dialogue. Rather, he makes use of the myth and only in addition to this he states the adequacy of this form of presentation for the present addressee. As already cited, the myth is a mere 'child's play' (*paidia*: 268d–e), yet the ludic form cannot be due only to the person of young Socrates.

[vii] According to a final interpretation of the instrumental type the myth of our dialogue could have an authenticating or authorizing function by justifying a certain point of view by recourse to *common sense*. If this were the correct reading, it would have to represent a generally accepted, collective truth not requiring any further justification. Yet this also seems to lack plausibility because the myth (as I intend to show) heavily leans on argumentative premises. Moreover, the Eleatic stranger points out that he tells the present myth for the first time. Thus he claims to have invented

or at least reshaped it (269b–c). He does indeed tie it to something already known by asking Socrates about the myth of Atreus and Thyestes (268e10–11). Yet he then goes on to tell, as he himself emphasizes, unknown aspects of this story, and he links it with the Cronos tale of the Golden Age and with the traditional idea of autochthony. What is characteristic of the *Statesman* myth is its free use of the narrative material, not the recourse to what is authoritative, self-evident, or generally shared.[10]

Up until now we have traced the various forms of interpretation according to which the *Statesman* myth has a cognitive value, that is: either a substantial or an instrumental significance. There remains one further possible reading which cannot be clearly allocated to either side, but combines both aspects.[11]

[viii] It is possible that the myth is a surrogate. It may owe its existence to the difficulty that, according to Plato, no strict method is applicable in circumstances where conditions are non-ideal and the objects of knowledge fluctuate. Viewed in this way the myth would, while epistemically unsatisfactory, at the same time offer a relatively adequate (perhaps even the best possible) form of knowledge for states of affairs which are hard to grasp, e.g. because they lie in the distant past, or for objects which have an inferior ontological status (i.e. those of the world of experience). As is well known, Plato did not regard the reality given to us by the senses as a possible object of genuine knowledge (*epistêmê*), but merely of opinion (*doxa*).[12] Plato concedes that a true and firmly rooted *doxa* does indeed enjoy a certain epistemic status (*Polit.* 309c; cf. *Men.* 97a–98a). Such a surrogate function seems to be what is referred to in his exposition in the *Timaeus*, where the description of the origin of the world is identified as an *eikôs muthos* (29d2). However, we need to caution against a possible confusion at this point: the fact that Plato can refer to scientific and philosophical positions as *muthoi* does of course not imply that he would accept as philosophical theories what we

---

[10] In general, Plato's intention in the use of myths does not seem to be to use conventional stories and traditional motives as confirmations of his philosophical theories. Thus, with regard to the criticism of myths in the *Republic*, Annas (1982), 121–122 has made it plausible that his intention has to lie, to the contrary, in the rejection of conventional mythical examples.

[11] One additional solution proposed by Colloud-Streit (2005), 184–223 seems to me extremely unlikely: namely that Plato, in the *Statesman*, might have suspended the opposition between narrative myth and philosophical argument as an inadequate distinction. This distinction, however, is of basic importance for Plato.

[12] Cf. esp. *Rep.* V, 474b–480a.

call myths (i.e. archaic tales about gods, heroes and families). One may certainly maintain that the *Statesman* myth, insofar as it makes—similar to the *Timaeus*—assumptions about cosmology, historical epochs or cultural history, represents a philosophically acceptable form of theory, even though this does not constitute a methodically adequate procedure. The merely narrative elements of the myth can, by contrast, not be given any meaning via this interpretation.

I think that our overview of the various interpretations [i]-[viii] leads to the result that Plato can have regarded mythological tales, especially the myth under discussion, at best as pejorative modes of abstract and rational forms of presentation. Yet if this assessment is correct, why does he give so much room to a myth as in the case in the *Statesman*? And why does he grant a narrative, of all things, such an important cognitive function for the further development of the dialogue? The first thing to note is that these questions only present themselves if we accept that the Eleatic stranger, as the leader of the discussion of the Statesman, appears in the name of Plato. What seems to me to support such a view is, among other things, the fact that in the *Sophist* the Eleatic stranger already acts as the accepted leader of the dialogue and that the *Statesman* develops a philosophy of the state which can be regarded as Platonic. Why then such a long myth in the middle of a methodical *dihairesis*?

In my view, the possible interpretations mentioned above, with the exception of the variant [viii] considered last, contribute little to the elucidation of the *Statesman* myth. Yet even this interpretation does not do more than merely partially characterize the uniqueness of this myth. What Plato presents in the myth under discussion seems to me to be no less than a concentrated, narrative version of important elements of his theology, cosmology, theory of history, and political philosophy. Therefore I believe that the *Statesman* passage is of much greater doctrinal importance than the afterlife myths of the *Gorgias*, *Phaedo*, *Phaedrus*, and in *Republic* X. The *Statesman* myth has a didactical character, and it plays an important part in the context of the argument. I thus want to call the *Statesman* text a 'doctrinal myth'— whereby I do not want to claim that all its details reflect Plato's views, least of all, that it points to insights which could not be reached by way of argument. However, it seems that the text does indeed make a serious and even far-reaching claim to truth and explanatory power.

In support of my thesis I appeal to the observation that the mythological narrative is linked with a surprisingly large number of accompanying reflections. In at least five places the origin, content, credibility and the

gain of the myth are discussed.[13] The first thing to note is that the Eleatic
stranger, according to his own testimony, makes use of the conventional
tradition in an instrumental way (cf. the expression *prochrêsasthai*: 268d9),
i.e. he takes advantage of it in a philosophical context. It is noteworthy that
he wants to integrate the myth directly into the dihairetic procedure. He
does this by giving the methodological instruction that one would have to
take away from the narrative 'bit by bit' (*meros aei merous aphairoumenous*:
268e1).[14] Moreover, the Eleatic stranger claims about his story that it provides the unifying background for three existing mythical subject matters,
i.e. for the topic of the reversal of the cycles of cosmic movement, for the
topos of the Golden Age under Cronos and for the motive of the births
out of the earth (269b5 f.). He also contends that he gives the first comprehensive exposition of a connection of these mythical materials (269b9 f.),
more specifically, in the sense of a first revelation. Further evidence for the
fact that the *Statesman* myth makes a claim to truth and that it corrects
traditional mythical narratives comes in the form of a few small remarks
in the text. Thus we find the claim that the current narrative for the first
time names 'the cause of the astonishing phenomena' (*tôn thaumastôn
aition*: 270b4; this refers to the Golden Age and the earth births). In another
place (271c1) we read that the name (*onoma*) and the whole story (*logos*)
about the earthborns must be traced back to the myths related here. A
similar remark is made in the context of the motive of the Golden Age.
About this the Eleatic stranger also claims that the tales of an easy ('automatic') life are based on the facts the myth told by him relates adequately
for the first time (271e3–5). Moreover, when describing the epoch of Zeus
reference is made to the Prometheus myth and related 'ancient tales' (*ta
palai lechthenta*: 274c5 f.). It is characteristic for the intention of the Eleatic
stranger that the traditional stories are here put into their proper context for the first time. Later the Eleatic stranger will criticize himself for
having told more than is required in the context of the present intention
(277a–c). This again implies that what is told does not merely meet narrative but also philosophical standards. The text also contains an authenticating passage which says that the common stories (of the two epochs),

---

[13] Cf. *Rep.* 268d–269c; 271d–e; 273e–274e; 275b, as well as 277a–c.

[14] The expression *aphairein* is used in the *Statesman* in a semi-technical sense to denote
whatever is the uninteresting side of a *dihairesis*. Lane (1998), 120–121 argues, with respect
to 277b4, for the view that the myth is abandoned as 'too large a paradeigma'. However, in
my own view, the passage merely realizes the announcement that the myth is to be included
into the *dihairesis*.

although doubted by many, could nevertheless be traced back to reliable 'reporters' (*kêrukes*), which had survived the reversal of the cosmic cycle (271b2–4).

As the analysis of the accompanying reflections shows the Eleatic stranger uses the mythical material to support a philosophical argument. The reflections determine the character of the text to such an extent that the whole passage from 268d to 274e might be more correctly called a philosophical explanation, classification, and correction of conventional myths than a narrative presentation itself. The numerous reflections that accompany this myth turn out invariably as confirmations of its content. The contradiction of this assessment by a self-reflective passage in the context of the story about the epoch of Cronos is only an apparent one: in 272b–c the Eleatic stranger leaves it an open question whether or not the people of this epoch had engaged in philosophical debate. However, he goes on to state that they would, when saturated an inebriated, have told each other and the animals stories (*muthoi*), 'as they are still being told about them' (272c7 f.). This is undoubtedly a clear degradation of the mythical form of narration. But nothing forces us to conclude that the passage contains an ironic self-destruction of what is being narrated. For the *Statesman* myth is hardly a story which can be appreciated in the lethargic state of culinary saturation and alcoholic intoxication. It is much too complex and theoretic for that. The point Plato is advancing here can instead be described as follows: philosophy is so much more valuable than are mere stories that it would make the worse contemporary epoch of Zeus even better than the epoch of Cronos, should no philosophy have been practiced at that time (which is unknown to us).

Indeed, how laden with theory the *Statesman* myth is also shows itself in the fact that the Eleatic stranger seems to have constructed the idea of two opposite cosmic cycles in rationalistic fashion, more specifically on the basis of the following four metaphysical considerations:[15]

- Something, which is not divine, but corporeal, cannot enjoy complete changelessness or uniformity (269d5–7).
- The heavens or the cosmos, while excellently endowed by its maker, cannot be free of all change due to its being corporeal (269d7–e2).
- As far as possible the cosmos tries to maintain a uniform circular motion in one direction, for this is the smallest deviation from self-motion (269e2–5).

---

[15] Compare the slightly different reconstruction of the argument in Lane (1998), 102.

– He who moves himself may not move in opposite directions; pure self-motion is a feature of the God alone, who steers everything which is in motion (269e5–7).

The Eleatic stranger concludes from these considerations on the one hand that the world cannot move itself, and on the other hand that it cannot always be controlled by the God. Furthermore, he considers it to be impossible that it is moved in opposite directions by two different Gods (269e–270a). This only leaves the possibility that the cosmos moves in two opposite directions: the one under the control of the demiurge, and the other as a result of its self-movement (270a). The young Socrates agrees with what has been explained as 'very plausibly said' (*mala eikotôs eirêsthai*: 270b1). Therefore, not only is the myth of the *Statesman* not told merely with the claim to correct and put right traditional myths, it also turns out to derive from serious metaphysical premises. It is, as we saw earlier, a narrative critically selected from material handed down by the tradition, and it is, as has become clear now, a narrative constructed from metaphysico-cosmological background assumptions.

Remarkably, the myth told in the closest parallel passage to our myth in *Laws* IV (713a–714b) is also claimed to be reporting the truth (cf. *alêtheia chrômenos*: 713e4). Its credibility is also underlined by the fact that there is talk about a necessity to believe in it (cf. *anankê dêpou peithesthai*: 714b2). The crucial passage in which we find a resumption and continuation of our myth is the following:

> So the story teaches us today, and teaches us truly, that when a community is ruled not by God but by man, its members have no refuge from evil and misery. We should do our utmost—this is the moral—to imitate (*mimeisthai*) the life of the age of Cronos and therefore should order our private households and our public societies alike in obedience to the immortal element within us, giving the name of law to the appointment of understanding.
> (713e3–714a2; trans. A.E. Taylor, slightly changed)

The Athenian stranger from the *Laws* represents, with a high degree of probability, Plato's own late political philosophy. In case this is as correct as the presence of Platonic convictions in the *Statesman* myth, the following conclusion regarding the common intention of both texts suggests itself: both texts set two cosmological and historical epochs against each other, the main difference between which lies in the fact, that in the first epoch the God (Cronos) guarded humanity, whereas in the second humans rule over humans. The human forms of state necessary in the second epoch can imitate (*mimeisthai*) the regiment of Cronos in better or worse ways.

2. How Many Epochs
Are Involved in the Myth of the *Statesman*?

How many cosmological and historical epochs have to be distinguished in the *Statesman* myth? As already mentioned I will challenge the interpretation of Brisson and Rowe[16] who both reach the conclusion that the passage talks about not two but three epochs. In my opinion there is a good *prima facie* argument against this interpretation: the *mythological* passage is supposed to explain why the definition of the statesman as the pastor of humans has become unusable (cf. *Rep.* 274e) in the current age. The passage can fulfil this purpose in a plausible way only if it is based on a *simple antithesis* between the current and an earlier epoch. To mention more than two epochs and to embellish each with colourful descriptions would be uneconomical compared to this overall intention, if not misleading, for the function of the myth is to illustrate the fundamental difference of the current age. Indeed, we find in the text an explicit juxtaposition of two ages: the one of the 'current rotation' (*hê nun periphora*: 274e9) and of the 'opposite rotation' (*hê enantia perihodos*: 274e10 f.). Even if one might object that according to Plato's view of history we have to assume more than two historical epochs, it would still remain the case that to list them would run against the overall intention. In the context of the *Statesman* debate the only thing relevant is the aspect in which the current state differs from one, several or all earlier situations, not a general theory of history. Against this reading Brisson and Rowe would have to show which relevance a tripartite presentation could have for the definition of the statesman, and in my view they have not succeed in doing this, nor does it look at all promising.

This *prima facie* argument is connected to the observation that the narrative from 268d to 274e can most naturally be understood as a unity of four elements, i.e. of the [A] cosmological, [B] theoretical, [C] anthropological and [D] cultural-historic and political level. As already suggested at the beginning of this essay (see page 394 above) I think that the myth can be reconstructed in such a way that it presents a simple antithesis according to which the God either holds the steering wheel of the cosmos in his hands or has withdrawn to his observation tower. If the first is the case the cosmos revolves in the direction intended by God, and humans are living in the paradise-like age of Cronos: they are born out of the earth and guided

---

[16] The vast majority of interpreters argues against this line of interpretation: e.g. Lane (1998), Delcomminette (2000), Ricken (2008) and Kahn (2009).

by the divine shepherd of humanity. If the second is the case the cosmos revolves autonomously in the opposite direction. Humans are then living in the toilsome age of Zeus, come into existence by sexual intercourse and grow old until they finally die. They have to guide themselves and establish a political power structure. Thus according to my interpretation, the Eleatic stranger advocates a *connection thesis*. This claims that one has to assume a sharp contrast between two epochs which are each characterized by a fourfold connection: in epoch I [a] the cosmos is moving in an ideal, divinely ordained direction, [b] Cronos is ruling (however this might be meant), [c] the biographical development runs from old age to childhood, and [d] a Golden Age of divine-daemonic guidance obtains. Epoch II, on the other hand, is characterized by the facts that [a'] the opposite direction of cosmic movement occurs, [b'] Zeus rules, [c'] biographies run in the familiar direction and that [d'] self-sufficiency and political structures are required. Viewed in this way the *Statesman* myth explains these processes monocausally: the features of both ages can be explained just due to the presence of God at the steering wheel or due to his absence. Based on their reading, Brisson and Rowe would thus also have to provide an answer to the question: according to which overall principle is the historical sequence being told?

It is surely the greatest weakness of the three-epochs-interpretation that it is forced to reject the connection thesis. Yet if someone denies the connection of [a], [b], [c], and [d] or of [a'], [b'], [c'], and [d'] they get into conflict with the statement that all changes can be traced back to one and the same cause (*tauta toinun esti men sumpanta ek tautou pathous*: 269b5–6; cf. c1). Epoch I differs from epoch II precisely by the God's presence at or absence from the steering wheel.

According to the reading defended by Brisson and Rowe the ages of Cronos and Zeus are not congruent with the antithesis of the two directions of cosmic rotation. Rather Brisson and Rowe assume two cosmic reversals (269c–d and 273e) and consequently arrive at positing a third age: this is supposed to lie between the ages of Cronos and Zeus and is supposed to have been completely abandoned by God and the daemons. Thus one could talk of a sandwich model. In the interim phase to be assumed by this reading the direction of cosmic rotation is contrary to the one of the age of Cronos and likewise contrary to the direction familiar to us, whereas in our present cosmic, anthropological and political situation we are living in a third epoch in which God (i.e. now Zeus) is governing the course of the world while the daemons responsible for the different regions are presumed not to have returned.

For an initial criticism of the three-stages-interpretation it is irrelevant that a closer look at the positions of Brisson and Rowe shows that they differ in many details from one another. However, the following can already be argued: if the god-forsaken age were not identical to the age of Zeus, a confused picture of the features of the epochs distinguished in the text would result. This picture would be of doubtful argumentative value, for on the one hand the cosmic and biographical directions of rotation or development would no longer be correlated. On the other hand, only the cosmic, yet not the socio-political harmony would be restored in the present time. If one follows Brisson and Rowe and gives up the connection thesis, one cannot explain any more why the current cosmological conditions should still have a ruinous influence on the state of politics. For one would have to give a reason why it should be the case that the God (i.e. Zeus), when he resumed power, corrected the direction of the cosmic rotation, but was not willing or able to comprehensively care for humans once again. As far as I can see the text offers no explanation at all for why it is that despite the divine government men (and not God, gods or daemons) rule over men and why humans at present still have to toil for their livelihood. The text does not even concede that an explanatory gap exists at all—something one might clearly expect assuming the reading of Brisson and Rowe.

That the *Statesman* myth is based on the connection thesis can be corroborated with some further observations. First, one might point to the fact that the two opposite directions of rotation are supposed to alternate (270b7–8); according to the text the changes of direction cause the greatest transformations (*megistas ... metabolas*: 270c4–5). This cannot simply mean that each change of direction leads to catastrophes, for immediately afterwards it says that these many great *metabolai* would harm living things, thus that they *cause* these catastrophes (270c7–9). Thus we must regard the *metabolai* as follow-on effects of the changed rotation which profoundly effects the living conditions on earth. This allows us to conclude that the direction of rotation is of decisive importance for the living conditions of the relevant epoch. And if there are exactly two such directions of rotation there also have to be precisely two sets of living conditions. Confirming this one could note that according to the claims of 271b7–8 and 274d7–8 humans imitate the cosmos and follow it in each of the two epochs insofar as at the one time they live and grow in one way and at the other time in the other way. Here too we clearly have a dichotomous juxtaposition and a connection of the cosmological and anthropological situation. One must also take an inquiry of young Socrates into account where there is talk of exactly two rotations (271c4–7); it is answered by the allocation of the 'autonomous' life to the epoch of Cronos (cf. *panta automata gignesthai tois anthrôpois*: 271d1). The answer implies, like the question, a two-part alternative. A little later a historical dichotomy is set up again in which the ages of Cronos and Zeus are contrasted (272b1–3). The epoch of Zeus is the current one (*ton nuni*: 272b2) and the dialogue partners have to decide the question which of the *two* ages is the happier one (*krinai d'autoin ton eudaimonesteron ktl.*: 272b3–4). Now, one might perhaps think that only the two epochs governed by gods were compared with each other. Yet in that case: would one not also at least expect that the fact that an evaluation of the third epoch is not given were at least mentioned? Anyhow, an explanation would seem to be required for why the Eleatic Stranger nowhere makes an explicit reference to the assumption of three ages. The parallel passage from *Laws* IV mentioned earlier does not contain any such reference either. Finally, there are two more passages which can be quoted as indications for the two-epoch-interpretation. On the one hand the passage 271a8–b2 talks about 'our ancestors' who are supposed to have survived the change of the epochs and who—as already mentioned—can be regarded as credible reporters (*kêrukes*) of the earth births. However, if our epoch borders on the epoch of the earlier earth births there can be only two epochs. On the other hand 274c–d describes the help of the gods in crafts and other skills which in our epoch is supposedly necessary for our self-sufficiency. Yet in 274c1–4 it is stated that humans were initially helpless because unlike before they now had to provide their food for themselves. However, if between the times of Cronos and Zeus there were a god-forsaken epoch, as Brisson and Rowe assume, it would be inexplicable why humans were helpless at the beginning of our time—after they had already lived through an arduous time. From this we can also conclude that the life under Cronos must border directly on our current epoch.

What makes the thesis of the existence of three stage seem attractive (at least to a certain extent) is the fact that the myth incorporates a number of details which are traditionally hard to interpret. If one follows Brisson [1995] his new interpretation of the *Statesman* myth succeeds in solving four difficulties which are supposedly unsolvable in the old reading. First difficulty: why should the god-forsaken age be also describable as the age of Zeus (according to 272b–d)? How could Prometheus, Hephaestus and others come to the help of humans if we were dealing with a god-forsaken age (according to 273e–274e)? Why should the age of Zeus, because of the technical and philosophical use of reason that occurs in it, be regarded as possibly even higher than that of Cronos (according to 272b)? Second difficulty: if only two epochs were referred to, a tension would result in the description of those circumstances which obtained at the beginning of the second epoch. For on the one hand, it says that 'initially' the god-forsaken cosmos was still in a good state because it remembered the teaching (*didachê*) of its 'demiurge and father' (273b2 ff.). On the other hand there is talk of the fact that 'in the earlier times' humans suffered from lack of protection and hunger, since they had to survive without techniques of self-sufficiency (274b–c). Third difficulty: in the age of Zeus humans originate in a sexual way. If this were the reversal of the time of Cronos we would have an asymmetry since the humans originating from the earth simply vanish. According to Brisson the text offers no clues regarding the fact that the origin of life and the direction of its course are correlated to the direction of the cosmic rotation. Fourth difficulty: Brisson brings together three passages in order to show that the age of Zeus is a time of divine guidance, yet not of daemonic providence. According to the first one (271d3–6) God had (in the epoch of Cronos) cared for the rotation of the universe as a whole, 'like now also'.[17] The second passage (272e6–273a1) states that the daemons abandoned their regional duty of care together with the God. Finally, the third passage (274d2–5) talks of the lack of daemonic care under present circumstances, with the consequence that humans had initially suffered hardship. Brisson concludes from this that the third age, that of Zeus, has again a God as a ruler of the world, but does not include daemonic care for humanity.

I think Brisson's reservations can be responded to as follows. It is correct that the traditional reading must claim that the god-forsaken age is at the same time the age of Zeus. However, this does not lead to a problem, because the Cronos-Zeus-antithesis has a purely conventional character.[18] This juxtaposition based on Hesiod does not contain more than a labelling of the two epochs—and no factual characterization. If the Eleatic stranger were to understand it literally this would lead to a problem for Brisson also: why does the myth always talk of only *one* God or demiurge, if it actually intended to bring both Cronos and Zeus into the picture? It is said of one, not of two Gods that he withdraws to the vantage point and that he returns to the steering wheel when the threat to the cosmos becomes too great. Brisson tries to solve this difficulty by suggesting that we should take 'Cronos' and 'Zeus' as two epoch-specific names for one and the same God.[19]

---

[17] However, at this point (d4) the dialogue poses serious text-critical problems, so that we are not compelled to see a comparison with the present time here.

[18] Cf. Erler already in (1995), 377. Moreover, Erler draws attention to the distancing which lies in the phrase *tonde d'hon logos epi Dios einai* (272b2).

[19] Brisson (1995), 350, n. 4.

However, like the reading advocated in this essay, this solution assumes that the use of the Cronos-Zeus-antithesis has a purely conventional character. Thus Brisson's doubts lose their argumentative force.

This leads us to the second of Brisson's difficulties: how can a single epoch be characterized by a successive decline following an initially well-ordered state on the one hand and by technical achievements and philosophy after an initial time of hardship on the other? It seems to me that there is nothing problematic about this. If one takes into consideration that the decline depicted is that of the cosmos whereas the opposite tendency of technical and philosophical progress is a (divinely assisted) achievement of humanity, nothing speaks against the possibility that these are two opposed, yet not incompatible phenomena of a single epoch. Indeed, it seems plausible to assume that human living conditions took a sudden turn for the worse when the God withdrew, whereas the rational, divinely instructed cosmos was merely subject to a slow process of decline. Again, there is nothing absurd in the assumption that at present the cosmos degenerates further and further until the time of its restitution by the God has arrived, while there is a parallel progress of human cultural development and autonomy. Especially in an age in which divine guidance of the world is lacking and only in the face of increasing cosmic decline does it make good sense that individual divine assistants support humanity with technical devices. On the contrary: if the so-called age of Zeus could be equated with the return of the God to cosmic control then this form of situational assistance would not be understandable. Thus the long sentence 274d2–8 following the mention of the help by Prometheus and Hephaestus explicitly refers to the absence of divine care. Moreover, it has to be noted that the God and the individual daemons have neither died nor disappeared. They have merely temporarily distanced themselves from a complete care for the world. Thus nothing speaks against the possibility that in an area of decline individual intervention occurs and thus partial progress can happen. Also with regard to the role of philosophy one can argue that it receives its full importance only when it is practiced under disadvantageous circumstances.

As to the third difficulty, i.e. the question regarding the correlation of the ages with the origin of the humans living through them: in the decisive passage on this problem (272d6–e3) it is stated that at the time of the reversal of the direction of cosmic rotation 'the race born from the earth' had already been completely destroyed after 'each soul had run through its appointed number of births and had returned as seed to the earth as many times as had been ordained for it'. Is what is talked about here a kind of human being different from the earthborn ones mentioned at 271a–c, as is assumed by Rowe because of the idea of seed which had previously not been mentioned?[20] I would want the following to be considered: if completely different humans were referred to it would be confusing that the earth race is signified by the definite article (*to*), which would seem to refer to the earthborns previously mentioned. The idea of an earthly birth and that of a seed do not exclude one another, especially as the text leaves it open in which way the earthborns meet their end. It simply says that they 'vanish' (*exêphanizeto*: 270e9). For example, it would be possible that the souls of those earthborns who have died fall back into the earth as seeds, in this way preparing a new incarnation. To conclude that there are two kinds of earthborns is therefore not especially plausible. It certainly does not provide a conclusive argument for the three-stages-argument.

Finally, let us turn to the fourth difficulty: in my view it is possible to rebut Brisson's reference to the three passages mentioned by indicating the compatibility of the last statements. It seems to me that the question whether Brisson rightly contends that the passage 273e marks a transition from the second to the third cosmic period, is of central importance in this context. I want to make a few observations about this claim. The text surrounding the passage contains no evidence whatsoever that, according to the Eleatic stranger, the God would have already left the vantage point (*periopê*: 272e5) he climbed in order to take up his position at the steering wheel again. And neither do we find any hint that the historic low point is at the present time already left behind, i.e. that currently humanity is living in a post-catastrophic era. The only thing that is stated is that the cosmic chaos was finally so great that there was an impending threat that the cosmos would be 'dissolved in the bottomless abyss of unlikeness' (*eis ton tês anhomoiotêtos apeiron onta ponton duêi*: 273d6–e1). I interpret this as the declaration of regularity and that means in this context: as a historical prognosis of the return of God which will occur at the moment of greatest danger. At that time the God will re-establish the earlier direction of rotation and restore the original state of the cosmos designed by him. Some evidence for the reading that no reference is made here to any previous event, but rather that a cosmic regularity is portrayed, can be seen in the use of the present tense in the passage under discussion. Interpreted in this way the passage 273e4 does not mark any decisive turning point, contrary to what Brisson and Rowe assume. A break occurs at this point only insofar as the attention returns to the topic of politics. Thus the text can be read in such

---

[20] Rowe (1995a), 194.

a way that beginning with 273e4 the political circumstances of our epoch are discussed from the viewpoint of the cosmic regularity of the changing of two epochs.

Rowe's argument emphasizes other aspects than Brisson, yet he shares the latter's basic interpretative model. He too wants to refer the asexual earth births and the backwards running biographies (270d6–271c2) to the phase beginning when the God lets go of the cosmos (see also Rowe [2002]). This phase is supposed to precede our own age. Our epoch is therefore characterized by the fact that the cosmos is again guided by the God. Thus Rowe thinks that the Golden Age of Cronos (271c8–272d4) belongs to an even older era so that between it and our Zeus epoch lies the interim phase which is marked by a change of the cosmic rotation. Consequently for Rowe the times of Cronos and Zeus share the same direction of cosmic rotation: the direction from east to west we are used to. The time of Cronos is also asexual for him, yet in contrast to the interim phase it is characterized by the idea of seeds. In Rowe's interpretation the end of the time of Zeus marks the beginning of a new overall cycle. Thus it is followed by a new return to the time of Cronos. Between the current epoch of Zeus and the age of Cronos following it there will be no change of cosmic direction (273d4–e4). If one follows Rowe's reading further, the decisive disadvantage of a two-stage-interpretation lies in the need to assume that a divinely governed age implies (in contrast to our present godless age) an inverted biographical development as well as asexuality—which is a bizarre assumption, as it is impossible to connect any discernible advantages with these features. He objects to the two-epochs-interpretation on the additional ground that according to it young Socrates would not really have to ask to which direction of cosmic rotation the time of Cronos belongs (271c), because it would have to be obvious that it belongs to the phase of reversed movement. Against this the most important advantage of a three-stage-interpretation would lie in the fact that it allows us to make better sense of the portrayal of the corporeal and yearning cosmos.

The first question one will naturally ask is: why should it, according to Rowe's opinion, not be equally unproblematic (or even easier) to interpret the corporeal-yearning cosmos within the framework of a two-stage-theory? The fact that the cosmos has 'its destined and own inborn urge' (272e6) does not imply Rowe's interpretation, according to which the cosmos (comparable to a human being) can learn or lose intellectual self-control. On the contrary, according to Rowe's reading it is not clear due to which circumstances the cosmos either assumes a positive order or lapses into chaos. Furthermore, it seems questionable to me why Rowe regards the interpretation as bizarre according to which Zeus' time of decline is characterized by sexuality and ageing whereas the positively evaluated time of Cronos is marked by the features of asexuality and increasing rejuvenation in the course of life. Thus also according to Rowe's reading Plato (provided he is not speaking ironically) must have seen something positive in these features—difficult as it may be for us to comprehend this. If asexuality and rejuvenation are to be part of the epoch of Cronos as well as of the interim phase (if with certain differences in the details) this will of course break the connection I have argued for earlier. Cosmology and anthropology will in this case not be correlated. Yet is that not precisely the intention of the myth? Equally problematic about Rowe's interpretation, it seems to me, is the fact that it can neither explain the less than optimal living conditions in the epoch of Zeus nor their gradual decline. How is it possible that we live at a time of disadvantageous political circumstances—although the God is at the steering wheel of the cosmos? In what sense can it be understood that at the return of the age of Cronos the God reassumes the government of the world? Is it really possible to weaken the Cronos-Zeus-antithesis to such a degree that two subsequent partial epochs exist within two cosmic major epochs? Is not the explanatory function of the *Statesman* myth precisely to spell out the difference between the relations of power in the ages of Cronos and Zeus? How is this difference interpreted in Rowe's model? And why would the myth bring in the cosmic dimension if it fails to explain the difference between the epochs? In particular, I think that Rowe's reading is very difficult to reconcile with the passage 269b5–6 already quoted (*tauta toinun esti men sumpanta ek tautou pathous*). For this statement also refers to the Cronos myth (cf. 269a7–8). Thus the character of this age must be explicable in terms of the direction of cosmic rotation. However, it seems to me that it follows from this that the epochs of Cronos and Zeus differ from each other by a change in the direction of cosmic rotation. As far as the literal textual basis is concerned, the greatest difficulty arises from a contrasting of *hê nun ... kathestêkuia phora* and *hê emprosthen* (271d2–3). While Rowe acknowledges this problem, in my view, he does not offer a convincing solution to it.

3. What Role Might the Myth
of the *Statesman* Play in Plato's Political Philosophy?

In conclusion I want to briefly touch on the question of the meaning of the myth for the political philosophy Plato develops in the *Statesman*. This much is clear: according to the view of the Eleatic stranger it is impossible

under contemporary conditions to simply equate the figure of the statesman with that of a shepherd of humans. The cosmic conditions have wors-
ened too dramatically for that. In the course of the *Statesman* the one
who possesses *politikê epistêmê* appears as the best possible replacement.
Political knowledge is defined as the 'regal art of weaving,' which comprises a number of individual partial competences which the artists knows
how to combine (305e). This integrative form of knowledge is possessed by
the 'kingly man, gifted with insight' (*andra ton meta phronêseôs basilikon*:
294a8). Only secondarily, the *Statesman* pleads for the rule of laws. On a
closer reading the dialogue even adopts an ambivalent position towards the
value of laws: on the one hand they are said to be deficient because they are
incapable of specifying what is at the same time the best and the most just
for all affected by the law. In the light of the multiplicity of people and situations the laws are rigid and unchangeable (294a–b). On the other hand they
do have two advantages. For one thing, a philosophically uneducated ruler
not governed by insight is incapable of giving each individual citizen precise
direction for an adequate way of life. The generality of laws is an immense
simplification of his task. On the other hand laws are necessary if a ruler
guided by insight is temporarily absent. Even if the topic of the philosopher
king of the *Republic* is not literally continued it is essentially present in the
rule of the *basilikos*. Thus the dialogue *Statesman* repeats the characterization of this form of government as an extremely unlikely exceptional case.

At this point one will obviously ask which feature it is that the royal
ruler has in common with the guiding God of the age of Cronos and what
is imitated by the laws in a less than perfect manner. Wherein lies the
characteristic which, according to Plato, the contemporary politician would
have to try to attain in order to approximate as much as possible the
example of the age of Cronos?

In order to answer this question I will choose the following detour: if
one compares the motifs used in the *Statesman* myth with the theories and
models employed by Plato elsewhere the strange motif of the asexual origin
and the increasing rejuvenation of the inhabitants of the age of Cronos is
particularly striking. It is virtually without parallel in Plato's other works.[21]
It seems curious, if not absurd, and only to be interpretable as a comical
element. By contrast, it is beyond doubt that the theological aspects of the
myth, for example, come close to Plato's actual views. The statements about
God (*theos*), the demiurge (*demiourgos*) as well as the father (*patêr*) of the

---

[21] The autochthony motif in *Menx.* 237c–238b belongs to a myth about origins, not to a
cosmological myth about two stages.

cosmos can be closely paralleled with those from the *Timaeus*. Moreover, there is a marked correspondence between the *Statesman* and the *Timaeus* in the kind of two-principles-conception which in both texts leads to the assumption that the universe is ordered insofar as the God has created it or governs it, but at the same time chaotic and unordered, insofar as it is left to itself and of a corporeal or bodily nature. Moreover, it seems plausible that in our myth Plato wants to offer a serious outline of his own cosmology. Admittedly: neither in the *Timaeus* nor in any other place in Plato's works is there any talk of two opposite cosmic rotations. Yet in numerous other details our myth agrees with the cosmology of the *Timaeus*.[22] Finally, there are good reasons for the assumption that the idea of different historical epochs and of an initial Golden Age was part of Plato's convictions. Thus Brigitte Wilke [1997] has compiled extensive material which shows that Plato saw the past as a norm and reference point for a proper political order.

This gives rise to the following question: is it convincing to assume that the four elements listed earlier—i.e. Plato's theology, his theory of principles, his cosmology and theory of history—are treated seriously in the *Statesman* myth, whereas the motif of the increasing rejuvenation in the course of life is the only one to be understood in an ironic and comic way? In my view, this seems not very credible, since in that case seriousness and jest would form a logically inconsistent synthesis. Should the most distinctive and striking features of the narrative be the one that was intended as a joke? It would in my view be much more preferable to adopt an interpretation which could give the asexual origin and the reverse biographical development a positive meaning.

I therefore propose to regard the divine provision, planning, order and determination which exists in the case of biographies during the age of Cronos as the decisive advantage Plato is aiming at. For the fact that human biographies develop in reverse direction firstly implies that the time of the end of their lives (their disappearance) is foreseeable for them. The reincarnation of those concerned seems to be equally foreseeable. Since no other causes of death are mentioned we can conclude that in the time of Cronos there are no untimely deaths. Given the presence of a divine protector physical threats to humans would be unlikely anyway. The motif of asexuality could be correspondingly interpreted as the freedom of violent

---

[22] Also according to *Tim.* 36c, the cosmos comprises two circles, an inner and an outer one. The outer is in a state of uniform movement because it participates in 'the nature of the same', the inner is in a state of non-uniform movement because it participates in 'the nature of the diverse'. For further conformities with the *Timaeus* see Rowe (1995a), 188.

desires. It thus seems plausible to assume that people living during the time of Cronos would not only have lead a peaceful and unproblematic, but also a rule-governed, anticipatable, and regular life free of consuming passions. By contrast the suboptimal age of Zeus is depicted as an epoch where there is work and a scarcity of goods, war and aggression, the wildness of animals, sexuality, death, and the formation of families and states. Humans are left to their own devices, subject to conflicts, threatened by early death, permanently exposed to the dangers of life as well as to violent desires. Although we may find it confusing that Plato has a more positive view of the divine paternalism of the herdsmanship of the 'flock' of humanity than of individual autonomy, it is obvious that in Plato we cannot expect to find a form of political liberalism. The characteristic which matters most for a statesman is therefore his ability to regulate, plan, determine and order. If he is not governed by insight he should take recourse to the surrogate of a legal order which regulates human life as far as this is possible.

This view is supported by an interesting article: for the detail of the earth birth G.R.F. Ferrari (1995) has developed a very similar interpretation. According to Ferrari, what distinguishes the biographies in the epochs of Cronos and Zeus is the lack of a historical memory in the first and its presence in the second case. Accordingly, the political situation in the age of Zeus is characterized by the fact that political power reaches an acceptable standard only by the strict adherence to a tradition of laws. This observation seems correct to me. Under current conditions of life humans have an open future, are autonomous, but have only limited insight. The only guarantee for a reasonably appropriate political orientation then is a strong sense of tradition.

Viewed in this way the point of the *Statesman* myth lies in the fact that it offers an explanation for how it was possible that an age like the present one, which is marked by a reduced cosmic and political harmony, could arise and how this situation can be properly remedied. The decisive consequence of the myth therefore seems to consist in the fact that political philosophy has to take account of a situation of decline. It is possible to describe the myth (admittedly somewhat pointedly) as a kind of theory of modernity because it tries to derive the current socio-political conditions of Plato's days from a general historical development and to characterize them as specifically topical. If we compare Plato's causal analysis of the current non-ideal living conditions with the biblical story of the fall or with the gnostic myth of the fall of the soul it is conspicuous that neither human failure nor a divine drama play any part in it. Rather, what is depicted is a law-governed, quasi-natural process. Plato perhaps tries to avoid the idea of a divine mistake which in the sophistical *Protagoras* myth is attributed to Epimetheus, and to stabilize his rationalist theodicy of the *Republic*. Moreover, we have to take note of the fact that Plato cautiously reaches a positive view of the age of Zeus which is characterized by developments in the crafts and an increase in technical knowledge, by growing autonomy and philosophy as compensations of a situation marked by deficiencies. However, this does not change the fact that Plato prefers conditions in which such compensations are not required.

CHAPTER TWENTY

THE DELPHIC ORACLE ON SOCRATES' WISDOM: A MYTH?

Louis-André Dorion

The title of this study raises a question: that of knowing whether the story of the oracle in the *Apology* can be considered a myth. But before answering that question, I will endeavour to answer another, prior question, which appears to me preliminary, namely: can we consider that the story of the oracle in the *Apology* is a Platonic invention and that it is thus a fictitious account? It is only after having answered this first question that I will be able to answer the one asked in the title of this study, for while it is evident that every myth has a fictional dimension, it does not follow that every fictitious account is a myth, so that in the event that the oracle story be fictitious, it would still remain to be determined if it can also be seen as a myth.

1. The *Apology* as a *Logos Sokratikos*

More and more commentators consider the *logos sokratikos* to be a literary genre allowing its author a broad freedom of invention, both as regards the staging and content of the remarks attributed to the various characters, including Socrates. Under these conditions, given that the very genre of the *logos sokratikos* authorizes and encourages fictionality, it is not at all astonishing that Plato might have fabricated not only the circumstances of such and such a discussion, 'reported' in the dialogues, but also the discussion's theme, as well as the remarks lent to the various characters taking part in the discussion. If the *Apology* is a *logos sokratikos*, just as are the other dialogues, nothing, at least in theory, prevents Plato's having also imagined certain scenes or certain exchanges reported in the *Apology*, including perhaps the story of the oracle. However several commentators refuse to consider the *Apology* to be a *logos sokratikos*. Although he insisted greatly on the fictional dimension of the *logoi sokratikoi* and on the impossibility of reconstituting the thought of the historical Socrates based on the *logoi sokratikoi*, C. Kahn maintains that the Platonic *Apology* is a case apart inasmuch as it is the text which is most likely to correspond to a 'quasi-historical document'[1] and to an 'historical account'[2] of Socrates' philosophy. This position is not just Kahn's; in fact many commentators[3] consider that the *Apology* is not a *logos sokratikos*, since therein Plato reports on a speech which has the status of an historical event several hundreds of people were witness to; this would have kept him from dealing as he pleased with historical truth and would have constrained him to report, if not the letter, then at least the spirit of the defence Socrates pronounced before the court. But if the *Apology* is not a fictional work, like Plato's *logoi sokratikoi*, it would then be possible, at least in principle, to reconstitute the philosophy of Socrates based on the *Apology*.[4] However there is no reason for refusing the *Apology* the status of *logos sokratikos*[5] and for considering that it does not contain what may amount to a considerable fictional element. Moreover, the very existence of several *Apologies* by different authors confirms that the theme of Socrates' trial and defence was no less a subject of rivalry, among the Socratics, than other themes on which they competed in writing dialogues.[6] If the Platonic *Apology* were a faithful report of the trial of Socrates, we would then have to consider that other, rival accounts of the trial of Socrates, among them the *Apology* by Xenophon, are not faithful, which amounts to affirming the superiority of Plato's testimony over Xenophon's, as was done in the heyday of the Socratic question. Will we seriously assert that only the Platonic *Apology* is a faithful report and that the other *Apologies* are fictions? If the *Apology* is a *logos sokratikos*, just as are the other dialogues, then, theoretically, nothing prevents the story of the oracle being partially or completely fictitious.

---

[1] Kahn (1996), 88.

[2] Kahn (1992), 257; cf. also 240, n. 9.

[3] Cf. Taylor (1932), 28; Ross (1933), 15, 22–23; Guthrie (1971), 158, n. 1 and the references indicated by Montuori (1981), 42–43.

[4] Basing himself on the *Apology*, which he presents as 'our measure for the historical Socrates' (95), Kahn (1996), 88–95 proposes a 'minimal view' of the historical Socrates. For another attempt at reconstituting the thought of the historical Socrates based on the *Apology*, cf. Döring (1987).

[5] Cf. Joël (1894), 480; Stokes (1992a), 57; Vander Waerdt (1993), 40, n. 107; Morrison (2000), 239 whose study is a methodical refutation of all those—notably Kahn and Döring (cf. the preceding note)—who consider that the Platonic *Apology* can serve as a 'document' for reconstituting the thought of the historical Socrates.

[6] Cf. Dorion (2005).

2. The Story of the Oracle Seen as a Fictitious Story

Historians and commentators have long suspected that the story of the oracle is a Platonic invention.[7] Since Antiquity authors have voiced doubts about its authenticity. Plutarch reports in these terms the incredulity expressed by the Epicurean Colotes:

> At the very outset Colotes throws in his reserves: after relating that Chaerephon returned from Delphi with the oracle about Socrates that we all know, he comments: 'we shall dismiss this business of Chaerephon's, as it is nothing but a cheap and sophistical tale'.[8]
>
> (*Adv. Colotem*, 1116e–f; trans. Einarson & De Lacy)

Athenaeus was just as sceptical, not only because he noticed that the Pythia's answer is not the same depending on whether we consider Plato's *Apology* or Xenophon's, but also because the question Chaerephon puts to the Pythia appears absurd and implausible to him:

> How, then, is it reasonable or probable that Socrates, who confessed that he knew nothing, should have been proclaimed by the god who knows all things as the wisest of all men? For if that is wisdom, to know nothing, then to know all things must be stupidity. And what was the use in Chaerephon's bothering the god by his question about Socrates? For Socrates was himself entitled to credence when he said on his own behalf that he was not wise.[9]
>
> (V, 218e–f; trans. Gulick)

Obviously a simple suspicion will not be satisfactory because, as it happens, the suspicion is hardly more than a vague intuition of the ahistorical or

---

[7] Cf. Schanz (1894), 599; Joël (1921), 759–761 ('Das Unglaublichste an dieser Geschichte ist wohl, daß sie geglaubt wurde und noch heute vielfach geglaubt wird'); Robin (1942), 115, n. 2; Fontenrose (1978), 34 ('Or could this response [*scil.* the Pythia's response] be a pious fiction of the Socratic circle? That is not impossible, though perhaps incredible'), 245–246; Montuori (1981), 57–66, 140–143; (1988), 52–53; (1990); Stokes (1992a), 51–55; Vander Waerdt (1993), 8, 12, n. 38, 27 sq.; (1994), 64, n. 59 ('of course one must bear in mind the possibility that Plato's story of the oracle is a literary fiction'); Danzig (2003), 304; Waterfield (2004), 94 ('Now, this story is certainly a Platonic fiction').—Without really taking a position on the oracle's historicity, Zeller (1868), 55, n. 2 affirms that the oracle's historical character 'certainly cannot be very rigidly proved'.

[8] Εὐθὺς οὖν τὸν ἀφ' ἱερᾶς κεκίνηκεν ὁ Κωλώτης, καὶ διηγησάμενος ὅτι χρησμὸν ἐκ Δελφῶν περὶ Σωκράτους ἀνήνεγκε Χαιρεφῶν, ὃν ἴσμεν ἅπαντες, ταῦτ' ἐπείρηκε· τὸ μὲν οὖν τοῦ Χαιρεφῶντος διὰ τὸ τελέως σοφιστικὸν καὶ φορτικὸν διήγημα εἶναι παρήσομεν.

[9] Πῶς οὖν εὔλογον ἢ πιθανὸν Σωκράτη τὸν ὁμολογοῦντα μηδὲν ἐπίστασθαι σοφώτατον ἁπάντων ὑπὸ τοῦ πάντα ἐπισταμένου θεοῦ ἀναρρηθῆναι; εἰ γὰρ τοῦτό ἐστι σοφία, τὸ μηδὲν εἰδέναι, τὸ πάντα εἰδέναι φαυλότης ἂν εἴη. Τίς δ' ἦν χρεία τῷ Χαιρεφῶντι παρενοχλεῖν τὸν θεὸν περὶ Σωκράτους πυνθανόμενον; αὐτὸς γὰρ ἦν ἀξιόπιστος ὑπὲρ αὐτοῦ λέγων ὡς οὔκ ἐστι σοφός.

fictitious character of the oracle story. If we want to get beyond mere suspicion, we must produce specific arguments that either cast doubt on the
historicity of the oracle story or provide evidence of its fictitious character. There are several such arguments. I will briefly sketch out the main
arguments which have been advanced so far by critics of the oracle's historicity:

a) Whereas Chaerephon is a character who was often satirized by Aristophanes and other comic authors,[10] and whereas Socrates had himself been
the target of several comic authors, the authors of Ancient comedies never
make mention of the oracle, which is quite astonishing for it is just the sort
of subject that would attract the comic authors' attention.[11]

b) Since the oracle provides a divine sanction for Socrates' philosophical
mission, and is at the very origin of Socrates' philosophical way of life—I
shall return to this point later—, we might expect, because of its importance, that it would be mentioned by writers and philosophers contemporary with Plato. However we find no mention of this oracle,[12] neither in
authors of the last quarter of the 5th century, nor among contemporaries
of Plato—except for Xenophon (*Ap.* 14–15). And since some date the oracle back to 430,[13] since Socrates was already practicing refutation when he
returned from the siege of Potidea,[14] Chaerephon and Socrates would have
had to have kept the oracle secret for about thirty years. In reading the *Apology* (21a), one indeed gets the impression that the oracle's answer is known
only to Chaerephon, his brother Cherecrates and Socrates. Why would they
have kept the secret for so long? Is it plausible that what is at the very source

---

[10] Cf. Aristophanes, *Nub.* (*passim*); *Av.* 1296, 1564; *Ran.* 1335; fr. 291, 377, 539, 573 Kock (=
fr. 295, 393, 552, 584 Kassel-Austin); Eupolis, fr. 165, 239 Kock (= fr. 180, 253 Kassel-Austin).

[11] Cf. Robin (1942), 144; Montuori (1981), 66; (1990), 256; Stokes (1992a), 55: 'granted the
majority dating of the oracle before the Peloponnesian War, how could the oracle fail to
become known to the comic poets who made Socrates the butt of so many jokes? Was
there no material for comedy in the man who was wiser than others with Socrates' strange
"wisdom"?'

[12] Cf. Döring (1895), 57; Stokes (1992a), 55: 'the absence of the oracle from the whole extant
literature of Socrates' lifetime and from all but two related works [*scil.* Plato's *Apology* and
that by Xenophon] of the next generation is, humanly speaking, extraordinary. Was it really
the best-kept secret of a lifetime? It seems to me improbable'. See also Waterfield (1994), 94;
Danzig (2003), 55.

[13] Cf. Vander Waerdt (1993), 28–29.

[14] See the beginning of the *Charmides.*

of Socrates' philosophical mission would be kept secret and in silence for so long,[15] even to the point that Socrates' disciples knew nothing of its existence?

c) Not only do Aristophanes and authors contemporary with Plato, excepting Xenophon, never mention the oracle, but there is no reference to it in the other dialogues of the Platonic corpus either.[16] Similarly, Xenophon only mentions the oracle in the *Apology*, and never in the *Memorabilia* or in his other Socratic writings (*Symposium* and *Oeconomicus*). Plato's silence in the other dialogues on the oracle's answer remains mysterious if we think of the bond between the oracle's answer and the form of argumentation (the *elenchus*) favoured by Socrates: on certain occasions, he might very well have invoked the oracle either to justify his putting his interlocutors to the test, or else to justify himself in having no knowledge of the subjects on which he questioned his interlocutors. Is it not precisely because he admits to not knowing anything about the most important subjects that the oracle proclaimed him the wisest of men?

d) Given that it is the oracle's answer which is at the source of Socrates' philosophical mission—I will return to this in the next section—and which makes him understand in what sense he is wise and distinguished from other men, it is hard to understand why Chaerephon and the Pythia herself already attribute that wisdom to Socrates, since nothing, prior to the refutations set in motion by the oracle, justifies attributing such wisdom to Socrates.[17] In other words, Chaerephon and the Pythia can only consider that Socrates is distinguished from other men in his relationship to *sophia* if Socrates has himself already become aware, by means of the *elenchus* he practised upon his interlocutors, that he possesses a *sophia* which distinguishes him from other men; however it is precisely the oracle's answer that is at the origin of his practice of the *elenchus* and of his awareness that he has a form of *sophia* distinguishing him from other men.[18]

---

[15] Cf. Montuori (1990), 255: 'we must ask whether it is likely that the impetuous Chaerephon was silent with everyone for so many years about the answer given by the Pythia, even during the nostalgia of exile, and that it was to his brother alone that he revealed it in secret'. Cf. also Daniel & Polansky (1979), 83: 'Surely it is strange both that Socrates speaks as if hardly anyone present in the court has ever heard about the Pythia's utterance and that he never refers to it again in any other dialogue'. See also Danzig (2003), 55.

[16] Cf. de Strycker (1975), 46; Montuori (1981), 66; (1990), 256; Vander Waerdt (1993), 29; de Strycker & Slings (1994), 78; Brisson (1997), 67.

[17] Cf. Schanz (1894), 599; Danzig (2003), 304.

[18] Cf. Waterfield (2004), 94: 'It [*scil.* the oracle story] is riddled with inconsistencies,

These are the main arguments in favour of the oracle story's fictitious nature. To these arguments can be added those aimed at showing that the oracle story is not only fictitious, but that it also has things in common with a myth. As I underlined at the beginning of this study, these are two distinct questions; but while several commentators today support the view that the oracle story is fictitious and that it is a Platonic invention, there is nobody, to my knowledge, who also considers it to be a myth.

3. THE ORACLE STORY AS A MYTH OF ORIGIN

On the assumption that the oracle story is fictitious, do we also have the right to see it as a myth? As everyone knows, the occurrences of the term *muthos* are very rare in the early dialogues[19] and, moreover, there are none in the *Apology*. But the scarcity of the occurrences of the term *muthos* in the early dialogues is not the main reason why Plato cannot *openly* recognize the mythical dimension of the oracle story. The main reason is obviously due to the very context of the *Apology*: since the oracle story is a key element in the defence of Socrates, and since Socrates presents that episode as an objective datum and an authentic fact of his own life, he would ruin his own defence if he implied that that account is an invention or a myth. Plato of course recognizes elsewhere that there are 'true' myths,[20] in that they corroborate, confirm or supplement the teaching of philosophy on the same subjects, but he cannot describe the oracle story as a true myth because that would immediately cast doubt on the veracity and authenticity of that episode in Socrates' life.

If during the trial Socrates cannot recognize the mythical character of the oracle story, we still need not exclude the possibility that Plato gave the reader all the clues necessary for the story to be read as a form of myth. With that in mind, we need only determine whether the oracle story has

---

not the least of which is that there could have been no reason for Chaerephon to have approached the oracle with his question in the first place if Socrates were not already famous as a philosopher. [...] in other words, he was famous as the person in Athens who went around questioning people and finding out if they could define the moral concepts they claimed to understand. But this is precisely the kind of questioning that was supposed to have been triggered by the oracle, not the background to the oracle'.

[19] See the statistics compiled by Brisson (1982), 178–179. There are only nine occurrences of the term *muthos* in the early dialogues and they are divided up as follows: five in the *Protagoras* (320c3, c7, 324d6, 328c3, 361d2), three in the *Gorgias* (505c10, 523a2, 527a5) and one in the *Cratylus* (408c8).

[20] Cf. *Gorg.* 523a, 527a.

certain characteristics usually found in myths. Indeed, in what follows I propose to show that the oracle story satisfies all the criteria that G. Most[21] has enumerated with the goal of identifying accounts which can be seen as myths. I will take up the eight criteria suggested by Most, one by one, and will try to demonstrate that the oracle story fully satisfies each of them.

– 1st criterion: '*Platonic myths are almost always monological*' (16). According to Most, 'the myths are differentiated in the first instance by the fact that they are presented orally by a single speaker without any interruption at all by his listeners from beginning to end' (16).—The oracle story easily satisfies this criterion: from the story's beginning until its end (20d–23c), Socrates delivers an oral monologue that is never interrupted.

– 2nd criterion: '*Platonic myths are probably always recounted by an older speaker to younger listeners*' (16).—This is also the case of the oracle story: at the time of his trial, Socrates is 70 years old and the listeners he addresses are, in the vast majority, younger. Addressing his judges at the beginning of the trial, Socrates refers to his first accusers, saying 'they got hold of most of you from childhood' (18b5). Since the *Clouds* was performed in 423, and the trial takes place in 399, the judges who were warned away from Socrates, from their childhood onward, were hardly over 10 years old at the time of the *Clouds*' performance, so that they would be between 30 and 35 years old at the time of the trial. The public Socrates addresses on his trial day is also composed of young people in the habit of following him, as well as their families (33d–34b).

– 3rd criterion: '*Platonic myths go back to older, explicitly indicated or implied, real or fictional oral sources*' (17).—The oracle story satisfies that criterion too, because Socrates states expressly that he has it from his friend Chaerephon (20e–21a). Thus we are dealing with an oral source who is mentioned explicitly and, although Socrates presents him as a real source, everything leads us to believe that it is fictitious.

– 4th criterion: '*Platonic myths always deal with objects and events that cannot be verified*' (17).—In fact, an essential characteristic of myth is its unverifiability, i.e. nobody is able either to confirm or disprove its content.[22] And the oracle story is also unverifiable: as Socrates prepares to relate the oracle

---

[21] Cf. *supra*, 16–19.
[22] On the unverifiable character of myth, cf. Brisson (1982), 12, 28–29, 126.

story to his judges, he carefully underlines that Chaerephon is dead (21a). Now it is Chaerephon who went to consult the Pythia in Delphi in connection with Socrates and it seems that he was alone when the Pythia answered him.[23] Because Chaerephon is the only witness to the oracle's answer, and because he is already dead by the day Socrates renders the answer public, apparently for the very first time,[24] the story of the oracle seems to me, in the absence of any direct witness to the answer, unverifiable. According to the conditions of verifiability proposed by Brisson,[25] the oracle story would seem to be verifiable at least for Socrates, since he had the possibility of verifying the content with Chaerephon. However it is not clear that Socrates was really able to verify the account Chaerephon related to him because the latter was the only witness to the oracle's answer, so that Socrates was obliged to take his word for it, without being able to verify the truth of Chaerephon's account. As for the Athenians present at the trial, and who hear the oracle story for the first time, they have no means of verifying its authenticity either, since Chaerephon is dead and since his brother, as well as Socrates, are at best only indirect witnesses to the oracle's answer. The story of the oracle, as told by Socrates, is thus unverifiable. I therefore disagree with those who, on the contrary, consider that Chaerephon's brother's testimony attests to the oracle's historicity: 'But within the dialogue itself, Socrates does appeal to Chaerephon's brother, since Chaerephon is dead, to confirm his report of the oracle's message (21a7–8). This reference to

---

[23] Xenophon, on the contrary, insists on the presence of numerous witnesses: 'Once on a time when Chaerephon made inquiry at the Delphic oracle concerning me, in the presence of many people (πολλῶν παρόντων), Apollo answered that no man was more free than I, or more just, or more prudent.' (Ap. 14; trans. Todd). The presence of numerous witnesses has the effect of providing the oracle a 'publicity' it does not possess for Plato.

[24] Cf. Montuori (1990), 255: 'it was only in the presence of his judges, in order to defend himself, that Socrates decided to reveal to the Athenians the pronouncement about his wisdom which Apollo made through the Pythia, *and which until then no one knew, not even his friends*. If this is the case, we must ask whether it is likely that the impetuous Chaerephon was silent with everyone for so many years about the answer given by the Pythia, even during the nostalgia of exile, and that it was to his brother alone that he revealed it in secret.' (italics mine). Cf. also Vander Waerdt (1993), 29; de Strycker & Slings (1994), 75–76.

[25] Cf. Brisson (1999 [1982]), 21: 'The events with which the myths are supposed to deal must have unfolded long enough ago that the person who relates them finds it impossible to verify their validity, either directly, by having witnessed them, or indirectly through the mediating agency of someone who did'. See also 101: 'Indeed, the adequacy or inadequacy of such a discourse to its referent can only be falsified if this referent can be perceived. For a referent to be perceptible, however, it must be situated, in relation to the percipient, in the present, or in a past recent enough for the individual in question to have had an experience of it, or to have been informed of it by someone who has had a direct experience of it'.

a witness present in the court prevents our believing Plato intends his readers to view the episode as totally invented'.[26] But if that is the case, why do we have to be reminded that the principal witness is dead and that Chaerephon's brother was not in Delphi?[27] That amounts to saying that there are no more witnesses and that there is thus no means of verifying the oracle's authenticity on the trial day. Vlastos' position on the value of Chaerephon's brother's testimony appears contradictory. After having affirmed that in the *Apology* 'a well qualified witness is in court to attest the story',[28] he then affirms, on the assumption that Chaerephon had consulted the oracle according to the procedure of cleromancy, that 'Chaerephon could have kept it [*scil.* the oracle's answer] to himself and divulged *it only to Socrates*'.[29] If the oracle's answer has been revealed to Socrates alone, how could Chaerephon's brother be a good witness? Moreover, since we have the impression that Socrates is telling the oracle story for the first time on the day of his trial, as Vlastos (p. 289) rightly underlines,[30] the assumption is reinforced that the oracle was known only to Socrates and Chaerephon. The other witness Socrates calls upon to attest to his possessing a *sophia* of a certain type is just as far as Chaerephon's brother from any possibility of verification: indeed it is Apollo himself and we have no choice but to take his word for it![31]

Before examining the fifth criterion Most proposes, I would like to make a short digression here. One aspect contributing strongly to the myth's unverifiable character is the temporal indetermination of the facts and actions the myth reports. Most myths report facts and actions reaching back to a very distant past that is impossible to date accurately. Brisson stresses that the absence of any exact dating is a characteristic of myth: 'Myth is distinguished from true discourse about the past by its inability to precisely state when the events which it mentions took place'.[32] But in a certain way,

---

[26] Daniel & Polansky (1979), 83. Cf. 21a5–8: '[Socrates] he (*sc.* Chaerephon) asked if any man was wiser than I, and the Pythian replied that no one was wiser. Chaerephon is dead, but his brother will testify to you about this'. (trans. Grube).

[27] Cf. Burnet (1911) *ad* 21a7: 'Schanz imagines that the calling of Chaerepho's brother shows that the oracle was not generally known, and suggests that it is a hint of the fictitious character of the whole story. I cannot follow reasoning of this kind'.

[28] Vlastos (1991), 289.

[29] Ibid. (italics mine).

[30] Ibid.

[31] Cf. *Ap.* 20e6–8: '[Socrates] but I will refer you to a trustworthy source. I shall call upon the god at Delphi as witness to the existence and nature of my wisdom, if it be such' (trans. Grube).

[32] Brisson (1999 [1982]), 24.

the same goes for the oracle story; admittedly, it is not a question of a very distant past, in the sense that it is said to be about an event in the life of Socrates, and not, as with myths, about facts or actions preceding the time when the narrator relates the myth by several generations. While this is indeed a point of divergence between the oracle story and myth, still we cannot help noticing that Socrates provides no indications which would allow us to date the Pythia's answer to Chaerephon's question. This temporal indetermination is all the more surprising when we consider that a determining episode in the life of Socrates is at issue, since everything proceeds as if it were the oracle's answer that marked the starting point of Socrates' philosophical engagement. It is significant that Plato gives no indication which would allow us to even approximately determine the date the Pythia delivered her oracle. That has the effect of accentuating the story's mythical dimension. When did Chaerephon go to Delphi to consult the Pythia? At what period in his life did Socrates start practicing refutation? By purposefully leaving the date when the events reported were said to have occurred unspecified,[33] Plato prohibits our ever being able to answer these questions and even seems to indicate in advance that they are of little importance. The various attempts at determining the oracle's date[34] are doomed to failure from the start and all sin by naivety insofar as they seek an accurate dating of an episode in Socrates' life for which Plato himself, in failing to provide the required chronological bearings, avoids underlining the historical character.

– 5th criterion: *'Platonic myths generally derive their authority not from the speaker's personal experience but from the tradition.* For this very reason they are not subject to rational examination by the audience' (18).— Despite appearances, the story of the oracle draws its authority, not from Socrates' personal experience—he was not in Delphi—, but rather from Chaerephon's testimony. Thus the oracle story does not draw its authority from tradition, but the consequence is exactly the same: given that Chaerephon is dead, the account cannot be the subject of a rational examination by Socrates' listeners.

---

[33] Cf. Brisson (1997), 67: 'Aucune date ne peut être assignée à cet événement auquel il n'est fait allusion dans aucun autre dialogue de Platon'.

[34] Cf. Burnet (1914), 136; Horneffer (1922), 98–101; Taylor (1932), 78; Parke & Wormell (1956), I, 401–402; Ferguson (1964), 70–73; Guthrie (1971), 85–86; Brickhouse & Smith (1989), 94–95; de Strycker & Slings (1994), 75; Vlastos (1991), 252, n. 60, etc. On the impossibility of dating the oracle with precision, cf. Montuori (1981), 87–95; Brickhouse & Smith (1989), 94, n. 76.

– 6th criterion: *'Platonic myths often have an explicitly asserted psychagogic effect'* (18).—Most mentions several passages[35] where it is explicitly stated that hearing a myth procures a goodly amount of pleasure. On the contrary, however, the oracle story risks irritating the judges and Socrates is perfectly aware of it: 'Do not create a disturbance, gentlemen, even if you think I am boasting'.[36] Does that mean that the oracle story has no psychagogic effect? I do not believe so. We should distinguish two categories of listeners present at the trial: judges and Socrates' friends. While most of the judges were undoubtedly deeply irritated by the story of the oracle, Socrates' friends, on the other hand, were certainly delighted to hear it for this first time. What a pleasure to learn, straight from their Master's mouth, that he had been proclaimed the wisest of men by Apollo! Moreover, the pleasure the myth procures for his listeners is not only, nor even, the principal psychagogic effect it produces: 'But the myth's appeal to its listeners' emotions goes beyond providing them with delightful entertainment: it can also supply them with a strong motivating impulse towards performing action, one capable of surpassing any form of rational persuasion' (18). In addition to the pleasure of hearing the oracle story, it certainly provides Socrates' friends with the motivation necessary for continuing the philosophical way of life. Moreover, Socrates counts on them to go on questioning the Athenians after his death so that they render an account of their lives[37] and we can easily imagine that the purpose of the oracle story is also, on the day they see Socrates paying for his engagement in philosophy with his life, that of procuring the motivation they need for surmounting this ordeal and strengthening their determination to lead lives dedicated to philosophy, meaning to the examination of others and themselves. As for the judges, those among them who have voted for acquittal must have been affected by his account and we can thus assume that they felt the kind of psychagogic effects aimed at by myth. And the fact that, at the end of the *Apology*, Socrates invites them to examine his own children to see if they neglect the care of their souls,[38] leads us to think that the oracle story has exerted a psychagogic effect on these judges, inclining them favourably towards the *elenchus*.

– 7th criterion: *'Platonic myths are never structured as dialectic but as description or narration.* [...] the Platonic myths are structured either synchroni-

---

[35] Cf. *Prot.* 320c, *Phd.* 108d, *Symp.* 193e, *Rep.* X, 614b.
[36] 20e4–5 (trans. Grube).
[37] Cf. 39c–d.
[38] Cf. 41e.

cally as the description of the co-existing parts of a place (so in the *Phaedo*, *Gorgias*, and *Republic*) or, more often, diachronically as the narration of the successive episodes of one or more larger actions' (18).—The oracle story also satisfies this criterion since it is very clearly structured according to a diachronic perspective: Socrates first relates the oracle's answer, then his reaction to that answer, and finally the round of investigations he has decided to undertake in order to penetrate the oracle's meaning.

– 8th criterion: '*Platonic myths are always found either (a) at the beginning of an extended dialectical exposition, or (b) at the end of one*' (18).—The story of the oracle (20d–23c) immediately precedes the dialectical passage wherein Socrates questions Meletus in order to refute him (25c–28a). The short passage (23c–25c) situated between the oracle story and his interrogation of Meletus is in fact a prolongation of the story: Socrates continues his monologue there and describes the consequences the oracle has had on his life and on how his fellow-citizens have perceived him. There is neither an exchange nor a dialectical passage between the oracle story and the interrogation of Meletus.

Applying these eight criteria has allowed Most to identify fourteen accounts which may be regarded as myths.[39] Most readily acknowledges that this group of fourteen accounts is not definitively closed and that it might possibly be expanded to include other accounts satisfying the criteria he proposes. However, because the oracle story easily satisfies the eight criteria defined by Most, I see no reason not to include it in the group of accounts which have the status and function of a myth.

It seems to me important to stress that the oracle story has a function which corresponds in all points to that of a myth of origin. According to Most, '[e]ither the myths deal with the very first things, deriving present circumstances aetiologically from the earliest times [...] Or else they deal with the very last things, supplying an eschatology for events after death' (17). The oracle story corresponds to myths of the first kind: it obviously deals with 'first things' and it is just as obvious that it is used to justify the present, in this case, Socrates' practice of the *elenchus*, in light of the past, namely the oracle from which Socrates derives his 'mission'. The function of the oracle story is thus comparable to that of myths of origin, namely myths which, at

---

[39] Cf. *supra*, 16, 24 (Appendix B): *Prot.* 320c–323a, *Gorg.* 523a–527a, *Men.* 81a–c, *Phd.* 107c–114c, *Symp.* 189c–193d; 203b–204a, *Phdr.* 246a–257a; 274b–275b, *Rep.* X, 613e–621d, *Pol.* 268e–274e, *Tim.* 20d–25e; 29d–92c, *Crit.* 108e–121c, *L.* IV, 713a–e.

the same time that they reveal the origin of a practice, a habit or a technique whose origin is in fact lost in the mists of time, have as their goal justifying and legitimizing that practice or that technique. Here the story indeed accomplishes the function of a myth of origin, since this story, at the same time that it reveals the origin of the philosophical activity of Socrates, and even of philosophy itself, has the goal of justifying and legitimizing philosophy and those who are devoted to it. Numerous commentators have noticed that the *Apology* sees the oracle story as the source of Socrates' philosophical life and, more precisely, of his investigations by means of refutation,[40] since philosophy, for the Socrates of the *Apology*, essentially consists in examining oneself and examining others by means of the *elenchus* (cf. 28e, 29d, 30a, 33c, 38a). The sole reason why Socrates carries out his investigations among politicians, poets and craftsmen is that he sees in it the best way of testing the oracle and shedding light on its deep and hidden meaning. Without the Pythia's answer to Chaerephon, Socrates would seemingly never have felt the need to determine whether the alleged wisdom of his fellow-citizens was real. Commentators who establish a link between the Pythia's answer and the source of Socrates' practice in the matter of refutation are however wrong in not being astonished that Socrates spontaneously set about refuting, whereas he probably knew nothing about this practice. It all takes place as if Socrates had never questioned people before this celebrated oracle, nor looked into their opinions; in short, it is as if he had never practiced refutation before the day his friend Chaerephon brought him the Pythia's reply. In reading Plato's account, we get the impression that the Socratic

---

[40] Cf. Zeller (1868), 55, n. 2: 'If then he speaks in the Apology as though the Delphic oracle had first aroused him to sift men, this must be an oratorical figure.' Hackforth (1933), 102: 'it was the oracle that had been the occasion of Socrates' embarking upon his 'elenctic' task'; Robin (1942), 143–144: 'Cependant l'oracle de Delphes, en répondant à Chéréphon que Socrate est le plus sage des hommes, vient déterminer dans la carrière de Socrate un nouveau changement: il commence à pratiquer cette sorte d'enquête publique sur la valeur et les fondements des compétences affirmées et reconnues, cette méthode d'ἐξέτασις dont il est tant question dans l'*Apologie*'. E. de Strycker (1975), 40: 'Socrates' elenctic activity is depicted as starting after the oracle'; West (1979), 107: 'he [*scil.* Socrates] only began his questioning examinations after the oracle was delivered'; Rankin (1983), 149: 'In the *Apology* Plato makes him [*scil.* Socrates] say that the Delphic oracles' reply to Chaerephon struck him so forcibly that he decided to find whether it was true. Convinced that he himself knew nothing, *he embarked on a career of questioning people*' (italics mine); Reeve (1989), 21: 'Socrates began his elenctic mission sometime after the oracle to Chaerephon'; Vander Waerdt (1993), 33: 'the Platonic Socrates traces—in some sense—his practice of the *elenchus* to the divine command of Apollo which he finds implicit in the oracle's pronouncement.'; Brisson (1997), 71: 'cette nouveauté [*scil.* dialectical refutation], Platon la présente comme absolue, en lui déniant toute autre origine que la réponse de l'oracle'.

practice of refutation was born spontaneously, as if by enchantment, and was not inspired by any former practice. What a thing to believe, dialectical refutation appeared just like that, as if by magic, almost by spontaneous generation! It is frankly at the very least implausible that Socrates would have created the technique and practice of refutation *ex nihilo*. The oracle of Delphi episode bears a strong resemblance to a myth of origin, meaning a story which assigns a divine origin to a practice which, while being eminently illustrated by Socrates, was certainly inspired by former practices.[41]

Assigning a divine origin to Socrates' philosophical activity, which is identified in the *Apology* with the practice of the *elenchus*, serves a dual purpose: on the one hand, it seeks to erase the bonds of filiation between the Socratic practice of refutation and similar practices by philosophers contemporary with Socrates or earlier; in addition, it aims at giving a divine sanction to those devoted to refutation, facilitating the justification of this practice in the eyes of Athenians and granting a complement of legitimacy and motivation to those practicing it.

The oracle story's status and function are connected to those of myth, and particularly the myth of origin, to such an extent that I am inclined to consider that this story is not only a Platonic fiction, but also a Platonic myth.

Conclusion

What conclusions can we draw from the fact that the oracle story is not only fictitious, but also a type of myth of origin? Firstly, we can conclude that the *Apology* is not a 'historical document' based on which we might attempt to reconstitute the thought and doctrines of the historical Socrates. Given the central role the oracle story plays in the economy of the *Apology*, demonstration of the fictitious and mythical nature of this story prevents any attempt at reconstituting the thought of the historical Socrates based on the Platonic *Apology*.[42]

A second conclusion relates to identifying other accounts, in the dialogues, that can be considered to be myths. Interpreters do not always agree on the criteria which allow us to identify the myths in the dialogues,[43] with the result being that the identity and number of accounts which may be

---

[41] Cf. Dorion (1990), 334.
[42] Cf. Montuori (1990); Dorion (2011).
[43] Cf. Pradeau (2004), 27.

described as 'myths' remain vague.[44] But if we must conclude that the oracle of Delphi story has much in common with myths, in relation to both its status and function, we may envisage that other accounts, present in the early dialogues, may also be seen as myths. Thus we would be wrong in considering, with Edelstein,[45] that the early dialogues, except for the *Protagoras*, contain no myths.

Lastly, if the Pythia's response to Chaerephon marks the starting point of Socrates' practice of refutation, and if the oracle story is, moreover, mythical, it follows that Plato assigns a divine and mythical origin to the Socratic *elenchus*. This interpretation is confirmed by another passage of the *Apology*:

> You have heard why, men of Athens; I have told you the whole truth. They enjoy hearing those being questioned who think they are wise, but are not. And this is not unpleasant. To do this has, as I say, been enjoined upon me by the god, by means of oracles and dreams, and in every other way that a divine manifestation has ever ordered a man to do anything.[46]
>
> (*Ap.* 33c1–7; trans. Grube)

This task that the gods prescribed for Socrates is nothing but the examination of the opinions of others by means of the *elenchus*. Rather than considering, like Aristotle, that the practice of refutation is lost in the mists of time and that it is hence vain to seek an exact origin of it, since men have always sought to refute one another,[47] and rather than shed light on the filiation between the legal *elenchus* and the dialectical *elenchus*,[48] Plato acts as if the dialectical *elenchus* were a form of argumentation that Socrates began to practice spontaneously as soon as he learned of the oracle. The *Apology* is not the only text where Plato assigns a mythical origin to the *elenchus*. In the prologue to the *Charmides* (155e–157c), Socrates says that he learned from a Thracian doctor claiming to be a follower of Zalmoxis, a remedy and incantation allowing him to cure headaches. Thus, in the final analysis, Socrates is claiming to have learned a remedy and incantation allowing him to cure Charmides' headache from a mythical character, Zalmoxis. But since

---

[44] As Most (2002), 10–11 himself recognizes.

[45] Cf. Edelstein (1949), 463: 'The early dialogues, with the exception of the *Protagoras*, do not contain any mythical tale at all'.

[46] ἀκηκόατε, ὦ ἄνδρες Ἀθηναῖοι, πᾶσαν ὑμῖν τὴν ἀλήθειαν ἐγὼ εἶπον· ὅτι ἀκούοντες χαίρουσιν ἐξεταζομένοις τοῖς οἰομένοις μὲν εἶναι σοφοῖς, οὖσι δ' οὔ. ἔστι γὰρ οὐκ ἀηδές. ἐμοὶ δὲ τοῦτο, ὡς ἐγώ φημι, προστέτακται ὑπὸ τοῦ θεοῦ πράττειν καὶ ἐκ μαντείων καὶ ἐξ ἐνυπνίων καὶ παντὶ τρόπῳ ᾧπέρ τίς ποτε καὶ ἄλλη θεία μοῖρα ἀνθρώπῳ καὶ ὁτιοῦν προσέταξε πράττειν.

[47] Cf. *Soph. Ref.* 11, 172a30–35; *Rhet.* I, 1, 1354a3–7.

[48] Cf. Dorion (1990).

'incantation' (*epôidê*) is a metaphor designating refutation,[49] it follows that Plato has again made appeal to a myth, or more exactly to a mythical character, in assigning the Socratic practice of *elenchus* an origin. From which we see that assigning a divine or mythical origin to dialectics, as we see, for example, in the *Philebus* (16c), is not a characteristic of the later dialogues, since it is already expressed in the early dialogues.

---

[49] Cf. Dorion (2004), 119, n. 37.

REFERENCES

Adam, J. (1902), *The* Republic *of Plato*, edited with critical notes, commentary, and appendices, two volumes, Cambridge, Cambridge University Press.

Adkins, A.W.H. (1960), *Merit and Responsibility: A Study in Greek Values*, Oxford, Clarendon Press.

Allen, D. (2000), *The World of Prometheus: The Politics of Punishing in Democratic Athens*, Princeton, Princeton University Press.

Allen, R.E. ed. (1965), *Studies in Plato's Metaphysics*, London, Routledge & New York, Kegan Paul, The Humanities Press.

Ambuel, D. (2007), *Image & Paradigm in Plato's* Sophist, Las Vegas/Zurich/Athens, Parmenides Publishers.

Anceschi, B. (2006), *Die Götternamen in Platons* Kratylos: *Ein Vergleich mit dem Papyros von Derveni*, Frankfurt-am-Main, Peter Lang.

Annas, J. (1982), 'Plato's Myths of Judgement', *Phronesis* 27.2, 119–143.

Annas, J. and Waterfield, R. (1995), *Plato. Statesman*, Cambridge, Cambridge University Press.

Archer-Hind, R.D. (1894 [1883]), *The* Phaedo *of Plato* (London, Macmillan and Co.).

Ashbaugh, A.F. (1988), *Plato's Theory of Explanation. A Study of the Cosmological Account in the* Timaeus, Albany, State University of New York Press.

Asmis, E. (1986), '*Psychagogia* in Plato's *Phaedrus*', *Illinois Classical Studies* 11, 153–172.

Ausland, H.W. (2002), 'Forensic Characteristics of Socratic Argumentation', in: Scott, G.A. (ed.), *Does Socrates Have a Method: Rethinking the* Elenchus *in Plato's Dialogues and Beyond*, University Park, Pennsylvania State University Press, 36–60.

Babut, D. (1983), 'L'unité du livre X de la *République* et sa fonction dans le dialogue', *Bulletin de l'Association Guillaume Budé*, 31–54.

Barbarić, D. (1999), *Anblick, Augenblick, Blitz: Ein philosophischer Entwurf zum Seinsursprung*, Tübingen, Attempto.

Bees, R. (1993), *Zur Datierung des Prometheus Desmotes*, Stuttgart, Teubner (Beiträge zur Altertumskunde; 38).

Belfiore, E. (2006), 'Dancing with the Gods: The Myth of the Chariot in Plato's *Phaedrus*', *American Journal of Philology* 127, 185–217.

Benson, H. (1987), 'The Problem of the *Elenchus* Reconsidered', *Ancient Philosophy* 7, 67–85.

Berti, E. (1997), 'L'oggetto dell'*eikôs muthos* nel *Timeo* di Platone', in: Brisson, L. and Calvo, T. (eds), *Interpreting the* Timaeus—Critias. *Proceedings of the IVth Symposium Platonicum. Selected Papers*, Sankt Augustin, Academia Verlag, 119–131.

Blank, D. (1991), 'The Fate of the Ignorant in Plato's *Gorgias*', *Hermes* 119, 22–36.

—— (1993), 'The Arousal of Emotion in Plato's Dialogues', *Classical Quarterly* 43, 428–439.

Blondell, R. (2002), *The Play of Character in Plato's Dialogues*, Cambridge, Cambridge University Press.

Blössner, N. (1997), *Dialogform und Argument: Studien zu Platons* Politeia, Stuttgart, Steiner (Abhandlungen der Geistes- und Sozialwissenschaftlichen Klasse/Akademie der Wissenschaften und der Literatur Mainz; 1).

―― (2007), 'The City-Soul Analogy', in: Ferrari, G.R.F. (ed.), *The Cambridge Companion to Plato's* Republic, Cambridge, Cambridge University Press, 345–385.

Blumenberg, H. (2005), *La Raison du mythe*, Paris, Gallimard, coll. "Idées" [trans. S. Dirschauer of 'Wirklichkeit und Wirkungspotential des *Muthos*', in *Ästhetische und metaphorologische Schriften*, Frankfurt-am-Main, Surhkamp Verlag, 2001].

Bobonich, C.J. (1995), 'The Virtues of Ordinary People in Plato's *Statesman*', in: C.J. Rowe (ed.), *Reading the* Statesman. *Proceedings of the IIIrd Symposium Platonicum*, Sankt Augustin, Academia Verlag, 313–329.

―― (2002), *Plato's Utopia Recast: His Later Ethics and Politics*, Oxford, Clarendon Press.

Bordo, S. (1993), *Unbearable Weight: Feminism, Western Culture and the Body*, Berkeley, University of California Press.

Bostock, D. (1986), *Plato's* Phaedo, Oxford, Clarendon Press.

Bowden, H. (2005), *Classical Athens and the Delphic Oracle: Divination and Democracy*, Cambridge/New York, Cambridge University Press.

Boys-Stones, G.R. and Haubold, J.H., eds. (2010), *Plato and Hesiod*, Oxford, Oxford University Press.

Bremmer, J. (1988), 'La plasticité du mythe: Méléagre dans la poésie homérique', in: Calame, C. (éd.), *Métamorphoses du mythe en Grèce antique*, Genève, Labor & Fides, 37–56.

Brickhouse, T.C. and Smith, N.D. (1984), 'Vlastos on the *Elenchus*', *Oxford Studies in Ancient Philosophy* 2, 185–195.

―― (1989), *Socrates on Trial*, Oxford, Oxford University Press.

―― (1991), 'Socrates' Elenctic Mission', *Oxford Studies in Ancient Philosophy* 9, 131–159.

―― (1997), 'The Problem of Punishment in Socratic Philosophy', in: McPherran, M.L (ed.), *Wisdom, Ignorance and Virtue: New Essays in Socratic Studies, Apeiron* 30.4, 95–107.

―― (2002), 'Incurable Souls in Socratic Psychology', *Ancient Philosophy* 22.1, 21–36.

Brisson, L. (1974), *Le Même et l'autre dans la structure ontologique du* Timée *de Platon. Un commentaire systématique du* Timée *de Platon*, Paris, Klincksieck; seconde édition revue, pourvue de *Corrigenda*, d'*Addenda*, d'Index révisés et surtout d'une Bibliographie analytique nouvelle, Sankt Augustin, Academia Verlag, 1994; troisième édition revue, pourvue de *Corrigenda*, d'*Addenda*, d'Index révisés et surtout d'une Bibliographie analytique nouvelle, Sankt Augustin, Academia Verlag, 1998.

―― (1975), 'Le mythe de Protagoras: essai d'analyse structurale', *Quaderni Urbinati di Cultura Classica* 20, 7–37.

―― (1982), *Platon, les mots et les mythes. Comment et pourquoi Platon nomma le mythe?*, Paris, François Maspero; 2ᵉ éd. revue et mise à jour, Paris, La Découverte,

1994; trans. G. Naddaf, *Plato the Myth Maker*, Chicago/London, University of Chicago Press, 1999.

—— (1992), *Platon: Timée. Critias*, traduction inédite, introduction et notes, avec la collaboration de M. Patillon pour la traduction, Paris, Flammarion; 2ᵉ éd. corrigée et mise à jour, 1999, Paris, GF Flammarion.

—— (1995), 'Interprétation du mythe du *Politique*', in: Rowe C.J. (ed.), *Reading the Statesman. Proceedings of the IIIrd Symposium Platonicum*, Sankt Augustin, Academia Verlag, 349–363.

—— (1997), *Platon. Apologie de Socrate. Criton*, Paris, GF Flammarion.

—— and Calvo, T., eds. (1997), *Interpreting the* Timaeus—Critias. *Proceedings of the IVth Symposium Platonicum*, Sankt Augustin, Academia Verlag.

—— (2004), 'Vie théorique et vie pratique: la critique de Platon par Aristote', in: Lisi, F.L. (ed.), *The Ways of Life in Classical Political Philosophy. Papers of the 3rd Meeting of the Collegium Politicum, Madrid*, Sankt Augustin, Academia Verlag (*Studies in Ancient Philosophy*, 5), 85–94.

—— (2006a), 'Platon et la cosmologie', *Cahiers critiques de philosophie* 3, 31–43.

—— (2006b), 'Plato's Natural Philosophy and Metaphysics', in: Gill, M.L. and Pellegrin, P. (eds.), *A Companion to Ancient Philosophy*, Oxford/Malden (Mass.), Blackwell (= Blackwell Companions to Philosophy; 31), 212–231.

Broackes, J. (2009), 'Αὐτὸς καθ' αὑτόν in the Clouds: Was Socrates Himself a Defender of Separable Soul and Separate Forms?', *Classical Quarterly* 59.1, 46–59.

Broadie, S. and Rowe, Ch. eds. (2002), *Aristotle. Nicomachean Ethics*, Oxford/New York, Oxford University Press.

Brochard, V. (1974), 'Les mythes dans la philosophie de Platon', in: *Études de philosophie ancienne et de philosophie moderne*, 4ᵉ éd., Paris, Vrin (= *L'Année philosophique*, 11 [1901]), 46–59.

Buccioni, E.M. (2002), 'The Psychical Forces in Plato's *Phaedrus*', *British Journal for the History of Philosophy* 10, 331–357.

Burnet, J. (1911), *Plato's* Phaedo, Oxford, Clarendon Press.

—— (1914), *Greek Philosophy: Thales to Plato*, London, Macmillan & Co.

Burnyeat, M.F. (1990), *Plato. Theaetetus*, introduction to the translation by M.J. Levett, Indianapolis, Hackett.

—— (2005), '*Eikôs muthos*', *Rhizai* 2, 143–165.

—— (2009), '*Eikôs muthos*', in: Partenie, C. (ed.), *Plato's Myths*, Cambridge, Cambridge University Press, 167–186.

Buxton, R. (1994), *Imaginary Greece. The Contexts of Mythology*, Cambridge, Cambridge University Press.

Calame, C. (1996), *Mythe et histoire dans l'Antiquité grecque. La création symbolique d'une colonie*, Lausanne, Payot; trans. D.W. Berman, *Myth and History in Ancient Greece: The Symbolic Creation of a Colony*, Princeton/Oxford, Princeton University Press, 2003.

—— (2000), *Poétique des mythes dans la Grèce antique*, Paris, Hachette.

—— (2006), 'La fabrication historiographique d'un passé héroïque en Grèce classique: *arkhaîa* et *palaiá* chez Hérodote', *Ktèma* 31, 39–50.

—— (2010), *Prométhée généticien: profits techniques et usages de métaphores*, Paris, Les Belles Lettres.

Cameron, A. (2004), *Greek Mythography in the Roman World*, Oxford, Oxford University Press.

Černý, J. (1948), 'Thoth as Creator of Languages', *Journal of Egyptian Archaeology* 34, 121–122.

Chambry, É. (1932), *Platon. Œuvres complètes*, tome VI: La *République*, 3 vols, édition et traduction d'É. Chambry, avec une introduction d'A. Diès.

Cerri, G. (1996), *Platone sociologo della communicazione*, 2nd edition, Lecce, Argo (1st edition, 1991).

Chantraine, P. (1968), *Dictionnaire étymologique de la langue grecque*, Paris, Klincksieck.

Cherniss, H.F. (1944), *Aristotle's Criticism of Plato and the Academy*, I, Baltimore, The Johns Hopkins University Press.

―― (1977 [1936]), 'The Philosophical Economy of the Theory of Ideas' [1936], reprint in Tarán, L. (ed.), *Selected Papers*, Leiden, Brill.

―― (1977 [1954]), 'A much misread Passage of the *Timaeus* (*Timaeus* 49c7–50b5)' [1954], reprint in Tarán, L. (ed.), *Selected Papers*, Leiden, Brill.

Cherubin, R. (2009), '*Aletheia* from Poetry into Philosophy: Homer to Parmenides', in: Wians, W. (ed.), Logos *and* Muthos: *Philosophical Essays in Greek Literature*, Albany, SUNY Press.

Cholbi, M.J. (2002), 'Dialectical Refutation as a Paradigm of Socratic Punishment', *Journal of Philosophical Research* 27, 371–379.

Clark, A. (2003), *Natural Born Cyborgs: Minds, Technologies, and the Future of Human Intelligence*, Oxford, Oxford University Press.

―― (2008), *Supersizing the Mind: Embodiment, Action, and Cognitive Extension*, Oxford, Oxford University Press.

Clay, D. (1985), 'The Art of Glaukos (Plato, *Phaedo* 108d4–9)', *The American Journal of Philology* 106.2, 230–236.

Clay, D. (2007), 'Plato *Philomuthos*', in: Woodard, R.D. (ed.), *The Cambridge Companion to Greek Mythology*, Cambridge, Cambridge University Press, 210–236.

Clayton, E. (2008), 'Aesop, Aristotle, and Animals: The Role of Fables in Human Life', *Humanitas* 21, 179–200.

Collobert, C. (2011), 'Poetry as Flawed Reproduction: Possession and *Mimesis* in Plato', in: Destrée, P. and Herrmann, F.-G. (eds), *Plato and the Poets* (*Mnemosyne Suppl.*, vol. 328), 41–61.

Colloud-Streit, M. (2005), *Fünf platonische Mythen im Verhältnis zu ihrem Textumfeld*, Fribourg, Academic Press.

Cooper, J. and Hutchinson, D.S., eds. (1997), *Plato. Complete Works*, Indianapolis/Cambridge, Hackett Publishing Company.

Coulter, J.A. (1976), *The Literary Microcosm: Theories of Interpretation of the Later Neoplatonism*, Leiden, Brill.

Cordero, N.-L. (1993), Le *Sophiste*, Paris, GF Flammarion.

Cornford, F.M. (1935), *Plato's Theory of Knowledge*. The *Theaetetus* and the *Sophist* of Plato, translated with a running commentary, London, Routledge & Kegan Paul.

―― (1952 [1937]), *Plato's Cosmology. The* Timaeus *of Plato*, translated with a running commentary, London, Routledge & Kegan Paul.

Cossutta, F. (2001), 'La joute interprétative autour du poème de Simonide dans le *Protagoras*: herméneutique sophistique, herméneutique socratique', in: Cossutta, F. and Narcy, M. (eds.), *La Forme dialogue chez Platon: Évolution et réceptions*, Grenoble, Jérôme Millon, 119–154.

Couturat, L. (1896), *De Platonicis mythis*, Paris, F. Alcan.

Croiset, A. (1895), *Histoire de la littérature grecque*, vol. 4, Paris, E. Thorin.

—— (1896), 'Compte rendu de la soutenance de thèse de Couturat', *Revue de métaphysique et de morale* 6.4, 401–421.

Crotty, K. (2009), *The Philosopher's Song: The Poets' Influence on Plato*, Lanham (MD), Lexington Books.

Dalfen, J. (1998), 'Wie, von wem and warum wollte Platon gelesen werden?', *Grazer Beiträge* 22, 29–79.

—— (2004), *Platon, Gorgias: Übersetzung und Kommentar (Platon Werke, 3)*, Göttingen, Vandenhoeck & Ruprecht.

Daniel, J. & Polansky, R. (1979), 'The Tale of the Delphic Oracle in Plato's *Apology*', *Ancient World* 2, 83–85.

Danzig, G. (2003), 'Apologizing for Socrates: Plato and Xenophon on Socrates' Behavior in Court', *Transactions of the American Philological Association* 133, 281–321.

Delattre, C. (2009), '*Aitiologia*: mythe et procédure étiologique', *Mètis* n. s. 7, 341–357.

Delcomminette, S. (2000), *L'Inventivité dialectique dans le* Politique *de Platon*, Bruxelles, Ousia.

De Luise, F. (2007), 'Il mito di Er: significati morali', in Vegetti, M. (ed.) *La Repubblica, libro X*, Napoli, Bibliopolis, 311–366.

Deman, T. (1942), *Le Témoignage d'Aristote sur Socrate*, Paris, Les Belles Lettres.

Demont, P. and Trédé, M. (1993), *Platon. Protagoras*, traduction nouvelle, introduction et commentaires, Paris, Le Livre de Poche.

Derrida, J. (1972), 'La pharmacie de Platon', in: *La Dissémination*, Paris, Seuil, 71–197.

Derrida, J. (2010), *La Naissance du corps: Plotin, Proclus, Damascius*, Paris, Galilée.

Desclos, M.-L. (1992), 'Autour du *Protagoras*: Socrate médecin et la figure de Prométhée', *Quaderni di Storia* 36, 105–140.

—— (2001), 'L'interlocuteur anonyme dans les *Dialogues* de Platon', in: Cossutta, F. and Narcy, M. (eds), *La Forme dialogue chez Platon: Évolution et réceptions*, Grenoble, Jérôme Millon, 69–97.

Destrée, P. (2010), 'Happiness, Justice, and Poetry in Plato's *Republic*', *Proceedings of the Boston Area Colloquium in Ancient Philosophy* 25, 243–269.

Detienne, M. et Vernant, J.-P. (1974), *Les Ruses de l'intelligence: La* mètis *des Grecs*, Paris, Flammarion.

Detienne, M. (1981), *L'Invention de la mythologie*, Paris, Gallimard.

Dillon J. (1973), *Iamblichi Chalcidensis in Platonis Dialogos Commentariorum Fragmenta*, Leiden, Brill.

—— (1995), 'The Neoplatonic Exegesis of the *Statesman* Myth', in: Rowe, Ch. (hg.), *Reading the* Statesman. *Proceedings of the IIIrd* Symposium Platonicum, Sankt Augustin, Academia Verlag, 364–374.

Dirlmeier, F. (1962), *Merkwürdige Zitate in der* Eudemischen Ethik *des Aristoteles*, Heidelberg, C. Winter.

Dixsaut, M. (1990), 'La rationalité projetée à l'origine, ou: De l'étymologie', in: Mattéi, J. (éd.), *La Naissance de la raison en Grèce*, Paris, Presses Universitaires de France, 59–70.

—— (1991), *Platon. Phédon*, trad. nouvelle, introduction et notes, Paris, GF-Flammarion.

—— (1999), 'What is it Plato calls thinking?', *Boston Area Colloquium in Ancient Philosophy* 13, 1–26.

—— (2000), *Platon et la question de la pensée*, Paris, Vrin.

—— (2001), *Métamorphoses de la dialectique dans les dialogues de Platon*, Paris, Vrin.

—— (2003), 'Divination et prophétie (*Timée*, 71a–71d)', in: Natali, C. and Maso, S. (eds), *Plato Physicus*, Amsterdam, Hakkert (*Lexis*, suppl. 17), 275–291.

Dodds, E.R. (1959), *Plato. Gorgias*, a revised text with introduction and commentary, Oxford, Clarendon Press.

Donini, P. (1988), 'Il *Timeo*: unità del dialogo, verosimiglianza del discorso', *Elenchos* 9, 5–52.

Döring, A. (1895), *Die Lehre des Sokrates als soziales Reformsystem. Neuer Versuch zur Lösung des Problems der sokratischen Philosophie*, Munich, Beck.

Döring, K. (1987), 'Der Sokrates der Platonischen Apologie und die Frage nach dem historischen Sokrates', *Würzburger Jahrbücher für die Altertumswissenschaft* 14, 75–94.

Dorion, L.-A. (1990), 'La subversion de l'*elenchos* juridique dans l'*Apologie de Socrate*', *Revue philosophique de Louvain* 88, 311–344.

—— (1995), *Aristote. Les Réfutations sophistiques*, Paris, Vrin/ Presses de l'Université Laval.

—— (2004), *Platon. Charmide, Lysis*, Paris, GF Flammarion.

—— (2005), 'The *Daimonion* and the *Megalêgoria* of Socrates in Xenophon's *Apology*', in: Destrée, P. and Smith, N.D. (eds), *Socrates' divine Sign: Religion, Practice, and Value in Socratic Philosophy*, Apeiron 38. 2, 127–142.

—— (2011), 'The Rise and Fall of the Socratic Question', in: Morrison, D.R. (ed.), *The Cambridge Companion to Socrates*, Cambridge, Cambridge University Press, 1–23.

Dorter, K.N.M. (1969–1970), 'The Dramatic Aspect of Plato's *Phaedo*', *Dialogue* 8, 564–580.

—— (1982), *Plato's* Phaedo: *An Interpretation*, Toronto, University of Toronto Press.

—— (1994), *Form and Good in Plato's Eleatic Dialogues. The* Parmenides, Theaetetus, Sophist, *and* Statesman, Berkeley, University of California Press.

Droz, G. (1992), *Les Mythes platoniciens*, Paris, Éditions du Seuil.

Druet, F.-X. (1998), 'Les niveaux de récit dans le mythe d'Er: Platon *Rép.* X, 613e–621d', *Les Études classiques* 66, 23–32.

Duke, E.A., Hicken, W.F., Nicoll, W.S.M., Robinson, D.B., Strachan, J.C.G., eds. (1995), *Platonis Opera*, vol. I, Oxford, Clarendon Press.

Edelstein, L. (1949), 'The Function of the Myth in Plato's Philosophy', *Journal of the History of Ideas* 10, 463–481.

Edmonds III, R.G. (2004), *Myths of the Underworld Journey: Plato, Aristophanes, and the 'Orphic' Gold Tablets*, Cambridge, Cambridge University Press.

Edmunds, L. (1993), *Myth in Homer: A Handbook*, 2nd ed., Highland Park (NJ), Mill Brook Press.

Else, G.F. (1972), *The Structure and Date of Book 10 of the* Republic, Heidelberg, C. Winter.

Eliade, M. (1963), *Aspects du mythe*, Paris, Gallimard, coll. "Idées".

Erler, M. (1995), 'Kommentar zu Brisson und Dillon', in: Rowe, Ch. (hg.), *Reading the* Statesman. *Proceedings of the IIIrd Symposium Platonicum*, Sankt Augustin, Academia Verlag, 375–380.

Ferguson, J. (1964), 'On the Date of Socrates' Conversion', *Eranos* 62, 70–73.

Ferrari, G.R.F. (1987), *Listening to the Cicadas*, Cambridge/New York, Cambridge University Press.

—— (1995), 'Myth and Conservatism in Plato's *Statesman*', in: Rowe, Ch. (hg.), *Reading the* Statesman. *Proceedings of the IIIrd Symposium Platonicum*, Sankt Augustin, Academia Verlag, 389–397.

—— (1999), 'Aristotle's Literary Aesthetics', *Phronesis* 44.3, 181–198.

—— (2003), *City and Soul in Plato's* Republic, Sankt Augustin, Academia Verlag [repr. Chicago, University of Chicago Press, 2005].

—— (2007), 'The Three-Part Soul', in: Ferrari, G.R.F. (ed.), *The Cambridge Companion to Plato's* Republic, Cambridge, Cambridge University Press, 165–201.

—— (2008), 'Socratic Irony as Pretence', *Oxford Studies in Ancient Philosophy* 34, 1–33.

—— (2009), 'Glaucon's Reward, Philosophy's Debt: The Myth of Er', in: Partenie, C. (ed), *Plato's Myths*, Cambridge, Cambridge University Press, 116–133.

Festugière, A.J. (1973), *Les trois 'protreptiques' de Platon. Euthydème, Phédon, Epinomis*, Paris, Vrin.

Finamore, J.F. (1985), *Iamblichus and the Theory of the Vehicle of the Soul*, Chico (CA), Scholars Press (= *American Classical Studies*, 14).

Findlay, J.N. (1978), 'The Myths of Plato', *Dionysius* 2, 19–34.

Fine, G. (2003), *Plato on Knowledge and Forms*, Oxford, Oxford University Press.

Fodor, J. (2009), 'Where is my Mind?', *London Review of Books* 31.3, 12 February, 13–15.

Fontenrose, J. (1978), *The Delphic Oracle, its Responses and Operations, with a Catalogue of Responses*, Berkeley, University of California Press.

Ford, A. (2009), 'The Beginnings of Dialogue Socratic Discourses and Fourth-Century Prose', in: Goldhill, S. (ed.), *The End of Dialogue in Antiquity*, Cambridge, Cambridge University Press, 29–44.

Friedländer, P. (1954), *Platon*, Band I: *Seinswahrheit und Lebenswirklichkeit*, Berlin, De Gruyter; *Plato*, vol. 1: *An Introduction*, trans. H. Meyerhoff, New York, Pantheon Books, 1958; *Plato*, vol. I: *An Introduction*, 2nd ed. revised, Princeton, Princeton University Press, 1969.

Friedman, M. (1993), *What Are Friends For? Feminist Perspectives on Personal Relationships and Moral Theory*, Ithaca, Cornell University Press.

Frutiger, P. (1930), *Les Mythes de Platon. Étude philosophique et littéraire*, Paris, F. Alcan (repr. New York, Arno Press, 1976).

Gagarin, M. (1996), 'The Torture of Slaves in Athenian Law', *Classical Philology* 91, 1–18.

Gaiser, K. (1959), *Protreptik und Paränese bei Platon. Untersuchungen zur Form des platonischen Dialogs*, Stuttgart, W. Kohlhammer.

—— (1968), *Platons ungeschriebene Lehre*, Stuttgart, Klett, 2nd edition (1st edition 1963).

—— (1984), *Platone come scrittore filosofico. Saggi sull'ermeneutica dei dialoghi platonici*, Napoli, Bibliopolis.

Gallagher, R.L. (2004), 'Protreptic Aims of Plato's *Republic*', *Ancient Philosophy* 24.2, 293–319.

Gallop, D. (1975), *Plato Phaedo, Translated with Notes*, trans. with commentary, Oxford, Clarendon Press; 2nd ed., Oxford/New York, Oxford University Press, 1993.

Goldberg, L. (1983), *A Commentary on Plato's* Protagoras, New York/Berne/Frankfurt-am-Main, Peter Lang.

Gonzalez, F.J. (2003), 'Perché non esiste una "teoria platonica delle idee"', in Bonazzi, M. and Trabattoni, F. (cur.), *Platone e la tradizione platonica. Studi di filosofia antica*, Milano, Cisalpino, 31–67.

—— (2009), *Plato and Heidegger: A Question of Dialogue*, University Park, Pennsylvania State University Press.

Gordon, J. (2007), 'In Plato's Image', in: Scott, G.A. (ed.), *Philosophy in Dialogue: Plato's Many Devices*, Evanston, Northwestern University Press, 212–237.

Griffith, M. (1983), *Aeschylus, Prometheus Bound*, Cambridge, Cambridge University Press.

Griswold, C.L. (1986), *Selfknowledge in Plato's* Phaedrus, New Haven, Yale University Press.

Guthrie, W.K.C. (1971), *Socrates*, Cambridge, Cambridge University Press.

—— (1975), *A History of Greek Philosophy*, vol. IV: *Plato: The Man and his Dialogues—Earlier Period*, Cambridge, Cambridge University Press.

Hackforth, R. (1933), *The Composition of Plato's* Apology, Cambridge, Cambridge University Press.

—— (1972 [1952]), *Plato's* Phaedrus, translation with an introduction and commentary, Cambridge, Cambridge University Press.

—— (1955), *Plato's* Phaedo, translation with commentary, Cambridge, Cambridge University Press.

Hadot, P. (1983), 'Physique et poésie dans le *Timée* de Platon', *Revue de Théologie et de Philosophie* 115, 113–133.

Halliwell, S. (2002), *The Aesthetics of Mimesis*, Princeton, Princeton University Press.

—— (2007), 'The Life-and-Death Journey of the Soul. Interpreting the Myth of Er', in: Ferrari, G.R.F (ed.), *The Cambridge Companion to Plato's* Republic, Cambridge, Cambridge University Press, 445–473.

Hamilton, E. and Cairns, H. (1961), *The Collected Dialogues of Plato*, Princeton, Princeton University Press (Bollingen Series, LXXI).

Harte, V. (2006), 'Beware of Imitations: Image Recognition in Plato', in: Herrmann, F.-G. (ed.), *New Essays on Plato. Language and Thought in Fourth-Century Greek Philosophy*, Swansea, Classical Press of Wales, 21–42.

Havelock, E. (1962), *Preface to Plato*, Cambridge (Mass.), Harvard University Press.

Hawtrey, R.S.W. (1983), '*Pan*-Compounds in Plato', *Classical Quarterly* 33, 56–65.

Hegel, G.W.F. (1832–1887), *Vorlesungen die Geschichte der Philosophie*, in: *Werke*, 19Bd., Berlin, 1832–1887, vol. XIV [*Leçons sur l'histoire de la philosophie*, P. Garniron (trad.), vol. 3, Paris, Vrin].

Heidegger, M. (1992), *Parmenides, Gesamtausgabe* 54, 2nd ed., Frankfurt-am-Main, Vittorio Klostermann.

Heitsch, E. (1997), *Platon Werke*, Band III 4: *Phaidros*, Göttingen, Vandenhoeck & Ruprecht.

Herter, H. (1975 [1958]), 'Gott und die Welt bei Platon. Eine Studie zum Muthos des *Politikos*', in: Vogt, E. (hrsg.), *Kleine Schriften*, München, Wilhelm Fink, 316–358.

Heyes, C. (2007), *Self-Transformations. Foucault, Ethics, and Normalized Bodies*, Oxford, Oxford University Press.

Hirsch, W. (1971), *Platons Weg zum Muthos*, Berlin/New York, Walter de Gruyter.

Hoffman, Ph. (2003), 'Le travail antique selon Jean-Pierre Vernant, ou de Marx à Aristote et à Platon', in: Balansard, A. (ed.), *Le Travail et la Pensée technique dans l'Antiquité classique. Lecture et relecture d'une analyse de psychologie historique de Jean-Pierre Vernant* (= *Technologie, Idéologie, Pratiques. Revue d'anthropologie des connaissance*, 15), 23–38.

Horn, Ch. (2002), 'Warum zwei Epochen der Menschheitsgeschichte? Zum *Muthos* des *Politikos*', in: Janka, M. and Schäfer, Ch. (eds), *Platon als Mythologe. Neue Interpretationen zu den Mythen in Platons Dialogen*, Darmstadt, Wissenschaftliche Buchgesellschaft, 137–159.

Horneffer, E. (1922), *Der junge Platon*, Giessen, Töpelmann.

Howald, E. (1922), '*Eikôs logos*', *Hermes* 57, 63–79.

Humphreys, S. (1985), 'Social Relations on Stage: Witnesses in Classical Athens', *History and Anthropology* 1.2, 313–369.

Imbert, C. (1999), *Pour une histoire de la logique, un héritage platonicien*, Paris, Presses Universitaires de France.

Inwood, M. (2009), 'Plato's Eschatological Myths', in: Partenie, C. (ed.), *Plato's Myths*, Cambridge, Cambridge University Press, 28–50.

Irwin, T. (1979), *Plato. Gorgias*, translated with notes, Oxford, Clarendon Press.

Jackson, K.R., Lycos, K. and Tarrant H. (1998), *Olympiodorus: Commentary on Plato's Gorgias*, Leiden, Brill.

Janaway, Ch. (1995), *Images of Excellence. Plato's Critique of the Arts*, Oxford, Clarendon Press.

Janka, M. and Schäfer, C. eds. (2002), *Platon als Mythologe. Neue Interpretationen zu den Mythen in Platons Dialogen*, Darmstadt, Wissenschaftliche Buchgesellschaft.

Jentel, M.-O. (1988), 'Glaukos I', in Boardman, J. et al. (eds), *Lexicon Iconographicum Mythologiae Classicae*, 4.1, Zürich, Artemis Verlag, 271–273.

Joël, K. (1894–1896), 'Der λόγος Σωκρατικός', *Archiv für Geschichte der Philosophie* 8 (1894), 466–483; 9 (1896), 50–66.

—— (1921), *Geschichte der antiken Philosophie*, Tübingen, Mohr.

Johansen, T.K. (2004), *Plato's Natural Philosophy. A Study of the* Timaeus-Critias, Cambridge, Cambridge University Press.

Jordan, M.D. (1986), 'Ancient Philosophic Protreptic and the Problem of Persuasive Genre', *Rhetorica* 4. 4, 309–333.

Jowett, B. (1892), *The Dialogues of Plato translated into English with Analyses and Introductions*, 3rd edition revised and corrected, Oxford, Oxford University Press.

Kahn, C.H. (1984), 'Drama and Dialectic in Plato's Gorgias', *Oxford Studies in Ancient Philosophy* 1, 75–121.

—— (1992), 'Vlastos's Socrates', *Phronesis* 37, 233–258.

—— (1996), *Plato and the Socratic Dialogue: The Philosophical Use of a Literary Form*, Cambridge, Cambridge University Press.

—— (2009), 'The Myth of the *Statesman*', in: Partenie C. (ed.), *Plato's Myths*, Cambridge, Cambridge University Press, 148–166.

Keyt, D. (1971), 'The Mad Craftsman of the *Timaeus*', *Philosophical Review* 80, 230–235.

Kingsley, P. (1995), *Ancient Philosophy, Mystery and Magic*, Oxford, Clarendon Press.

Kouremenos T., Parassoglou G.M., and Tsantsanoglou K., eds. (2006), *The Derveni Papyrus*, Firenze, Olschki (*Studi e testi per il corpus dei papyri filosofici*, 13).

Kraut, R. (1983), 'Comments on Gregory Vlastos, 'The Socratic *Elenchus*'', *Oxford Studies in Ancient Philosophy* 1, 59–70.

Kurke, L. (2006), 'Plato, Aesop, and the Beginnings of Mimetic Prose', *Representations* 94, 6–52.

Laín-Entralgo, P. (1970), *The Therapy of the Word in Classical Antiquity*, ed. and trans. by L.J. Rather and J.M. Sharp, New Haven, Yale University Press.

Laird, A. (2001), 'Ringing the Changes on Gyges: Philosophy and the Formation of Fiction in Plato's *Republic*', *The Journal of Hellenic Studies* 121, 12–29.

Laks, A. (2004), ''Qu'importe qui parle?': sur l'anonymat platonicien et ses antécédents', in: Calame, C. and Chartier, R. (eds), *Identités d'auteur dans l'Antiquité et la tradition européenne*, Grenoble, Jérôme Millon, 99–117.

Lane, M.S. (1998), *Methods and Politics in Plato's* Statesman, Cambridge/New York, Cambridge University Press.

Larivée, A. (2003), 'L'incarnation législative du souci de l'âme dans les *Lois*: un héritage socratique', in: Brisson, L., and Scolnicov, S. (eds), *Plato's Laws: From Theory into Practice. Proceedings of the VIth* Symposium Platonicum, Sankt Augustin, Academia Verlag, 98–102.

—— (2009), 'Avoir choisi sa vie. Le mythe d'Er comme expérience de pensée', *Revue de philosophie ancienne* 27. 1, 87–108.

—— (2011), 'Le *Philèbe*, un protreptique?', *Phoenix*, forthcoming.

Lear, J. (2006), 'Allegory and Myth in Plato's *Republic*', in: Santas, G. (ed), *Blackwell's Companion to Plato's* Republic, Oxford, Blackwell Publishers, 25–43.

Lebeck, A., (1972), 'The Central Myth of Plato's *Phaedrus*', *Greek, Roman and Byzantine Studies* 13, 267–290.

Lee, D. (2003 [1955]), *Plato. The Republic*, translated with an introduction, 2nd ed., London, Penguin Books.

Lee, H.D.P. (1952), *Aristotle. Meteorologica*, English translation, Cambridge, Mass./ London, Harvard University Press.

Leroux, G. (2002), *Platon. La* République, traduction et présentation, Paris, Garnier-Flammarion.

Lesher, J. (2002), 'Parmenidean *Elenchos*', in: Scott, G.A. (ed.), *Does Socrates Have a Method: Rethinking the* Elenchus *in Plato's Dialogues and Beyond*, University Park, Pennsylvania State University Press, 19–35.

Levi, A. (1946), 'I miti platonici', *Rivista di Storia della filosofia* 1, 197–225.

Levi, P. (2005 [1947]), *Se questo è un uomo*, Torino, Einaudi.

Lévinas, E. (1971), *Totalité et infini. Essai sur l'extériorité*, La Haye, Martinus Nyjhoff.

Lieb, I.C. (1963), 'Philosophy as Spiritual Formation: Plato's Myth of Er', *International Philosophical Quarterly* 3, 271–285.

Loewenclau, I. von (1958), '*Muthos* und *Logos* bei Platon', *Studium Generale* 11, 731–741.

Long, A.A. (1992), 'Stoic Readings of Homer', in: Lamberton, R. and Keaney, J.J. (eds), *Homer's Ancient Readers*, Princeton, Princeton University Press, 58–84.

Long, H.S. (1948), *A Study of the Doctrines of Metempsychosis in Greece from Pythagoras to Plato*, Princeton, Princeton University Press.

Lorenz, H. (2006), *The Brute Within. Appetitive Desire in Plato and Aristotle*, Oxford/New York, Oxford University Press.

Mackenzie, M.M. (1981), *Plato on Punishment*, Berkeley, University of California Press.

Maguire, J.P. (1977), 'Protagoras ... or Plato?—II. The *Protagoras*', *Phronesis* 22.2, 103–122.

Manuwald, B. (2003), 'Der *Muthos* im *Protagoras* und die Platonische *Mythopoiie*' in: Havlíček, A. and Karfík, F. (eds), *Plato's Protagoras. Proceedings of the IIIrd Symposium Platonicum Pragense*, Prague, Oikoumenè, 39–59.

Martijn, M. (2006), 'The *eikôs muthos* in Proclus' *Commentary on the* Timaeus', in: Tarrant, H. and Baltzly, D. (eds), *Reading Plato in Antiquity*, London, Duckworth, 151–167.

Martin, R.P. (1987), *The Language of Heroes: Speech and Performance in the* Iliad, Ithaca/London, Cornell University Press.

Mattéi, J.F. (2002), *Platon et le miroir du mythe*, Paris, Presses Universitaires de France.

May, H.E. (1997), 'Socratic Ignorance and the Therapeutic Aim of the *Elenchos*', in: McPherran, M.L. (ed.), *Wisdom, Ignorance and Virtue: New Essays in Socratic Studies, Apeiron* 30.4, 37–50.

McCoy, M. (2008), *Plato on Rhetoric of Philosophers and Sophists*, Cambridge, Cambridge University Press.

McKim, R. (1988), 'Shame and Truth in Plato's *Gorgias*', in: Griswold, C.L. Jr. (ed.), *Platonic Writings, Platonic Readings*, New York, Routledge; London, Chapman & Hall, 34–48.

Mesch, W. (2002), 'Die Bildlichkeit der platonischen Kosmologie. Zum Verhältnis von *Logos* und *Muthos* im *Timaios*', in: Janka, M. and Schäfer, C. (eds), *Platon als Mythologe. Neue Interpretationen zu den Mythen in Platons Dialogen*, Darmstadt, Wissenschaftliche Buchgesellschaft, 194–213.

Meyer-Abich, K.M. (1973), '*Eikôs Logos*. Platons Theorie der Naturwissenschaft', in: Scheibe, E. and Süßmann, G. (eds), *Einheit und Vielheit. Festschrift für Carl Friedrich von Weizsäcker*, Göttingen, Vandenhoeck & Ruprecht, 20–44.

Miller, C. (1978), 'The Prometheus Story in Plato's *Protagoras*', *Interpretation* 7, 22–32.

Miller Jr., M.H. (1980), *The Philosopher in Plato's* Statesman, The Hague, Martinus Nijhoff.

Milliat-Pilot, I. (2009), 'Représentation d'une illusion. Les sophistes du *Protagoras*: tensions poiétiques dans le monde du texte', in: Milliat-Pilot, I. (ed.), *Texte du monde. Monde du texte*, Grenoble, Jérôme Millon, 279–314.

Moline, J. (1978), 'Plato on the Complexity of the *Psyche*', *Archiv für Geschichte der Philosophie* 60, 1–26.

Montuori, M. (1981), *Socrates. Physiology of a Myth*, Amsterdam, J.C. Gieben.
—— (1988), *Socrates. An Approach*, Amsterdam, J.C. Gieben.
—— (1990), 'The Oracle given to Chaerephon on the Wisdom of Socrates. An Invention by Plato', *Kernos* 3, 251–259.
Morgan, K.A. (2000), *Myth and Philosophy from the Presocratics to Plato*, Cambridge/New York, Cambridge University Press.
Morgan, M.L. (1990), *Platonic Piety*, New Haven/London, Yale University Press.
Moors, K. (1988), 'Named Life Selections in Plato's Myth of Er', *Classica et Medievalia* 39, 55–61.
Morrison, D. (2000), 'On the Alleged Historical Reliability of Plato's *Apology*', *Archiv für Geschichte der Philosophie* 82, 235–265.
Morrison, J.S. (1959), 'The Shape of the Earth in Plato's *Phaedo*', *Phronesis* 4. 2, 101–119.
Morrow, G.R. (1960), *Plato's Cretan City. A Historical Interpretation of the* Laws, Princeton, Princeton University Press.
—— (1965), 'Necessity and Persuasion in Plato's *Timaeus*', in: Allen, R.E. (ed.), *Studies in Plato's Metaphysics*, London, Routledge & Kegan Paul, 421–437.
Most, G.W. (1994), 'Simonides' *Ode to Scopas* in Contexts', in: de Jong, I.J.F. and Sullivan, J.P. (eds), *Modern Critical Theory and Classical Literature*, Leiden/New York/Cologne, Brill, 127–152.
—— (1999), 'From *Logos* to *Muthos*', in Buxton, R. (ed.), *From Myth to Reason? Studies in the Development of Greek Thought*, Oxford, Oxford University Press, 25–47.
—— (2002), 'Platons exoterische Mythen', in: Janka, M. and Schäfer, C. (eds), *Platon als Mythologue. Neue Interpretationen zu den Mythen in Platons Dialogen*, Darmstadt, Wissenschaftliche Buchgesellschaft, 7–19.
Murray, P. (1999), 'What is a *Muthos* for Plato?', in Buxton R. (ed.), *From Myth to Reason? Studies in the Development in Greek Thought*, Oxford, Oxford University Press, 251–262.
Nagy, G. (1990), *Pindar's Homer: The Lyric Possession of an Epic Past*, Baltimore/London, The Johns Hopkins University Press.
—— (1996), 'Myth as Exemplum in Homer', in: *Homeric Questions*, Austin, University of Texas Press, 113–152.
Narcy, M. (1995), 'La critique de Socrate par l'Étranger dans le *Politique*', in: Rowe C.J. (ed.), *Reading the* Statesman. *Proceedings of the IIIrd Symposium Platonicum*, Sankt Augustin, Academia Verlag, 227–235.
Nicholson, P. and Rowe, C., eds. (1993), *Plato's* Statesman. *Selected Papers from the IIIrd Symposium Platonicum*, in: *Polis. Newsletter of the Society for the Study of Greek Political Thought* 12.
Nightingale, A.W. (1995), *Genres in Dialogue. Plato and the Construct of Philosophy*, Cambridge/New York, Cambridge University Press.
—— (2002), 'Distant Views: 'Realistic' and 'Fantastic' *Mimesis* in Plato', in: Rowe, C. and Annas, J. (eds), *New Perspectives on Plato, Modern and Ancient*, Cambridge (Mass.), Harvard University Press, 227–262.
—— (2004), *Spectacles of Truth in Classical Greek Philosophy. Theoria in its Cultural Context*, Cambridge, Cambridge University Press.

Notomi, N. (2001), *The Unity of Plato's Sophist: Between the Sophist and the Philosopher*, Cambridge, Cambridge University Press.

—— (2010), 'Glaucon's Challenge', in: Bosch-Veciana, A. and Monserrat-Molas, J. (eds), *Philosophy and Dialogue. Studies on Plato's Dialogues II*, Barcelona, Barcelonesa d'Edicions-Societat Catalana de Filosofia, 35–50.

Notopoulos, J.A. (1938), 'Mnemosyne in Oral Literature', *Transactions and Proceedings of the American Philological Association* 69, 465–493.

Nussbaum, M.C. (1986), *The Fragility of Goodness: Luck and Ethics in Greek Tragedy and Philosophy*, Cambridge, Cambridge University Press.

Ober, J. (1989), *Mass and Elite in Democratic Athens. Rhetoric, Ideology and the Power of the People*, Princeton, Princeton University Press.

O'Connor, D.K. (2007), 'Rewriting the Poets in Plato's Characters', in: Ferrari, G.R.F. (ed.), *The Cambridge Companion to Plato's* Republic, Cambridge, Cambridge University Press, 55–89.

Olsen, H. (2000), 'Socrates Talks to Himself in Plato's *Hippias Major*', *Ancient Philosophy* 20, 265–287.

Pachet, P. (1993), *Platon. La* République, trad., Paris, Gallimard, coll. "Folio/ Essais".

Parfit, D. (1984), *Reasons and Persons*, Oxford, Oxford University Press (reprinted with further corrections, Oxford, Clarendon Press, 1987).

Parke, H.W. and Wormell, D.E.W. (1956), *The Delphic Oracle*, 2 vol., Oxford, Blackwell.

Parker, R. (1996), *Athenian Religion: A History*, Oxford, Clarendon Press.

Partenie, C. ed. (2009), *Plato's Myths*, Cambridge, Cambridge University Press.

—— (2009a), Introduction to *Plato's Myths*, Cambridge, Cambridge University Press.

Pender, E.E. (1999), 'Plato's Moving *Logos*', *Proceedings of the Cambridge Philological Society* 45, 75–107.

—— (2000), *Images of Persons Unseen. Plato's Metaphors for the Gods and the Soul*, Sankt Augustin, Academia Verlag.

—— (2003) 'Plato on Metaphors and Models', in: Boys-Stones, G.R. (ed.), *Metaphor, Allegory, and the Classical Tradition: Ancient Thought and Modern Revision*, Oxford, Oxford University Press, 55–81.

Penner, T. (1991), 'Desire and Power in Socrates: The Argument of *Gorgias* 466a–468e that Orators and Tyrants Have no Power in the City', *Apeiron* 24, 107–202.

Penner, T. and Rowe, C. (2005), *Plato's* Lysis, Cambridge, Cambridge University Press.

Pépin, J. (1990), *Mythe et allégorie. Les origines grecques et les contestations judéo-chrétiennes*, Aubier, Paris (1st ed. 1958).

Pieper, J. (1965), 'Über die Wahrheit der platonischen Mythen', in: Oehler, K. and Schaeffler, R. (eds), *Einsichten. Gerard Krüger zum 60. Geburtstag*, Frankfurt-am-Main, Klostermann, 289–296.

Pisi, P. (1980), *Prometeo nel culto attico*, Roma, Ateneo.

Pradeau, J.-F., ed. (2004), *Les Mythes de Platon: Anthologie*, Paris, GF Flammarion.

Racionero, Q. (1998), '*Logos*, Myth and probable Discourse in Plato's *Timaeus*', *Elenchos* 19, 29–60.

Rankin, H.D. (1983), *Sophists, Socratics, and Cynics*, London/Canberra, Croom Helm, Totowa (NJ), Barnes & Noble.

Reale, G. (2004), "Il mito in Platone con particolare riguardo al mito nel *Protagora*", in: Casertano, G. (ed.), *Il* Protagora *di Platone: struttura e problematiche*, Napoli, Loffredo Editore, 128–144.

Reeve, C.D.C. (1989), *Socrates in the* Apology. *An Essay on Plato's* Apology *of Socrates*, Indianapolis, Hackett.

—— (2004), *Plato. Republic*, translated by G.M.A. Grube, revised by C.D.C. Reeve, Indianapolis, Hackett.

Reinhardt, K. (2007), *Les Mythes de Platon*, Paris, Gallimard [trans. A.-S. Reineke of 'Platons Mythen', in: Vermächtnis der Antike. *Gesammelte Essays zur Philosophie und Geschichtschreibung*, Göttingen, Vandenhoeck & Ruprecht, 2. Auflage, 1989].

Renaud, F. (2002), 'Humbling as Upbringing: The Ethical Dimension of the *Elenchus* in the *Lysis*', in: Scott, G.A. (ed.), *Does Socrates Have a Method: Rethinking the* Elenchus *in Plato's Dialogues and Beyond*, University Park, Penn State University Press, 183–198.

Ricken, F. (2008), 'Platon, *Politikos*', in: *Platon Werke*, II 4, Übersetzung und Kommentar, Göttingen, Vandenhoeck & Ruprecht.

Ricœur, P. (1975), *La Métaphore vive*, Paris, Éditions du Seuil.

Rivaud, A. (1925), *Platon. Œuvres complètes*, t. X, *Timée. Critias*, texte établi et traduit, Paris, Les Belles Lettres.

Robin, L. (1942), *La Pensée hellénique des origines à Épicure*, Paris, Presses Universitaires de France.

—— (1955), *Platon. Œuvres complètes*, I, nouvelle traduction par L. Robin en collaboration avec M.-J. Moreau, Paris, Gallimard.

—— (1985), *Platon. Phèdre*, Paris, Les Belles Lettres.

Robinson, T.M. (1970), *Plato's Psychology*, Toronto, University of Toronto Press.

—— (1993), 'The World as Art-Object: Science and the Real in Plato's *Timaeus*', *Illinois Classical Studies* 18, 99–111.

Romilly, J. de (1975), *Magic and Rhetoric in Ancient Greece*, Cambridge (Mass.), Harvard University Press.

—— (1982), 'Les conflits de l'âme dans le *Phèdre* de Platon', *Wiener Studien* n.s. 16, 100–113.

Roochnik, D. (2003), *Beautiful City: The Dialectical Character of Plato's* Republic, Ithaca, Cornell University Press.

Rosen, S. (1979), 'Plato's Myth of the Reversed Cosmos', *Review of Metaphysics* 33, 59–85.

—— (1983), *Plato's* Sophist. *The Drama of the Original and Image*, New Haven/London, Yale University Press.

—— (1995), *Plato's* Statesman. *The Web of Politics*, New Haven, Yale University Press.

Ross, W.D. (1933), 'The Problem of Socrates', *Proceedings of the Classical Association* 30, 7–24.

Rowe, C. (1986), *Plato. Phaedrus*, Warminster, Aris & Phillips.

—— (1993), *Plato. Phaedo*, Cambridge, Cambridge University Press.

—— (1995a), *Plato. Statesman*, edited with an introduction, translation and commentary, Warminster, Aris & Phillips.

—— ed. (1995b), *Reading the* Statesman. *Proceedings of the IIIrd Symposium Platonicum*, Sankt Augustin, Academia Verlag.

—— (1998), 'Myth, History, and Dialectic in Plato's *Republic* and *Timaeus-Critias*', in: Buxton, R. (ed.), *From Myth to Reason? Studies in the Development of Greek Thought*, Oxford, Oxford University Press, 263–278.

—— (1999), *Plato. Statesman*, Indianapolis, Hackett.

—— (2002), 'Zwei oder drei Phasen? Der Muthos im Politikos', in: Janka, M. and Schäfer, Ch. (eds), *Platon als Mythologe. Neue Interpretationen zu den Mythen in Platons Dialogen*, Darmstadt, Wissenschaftliche Buchgesellschaft, 160–175.

—— (2003), 'The Status of the Myth in Plato's *Timaeus*', in: Natali, C. and Maso, S. (eds), Plato Physicus: *Cosmologia e antropologie nel* Timeo, Amsterdam, Adolf Hakkert, 21–31.

—— (2005), 'The Good and the Just in Plato's *Gorgias*', in: Barbarić, D. (ed.), *Platon über das Gute und die Gerechtigkeit*, Würzburg, Königshausen & Neumann, 73–92 (reprinted in revised form in *Philosophical Inquiry* 30.3–4 (2008), 55–75).

—— (2006), 'The *Symposium* as a Socratic Dialogue', in: Lesher, J.H., Nails, D. and Sheffield, F. (eds), *Plato's* Symposium: *Issues in Interpretation and Reception*, Cambridge (Mass.), Harvard University Press (= *Hellenic Studies*, 22), 9–22.

—— (2007a), *Plato and the Art of Philosophical Writing*, Cambridge, Cambridge University Press.

—— (2007b), 'A Problem in the *Gorgias*: How is Punishment supposed to help with intellectual Error?', in: Bobonich, C. and Destrée, P. (eds), Akrasia *in Greek Philosophy: From Socrates to Plotinus*, Leiden, Brill, 19–40.

—— (2007c), 'The Moral Psychology of the *Gorgias*', in: Erler, M. and Brisson, L. (eds), Gorgias-Menon: *Selected Papers from the VIIth Symposium Platonicum*, Sankt Augustin, Academia Verlag, 90–101.

—— (2009), 'The Charioteer and his Horses: An Example of Platonic Myth-making', in: Partenie C. (ed.), *Plato's Myths*, Cambridge, Cambridge University Press, 134–147.

Rutherford, I. (1990), 'Μνήμης ... Φάρμακον in Plato *Phaedrus* 274e–275a: An Imitation of Euripides fr. 578?', *Hermes* 118.3, 377–379.

Rutherford, R.B. (1995), *The Art of Plato*, London, Duckworth.

—— (2002), 'Comments on Nightingale' (= on Nightingale [2002]), in: Rowe, C. and Annas, J. (eds), *New Perspectives on Plato, Modern and Ancient*, Cambridge (Mass.), Harvard University Press, 249–262.

Saïd, S. (1985), *Sophiste et tyran, ou le problème du* Prométhée enchaîné, Paris, Klincksieck.

—— (1987), 'Deux noms de l'image en grec ancien: idole et icône', *Comptes rendus de l'Académie des Inscriptions et Belles Lettres*, 309–330.

Santa Cruz, M.I. (1997), 'Le discours de la physique: *eikôs logos*', in: Brisson, L. and Calvo, T. (eds), *Interpreting the* Timaeus—Critias. *Proceedings of the IVth Symposium Platonicum*, Sankt Augustin, Academia Verlag, 133–139.

Saunders, T.J. (1991), *Plato's Penal Code: Tradition, Controversy, and Reform in Greek Penology*, Oxford, Clarendon Press.

—— (1992), 'Plato's Later Political Thought', in: Kraut R. (ed.), *The Cambridge Companion to Plato*, Cambridge, Cambridge University Press, 464–492.

Schanz, M. (1894), 'Sokrates als vermeintlicher Dichter', *Hermes* 29, 597–603.

Scheid-Tissinier, É. (1994), *Les Usages du don chez Homère: vocabulaire et pratiques*, Nancy, Presses Universitaires de Nancy.

Schicker, R. (1995), 'Aspekte der Rezeption des *Politikos* im Mittel- und Neuplatonismus', in: Rowe, C. (ed.), *Reading the* Statesman. *Proceedings of the IIIrd* Symposium Platonicum, Sankt Augustin, Academia Verlag, 381–388.

Schofield, M. (2007), 'Metaspeleology', in: Scott, D. (ed.), *Maieusis: Studies in Ancient Philosophy in Honour of Myles Burnyeat*, Oxford, Oxford University Press, 216–231.

Scodel, H.R. (1987), 'Diaeresis and Myth in Plato's *Statesman*', Göttingen, Vandenhoeck & Ruprecht (= *Hypomnemata*, 85).

Scott G.A., ed. (2002), *Does Socrates Have a Method: Rethinking the* Elenchus *in Plato's Dialogues and Beyond*, University Park, Pennsylvania State University Press.

Sedley, D.N. (1989), 'Teleology and Myth in the *Phaedo*', *Proceedings of the Boston Area Colloquium in Ancient Philosophy* 5, 359–383.

—— (1995), 'The *Dramatis Personae* of Plato's *Phaedo*', *Proceedings of the British Academy* 85, 3–26.

—— (2007), *Creationism and its Critics in Antiquity*, Berkeley/Los Angeles/London, University of California Press.

—— (2009), 'Myth, Punishment and Politics in the *Gorgias*', in: Partenie, C. (ed.), *Plato's Myths*, Cambridge, Cambridge University Press, 51–76.

Sharp, K. (2006), *Socrates and the Second Person: The Craft of Platonic Dialogue*, Ph.D. diss., Chicago, University of Chicago.

Shorey, P. (1901), 'Plato, Lucretius, and Epicurus', *Harvard Studies in Classical Philology* 12, 201–210.

—— (1933), *What Plato said*, Chicago, University of Chicago Press; Cambridge, Cambridge University Press.

Skemp, J.B. (1987 [1952]), *Plato's* Statesman. *A Translation of the* Politicus *of Plato with Introductory Essays and Footnotes*, Bristol, Bristol Classical Press.

Slaveva-Griffin, S. (2003), 'Of Gods, Philosophers, and Charioteers: Content and Form in Parmenides' *Proem* and Plato's *Phaedrus*', *Transactions of the American Philological Association* 133, 227–253.

Slings, S.R. (1995), 'Protreptic in Ancient Theories of Philosophical Literature', in: Abbenes, J.G.J., Slings, S.R. and Sluiter, I. (eds), *Greek Literary Theory after Aristotle. A Collection of Papers in Honour of D.M. Schenkeveld*, Amsterdam, VU University Press, 173–192.

Smith, J. (1985), 'Plato's Myths as "Likely Accounts", Worthy of Belief', *Apeiron* 19. 1, 24–42.

Smith, N. (1999), 'How the Prisoners in Plato's Cave are "like us"', *Proceedings of the Boston Area Colloquium in Ancient Philosophy* 13, 187–204.

Smith, R. (1997), *Aristotle: Topics, Books I and VIII*, Clarendon Aristotle Series, Oxford, Clarendon Press.

Sontag, S. (2001 [1966]), *Against Interpretation, and Other Essays*, New York, Picador.

Speliotis, E. (2007), 'Image, Myth, and Dialectic in Plato', *The European Legacy* 12, 211–223.

Spence, L. (1990), *Ancient Egyptian Myths and Legends*, Mineola (NY), Dover (1st ed., *Myths and Legends in Ancient Egypt*, London, G. Harrap, 1915).

Stalley, R. (2009), 'Myth and Eschatology in the *Laws*', in: Partenie, C. (ed.), *Plato's Myths*, Cambridge, Cambridge University Press, 187–205.

Steiner, D.T. (1994), *The Tyrant's Writ: Myths and Images of Writing in Ancient Greece*, Princeton, Princeton University Press.

Stewart, D.J. (1972), 'Socrates' Last Bath', *Journal of the History of Philosophy* 10, 253–259.

Stewart, J.A. (1905), *The Myths of Plato*, London/New York, Macmillan (repr. Carbondale, Southern Illinois University Press, 1960).

Stewart, R. (1989), 'The Epistemological Function of Platonic Myth', *Philosophy and Rhetoric* 22, 260–280.

Stöcklein P. (1937), *Über die philosophische Bedeutung von Platons Mythen* (= *Philologus*, Suppl. 30.3), Leipzig, Dieterich'sche Verlagsbuchhandlung.

Stokes, M.C. (1992a), 'Socrates' Mission', in: Gower, B.S. & Stokes, M.C. (eds), *Socratic Questions. New Essays on the Philosophy of Socrates and its Significance*, London, Routledge, 26–81.

—— (1992b), 'Plato and the Sightlovers of the *Republic*', in: Barker, A. and Warner, M. (eds), *The Language in the Cave, Apeiron* 25. 4, 103–132.

Strycker, E. de (1975), 'The Oracle given to Chaerephon about Socrates (Plato, *Apology*, 20e–21a)', in: Mansfeld, I. & Rijk, L.M. de (eds.), *Kephalaion. Studies in Greek Philosophy and its Continuation offered to Professor C.J. de Vogel*, Assen, Van Gorcum, 39–49.

—— & Slings, S.R. (1994), *Plato's Apology of Socrates*, Leiden, Brill.

Talisse, R.B. (2002), 'Misunderstanding Socrates', *Arion* 9.3, 46–56.

Tarán, L. (1971), 'The Creation Myth in Plato's *Timaeus*', in: Anton, J.P. and Kustas, G.L. (eds), *Essays in Ancient Greek Philosophy*, Albany, State University of New York Press, 372–407.

Tarrant, D. (1952), 'Metaphors of Death in the *Phaedo*', *Classical Review* n.s. 2, 64–66.

Tarrant, H. (1998) 'Myth as a Tool of Persuasion in Plato', *Antichton* 24, 19–31.

—— (2002), '*Elenchos* and *Exetasis*' in: Scott, G.A. (ed.), *Does Socrates Have a Method: Rethinking the* Elenchus *in Plato's Dialogues and Beyond*, University Park, Penn State University Press, 61–77.

—— (2007), *Proclus. Commentary on Plato's* Timaeus, *Volume 1, Book I: Proclus on the Socratic State and Atlantis*, Cambridge, Cambridge University Press.

Taylor, A.E. (1926), *Plato: The Man and his Work*, London, Methuen.

—— (1928), *A Commentary on Plato's* Timaeus, Oxford, Clarendon Press & Humphrey Milford.

—— (1932), *Socrates*, London, P. Davies.

Taylor, C. (1991), *Ethics of Authenticity*, Cambridge (Mass.), Harvard University Press.

Thayer, H.S. (1988), 'The Myth of Er', *History of Philosophy Quarterly* 5.4, 369–384.

Thein, K. (2001), *Le Lien intraitable. Enquête sur le temps dans la* République *et le* Timée *de Platon*, Paris, Vrin.

Thesleff H. (1982), *Studies in Platonic Chronology*, Helsinki, Acta Societatis Fennicae (*Commentationes Humanarum Litterarum*, 70).

—— (2007), 'The *Gorgias* rewritten—why?', in Brisson, L. and Erler, M. (eds.), Gorgias—Menon: *Selected Papers from the VIIth Symposium Platonicum*, Sankt Augustin, Academia Verlag, 78–82.

Thomas, R. (2000), *Herodotus in Context: Ethnography, Science and the Art of Persuasion*, Cambridge, Cambridge University Press.

Thoreau, H.D. (2004 [1854]), *Walden*, Princeton, Princeton University Press.

Todd, S. (1990), 'The Purpose of Evidence in Athenian Courts', in: Cartledge, P., Milett, P. and Todd, S. (eds), *NOMOS: Essays in Athenian Law, Politics and Society*, Cambridge, Cambridge University Press, 19–40.

Trabattoni, F. (1985–1986), 'Sul significato dello Jone platonico', *Sandalion* 8–9, 27–57.

—— (2000), *Platone, Gorgia, Parola e Ragione*, Milano, Unicopli.

—— (2004), Platone, *Ione*, Firenze, La Nuova Italia.

—— (2006), 'L'intuizione intellettuale in Platone. In margine ad alcune recenti pubblicazioni', *Rivista di storia della filosofia* 61, 701–719.

—— (2007), 'Esiste, secondo Aristotele, una "dottrina platonica delle idee"?', in *Méthexis* 20, 159–180.

—— (2008), 'Platone, Martha Nussbaum, e le passioni', in Giardina, G.R. (cur.), *Le emozioni secondo i filosofi antichi*, Catania, Cluecm, 39–61.

—— (2010), 'Fondazionalismo o coerentismo? In margine alla terza definizione di ἐπιστήμη del *Teeteto*', in Mazzara, G. & Napoli V. (eds), *Platone. La teoria del sogno nel* Teeteto, Sankt Augustin, Academia Richarz, 295–317.

Tulin, A. (2005), 'On the Refutation of Polemarchus: Analysis and Dialectic in *Republic* I', *Elenchos* 26.2, 277–316.

Turrini, G. (1977), 'Contributo all'analisi del termine *eikos*. I. L'età arcaica', *Acme* 30, 541–558.

—— (1979), 'Contributo all'analisi del termine *eikos*. II. Linguaggio, verosimiglianza e immagine in Platone', *Acme* 32, 299–323.

Usener, S. (1994), *Isokrates, Platon und ihr Publikum. Hörer und Leser von Literatur im 4. Jahrhundert v.Chr.*, Tübingen, G. Narr (= *ScriptOralia*, 63).

Valéry, P. (1957), 'Petite lettre sur les mythes', in: *Œuvres, Variétés I*, Paris, Gallimard, Bibliothèque de "La Pléiade", 961–967.

Vamvouri Ruffy, M. (to be published), 'Hermès: double divin du sophiste Protagoras? Lecture intertextuelle de l'*Hymne homérique à Hermès* et du *Protagoras* de Platon'.

Van Der Merren, S. (2002), 'Le protreptique en philosophie: essai de définition d'un genre', *Revue des études grecques* 115.2, 591–621.

Vander Waerdt, P. (1993), 'Socratic Justice and Self-Sufficiency. The Story of the Delphic Oracle in Xenophon's *Apology of Socrates*', *Oxford Studies in Ancient Philosophy* 11, 1–48.

—— ed. (1994), *The Socratic Movement*, Ithaca, Cornell University Press.

Vasiliu, A. (2008), *La Parole visible du* Sophiste, Paris, Vrin.

Verdenius, W.J. (1949), *Mimesis: Plato's Doctrine of Artistic Imitation and its Meaning to Us*, Leiden, Brill.

Vernant, J.-P. (1965), 'Le fleuve *Amélès* et la *mélétè thanatou*', in: *id., Mythe et pensée chez les Grecs*, vol. I, Paris, Maspero, 79–94.

Vidal-Naquet, P. (2007), *The Atlantis Story: A Short History of Plato's Myth*, trans. by J. Lloyd, Exeter, University of Exeter Press [*L'Atlantide. Petite histoire d'un mythe platonicien*, Paris, Les Belles Lettres, 2005].

Vlastos, G. (1965a), 'The Disorderly Motion in the *Timaeus*', *Classical Quarterly* 33 [1939], 71–83, reprint in Allen, R.E. (ed.), *Studies in Plato's Metaphysics*, London/New York, Routledge & Kegan Paul, 379–389.

—— (1965b), 'Creation in the *Timaeus*: is it a Fiction?', in: Allen, R.E. (ed.), *Studies in Plato's Metaphysics*, London/New York, Routledge & Kegan Paul, 401–419.

—— (1983), 'The Socratic *Elenchus*', *Oxford Studies in Ancient Philosophy* 1, 27–58.

—— (1991), *Socrates: Ironist and Moral Philosopher*, Ithaca, Cornell University Press.

Vries, G.J. de (1969), *Commentary on the* Phaedrus *of Plato*, Amsterdam, Hakkert.

Waterfield, R. (2004), 'Xenophon's Socratic Mission', in: Tuplin, C. (ed.), *Xenophon and his World. Papers from a Conference held in Liverpool in July 1999* (= *Historia Einzelschriften*, 172), Stuttgart, 79–113.

Weil, S. (1941/1951), 'Expérience de la vie d'usine', in: *id., La Condition ouvrière*, Paris, Gallimard.

Werner, D.S. (2005), 'Myth and Philosophy in Plato's *Phaedrus*', Ph.D diss., Bloomington, Indiana University Press.

West, T.G. (1979), *Plato's* Apology of Socrates, Ithaca, Cornell University Press.

White, N. (2006), 'Plato's Concept of Goodness', in: Benson, H. (ed.), *A Companion to Plato*, Malden (Mass.), Blackwell Publishing Ltd, 356–372.

Whitehead, A.N. (1929), *Process and Reality*, Cambridge, Cambridge University Press.

Wilke, B. (1997), *Vergangenheit als Norm in der platonischen Staatsphilosophie*, Stuttgart, Steiner.

Winkler, J.J. (1990), 'Laying Down the Law: The Oversight of Men's Sexual Behavior in Classical Athens', in: Halperin, D.M., Winkler, J.J. and Zeitlin, F.I. (eds.), *Before Sexuality: The Construction of Erotic Experience in the Ancient Greek World*, Princeton, Princeton University Press, 257–308.

Williams, B. (1981), *Moral Luck*, Cambridge, Cambridge University Press.

—— (1993), *Shame and Necessity*, Berkeley/Los Angeles/London, University of California Press.

Witte, B. (1964), 'Der *eikôs logos* in Platos *Timaios*. Beitrag zur Wissenschaftsmethode und Erkenntnistheorie des späten Plato', *Archiv für Geschichte der Philosophie* 46, 1–16.

Yunis, H. (2007), 'The Protreptic Rhetoric of the *Republic*', in: Ferrari, G.R.F. (ed.), *The Cambridge Companion to Plato's* Republic, Cambridge, Cambridge University Press, 1–26.

Zanker, G. (1981), '*Enargeia* in the Ancient Criticism of Poetry', *Rheinische Museum* 124, 297–311.

Zaslavsky, R. (1981), *Platonic Myth and Platonic Writing*, Washington, University Press of America.

Zeller, E. (1868), *Socrates and the Socratic Schools*, trans. O.J. Reichel, London, Longmans, Green & Co.

—— (1888), *Plato and the Older Academy*, 3rd ed., trans. S. Frances Alleyne and A. Goodwin, London, Longmans.

INDEX LOCORUM

The more meaningful an *index locorum* is to be, the more imprecise an art is the exercise of compiling it. In this index, we have, by and large, left out all those place where an author or a work are just mentioned, without precise citation. Where portions of a work or a work as a whole are the **topic of discussion**, page numbers appear **in bold type**, without additional listing of individual references/citations. Where passages are *quoted*, page numbers are in *italics*. Where passages are merely cited, as parallels in footnotes, or with little discussion, or without discussion altogether, standard roman type has been used. There has been some telescoping and simplification in referencing to reduce the bulk of entries. Judgement in these matters must to some extent be subjective. A balance had to be struck between being comprehensive and being useable.